TEACHING STUDENTS WITH MILD DISABILITIES

WILLIAM N. BENDER

University of Georgia

ALLYN AND BACON

Boston London Toronto Sydney Tokyo Singapore

Senior Editor: Ray Short
Editorial Assistant: Christine Svitila
Production Administrator: Rob Lawson
Cover Administration: Suzanne Harbison
Manufacturing Buyer: Megan Cochran
Editorial-Production Service: Electronic Publishing Services Inc.

A Simon & Schuster Company
Needham Heights, Massachusetts 02194

Photo Credits: Courtesy of Edmark: pp.: 162, 163; Will Faller: pp.: 1, 35, 61, 156, 184, 350; Robert Harbison: pp.: 205, 309, 368; Jim Pickerell: p. 328; Stephen Marks: p. 114; Brian Smith: pp.: 82, 142, 230, 258, 288.

Library of Congress Cataloging-in-Publication Data

Bender, William N.
Teaching students with mild disabilities / William N. Bender
p. cm.
Includes index.
ISBN 0-13-892720-0
1. Handicapped children—Education—United States. 2. Special education—United States. I. Title.
LC4031.B417 1996
371.91'0973—dc20 95-37933
CIP

Printed in the United States of America

10 9 8 7 6 5 4 3 2 1 98 97 96 95

CONTENTS

PART FOUR
INDIRECT INSTRUCTIONAL RESPONSIBILITIES

PREFACE

This text is intended to acquaint you with multiple strategies for dealing with students with mild and moderate disabilities in the most common instructional settings. Particular attention is given to the inclusive instruction and consultation responsibilities for working with students with disabilities.

Each section presents instructional suggestions and ideas ranging from the initial setup of the classroom, to classroom management, to specific suggestions for highly technical instructional techniques such as learning strategies, precision teaching, metacognitive instruction, and self-monitoring. Because of the fundamental importance of secondary preparation in the lives of students with disabilities, particular attention is given to vocational skills development for students with disabilities.

Working with students with special needs has always been more complex than merely applying correctly the latest teaching idea. These students need instruction in curriculum areas that are not routinely covered for students without disabilities. In working with these students, you will be expected to implement a social skills curriculum, which typically is not included in the traditional elementary or secondary class. Also, you will have responsibilities for working with parents and other teachers who are unique to special education. This book is intended to provide you with the initial foundation for all of these tasks.

Of course, no text—for that matter no single course—can prepare you for these extended responsibilities. You will be mastering these skills for at least your first five years in the classroom. However, this text does present the framework to begin your understanding of the complex demands that will be made on you.

Part One presents the basis for effective instruction. Suggestions are included about initial classroom setup and planning disciplinary options for students with special needs. Also, the concepts of inclusive instruction and consultation are introduced. These two concepts seem to be the guiding principles in current instructional thought for special students.

Part Two presents several specialized instructional areas. Behavioral and metacognitive instructional models and techniques are explained. Also, tutoring, cooperative instruction, and computer-based instruction are presented. Although any one of these instructional approaches could be (and in many cases is) a separate course in the teacher preparation curriculum, the introduction sections here are intended to present these approaches in an integrated fashion, with an eye toward helping you to set up your own class.

Part Three presents the instructional strategies for the curriculum content areas. Instruction must be grounded in the curriculum that is common to both students with special needs and students without disabilities. These chapters cover instruction in the traditional content areas for both elementary and secondary education.

Part Four presents information on indirect instructional responsibilities. Teachers of students with disabilities often interact much more frequently with parents than do teachers in the traditional classes, and these indirect responsibilities can be a real success for you, or your biggest failure. Take care to read and study these suggestions for working with parents and informing them about unproven instructional techniques.

With your studies in special education, you have begun a commitment to students with disabilities. This is a very serious undertaking, and can be your greatest joy. Students with disabilities suffer under a great deal of pressure and expectations of failure, and these can lead to poor attitudes. If, through these techniques, you find a way to gain their confidence, respect, and effort towards learning, you will have succeeded for those students and for yourself. There is no greater personal reward in life than helping students discover their own learning potential and seeing them become excited about their own possibilities again. With that goal in mind, and these techniques and strategies in hand, you are ready to begin an exciting and challenging career. Good luck to you.

INVITATION TO CONTRIBUTE

The evaluation information below is sought by the author of this text. Please take a moment to complete this invitation to contribute to the continuing development of this text by completing the questions and mailing this form to William N. Bender, 577 Aderhold Hall, UGA, Athens, GA 30602. All input is considered, and if the volume of the response prevents a personal thank you, please know that the author appreciates your input.

	Strongly Agree				*Strongly Disagree*
This text was helpful to me	1	2	3	4	5
The text seemed complete	1	2	3	4	5
The artwork was helpful	1	2	3	4	5
More explanations were needed	1	2	3	4	5
The book was well edited	1	2	3	4	5
More explanations of research would help	1	2	3	4	5

Please write additional comments below or on the back of this form.

CHAPTER 1

EFFECTIVE TEACHING IN SPECIAL EDUCATION

OBJECTIVES

Upon completion of this chapter, you should be able to:

1. Identify the types of research studies that make up the effective teaching research.
2. Define pacing, monitoring, feedback, academic learning time, and other terms from the effective teaching literature.
3. Discuss an intervention study that demonstrates the relationship between time-on-task and achievement.
4. Identify three types of research thrusts in the research on teaching.
5. Discuss the reasons for the development of the resource rooms within the context of mainstreaming.
6. Describe five separate types of resource rooms.
7. Describe the three most common types of curricular content in resource rooms.
8. Discuss the daily activities common in a self-contained class.
9. Discuss the purpose of the instructional areas within the room and the types of instruction recommended for each area.
10. Identify three aspects of individualized instruction.
11. Discuss the types of activities for which group instruction is appropriate.
12. Define a task card approach to individualized instruction and draw several task card formats.
13. Identify the grading options for special education teachers who must give grades on report cards.
14. Identify the components of an individualized education plan (IEP).

KEYWORDS

effective teaching
Carroll's model
time-on-task
engaged time
opportunity to learn
BTES
quality of instruction
content coverage
pacing
academic learning time
monitoring
student accountability
feedback
higher level questions
small group
Cascade of Services
resource room
self-contained
cross-categorical
basic skill approach
tutorial approach
functional curriculum
consultation
engineered classroom
learning center
task card approach
components of individual education plans (IEPs)

EFFECTIVE TEACHING BEHAVIORS

Teachers are born, not made.

Teaching is an art, not a science.

Teaching is a matter of personality, not grades in school.

You learn to teach by teaching, not in a college class.

As a student in a methods course in special education, you have, no doubt, heard some of these remarks or others like them. Needless to say, these are the remarks you hear in the hallway before the materials and methods class begins, rather than in the class itself. Although there may have been some truth to these remarks when education was in its infancy, today we can state that these are at best half-truths. In fact, unlike 30 years ago, we now know what types of behaviors effective teachers engage in to increase the academic achievement of the students in their classes. Although teaching does frequently call for informed professional judgement, many of the decisions may be guided by scientific evidence concerning the types of options a teacher has built into the classroom environment. Finally, individuals who enter the classroom without appropriate preparation in methods classes, taught by an informed and experienced teacher, generally do not last long in the class before losing control completely. Although laboratory experiences (both pre-student teaching and student teaching itself) are crucial, the material concerning effective teaching that can be learned from methods and materials classes is also crucial.

This chapter explores the research on effective teaching behaviors. Although most of this research has been done in elementary classrooms, the findings are important for special education teachers in inclusive classes, consultative instructional roles, self-contained classes, and resource classes. Given the wealth of this knowledge and the information that can now be provided for preservice and inservice teachers, any text used in a methods course must begin with a review of this information.

Thus this chapter begins with a general discussion on the direction of research on teaching over the last three decades. Then the specific findings on the research on teaching are reviewed, in order to provide guidelines for structuring educational time in the classroom. Finally, a discussion on effective strategies for use in inclusive classes and various special education classes is presented, in order to identify potential differences in the behaviors teachers should use.

Research on Teaching

Three Different Approaches. Although it is difficult to imagine a doctor, lawyer, or engineer dismissing the importance of the courses that taught practical methods in their respective fields, it is somewhat more common for preservice and inservice teachers to denigrate the materials and methods courses as less than effective in communicating useful knowledge about how to teach. Unfortunately, a brief look at the research on teaching will lend some support to this perspective.

Research on educational practices in the classroom has generally involved attention to three distinct areas: teacher personality, curriculum, and teacher behavior (Bloom, 1980; Brophy, 1976, 1986; Greenwood, 1991; Lanier & Glassberg, 1981; Wyne & Stuck, 1982). Research in the first area—teacher personality—was conducted initially, and attention to that area has not been particularly helpful in suggesting effective ways to teach.

During the early years of this century, educational research generally included attempts to delineate the personalities of effective teachers (Bloom, 1980). For example, the evaluations of teachers' effectiveness completed by supervisors would be correlated with various personality measures (Lanier & Glassberg, 1981). Such research studies are clearly founded on the assumption that "teachers are born, not made." Numerous studies demonstrated only very tentative results, however, and during the late 1960s this type of research study became less frequent (Lanier & Glassberg, 1981). Simply put, this type of research produced very little useful knowledge.

A second area of research consisted of studies on the curriculum (Brophy, 1976). It is quite clear that a student's exposure to particular areas of knowledge does affect what that student learns. However, during the early years, this area of research tended to concentrate on major curricular content areas, not on specific curricular design features that might improve learning. Consequently, like the earlier research on personality, early research on curriculum did not yield guidelines for what a teacher should actually do in a classroom to increase student performance.

The third area of research has proven much more useful in providing guidelines for teachers. Researchers in the 1960s began to concentrate on what teachers actually did in the class. This body of research is sometimes referred to as process–product research because teacher behavior—the teaching process—is assumed to affect the students' learning—the educational product (Brophy, 1986). In fact, a number of studies done within the last 20 years have clearly demonstrated the effectiveness of certain types of teaching behaviors for improving student achievement. As a result of this research, we can now stipulate the types of things an effective teacher should do in class. This body of research tended to focus on teacher behaviors in terms of time, and is still very influential in education today (Greenwood, 1991).

Historical Roots: Time and Learning. Many scholars associate the process–product research with John Carroll's theoretical model of time and learning (Greenwood, 1991; Kavale & Forness, 1986; Wyne & Stuck, 1982). In 1963, Carroll presented a novel definition of learning aptitude in which he defined aptitude as a function of time spent learning in relation to the time needed to learn.

APTITUDE = TIME SPENT/TIME NEEDED

Each of the variables was further refined over the last 35 years. For example, time spent learning represents a combination of opportunity to learn material—related to the curriculum research discussed earlier—and the students' perseverance in learning. Student perseverance is sometimes called time-on-task or engaged time. Interest Box 1.1 identifies the two types of research studies that

INTEREST BOX 1.1
Time-on-Task and Learning

Time-on-task is one of the most important variables for increasing achievement in public school classes. Two different types of research studies have demonstrated this importance. First, a number of "correlation studies" have shown the relationship between time-on-task and achievement (see Hoge and Luce, 1979). Correlation studies demonstrate a mathematical relationship between different scores for a given group of subjects. Generally, in the early correlation studies researchers would conduct an observation of a student's time-on-task behavior in the classroom and relate these scores to student achievement. Those studies consistently demonstrated that the higher the on-task behavior of the students, the higher the achievement. Correlations between these two variables generally range between .30 and .60 (Hoge and Luce, 1979), which compare favorably to the relationship between IQ and achievement—one of the strongest relationships in educational research.

One problem with correlation studies is that they demonstrate only relationships. They cannot be used to show that one variable causes change in another variable. For that purpose experimental or "treatment" studies are needed. In an experimental treatment study, subjects are randomly assigned to a treatment or a control group, and the independent variable is directly manipulated. The treatment studies in the time-on-task literature generally use a behavioral treatment in which the student is rewarded for on-task behavior (see Wyne and Stuck, 1979), and these studies have shown that when time-on-task increases, achievement increases.

demonstrate the importance of engaged time in changing student achievement.

The time needed to learn is composed of three variables. First, each student requires a different amount of time to learn a particular task, and this is defined as an individual learner's aptitude. Second, the ability to understand instructions represents a student's ability to verbally understand the requirements of the task. Finally, the quality of instruction represents the teacher's ability to present information in a manner understandable to the individual student.

Many of the studies in research on teaching may be related conceptually to the several variables in this model of learning aptitude (Greenwood, 1991; Wyne & Stuck, 1982). Interest Box 1.2 presents information on one of the historically important studies in this area.

Although this chapter is not intended to be a review of this entire area, you will want to note the relationship between the recommended behaviors and the variables in this conceptual model. Beginning with the research on teaching effectiveness, educators have the opportunity to learn a great deal about how effective teaching takes place. The degree to which our field implements this knowledge will affect our success in teaching our students and may affect the status of our profession as a whole.

Effective Teacher Behaviors

Opportunity to Learn. In order for students to learn material they must be provided with ample opportunity in which to learn it. A task such as double-digit addition must be introduced appropriately for each individual student, and the student must be provided with enough time to master that task before going on to double-digit addition with regrouping. Thus, opportunity to learn includes the concept of content coverage—actual exposure of the student to the concept or task to be learned—and pacing, or the presentation of new material with appropriate regularity (Brophy, 1986).

The concerns for content coverage and teacher accountability have led to time charting practices in which teachers document the instructional time allocated to particular curriculum material in an effort to demonstrate that the students have been exposed to the content. For example, Greenwood (1991) recently used longitudinal

INTEREST BOX 1.2
BTES Study

The Beginning Teacher Evaluation Study (BTES) (Lambert & Hartsough, 1976) was a study of the teaching effectiveness of beginning teachers in the state of California. Forty-one second grade teachers and 54 fifth grade teachers participated in Phase II of this project. These teachers allowed researchers to visit their classes and to observe the classroom processes systematically. Student behaviors, teacher behaviors, and academic progress for the students in the classes were measured. The results demonstrated that productive on-task behavior was related to achievement in reading and math in both the second and the fifth grade. Also, the proportion of productive time in individual contexts was small, indicating that students need to be monitored by the teacher. In fact, the frequency of independent group and independent individual instruction was negatively related to achievement at both the second and the fifth grade level. This result strongly suggests that the less time students spend in individual seatwork (as compared to teacher-led instruction), the higher their academic progress will be. Clearly, students need to be closely monitored by the teacher in order to maximize the improvement in achievement.

data to demonstrate that students who were at risk for academic problems received less daily instructional time in academic areas than did a comparison group of students who were not at risk. Clearly, this deprivation of academic instructional time may create a retardation in academic progress.

Further, this concern for content coverage has focused awareness on the match between curricular content and the content of tests used in special and remedial education. Obviously, the most effective assessment procedures cover only what the curriculum covers and nothing else.

Pacing the material and the flow of lessons is a skill that requires continued practice. Generally, you should set a brisk pace for the introduction of new material; a task-oriented, no-nonsense approach toward the instructional lessons, and this expectation will be the guiding criterion for student behavior. Keep directions to a minimum, simple and sequential. You may wish to list them on the blackboard and go over them only once. You should instruct the students to begin the assignment only after all the instructions have been completed. Finally, as soon as a student has mastered a task, that student should move on to another task and not waste instructional time on endless review while other members of the group "catch up."

Wyne and Stuck (1982) provide several guidelines that tend to increase the opportunity to learn. The teacher should be time conscious and begin and end lessons precisely on time. Transition time between instructional activities should be kept to a minimum. Activities such as advanced planning, preparation of demonstration problems (on the blackboard or flip chart) prior to the lesson, and rewarding students for beginning tasks on time will effectively increase the time for instruction. Also, the students perceive that the teacher is concerned with effective use of instructional time, thus making the teacher an effective role model.

Monitoring. The importance of monitoring is demonstrated when one considers the student's time-on-task. This time-on-task variable is related to the perseverance variable in Carroll's model and is one of the most important variables in effective teaching research. Also, time-on-task (or engaged time) was the first variable conceptualized in that body of research. However, research quickly demonstrated that students learned more when a fairly high level of success was built into the task. Consequently, researchers developed the concept of academic learning time or the time during which a student is engaged with a learning task at an appropriate level of difficulty. This concept is readily understood in relation to the pacing of material discussed earlier. Although new material should be introduced at a fairly brisk pace, the teacher should not move to another task until the student has demonstrated a high level of success on the present task, because that task is usually a prerequisite for later tasks. The student's lack of knowledge on the first task may lead to failure on later tasks in the series. The student will probably not try these later tasks because they will be too difficult. In contrast, if a student's success rate on a set of problems is too high, the teacher is wasting the student's learning time. An appropriate success rate for most learners is around 80 to 95 percent.

Monitoring comprises a set of teacher behaviors that encourages close scrutiny of the student's behavior and work in an effort to increase academic learning time (Greenwood, 1991; Kounin, Friesen, & Norton, 1966; Wyne & Stuck, 1982). The teacher should monitor both the engaged time of the student and the difficulty the student is having with a particular type of problem. Generally, when students are completing seatwork, the effective teachers are walking quietly through the class, assisting different students with the assignment as required; that is, they are individually monitoring the student's engagement with the academic lesson. The teacher should note the level of success demonstrated by a student's work and should carefully monitor the student's eye contact with the learning task (Wyne & Stuck, 1982). Interest Box 1.3 presents suggestions for effective monitoring of student work.

Quality of Instruction. Improving the quality of instruction must be the concern of every effective teacher. The teacher must make sure that the task

INTEREST BOX 1.3
Monitoring Behaviors

1. Move through the class when the students are doing seatwork, and observe the success rate of the students and their time-on-task.
2. Use frequent verbal cues to bring a student back to task without being overly punishing. Ask a student the next question and "give a hint," including the page on which the answer can be found.
3. Use physical proximity as a cue to get back on task. Merely keep speaking (or doing whatever you were doing) and gradually move to the side of the student who is off-task. This will usually result in the student beginning the task again.
4. Eliminate reinforcement for being off-task. Move students away from others with whom they frequently whisper.
5. Reinforcement of on-task behavior will often increase such behavior in others. If Billy is off-task, reinforce Martina who sits next to Billy with two extra minutes of free time. This will usually result in Billy choosing to return to task.
6. Never allow yourself to be overly distracted by one student's work. Even while you are helping a student with a seatwork problem, you should continually scan the room at frequent intervals and verbally cue other students to return to task.

to be learned is consistent with what the student needs. This may be particularly difficult in special education settings that, by definition, include a number of students functioning at widely discrepant grade levels in almost every subject. However, certain curricular materials that are currently available on the commercial market do facilitate the appropriate match between learners in special education classes and curricular needs. Scholars who specialize in direct instructional techniques have concentrated on design features of curriculum materials for various special education populations, thus increasing the effective instructional behaviors of the teachers. Complete discussion of this instructional approach is presented in Chapter 4.

There are guidelines for teachers that emphasize methods of improving the quality of instruction (Kavale & Forness, 1986; Wyne & Stuck, 1982). First, the teacher should communicate with the student concerning the expectations for the task. Learning tasks should be selected by the teacher rather than by the student. These tasks should be selected at an appropriate level of difficulty that will yield a high success rate, but not a perfect score.

Student Accountability. One of the most important aspects of effective instruction is the responsibility the student feels for the learning. Students must "own" the learning in order to realize academic gain, and teachers can encourage this ownership of responsibility by students. Students should be apprised of the usefulness of the learning task in real life situations. If you, as the teacher, cannot justify to a student the need to learn something, do not teach it. Some type of frequent, active student response should be built into every lesson, and this should be viewed as an opportunity for rewarding correct responses. Students should be required to hand in regular products of learning such as homework, written work in class, and class notes to be checked. These frequent assignments become the vehicle for communication between student and teacher concerning the strengths and weaknesses of the work and providing further clarification of the teacher's expectations. Also, regular assignments give the student the belief that learning is occurring, and they identify these products as evidence of learning.

Finally, students should be constantly shown evidence of their own progress. For example, a student-maintained record of spelling test scores for each weekly test throughout the year will facilitate communication between the teacher and student and may serve as a motivator for student improvement.

Feedback for the Student. Several of the suggestions mentioned above deal with learner feedback. A student needs effective feedback in order to know that his or her work is progressing as the teacher would like. Also, one of the most important aspects of education is providing feedback to the learner when things are not going well. It may come as a shock to many teachers, but teachers can teach most effectively when students make errors. If a student completes a math worksheet perfectly, that student did not need instruction from the teacher. Similarly, a student who makes errors on every second problem on the math worksheet is probably completing a worksheet written at a level too advanced for that student. However, the student who experiences a high enough success rate to maintain his or her motivation to complete the work, but still makes several errors, is appropriately placed in relation to the difficulty of the work; that student is ready for instruction. The effective teacher will praise the student for the high success rate (and such praise will sound substantive rather than hollow), and then proceed to discuss the problems on which the student made errors. Those are the problems that illustrate the student's lack of understanding of the task, and that is where feedback should be concentrated.

In some sense, the most effective instruction may be viewed as a continuing dance between learner, task, and teacher's feedback. Effective instruction is individually planned to yield the necessary success rate (80 to 95 percent) and the necessary error rate (5 to 20 percent). Feedback should concentrate on the task (without denigrating the learner) and provide information on how the errors may be corrected. When such correction takes place, the student should receive full credit for the work as a reward for work well done. The learner should typically receive as much or more praise for redoing problems with errors as for doing the problems correctly the first time, because the problems with errors have to be done twice. Feedback should make the learner feel successful in progressing toward personal learning goals.

Questioning Strategies. One specialized form of feedback is the questioning strategy employed by teachers (Brophy, 1986). For example, the questions that teachers ask students in verbal interchange can generally be grouped into two distinct types: lower-level questions (basically rote recall of factual material, etc.), and higher-level questions (questions that involve synthesis, drawing conclusions, or inference). Originally, the assumption was made that higher-level questions would elicit higher-level thinking among students. However, research has shown mixed results (Brophy, 1986), and a combination of higher- and lower-level questions is probably most appropriate.

The sequencing and timing of questions is probably also of importance. For example, if the teacher wishes to probe for a new idea, a higher-level question followed by several lower-level questions to follow up on the details may be the most appropriate sequence (Brophy, 1986). Also, prior to asking a second question, the teacher should provide ample waiting and thinking time. Many student teachers rush through questions without waiting for the students to answer, with the result that students train such teachers to quickly provide the answers to their own questions. This is obviously not effective instruction. Awareness of these issues during questioning periods will probably heighten your effectiveness as a teacher. Also, you will wish to remain cognizant of the continuing research on questions and appropriate question formats.

Instructional Grouping. One question faced by every teacher concerns the identification of appropriate groups for instruction. Generally, the type of task will provide some indication for the instructional group in large, inclusive mainstream classes. For example, new material in subject content areas (history, science, health, etc.) is usually introduced to the entire class as a whole group activity. This is typically followed by individual seatwork and homework that is used to monitor comprehension. In certain basic skill subjects such as reading and math, the typical elementary class includes several smaller instructional groups at different achievement levels.

Research on effective teaching has demonstrated that elementary students learn best when they are taught in small groups led by the teacher (Brophy, 1986; Glass & Smith, 1979). This is probably a function of low levels of time-on-task in both whole group activities (where the teacher must monitor the on-task behavior of 25 or 30 students) and individual seatwork (in which on-task behavior is not monitored). The teacher should be the active agent in presenting information to the small group. This should be done in a brisk, businesslike fashion, without leaving anyone behind. Obviously, the mandate for individualized instruction upon which special education is built has some bearing on the degree of whole group instruction in special education classes. This issue is explored further in the discussion of task card instruction.

Effective Teaching Research for Special Education

Each of the recommendations that has been made is based on research in elementary mainstream classes, and the numerous differences between these classes and special education classes or today's inclusive mainstream classes in the school indicate the need to view these recommendations with some caution. For example, the cognitive level of a self-contained class for pupils with mild intellectual disabilities may have some bearing on the types of question formats a teacher chooses to use. Also, a resource class or inclusive class that includes children with emotional or behavioral disabilities may have to make certain adjustments in the recommendations concerning student responsibility.

Still, it is important to remember that most children and youth with mild to moderate disabilities are more similar to average functioning children than they are different. For example, the recommendations concerning monitoring are just as appropriate in special education classes as they are in mainstream elementary classes. When you organize your class and get to know your students, you will begin to develop an understanding of the effective teaching behaviors discussed in this section, and you will then be able to decide which behaviors to increase and which to decrease in order to facilitate a healthy learning atmosphere in your class.

TYPES OF SPECIAL EDUCATION INSTRUCTIONAL SETTINGS

With some grasp of effective instructional behaviors, the beginning teacher should next investigate the types of special education instructional settings used in schools today. Historically, the responsibility of the special education teacher generally centered around the special education class itself (Evans, 1981), though this is changing with the new emphasis on inclusion of children with disabilities in mainstream classes (Tindal, Parker, & Germann, 1990). Because of this new emphasis, many special education teachers also have some responsibility for consultation with mainstream teachers. Consequently, it is important for new teachers to have some understanding of the types of instructional responsibilities typically used in schools today for delivery of services to students with mild and moderate disabilities. Also, understanding of the rationale for the development of these diverse special education instructional settings will help clarify the types of curriculum thrusts included in each type of setting.

During the 1960s and early 1970s, various courts throughout the United States assertively stated that children with disabilities have a right to education at public expense. Although some schools did include full-time special education classes—now known as self-contained classes—others did not. The law that mandated services for all children with disabilities was already being discussed and would be enacted in 1975. In short, it was quite apparent that the public schools needed some conceptual framework from which to formulate a range of options for educating children with disabilities.

In this political context, Deno (1970) proposed a model of special education practices that has become known as a "cascade of services." This model specified 7 types of educational settings for children with disabilities, ranging from maintenance in a hospital setting to full-time mainstream placement. This article by Deno is crucial historically, and all students of the field should have some familiarity with its concepts. Within the model of services, two types of nonmainstream classes were recommended for in-school placements. These became the resource room and the self-contained class, and the vast majority of students with mild and moderate disabilities have been served in these two special education placements for the last two decades.

The Self-Contained Class

As mentioned previously, the self-contained class was one of the earlier types of educational settings used to serve children and youth with disabilities. Although the legal thrust to mainstream children with disabilities has decreased the frequency of self-contained classes as compared to resource rooms and inclusive mainstream classes, many children are still served in self-contained classes. For example, according to many teachers in special education, the student with severe behavioral disorders, one who occasionally suffers from "hearing voices," and the autistic child who is self-abusive can rarely be mainstreamed. However, these children clearly do not need programs as restrictive as the home-based or hospital-based programs portrayed in Deno's (1970) cascade of services. Consequently, many practitioners believe that the self-contained class is a necessary educational option in these situations, and most school districts have at least some children with disabilities served in this type of instructional setting.

Generally, if children's disabilities are severe enough to warrant placement in a self-contained class, they are probably severe enough to necessitate instruction designed specifically for that type of disability. Although Bender, Scott, and McLaughlin (1993) have recommended grouping children with mild disabilities together for instruction, few scholars would support such grouping of students with severe disabilities. Even in states like North Carolina, where a noncategorical model of service delivery is the norm for resource room programming, the self-contained classes are identified with particular disabilities. This is understandable, as it would clearly be difficult for one teacher to educate a child with a severe learning disability, a child with autism, and a child with severe behavioral disabilities in the same class.

For this reason, any description of curriculum content of self-contained classes will vary considerably with the populations served in each class. Also, much of the curricular emphasis in self-contained classes has no counterpart in the general curriculum. For example, a class for children with behavioral disabilities or emotional disturbances may include values clarification training and emotional crisis intervention, whereas classes for students with autism usually include basic language development activities.

The Daily Schedule. Although the curriculums in self-contained classes may be very diverse, the schedule for self-contained classes generally follows a predetermined plan. Interest Box 1.4 presents a sample daily schedule of a self-contained class.

The schedule includes several components that provide both group and individual instructional time. Also, the noninstructional time, such as recess, lunch, and toilet activities are included so that the teacher can tell students in advance what to expect. This type of structuring can reduce the uncertainty for many students with disabilities, and may alleviate some students' behavior problems.

Although such scheduling seems rather elementary to the beginning teacher, one must realize

INTEREST BOX 1.4
A Sample Daily Schedule for a Self-Contained Class

Activity	Time
Opening Exercises	8:30 – 9:00
Instructional Period	9:00 – 9:30
Instructional Period	9:30 –10:00
Recess	10:00 –10:30
Group Sharing Time	10:30 –11:15
Instructional Period	11:15 –11:45
Instructional Period	11:45 –12:05
Lunch	12:05 –12:40
Class Project	12:40 – 1:45
Instructional Period	1:45 – 2:15
Instructional Period	2:15 – 2:45
Closing Exercises	2:45 – 3:15

Note: Each set of instructional periods is preceded by an in-class activity that requires talking and social exchange. This provides some time for students to "calm down" after activities on the playground or lunch period.

that the types of students who are in self-contained programs are likely to need this structural congruence from one day to the next. Students need to be aware of the anticipated lunch or the next instructional activity, because this will generally lead to some degree of security in the routine. For this reason, it is advisable to put the daily schedule on a chart and display it in front of the class. You may wish to refer to it several times each day, and ask children what activity comes next as you point to the next task on the chart. Finally, principals and supervisors tend to view such a daily plan as one indication of effective instruction and will generally base their observations of new teachers on the plan presented to them.

The Opening Exercises. The opening exercises generally include activities that the child completes upon arrival in the morning. Depending on the ability levels of the children, the teacher may need to be involved in removing coats from the students and seating them in the appropriate area. When the children are seated, the group exercises may begin. These typically include counting lunch money, saluting the flag, discussion of the weather outside, the day of the week, holidays that are approaching, or activities that the students engaged in over the last weekend. Many teachers find that visual aids prepared for this purpose assist in the morning exercises. Flannel boards that depict various "weather clothes" and a flag may be helpful. A large calendar may also be used.

Morning exercises are conducted at the discretion of the teacher, though some type of morning exercise is recommended for a variety of reasons. First, the exercises give the students a brief time to calm down and get used to the school classroom again. Such an orientation period is required by some students. Second, the activities are generally done as a group, and can provide opportunity for social interaction between the students. Finally, the exercises can provide a brief opportunity for the use of academic skills. For example, a calendar activity may be used for children who can count to ten, with a student pointing at each of the days until an approaching holiday.

Instructional Periods. During the various instructional periods the teacher and the paraprofessional may find themselves working with one child or several. Generally, the student/teacher ratio prevents a teacher from concentrating exclusively on one child for an entire instructional period, though this can be done for more brief periods of time. In short, the teacher should work individually with a child in situations where assessment is involved or in situations where the child's behavior and actions require such a one-to-one instructional situation. On other occasions, the paraprofessional may work with the child or the child may work as a member of an instructional group.

Instructional sessions should be planned to take 20 to 30 minutes, as this time length gives the teacher the maximum amount of flexibility in planning without becoming overworked. Shorter times would require more activities per day, whereas longer time periods are unrealistic given the attentional capabilities of most children and youth with moderate disabilities. Finally, if a particular student requires more brief assignments and activities, that student can easily be given two activities of 15 minutes each during the structured 30-minute instructional time.

Group Sharing Time. Many teachers find that a group sharing time is useful in order to "put the students on stage." Such a time can be used to discuss the family activities the previous night or a recent weekend trip by class members. The teacher may wish to "share" certain class projects that particular class members did well. Students should be encouraged to actively participate and share their sources of pride and accomplishment. This activity will quickly become one to which the students look forward.

Class Project. A class project should be a regular part of the school day. It can be a brief movie or a long-term project for display at parent–teacher meetings or in the school display case. It should be something that the students want to do and in which they take pride. For example, in one self-contained class for students with behavioral disorders, the class studied dinosaurs and made a large model from plaster and newspaper (6 ft. tall). These third through sixth graders then assisted in judging the "Dinosaur Contest," in which each class in the school entered a similar project. Such a visible activity, with judging done in front of the whole school, did a great deal for the morale of the students in this class. This teacher had used a class project to combat the negative effects of labeling and gave the class a positive identity as judges of the contest.

Closing Exercises. Closing exercises may be thought of as the opening exercises in reverse. Generally, teachers use the closing exercise period as a time for orientation to the task of going home. First, students must put on their weather clothes, and teachers may wish to discuss the weather outside and how it may have changed during the day. Some teachers have to remind students each day of the bus number or walk students to the bus. Others may discuss what color the parent's car is and where it will be parked. The exercises are designed to not disrupt the continuity of the day for the children, even though the setting is changing.

Effectiveness of Self-Contained Classes. Both the early research and more modern comparisons have demonstrated that students in self-contained classes do not do as well as students maintained in mainstream classes (Glass, 1983; Dunn, 1968). Such results are contrary to the results discussed later regarding effectiveness of the resource room (Sindelar & Deno, 1978). This is because most students in resource rooms were also mainstreamed usually for four-fifths of the instructional time each day and the influence of higher expectations and better role models in the mainstream class is shown in the student's achievement. However, the student in the self-contained class has role models that are not optimal and is functioning in an environment where the expectations for academic growth may be lower. Therefore, the academic growth will probably be lower.

Research outcomes such as this one cannot be used to argue that all children should be mainstreamed, as mainstream classes may be inappropriate for some children and youth with severe disabilities unless a great deal of support for the teacher is provided. However, both the research results and legal statute demonstrate that children and youth with disabilities should be maintained in the least restrictive environment. Teachers should be aware of this legal mandate and be prepared to challenge, in a professional manner, any placement that seems unduly restrictive. A student should be given every opportunity and every support in order to be maintained in an inclusive placement or the mainstream/resource combination before being placed in a self-contained class.

The Resource Room

The resource room is a concept that has historical roots in both special education and remedial education for slow learners (Cohen, 1982). Basically, the resource room was developed in response to the need for some specialized training for students with mild to moderate disabilities who were mainstreamed during the majority of the school day. The resource room was identified as a short-term intervention, initially conceived of as an adjunct placement to the regular mainstream class. Also, the curricular emphases in the resource rooms are very similar to the general curriculum. Children in resource room placement generally go to the resource room for one or two periods each day, though such time arrangements generally remain flexible. Today, resource placement is by far the most common type of placement for students with mild disabilities, although the number of placements in inclusive classes seems to be growing. These inclusive placements are described in Chapter 2.

Because students who are in resource rooms are generally in mainstream classes for the majority of the day, this is one level of special education where special educators and mainstream teachers must interact closely to provide an appropriate educational program. For this reason, it is crucial that special education resource teachers understand the interaction with mainstream teachers, discussed below and in Chapter 2.

Types of Resource Rooms. D'Alonzo, D'Alonzo, and Mauser (1979) identified five separate types of resource room programming for children with disabilities. These are presented in Interest Box 1.5. As these definitions indicate, the concept of resource room programming is a multifaceted theoretical concept, and various states use different types of resource placement. For example, in some states—New Jersey, Virginia, and West Virginia are examples—children and youth with mild intellectual disabilities, learning disabilities, and emotional or behavioral disabilities will be placed in the same cross-categorical resource room program in addition to their mainstream class placement. In other states, these students may be in the same mainstream class while attending separate, categorical resource programs.

Curricular Content in Resource Rooms. Given these differences in the available types of resource programming, there is every reason to expect a certain degree of confusion about the appropriate content areas for resource rooms, as well as the appropriate theoretical focus for the resource programs. In one of the few data-based studies available, Deshler, Lowrey, and Alley (1979) surveyed 98 secondary teachers from 48 states to identify the curricular content in special education classes. The most popular curricular approach, found in 45 percent of the classes, was a basic skill remediation approach. In other words, regardless of the administrative structure of these programs, the curriculum emphasized basic skills instruction using materials and strategies from reading and math instructional theories for lower-achieving students.

A tutorial approach—where resource teachers actually tutor students in subject areas from secondary classes—was the second most popular approach, with 24 percent of the classes using this curriculum thrust. Finally, an approach that stressed functional or "survival" curriculum, including survival words, driver's education, job applications, and other survival skills from various life situations, was the third most popular curriculum thrust, with 17 percent of the sample indicating that this model was in use.

Most common is the resource room, which uses a combination of these curriculum thrusts.

INTEREST BOX 1.5
Resource Room Types

- *Categorical resource rooms* serve only students who have one particular disability. A resource room for students with learning disabilities would include only those students; students with mental retardation would go to another resource room. New York uses this type of program.
- *Cross-categorical resource rooms* serve groups with several disabilities functioning at about the same gross achievement levels. Learning disabled, educable mentally retarded, and behaviorally disordered are often placed together in this type of resource room. North Carolina and Virginia use this type of resource room organization.
- *Noncategorical resource rooms* serve as the resource room for all children with disabilities in states that do not recognize categorical distinctions. New Jersey is considering a new state plan for special education in which students would be identified as "needing resource placement" rather than categorized by handicapping condition.
- *Specific skills resource rooms* aim their curricular content at one basic skill area (usually reading or math) and may serve the mildly handicapped and other low achievers. Texas, Tennessee, and Georgia use this type of program.
- *Itinerant resource programs* are programs in which student visits to the resource room are not scheduled on a daily basis. Rural areas with very small schools in difficult to reach locations may provide one resource teacher for several schools, which he or she visits every other day. Mountainous states such as West Virginia and Kentucky use this model of resource service.

Source: D'Alonzo, D'Alonzo, and Mauser (1979).

However, the question of which content areas should be stressed in a resource room will remain unresolved for the immediate future (Haight, 1985). Each of the three curriculum thrusts has proponents and critics. The advantages and criticisms for each are presented in Interest Box 1.6 (Carlson, 1985; Haight, 1985).

Effectiveness of Resource Rooms. Research has shown that resource room placement is an effective educational alternative for many students with mild and moderate disabilities (Sindelar & Deno, 1978). Specifically, the studies that compared the mainstream placement alone to the combination of mainstream and resource placement suggest that the latter is more effective in increasing academic achievement among children and youth with mild disabilities. However, the research, as reviewed by Sindelar and Deno (1978), is more supportive of resource programming for students with learning disabilities or behavioral disabilities than for students with intellectual disabilities.

A second concern in the research is lack of support for resource room placement in increasing personal and social adjustment (Sindelar & Deno, 1978). Since one of the original goals of mainstreaming was to provide nonhandicapped role models for children and youth with disabilities in order to increase their social skills, this lack of support in increasing social adjustment is of great concern. Clearly, more emphasis on social skills and social adjustment is needed in many special education resource classes.

INTEREST BOX 1.6
Advantages and Disadvantages of Various Curricula

Approach	Advantages	Disadvantages
Basic Skills	stresses basic reading and math skills, which improve success in mainstream classes	turns special educator into a basic skills tutor or reading tutor
	emphasizes only skills necessary for success in school	eliminates teaching of specialized methods, which are replaced by remedial instruction
	easily modeled on the elementary curriculum	
Tutorial in Subject Areas	complements the entire school curriculum rather than just basic skills	forces special teacher to teach subjects for which the teacher may not be certified
	mainstream subject area teachers usually appreciate the help	may overlook skills essential for life in order to cover the subject areas
	usually consistent with state-adopted curriculum requirements	
Functional	stresses essential skill areas used later in life	represents a view of potential which is pessimistic
	handicapped kids see the relevance of this content	students may miss certain skills

Source: Carlson (1985).

Consultation and Inclusive Mainstream Instruction

During the past several years, a number of consultative services have been provided for students with mild to moderate disabilities within the mainstream class (Tindal, Parker, & Germann, 1987). In a consultant service model, a person with specialized training in special education instruction will serve as a consultant to the mainstream teacher, and that person may even enter the mainstream class while the class is in session in order to instruct the students with disabilities in the class. The consultant may also have the responsibilities of providing instructional suggestions that the mainstream teacher can implement with particular students.

Further, since 1990 a number of professionals have participated in inclusive mainstream instruction, in which both a special education teacher and a mainstream teacher actually co-teach in the mainstream environment on a daily basis. Because these types of special education service delivery are relatively recent, an entire chapter in this volume (Chapter 2) has been devoted to inclusive instruction and consultation responsibilities for working with mainstream teachers.

ARRANGEMENT OF THE CLASS

Considerations of room organization for special education classes must be guided by concerns about the types of activities planned. This section should enable you, as a teacher, to consider the types of educational activities that may be conducted in various areas in your room. Also, both resource and self-contained classes are physically arranged in a similar manner, and the discussion below presents suggestions appropriate for both. Many of these concepts in room arrangement can be traced back to Frank Hewett (1967), who recommended certain arrangements in his "engineered classroom." In this framework, the class was designed to be an environment that facilitated (engineered) the growth of the child through availability of appropriate rewards. The class environment included areas for mastery work on basic skills as well as secluded areas for individual study, based on the demonstrated attention problems of some students with disabilities. The class was intended for students with emotional disabilities, though more recent adaptations of these ideas may be found in many texts on instructional methods for students with various disabilities. Figure 1.1

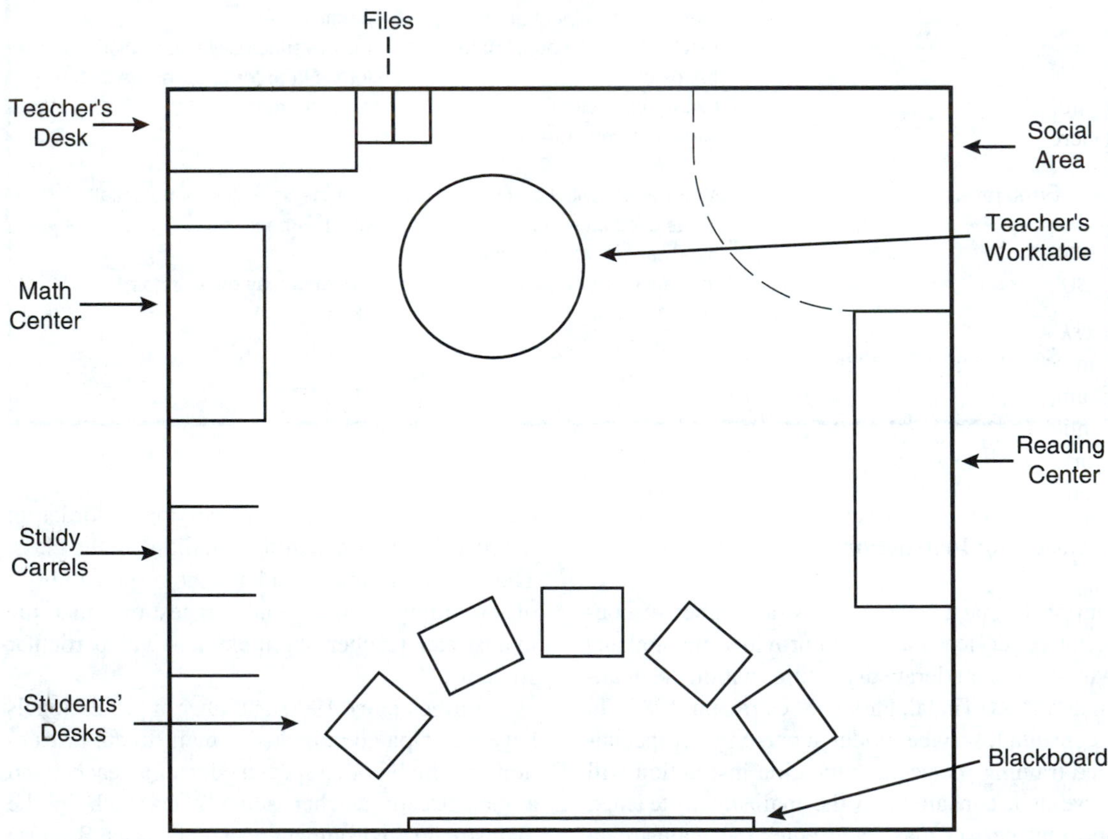

FIGURE 1.1 Recommended Classroom Arrangement

presents a diagram of a classroom arrangement that includes the various necessary instructional and noninstructional areas.

Large- and Small-Group Instruction

Because special education law mandated individualized instructional procedures, large- and small-group instruction should involve only a small percentage of the child's instructional time. For example, Westling, Koorland, and Rose (1981) report that special education teachers who were rated as superior used large-group instruction much less than special education teachers who were rated average. However, such activities as morning exercises, simulation games, sharing time, audiovisual instruction, or social skills instruction may require an area that allows all of the students to attend to the teacher at the same time. If this area is furnished with individual desks (rather than tables, for example) the area may also double for individual seat work or worksheets. There should be enough desks for each student to have a place to use as a home base.

Furniture Arrangements and Instructional Areas

Desk Arrangement. The arrangement of desks can facilitate the management of the class. For example, if all of the desks face the board in a semicircular pattern, the teacher can monitor the work of the entire group and assist particular children by walking around the outside of the semicircle. This arrangement allows the teacher to face all members of the class. The obvious disadvantage is that each child is facing the other children and this may cause inattentive behavior. You, as the teacher, should consider the advantages and disadvantages of the semicircular arrangement compared to the more traditional straight-row arrangement, and make the choice that seems more comfortable to you and your class.

Learning Centers. Learning centers may be included at the inclination of the teacher. Because such a high percentage of time is spent on basic skills, centers in both reading/language arts and math seem to be a minimum. Other teachers, depending on their class maturity and teaching responsibilities, also include a center for science, social science, and/or other subject areas. Materials that should be included in various learning centers are discussed below.

Teacher's Worktable. The teacher should have a worktable located such that the teacher can scan the entire room while working with one student at a time. Although this requires that the worktable be located somewhere at the front of the room, it does not have to be the focal point of the front area. Also, many special education teachers find that they prefer not to use the teacher's desk as a worktable. The desk is used for writing assignments and grading papers at the end of the day, along with bookkeeping matters, such as lunch money collection and attendance records. Consequently, desks tend to have a lot of noninstructional material on them. The worktable, on the other hand, can be kept clear of everything except the instructional materials in use.

Social Area. Many social activities, such as sharing time, group games, or class projects, require a nonfurnished area. This area may be partially carpeted and generally includes some nearby shelves. A screen for viewing films together may also be placed here.

Time-Out Area. A small area, removed from the class, should be designated as the time-out area. This is a space where a student can be isolated from any possibility of reinforcement for brief periods of time. It should not be a space in the hall, because hallways can be one of the more interesting spaces in a school building, and because it should be located in a manner that allows you to monitor the child who is in time-out. Time-out procedures are discussed in more detail in Chapter 3.

Study Carrels. Study carrels are essential in many special education classes, because of the high levels of distractibility demonstrated by many students with disabilities. Generally, these can be lined up along one wall and may be used for seatwork. In some cases, the students feel better about using these areas if they are labeled "office" (Hewett, 1967). These can easily be constructed by cutting out the bottom and one side from a cardboard box, and, after the student decorates the remaining portion, taping it around the top of the individual desk. One important fact to remember is that if a student needs a place to work that is free of visual distraction, one must be provided in order to assist the student to remain task oriented.

Furthermore, some students are also disturbed by auditory distraction. Consequently, soft music played continuously in class becomes a type of background noise (white noise) and may facilitate higher work output. However, one person's relaxation music is another person's distraction. In some instances, you may wish to provide soft music through earphones to only one or two students. Regardless of how you resolve this, you must be careful of the effects of such music on all of the students in your class.

The Learning Centers

Both self-contained classes and resource room programs use the learning center instructional organization. Also, many inclusive mainstream classes utilize learning centers. The center provides a set of materials that students can use as a group or individually.

Learning Center Materials. The materials that should be included in each learning center should be obtained before school begins, and a list of desired materials for each center should be kept. Constraints on the budget often have as much bearing on the materials as the preferred materials list. However, principals and media center persons often have some "leftover" money at year's end, and they will request from teachers a list of desired instructional materials. Keeping a list throughout the year is much more useful than preparing one when asked to do so.

You should obtain several complete sets of basal reading and basal math texts used in your school district. Because the eventual goal of special education is to be able to mainstream all children with disabilities, the availability of mainstream materials can facilitate this process. If students are working on reading and/or language arts, they should read a story at their reading comprehension level every day, as well as complete some type of reading comprehension and language arts activity. The overall goal is to have the students working at or near their grade level with the same materials used in the mainstream class. You may also want to get other texts that a number of your students use, particularly in departmentalized schools. Also, this enables you, as the special education teacher, to become more familiar with the general education curriculum, which will assist you with your consultative and/or inclusive teaching responsibilities. This familiarity with the school curriculum has been identified as a desirable characteristic of the "superior" special education teacher because it facilitates consultative communication (McLaughlin & Kelly, 1982).

Next, inventory your class to get some idea of the educational materials already available. These may include computer software, educational games and manipulatives, and gameboards for multiple uses. Remember to seek out the media specialist/librarian and inquire whether materials are available for long- or short-term loan to a particular class. In many cases, with special permission you may be able to check out materials for use for a week or a month. Also, obtain some materials for students with disabilities who have no measurable reading skills. Most students with disabilities can match the written assignment instructions with the labels of the various centers in your class, and you will want some materials for them. This will enable most students to obtain their own assignments.

Learning Center Organization. Centers are usually organized around subject areas, with one center for reading/language arts and one for mathematics. The learning center should be set up in such a way that, with three (or fewer) pieces of information, any child can find the correct assignment. Obviously, with certain learners, the expectation that they obtain their own materials is inappropriate. However, for the vast majority of students with disabilities, this is a valid expectation that encourages children to take responsibility for their own work. Also, this organizational arrangement frees the teacher from having to give out educational materials and results in more teacher-led instructional time. Finally, the student learns some schema for organization from the mechanics of the classroom itself.

A student should be able to obtain an assignment from accurately labeled materials with three pieces of information: (1) the learning center (e.g., Reading Center, Math Center), (2) the type of material (e.g., Language Cards, Time Cards, Activity Box 1), and, finally, (3) the specific assignment (e.g., Red Cards 1–5) must be identified. Such precise sets of instructions can be followed by almost all students with mild disabilities after a few days (or weeks) of practice. This type of instruction can also be followed by third grade students with intellectual disabilities who have no measurable reading skills because they will be able to match the assignments to the labels on each center, each box of materials in each center, and each file folder in each box.

Are You Ready?

Unlike many of the problems faced in teaching, the problem of organization of the room can be dealt with before the children arrive. The beginning teacher may use the list of activities in Interest Box 1.7 as a set of objectives for the first several days of the first year. Completion of these activities will take several days, but your room will be ready, and you will have activities for the first day of school.

INTEREST BOX 1.7
Activities and Preparations for School Opening

1. Prepare learning center materials in reading and math such that students can access them with three specific directions.
2. Arrange the room to facilitate eye contact with each student from the teacher's worktable.
3. Label everything in the room (desk, worktable, file, etc.); students will master an amazing array of nouns over the year.
4. Set up equipment with one or two filmstrips "at the ready," in case you misjudge the time required for a particular educational activity during the first days.
5. Plan for the opening exercises by gathering materials for discussions of weather, the flag, or other topics.
6. Prepare sight word and essential skills word lists for each student to master.
7. Set up an individual work folder for each student.
8. Gather basal reading and elementary math books from the mainstream classes for use in the learning centers.
9. Arrange a long-term checkout for library materials with the media specialist (long-term checkout for equipment also, if possible).
10. Verify the list of students who will attend and arrange schedule with their other teachers. Almost every veteran special education teacher has discovered a new student in their class on the first day of school when no plans have been made for that student.
11. Prepare to begin a job that you will enjoy!

INDIVIDUALIZED INSTRUCTION IN SPECIAL EDUCATION

Once the room and materials are arranged in an appropriate fashion and some type of organizational schedule is worked out for student instructional time, you must prepare for the instruction of the students. Instruction in special education must be individualized and based on the needs of the individual learner. In many cases, an individual educational plan (IEP) has already been prepared for each student, so that the teacher's task is to translate the goals and objectives on the IEP to daily work.

This section is designed to let you know how to make this transition between the IEPs and instructional tasks for the students in your class. First, a discussion of the meaning of individualized instruction is presented. Then, a discussion of a task card approach to individualized instruction is followed by the selection criterion for choosing individual or small-group instructional settings for various types of activities. Finally, a discussion of grading procedures in an individualized instructional system is presented.

Individualized Education Plans

Individualized instruction, based on an individualized education plan, is mandated by law for special education students. However, no further definition of individualized instruction has ever been specified by the federal special education legislation. This leaves many potential types of individualized education programs that may or may not meet the intended criteria for individualized education.

Components of an Effective IEP. Turnbull, Strickland, and Hammer (1978b) list seven components that must be included in an IEP. These are listed in Interest Box 1.8, along with several other items that should be included in the IEP.

INTEREST BOX 1.8
Components of an Individualized Education Program

Turnbull, Strickland, and Hammer (1978b) list seven components of an IEP based on federal legislation. These include: (1) the student's current level of functioning; (2) goals the student is expected to accomplish by the end of each school year; (3) short-term objectives stated in behavioral terms outlining intermediate steps to reach annual goals; (4) the dates on which the services will be initiated and terminated; (5) documentation of the extent to which the student will be included in the regular education program; (6) special education services needed by the student (commonly called related services); and (7) evaluation criteria and procedures to be used for determining mastery of goals and objectives on at least an annual basis.

In the national survey of IEPs, Pyecha (1980) identified two mandated areas frequently left out of IEPs, including proposed evaluation criteria and the extent of participation in the regular education program. As a teacher, you will wish to review each IEP to which you contribute in order to assure that each of the mandated areas is included in a manner that results in increased individualization for the student.

Pyecha (1980) indicated that many IEPs include, in addition to the required components, other relevant nonmandated information. These areas include student descriptors (age, sex, race, grade level, etc.), information about student assessment, general educational history, and the process whereby the IEP was developed. Information of this nature is not necessary but, on occasion, may aid in better understanding of the student.

Generally, these items may be identified as either items for which the special education teacher is responsible or items for which other professionals in the school take responsibility. For example, the special education teacher and mainstream teachers would assume the responsibility for instruction related to the short-term objectives and long-term goals included in the IEP, whereas an assistant principal may assume responsibility for assigning alternative transportation and the guidance counselor may assume responsibility for weekly counseling sessions.

Generally, an IEP should provide a weekly plan for instruction throughout the year. Such a plan would include yearly goals and sequenced objectives for each goal, with at least one objective specified in every area for every week of the school year. A set of objectives from an IEP of this nature is presented in Interest Box 1.9.

This type of IEP is very detailed and will help the teacher to select appropriate instructional materials and worksheets during each week of the academic year. The special education teacher consults the IEP weekly to decide what instructional worksheets and materials to use with a particular child for the coming week. Clearly, the IEP was intended to be a regularly consulted plan for instruction and teachers should keep these in their classes in order to make them useful for instructional planning.

Problems With IEP Utilization. There are several types of problems with the manner in which some school systems develop and use IEPs. As a special education teacher, you should be aware of these problems and work to realize the initial intentions behind the IEP process as described above.

First, many school districts have assumed that individualized education is synonymous with individualized assessment. In other words, if a child is tested individually and placed in a special class, it is presumed that the child is receiving individualized education. However, one look at some special classes would reveal small-group instruction for the entire school day. Is that individualized instruction? Haven't students with mild and moderate disabilities already failed in small-group instructional situations in mainstream classes? Clearly, individualized instruction must go beyond merely individual testing, and instruction in the special education setting should be, at least in part, individualized.

Apparently, some school districts accept the idea that the IEP is merely a paper-wasting exercise and should be done with as little effort as possible. For example, Pyecha (1980), in a national survey of IEPs, presented information that suggested that around 60 percent of the IEPs were not informative for instructional purposes. Many IEPs are merely one or two pages with few detailed objectives and only general goal statements (Pyecha, 1980). Although this may have changed somewhat during the last 15 years, it does seem clear that IEPs of this nature will not be helpful in planning the daily instruction for children and youth with disabilities. The self-fulfilling nature of this premise is obvious: If school personnel believe that IEPs represent wasted time, those personnel will invest very little effort in preparation of the IEPs. Consequently, the IEPs will be very poorly prepared and will not include useful information; this suggests that those IEPs will represent wasted time.

Another type of IEP that may violate the intention for individualized instruction is the standard course IEP. For example, in many secondary schools, students with mild and moderate disabilities are mainstreamed into a standard set of courses that typically include lower-level English classes, general math classes, general sciences classes, and vocational classes. Instead of writing an individual plan for each of the students, the school system has chosen to prepare a list of objectives for each of the courses in the standard "lower-level" curriculum, and when a student with disabilities is mainstreamed into that course, the list of objectives is merely appended to the IEP. These classes are generally taught in group settings, and, in many cases, no individual differentiation is made for any student in these classes. Such a standard course system probably violates the intention behind the individualized instruction provisions of the law.

INTEREST BOX 1.9
A Sample Individualized Educational Program

Identification Information:

Student Name: Benjamin Claxton Grade Level 2 Age 8

Date of IEP 5/6/89 Mainstream Teacher Ms. Jasper

Parents John and Rene Johnson, 105 Ashwood Drive, Berrywells, NC

Home Phone 228-2942 School Woodcliff Elementary

Referral and IEP Conference Information:

Referral by Ms. Jaspers Date Parents were informed 4/12/89

Assessment Information Presented: A grade equivalent score of 1.8 in reading recognition, 1.9 in decoding unknown words, 1.5 in reading comprehension, 2.9 in math, and 2.1 in spelling from formal assessments and supported by criterion referenced assessment

Placement Recommendation: Resource Room for one period per day for work in reading and language arts with the remainder of the time (83%) in mainstream third grade

Additional Services Necessary: Counseling one day per week by guidance counselor for work on improving self-concept

Date of Initiation of IEP 9/1/89 To be reviewed/revised 5/90

Committee Members Present

See attached goals and objectives

GOAL: Improve spelling through third grade level spelling lists. Each spelling objective to begin at the first of the year and continue all year.

Objectives

1. When presented with diagnostic spelling lists at the 2.1 to the 3.1 grade levels, including predictable words from the mainstream spelling curriculum at a rate of 10 words per week, Benny will spell the words by outlining the letters with his finger on sandpaper, and/or writing the words on paper with 80 percent accuracy. Task to be completed *daily*. Criterion Assessment *each Friday*.
2. When presented with diagnostic spelling lists or regularly spelled words at the 2.1 to the 3.1 grade level, the student will look up the meaning of the word in the dictionary and copy the first definition. Task to be completed *weekly*.
3. When presented with words with similar consonant–vowel–consonant patterns (one of three patterns: CVC, CVCe, or CVCCVC), Benny will state the pattern with 100 percent accuracy. Task to be completed *twice per week*. Criterion Assessment *every other week*.

GOAL: Improve punctuation in sentences.

Objectives

1. When presented with 10 sentences requiring periods or question marks, the student will correctly punctuate the sentences with 90 percent accuracy. Assignment to be completed *twice per week*. Criterion tests *every week*. Begin this objective 9/1/89.
2. When presented with 10 sentences requiring a comma or a semicolon, the student will correctly punctuate the sentences with 90 percent accuracy. Assignment to be completed *twice per week*. Criterion tests *every week*. Begin this objective 11/1/89.
3. When presented with 10 sentences requiring all punctuation, the student will punctuate the sentences with total accuracy on 9 of the 10 sentences. Assignment to be completed *twice per week*. Criterion tests *every week*. Begin this objective 1/1/90.

GOAL: Improve sentence formation.

Objectives

1. When presented with 10 simple sentences, the student will underline the complete subject once and the complete predicate twice with 90 percent accuracy. Assignment to be completed *three times per week*. Criterion tests *every week*. Begin assignment on 9/1/89.
2. When presented with 10 simple sentences, the student will underline the simple subject once and simple predicate twice with 90 percent accuracy. Assignment to be completed *three times per week*. Criterion tests *every week*. Begin assignment on 10/1/89.
3. When presented with 20 sentences, 10 of which include a direct object, the student will identify each by circling the direct object with 90 percent accuracy. Assignment to be completed *three times per week*. Criterion tests *every week*. Assignment to begin 11/1/89.
4. When presented with 10 partial sentences lacking a direct object, the student will complete the sentences by supplying the direct object with 90 percent accuracy. Assignment to be completed *three times per week*. Criterion tests *every week*. Assignment to begin 1/1/90.
5. When instructed to do so, the student will write 10 complete sentences and check completion by identification of subjects, predicates, and direct objects with 90 percent accuracy. Assignment to be completed *three times per week*. Criterion tests *every week*. Assignment to begin 3/1/90.

(continued)

INTEREST BOX 1.9 Continued

6. When presented with a paragraph including simple sentences and sentences with direct objects, the student will check the completion of each sentence by identification of subject, predicate, and direct object with 90 percent accuracy. Assignment to be completed *three times per week*. Criterion tests *every week*. Assignment to begin 4/1/90.

GOAL: To improve skill in recognition of basic sight words.

Objectives

1. When presented with 10 sight words that Benny has trouble reading (selected from a sight word list), he will write each word five times each day and then read the words to the teacher. The words will be changed every two weeks. Assignment to begin 9/1/89.
2. When presented with 10 sight words, Benny will look up the words and copy one definition for each word. Assignment to be completed *every two weeks*. Assignment to begin 9/1/89.

GOAL: To improve reading skill.

Objectives

1. When presented with a two-paragraph sequence from a basal reading story at appropriate grade levels (1.5, 2.0, 2.5, 3.0), the student will write the main idea and two important supporting details for each paragraph. Assignment to be completed *daily*. Criterion tests by *daily records*. Assignment to begin 9/1/89.
2. When presented with a multi-paragraph sequence (2 to 5) from a reading section written at appropriate grade levels (1.5, 2.0, 2.5), the student will identify the appropriate conclusion from four possible options. Assignment to be completed *every other day*. Criterion tests *every other week*. Assignment to begin 9/1/89.
3. When presented with a story from a basal reader (grade levels 1.5, 2.0, 2.5, and 3.0), the student will read the story and answer the five "W" questions (who, what, when, where, and why) as a method of summarizing the story. Assignment to be completed *every other day*. Criterion tests by *records collected from each assignment*. Assignment to begin 9/1/89.
4. When presented with a reading paragraph from a textbook at appropriate grade levels (2.0, 3.0) the student will read the paragraph and write the main idea and two supporting details. Assignment to be completed *every other day*. Criterion tests *every other week*. Assignment to begin 10/1/89.

One factor that influences the usefulness of IEPs is the active participation of the persons responsible for implementation of the IEPs. For example, in certain states (such as New Jersey and West Virginia) special education teachers are not required to be members of the child study team that prepares the IEP. Consequently, IEPs are written that do not take advantage of the teacher's unique knowledge of the student. Also, the objectives in that instance will not be written with the curriculum materials the teacher has in mind. With this type of practice, it is not surprising that some teachers have not seen the usefulness of IEPs in program planning (Hoy & Retish, 1984; Thurlow & Ysseldyke, 1982).

Individualized Education: A Definition

With continued use of these questionable practices, it is necessary to begin a discussion of the meaning of individualized education. For our purposes, individualized instruction will be defined in terms of three components: individualized assessment leading to an individualized plan, individualized teaching, and individualized student responsibility for learning.

Individualized assessment for students in special education classes is mandated by law and has been done in most instances (Pyecha, 1980; Ysseldyke, 1983). For example, Pyecha (1980) reported that IEPs generally included a number of individualized objectives (the mean number was 26) based on individualized assessment of the student. One aspect of the federal legislation was this emphasis on individualized assessment and on instructional objectives resulting from that assessment (Turnbull, Strickland, & Hammer, 1978a, 1978b). However, only one third of the objectives in a typical IEP included measurable evaluation criteria (Pyecha, 1980). Also, many of the tests used for individualized assessment are not acceptable tests in terms of technical criteria (Lehr, Ysseldyke, & Thurlow, 1987; Ysseldyke, 1983). Although there are problems with this aspect of individualized assessment, generally, school districts have attended to the requirement for individualized assessment and individualized educational plans, and in 1980, 93 percent of the students receiving special education services had some type of IEP (Pyecha, 1980). That figure is probably somewhat higher now.

The requirement for individualized instruction was never specified in the law, though the federal legislation certainly included the assumption that students in special education placements would be instructed individually. This does not mean that no group instruction should be allowed in special classes, but that the administrative reasons for instruction of groups of children should be secondary to the needs of each individual in those groups. This is a concern in many special education classes because many of these include only small-group instruction to the exclusion of individualized instruction, and that was clearly not the intention behind the legislation.

This emphasis on small-group instruction may also be related to the method in which teachers were trained. For example, immediately after state and federal legislation was passed mandating special education, many elementary teachers elected to become special education teachers. An elementary teacher is trained to think of individualizing the instruction in a class of 25 to 30 pupils by formation of small instructional groups, because in classes of that size, individual assignments for each student would be impossible to manage. This understanding of the term "individualization" was carried over into special classes during the 1970s and 1980s. However, with only 5 or 6 students in the special education class, different assignments for each student can easily be structured and managed (the task card approach, discussed below, will tell you how). Clearly, the intention behind special education legislation was that each student in special education placements or each special education student in inclusive mainstream placements requires individual assignments and individual instruction, at least part of the time.

A third aspect of individualized education is the need to have the student assume individual responsibility for learning. Unlike the two requirements discussed above, this requirement was not stated explicitly in the law nor was this an assumption behind the legislation. However, recent research in several areas has shown that this requirement should now be added to the other stipulations because research has shown that, unless students take personal responsibility for learning, they will not achieve commensurate with their maximum potential. Research in diverse areas, including effectiveness of student initiated goals, self-monitoring of behavior, precision teaching, and learning strategies instruction, all indicate the effectiveness of having the student "own" the responsibility for learning. Research in these areas is presented in other sections of the text, and for our purposes here, it is sufficient to indicate that the requirement for students to take responsibility for their own learning seems to be a major determinant of instructional effectiveness. Consequently, as conceptualized in this text, individual responsibility for learning is the third component of individualized education. The IEP process, as well as instruction in the special education and mainstream classes, should accentuate this personal responsibility.

INSTRUCTIONAL TIME ORGANIZATION

Generally, special education classes include from 4 to 8 students at a time for each adult in the class (some classes have a teacher and a paraprofessional). The problem, then, is to structure an instructional situation where one adult can monitor the instruction of 6 to 8 children at a time, even when all 8 are doing different assignments. In the context of the special class and/or the special education resource room, the teacher has two general options for managing the education of the students in the class: task card approaches and small-group instruction.

The Task Card Approach

Use of a task card approach is the method of choice for individualized education in special classes. A task card is prepared each day for every student in the special education class, and it lists the tasks that each student is supposed to complete during that day. Numerous types of task cards are available in the literature (Manley & Levy, 1981; Sugai, 1985). Also, Interest Box 1.10 presents a sample task card for a self-contained class.

As you can see, the task card lists (in very simple instructions) the location for the work the student is to complete first, second, and so forth, during the school day. During the several periods of individual instruction throughout the school day, each student gets his or her task card folder from a shelf, pulls the materials listed as the first activity, and begins the activity. The teacher wanders around the circle of student desks assisting students as needed. When a student completes an activity, he or she signals the teacher and requests that the teacher check the work. The teacher may then check that student's work or request that the student begin the next activity while the teacher finishes work with another student. During the checking, the teacher should move to the desk of the student, provide praise and corrective feedback, and instruct the student to begin the next assigned task. The student then returns any materials from the first task to the correct location, pulls materials for the next assignment, and begins the work. Also, during this instructional period, the teacher monitors the on-task behavior of the other students in the group.

A task card approach may also be used in a special education resource room. Figure 1.2 presents a week-long task card used by this author in a junior high school resource room for students with learning disabilities.

At the beginning of each period, the teacher instructs the students to get their folders and their assigned work. For students without the appropriate skills (or the experience) to read the assignments, the teacher merely places the worksheets, manipulative materials, and other materials directly in the student's folder on top of the task card. Generally, the three-step instructions in locating assignments are kept simple, so that even second and third grade students with very low reading levels can eventually learn to take responsibility for obtaining their own materials. The students should be expected to complete the assignments and return materials to their appropriate location. Also, the peer pressure (of everyone else being "old enough" to get their own materials) generally encourages pupils to get used to this system.

There are several guidelines for using a task card approach. First, the instructions should include three short statements that enable a child to locate an assignment (e.g., Reading Center, Box 4, Spelling Activity Number 13). Second, any manipulative, computer work, or audiovisual materials should be set up in advance, because some students may not be able to load software or

INTEREST BOX 1.10
Sample Daily Task Card for a Self-Contained Class

8:15–8:30	Students Arrive, Lunch Money, Games
8:30–8:45	Opening Exercises
8:45–9:50	Individual Work
9:50–10:00	Clean up Materials (recess begins early for those who clean up first)
10:00–10:30	Recess
10:30–10:45	Sharing Time (tell interesting stories to the class)
10:45–11:30	Individual Work
11:30–12:15	Lunch
12:15–1:00	Group Story Time (a teacher-read story)
1:00–1:45	Art Activity/Music Activity (alternative days)
1:45–2:15	Individual work
2:15–2:45	Physical Education
2:45–3:00	Closing Exercises

to insert a filmstrip into a filmstrip viewer. Third, because of the tendency toward distractibility among many students with mild disabilities, assignments should be given that take approximately 5 to 15 minutes to complete (try to increase this length of time through the year). Fourth, the use of self-checking materials should be allowed among those students who will use them correctly. Always remember, however, that praise from the teacher is a powerful reinforcer for many students with disabilities, and the teacher should attend to every assignment when it is completed. Fifth, remember to include work from mainstream classes on task cards. For example, if a student's objectives for a particular week include dictionary usage and a mainstream science teacher has provided a list of terms for the present science unit, use instructional time in the dictionary to look up and write science term definitions. Next, allow the students some time to get used to being responsible

NAME: Julian Gibbs	DATE: 3/18/90
MONDAY	TUESDAY
Reading Center .15 Story Book, Next Story .15 Write Paragraph about the Story .05 Spelling Cards, Red 10+11 Math Center .10 Time Cards, 1-5 .10 Box 1, Folder 1 .55	Reading Center .15 Story Book, Next Story .15 Write Paragraph about the Story .05 Box 1, Folder 3 Math Center .10 Time Cards, 5-10 .10 Box 1, Folder 2 .55
WEDNESDAY	THURSDAY
Math Center Box 1, Folder 2	
FRIDAY	OBJECTIVES
	Double Digit Addition Telling Time Story Comprehension (3rd Grade) Sentence Construction

FIGURE 1.2 Resource Room Task Card

for their own work. Be patient at the beginning of the year, and be prepared to help them through finding their materials for the first several weeks of school. Also, be prepared to accept more noise and movement in your class than in the traditional teacher-led class. Finally, do not accept work from students that includes errors. Give instructional feedback to the students and ask that the errors be corrected and that the corrected work be recopied for display on the wall—another powerful reinforcer for many students with disabilities.

The advantages of the task card approach are numerous. First, under this system the teacher becomes instructional personnel rather than a mere organizer who must hand out and collect assignments. Second, the assumption of responsibility by the students for their own work probably has positive effects for the students' self-concept. Third, this approach makes totally individualized assignments possible with as many as 8 children at once. Also, assignments may be more varied in terms of length of completion, and the entire class doesn't have to wait for the slower children to complete every item. In short, assuming appropriate assignment selection and appropriate monitoring of students, wasted time is minimized. These advantages clearly indicate that the task card approach is the method of choice for special education instruction in resource classes.

However, there are several disadvantages to using this approach. First, some types of instructional activities simply require involvement from several students. Activities such as educational games, computer work, class meetings, and social skills instruction may require participation of the whole class. Second, in self-contained classes (which include a great deal of initial instruction) group instruction may be needed to introduce a new concept or type of problem to several students at once. Finally, small-group instruction monitored by the teacher is one of the more effective types of instruction because students often learn from the mistakes of others if corrective feedback is offered in a supporting manner. These disadvantages suggest the necessity to include some small-group instruction in the resource and self-contained settings.

Small-Group Instruction

Small-group instruction may involve several members of the class or the entire special education class. Also, small-group instruction can work in tandem with the task card approach. For the students who will participate in the small-group instruction, merely assign "group instruction" as the first activity for a particular period or a particular day. These individuals will then group themselves together and work for the allotted time. The teacher should be prepared to monitor this work and will, therefore, have less time to provide feedback to the others in the class. Instruction of small groups under these conditions is very similar to instruction of small groups in the elementary class.

Small-group instruction in the special education class has several advantages. First, it makes group instruction possible during the initial instruction on a new topic. Instruction in social skills, feelings, and social relationships is also possible. Group projects in subject areas such as science fair projects and history projects are possible. Also, role play, debate, and theater production projects may be done in this format.

Selection of the Instructional Setting

One issue raised by this discussion is what degree or percentage of time students with disabilities should spend in small-group instruction and totally individualized instruction within the special education class. Although only general guidelines may be offered, you must remember that the special education student has probably already failed in lower-level small-group instruction in the elementary class. Consequently, this suggests that more individualized instruction may be necessary. Perhaps 40 to 90 percent of the special education instructional time should be spent in totally individualized instruction, closely monitored by the teacher.

However, this percentage is a function of the types of objectives on the IEP and the reasons for placement. For example, a child with an emotional or behavioral disability who is in a resource room for two periods per day may be on grade level in reading and math, and the IEP would indicate only behavioral objectives to increase appropriate classroom and social behavior. Although some individualized instruction is necessary in basic skill areas, this student may need to spend 60 percent of his or her time in group work, social skills training, and role playing to increase awareness of the feelings of others. Likewise, a child with a learning disability with major deficits in phonics and reading comprehension may need as much as 90 percent of the time on individualized worksheets, computerized reading software, or other reading comprehension activities.

GRADING SPECIAL EDUCATION WORK

One final aspect of instructional decision-making on an individualized basis is the assignment of graded or ungraded reports for the work a student completes in special education. For example, certain students with disabilities receive all of their instruction in reading from the special education teacher, whereas grades are assigned by the mainstream teacher. In that instance, it would not be unusual for a fifth grade boy to be successfully completing reading projects at an *A* level in the special education resource room, because the reading assignments would be selected from second and third grade reading level materials. If that student received *C*s on every subject in the mainstream and an *A* on reading, the parents may become confused. Also, the mainstream teacher may be upset because his or her teaching does not look successful. Does this student's *A* somehow invalidate the *A* that other students in the fifth grade class received?

In order to prevent this type of problem, some school districts have adopted a policy that no student in special education can earn above a *C* on any work done predominantly in the special education setting. However, such a policy solves only one aspect of the problem. This type of policy may lead to a lack of motivation on the part of some students. If a student receives less than an *A* on work that was difficult to do, why should further attempts at difficult work be made?

Bender (1984) recommended that grading practices be based on giving the student the highest grade possible (up to an *A*) based on success and effort. A notation can be made in writing to the parents explaining that the *A* represents success on lower-grade-level work in the special education class, and a copy of this notation should be included on the IEP. Many IEP forms today have a section in which specialized grading restrictions may be described.

A further restriction may be the necessity to pass certain minimum competency tests at various grade levels (Bender, 1984). As a teacher, you may not wish to see a student whose entire report card reflects an *A* to *B* average fail the minimum basic skills test. Consequently, an alternative recommendation is to base the grades a student receives on the objectives on the minimum competency test.

Finally, most states allow for exemptions from minimum competency testing for students with disabilities. Under these conditions, you may wish to base your grades on the level of performance in relation to the objectives on the student's IEP (Bender, 1984). In each case, documentation of communication with the parents concerning instructional grading practices is essential.

SUMMARY

The conventional wisdom concerning teacher preparation must now yield to research evidence on effective teaching. Clearly, research has demonstrated the effectiveness of a number of teaching behaviors and organizational strategies. These should be employed by every teacher in the school to the degree allowed by the specifics of the class type and situation.

For example, every teacher should actively monitor student seatwork at all times. Effective and timely feedback should be provided to the learners for every task. Questions and questioning strategies should be planned in advance to include a number of higher-level and a number of lower-level questions, depending on the overall goals the teacher has for that specific situation. Finally, students should be held accountable for learning through regularly required assignments, which become the focus of corrective feedback.

In a larger philosophical sense, the research has demonstrated that effective teaching can be a product of effective education for teachers. Teachers should be well trained in the effective teaching behaviors and demonstrate these behaviors in numerous laboratory placements, student teaching placements, and beginning teacher programs. To some degree, teaching can become a "science" in that use of these teaching behaviors will result in increased student achievement. At any rate, effective teaching can proceed only from a healthy understanding of the effective teaching research. Within this framework, the next task becomes organization of the physical aspects of the classroom and curriculum to facilitate instruction.

The delivery of instruction in special education can be organized in a number of ways, including the self-contained class, the resource class, consultation services, and inclusive mainstream instruction. Several of these service delivery arrangements have been used since Deno (1970) first suggested the cascade of services, though consultation and inclusive service delivery are more recent. Although the resource room is still the most frequently used instructional model for most students with mild disabilities, inclusive instructional services have been widely recommended during the last several years.

The individualized education plan (IEP) should form the backdrop for decisions concerning individualized instruction and individualized grading practices. However, merely testing a student individually and writing a few objectives does not constitute individualized education. In addition, the student should receive some individualized instruction directly related to his or her needs and should be encouraged to assume personal responsibility for the goals and objectives on the IEP as well as the daily written assignments related to those goals.

Given this optimistic definition of individualized education, you, the teacher, are still confronted with the need for a scheduling mechanism that will allow you to deal with numerous students at the same time. The task card approach to individualization will allow one adult to work with as many as 8 students completing different assignments. When coupled with some small-group instructional activities, the task card approach is the most effective method for organizing individual instruction in special education settings.

Summary Points

- Teachers must demonstrate effective teaching behaviors in order to facilitate students' achievement.
- Teachers must monitor students' attention to task, and assure that the task is structured at an appropriate level of difficulty.
- Teachers must assure correct pacing of instruction by introducing new material at appropriate intervals.
- Teachers should require regular student products in order to effectively monitor their learning.
- Teachers must provide appropriate, timely, and frequent feedback on student work.
- Special education instruction takes place in a number of different instructional settings: self-contained classes, resource rooms, mainstream classes with consultation, and inclusive classrooms.
- The special class is typically used for students with moderate disabilities who cannot profit from instruction in less restrictive environments.
- The resource room is, by far, the most commonly used instructional setting for students with mild disabilities.
- Curricula emphases do differ somewhat, depending on the type of instructional setting.
- The mandate for individualized education includes three components: individualized assessment, individualized instruction, and individualized responsibility for learning.
- Instructional planning in the context of special education must allow for numerous students doing different types of work in the class at the same time. A task card instructional arrangement can facilitate such planning.
- Grading special education work should involve assigning the highest grade possible, given the student's abilities, effort, and level of success. Adapted grading systems should be explained on the IEP for each student.

QUESTIONS AND ACTIVITIES

1. List the recommendations for increasing academic learning time. Can you think of others?
2. Why is monitoring so important? How does one teacher effectively monitor a group of students?
3. Explain Carroll's model of learning aptitude, and tell why it can be considered a more optimistic model than traditional models of learning potential.
4. What is the relationship between time-on-tasks and academic learning time?
5. What cognitive, emotional, and effective consequences occur if the success rate for a student falls to 50 percent?
6. Explain methods to increase student accountability.
7. What is the relationship between the space arrangement in the class and the types of instruction that can be conducted?
8. What were the political events of the 1960s and 1970s that had a bearing on the development of the idea of mainstreaming? How were the rights of students with disabilities logically connected to other human rights movements, such as civil rights, or women's rights?
9. Discuss the responsibilities of special education teachers in the nonschool settings presented by Deno's cascade of services.
10. Read Dunn's 1968 article and note any current themes relative to pulling students out of mainstream classes.
11. What types of learning centers would be needed in a resource room in a high school? Can you locate materials in your local curriculum laboratory that would be appropriate for these centers?
12. As a class, design a learning center for reading and language arts. Collect the materials and make certain that the assignments can be located by the students.
13. How much time do special education students in your local area spend in individualized instruction in the special class settings? How much time in small-group instruction? Are these percentages of time appropriate for the goals of the student?
14. Report on the several references in the text that explain how to use an IEP to plan and organize instruction in the special education setting. In what sense are these approaches task card approaches?
15. Identify additional areas in which small-group instruction may be appropriate in special education settings.
16. Interview teachers in the local schools concerning their views on small-group instruction and individual instruction. Do these teachers accept the three-component definition of individualization offered here? Do their classes reflect this definition?

REFERENCES

Bender, W. N. (1984). Daily grading in mainstream classes. *The Directive Teacher, 6* (2), 4–5.

Bender, W. N., Scott, K. S., & McLaughlin, P. (1993). A model for noncategorical service delivery for students with mild disabilities. In P. McLaughlin and P. Wehman (Eds.), *Issues in Special Education.* Boston: Andover Medical Publishers, pp. 82–95.

Bloom, B. S. (1980). The new direction in educational research: Alterable variables. *Phi Delta Kappan, 61,* 382–386.

Brophy, J. E. (1976). Teacher behavior and its effects. *Journal of Educational Psychology, 71,* 733–750.

Brophy, J. E. (1986). Teacher influences on student achievement. *American Psychologist, 41,* 1069–1077.

Carlson, S. A. (1985). The ethical appropriateness of subject matter tutoring for learning disabled adolescents. *Learning Disability Quarterly, 8,* 310–314.

Carroll, J. B. (1963). A model of school learning. *Teachers College Record, 64,* 723–733.

Cohen, J. H. (1982). *Handbook of Resource Room Teaching.* Rockville, MD.: Aspen.

D'Alonzo, B., D'Alonzo, R., & Mauser, A. (1979). Developing resource rooms for the handicapped. *Teaching Exceptional Children, 11,* 91–92.

Deno, E. (1970). Special education as developmental capital. *Exceptional Children, 37,* 229–237.

Deshler, D. D., Lowrey, N., & Alley, G. R. (1979). Programming alternatives for LD adolescents: A nationwide survey. *Academic Therapy, 14,* 389–397.

Dunn, L. M. (1968). Special education for the mildly retarded—Is much of it justifiable? *Exceptional Children, 35,* 5–22.

Evans, S. (1981). Perceptions of classroom teachers, principals, and resource room teachers of the actual and desired roles of the resource teacher. *Journal of Learning Disabilities, 14,* 600–603.

Glass, G. V. (1983). Effectiveness of special education. *Policy Studies Review, 2,* 65–78.

Glass, G. V., & Smith, M. E. (1979). Meta-analysis of research on class size and achievement. *Educational Evaluation and Policy Analysis, 1,* 2–16.

Greenwood, C. R. (1991). Longitudinal analysis of time, engagement, and achievement in at-risk versus non-risk students. *Exceptional Children, 58,* 521–535.

Haight, S. L. (1985). Learning disabilities resource room teachers and students: Competent for what? *Journal of Learning Disabilities, 18,* 442–448.

Hewett, F. (1967). Educational engineering with emotionally disturbed children. *Exceptional Children, 33,* 459–467.

Hoge, R. D., & Luce, S. (1979). Predicting academic achievement from classroom behavior. *Review of Educational Research, 49,* 479–496.

Hoy, M. P., & Retish, P. M. (1984). A comparison of two types of assessment reports. *Exceptional Children, 51,* 225–229.

Kavale, K. A., & Forness, S. R. (1986). School learning, time and learning disabilities: The dissociated learner. *Journal of Learning Disabilities, 19,* 130–138.

Kounin, J. S., Friesen, W. V., & Norton, A. E. (1966). Managing emotionally disturbed children in regular classrooms. *Journal of Educational Psychology, 57,* 1–13.

Lambert, N. M., & Hartsough, C. S. (1976). *Beginning Teacher Evaluation Study: Phase II. Final Report, Vol. III.1.* Princeton, NJ.: Educational Testing Service.

Lanier, J. E., & Glassberg, S. (1981). Relating research in classroom teaching to inservice education. *Journal of Research and Development in Education, 14,* 22–33.

Lehr, C. A., Ysseldyke, J. E., & Thurlow, M. L. (1987). Assessment practices in model early childhood special education programs. *Psychology in the Schools, 24,* 390–399.

Manley, S. C., & Levy, S. M. (1981). The IEP organizer: A strategy for turning IEPs into daily lesson plans. *Teaching Exceptional Children, 14,* 70–74.

McLaughlin, J. A., & Kelly, D. (1982). Issues facing the resource teacher. *Learning Disability Quarterly, 5,* 58–64.

Pyecha, J. N., Project Director (1980). *Final Report: A National Survey of Individualized Education Programs (IEPs) for Handicapped Children, Vol. 1.* Research Triangle Park, NC.: Research Triangle Institute.

Sindelar, P. T., & Deno, S. L. (1978). The effectiveness of resource programming. *Journal of Special Education, 12,* 17–28.

Sugai, G. (1985). Case study: Designing instruction from IEPs. *Teaching Exceptional Children, 17,* 233–239.

Thurlow, M. L., & Ysseldyke, J. E. (1982). Instructional planning: Information collected by school psychologists vs. information considered useful by teachers. *Journal of School Psychology, 20,* 3–10.

Tindal, G., Parker, R., & Germann, G. (1990). An analysis of mainstream consultation outcomes for secondary students identified as learning disabled. *Learning Disability Quarterly, 13,* 220–229.

Turnbull, A. P., Strickland, B., & Hammer, S. E. (1978a). The individualized education program—Part 1: Procedural guidelines. *Journal of Learning Disabilities, 11,* 40–46.

Turnbull, A. P., Strickland, B., & Hammer, S. E. (1978b). The individualized education program—Part 2: Translating law into practice. *Journal of Learning Disabilities, 11,* 67–72.

Westling, D. L., Koorland, M. A., & Rose, T. L. (1981). Characteristics of superior and average special education teachers. *Exceptional Children, 47,* 357–363.

Wyne, M. D., & Stuck, G. B. (1979). Time-on-task and reading performance in underachieving children. *Journal of Reading Behavior, 11,* 119–128.

Wyne, M. D., & Stuck, G. B. (1982). Time and learning: Implications for the classroom teacher. *The Elementary School Journal, 83,* 67–75.

Ysseldyke, J. E. (1983). Current practices in making psychoeducational decisions about learning disabled students. *Journal of Learning Disabilities, 16,* 226–233.

Chapter 2

INCLUSION AND CONSULTATION WITH MAINSTREAM TEACHERS

OBJECTIVES

Upon completion of this chapter, you should be able to:

1. Describe the rationale for mainstreaming.
2. Describe inclusive instruction.
3. Discuss the resistance toward modification of mainstream classes.
4. Describe the types of modifications teachers are encouraged to make in order to accommodate students with disabilities.
5. Discuss the components of the ALEM model.
6. Describe the Regular Education Initiative.
7. Describe an evaluation of mainstream class instructional strategies, and state how such evaluation efforts may improve mainstream practices.

KEYWORDS

modifications
consultation
Adaptive Learning Environments Model (ALEM)
inclusion
Regular Education Initiative (REI)
mainstreaming
pull-out programs
co-teaching
BCSQ

Mainstreaming has been an emphasis in special education for the last several decades and scholars are still seeking the most functional mainstream instructional techniques. More recently, the term "inclusion" has been utilized to indicate the desire to include all students with disabilities into various aspects of school life (Fuchs & Fuchs, 1994). Although many educators are nervous about inclusion of all students—even those with severe disabilities—the early research has indicated that there are many positive benefits from such inclusion, such as more tolerant attitudes on the part of other students (York, Vandercook, MacDonald, Heise-Neff, & Caughey, 1992). Although these data are still tentative, it seems clear that increased inclusive efforts will be apparent in the future for many children with disabilities.

One plan to facilitate the success of these inclusion efforts is the provision of assistance to mainstream teachers when educational problems arise for students with disabilities in mainstream classes. Consequently, one type of instruction many special education teachers provide is referred to as co-teaching, in which a mainstream teacher and a special education teacher jointly teach a mainstream class that includes a number of students with disabilities.

Alternatively, the current resource room plus mainstream placements will also continue, and many special education teachers will be expected to provide consultative services for mainstream teachers in order to assist them in modifying the mainstream class to accommodate the needs of the learners with disabilities in that class. The process whereby a special education teacher provides consultation assistance can vary considerably from school to school or even from teacher to teacher, and these services can be described only in fairly broad terms. Nevertheless, this type of service delivery support is very important;

research has demonstrated that 90 percent of mainstream teachers desire consultation in order to facilitate mainstreaming (Myles & Simpson, 1989), and you should expect to be called upon to fulfill that consultative role in your teaching career.

This chapter provides some essential information that should facilitate your efforts at inclusive instruction and/or consultation. First, the history of mainstreaming is reviewed briefly in order to assist you in understanding the development of the current "resource plus mainstream class" placement that is used for the majority of students with disabilities. Next, the role of the consultant teacher is briefly discussed in the context of supportive services for mainstream teachers.

Next, information is provided on the Adaptive Learning Environments Model (ALEM), which is intended to facilitate meaningful instruction that is adapted to the needs of each individual learner with special needs in mainstream classes. This instructional process is receiving increased research attention, and you should be aware of these potential mainstream adaptations.

A discussion of the types of modifications made by mainstream teachers in their classes is presented next. Also, a list of recommended modifications is presented in order to facilitate mainstreaming and inclusive educational programs. As a consultant, you will frequently share these modification suggestions with mainstream teachers.

Next, information of the recent development of inclusive classrooms is presented. Coteaching and other inclusion options are discussed, along with the stated concerns about the wisdom of inclusion that have been voiced by many researchers in the field. Finally, information on evaluation of mainstream classes is presented. In an effort to ensure that students with disabilities are receiving meaningful education in mainstream classes and that the appropriate instructional techniques are utilized, several scholars have recommended evaluation of those classes.

THE RATIONALE FOR MAINSTREAMING

Most teachers do not understand the concept of mainstreaming, and this lack of understanding encourages them to apply the same standards of judgement and evaluation to children with disabilities as to nondisabled children in the mainstream class. In fact, when one understands the original rationale for mainstreaming, one is better prepared to provide instruction for all children in the mainstream, and to participate in either consultative services or inclusive instruction in mainstream classes. Also, teachers who understand mainstreaming generally see the overall success of mainstream programs in a more favorable light. As a consultant to mainstream teachers, or in inclusive instructional roles, you may wish to share the following rationale for mainstreaming to elicit the mainstream teachers' support for your instructional recommendations.

First of all, mainstreaming must be understood as an attempt on the part of individuals with disabilities and their families to secure their human and civil rights. Students with disabilities were denied education in this nation until recently, and the movement for mainstream education for these students came in the wake of the movement among African-American individuals to secure their civil rights and in the same decade as the growing concern for the civil rights of women in our society. Native Americans also demanded their rights as members of our society during the time period between 1965 and 1975.

Mainstreaming, and improved treatment for students with disabilities overall, must be understood in this historical context as an attempt to secure the rights offered by our society for individuals with disabilities—a movement that was and is related to a number of other civil rights movements. Explaining this historical cause for mainstreaming can place you on the moral "high ground" in your initial consultation efforts with some mainstream teachers. If those teachers understand that mainstreaming was undertaken by our society in order to provide civil and educational rights fairly to individuals with disabilities, the teachers may be more willing to assist you in modifying the curriculum.

Proponents of mainstreaming viewed separate classes for students with disabilities as ineffective and unequal. As discussed in Chapter 1, research data on the effectiveness of the self-contained class is lacking (Dunn, 1968). There is little reason to believe that separate classes facilitate meaningful educational gains among these students, and the separation of students with disabilities from the general population may provide a negative stigma to the self-contained class. Consequently, placing students with disabilities in mainstream placements that could be modified to meet their individual needs seemed the most attractive alternative.

Next, the mainstream classes offered the advantage of learning social skills through observation of one's peers. Clearly, self-contained classes offered peer role models that represented only "handicapped" behavior, whereas the mainstream class provided numerous peer role models that were normal in terms of their social and adaptive behavior. As Coleman, Pullis, and Minnett (1987) indicated, the impetus for mainstreaming has always been more related to facilitating social competence than to enhancing academic performance. Proponents of mainstreaming and, more recently, inclusion have argued that provision of normal role models was an important advantage for mainstream placement, independent of potential gains in academic achievement.

Finally, the combination of these arguments resulted in a move for mainstream education. The overall argument followed this logic: Mainstream classes at least offer normal behavioral role models, and self-contained classes were not notably more effective in securing educational achievement gains among students with disabilities. Therefore, the arguments seemed to suggest mainstream placement as the option of choice, in spite of the fact that many students with disabilities may not master the academic curriculum as quickly as, or using the same instructional techniques as, nondisabled learners.

It may be interesting to note here that the arguments for mainstreaming are intriguing because of what they did not say. Proponents of mainstreaming did not believe that mainstreaming would result in the same level of achievement gain for students with and without disabilities, nor did proponents of mainstreaming ever suggest that effective mainstreaming would be easy. Clearly adaptations would have to be made in the mainstream class environment for mainstreamed learners. Still, its proponents pointed out that mainstreaming would probably not hurt learners with disabilities academically, and it may provide some social and behavioral benefits.

Clearly, this logic must be shared with mainstream teachers, who are trained to view their own success, in part, in terms of student achievement gains. In simplified terms, the mainstream teacher sees his or her job as "moving" a group of children from a 2.0 grade equivalent score in reading to a 3.0 grade equivalent score. Clearly, some children with disabilities cannot be expected to make those types of academic gains, and a gain of .6 grade equivalent for a child with a learning disability or a child with mild intellectual disabilities should be viewed as a success. Unfortunately, that view of "success" is rarely shared with mainstream teachers. As a result, many mainstream teachers attempt to encourage major academic gains among students with disabilities—an attempt that, for some children, is doomed to failure. Once that failure has occurred, those teachers begin to feel that mainstreaming is an unfair burden under which they must labor. They may then begin to feel that they do not have adequate mainstreaming instructional skills (Graham, Hudson, Burdg, & Carpenter, 1980). The burden of mainstreaming is particularly unrewarding because few mainstream teachers understand the crucial importance of even the smallest academic and social/behavioral gain.

You may find that, in working with various mainstream teachers, you need to explain that a child with a disability is receiving much more benefit from the mainstream placement than his or her reading/math scores indicate. You should attempt to assist mainstream teachers in understanding the importance of small academic gains and highlight the less tangible benefits of mainstream placement for those teachers. Those benefits include normal social role models and a more "typical" lifestyle than would be possible in a self-contained class. In order to assist you in this crucial task, a set of sample statements that you could make to mainstream teachers that will help them to value the benefits of mainstream placements appropriately is presented in Interest Box 2.1. In a real sense, you must become the advocate for inclusion and increased use of mainstream placements, and your first task in consultation is often to help the mainstream teacher see the advantages of mainstreaming and/or inclusion for the child.

THE CONSULTATION PROCESS

Consultation as a Job Responsibility

In the context of many special education instructional positions, special education teachers are expected to provide consultation of one type or another to mainstream teachers. Even special education teachers in self-contained classes may be requested to provide consultative assistance to nonacademic personnel regarding a child's

INTEREST BOX 2.1
Sample Statements Supportive of Mainstreaming and Inclusion

When mainstream teachers indicate some dissatisfaction with mainstreaming, the following types of statements may help.

- "Well, I hear that you are having a problem because Billy doesn't finish his worksheets, but I'm sure he's doing his best. He always does in my class. Maybe you and I can look at the worksheets together and come up with some ideas to change them some."
- "You know, children are mainstreamed to provide normal behavioral role models, and not only to improve their academic performance. I think Alonzo is receiving a lot of benefits from your class in that area, and I'm not sure he'd do any better academically if he were in the self-contained special education program."
- "Yes, hyperactive behavior is a real problem. Maybe we can get together during lunch and talk about ways to offer Shannon a behavior contract to make her want to stay in her seat and complete her work.
- "Yes, sometimes children do ask why a particular child gets different treatment, but I just tell my class that I treat them all differently, depending on their needs. It's not my job to treat them all the same, but rather to teach each of them, and I sometimes have to spend more time, or do something different with one or the other. It usually helps if I can point out several examples where I've treated students differently."

Note that each of these statements emphasizes the special education teacher's desire to assist the mainstream teacher in dealing with the problem. That type of assistance, freely and frequently offered, can be the most important component of an effective consultation relationship with a mainstream teacher.

behavior. For example, the principal may request that the self-contained special education teacher consult with the bus driver regarding a particular child's behavior on the bus.

Obviously, the teacher in the self-contained class will be called for consultative services less frequently than a teacher in a resource class, because the children in the resource room spend a high percentage of their day in mainstream classes, and the mainstream teachers responsible for those students will frequently request assistance. Nevertheless, all special education teachers will be expected to provide consultative assistance at some time.

Process of Consultation

The consultative process involves any number of services that may be required of the consultant teacher (Idol, 1993). Consequently, it would be very difficult to provide an exhaustive list of services that may be required in any particular situation. Typically, consultant teachers are expected to schedule some brief time with each mainstream teacher for whom consultation is necessary in order to check on the academic and behavioral progress of the children with disabilities in the mainstream class. These meetings are usually held on a weekly or twice-weekly basis. Ideas for adapted strategies for instruction and behavioral interventions should be made available to the mainstream teachers, along with specific instructions on implementation.

In some cases, it may be necessary and desirable for the consultant to actually enter the mainstream class occasionally and demonstrate a particular instructional methodology for the mainstream teacher (Idol, 1993; Schulte, Osborne, & McKinney, 1990). This type of demonstration lesson should be viewed as an educational experience for the mainstream teacher, and every effort should be made to turn over the new instructional approach to the mainstream teacher as soon as possible.

For example, Schulte, Osborne, and McKinney (1990) described a consultation program in which the consultant teacher was expected to meet with the mainstream teacher on a weekly basis to plan instructional and behavioral interventions. The consulting teacher's responsibilities included developing alternative instructional materials, modeling teaching strategies, and monitoring reinforcement programs. These types of responsibilities are considered typical of the consultation process.

Perhaps the overriding concern in the consultation process is the provision of effective suggestions that can be easily implemented in the mainstream class. The later sections of this chapter provide a host of suggestions that may be made to mainstream teachers in particular situations. In order to be an effective consultant, one must first make certain that he or she has something meaningful to contribute to the mainstream teacher in the way of practical, workable suggestions. Although a particular instructional idea may be perfect for a particular child in the mainstream class, time constraints may prohibit the mainstream teacher from implementing that idea, and the effective consultant teacher will be sensitive to the limitations imposed on the mainstream teachers when suggesting particular strategies.

Documentation of Consultation

Some type of notation log of each contact between the consultant and the mainstream teacher should be kept that indicates the topics of discussion, the level of implementation of the proposed ideas, and the outcome of the new strategies that have been implemented. These logs range from simple parenthetical notations to fairly involved sets of behavioral data collected on a daily basis.

Tindal, Parker, and Germann (1990) described a Mainstream Consultation Agreement between the special education teacher and the mainstream teacher. This type of agreement should specify the types of responsibilities that will be assumed by each teacher. These agreements thus can serve two functions: clear communication between the teachers regarding each teachers' responsibilities, and increased commitment to fulfill the responsibilities assumed by each teacher.

Efficacy of Consultation

To date, there has not been a great deal of research on the effectiveness of consultation for students with mild disabilities in mainstream classes (Idol, 1993). Unfortunately, the research available is equivocal with some studies supporting the efficacy of consultation (Fuchs, Fuchs, Hamlett, & Ferguson, 1992; Gottlieb, Alter, & Yoshida, 1990; Schulte, Osborne, & McKinney, 1990; Wesson, 1991) and others showing little improvement resulting from consultation (Tindal, Parker, & Germann, 1990).

Schulte, Osborne, and McKinney (1990) collected pretest and posttest achievement test scores for 67 children with learning disabilities who were receiving special education services in one of four conditions: one period of resource room service per day, two periods of resource room service per day, consultative service combined with in-class instruction, and consultative service alone. The students were randomly assigned to the treatment conditions, which, although difficult to do in applied research designs such as this, does tend to result in more defensible research results. The data indicated that students who received consultation services in addition to mainstream class instruction provided by the special education teacher/consultant outperformed students who received one period per day in the resource room. This study tentatively suggests the effectiveness of consultative services when those services are combined with some instruction time provided by the special education teacher in the mainstream class.

With this type of tentative research support, it is a certainty that additional research will be forthcoming. Also, because of the current research interest in consultation, most special education teachers will probably be expected to lend their expertise to other teachers in the school. Consequently, any information that can be given to mainstream teachers to facilitate instruction of children with disabilities in the mainstream is beneficial.

ADAPTING INSTRUCTION

Resistance to Instructional Adaptations

One issue that must be confronted in consultation with mainstream teachers is the necessity to diversify the instruction in the mainstream, or to adapt the mainstream classroom to assure both social gains and academic success of individuals with disabilities. Some type of adaptation is necessary for almost every child with a disability, though many mainstream teachers resist instituting the necessary modifications (Margolis & McGettigan, 1988). Teachers are very concerned about the amount of time that must be devoted to diversification efforts, and adaptations do, initially, take some time. Consequently, you will need to deal with this issue in your consultation efforts.

There are several arguments to make if a mainstream teacher confronts you with the belief that it takes too much "extra time to mainstream." First, point out that modifications typically result in diversifying the types of educational activities in the class and, by diversifying the class, the teacher will assist not only the students in the class with the identified disabilities, but also the other children at risk, the low achievers, and the gifted children. Diversification of curriculum, tests, assessment formats, and so forth, leads to a class that is more individualized overall, and some teachers have indicated that, having been through this diversification process, they felt themselves to be more effective teachers.

Next, indicate that any additional planning will also be of benefit next year. In all probability the same mainstream teacher will again be faced with highly divergent needs among the students in the class, and the planning, lesson plans, worksheets, and units that are organized on a diversified manner this year will be appropriate next year too. This has the effect of spreading the additional planning time across several years, and this can be one effective argument in favor of implementing such modifications.

Finally, remind teachers of the moral imperative of mainstreaming. No student with a disability should be denied access to normal social role models if such access will assist that child in developing more normal social behaviors, and often the only school environment in which to find those appropriate social role models is the mainstream class. Parents, in particular, are acutely aware of the advantages of providing appropriate social role models for students with disabilities, and most parents support mainstreaming efforts with consultative support (Idol, 1993).

Frequency of Mainstream Modification

Unfortunately, the research has indicated that many mainstream teachers do not adapt their classes in ways that would allow for successful mainstreaming (Baker & Zigmond, 1990; Bender, 1986; Margolis & McGettigan, 1988; Munson, 1987). For example, in a very thorough study on this topic, Baker and Zigmond (1990) used a case study approach in which numerous variables in one elementary school were assessed. These included observations of instructional activities in every class, students' behavior, grouping arrangements for instruction, reinforcement techniques, and interviews with parents, students, and teachers. The results revealed that mainstream classrooms seemed orderly and generally had a positive atmosphere. Each classroom had classroom rules posted, and students were frequently reinforced with food items for correct academic work and good behavior. The demographic results indicated that this school could be viewed as moderately effective, a suggestion supported by the fact that 43 percent of the students tested at or above the 50th percentile on a nationally normed achievement test.

However, even in schools that are generally effective, few significant mainstream modifications are noted. For example, even in a crucial basic skill such as reading, the Baker and Zigmond (1990) study indicated that teachers did very little beyond the activities recommended in the teachers' manual. Teachers aimed at completing a year of instruction during the school year, and were apparently unaware that many students with mild disabilities cannot be expected to manage that level of academic growth. In every kindergarten, first, and second grade class each reading lesson was taught to the entire class, with no grouping for instruction and no differentiated pacing or diversification of assignments. This is a particular disappointment, since grouping children for educational attainment has been shown to result in improved efficacy of instruction. Clearly, these results do not indicate that this school is prepared to accommodate learners with disabilities in the mainstream, and significant modifications would be necessary to assure success of students with disabilities in this school.

Munson (1987) conducted a structured interview with 26 mainstream teachers in grades 1 through 6. The results indicated that two distinct types of modifications were made in mainstream classes; modifications the teacher might make for any student in the class—referred to as "typical" modifications, and modifications that would be used only for learners identified as disabled—referred to as "substantive" modifications. Interest Box 2.2 identifies the various types of modifications found.

Only two types of modifications—format of directions and assignments, and testing procedures—were considered typical (Munson, 1987). Of the twenty-six teachers interviewed, seventeen indicated that they used these two modifications when necessary for all students. Few teachers made any substantive modifications that involved diversification of curriculum, grading, or provision of individualized instruction. Clearly, many more substantive modifications are essential if mainstreaming is to succeed. Other research has further documented that mainstream teachers do not modify the learning activities a great deal (Bender, 1986; Munson, 1987; Ysseldyke, Thurlow, Wotruba, & Nania, 1990). Elementary teachers assign individualized work to students with mild disabil-

INTEREST BOX 2.2
Examples of Typical and Substantive Modifications

The typical modifications that Munson (1987) found involved those that a mainstream teacher may make for any student. They included variations of directions for assignments and variations in administration procedures for classroom tests. These were the most frequently reported modifications utilized by the mainstream teachers in Munson's study. For example, 25 of 26 mainstream teachers indicated that they varied the format of directions and assignments for various students in the class. Also, 24 of 26 teachers indicated that some variations in testing procedures were used.

Munson also described several "substantive" modifications, including modifications made only for children who were identified as disabled. These included allowing the child to take the test in the special education room, altering the difficulty of the task, using lower grade-level texts, altering the teacher presentation mode or the student response mode, altering teaching strategies, altering curriculum and/or instructional materials, and provisions of individualized instruction. Unfortunately, these substantive modifications were made much less frequently than the typical modifications discussed above. Only 5 of 26 mainstream teachers indicated that they varied the instructional material for students with disabilities. Also, 5 of 26 teachers indicated that they varied the grading requirements. These results indicate that mainstream teachers do not use the types of modifications likely to assist students with disabilities in mainstream classes.

ities only 10 percent of the time, and secondary teachers assign such work less than 2 percent of the time (Bender, 1986). Also, a teacher's age and teaching experience negatively relate to the number of modifications implemented, so that older, more experienced teachers modify their class less often (Munson, 1987). Finally, research by Ysseldyke and his co-workers (1990) indicated that teachers thought it was difficult to make adaptations in the mainstream even though such adaptations seemed desirable.

These results strongly suggest that many mainstream teachers are not positively disposed to modifying the mainstream class to accommodate learners with disabilities (Margolis & McGettigan, 1988). For this reason, part of the job responsibilities of the special educator may be to promote mainstream class modifications in spite of this hesitancy on the part of mainstream teachers. These studies make clear the need to inform mainstream teachers, not only of the desirability of modifying their classes, but of effective and efficient ways of doing so.

Modification Preferences

Several recent studies have been conducted to ascertain the types of modification preferences desired (Cohen, 1988; Myles & Simpson, 1989, 1990). Myles and Simpson (1989) conducted a study in which 100 practicing mainstream teachers read brief vignettes describing children with various exceptionalities. The teachers were asked to describe the types of modifications they would desire in order to accommodate students with disabilities in their class. Seventy-eight percent of the teachers requested additional support services and modified class size. The mainstream teachers indicated a strong preference for receiving consultative assistance from special education teachers and/or psychologists, as compared to crisis teachers and counselors. When asked to identify specific types of information that should be made available through support services, teachers seemed to prefer hands-on techniques such as behavior management and instructional suggestions, rather than information on the characteristics of the various disabilities. Also, 55 percent of the teachers indicated that additional planning time would help. The overall results suggested that, if certain administrative modifications are possible—class size reductions, support services, availability of a teacher's aide, etc.—most mainstream teachers would be willing to consider placing children with disabilities in their class and modifying the class in an appropriate fashion.

However, these results do have a negative aspect, at least from the perspective of the consultant special education teacher. The types of modifications that mainstream teachers prefer center around administrative changes, which mainstream teachers and special educator consultant teachers cannot make without administrative approval and additional resources. When the special education teacher is called in for consultation, hiring an aide, granting a teacher an additional planning period, or reduction of class size are not usually options that can be considered. As one may surmise, these are options that must be initiated from the administrator's office—either the principal or the special education director. Consequently, the special education teacher will frequently find himself or herself in the position of attempting to elicit meaningful change in the learning environment without additional resources. Although these administrative modifications are not unreasonable, selection of these options may indicate that mainstream teachers desire to absolve themselves of responsibility to meaningfully modify the instruction in their classes.

Myles and Simpson (1990) also investigated the types of modification options preferred by parents of children with disabilities. Using a survey instrument, these researchers contacted 374 parents, and 35 percent of that group responded. Reductions in class size again headed the list of preferred options, with 70 percent of the parents indicating that such an option would assist their child. Provision of support services, consultation, and use of paraprofessionals were also highly desired. Overall these results seem to support the modifications selected by the mainstream teachers themselves.

Several studies have addressed student preferences for educational services (Cohen, 1988; Jenkins & Heinen, 1989). Jenkins and Heinen (1989) interviewed 686 students, including 101 special education students, and the results indicated that the students with disabilities preferred to receive instructional help from the mainstream teacher rather than from a specialist or special educator who visits the class to offer assistance. If modifications are to be made, the students do not wish to be singled out by having a specialist, an aide, or a tutor assigned to them. Although understandable, this clearly contradicts the desire on the part of both teachers and parents to use such support services from other adults.

Cohen (1988) interviewed 25 college students with learning disabilities concerning the coping strategies those students used to assist them in mastering a college curriculum. The strategies those students selected may give some indication concerning the types of modifications those students desire. The results indicated that many students depended on purchase of previously highlighted books, subvocalizing during reading, and heavy use of teaching assistants. These are reasonable modifications that can be implemented with little effort in mainstream classes in public schools, and mainstream teachers should be encouraged to make these options available to students with disabilities.

Recommended Modifications

In discussion of modifications necessary to facilitate mainstreaming, it is essential to determine initially if the most recently developed instructional ideas are being applied in the mainstream class. Clearly, one imperative for mainstream teachers is the implementation of effective instructional methods for all students.

As indicated in Chapter 1, only 20 years ago, educational researchers knew very little about the types of teaching behaviors and activities that lead to increased achievement gains. Today, however, definitive research is available, and numerous specific teaching techniques can be stipulated. Unfortunately, much of this research is very recent, and mainstream teachers may not yet be implementing the specific "effective teaching behaviors" suggested by this research. Consequently, when considering modification of mainstream classes, you should initially ascertain the extent to which the mainstream teacher is using effective instructional behaviors. Gersten and Woodward (1990) have provided a synopsis of these effective instructional behaviors, presented in Interest Box 2.3.

Additional Modification Suggestions

In addition to the general categories of modifications described above, a special education teacher needs numerous specific examples of the types of modifications that may facilitate successful mainstreaming. Although a list of potential modifications would be almost endless, Interest Box 2.4 provides an extended description of various modifications that are frequently made. You should review these ideas and share them with mainstream teachers, as necessary. Finally, when a particular problem arises, you should feel free to brainstorm and develop additional adaptive ideas to facilitate mainstreaming.

THE ADAPTIVE LEARNING ENVIRONMENTS MODEL

As researchers became aware that more mainstream modifications were desirable, a group of

INTEREST BOX 2.3
Effective Teaching Behavior

1. Gains in academic learning are consistently correlated with the amount of time students are actively engaged in relevant academic activities. The teacher should frequently monitor each child's on-task time.
2. Learning is optimal when all students respond to many questions during the course of a lesson. Typically, asking focused questions leads to results that are superior. But it is essential to have all students respond during each segment of each lesson.
3. Learning is maximized for low-performing students when their error rate is minimal (no higher than 20 percent for initial presentation of new concepts, and no higher than 10 percent on independent work assignments).
4. The teacher's strategy for responding to student errors is significantly correlated with student learning. When teachers provide strategy feedback to students—when they remind students of essential parts of a problem-solving strategy—student academic growth is maximized.
5. Students learn best when the instructor provides a clear, detailed, step-by-step model of all steps in the problem-solving or comprehension process and gradually fades the model.
6. The teacher follows modeling with brief opportunities for students to practice the concepts through further examples.
7. In teaching comprehension, teachers make use of scaffolded instruction. Teachers work with students on skills that are emerging in their repertoire, but are immature. Teachers often "think aloud," explaining to students how they reached a conclusion.
8. The teacher provides relevant independent seatwork activities in which students apply concepts recently taught. The teacher actively monitors student work, providing individualized, corrective feedback.
9. When appropriate, teachers set up cooperative learning situations.

Source: Adapted from the list compiled by Gersten and Woodward (1990).

INTEREST BOX 2.4
Modifying the Mainstream Environment

Some research is available on the types of modifications made by mainstream teachers in order to accommodate students with disabilities (Bender and Ukije, 1989; Cohen, 1988; Munson, 1987; Myles and Simpson, 1989). The partial lists that follow are intended to give some examples of the types of modifications that may be required. In addition to using this list, special and mainstream educators are encouraged to be creative in developing innovations that improve the likelihood of successful mainstream class participation.

Academic Modification Strategies

1. Use a peer tutor/teacher's aide to read with students with disabilities. Instruct the person in comprehension monitoring skills.
2. Use cooperative instructional groups to facilitate learning and interaction between students with and without disabilities.
3. Diversify the reading materials for each instructional unit by selecting materials from several different grade levels on the same topic. If the unit involves study of the solar system for a sixth grade class, obtain some materials written at the fourth grade level and some at the eighth grade level to supplement or replace the sixth grade level book. Assign children (both gifted and disabled) to a text based on their reading comprehension ability.
4. Always write examples on the blackboard so that children may see the examples as it is being discussed.
5. Use audio tapes to allow students to rehear lecture/discussion material.
6. Check students' notebooks in order to assure they have notes on the necessary material and those notes are in readable form.
7. Build movement activities into your classwork for younger hyperactive children, between every seatwork activity.
8. Use audiovisual materials to display the main unit ideas for the entire class throughout the unit. Show the students, in a very direct fashion, the relationship between the display materials and their unit content. Do not assume that the relationships that are obvious to average learners are obvious to students with disabilities.
9. Use various art projects, or creative works, to allow students to demonstrate knowledge of a subject.
10. Assign different levels of classwork for different students in the class. Be variable, and include four or five different assignments, with each assignment varying in the number of problems required. Explain to the children that you are attempting to be more fair for those who do some problems more slowly, and point out how you frequently vary assignments.
11. Use graphic organizers and advanced organizers to help students understand the structure of lessons as they complete them.
12. Set up various learning centers in your class, where students choose the work assignments they wish to complete with your guidance.
13. Encourage students to compare notes and form study groups for unit quizzes.
14. Differentiate homework assignments by requiring certain types of work from groups of students and letting the group decide who does what work.
15. Use reading material that is available on audio tape and allow students to listen and read at the same time.

16. Encourage gifted students to "highlight" the textbook this year and assign the highlighted book to a student with a disability next year. Instruct that student to read and think about only the highlighted sections.
17. Provide instruction on reading competency that involves active interaction with the reading material—self-questioning, or paraphrasing strategies (as discussed in Chapter 5).
18. Make videotapes and films available that parallel the text.
19. Use computer simulations to demonstrate historical, political, or mathematical processes.
20. Vary the directions for assignments to assure that each student understands the work required. Privately verify that particular students with disabilities have understood the instructions for the assignment.
21. Review class papers when they are returned so that each test and homework assignment becomes a learning experience rather than merely a practice or assessment experience.
22. Plan the instructional activities with the special educator so that the student can receive instruction on the same task at the same time in both the mainstream and the resource class.
23. Use manipulatives in math and science to illustrate points. Encourage the students to use counting aides, calculators, etc., as necessary.
24. Diversify the instructional groups in the class. Use a variety of instructional groups and change group membership frequently to assure the students contact with various class members. This promotes both academic and social skills gains.
25. Diversify the instructional unit while planning the unit. If a lesson requires a worksheet, prepare three worksheets at three different levels. Likewise, prepare several versions of laboratory sheets and tests. Balance this planning time over a period of several years, and use these different level unit materials throughout the next few years.

Testing Modification Strategies

1. Use several levels of testing for each instructional unit.
2. Allow students to take tests in the resource room, where the special education teacher can administer the questions individually to ensure understanding.
3. Accept different types of information as indicative of understanding.
4. Extend the time allotments for students as necessary.
5. Vary the number of questions required for various students in the class.
6. Give assessments orally, as necessary.
7. Vary the question format on tests.
8. Instruct the students in various test-taking strategies to help them understand the various question types.
9. Eliminate large unit tests and grade students on daily work, including homework, classwork, and frequently administered quizzes.
10. Vary the grading requirements for various students. Remember to note these variations on the IEPs of the students with disabilities.

Behavior Management Modification Strategies

1. Implement a token economy to reinforce appropriate behaviors such as readiness for class (paper, books, and pencils out, etc.), completing work on time, and neatness. Use class privileges such as five minutes of free time at the end of class to redeem tokens.
2. Reinforce groups of students for projects done together.
3. Institute group time-out procedures.

(continued)

INTEREST BOX 2.4 Continued

4. Use behavior contracts for behavior/academic gains and to assist the student in celebrating mastery of difficult curriculum.
5. Instruct the students with disabilities who have attention problems in self-monitoring skills, as discussed in Chapter 8.
6. Use assertive disciplinary planning, involving posted rules and stated consequences for rule violation.
7. Include some type of "peer pressure" intervention in your class whereby the class is trained to meaningfully discuss the disciplinary transgressions of class members to get them back on task.

researchers developed the Adaptive Learning Environments Model (ALEM) (Wang & Birch, 1984; Wang & Zollers, 1990). It is composed of a set of recommendations concerning modifications of typical mainstream classes to facilitate the success of all learners—both disabled and nondisabled—in those classes (Wang & Birch, 1984; Wang & Zollers, 1990). The model focuses on numerous factors that affect a student's educational progress, ranging from administrative organization of the school to family characteristics of the student. The primary concern of the model is to allow and encourage classroom teachers to adapt instruction to meet the needs of all the students in the classroom. The conceptual model is presented in Figure 2.1.

The six components of ALEM focus on major adaptations in the organization of school classrooms. In each of the six components, the variables listed interact with each other and with those variables in the other components to determine how a student learns. Consequently, the model must be conceptualized and implemented for the entire school, rather than merely for change in a single classroom (Wang & Zollers, 1990).

ALEM and Mainstream Adaptations

From the individual teacher's perspective, the core of the ALEM program is adaptation of instruction for each individual learner in the classroom. For example, in a classroom that has implemented the ALEM program, every learner is assessed individually, using criterion-referenced, curriculum-based assessments to concretely and adequately identify the student's level of skill. This regular assessment involves a diagnostic–prescriptive monitoring system designed to yield specific information on which to base the learner's instruction (Wang & Zollers, 1990). This type of assessment process is notably similar to the most effective instructional planning assessments currently used in special education. You may wish to read the discussion of curriculum-based assessment in Chapter 4.

In addition to the assessment process in the ALEM class, each learner also has an individualized progress plan that includes a prescriptive component for basic skills mastery. This contains specific individual objectives for each of the basic skills areas. Each learner also has an individualized plan for development of social and personal/emotional skills (Wang & Zollers, 1990). In effect, the ALEM model recommends that every student in the elementary class, disabled and nondisabled, should be provided with an individualized progress plan similar to the IEP currently mandated for students in special education classes.

Finally, the ALEM model includes a classroom instruction learning management system

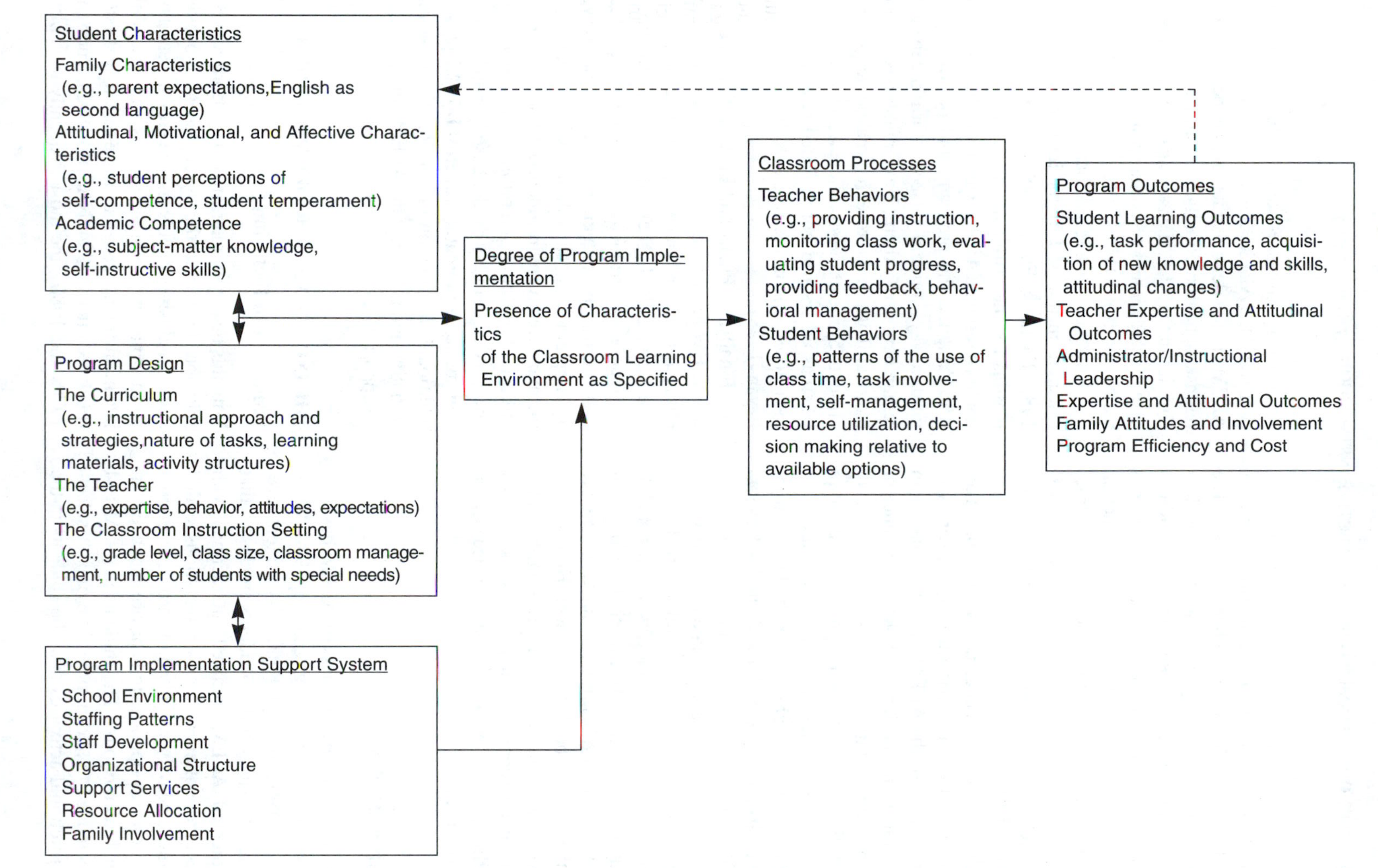

FIGURE 2.1 The Adaptive Learning Environments Model

referred to as Self-Schedule System. In other words, each student is individually responsible for his or her schedule, with teacher guidance. The teachers circulate among the students providing instruction and evaluative feedback to individuals and small groups. In effect, the teacher has become a facilitator and monitor of instruction rather than the primary delivery agent for instruction (Wang & Zollers, 1990). Lectures and whole-class teacher-led discussions tend to be less frequent in ALEM classes.

The use of the teacher as a facilitator rather than a lecturer or discussion leader is a very significant aspect of the ALEM model of classroom instruction. Many teachers feel that the presence of even one student with a disability in a mainstream class will slow down the progress of the entire class (Graham, Hudson, Burdg, & Carpenter, 1980) and that is probably true if all of the instruction is delivered in the traditional whole-class format. When teachers lecture or initiate whole-class discussions, the concepts and intellectual demands of the class activities are generally aimed at the average level student, and students with lower ability may be left behind. If a teacher realizes that several students are being left behind, the teacher may then slow the lesson down. However, in ALEM classes, the students take responsibility for their own instruction, which allows the teacher flexibility to accommodate individual learners at their own pace.

Effectiveness of ALEM

Research on the effectiveness of ALEM has generally been positive (Wang & Birch, 1984; Wang & Zollers, 1990), though the results are tentative. Early results suggest that students in classes that implemented ALEM initiated interactions with teachers more often, and those interactions tended to be more heavily weighted toward instructional interactions (as opposed to behavior management or social interactions). The students in the ALEM classes tended to spend more time on self-selected instructional activities than the students in the comparison classes. Student attitudes were more positive in the ALEM classes. Also, students in the ALEM classes demonstrated higher percentages of on-task behavior. Finally, the students with disabilities in the ALEM classes gained more on academic achievement tests than similar students in the comparison classes (Wang & Birch, 1984).

However, some researchers have criticized the research on the ALEM model (Bryan & Bryan, 1988; Fuchs & Fuchs, 1988). There are several reasons for the criticisms. First, the research has not been replicated by researchers other than those who designed the program, and positive results must always remain suspect until independent researchers verify them. Next, numerous methodological flaws in the research make interpretation difficult. Some of the studies had no control group, whereas others had not included random assignment to groups in the research design (Bryan & Bryan, 1988).

Finally, as Fuchs and Fuchs (1988) indicate, the ALEM has become the focus for the recently initiated Regular Education Initiative, sometimes referred to as REI. That initiative is an attempt by the federal government to change special education services by reducing resource room service and implementing consultation with adaptations in the mainstream environment. As Fuchs and Fuchs indicate, formation of a public policy change to a new service delivery model based on only three or four studies is premature. Interest Box 2.5 presents additional information on the Regular Education Initiative and the use of the ALEM efficacy data as a support base.

THE INCLUSIVE SCHOOLS MOVEMENT

From REI to Inclusion

With this history of mainstreaming efforts and consultation in mind, the more recent movement toward inclusive schools and the growing emphasis on the total inclusion of students with disabilities into mainstream classes are more easy to understand (Fuchs & Fuchs, 1994; NASBE, 1992). During the 1970s and 1980s, the most frequently used place-

INTEREST BOX 2.5
The Regular Education Initiative (REI)

Recently, the federal government indicated a desire to place more children with disabilities in mainstream environments and to end the typical type of resource room support that is frequently offered (Carnine and Kameenui, 1990; TED, 1987; Will, 1988). Because special education services in resource rooms cost more than mainstream educational placements, and because data that demonstrates effectiveness of combined mainstream and resource placement is equivocal (Coleman, Pullis, and Minnett, 1987), several leaders in the Department of Education in Washington indicated that schools may need to consider ending resource room services and using more resources to provide consultative services for mainstream teachers (Will, 1988). Services that took place outside the mainstream class have been labeled "pull-out" services, and Will (1988) argued that these services had a tendency to break down the continuity needed for meaningful instruction. This initiative suggested the provision of more support services for mainstream teachers rather than pull-out programs, in spite of the fact that students consider pull-out programs for special assistance to be less embarrassing than having a specialist come into the room (Jenkins and Heinen, 1989).

The ALEM model was frequently cited as one method whereby mainstream classes may be adapted to accommodate learners with disabilities (Fuchs and Fuchs, 1988). The initial research on the efficacy of ALEM suggested that teachers could modify the learning environment such that students took responsibility for their own studies and progressed at their own pace. This strongly suggests the possibility that students with disabilities can succeed in ALEM classrooms.

However, numerous scholars have raised questions concerning the efficacy of the ALEM research, as discussed above (Fuchs, and Fuchs, 1988). These individuals indicate that research is at best incomplete. Also, other researchers have argued that no demonstrable evidence indicates the effectiveness of adaptations in facilitating success in full-time mainstream programs (Carnine and Kameenui, 1990). Clearly, this debate will continue for a period, and prospective special education teachers should be aware of the various positions on the Regular Education Initiative.

ment for the vast majority of students with disabilities was a "resource placement" in which the student spent most of the day in the mainstream class, coupled with one or two periods per day in a resource room. Thus, these students were "pulled out" of the mainstream for one or two periods. However, during the late 1980s, various special education administrators became concerned about the ever increasing cost of special education "pull out" programs (Fuchs & Fuchs, 1994; Will, 1988) and began to investigate how, through the REI mentioned above, some degree of increased mainstreaming (which costs less than special education pull out programs) could take place.

More recently, the term "inclusion" has been used to indicate a need to incorporate more students with disabilities in mainstream classrooms. For some researchers, inclusion means the wholesale placement of all students with disabilities into the mainstream class 100 percent of the time (Fuchs & Fuchs, 1994; NASBE, 1992), whereas other researchers have taken a more moderate approach and viewed inclusion as one option on the continuum of services, originally represented by Deno's cascade of services (discussed in Chapter 1). Further, some researchers tend to view the REI movement as separate from the inclusive schools movement, whereas other researchers view the latter as a logical outgrowth of the former (Hallahan & Kauffman, 1994). For the purposes of this text, it seems that the logical context for each of these is the historical emphasis of increasing mainstream instruction. Fuchs and Fuchs (1994) provide a helpful review of the inclusive schools movement in special education, and you may wish to read that article.

As a teacher you should attempt to make certain of the definitions different persons may use for inclusion or inclusive instruction. For example, on your first job interview, if a principal asked how you feel about inclusion, you should quickly inquire what, exactly, that principal means by the term and how the term is operationalized in that district. The discussion below should help you understand the possibilities and drawbacks of inclusion.

The *Winners All* Report

Inclusive instruction received a real boost in 1992, when the National Association of State Boards of Education (NASBE, 1992) released the report titled *Winners All: A Call for Inclusive Schools.* This document was an endorsement of inclusive instruction for all students, utilizing immoderate phrases in support of the inclusive schools concept, such as "All means all!" Perhaps in response to the intemperate language utilized in this document, some researchers began to feel that proponents of inclusion wished to end special education altogether (Fuchs & Fuchs, 1994). In reply, a number of professional advocacy groups have recently expressed some reservations about the wisdom of total inclusion for all students with all types of disabilities in mainstream classes (Council for Exceptional Children, 1993; Learning Disabilities Association, 1993). The typical tone of these reports encourages inclusive instruction as one service delivery option, but not the only one.

What Does Inclusion Look Like?

Students with Severe Disabilities. Inclusive classrooms may vary widely, given the wide range of definitions of inclusion discussed previously. For example, for many students with severe disabilities, inclusion may mean moving the students into the mainstream class for the entire day, and providing a full-time paraprofessional to assist the teacher and that particular student. In other cases, a paraprofessional may be provided for every two students with disabilities, depending upon the need for assistance of this type. However, some researchers have argued that the concept of inclusion doesn't necessarily mean total inclusion of all students for 100 percent of the day. Again, there are a very wide variety of inclusive instructional programs in the various states and little consensus has emerged upon what the terms really mean (Friend & Cook, 1994; Fuchs & Fuchs, 1994).

The Co-Teaching Experience. Many practitioners are excited about the service delivery possibilities embodied in the inclusive schools movement for students with mild and moderate disabilities (Friend & Cook, 1994, 1992; Fuchs & Fuchs, 1994). In order to end pull out programs, some have recommended that special education teachers be assigned to various mainstream classes for one or two periods per day, during which the special educator and the mainstream educator would co-teach. Using this model, the special education teachers would no longer have their own classroom; rather they would serve several classes.

Friend and Cook (1994, 1992) defined co-teaching as two teachers planning lessons and delivering instruction together. These two teachers would be involved in planning all of the students' instruction, and would typically both be present in the same classroom. At times, one teacher would teach a large group of students, including students both with and without disabilities; the other would teach a small group—again, including students both with and without disabilities. At other times, the teachers might divide the class in half for instruction, or one teacher might teach only one child while the other teacher instructs the remainder of the group. From the students' perspective, there should be no difference between the two teachers; that is, the students may not even be able to tell who is the mainstream teacher and who is the special education teacher. Interest Box 2.6 provides some suggestions about how the teachers should work together.

In inclusive classes of this nature, the teachers work very closely together, and sometimes personality problems can result (Friend & Cook, 1992). Obviously, this is less likely when both teachers choose to participate in inclusive instruction, and in situations where they respect each other. If one teacher is viewed as the "real" teacher, while the other teacher is viewed as a highly skilled teacher's aide, problems will typically result. Under the best of circumstances, the teachers will quickly learn to

INTEREST BOX 2.6
Tips for Successful Co-Teaching

1. *Planning is the key:* Make time to plan lessons and discuss exactly how to work together throughout the co-teaching experience. Set aside a lunch period each week or meet biweekly after school. If possible, set aside a planning period together.
2. *Discuss your views on teaching and learning:* What are your common goals for the students in the lessons? Do you expect all students to master those materials? Effective co-teachers agree that teachers should share basic beliefs about instruction.
3. *Attend to details:* When another professional is teaching with you, you'll need to clarify such classroom rules and procedures as:
   —class routines for leaving the room, using free time, turning in assignments;
   —disciplinary matters;
   —division of chores, such as grading student work or making bulletin boards;
   —pet peeves, such as gum chewing.
4. *Prepare parents:* A few parents may wonder what co-teaching means for their children. Does this mean you'll be teaching less? Will expectations for behavior be lower? Does the special education teacher work with all children? The answers to these questions should be, "No," "No," and "Yes!" Explain to the parents that having two teachers in the class gives every child the opportunity to receive more attention that before.
5. *Make the special education teacher feel welcome:* Clear a place in your room for the other teacher's belongings and be sure to display his or her name. Also, plan how you will introduce the special education teacher to students. Many co-teachers decide that the special education teacher can be described as a teacher who helps students learn how to learn.
6. *Avoid the "paraprofessional trap:"* The most common concern about co-teaching is that the special education teacher may become a classroom helper. This quickly becomes boring for that teacher. More important, it is a very limited use of the talents of two professionals. Having two teachers in the class opens teaching opportunities you may never have had before; the excitement of co-teaching comes from taking advantage of these.
7. *When disagreements occur, talk them out:* To have some disagreements is normal. What is important is to raise your concerns while they are still minor, and to recognize that both of you may have to compromise to resolve them.
8. *Go slowly:* If you begin with co-teaching approaches that require less reliance on one another, you have a chance to learn each other's styles. As your comfort level increases, you will try more complex co-teaching approaches. Above all else, stop periodically to discuss with your co-teacher what is working and what needs revision.

Source: (Friend and Cook 1992, 1994).

serve as a resource person for each other. Although special education teachers may be more highly trained in modification of curriculum materials and individualized instruction, the mainstream teacher is typically more skilled at pacing the class as a whole to master the curriculum according to the areas that need to be covered during the year. These two types of teachers, working together based on their respective strengths, can mutually support each other. In situations of that nature, the practitioners who have experienced inclusive instruction love it, because they feel supported by another professional, another co-worker whom they respect.

Inclusive Schools in the Future

There are as many different opinions concerning the future of inclusive instruction as there are special educators. A number of practitioners, however, have enjoyed their inclusive instructional experience and believe that this is very beneficial for at least some students with disabilities. To date, other than the research base cited above for ALEM classrooms, there is no research base to demonstrate that inclusive instruction works. Typically, proponents of inclusive instruction utilize that research base to document the efficacy of inclusion and, as mentioned previously, serious concerns have been raised about the limited research data supportive of ALEM. Still, given the momentum of this growing movement, you may well see inclusive instructional responsibilities as one component of your job.

EVALUATIONS OF MAINSTREAM CLASS PLACEMENTS

Rationale for Evaluation of Mainstream Classes

Because of the importance of education in the mainstream class, and the tendency for increased mainstream placement, several researchers have recommended evaluation of mainstream educational environments in conjunction with placement decisions (Bender, 1987; Bender, Smith, & Frank, 1988; Bender & Ukije, 1989; Hoier, McConnell, & Pallay, 1987; Ysseldyke & Christenson, 1987). Although most students with mild disabilities spend one or two instructional periods each day in a special education class, the same students spend four or five instructional periods each day in the mainstream. Further, if the inclusive schools concept gains influence, students with disabilities will be spending more and more time in mainstream classes. Clearly, if education is to be effective for those students, the educational environment within the mainstream must be an environment that utilizes the techniques, strategies, and modifications that facilitate learning among individuals with disabilities. As the data on modifications in mainstream classes demonstrate, mainstream teachers do not adequately modify their classes to facilitate mainstreaming, and some type of informal evaluation of their class environment may provide the impetus for the desired modification (Bender, 1992).

From an ecological assessment perspective, evaluation of the learning environment makes sense (Bender, 1992). Ecology represents the study of organisms within their native habitat, and assessment of students with disabilities is not complete without some assessment of the "native habitat" in which most of their education takes place. Although special educators have long practiced in-depth assessment of the learning problems of a particular child, there has been little organized effort at assessing the learning problem in relation to the instructional environment.

Perhaps, in certain instances, assessment of the types of instructional activities offered—and some modification of those activities—will alleviate the learning problem without the need to identify a child as disabled. After decades of individualized child-centered assessment, it seems clear that assessment of a child will provide only part of the explanation for a learning problem. At the very least, some knowledge about how a mainstream teacher teaches will give consultant special education teachers insight on the types of methods that have not been successful with that child. Furthermore, such assessment may yield understanding of the future likelihood of successful mainstreaming in that teacher's class (Bender, 1987).

Evaluation Approaches

The research on evaluation of mainstream class learning environments is still embryonic, and only a few ideas on evaluation methods have been forthcoming (Bender, 1987; Hoier, McConnell, & Pallay, 1987; Ysseldyke & Christenson, 1987). One concept is actual observations of "average" children in the mainstream class in order to determine the "typical" behaviors within the context of that class. Hoier, McConnell, and Pallay (1987) recommend that consultants attempt to match a particular child with a disability to a particular class or learning environment, based on a comparison between the behavioral profiles of the referred child and the "average" child from that mainstream class. However, these authors readily admit that the behavioral assessment technology to accomplish this is not available at present.

Other researchers have suggested some type of self-evaluation, in which the mainstream teacher uses a checklist or scale to identify the instructional strategies in use in the mainstream class (Bender, 1987; Bender & Ukije, 1989; Ysseldyke & Christenson, 1987). Several self-evaluations of this nature are available in the literature or commercially (Bender & Ukije, 1989; Ysseldyke & Christenson, 1987), and use of this self-evaluation format has several advantages. First, mainstream teachers are less likely to feel threatened by this type of evaluation, and may see the evaluation as a method of improving consultative services for their class. Also, the indicators on the evaluation instrument may provide some hints to the mainstream teacher concerning the types of modifications that should be utilized. In that sense, a self-evaluation may serve as an instructional tool for the mainstream teachers.

Figure 2.2 presents a mainstream evaluation instrument that has been used in several research studies (Bender & Ukije, 1989; Bender, Smith, & Frank, 1988). You may wish to read through the indicators included and think about using this instrument as a catalyst for consultation services, or as a "conversation starter," when you sit down with a mainstream teacher to solve his or her problem in educating a student with a disability in the mainstream class.

SUMMARY

Consultation with mainstream teachers is one responsibility of many special education teachers, and that responsibility will only increase in inclusive classrooms involving co-teaching responsibilities. Often a teacher's personal job satisfaction is partially dependent on development of good relationships with mainstream teachers in order to positively influence the education of students with disabilities in mainstream classes. Also, special education teachers are being called on more frequently for consultative services today than in the past.

The rationale for mainstreaming is based on the provision of "normal" social role models for students with disabilities, rather than perceived academic gains associated with mainstream placement. When a mainstream teacher is acquainted with this fact, that teacher can better structure the mainstream class to accomplish meaningful educational growth.

Unfortunately, the research has indicated that many mainstream teachers do not modify the mainstream class a great deal to accommodate students with disabilities. Also, the modifications made are not the type of substantive modifications that would facilitate the education of students with disabilities. One role that many special educators have to perform is attempting to entice the mainstream teachers to implement more modifications.

The ALEM is one body of information that may be useful in advocating for modifications. Research has tentatively suggested that this model is effective in transforming the typical

BENDER CONSULTATION STRATEGIES QUESTIONNAIRE

Name ______________________ School ______________________ Date ______________

This rating is designed to measure various aspects of instructional environments in order to help the placement team make useful recommendations to you. It will take about 15 minutes to complete. Please fill in each blank below, then rate each question on the 5-point scale ranging from *only rarely* (less than once a month) to *almost always* (every day). You are welcome to inquire about the instructional strategies mentioned below for use with children with disabilities in your class.

How many years have you taught school? ______________________

How many years did you have students with disabilities in your class? ______________________

Please list current certification areas. ______________________

____

What is your highest earned degree? ______________________

How many courses specifically on teaching students with disabilities have you completed? ______________

How many children with disabilities are in the mainstream class for which this rating was completed? ______

How many students (total) are in that class? ______________________

	Only rarely				Almost always
I keep the lesson moving along quickly.	1	2	3	4	5
The class reviews assignment papers when I return them.	1	2	3	4	5
Several students may be walking around in my class at any one time retrieving materials.	1	2	3	4	5
Students receive verbal praise from each other.	1	2	3	4	5
I encourage students to share various techniques that may help them memorize facts in class.	1	2	3	4	5
The class emphasizes correction of worksheets.	1	2	3	4	5
Students must raise their hands before standing.	1	2	3	4	5
I ask, "How did you learn that?" or some other question to focus on learning strategies.	1	2	3	4	5
I insist that doors be shut and students remain in their seats to minimize distractions.	1	2	3	4	5
New material is introduced fairly rapidly.	1	2	3	4	5
I suggest particular methods of remembering.	1	2	3	4	5
Peer tutoring is used to assist slow learners.	1	2	3	4	5
I emphasize the importance of working quietly.	1	2	3	4	5
I determine early in the year if a student needs the same concepts covered in several different ways.	1	2	3	4	5
I use physical touch, such as a pat on the back, as a reinforcer.	1	2	3	4	5
I praise students for successful work whenever possible.	1	2	3	4	5

	Only rarely				Almost always
Students are encouraged to help each other informally on learning tasks.	1	2	3	4	5
I try to determine how students learn best.	1	2	3	4	5
I use reading materials that highlight the topic sentence and main idea for slow learners.	1	2	3	4	5
I individualize in my class when necessary.	1	2	3	4	5
Students are taught to use their own inner language to give themselves silent task instructions.	1	2	3	4	5
I use class privileges as rewards for work.	1	2	3	4	5
I use a specialized grading system that rewards effort for pupils with disabilities.	1	2	3	4	5
I use several test administrations options such as oral tests or extended time tests.	1	2	3	4	5
Directions for educational tasks are kept simple and are demonstrated to achieve clarity.	1	2	3	4	5
Differential curriculum materials are selected based on the learning characteristics of particular students in my classes.	1	2	3	4	5
I routinely vary the instructional level for different-ability children doing the same task.	1	2	3	4	5
Instructional materials are varied for different students in my classes.	1	2	3	4	5
I constantly monitor the on-task behavior of my students.	1	2	3	4	5
I individualize my class for low-ability students.	1	2	3	4	5
I use visual displays and transparencies in class to aid comprehension.	1	2	3	4	5
Students use self-monitoring to record daily academic and behavioral progress.	1	2	3	4	5
I use a token economy for reinforcement.	1	2	3	4	5
I use the blackboard frequently to explain concepts.	1	2	3	4	5
I have an assertive discipline plan in effect.	1	2	3	4	5
Cooperative learning groups are frequently used.	1	2	3	4	5
I use individual behavioral contracts with students to improve behavior.	1	2	3	4	5
I use advance organizers to assist students in comprehension of difficult concepts.	1	2	3	4	5
Students complete direct daily measures of academic progress in class.	1	2	3	4	5
A set of class rules is on display in my class.	1	2	3	4	5

FIGURE 2.2 Bender Classroom Structure Questionnaire

mainstream class into a highly flexible learning environment that can accommodate various learners.

Based on the ALEM research, a number of researchers have recommended inclusive schools where teachers co-teach in the mainstream learning environment. Although research on this instructional option is limited, you can expect to hear a great deal about inclusion in the near future.

Another tool that may be used is the checklist for evaluation of mainstream environments. Several of these are available and may provide some insight into how mainstream teachers currently teach their classes. Also, these self-evaluation checklists can provide some impetus for mainstream teachers to remain abreast of the newly emerging instructional strategies that facilitate mainstreaming.

Summary Points

- Mainstream predated inclusive classes, and differs from inclusive school programs because, the co-teaching that characterizes inclusive teaching is not typical in mainstream classes, even though consultative services may be available in mainstream classes.
- Consultation is a growing type of service delivery in which the special education teachers enter the mainstream class on an occasional basis to provide assistance to mainstream teachers in dealing with children with disabilities.
- Historically, mainstreaming may best be explained as one of the civil rights movements in our nation's recent history in which individuals with disabilities and advocates for that group became active and demanded the rights of education in the least restrictive environment that would meet the needs of the learner.
- Inclusive classes make sense from the perspective of providing effective social role models to students with disabilities. Students with disabilities do not suffer academically in mainstream classes and they are exposed to more appropriate social role models.
- Numerous professional groups have expressed some concern over inclusion because of the fear that supportive services will not be provided to mainstream teachers.
- The ALEM model involved modifications to the learning environment at the school and classroom level in order to accommodate the needs of more diverse groups of learners.
- Accommodations to the class may be more easily explained if it is considered that modifications made this year will facilitate instruction for the next several years, or until the school curriculum changes.
- Environmental evaluation involves evaluation of the instructional strategies used in mainstream classes in order to facilitate mainstreaming. Several instruments are available for this type of self-evaluation.

QUESTIONS AND ACTIVITIES

1. What differences exist between inclusion and mainstreaming? How much time does a special education teacher spend in the mainstream classroom in each type of setting?
2. If schools in your area provide inclusive instruction, you may wish to bring in two teachers who teach in an inclusive class and have them describe the problems such teaching involves.
3. Describe the ALEM and the research support that has been provided for this type of instruction.
4. What rationale can you provide for self-evaluation of the instructional strategies used in mainstream classes?
5. Have members of the class share experiences from their early field placements in which they heard teachers criticize the concept of mainstreaming.

REFERENCES

Baker, J. M., & Zigmond, N. (1990). Are regular education classes equipped to accommodate students with learning disabilities? *Exceptional Children, 56,* 515–526.

Bender, W. N. (1986). Instructional grouping and individualization for mainstreamed learning disabled children and adolescents. *Child Study Journal, 16,* 207–215.

Bender, W. N. (1987). Effective educational practices in the mainstream setting: Recommended model for evaluation of mainstream teacher's classes. *The Journal of Special Education, 20,* 475–486.

Bender, W. N. (1992). The Bender Classroom Structure Questionnaire: A tool for placement decisions and evaluation of mainstream learning environments. *Intervention in School and Clinic, 27,* 307–312.

Bender, W. N., Smith, J. D., & Frank, J. N. (1988). Evaluation of mainstream classes: A scale for determining appropriate class placements. *Education, 108,* 540–545.

Bender, W. N., & Ukije, I. C. (1989). Instructional strategies in mainstream classrooms: Prediction of the strategies teachers select. *Remedial and Special Education, 1* (2), 23–30.

Bryan, J. H., & Bryan, T. H. (1988). Where's the beef? A review of published research on the Adaptive Learning Environments Model. *Learning Disabilities Focus, 4* (1), 9–14.

Carnine, D. W., & Kameenui, E. J. (1990). The general education initiative and children with special needs: A false dilemma in the face of true problems. *Journal of Learning Disabilities, 23,* 141–144.

Cohen, S. E. (1988). Coping strategies of university students with learning disabilities. *Journal of Learning Disabilities, 21,* 161–164.

Coleman, J. M., Pullis, M. E., & Minnett, A. M. (1987). Studying mildly handicapped children's adjustment to mainstreaming: A systemic approach. *Remedial and Special Education, 8* (6), 19–30.

Council for Exceptional Children (1993, April). *Statement on Inclusive Schools and Communities.* Reston, VA: Author.

Dunn, L. M. (1968). Special education for the mildly retarded—Is much of it justifiable? *Exceptional Children, 34,* 5–22.

Friend, M., & Cook, L. (1992, March). The new mainstreaming. *Instructor,* 30–36.

Friend, M., & Cook, L. (1994, November 12). *Co-teaching principles, practices and pragmatics.* A paper presented at the annual meeting of the Council for Learning Disabilities, San Diego.

Fuchs, D., & Fuchs, L. (1988). Evaluation of the Adaptive Learning Environments Model. *Exceptional Children, 55,* 115–127.

Fuchs, D., & Fuchs, L. (1994). Inclusive schools movement and the radicalization of special education reform. *Exceptional Children, 60,* 294–309.

Fuchs, L. S., Fuchs, D., Hamlett, C. L., & Ferguson, C. (1992). Effects of expert system consultation within curriculum-based measurement, using a reading maze task. *Exceptional Children, 58,* 436–450.

Gersten, R., & Woodward, J. (1990). Rethinking the Regular Education Initiative: Focus on the classroom teacher. *Remedial and Special Education, 11* (3), 7–16.

Gottlieb, J., Alter, M., & Yoshida, R. K. (1990). *New York Department of Education: Evaluation of Consultant Teacher Program.* Larchmont, NY: Center for Educational Research.

Graham, S., Hudson, F., Burdg, N. B., & Carpenter, D. (1980). Educational personnel's perceptions of mainstreaming and resource room effectiveness. *Psychology in the Schools, 17,* 128–134.

Hallahan, D. P., & Kauffman, J. M. (1994). From mainstreaming to collaborative consultation. In J. M. Kauffman & D. P. Hallahan (Eds.), *The Illusion of Full Inclusion: A Comprehensive Critique of a Current Special Education Bandwagon.* Austin, TX: ProEd, pp. 208–243.

Hoier, T. S., McConnell, S., & Pallay, A. G. (1987). Observational assessment for planning and evaluating educational transitions: An initial analysis of template matching. *Behavioral Assessment, 9,* 5–19.

Idol, L. (1993). *Special Educator's Consultation Handbook: Second Edition.* Austin, TX.: ProEd.

Jenkins, J. R., & Heinen, A. (1989). Students' preferences for service delivery: Pull-out, in-class, or integrated models. *Exceptional Children, 55,* 516–523.

Learning Disabilities Association (1993, January). *Position Paper on Full Inclusion of All Students with Learning Disabilities in the Regular Education Classroom.* Pittsburgh, PA: Author.

Margolis, H., & McGettigan, J. (1988). Managing resistance to instructional modifications in mainstreamed environments. *Remedial and Special Education, 9* (4), 15–21.

Munson, S. M. (1987). Regular education teacher modifications for mainstreamed mildly handicapped students. *The Journal of Special Education, 20,* 489–502.

Myles, B. S., & Simpson, R. L. (1989). Regular educators' modification preferences for mainstreaming mildly handicapped children. *The Journal of Special Education, 22,* 479–491.

Myles, B. S., & Simpson, R. L. (1990). Mainstreaming modification preferences of parents of elementary-age children with learning disabilities. *Journal of Learning Disabilities, 23,* 234–239.

National Association of State Boards of Education (NASBE) (1992, October). *Winners All: A Call for Inclusive Schools.* Washington, DC: Author.

Schulte, A. C., Osborne, S. S., & McKinney, J. D. (1990). Academic outcomes for students with learning disabilities in consultation and resource programs. *Exceptional Children, 57,* 162–175.

Teacher Education Division (TED) (1987). A statement by the Teacher Education Division Council for Exceptional Children: October 1986. *Journal of Learning Disabilities, 20,* 289–293.

Tindal, G., Parker, R., & Germann, G. (1990). An analysis of mainstream consultation outcomes for secondary students identified as learning disabled. *Learning Disability, 13,* 220–229.

Wang, M. C., & Birch, J. W. (1984). Comparison of a full-time mainstreaming program and a resource room approach. *Exceptional Children, 51,* 33–40.

Wang, M. C., & Zollers, N. J. (1990). Adaptive instruction: An alternative service delivery approach. *Remedial and Special Education,* 11 (1), 7–21.

Wesson, C. L. (1991). Curriculum-based measurement and two models. *Exceptional Children, 57,* 246–256.

Will, M. (1988). Educating students with learning problems and the changing role of the school psychologist. *School Psychology Review, 17,* 476–478.

York, J., Vandercook, T., MacDonald, C., Heise-Neff, C., & Caughey, E. (1992). Feedback about integrating middle-school students with severe disabilities in general education classes. *Exceptional Children, 58,* 244–259.

Ysseldyke, J. E., & Christenson, S. L. (1987). Evaluating students' instructional environments. *Remedial and Special Education, 8* (3), 17–24.

Ysseldyke, J. E., Thurlow, M. L., Wotruba, J. W., & Nania, P. A. (1990). Instructional arrangements: Perceptions from general education. *Teaching Exceptional Children, 22* (5), 4–8.

CHAPTER 3

DISCIPLINARY OPTIONS FOR SPECIAL STUDENTS

OBJECTIVES

When you complete this chapter, you should be able to:

1. Identify four levels of disciplinary options in special classes.
2. Discuss behavioral change strategies in the classroom.
3. Identify the steps required in organization of a token economy and store.
4. Define assertive discipline.
5. Discuss the guidelines for moving from one level of disciplinary tactic to another.
6. List the reasons for taking a disciplinary matter beyond the classroom.
7. Describe a class meeting.
8. Identify the guidelines for conducting a life-space interview.
9. Present evidence on the effectiveness of several relaxation techniques.

KEYWORDS

assertive discipline	peer pressure	relaxation training
rule system	time-out	exercise program
token economy	life-space interview	turtle technique
behavioral contract	class meeting	response cost
fining	biofeedback	office visit report

The classroom environment is arranged, materials in order, student task cards are completed for the first few days of school, and the students arrive on the first day. It will not take you long, as a beginning teacher, to realize that your problems are not a result of having omitted preparation of materials or student task cards. The problems that both beginning teachers and experienced teachers most frequently identify as their most serious concerns are disciplinary, not instructional, matters. An inability to maintain discipline in the class is also one common reason for nonrenewal of beginning teachers' contracts. Consequently, you need to be well prepared to handle disciplinary problems.

Unfortunately, consistent success in discipline is a very difficult attainment. Although experience is the best teacher for disciplinary techniques, some beginning teachers undergo relatively inadequate preservice preparation for disciplinary matters. For example, many methods texts substitute a few chapters on behavior management for the required chapters on disciplinary techniques. Although behavioral strategies are effective and certainly should be included, these strategies must be translated into usable classroom form, enriched with other disciplinary strategies, and included in an overall plan that stipulates the appropriate types of interventions for specific problems. A knowledge of behavioral strategies is a necessary but not sufficient condition for becoming an effective disciplinarian in public school special education classes.

The assumption behind this section of the text is that you have had some extended exposure to behavioral strategies in earlier courses, laboratory experiences, and public school field experiences. Although this chapter does not present comprehensive discussion of the particulars of behavioral managements, such as the advantages of various reinforcement schedules, the translation of behavioral strategies into classroom disciplinary strategies is presented. Classroom applications of behavioral strategies include behavioral contracting, time-out, peer pressure, and token economies. However, these strategies are placed in the larger context of an assertive prioritized disciplinary plan. Finally, strategies are presented that are not behavioral in origin, including life-space interviewing, class meetings, and relaxation strategies. After reading this chapter you should put together the set of disciplinary techniques you select for use in your own class and further explore the research on those particular techniques.

ASSERTIVE DISCIPLINE

Assertive discipline is a term used to indicate the right and responsibility of every teacher to be (or become) assertive as an instructional leader and disciplinarian in the classroom (Canter, 1982). For example, as a teacher, you have the right to identify a level or noise, movement, and out-of-seat behavior in your class that you will allow. The choice is yours, and you make the decisions. If there are disciplinary problems in your class, students did not create them—you did. You set the expectations for behavior, the behavioral norms, and the limits of tolerable behavior in your class, and assertive disciplinary programs attempt to highlight the decisions you make as the teacher—unconsciously or consciously—that create the disciplinary tolerances in your classroom. According to this view, the responsibility for discipline rests squarely with the teacher—an empowering point of view for a teacher.

Numerous workshops, books, and pamphlets on assertive disciplinary techniques are available (Canter, 1982), and the techniques have received some research support (Mandlebaum, Russell, Krouse, & Gonter, 1983). However, the assertive disciplinary program has also been criticized as being punishment oriented and too restrictive (Hill, 1990).

In spite of this recent criticism, many beginning and experienced teachers find these techniques helpful. Although a full discussion of assertive discipline is beyond the scope of this book, several of the techniques discussed below are included in the assertive discipline literature, despite the fact that the research for these techniques predates the popularization of that term.

Rule Systems

As a first step in outlining a disciplinary plan for your class you should develop a set of rules for the class and insist that those rules be followed. The most effective manner for rule development is to encourage the students to assist in the formulation of the rules. This encourages ownership of the rules, and makes them seem less arbitrary. Also, the rules should be posted throughout the school year, in sight of each student. When an infraction occurs, you should indicate which rule was broken before assigning punishment. The fact that the rules are posted makes you seem less arbitrary as a disciplinarian (the student may even look over at the rules when you refer to them).

As in all disciplinary matters, consistency is the key; the rules should be applied to all students in the same manner on each day of the year. A teacher may be either very strict or very lenient with students in rule interpretation and still be an effective disciplinarian, as long as the teacher is consistent. Contrary to popular opinion, the sex and physical size of the teacher do not seem to matter either, in terms of who is effective in managing disciplinary matters in a classroom. Consistency is the key. A consistent disciplinarian will let students know what is expected and what is tolerated through the development and consistent application of classroom rules, and these limits will not change from day to day.

The rules should be stated in a positive manner, indicating what a student will do rather than what a student will not do ("Students will work quickly and quietly" and "Students will put materials away without disturbing others" are two rules from the system this author used in a junior high resource room). Rules should be brief, and generally four or five rules should be enough. In preparation of your rule system, do not try to cover every imaginable contingency; address only the most common problems. Finally, during the first several weeks of school, use each infraction of the rules as an opportunity to go over the rules with the class. Rosenburg (1986) presented research to indicate that a regular review of the class rules enhanced the effectiveness of the rules as a disciplinary aid. Review of the rules on a daily basis (at least at the beginning of the year) will let the class know that you take the rules seriously, and that they will apply throughout the year.

Outside Support

As the teacher, you have the right to seek support for your disciplinary decisions from authority figures outside your classroom. Both parents and school administrators should be expected to support your decisions, if those decisions are made in the best interests of the student, and if the appropriate communication has preceded the decision. Canter (1982) recommends sending an abbreviated copy of your rule system home to the parents. This letter should be phrased in a positive way and should let the parents know that you are willing to negotiate somewhat if a particular matter is problematic for their child. However, many parents today are demanding more firm disciplinary action from schools, and you should expect many more positive responses from the parents than negative ones. Interest Box 3.1 presents a form letter you could use to explain your disciplinary system to parents. This letter was modeled on the typical letter that Canter (1982) suggests as a communication with parents. At the beginning of each year, every parent should receive this type of letter as a way to elicit parental support for your disciplinary plans.

You also have the right to expect the support of the principal and the administrators in your district. Most principals explain early to beginning teachers the conditions under which they want to be involved in disciplinary situations. If your principal does not offer such guidance early in your beginning year as a teacher, you should request a brief conference in order to gain a better understanding of what is expected. The general guidelines for when to involve administrators in disciplinary actions are discussed below in the discussion of the four disciplinary options.

BEHAVIORAL STRATEGIES

There are numerous behavioral strategies in use in special education classes throughout the country, and these have, without exception, been very successful in assisting students with disabilities to function successfully in school classrooms (Katz, Reeder, Russell, & Salend, 1992; Minner & Knutson, 1980; Rosen, Gabardi, Miller, & Miller, 1990; Salend, Jantzen, & Geik, 1992; Stolz, Wienckowski, & Brown, 1975; White, 1986; Smith & Fowler, 1984). In fact, the very effectiveness of these interventions has resulted in a concern for "overcontrol" of students with disabilities and other students in certain instances (Gast & Nelson, 1977; Hill, 1990; Stolz, Wienckowski, & Brown, 1975). Given this level of effectiveness, it is difficult to imagine a special education class of any type that does not incorporate some behavioral strategies into the program. In this section several strategies are discussed that can easily be incorporated in almost any special education setting. These include token economies, behavioral contracting, response cost, time-out, and peer pressure. Precision teaching—another behavioral technique—is both a disciplinary and an instructional technique. As such, this technique is discussed in Chapter 4.

Token Economies

The token economy represents an attempt to provide a standard exchangeable reinforcement for

INTEREST BOX 3.1
Sample Letter on Disciplinary Procedures

Ms. Lillian Neihaus
9/4/96

Dear Parent:

I have your son or daughter in my class this year, and, as a group, the class has decided to identify some class rules that will allow us to work together more effectively. These are listed below.

1. We will work quietly and quickly.
2. When we need assistance, we will request it by silently raising our hand.
3. We will stay at our desks whenever possible so that others may work without being disturbed.
4. We will move quietly, without disturbing others, when we have to sharpen pencils, get books, or leave our desk for any other reason.
5. We will always respect the rights of others in the class.

These rules are posted in the classroom and will be used throughout the year. I will remind the class of these rules whenever necessary.

Although we do not anticipate problems, the principal and I have identified several steps to be taken should recurring disciplinary problems arise. First, a warning will be given by me. If the problem occurs again, I will discipline the student by removal of class privileges or rewards, previously earned. If the problem continues, I will request the principal's assistance and your assistance in order to prevent further disruption to the class. Please sign below, indicating your willingness to assist in this disciplinary plan, and to assure that every child has a good opportunity to learn. I thank you in advance for your support, and should any consistent problems arise, I will contact you to discuss them at length. I look forward to meeting you at the first parent-teacher conference.

Yours,

____

Ms. Lillian Neihaus,
Resource Room Teacher

I agree to work with Ms. Neihaus to assure that my child has the best possible opportunity to learn this year.

SIGNATURE: ________________________ Child's Name ________________________

Source: Modeled after Canter (1982).

appropriate behavior. It provides both the teacher and the student with disciplinary choices and increases the options for dealing with minor problem behaviors (Minner & Knutson, 1980; Stainback & Stainback, 1975). Also, token economies provide an easy method for reinforcing appropriate behavior or good work in class. For many students with mild and moderate disabilities, grades have lost their "reinforcing potency," since these students have received low grades for so long. A token economy offers a new reinforcement option for the teacher who wishes to motivate these students.

The initiation of a token system for your class involves three steps. First, you must select the tokens and introduce these to the class. Generally, "play money" that looks like real money is the choice because students will inadvertently learn such skills as counting change, addition and subtraction of money, and, in more advanced cases, checking and banking skills. The other option—plastic counters—does not encourage these skills to the same degree. The lowest denomination of tokens should be relatively cheap, such that a student may earn one to five "pennies" for a single math problem done well (teachers who use one token or sticker per day do not realize the full positive effects of a strong token economy, since many students with disabilities do not associate a sticker at the end of the day with good behavior or hard work during the writing activity they did at 9:30 that morning).

As a general guideline, pay each student for every assignment, or about every 10 minutes, and make the payment relative to the amount of work completed (shorter assignments or assignments done less than adequately receive only minimal payment). You must explain to the class that the tokens used are exchangeable for rewards in the class "store" on a daily or weekly basis. With younger children you may wish to give an additional reward, such as praise, or an edible reward when you first give tokens, as a way of strengthening the effects of the tokens.

Second, most token economies depend on the establishment of a "store" that provides the reinforcers for the economy. The items in the store may be purchased by the students with the money or tokens earned for good work and good behavior in the class. This store may be stocked with "yard sale" materials collected from other teachers (old records, jewelry, old books, magazines), edibles (raisins, nuts), materials collected from local merchants, necessary school materials (pencils, note pads, paper), and "privilege cards" that represent class privileges. Each of the items should be marked with a price relative to the value of other items in the store. At the beginning of the year, you may wish to take the students to the store each of the first three days in order to strengthen the reward aspects of the system.

Finally, you must establish procedures for payment and store visitations. After the economy is established, once-a-week visits should be sufficient to maintain the power of the reward system. For payment options, pay each student during the activity (for good effort), after the activity, or at the end of the day.

With some students who already count money and figure correct change, you may wish to establish a checkbook system (Minner & Knutson, 1980). For daily assignments, the student would receive rewards when the teacher indicates the amount a student earned for an assignment by writing the amount earned on the student's task card next to that particular assignment. This should be done as each assignment is checked. The actual presentation of money takes place at the end of class, after each student correctly adds his or her earned money for that day. For students in a checkbook, the teacher would wait until all work for each day is completed, and have the student add each daily sum to get a "weekly deposit" figure. Figure 3.1 presents a check system this author used in a token economy for junior high handicapped students. A deposit is made each week, added to the balance brought forward, and the student may write one check for each visit to the store.

Minner and Knutson (1980) recommend that older students who are capable with elementary money management go further. For example, balancing checkbooks (which pay interest), health insurance for absences, and charge cards may all be added to the token economy after students are used to the system. These additions make a token economy an instructional system rather than merely a reward system. However, with each increased

Brought Forward ______	____ ____ 19 ______
Deposit ______	Pay to The Order of ______ $______
	______ dollars
Total ______	Class Store Bank
	Neihaus Class
Check ______	Memo______ Signature ______
Total ______	

FIGURE 3.1 Token Economy Checks

use of the economy, you will increase the management problems, so beware of time usage allocated exclusively for the economy management. Also, the economy quickly becomes "real" for the students, and you will have some problems that include every major crime imaginable; theft, blackmail, bribery, and extortion are possible. As a result, only the teacher should have access to the money bank, and unused monies should be stored under lock and key.

Even with these problems, a good token economy can be very easy to manage and not time consuming. In the system described above, only the last two minutes or so of class will be spent on the token economy management, and that usually takes place while students put away materials and add their earnings. The teacher should check each student's addition to assure that the amount was correct (generally for seven or eight problems) and reward money to those who were not in checkbooks. Each week on Friday, the class should be allowed to go to the store for the last eight to ten minutes of the period.

This system offers numerous disciplinary options for relatively minor rule infractions. Such things as talkouts in class, playful hitting, or whispering may be handled easily using the economy. Perhaps 80 percent of the minor infractions in the junior high class that utilized this system were handled through the token economy. For example, when a student was off-task or mildly disruptive, one option was to reward everyone who was on-task, or everyone who got back on-task in the ensuing five seconds. This usually resulted in returning to on-task behavior. Personally, I used this system for each year I taught, and I could not imagine teaching in special education without some type of token economy.

Behavioral Contracting

The behavioral contract is an agreement between a student and a teacher. It specifies a task or set of tasks to be completed and a specific reward that will be earned. The task and the evaluation of task completion should be detailed, in order to prevent misunderstandings concerning task completion. Interest Box 3.2 presents a behavioral contract form that has been completed. You should copy this form (or a similar form), and fill in the blanks when you wish to establish a contract with particular students.

INTEREST BOX 3.2
The Behavioral Contract

I, ______________________________, agree to undertake and satisfactorily complete the following task: ____

____

____

The task will be judged to be completed under the following conditions.

____

____

____

I, ______________________________, value the task described above, and have entered into this agreement in order to find an appropriate opportunity to reward this student for achieving the described task. When the task is satisfactorily completed the student will receive the following rewards and class privileges.

____

____

____

____

We have entered into this agreement, which will be binding on each of us. We are fully aware of the intention of this agreement and understand the information provided here.

Signatures ______________________________ (Student)

______________________________ (Teacher)

The contract should be used as an additional measure, over and above the token economy. Students should be allowed to continue earning money and complete the contract at the same time. However, contracts should be used only in very special situations, offered when a student has shown particular motivation problems relative to a task. The student should understand that the contract is a personal agreement that he or she can reject before signing. However, after signing, the agreement becomes a "contract," and the assertive teacher has every right to expect it to be fulfilled.

Generally, contracts should specify longer-term goals, over a period of days or weeks, and the reward should be very costly in order to provide the special motivation for the student.

Response Cost (Fining)

When society wishes to reprimand a citizen for unlawful behavior, the court system may impose a fine, and money is frequently taken from the offender. Such a disciplinary option is also available in the token economy (or independent of it, as we shall see later). Either money or class privileges may be taken from students, based on the misbehavior. This system is referred to as fining or, more appropriately, response cost. Systems such as these should impose fines commensurate with the rule infraction, and they should be directly tied to the rule system on display in the room. Also, it may be advantageous for the teacher to keep the response cost separate from the earned rewards for work. Removal of one or two minutes of break or recess time is quite punishing for infractions that are slightly more than minor occurrences (verbal aggression that is not playful, shouting, cursing, etc.). Generally, you should remember that it is not the length of time a student has to remain inside that is punishing, but the fact that he or she may not go out when everyone else does. When I used this system, I frequently started with a two-minute fine, and if the student objected in a hostile fashion, I increased that to a five-minute fine. Such a fine could be increased again, to ten minutes, if the student did not calm down. Thus, the break period was used to construct several punishment options, rather than merely one punishment option. Using this strategy, the teacher can respond to a student's anger at imposition of the fine by reminding the student of the class rules and increasing the penalties each time the student responds negatively to the fine. This usually results in student compliance and acceptance of the fine at some point.

However, one problem with escalating response cost strategies is the potential for a resultant power struggle between teacher and student. Power struggles should be avoided, and if fining is likely to result in one for a particular student, you should choose another disciplinary procedure.

Peer Pressure

One fairly recent behavioral intervention is the use of peer pressure for decreasing negative behaviors in the classroom (Marandola & Imber, 1979; Salend, Jantzen, & Geik, 1992; Sandler, Arnold, Gable, & Strain, 1987; Smith & Fowler, 1984). For example, Sandler and his co-workers initiated a teacher directed peer confrontation behavior change program in a class for emotionally disturbed students, with very impressive results.

Implementation of such a procedure is very easy. First, a teacher should keep baseline data for a period of a few days. This can be done by merely counting and tallying the number of behaviors or by keeping a critical incidents log, which specifies the problem behavior, the events preceding the behavior, and the consequences of the behavior (see Sugai, 1986, for information on recording classroom events). Then, during the treatment phase, when a problem behavior is observed, the teacher should engage the other members of the class in a dialogue about the student emitting the problem behavior. The dialogue should specify the behavior that is considered problematic, and appropriate behaviors for the student to begin in order to alleviate the problem. Interest Box 3.3 presents some of the actual statements a teacher may use, though these may vary somewhat with the particular instance.

Although the early research demonstrated the efficacy of peer confrontation to alleviate a single student's behavior problems, Salend, Jantzen, and Geik (1992) used the peer confrontation system to alleviate the behavioral problems among two groups of students. In that intervention study a count was made of the specific behavior problems demonstrated by two groups of students with behavioral disabilities in a self-contained special

INTEREST BOX 3.3
Statements for Peer Pressure Strategy

The statements made during a peer pressure strategy session may vary somewhat because of the challenging uniqueness of disciplinary situations in the classroom. Sandler and his co-workers (1987) used the following statements in their work:

> Subject (student's name) seems to be having a problem. Who can tell (student's name) what the problem is?
> (Student response here)
> Good. Now can you tell (student's name) why that is a problem?
> (Student response here)
> Very good. Who can tell (subject's name) what he or she needs to solve the problem?

With this set of simple straightforward statements, the teacher has begun to use peer pressure in a directed way to manage disruptive behavior of the students. Other statements may need to be added, and if a playful or destructive remark is used by the peers when responding to the questions, you may need to repeat the question and/or ask another student. However, as you can see, this technique is very simple to use in the class, and research has demonstrated the effectiveness of this strategy.

Source: Sandler et al. (1987).

education classroom. For group A, the target goal was reduction of off-task behavior, whereas the goal for group B was reduction of inappropriate vocalizations. Each time a member of either group demonstrated a behavior problem, that student's peers were used to assist in identifying the problems and suggesting solutions to the student. The results indicated that peer confrontation was very effective in reducing these disruptive and off-task behaviors for both groups.

This is a more involved intervention than fining a student, because the work of other students is temporarily halted. Consequently, this intervention should be used only when verbal warnings or fining is not enough. This intervention is for relatively serious problems you wish to solve in class.

Time-Out

When a serious behavioral infraction occurs, and a student has temporarily lost control over his or her actions, a time-out intervention may be appropriate (Gast & Nelson, 1977). Time-out consists of the removal of the student from all sources of reinforcement. The assumption is that a brief removal from such reinforcement may result in the reestablishment of control over the behavior. Many special education settings are equipped with special time-out rooms where a student may be placed for brief periods. Such rooms are particularly effective because ideally the time-out intervention should remove the student from potential reinforcement from other students as well as from environmental stimuli in the class. Research has demonstrated that time-out can be a very effective intervention for students with mild and moderate disabilities.

Gast and Nelson (1977) presented several recommendations concerning the use of time-out. First, a verbal explanation should be provided to the student whenever he or she is placed in time-out. Notation should be made on the IEP as to the conditions under which time-out will be employed. Some teachers prefer to use a warning signal or verbal cue that placement in time-out is imminent unless the student's behavior changes. Generally time-out should not exceed a few minutes—five minutes is a typical recommendation—as more extensive removal from the classroom environment is quite punitive. Finally, time-out should not be the procedure of choice if the student finds time-out itself reinforcing. Time-out interventions each week before the weekly spelling test do not contribute to the long term well-being of the student, and time-out in the school hallway places students in one of the most interesting settings in the school, when there is action in the hall. These kinds of practices should be avoided.

SELF-AWARENESS STRATEGIES

A number of research studies have demonstrated the effectiveness of disciplinary strategies based on increased self-awareness of the problem, optional behavioral responses to the problem, and consequences of the alternative responses. These strategies, with the self-awareness component, have the potential to make the student an active participant in management of behavior problems, and this may have positive effects in numerous areas, including self-concept and locus of control. Most of these strategies come from the psychotherapy literature rather than the behavioral school of thought. These techniques include life-space interviewing, class meetings, relaxation techniques, and self-monitoring. Because the latter strategy may also be viewed as an instructional intervention, it is reviewed separately in Chapter 4.

Life-Space Interviews

The life-space interview consists of a discussion between the teacher and the misbehaving student designed to explore the entire life circumstances that may contribute to the problem (Demagistris & Imber, 1980; Morse & Small, 1959). Although almost all teachers have interviewed students concerning the reasons for behavior, few teachers have any systematic training in interviewing techniques. The life-space interview is intended as a directed interview in which the teacher, in a nonjudgmental fashion, assists the student to focus on the problem. When the student says something that is not a true statement about the problem, the teacher—again in a nonjudgmental way—corrects the student ("You say Tommy hit you first, but I was aware of you calling Tommy a bad name. What about that? How do you think Tommy felt?"). The teacher should elicit from the student an accurate description of the situation, alternative responses the student could have made, an assessment of the consequences of each potential response, and a commitment to attempt an appropriate response during the next similar situation. Punishment may or may not then be administered. Interest Box 3.4 presents several general guidelines for conducting the life-space interview.

Obviously, the life-space interview takes some time, and may take up as much as 15 minutes. Also, teachers with some counseling or psychotherapeutic training will have had much more experience in these types of interview techniques. However, the life-space interview may take as little as three or four minutes, and all teachers interview students about problem behavior in class. It makes sense to seek effective methods of conducting these interviews. Finally, research has tentatively demonstrated the effectiveness of this technique (Bender & Evans, 1989; Demagistris & Imber, 1980). Consequently, additional readings on applications of this technique are recommended for the beginning teacher. Also, teachers of children and youth with emotional/behavioral disabilities should take classes that further explore this interviewing technique and provide supervised field experiences in this strategy.

Class Meetings

Several researchers have recommended class meetings to discuss disciplinary problems (Bender & Evans, 1989; Dolly & Page, 1981; Marandola & Imber, 1979). The concept was developed by Glasser (1965) as a component of "reality therapy."

INTEREST BOX 3.4
Guidelines for a Life-Space Interview

There are several general guidelines for the life-space interview that provide an impression of the tone of the interview.

1. Be polite, but confront the student in a nonhostile manner with your knowledge of the facts of the problem, should the student's version of the facts stray from reality. Simply tell the student your perception of the facts and say, "What about that?"
2. Get the conversation going about the actual situation, and do not inquire "why" a student did something. It is often very difficult for students with behavior problems to clarify their emotions, and such clarification may not be necessary in order to resolve the immediate situation.
3. If guilt is overwhelming the student, help the student to address the problem by minimizing the importance of the problem, without detracting from the seriousness of your concern that the student find appropriate ways of dealing with future situations.
4. Help the student articulate his or her feelings whenever possible in order to understand the actions taken. Although feelings are not the primary concern of the interview, they must be dealt with at some point, and you may need to assist a child in labeling them.
5. Help the student to generate plans for similar future situations that would not result in problems. If he or she has an alternative idea, follow that through to the logical conclusion, and, if necessary, generate a more satisfactory plan.

The intentions of the class meeting are very similar to the life-space interview discussed above, in that the overall goal should be to increase awareness of potential alternative courses of action in various situations. However, the class meeting involves the entire class in generation of these alternatives. Glasser (1965) identified three reasons for class meetings; social problem-solving meeting, the open meeting concerned with a thought-provoking question, and the educational–diagnostic meeting dealing with student understanding of a curriculum concept.

The focus of the meeting is to develop a plan to allow peaceful resolution to future similar problem situations. There are several guidelines for this process. First, deal with present behavior by letting every student who wishes to discuss his or her perception of the situation. These discussions should emphasize behavior and not feelings, and the moderator must correct the student when misstatements are made that cloud the issues. No excuses are accepted. However, no punishment is given, because the subject must learn to accept responsibility for his or her own transgressions, and punishment is believed to "absolve" the student from that responsibility. Next, the involved students are asked to make a value judgement concerning the usefulness of their behavior. At this point a plan is prepared or suggested that seems to offer a method of resolving future similar problems. A commitment to the plan is then obtained from the students, and a brief statement of the plan may be written down. If students cannot honestly commit to the plan (the moderator should urge the student not to commit to something until he or she means it), another should be prepared. The meeting ends with a brief synopsis of the proposed plan by the moderator.

This type of strategy takes time away from other class activities, and teachers who use this technique generally have fairly extensive training. Also, although some research has supported the use of this technique in self-contained classes for children with emotional disabilities (Bender & Evans, 1989), not all of the research is positive (Shearn & Randolph, 1978; Welch & Dolly, 1980). As a teacher of students with disabilities—many of whom demonstrate behavior problems—you may wish to investigate this strategy further. Ask the psychologist in your district for information or a demonstration class meeting with your class. As with each of these disciplinary techniques for classroom use, additional preparation in the use of this technique will increase your likelihood of success.

Relaxation Exercises

An awareness approach that has received increasing research support is the relaxation intervention (Amerikaner & Summerlin, 1982; Carter & Russell, 1985; Robin, Schneider, & Dolnick, 1976; Fleming, Ritchie, & Fleming, 1983). There are several different relaxation techniques, and each of these is founded on the principle that awareness of stress or awareness of the onset of aggressive impulses can be controlled by brief periods of relaxation. The methods include biofeedback, relaxation training, exercise, and the turtle technique.

Biofeedback. Biofeedback is the use of sensors to detect the medical indicators of stress, which include heightened skin resistance to electricity, heart rate, and electrical activity in the brain. Once these sensors are attached to the subject, an unpleasant sound appears when stress increases and a pleasant sound appears when stress decreases. This procedure eventually leads to decreasing levels of stress. The usual treatment period is around twenty minutes, and this treatment is repeated daily or several times per week.

Research results have generally indicated positive effects for biofeedback training in increasing appropriate classroom behavior (Amerikaner & Summerlin, 1982; Bender & Evans, 1989; Omizo & Michael, 1982). Research has suggested that biofeedback induced relaxation resulted in increased attention to task. Other positive results include decreased problem behaviors, as perceived by classroom teachers, and reductions of impulsive behavior (Bender & Evans, 1989).

Relaxation Training. One major problem with biofeedback is the requirement for complicated machinery to implement the procedures and to measure the effects (Bender & Evans, 1989). Teachers will generally have access to this procedure only through a privately owned biofeedback center in the vicinity, or through local medical centers. For this reason, researchers have attempted to identify other methods of reducing stress among children and adolescents with disabilities.

One alternative available to teachers is the use of relaxation tapes: auditory tapes that describe a "journey" through a very peaceful and tranquil setting (Amerikaner & Summerlin, 1982). These tapes are commercially available (Lupin, 1977), and generally include a 16- to 18-minute description of a peaceful environment such as a mountainside, seashore, or peaceful valley. Suggestions for relaxation are interspersed throughout the tape, and students close their eyes and "imagine" the reality of the peaceful setting as described. Amerikaner and Summerlin (1982) demonstrated that relaxation sessions twice a week for six weeks resulted in reduced behavior problems in a class for children with learning disabilities.

Teachers can readily purchase these tapes and use them in their special education classes. Use of relaxation tapes is probably more practical in self-contained classes than in resource classes, because major time commitments must be made for the training itself, and this time will be taken away from instructional activities. However, for the hyperactive student, or the student with excessive behavior problems and general overresponsiveness, results of this program can be very positive. Also, although research has not yet demonstrated the generalized effects of this relaxation treatment, it is possible that the time commitment to relaxation training may create increases in on-task behavior that result in increased academic performance.

With particular problem children it may be more effective to initiate a combined relaxation treatment that starts with the student going to a biofeedback center several times to become aware of the "feelings" associated with stress, and maintaining a long-term program of relaxation intervention using the relaxation tapes at the school. Omizo and Michael (1982) used a combination of biofeedback and relaxation training to treat behavior problems. First, 32 boys identified as hyperactive were ranked according to their rating on a behavior rating scale. The subjects were taken in pairs, from the highest pair to the lowest, and one member of each pair was assigned to one of the experimental groups by a coin toss. One of the groups was then randomly chosen as the experimental group; the other group served as the control. The experimental group was subjected to four sessions of biofeedback-induced relaxation approximately two weeks apart. The biofeedback training was supplemented with relaxation tapes designed to "take a trip to . . ." a relaxing imaginary place, as described in the text. The dependent measures for the experiment consisted of measures of impulsive responding and locus of control (the sense of controlling one's fate and well-being). Although no difference was found on the latter measure, the measure of impulsive responding did show a favorable effect for the group that had undergone the relaxation training.

Relaxation training, used either independently or in combination with biofeedback, can be a useful tool in dealing with behavior problems in the special education classroom. Although this research is relatively recent, it has been positive, and practitioners have noted increased use of these treatments in the public school.

Exercise Programs. Recent research has demonstrated that periods of organized exercise can reduce certain types of behavior problems among students with mild to moderate disabilities (Evans, Evans, Schmid, & Penneypacker, 1985; Yell, 1988). For example, Yell (1988) arranged for students with behavioral disorders to take 30 minutes from their daily schedule in a self-contained class to participate in 5 minutes of stretching, and a jog/walk on a trail on the school grounds (approximately a third of a mile). For 5 of the 6 children in the single-subject study, the number of inappropriate behaviors observed in class—both talk-outs and out-of-seat behaviors—went down considerably. This indicates that even brief periods of exercise can have positive consequences on classroom behavior.

Of course, this technique, like the relaxation technique discussed earlier, is more appropriate for use in a self-contained class than in a resource room, since application of the exercise period takes some time. Teachers who have a child for a 55-minute resource period generally cannot give up 30 minutes for exercise. However, this technique should be considered in self-contained placements, or in situations where behavioral problems are a major reason for referral and the relevant student's learning schedule would allow for such an intervention.

Turtle Technique. One final relaxation technique is the turtle technique, for use with younger impulsive/aggressive children. During this technique, the children are taught to recognize signs of anger and hostility and to inhibit them by "becoming like a turtle going inside its shell. In the shell, no one can bother you." The student then slowly places his or her head on the desk while ignoring the stressing stimuli in the environment. With some practice, the student, the teacher, or peers of the student may request that the student "go turtle," whenever indicators of hostility or behavior problems arise. The child stays in the turtle posture for several minutes while the teacher rearranges the environment to remove the factors (or persons) causing the stress.

Several research studies have shown the effectiveness of this treatment (Fleming, Ritchie, & Fleming, 1983; Robin, Schneider, & Dolnick, 1976). If your special education class includes children in kindergarten or the early grades who need assistance in becoming aware of their behavior, you should find out more about this technique. Your school psychologist or guidance counselor may be of assistance. This technique may be readily applied in almost any classroom.

Need for Self-Awareness Strategies

Although the assertive disciplinary strategies and the behavioral strategies discussed previously have long been considered appropriate disciplinary strategies, most of the research on the efficacy of the self-awareness interventions is much more recent. Most of these interventions come from the literature on instruction for children and youth with behavioral disorders, and many teacher education programs have included little or no information on these strategies. However, experienced, effective teachers who have used the behavioral strategies for several years often report the need for something more than behavioral strategies with certain children. Self-awareness provides one method to give the student some control over his or her behavior, rather than you, as the teacher managing the problem behaviors through external contingencies. This is consistent with the proposition that individualized responsibility should be a major consideration in every child's individualized education plan, as discussed in Chapter 1.

As noted previously, almost all teachers conduct "interviews" with children with disabilities about the cause for disciplinary problems (e.g., "Fernando, why did you hit Billy?"). Therefore, knowledge of the life-space interview technique would better prepare teachers for this type of common disciplinary task. Likewise, although biofeedback may not be an option for every class in rural areas, relaxation tapes, exercise interventions, and/or the turtle technique can be applied in many classroom situations.

Unlike teachers in mainstream classes, part of your responsibility in special education classes is to successfully deal with high frequencies of behavior problems before seeking help from those outside the classroom. Therefore, you may wish to take additional psychology, education, or counseling courses that prepare you in these techniques.

THE INTEGRATED PRIORITIZED DISCIPLINARY PLAN

The Need for Planning Ahead

After this review of the numerous techniques available, you should begin to conceptualize a disciplinary plan that encompasses the strategies you wish to use in your classroom. As a beginning teacher, one of the most important preparations you can make is the delineation of your response options to disciplinary problems in some integrated and well planned format. Do not assume that you will be prepared to handle a problem "when the time comes" because many disciplinary situations may be unforeseen and unique. The best decision is to be prepared ahead of time with a list of actions that you, as the teacher, can take in any type of situation. Of course, these actions should be listed in order of the least severe to the most severe disciplinary measure, thus allowing you to fit the disciplinary response you select to the particular offense committed by the student.

A prioritized plan that integrates behavioral and nonbehavioral strategies will enable you to respond to a range of disciplinary situations in the class. We shall assume for the moment that you have created some type of token economy in your class, that you have communicated with the parents concerning your disciplinary system, and that your principal generally supports your disciplinary actions.

The Four Options

Your first major option may be thought of as the "no overt response" response. If a rule infraction is minor (playful hitting, whispering, or merely off-task behavior) you may respond by simply ignoring the behavior for several seconds to see if the behavior is terminated. You may wish to use physical proximity to remind the students to return to task—merely walk near the students or inquire about their work. In many instances minor behavior problems take care of themselves with this type of casual involvement from the teacher. As a beginning teacher (even when your supervisor is observing) do not assume that every minor behavioral infraction requires your immediate involvement. Many do not, and although it is sometimes difficult not to get involved when you yourself are being observed and evaluated, you must remember that for minor infractions overt involvement is not the option of choice.

Your second set of options involves use of the token economy. Because you manage the rewards for this economy, you control these disciplinary options. When a more serious infraction occurs (playful hitting that does not stop and may escalate, loud talking, disrupting others) you may issue a warning and then reinforce behavior of others. An alternative is to use a response cost procedure. If the student verbally responds to your decision in a hostile manner, increase the fine. The options range from minor loss of earned rewards to loss of all rewards a student has already earned. It is not advisable to "garnish" rewards a student is expected to earn, as this may defeat the purpose of the token economy system. Therefore, when fining, you must know how many rewards the student has, and not exceed this amount.

Your third set of disciplinary options consists of the techniques you employ in the class that are not dependent on the token economy. For example, suppose you decided to fine a student after a behavioral infraction, and rather than submit to that, the student reacted by throwing a textbook at you and cursing you. Clearly, the student is emotionally involved in some way, and the student's behavioral response may be highly exaggerated. In that situation, it would be completely inappropriate for you to use a response cost intervention and remove a small token reward. Little would be accomplished, other than increased anger on the part of the student, by increasing the level of the monetary fine under those conditions.

At that point, you should consider nontoken economy options. If fining within the token economy is ineffective at that moment, fine the student several minutes of his or her next break. You may ask the student, in a nonjudgmental way, to accompany you to a "quiet corner" of the room, where you then initiate a life-space interview, in order to find out what the problem is. Another response is to recommend that the student try to calm down, and offer him or her the option of listening to several peaceful minutes of the relaxation tapes.

The final set of solutions for disciplinary matters consists of seeking outside support. You may, on occasion, have to seek help from the principal, the guidance counselor, the school psychologist, other teachers, or the parents. For example, most principals wish to be personally involved when a student commits violence against another student, particularly if any type of weapon is used. If a particular, nonviolent problem is continuous and repetitive, many administrators wish to be consulted. Also, because the principal is the major legal authority in the school, any behavior that breaks the law must be taken to the principal. This may include weapons possession, illegal drug use or sales, violence, or other types of problems. As a beginning teacher, you should be provided with guidelines by your principal concerning what types of behavioral problems require attention from the "office." Also, do not assume that you have failed somehow if you choose to take a behavioral problem to the office on occasion. Once your principal has provided guidelines indicating the types of problems that should be handled in the office, you would be remiss in your responsibilities as a member of the educational team to refuse to take those problems to the principal. Although beginning teachers should not be found every other day in the principal's office, they should take disciplinary problems to the office several times during the first few months of teaching, at least to let students know that such a disciplinary option is possible. If a principal or school district chose to hire you, it is in the best interests of all concerned that they offer you support in disciplinary options, particularly during the first few years of teaching.

Guidelines for Seeking Support

Many beginning teachers do not have a well articulated set of guidelines to be used when requesting outside support. As discussed previously, the principal or supervisor may give you guidelines concerning *when* to seek support by listing the types of incidents that should be called to the attention of the office. However, this information does not tell you *how* to proceed should a serious rule infraction occur. Furthermore, after you decide you need help is usually the worst time to be informed of "procedures." At that point, you will be interested in immediate assistance and not in red tape or forms to complete. Consequently, the steps in seeking outside help should be well understood beforehand.

Several guidelines may be offered. First, before the school year begins, inquire about local district or school policies. Some principals require that a written note accompany each student during a disciplinary office visit. Other principals request that the teacher personally accompany the student to the office for infractions serious enough to warrant an office visit. Certain school districts have an "office visit" report that must be completed by the teacher. You should request guidelines concerning these from your principal, assistant principal, and supervisor.

Second, teachers must request help in a professional manner, and supplement that request with detailed, nonjudgmental information that includes the specifics of the problem. Many teachers are attended to minimally by school psychologists, counselors, or principals when the teacher appears at the office door and says, "You've got to remove Tyrone from my class. He's misbehaving constantly!" Contrast this lack of specificity to a statement by a teacher who presents the following information. "Tyrone is becoming a problem, and I need help. Within the last week, he has been in one fight, and has been out-of-seat on seven occasions. Also, he cursed at another student yesterday. Here are my notes on each instance." The information presented by the second teacher suggests that outside support is being requested in a professional manner, by maintaining a professional calm and imparting specific information in a nonjudgmental fashion. The latter report is much more likely to be attended to as a serious matter by office personnel, because of the professionalism of that teacher.

Finally, the written notes are a crucial support for persons in the office who must fully understand the problem. The problem must be understood before action can be taken by an authority figure outside the class, and such information should be provided based on the problems in the class. Brief notes taken during class on each incident are a good idea. Information on compilation of this type of "Critical Incidents Log" is provided in Interest Box 3.5.

The Total Disciplinary Plan

As you can see, formation of a disciplinary plan does not consist of delineating specific punishments or rewards for specific behaviors in advance. That type of preplanning locks you, the teacher, into a set of options that may not be appropriate for particular situations. If anything is consistent about disciplinary problems in public school classes, it is the total inconsistency of such problems. Every experienced teacher has numerous stories—some humorous, some tragic—involving completely unforeseen disciplinary situations. The disciplinary plan recommended above integrates numerous behavioral and nonbehavioral strategies into a cohesive whole, and provides a flexible set of prioritized options for you to use at your discretion. You should not allow yourself to become locked into particular, predictable methods of responding to problems, but you should be completely consistent in the level of your response.

LEGAL CONSIDERATIONS AS DISCIPLINARY CONSTRAINTS

Numerous legal challenges to specific disciplinary procedures have resulted in a restricted choice of disciplinary techniques in certain states (Gast & Nelson, 1977; Smith, Polloway, & West, 1979). For example, although some states allow corporal punishment (spanking, either on the posterior or on the palm of the hand), others do not, and others have detailed procedures for use when a student is to be spanked. Time-out procedures have been the subject of various legal rulings. Also, in certain states principals are not allowed to suspend or expel pupils with disabilities,

INTEREST BOX 3.5
The Critical Incidents Log

Sugai (1986) provided information of the format for providing information on critical behavioral incidents. He recommended a log format in which certain information is summarized concerning particular behaviors that seem to be a problem with certain students. The log consists of the date and time of the behavioral infraction, the antecedents (or possible causes that immediately preceded the problem) and specific behavior, and the consequences of the behavior. Also, with most students, only several specific behavioral problems are demonstrated, and these may be briefly summarized in a "legend" that names these frequent behaviors. The log below indicates the type of information that should be provided to office personnel and child study team members when you bring a recurring behavior problem to their attention. Such a log will make you seem more professional to your colleagues.

Legend:

Date	Time	Antecedents	Behavior	Consequences

Source: Sugai (1986).

because a fight or aggressive behavior that resulted in the proposed suspension may, in fact, be a component of the disability and thus not under the student's control.

As a beginning teacher, the safest course of action is to avoid these types of disciplinary options, because these are the most frequently challenged techniques, legally. Also, many scholars feel that these techniques include so many unhappy side effects (e.g., spanking is, in effect, responding to a problem by forcefully hitting another individual and thus modeling that response for the child) that these techniques should be avoided at all cost.

However, if you choose to use some of these techniques, ask your principal and supervisor about local rules and constraints. Another good idea is to get someone—perhaps a school counselor, principal, or supervisor—to demonstrate the technique. You should also include an explanation of the technique, the reasons for the technique, and conditions under which the technique will be employed on both the child's IEP and any office visit reports. Each use of the technique should be followed by a written log of the application of the technique. Finally, prior to using the technique, obtain professional insurance to protect yourself against legal action from the parents or guardian of the child.

SUMMARY

The disciplinary options you choose to employ in your class will structure the learning environment you establish. You cannot leave these disciplinary responses to chance, or the effectiveness of your instruction will be severely hampered. As the assertive discipline literature emphasizes, you set the expectations and levels of tolerance for each type of behavior students demonstrate in your class. At the risk of being repetitive, consistency is the key to effective discipline. Students must know what to expect from their actions should they choose to misbehave. Many of the strategies, such as rule systems, token economies, peer pressure, and the awareness techniques are presented here in order to give you the techniques that allow you to be consistent in your expectations yet still respond flexibly to disciplinary problems when a student looses control.

When beginning teachers fail during their first year of school, it is more likely to be the result of a lack of understanding of effective disciplinary techniques than a lack of understanding of effective instructional techniques. Also, when teachers fail to be offered a continuing contract, in most cases, it is because they cannot control the students in their class. Unfortunately, many "methods of teaching" texts foster this lack of understanding because a set of disjointed behavioral techniques are offered instead of concrete recommendations concerning an integrated prioritized disciplinary plan.

Specifying a prioritized disciplinary plan prior to the beginning of school is one of the most effective uses of your time during the early teacher workdays. A token economy should be established, a store set up, a rule system established (or generally planned for later discussion with the students) and plans made for alternative disciplinary options. Letters explaining the rule system for parents should be prepared.

You should avail yourself of the assistance of experienced school personnel in the preparation of these systems. Seek the guidance of the administrators, counselors, psychologists, and, most important, other teachers. Generally, persons who have a classroom background themselves will be more helpful than those who do not. Be prepared to change the plan as required by the situation, once the students arrive. Finally, when disciplinary solutions overwhelm you (as they will at some point during your first year teaching) seek the help and recommendations of the administrators, parents, and teachers in the building. These individuals have had the same failures and may be able to recommend ideas you have not considered. As an assertive disciplinarian, you have the right to their support.

Summary Points

- Consistency is the key to successful discipline for students with mild and moderate disabilities.
- Assertive discipline means that the teacher should be assertive in stating exactly what the expectations are for the class.
- A rule system, with three to five positively stated rules, can provide an effective basis for discipline.
- Regular review of rules lets the students know that you are very serious about compliance with the rules.
- A token economy is an effective method to motivate students.
- Token economies may be supplemented to include checkbooks, insurance, and interest payments.
- Behavioral contracting offers the possibility of motivating students, who would be willing to work for the reward specified in the contract.
- Response cost means that the teacher applies a mild punishment for misbehavior by fining the student some of the rewards.
- Peer pressure, or peer confrontation, is a system whereby the teacher uses social pressure from the peers in the class to help a child identify his or her behavioral infraction.
- Time-out represents the removal of the student from the possibility of reinforcement for a specified period of time.
- Life-space interviewing is an interview technique that assists the student in identifying the problem and several courses of action that may alleviate the problem.
- Biofeedback is the use of sensors placed on or near the body to assist the client to become aware of increasing stress. This intervention has been used successfully with children with disabilities.

- Relaxation training represents an intervention in which students are taught to relax in order to decrease behavioral problems.
- Exercise programs requiring jogging have been shown to reduce inappropriate behaviors among children with mild disabilities.
- The turtle technique involves teaching a child to withdraw into himself or herself whenever the child begins to loose control.
- A prioritized disciplinary plan suggests that the level of intervention on the part of the teacher should be keyed to the seriousness of the rule infraction by the student. Four options exist: subtle option, token economy options, nontoken economy options, and out-of-class options.

QUESTIONS AND ACTIVITIES

1. Ask experienced teachers to explain the types of disciplinary options they use. See if some type of unconscious hierarchy emerges.
2. Review the literature on assertive discipline. Consider attending a workshop that stresses this methodology.
3. Ask a psychologist from your campus to visit the education class and present some ideas on appropriate methods for conducting life-space interviews and class meetings.
4. Copy the behavioral contract forms you find in several different textbooks. How are these forms similar or different?
5. Review the peer pressure strategy with several experienced teachers. Have these teachers employed this strategy? Do these teachers have a negative attitude toward use of this strategy in their classroom? Why?
6. Interview special education teachers who have a token economy. Do these teachers use the economy merely as a reinforcement tool or as an instructional tool as well?
7. In your field placements, ask your cooperating teacher about the types of problems that should be taken to the office or discussed with parents. Ask if you can accompany a teacher when he or she takes a problem to the office.

REFERENCES

Amerikaner, M., & Summerlin, M. L (1982). Group counseling with learning disabled children: Effects of social skills and relaxation training on self-concept and classroom behavior. *Journal of Learning Disabilities, 15,* 340–343.

Bender, W. N., & Evans, N. (1989). Mainstream and special class strategies for managing behaviorally disordered students in secondary classes. *High School Journal, 72.*

Canter, L. (1982). *Assertive Discipline.* Santa Monica, CA.: Canter & Associates, Inc.

Carter, J. L., & Russell, H. L. (1985). Use of EMG biofeedback procedures with learning disabled children in a clinical and educational setting. *Journal of Learning Disabilities, 18,* 213–216.

Demagistris, R. J., & Imber, S. C. (1980). The effects of life space interviewing on academic and social performance of behaviorally disordered children. *Behavioral Disorders, 6,* 12–25.

Dolly, J. P., & Page, D. P. (1981). Reality therapy with institutionalized emotionally disturbed mentally retarded adolescents. *Journal for Special Educators, 17,* 225–232.

Evans, W. H., Evans, S. S., Schmid, R. E., & Penneypacker, H. S. (1985). The effects of exercise on selected classroom behaviors of behaviorally disordered adolescents. *Behavioral Disorders, 11,* 42–50.

Fleming, D. C., Ritchie, B., & Fleming, E. R. (1983). Fostering the social adjustment of disturbed students. *Teaching Exceptional Children, 15,* 172–175.

Gast, D. L., & Nelson, C. M. (1977). Legal and ethical considerations for the use of timeout in special education settings. *Journal of Special Education, 11,* 457–467.

Glasser, W. (1965). *Reality Therapy: A New Approach to Psychiatry.* New York: Harper & Row.

Hill, D. (1990, April). Order in the classroom. *Teacher Magazine,* pp. 70–77.

Katz, N., Reeder, W., Russell, T., & Salend, J. (1992). The effects of a dependent group evaluation system. *Education and Treatment of Children, 15,* 33–42.

Lupin, M. (1977). *Peace, Harmony, Awareness.* Austin, TX.: Learning Concepts.

Mandlebaum, L. H., Russell, S. R., Krouse, J., & Gonter, M. (1983). Assertive discipline: An effective classwide behavior management program. *Behavioral Disorders, 8,* 258–264.

Marandola, P., & Imber, S. C. (1979). Glasser's classroom meeting: A humanistic approach to behavior change with preadolescent inner-city learning disabled children. *Journal of Learning Disabilities, 12,* 30–34.

Minner, S., & Knutson, R. (1980). Using classroom token economies as instructional devices. *Teaching Exceptional Children, 12,* 167–169.

Morse, W. C., & Small, E. R. (1959). The life space interview. *American Journal of Orthopsychiatry, 29,* 27–44.

Omizo, M. M, & Michael, W. B. (1982). Biofeedback-induced relaxation training and impulsivity, attention to task, and locus of control among hyperactive boys. *Journal of Learning Disabilities, 15,* 414–416.

Robin, A., Schneider, M., & Dolnick, M. (1976). The turtle technique: An extended case study of self-control in the classroom. *Psychology in the Schools, 13,* 449–453.

Rosen, L. A., Gabardi, L., Miller, C. D., & Miller, L. (1990). Home-based treatment of disruptive junior high school students: An analysis of the differential effects of positive and negative consequences. *Behavioral Disorders, 15,* 227–232.

Rosenberg, M. S. (1986). Maximizing the effectiveness of structured classroom management programs: Implementing rule-review procedures with disruptive and distractible students. *Behavioral Disorders, 11,* 239–248.

Salend, S. J., Jantzen, N. R., & Geik, K. (1992). Using a peer confrontation system in a group setting. *Behavioral Disorders, 17,* 211–218.

Sandler, A. G., Arnold, L. B., Gable, R. A., & Strain, P. S. (1987). Effects of peer pressure on disruptive behavior of behaviorally disordered classmates. *Behavioral Disorders, 12,* 104–110.

Shearn, D. F., & Randolph, D. L. (1978). Effects of reality therapy methods applied in the classroom. *Psychology in the Schools, 15,* 79–83.

Smith, J. D, Polloway, E. A., & West, G. K. (1979). Corporal punishment and its implications for exceptional children. *Exceptional Children, 45,* 264–268.

Smith, L. K., & Fowler, S. A. (1984). Positive peer pressure: The effects of peer monitoring on children's disruptive behavior. *Journal of Applied Behavior Analysis, 17,* 213–227.

Stainback, W. C., & Stainback, S. B. (1975). A few basic elements of token reinforcement. *Journal for Special Educators of the Mentally Retarded, 11,* 152–155.

Stolz, S. B., Wienckowski, L. A., & Brown, B. S. (1975). Behavior modification: A perspective on critical issues. *American Psychologist, 30,* 1027–1048.

Sugai, G. (1986). Recording classroom events: Maintaining a critical incidents log. *Teaching Exceptional Children, 18,* 98–102.

Welch, F. C., & Dolly, J. (1980). A systematic evaluation of Glasser's techniques. *Psychology in the Schools, 17,* 385–389.

White, O. R. (1986). Precision teaching—precision learning. *Exceptional Children, 52,* 522–534.

Yell, M. L. (1988). The effects of jogging on the rates of selected target behaviors of behaviorally disordered students. *Behavioral Disorders, 13,* 273–279.

CHAPTER 4

BEHAVIORAL INSTRUCTION AND MONITORING STUDENT PERFORMANCE

OBJECTIVES

When you complete this chapter, you should be able to:

1. Describe a positive practice instructional procedure.
2. Implement a time-delay instructional procedure.
3. Draw and explain the behavioral model of learning.
4. Define errorless learning and give several examples.
5. Identify two definitions of direct instruction.
6. Discuss the research basis for the components of direct instruction.
7. List several criticisms of direct instruction.
8. Describe precision teaching.
9. Define three types of curriculum-based assessment and differentiate CBA from traditional assessment.
10. Explain a CBA system in which no postyear assessment is necessary.
11. Discuss the efficacy of precision teaching.
12. Identify methods whereby CBA may be implemented using both microcomputer-based methods and paper and pencil methods.

KEYWORDS

learning
antecedent
consequences
modeling
stimulus
errorless learning
prompt
time-delay
waits
anticipations
performance monitoring
ability deficits
curriculum based assessment
precision teaching
rate of behavior
aim line
record floor
flat data
phase change
rate sheet
word window
criterion referenced test
reading mastery
DISTAR
corrective reading
scripts
teacher-directed practice
positive practice
direct instruction

In a certain sense, Chapter 3 serves as an introduction to behavioral instructional techniques, because many of the techniques used to alleviate disciplinary problems are behaviorally based. In your preservice teacher preparation courses, you may have had a course on behavioral management. All of these experiences may have acquainted you with the strategies founded in behavioral psychology.

Still, numerous behavioral strategies are not exclusively disciplinary strategies. Rather, these techniques are used to instruct a student with mild or moderate disabilities in the assigned academic tasks. Some of these techniques have been around for a while; others are relatively new. The purpose of this chapter is to describe several instructional techniques that are founded on the behavioral model of learning.

THE BEHAVIORAL MODEL OF LEARNING

First, a brief description of the behavioral model of learning is provided. Next, there is a discussion of the several techniques, followed by information from the special education research on the efficacy of these recently developed instructional techniques.

Behavioral psychology grew from a frustration with concepts in general psychology that tended to be so vague as to be unmeasurable. At the outset, psychologists associated with behavioral psychology, such as B. F. Skinner, demanded that behaviors be defined in a way that allowed for accurate measurement. In this model, therefore, learning is defined as a measurable change in behavior, and all behaviors of concern must be readily observable and measurable.

The behavioral model of learning, then, focuses on behavior and on the creation of changes in behavior. The model further stipulates that antecedents and consequences control behavior. Antecedents are the environmental events that immediately precede a behavioral response; consequences are the environmental events that immediately follow a particular response. Therefore, the behavioral model of learning looks like the diagram below.

Antecedents ⟶ Behavior ⟶ Consequence

This model is the underlying foundation for all behavioral thought. Clearly, if a teacher can control or influence both the antecedents and consequences, the teacher can influence behavior. This model of learning, in many ways, is fundamental to a student's understanding of special education instruction. For example, in your assessment class, you have learned that IEPs must be written in terms of behavioral objectives—objectives that specify behavioral change and the precise measurement of that change. Likewise, many disciplinary techniques used in education today are founded on this model. The teacher's role in this model is one of a behavioral change agent who manipulates the environmental antecedents and consequences to elicit the appropriate behavioral change. Of course, several courses in your program of study in teacher education could be devoted exclusively to behavioral change strategies, and this text cannot discuss each of these. Still, there are a few behavioral change strategies founded on this model of learning that seem to underlie effective instruction, and some recent instructional ideas, discussed in later chapters, utilize many of these behavioral change techniques.

Modeling

One of the most effective instructional techniques developed from behavioral thought is the technique of systematic modeling (Biedmerman, Davey, Ryder, & Franchi, 1994; Espin & Deno, 1984; Johnson, Gutkin, & Plake, 1991; Kameenui, Carnine, Darch, & Stein, 1986; Karsh & Repp, 1992). Modeling involves the intentional manipulation of antecedents in order to structure the desired behavioral response. This method is applied by careful measurement of the effects of showing the student how to do a task, and helping the student through the task after the model is presented. This technique has been incorporated into numerous other instructional programs. For example, modeling has been incorporated into numerous instructional strategies discussed in later parts of this volume, including direct instruction, metacognitive instructional strategies, and social skills instruction (Kameenui et al., 1986; Schloss, Schloss, Wood, & Kiehl, 1986).

McIntyre, Test, Cooke, & Beattie (1991) provided one of the more recent examples of the use of a modeling instructional procedure. These researchers used modeling to teach a particular method of memorizing multiplication facts. A fourth grade student with learning disabilities was taught to use a "count-by" method. In that method, as one example, the student is encouraged to determine the multiplication fact (4 x 3) by learning to count by fours. The student would count by four, three times (i.e., by saying, "4, 8, 12; 4 x 3 = 12." For teaching this count-by method, the teacher first taught the correct count-by sequences. Then the teacher modeled the use of the procedure to solve math problems. The teacher verbalized each step as it was completed, and then verbalized the count-by procedure. The student received training in the count-by method on a daily basis, and then completed a series of mathfacts problems. Each session ended with a probe of the mathfacts in that set, and a count of corrects and errors was kept. The results indicated that this modeling procedure worked quite well, and assisted the student in mastery of the count-by method and in overall performance on the mathfacts. Even when the count-by model was withdrawn, the effects of this instruction were still apparent in student performance. In addition to the modeling procedure, teachers should begin to employ this count-by procedure with students with mild disabilities who have difficulty memorizing the times tables.

Rinne (1994) implemented a high-tech modeling program that employed computer technologies. The system uses a videocamera coupled with a computer to tape trainees in almost any task imaginable. Trainees then review the tape of their task performance, while comparing that performance to a model tape in which the task was performed by an expert. The computer technology assures that the tapes will be comparable, and presents the trainee's task performance video on half of the computer screen while the model tape is presented on the other half. Results of this high-tech modeling have been very positive.

The majority of research on the use of modeling demonstrates the effectiveness of this behavioral technique. For example, Schloss and his co-workers (1986) indicated that modeling has become one of the preferred instructional strategies for use in social skills instruction. As an instructional technique modeling has been shown to be useful for students at almost any age and almost any skill level. Also, numerous specific academic skills have been taught by using modeling procedures (Espin & Deno, 1984; McIntyre et al., 1991; Vail & Huntington, 1993).

Stimulus Variation

A stimulus is the environmental event that precedes and stimulates a behavior (i.e., an antecedent of behavior). In academic instances, the stimulus is usually the problem (e.g., the math, language arts, or science problem) presented to the student. Because variation in certain aspects of the stimulus can enhance learning, behavioral researchers have devised numerous ways to vary the stimulus to elicit the desired response. In stimulus variation, the characteristics of the stimulus are varied in order to create an increased likelihood for the desired behavioral response (Vail & Huntington, 1993). Two examples are presented below.

Stimulus Shaping. In stimulus shaping, the stimulus is re-formed to assist the student in performing the task. Vail and Huntington (1993) provided the following example. In teaching the word "CAR," the instruction would begin with the word itself written in the shape of a car over a pair of wheels, as illustrated in Figure 4.1. The student could then look at the picture, with recognition of the words, and indicate to the teacher that the stimulus said "CAR."

Stimulus Fading. In addition to shaping the stimulus, the teacher can begin with paired stimulus—that is, a picture of a car and the word "car" shown together, and gradually fade out the picture (Dorry, 1976; Knowlton, 1980). The instruction would proceed until the letters "CAR" in block form appeared over a pair of wheels, and the student would be asked to respond. Finally, the letters would appear in block form without the wheels. Using this instructional format, the teacher can take a nonreading student, work with the nouns from various sight word lists that can be easily pictured, and build a vocabulary for that reader fairly quickly.

In a similar technique, various aspects of the stimulus itself may be faded in order to create an increased likelihood of accurate responses. Figure 4.2 shows a "fading card" on which the picture of a dog is paired with the word "dog." A "cat" card and a "frog" card are also prepared in this fashion. The student should review this series of pictures while the relationship between the word and the

FIGURE 4.1 Picture of a Stimulus Shaping Card

picture is emphasized. Then, over a series of instructional sessions, the picture is gradually faded by using translucent plastic, such that the picture is only partly visible. Instruction on those words would terminate when the student can recognize them without any picture. Research has shown that this fading technique is very successful in teaching basic sight words to students with either mild intellectual disabilities or learning disabilities. This technique is called picture fading, and is discussed more completely in Chapter 8 (Dorry, 1976; Knowlton, 1980).

Errorless Learning Procedures

As behavioral psychologists became more aware of the rules that govern learning in children, it quickly became apparent that students required high levels of success in order to continue to be motivated for completion of work. Behavioral psychology indicates that students need to succeed at least 80 percent of the time in order for learning to take place, and that conclusion is remarkably similar to the conclusions of the researchers in the effective schools research. You may recall from Chapter 1 that academic learning time was defined in terms of the amount of time that a student was engaged on work that resulted in at least an 80 percent success rate.

With this emphasis on high levels of success, some theorists began to experiment with a number of techniques that resulted in even fewer errors. The theorists postulated that learning would be less painful and more fun if it could be constructed to result in almost no errors. The procedures developed came to be known as errorless learning procedures. An errorless learning procedure is an instructional procedure that precludes students from performing an incorrect response (Wolery, Bailey, & Sugai, 1988, pp. 220). Like all behavioral procedures, errorless learning is dependent upon accurate daily recording of the number of corrects and the number of errors a student achieves during the lesson. That count is necessary in order to assure that the student is learning the material in an errorless or near errorless fashion.

Wolery, Bailey, and Sugai (1988, p. 220) presented a number of reasons for using errorless learning procedures. First, errorless learning is very efficient in that time is saved. This procedure usually results in mastery of material in considerably

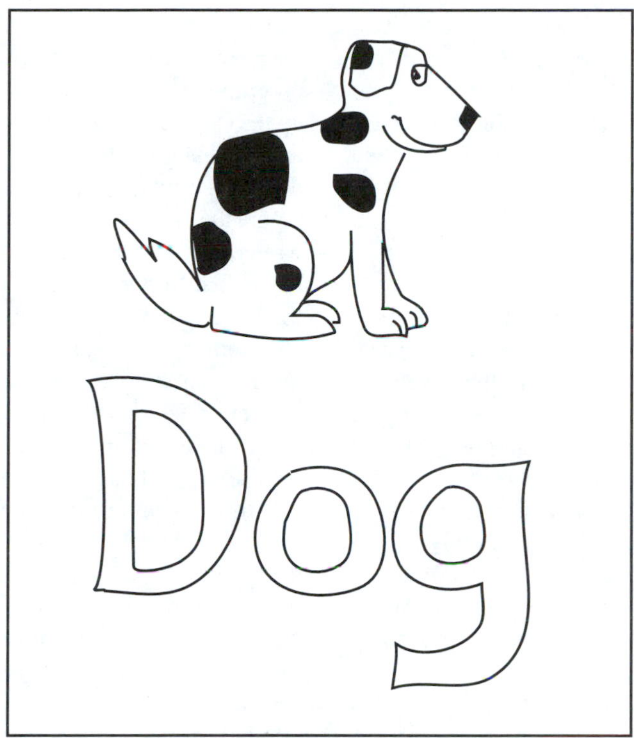

FIGURE 4.2 Picture of a Stimulus Fading Card

fewer instructional sessions than are required when other instructional procedures are in use.

Next, these researchers suggest that errorless learning promotes positive social interaction between students. Using these procedures, very few errors are made, and much less social stigma is associated with errors that do occur (Wolery, Bailey, & Sugai, 1988). For this reason, errorless procedures should certainly be considered an option of choice for special education students working in inclusive classrooms.

Finally, errorless learning tends to result in fewer instances of inappropriate behavior on the part of many children with disabilities (Wolery, Bailey, & Sugai, 1988). Presumably, when students make fewer errors, they enjoy learning more and are less likely to become disruptive.

Prompting. A prompt may be defined as teacher assistance before the behavioral response. Although prompts may be considered antecedent stimuli, they are not a part of the target stimulus. For example, the target stimulus may be a math problem (such as 4 + 5 =), whereas the prompt may be the teacher gently tapping the page on which the problem is written. Prompts may be either verbal or gestural, and systematic use of prompts can facilitate learning.

Prompts are used to increase the likelihood of correct response, and may be one component of an errorless learning procedure (Wolery, Bailey, & Sugai, 1988). For example, if enough prompts are used to all but eliminate any errors, and corrects are sufficiently rewarded, the student will master the behavior with very few errors.

An illustration may be helpful. If a student with mild disabilities is having difficulty with place value decisions (i.e., regrouping or carrying) in addition of whole numbers, the teacher will present a series of stimuli, such as double-digit addition problems written vertically like those found below.

25	44	62	47
+37	+19	+34	+39

The child would be required to discriminate between the problems that required regrouping and those that did not, as well as solve the problems. In assisting the child to complete the problems, if the child summed the digits in the ones' column and began to write a two-digit answer under that column rather than placing one digit at the top of the next column, the teacher could merely tap the paper at the top of the next column to prompt the student about where to write down the second (or "tens' place") digit. This prompting procedure would tend to eliminate most errors (presuming that the child had previously acquired the prerequisite skills in mathfacts addition), and errorless learning would result.

Time Delay. Time delay was introduced by Touchette (1971) as one method of structuring errorless learning. The time-delay procedure is implemented when increasing amounts of time are inserted between the task stimulus and the controlling prompt. The desired behavior is initially structured through immediate application of the prompt, and then a systematic fading through delaying the prompt for a specified period of seconds (Wolery, Cybriwsky, Gast, & Boyle-Gast, 1991; Schuster, Stevens, & Doak, 1990).

Schuster, Stevens, and Doak (1990) provided a clear example of this procedure. These researchers used time delay to teach students with mild disabilities a set of words and definitions. In planning the daily lessons, the teacher selected 30 unknown words and their definitions from material the student would soon cover in the mainstream class. During the first instructional session, a 0-second time delay was used. The teacher would hold up a flashcard with the word on it and immediately say the word and the definition for the student to repeat. During the remainder of the instructional sessions, a 5-second time delay was used. The teacher would hold up the card, wait 5 seconds, and then read the word and the definition for the student to repeat. The student was encouraged to read the word correctly before the teacher did, and reinforced if the answer was correct. If the student did not know the word, but waited for the teacher's prompt, and then read the word and definition correctly, the student was also reinforced. Results indicated that the students quickly mastered the words and definitions with near-errorless performance. Also, maintenance probes indicated that the students' mastery of the words was maintained for over three months.

In utilizing the time-delay instructional procedures, accurate records must be kept concerning the students' responses. The chart in Figure 4.3 presents a relatively standard recording format. Note that each type of student response is listed in the five columns so that the teacher can note the specific type of response made. "Waits" indicate that the child waited to hear the prompt from the teacher before responding; "non-waits" indicate that the child did not wait and answered the problem incorrectly. "Anticipations" indicate that the child responded without waiting for the prompt and that the response was correct. Obviously, the goal of the teacher is to increase corrects, particularly "anticipations," until the child performs with 100 percent accuracy and all of the corrects are anticipations rather than waits.

As you can see from the above example, this errorless learning procedure is fairly easy and can be implemented in almost any rote learning task. This includes memorization of such things as times tables, letters, word lists, and so forth. Also, more recent research has indicated that factual material from various curriculum areas can be mastered by the use of time delay. For example, Wolery and his co-workers (1991) recently used time delay to assist adolescents with learning disabilities in mastering factual material from their content secondary curriculum areas. These facts included the functions of federal offices, the ser-

Student Name ______________________________ Date ____/____/____

Trail/Stimulus	Corrects		Errors		
	Anticipations	Waits	Non-Waits	Waits	No Response
Totals					

FIGURE 4.3 Time-Delay Chart

vices provided by local offices and agencies, over-the-counter medications, and the effects of specific vitamins and minerals on the body. As these diverse topics indicate, any curricula that can be specified as isolated factual material can be structured as curricula for a time-delay procedure.

Research on the efficacy of time delay has been quite positive (Wolery, Bailey, & Sugai, 1988). As the studies reviewed above indicate, this technique can be applied at almost any age level. Other research has indicated that time delay can facilitate learning for preschool children (Alig-Cybriwsky, Wolery, & Gast, 1990), for students with severe intellectual disabilities (Browder, Morris, & Snell, 1981), and in peer tutoring instructional paradigms (Kowry & Browder, 1986). Time-delay instructional techniques may also be coupled with computer-assisted instruction (Kinney, Stevens, & Schuster, 1988). The consistency of these results indicates that time delay is an instructional strategy that should be applied much more frequently in special education and inclusive classroom settings.

Positive Practice. Positive practice means practice in successful completion of a particular behavioral response. Although many teachers use practice techniques, few use them in a systematic manner. For example, Wolery, Bailey, and Sugai (1988, p. 452) point out that many teachers require students who misspell words to write out these spelling words correctly a certain number of times. This positive practice typically results in correct spelling of the word in the future.

There are a number of different aspects to positive practice. The procedure typically includes telling the child that he or she behaved inappropriately, stopping the child's ongoing activity, providing systematic verbal instructions, and forcing practice of the desired forms of behavior. Research using this procedure has demonstrated its efficacy (Matson, Esveldt-Dawson, & Kazdin, 1982; Singh, Singh, & Winton, 1984; Trap, Milner-Davis, Joseph, & Cooper, 1978). For example, positive practice has been used to eliminate oral reading errors among children with mild intellectual disabilities (Singh, Singh, & Winton, 1984). Other researchers have used this technique to improve spelling and writing (Matson, Esveldt-Dawson, and Kazdin, 1982; Trap, Milner-Davis, Joseph, & Cooper, 1978).

Summary of Behavioral Techniques

This chapter has presented a very brief overview of several behavioral strategies used for academic instruction. The behavioral model that related antecedents, behavioral response, and consequences was presented as a backdrop for further elaboration of these techniques presented. Strategies such as modeling, prompting, and positive practice are useful techniques for the special education teacher in either a special education setting or an inclusive classroom, and research has demonstrated the efficacy of these techniques.

Unlike many of the behavioral techniques discussed in previous chapters, these deal with academic learning rather than modification of inappropriate behaviors. Also, these techniques have been shown to be quite effective when used with students who demonstrate mild disabilities. Finally, many of these techniques, because of this demonstrated effectiveness, have been incorporated into other instructional strategies that are covered in later sections of this chapter.

MONITORING STUDENT PERFORMANCE

Teachers must prepare for instruction by delineating a system of monitoring the academic and social development of the students with disabilities. Because the behavioral model of learning has been so influential in education, many monitoring systems are founded upon it. Also, although numerous norm-referenced assessments may be used to determine which students have mild or moderate disabilities, the types of assessment that facilitate instruction all have one thing in common: they concentrate on accurate measurement of student performance on specified curricular objectives. Thus, most classroom-oriented student performance monitoring systems are based on behavioral thought.

This concentration on frequent assessment of performance on curricular skills is a relatively new direction in assessment of the performance of students with mild and moderate disabilities (Fuchs & Deno, 1994; Fuchs, Fuchs, Hamlett, Phillips, & Bentz, 1994; Galagan, 1985; Wesson, 1991). Whereas traditional assessment often emphasized cognitive ability deficits (e.g., auditory perception, visual memory, or other disabilities that may hamper learning), the behavioral emphasis involves direct assessment of academic skills within the curriculum.

It may help to think of a commonplace example. When a student is assessed for special education, numerous tests are given, including tests of intelligence, visual perception ability, auditory perception ability, and other tests intended to describe a student's innate ability in various areas. These "ability" areas are not included in the school curriculum, because changing these abilities is not the purpose of instruction. Although we traditionally tested in these areas in order to identify the root problems a child may experience, we did not attempt to teach skills in these areas. Rather, these abilities were believed to enhance or limit the capacity of a child to master the academic skills in math, reading, and/or language arts.

Assessment of these noncurriculum abilities has been challenged repeatedly over the years (Coles, 1978; Linn, 1986; Galagan, 1985; Marston, Tindal, & Deno, 1984). For example, some theorists have argued that the tests used to measure innate ability are highly suspect on technical grounds (Coles, 1978; Galagan, 1985). Others have suggested that assessment should focus on skills that can be taught (Linn, 1986). Finally, other scholars suggested that through repeatedly measuring a child's progress on a particular set of skills, we obtain information that is much more useful for planning the next instructional tasks for that child (Marston, Tindal, & Deno, 1984; White, 1986). For these reasons, assessment based directly on the skills in the child's curriculum, measured on a repeated and frequent basis, seems to be the option of choice for the future (Galagan, 1985). This type of assessment is referred to as curriculum-based assessment, or CBA.

Scholars disagree on the frequency with which a child's behavior should be assessed in curriculum-based assessment models. For example, some theorists argue that a teacher-made assessment administered at three-week intervals may be sufficient (Peterson, Heistad, Peterson, & Reynolds, 1985), whereas others feel that student progress should be assessed every day (Jenkins, Deno, & Mirkin, 1979; White, 1986). The major points are that assessment should be based only on the skills listed in the child's curriculum, repeated regularly and frequently throughout the year, and used as the basis for educational decision making.

The last factor has proven to be a great advantage in favor of curriculum-based assessment. For example, most adults today can recall having a "trial test" on spelling words every Wednesday in elementary school, which represented an attempt to prepare us for the "final test" on the same words on Friday. This is a good instructional technique, as it allows the students to note their areas of deficiency. Also, on Thursday, the most effective elementary teachers would plan a spelling lesson that included the difficult words, as identified on the Wednesday test. In short, educational activities are most effective when they are based on recent data concerning the performance of the students.

Another example may be helpful. Imagine a teacher in the third grade basic skills class who introduces two-digit multiplication on a Monday. After teaching for two weeks through blackboard examples and seatwork, she tests her students on Friday. To her surprise, she determines that half her class has not mastered this skill. Further, although she may not realize it, several members of the class had mastered that skill in the elementary class last year, and did not need any additional instruction. Their participation over the last two weeks has been wasted time.

Suppose, however, that the same teacher had used the daily worksheets as a continuing assessment. After only one or two days, she would have discovered that some students had already mastered this skill. These students would have moved on to a more complex skill, while other students whose daily work indicated problems with comprehension of this task could have been instructed on a one-to-one basis until they mastered the work. Obviously repeated assessment, even when it is as informal as worksheets done in class, can be a very effective tool for instructional planning. Further, the more frequent the assessment (a daily basis seems to be the general consensus), the more responsive the instruction can be. Finally, if the assessment data is summarized in some readily interpretable form, this information is even more useful. Imagine the teacher having to look through all of the worksheets, and compare that with the teacher looking at a simple chart of correct and incorrect problems on a daily basis for each student; the latter summary of the data saves a great deal of time.

By basing instructional decisions on repeated measures of academic work, the traditional separation between "testing" and "teaching" becomes blurred. Theorists in curriculum-based assessment generally do not accept a distinction between assessment on the one hand and instruction on the other. In fact, with comprehensive curriculum-based assessment data, it is possible to envision a day when more traditional assessment of innate abilities or ability deficits becomes obsolete (Galagan, 1985).

PRECISION TEACHING

Curriculum-based assessment, in total, cannot be covered in one brief section such as this one, and the reader is referred to Monda-Amoya & Reed (1993) for a more comprehensive discussion. This section presents one model by which curriculum-based assessment can be conducted: an instructional, decision-making model called precision teaching, which is both an assessment method and a teaching method (White, 1986). Precision teaching is not the only available example of curriculum-based assessment. However, it is one method that incorporates daily assessment for instructional decision making, as well as a fairly simple method for charting daily performance. Familiarity with this performance-monitoring method will allow the teacher to structure his or her class for maximum achievement of the students. Also, the research evidence has shown that precision teaching works in both special education and mainstream class settings (White, 1986).

Precision teaching is a method that originated in the "behavioral school" of psychology (Lindsley, 1971). As you are aware, behavioral psychology emphasized readily observable behaviors, measured precisely, and antecedents or consequences that tended to increase or decrease these behaviors. When applying these behavioral principles to education, Lindsley (1971) enumerated five principles as having a direct bearing on educational success. Each of these principles, presented in Interest Box 4.1, related directly to the individual performance of students on learning tasks.

Given the emphasis on individual instruction, Lindsley began a method of instruction that focused on charting specific behaviors of a child. First, the behavior was pinpointed by stating an appropriate behavioral objective. Behavioral

INTEREST BOX 4.1
Five Principles of Precision Teaching

1. The learner knows best: This principle suggests that if the child is progressing, the teaching method is appropriate, whereas if the child is not progressing, some other procedure must be tried. In short, only the learner's actual progress is a valid measure of success or failure of a particular instructional method.
2. Focus on directly observable behavior: Lindsley demanded that teachers focus on behavior which is observable in order to glean a clear, unambiguous picture of progress.
3. Frequency as the measure of behavior: Because of the dissatisfactions with tabulation of correct responses as a measure of success, the focus in precision teaching is frequency or rate of the response (how many correct responses per minute the child demonstrates).
4. Use of a standard chart for measuring success: Charting has numerous advantages over merely saving the student's worksheets, as the example in the text demonstrates. Therefore, charts of pupil progress are a *must* for the precision teacher.
5. Description of environmental conditions: A teacher must understand the effect of the environment on the child's behavior, and be able to construct the appropriate antecedent and consequent conditions that shape behavior. Consequently, knowing what the child can do (prerequisite behaviors) facilitates the decision making for the present instructional sequence.

For a more complete description of these five principles, see Lindsley (1971) and White (1986).

objectives must stipulate three things: the task the student would perform, the conditions under which the student would perform the task, and the criteria used to evaluate the performance. An example of a behavioral objective would be:

> *When presented with 20 double-digit addition problems that do not involve regrouping, the student will complete the problems with 90 percent accuracy.*

With this type of objective in hand, the teacher's job becomes relatively easy. The student must be instructed in this skill and repeatedly assessed until he or she meets the criteria. Performance is charted on a daily basis on this skill and when the child reaches mastery for three consecutive days, he or she is ready to move on to the next skill—perhaps double-digit addition with regrouping.

However, Lindsley and his colleagues quickly realized that the problems of some students were not related to the correctness of their behavioral responses, but to their rate of response. Every teacher has had experience with a child who can correctly complete all twenty math problems if two hours of instructional time is allocated to one worksheet. Clearly, with some children, the problem is to get them to work both correctly and quickly. Therefore, behavioral objectives that specify a certain *rate* of behavior were introduced, as follows:

> *When presented with a page of double-digit addition problems that do not require regrouping, the student will successfully complete an average of 20 problems during each two-minute period.*

With this type of objective in hand, teachers were prepared to reward children who improved their rate of performance as well as their accuracy.

Precision Teaching: One-to-One

Precision Teaching Math Project. Figure 4.4 presents a behavioral chart recommended by Lindsley. In certain school districts around the country, precision teaching, utilizing this specific chart, is required of every special education teacher and every mainstream teacher. The chart represents Benito's performance on the objective above. The dots represent correct problems, and the x's indicate the number of errors for each day. As you can see, Benito answered 17 problems correctly and had 2 errors on Tuesday, September 22. You will note a shaded line on the "20" line. This represents the aim line, or the goal expressed in the objective. For most students, reaching the aim line for three days becomes a very rewarding experience. The shaded line on the "2" line is called the record floor. This indicates the length of the timed exercise as expressed in the objective.

The chart presents a great deal of information. You may notice that during the week of September 14 through September 18, Benito did not continue to make progress. Whenever three days of "flat data" are recorded, the teacher and the student must make some type of change, because the instructional exercises are not showing any results. This type of decision making is highly sensitive to the instructional needs of the student, when compared to the teacher discussed above, who had to wait two weeks for the unit test before changing the instruction.

Notice the "phase change" lines at the top of the chart. These indicate that instruction was adjusted, either because the warmup activities were not effective, or because Benito reached the aim. For example, during the week of September 14 through 18, the instructional activity was to use counters to complete the addition problems. On each of these days, Benito spent five to ten minutes working a page of problems using counters to represent each of the digits in the ones' column and each of the digits in the tens' column. After a warmup session, Benito would indicate that he was ready for the timing. The teacher would hand Benito a "rate sheet" (a worksheet of problems that included only the type of problem specified in the objective), and start a tape recorder that played a series of bell tones at two-minute intervals. Benito would start at one bell and finish at the next. The teacher and Benito jointly decided, on September 18, that the warmup activity was

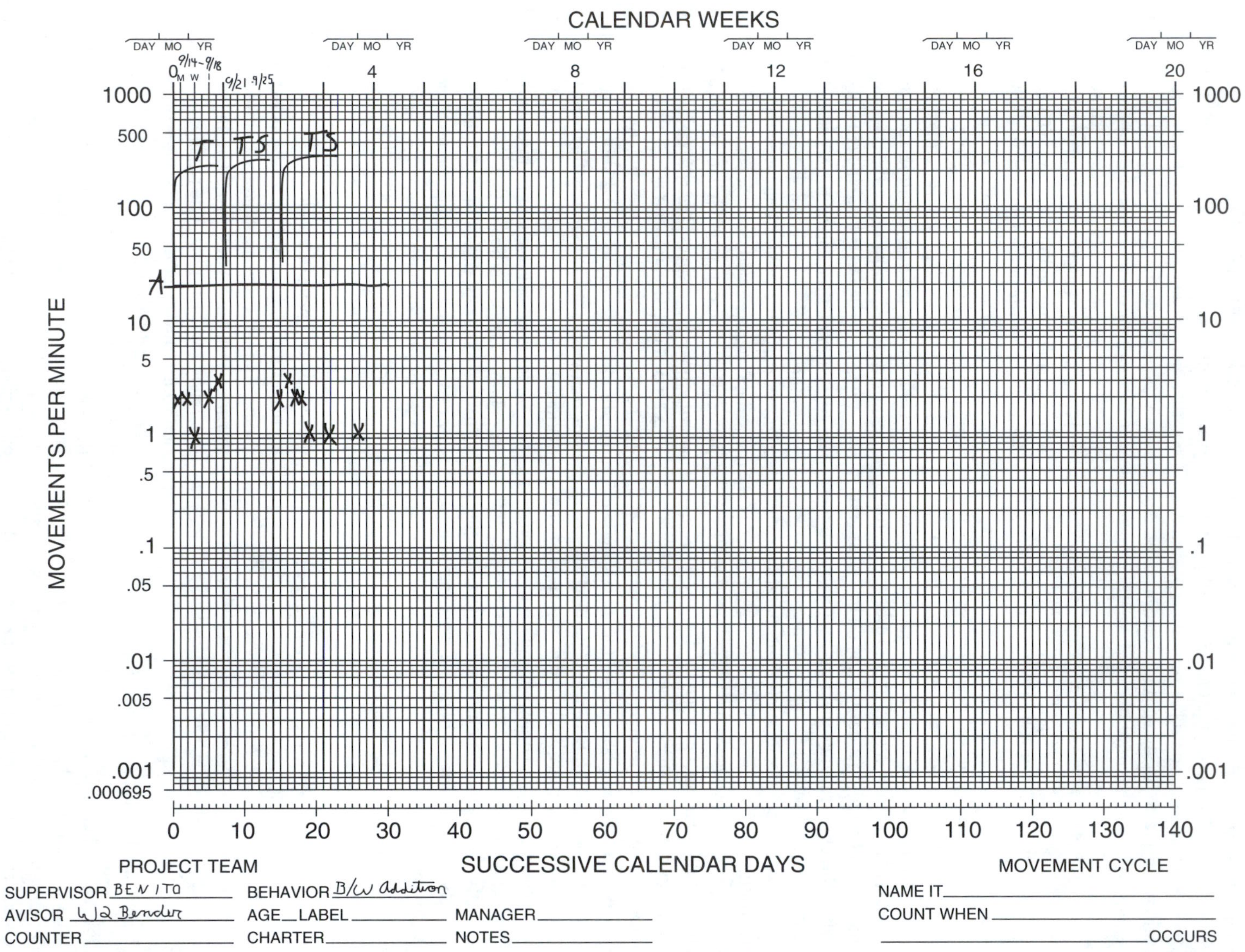

CALENDAR WEEKS

DAY MO YR — 0 — 4 — 8 — 12 — 16 — 20

9/14–9/18 9/21–9/25

M W

T TS TS

A

MOVEMENTS PER MINUTE

1000 500 100 50 10 5 1 .5 .1 .05 .01 .005 .001 .000695

0 10 20 30 40 50 60 70 80 90 100 110 120 130 140

SUCCESSIVE CALENDAR DAYS

PROJECT TEAM

SUPERVISOR BENITO

AVISOR W2 Bender

COUNTER

BEHAVIOR B/W addition

AGE LABEL

CHARTER

MANAGER

NOTES

MOVEMENT CYCLE

NAME IT

COUNT WHEN

OCCURS

FIGURE 4.4 Precision Teaching Chart

not helping Benito improve his work. Consequently, the phase change line on September 21 indicates a new warmup activity: completion of problems on a worksheet without using counters. Apparently, this activity worked out well because Benito reached aim for three days at the end of the next week. The next phase change line (September 28) indicates that Benito moved on to the next skill in the sequence.

Initiation of a Precision Teaching Project. Certain steps should be followed when initiating a precision teaching project. As a first step, you will need to pinpoint the behavioral objective for the project. You may ask what the child feels he or she needs to work on, or you may select an objective and then try to get the child to "buy into" the objective. Again, this effort to get the child to take responsibility for learning reflects the third aspect of individualized education: individual assumption of responsibility, as discussed in Chapter 1. You should not attempt to teach the child something for which he or she does not see the value. Any academic skill that can be stated as a measurable objective based on the rate of behavior is acceptable.

Second, you will need some graph paper, a set of rate sheets (usually worksheets from your usual curriculum will do, as long as they include only the specific type of problem stipulated in the objective). You will also need a timing device. In the example above, a bell tone was used, but some teachers have used egg timers. These things should be demonstrated for the child until he or she becomes familiar with them and can use them independently.

Next, you will need to establish a goal in order to set the aim line. Although precision teaching theorists have recommended different procedures for setting the aim, the simplest method is to have the child's performance timed for three days, and then use that information for an educated "guess" at an appropriate aim.

Finally, you should select a three- to five-minute instructional warmup activity directly related to the objective. For example, flash cards may be a good exercise for mathfacts. Likewise, "word window" exercises that reveal only one syllable of a multisyllabic spelling word may be appropriate for a spelling exercise. Note that precision teaching is really somewhat eclectic in that no particular teaching method is recommended. The teacher is free to choose anything that may work. The difference in using precision teaching is that instructional decisions are made based on two or three days of instruction rather than on a two-week instructional unit. This model of instruction is much more reactive to the individual needs of the students and gives the teacher the necessary data to make very frequent instructional decisions.

You may now begin your project. Have the student do the intended warmup and one timed exercise. You may also require the student to check his or her work. At first, you should check that student's skill in "checking" the work, then discuss the results with the student. Ask if he or she can do better, then allow a second timing and chart the best time. After several days you may turn the checking and charting over to the student. You should continually encourage the student by indicating the successes revealed by the chart.

In order to attain the maximum motivational benefit from the project, there are certain guidelines or decision rules intended to assure success. First, something about the project must change if three days' data are flat, and thus indicate no progress (i.e., the correct responses are not accelerating or the errors are not decelerating). You may change the warmup activity, identify a particular prerequisite behavior the student did not have, or provide tangible reinforcement for correct responses above a certain level. The point is that you, as the teacher, must change something if the data reveal that the present project is not working. Obviously, if the child attains aim (for three consecutive days), he or she should move to the next skill in the sequence.

The advantages of this system over traditional group instruction are numerous. First, each student is instructed as an individual, as mandated by special education law. Second, there is a direct relationship between the particular objectives on a student's IEP and the daily work in class, and this relationship can easily be communicated to parents; the chart serves to make the educational attainment very real to parents. Third, when a student's progress is graphically portrayed, the students tend to "own" more responsibility for achieving the goals set forth in their educational program. Achieving aim, in and of itself, becomes reinforcing for most students. Fourth, instructional decisions may be made on a daily basis, which minimizes the wasted time associated with two- or three-week unit tests. Finally, communication with other teachers is facilitated by showing progress.

Precision Teaching in a Group Setting

Management of precision teaching in group situations is easily handled. For example, in the typical special education resource or self-contained class, between 5 and 8 students are present. Thus, the teacher may wish to use precision teaching with the entire group. Of course, the recommendations given below allow teachers to use precision teaching in an inclusive environment also.

Students with an ongoing precision teaching project should be encouraged to move to a particular spot in the class whenever they complete a warmup exercise. For example, you may choose to have a "timing table" in one corner. In that location, a cassette tape may play continually, sounding a bell tone every minute. Students who are completing a two- or three-minute timing should ignore the first bell(s) and terminate their work at the appropriate time. Either the teacher or the teacher's aid would then help the student check the work and chart the results. After that, the student would return to his seat, locate the next assignment, and begin the work on that assignment. Such a flexible system would work, as long as there were not too many students at the timing table at once.

Another option is to do all of the timed work during the last 15 minutes of the period. For example, Benito may have the addition worksheet, a worksheet on identification of subjects and predicates, and a worksheet on punctuation. Other students would, likewise, have several timed rate sheets to complete, and the length of their various timings would probably vary. After checking to see that each student had the correct worksheets, the teacher would start the bell-tone tape and leave it running. When Benito finishes a two-minute timing, he could use the next couple of minutes to check his work and put the score on the math chart. When the next bell rings, he would begin his language arts worksheet for a one-minute timing. Clearly, given the small numbers of students in special education classes, this is a manageable instructional activity. With two teachers available in the inclusive class setting, this should also be manageable for most inclusive classes.

Research on Precision Teaching

The research on precision teaching has been unequivocal: precision teaching is a very effective method of instruction for every group of students with whom it has been tried (Jenkins, Deno, & Mirkin, 1979; Wesson, 1991; White, 1986). Unlike other areas of research in which conflicting results are present, every study that has utilized a precision teaching methodology for students with mild or moderate disabilities has shown that this method is highly successful.

For example, Bohannon (1975) utilized a precision teaching project for instruction in phonics. Fifteen resource teachers were included in the study and each of these teachers taught at least one student in the precision teaching group and one student in the control group. A total of 24 students comprised each group. The precision teaching group was instructed using the procedures outlined here; the other group was instructed in a traditional manner. After 28 days, the results strongly favored the precision teaching group, even though its instructional time was much less on a daily basis than that of the control group. Ninety-two percent of the precision teaching group had successfully remediated their phonics skills, compared to only 8 percent of the control group.

Other studies have demonstrated that precision teaching is effective in subjects including basic skills instruction in reading, math, language arts, vocabulary, and sight word acquisition (see White, 1986, for a review). Also, this method is useful in special education classes, mainstream classes, and basic skills classes (White, 1986).

Clearly, with this demonstrated effectiveness, use of precision teaching methods will be increasing during the next several years. The potency of daily charts of student performance as a motivational tool make this instructional methodology hard to resist. You may notice in Chapter 5 that the learning strategies instructional methodology also utilizes a charting procedure based on daily assessment as a motivational tool. Also, many educational materials that are commercially available today include strategies that involve daily charting of each student's performance on particular behavioral objectives. These commercial materials may not include the term "precision teaching" in their published advertisements, but they are based, at least in part, on the research results for precision teaching.

Problems with Precision Teaching

Every educational method has problems in implementation and precision teaching is no exception. First, both teachers and students will need help in rethinking their role in this particular instructional system. Students are not used to participating in aim setting or in assuming responsibility for their own learning, nor are teachers used to sharing these responsibilities.

Second, the record-keeping aspects of precision teaching will take some instructional time. This is particularly true during the first few weeks of precision teaching. However, if you choose to use precision teaching for several different projects over the year with one student (say, subtraction mathfacts, identification of subjects and verbs, sight word recognition, etc.), the charting skills will be the same for each project. Also, most children quickly learn the self-checking and charting skills that are necessary.

Third, the actual rate sheets should be carefully selected to include only the specific type of problem included in the objective. During the first year of implementation many teachers develop their own rate sheets for various activities, and this will take some time. However, various companies have commercially prepared rate sheets available and these can save the teacher's time. Interest Box 4.2 lists several companies you may wish to contact regarding rate sheets and other materials.

INTEREST BOX 4.2
Companies That Sell Precision Teaching Materials

Precision Teaching Project
Skyline Center
3300 Third St., Northeast
Great Falls, MT 59404

Regional Resource Center Diagnostic Inventories
Clinical Services Bldg.
University of Oregon
Eugene, OR 97403

Precision People
P.O. Box 17402
Jacksonville, FL 32216

Finally, after several projects, certain children may request a holiday from precision teaching. This is permissible if the student requests this in a mature manner and expresses a willingness to return to these procedures after a week or two on a new project. This is a fairly rare occurrence.

ALTERNATIVE CURRICULUM BASED ASSESSMENT MODELS

Criterion Referenced Testing

One alternative to the use of precision teaching is continuing and repeated use of criterion referenced tests (CRTs) as a basis for instructional decision making. As Howell and Morehead (1987) indicate, the purpose of the criterion referenced test is to identify specific skills that require additional instruction. A criterion referenced test is an assessment that lists sequenced behavioral skills in a particular area, such as whole-number addition. A test including the specific types of problems associated with each objective is then administered to the student until the student fails to reach criteria level on a particular skill. An example of a CRT is presented in Interest Box 4.3. Use of such testing is described more fully in assessment courses that most teachers of students with disabilities are required to complete as a component of their preservice training.

Use of a CRT on one occasion during the school year does not constitute curriculum-based assessment. Clearly, although CRT assessment is preferable to assessment of ability deficits as discussed previously, the last two components of curriculum-based assessment cannot be addressed if the CRT is administered only once. Curriculum-based assessment requires frequently repeated measurement in order to allow for instructional decisions based directly on student performance.

INTEREST BOX 4.3

Criterion Referenced Assessment for Whole Number Addition

1. When presented with five whole number addition problems involving mathfacts up to 10, the student will complete the problems with 80 percent accuracy.

2	5	6	3	7
+ 6	+ 4	+ 3	+ 5	+ 2

2. When presented with five whole number addition problems involving mathfacts up to 20, the student will complete the problems with 80 percent accuracy.

8	6	4	3	6
+ 5	+ 7	+ 9	+ 8	+ 5

3. When presented with five whole number addition problems involving double digit addition without regrouping, the student will complete the problems with 80 percent accuracy.

13	64	47	26	55
+ 26	+ 35	+ 21	+ 32	+33

4. When presented with five whole number addition problems involving double digit addition with regrouping, the student will complete the problems with 80 percent accuracy.

36	24	38	26	53
+ 25	+ 48	+ 37	+ 46	+ 39

Microcomputers in CBA

With the increasing presence of the microcomputer, scholars quickly seized the opportunity to use technology for the record-keeping aspects of curriculum-based assessment. Peterson, Heistad, Peterson, and Reynolds (1985) described an instructional model in which a student completed specific rate sheets each day, and the number of corrects and errors was placed in the computer such that a performance chart was generated. Today modern computerized systems can utilize information from the drill and practice work a student does at the computer terminal and generate a performance chart. Clearly, this use of computer technology will save instructional time by handling the various aspects of charting and checking work. Additional information on performance monitoring through the use of microcomputers is presented in Chapter 7. Also, you may wish to review the materials listed at the back of each content chapter in Part III of this volume, to ascertain if those computer assisted instructional materials are operated on the basis of daily curriculum-based assessment. You will find that many of the preferred materials have the capacity to generate daily performance charts that should assist you greatly in your instructional planning for students with disabilities.

DIRECT INSTRUCTION

Direct instruction is a set of behaviorally oriented instructional procedures. The term has several meanings, depending upon the theorists or practitioner using it. Perhaps the first person to use the term was Rosenshine (1976). At that point, the term meant the use of several specific behaviors on the part of the teachers that tended to lead to higher student achievement. These behaviors were specified in the body of research that has become identified as the effective teaching research, as discussed in Chapter 1. As mentioned there, teachers should directly lead the instruction of pupils, monitor the instructional outcomes on specific objectives, require regular products from the students based on new learning, provide constant and timely feedback to students regarding errors, and ascertain that each student has reached a mastery level on the particular skill before moving on to the next task. Under this definition of the term, "direct instruction" is roughly synonymous with effective teaching behaviors. Also, note the important relationship between direct instruction and the behavioral model of learning. Good (1983) used the term "active teaching" to indicate this same constellation of teaching behaviors that result in higher student achievement (Kameenui et al., 1986).

More recently, this definition was re-emphasized in an important theoretical article. Gersten, Woodward, and Darch (1986) used this comprehensive definition in a discussion of effectiveness of direct instruction, which included such components as curriculum design, classroom management, and teacher preparation. Other theorists have also used the term "direct instruction" to indicate all aspects of the effective teaching behavior research (Gersten & Carnine, 1984; Polloway, Epstein, Polloway, Patton, & Ball, 1986; Wilson & Sindelar, 1991), and when researchers say "direct instruction," this is probably the concept to which they are referring.

However, the term has been more narrowly defined by several theorists to include a prescribed set of instructional curriculum materials, including a teacher's script to be used with low-achieving children (Baumann, 1984). Such curriculum materials as *Reading Mastery,* originally known as *DISTAR* (Engelmann & Carnine, 1972), and *Corrective Reading* (Engelmann & Hanner, 1982), are written in order to assure that the teacher incorporates each of the effective teaching behaviors into the delivery of the lesson. These materials have very specific "scripts" that the teacher is to read word for word when conducting the lesson on a particular topic. The scripts include alternative teacher responses for correct and incorrect answers that students may give. Interest Box 4.4 shows a commercially prepared script (Engelmann, Osborn, & Hanner, 1989). An example of a script that is not commercially available is presented in Interest Box 4.5. This particular script comes from

INTEREST BOX 4.4
Direct Instruction Script

Lesson 13

GROUP ORAL WORK

EXERCISE 1 Definitions

1. Everybody, tell me the verb that means **end** or **figure out.** Pause. **Get ready.** Signal. *Conclude.*
   Tell me the **verb** that means **change food into fuel for the body.** Pause.
   Get ready. Signal. *Digest.*
   Tell me the **verb** that means **change.** Pause.
   Get ready. Signal. *Modify.*
   Tell me the **verb** that means **find fault with.** Pause. Get ready. Signal. *Criticize.*
   Repeat step 1 until firm.
2. Get ready to use those words in sentences.
3. Listen. Their new residence needs to be **changed**. Listen again.
   Their new residence needs to be **changed.** Say that sentence with a different word for **changed.** Pause. Get ready. Signal.
   Their new residence needs to be modified.
   Repeat step 3 until firm.
4. Listen. He **ended** work on the construction. Listen again. He **ended** work on the construction. Say that sentence with a different word for **ended.** Pause. Get ready. Signal.
   He concluded work on the construction.
   Repeat step 4 until firm.
5. Listen. Ann **changed** the steak **into fuel for her body.**
   Listen again. Ann **changed** the steak **into fuel for her body.**
   Say that sentence with a different word for **changed into fuel for her body.** Pause. Get ready. Signal.
   Ann digested the steak.
6. Listen. She **found fault with** Dan's selection of records. Listen again.
   She **found fault with** Dan's selection of records.
   Say that sentence with a different word for **found fault with.** Pause. Get ready. Signal. *She criticized Dan's selection of records.*
   Repeat step 6 until firm.
7. Listen. They are **changing** that old construction. Listen again. They are **changing** that old construction. Say that sentence with a different word for **changing.** Pause. Get ready. Signal.
   They are modifying that old construction.
   Repeat step 7 until firm.

Individual test

Repeat steps 3–7 with individual students.

EXERCISE 2 Information: body systems

1. Everybody, name the body system of nerves. Signal. *The nervous system.*
   Name the body system that changes food into fuel. Signal. *The digestive system.*
   Name the body system that brings oxygen to the blood. Signal. *The respiratory system.*
   Name the body system of muscles. Signal. *The muscular system.*
   Name the body system of bones. Signal. *The skeletal system.*
   Name the body system that moves blood around the body. Signal. *The circulatory system.* Repeat step 1 until firm.
2. Name the system that is made up of the central and peripheral systems. Pause. Get ready. Signal. *The nervous system.*
   Name the system that is made up of all the nerves leading to and from the spinal cord. Pause. Get ready. Signal.
   The peripheral nervous system.
   Name the system that is made up of the brain and the spinal cord. Pause. Get

ready. Signal. *The central nervous system.*

Repeat step 2 until firm.

Individual test

Repeat steps 1 or 2 with individual students.

Note: Pass out the workbooks.

WORKBOOK

EXERCISE 3 Writing directions

1. Open your workbook to lesson 13. I'll read the instructions for Part A. Write the instructions. Look at circle 1. Then look at item 1. The word in the parentheses after item 1 is **what.** That means that you have to tell **what** is shown by circle 1.
2. Everybody, **what** is shown by circle 1? Signal. *A vertical line.*
   Yes, tell me the **whole** instruction for item 1. Pause. Get ready. Signal. *Draw a vertical line.* Repeat until firm.
3. Look at circle 2. Then look at item 2. The words in the parentheses after item 2 are **what** and **where.** That means that you have to tell **what** is shown by circle 2 and **where** that thing is.

Lesson 14

THINKING OPERATIONS

EXERCISE 1 Same: review

The first Thinking Operation is Same.

1. We're going to name some ways that a jacket and a shoe are the same.
2. Can you point to jackets and shoes? Signal. *Yes.*
   So, are jackets and shoes objects?
   Signal. *Yes.*
3. So, name those three ways that a jacket and a shoe are the same.
   Hold up one finger. *They are objects.*
   Hold up two fingers. *They take up space.*
   Hold up three fingers. *You find them in same place.* Repeat until firm.
4. Listen. A jacket and a shoe are also the same because you do some of the same things with them. When I call on you, name some things that you do with them.
   Call on individual students.
   Praise reasonable responses; for example, wear them, buy them, clean them.
5. Listen. A jacket and a shoe are the same because they are in the same class. Everybody tell me that class. Signal. *Clothing.* Yes, they are clothing. How are they the same? Signal. *They are clothing.*
6. I'll name some ways a jacket is the same as a shoe. They are objects. They keep you warm. They keep you dry. When I call on you, see how many ways you can name that a jacket is the same as a shoe.
   Start with objects. Call on individual students. Each student is to name at least seven ways a jacket and a shoe are the same.

EXERCISE 2 Same: parts

1. We're going to name some ways that a squirrel and a lion are the same. Do a squirrel and a lion have some of the same **body parts?** Signal. *Yes.*
2. Name some of the same body parts that a squirrel and a lion have.
   Call on individual students.
   Praise reasonable responses; for example, fur, teeth, legs.
   So, a squirrel and a lion are the same because they have some of the same body parts.

EXERCISE 3 Definitions

The next Thinking Operation is Definitions.

1. **Modify** means change.
2. What does **modify** mean? Signal. *Change.*
   What word means **change?** Signal. *Modify.*
   Repeat step 2 until firm.
3. Listen. Writers often change their stories. Say that. Signal.

(continued)

INTEREST BOX 4.4 continued

Writers often change their stories.
Repeat until firm.
Now say that sentence with a different word for **change.** Pause. Get ready. Signal.
Writers often modify their stories.
Repeat until firm. Repeat step 3 until firm.

4. Listen. That camera needs to be modified. Say that. Signal.
That camera needs to be modified.
Repeat until firm.
Now say that sentence with a different word for **modified.** Pause. Get ready. Signal.
That camera needs to be changed.
Repeat until firm. Repeat step 4 until firm.
5. Listen. You should change the design. Say that. Signal. *You should change the design.* Repeat until firm.
Now say that sentence with a different word for **change.** Pause. Get ready. Signal.
You should modify the design.
Repeat until firm. Repeat step 5 until firm.

EXERCISE 4 Definitions

1. **Amble.** Pause. What does **amble** mean? Signal. *Walk slowly.* What word means **walk slowly?** Signal. *Amble.* Repeat step 1 until firm.
2. Listen. They walked slowly to school. Say that. Signal.
They walked slowly to school.
Repeat until firm.
Now say that sentence with a different word for **walked slowly.** Pause. Get ready. Signal. *They ambled to school.*
Repeat until firm. Repeat step 2 until firm.
3. **Lazy.** Pause. What's a synonym for **lazy?** Signal. *Indolent.*

Source: Engelmann, Osborn, and Hanner (1989).

a research article by Patching, Kameenui, Carnine, Gersten, and Colvin (1983), as quoted in Darch and Kameenui (1987).

As you can see, these scripts include the specific components of effective instruction as recommended by the effective instructional literature. For example, the teacher states explicitly the content to be learned and an example is given in order to demonstrate that content. Lessons also include guided practice, in which the student completes the work while receiving immediate teacher feedback about it, and independent practice for the student. Although many researchers indicate that the first definition is the only correct use of the term, many practitioners who use the term "direct instruction" would probably have this second definition (i.e., scripted lessons) in mind.

Components of Direct Instruction Programs

Specification of Objective. As mentioned previously, direct instruction curriculum materials are comprised of lessons, each of which includes a script. The intention of the script is to focus both the teacher and the student on the specific task, and the script reflects the appropriate effective instructional behaviors. The script states everything a teacher is supposed to say. These scripts start with a few statements of dialogue that let the students know what the lesson is about (Darch & Kameenui, 1987). The task is stated clearly and briefly so that students can understand. Instructions to the students are kept simple and given at a brisk pace to keep the lesson moving along smoothly (see the discussion of pacing in Chapter 1). Also, some discussion of the importance of mastering the objective is presented in order to help students understand the need to work hard on the material to be presented.

The proponents of direct instruction frequently indicate that the exact specification of the task, as well as the justification for learning the task, are relatively rare in most curriculum lesson plans (Gersten, Woodward, & Darch, 1986). For

INTEREST BOX 4.5
A Sample Direct Instruction Script

Teacher: Listen. Here's a rule. Just because someone important in one area says something is good or bad in another area, you can't be sure it's true. (Repeat.)

Teacher: When someone important in one area says something is good or bad in another area, can you be sure it's true?

Student: No.

Teacher: No, just because someone important in one area says something is good or bad in another area, you can't be sure it's true.

Teacher: OK, Listen. Terry Bradshaw (former quarterback for the Pittsburgh Steelers) says that Ford Mustangs are the best family cars.

Teacher: What do you know about Terry Bradshaw?

Student: He's an important person.

Teacher: In what area is Terry Bradshaw important?

Student: Football.

Teacher: And what's this important person saying?

Student: That Ford Mustangs are the best family cars.

Teacher: So what is the other area that Terry Bradshaw is talking about?

Student: Cars.

Teacher: Since we're learning to judge what people say, can you be sure what a quarterback says about Ford Mustangs is true?

Student: No.

Teacher: Why not?

(Or prompt with, "What can you say when someone important says something is good or bad?)

Student: (Student should give the rule or respond with something like,) You can't be sure it's true, and quarterbacks may not know very much about cars.

Teacher: Listen, if I tell you that Terry Bradshaw says that one good way to throw a football is by placing your fingers on the laces, can you be sure it's true?

Student: Yes.

(Correction Procedure: If a child answers "No," ask, "What do you know about the important person?" ["One good way to throw a football . . ."] "Yes, the quarterback is talking about one good way to throw a football. So, can you be sure what a quarterback says about one way of throwing the football is true? ("Yes.")

Teacher: Yes, you can be sure that's true. Why?

(Accept the answer in varying form, providing that the following information is provided: [1] he's a quarterback, [2] quarterbacks know about throwing the football, and [3] he's talking about one way to throw the football.

Source: This script is cited in Darch and Kameenui (1987). Other articles which present partial scripts include Baumann (1984); Gersten, Woodward, and Darch (1986); and Kameenui, Carnine, Darch, and Stein (1986).

example, as Kameenui and his co-workers (1986) discussed, the typical beginning of a lesson recommended by basal mathematics texts includes a wide array of interest activities and a daily review of previous lessons, but not necessarily a clear, explicit statement of what the current lesson is designed to teach and why that is important. Proponents of direct instruction demand that a clear objective be stated for the student in terms that the student can understand. This is seen as one method to encourage individual responsibility for learning on the part of the student.

Direct Instruction Phase. Next, the script would include a dialogue for the teacher to read that emphasized certain aspects of the task (Baumann, 1984; Darch & Kameenui, 1987). A sentence about the last lesson is sometimes included and the teacher would be instructed to model the first step of the task. Students would be asked questions about the task. Several tasks may be completed during this direct instruction phase, with the teacher assuming the major burden for the work.

The key distinction between direct instruction and other instructional programs is the explicit nature of instruction during this phase. The script instructs the teacher to present the examples, note problem areas, and model the task; each of these activities was identified as an effective teaching behavior in Chapter 1. Proponents of direct instruction note that most instructional techniques recommended by basal textbooks are far from explicit in this phase (Kameenui et al., 1986).

Teacher-Directed Practice. After the direct instruction phase involving modeling with student participation, several practice tasks are given to the student (Baumann, 1984). In these tasks, the teacher may verbally cue the students about the correct task procedure, but the responsibility for the task rests with the students. The script includes explicit questions that the teacher is supposed to ask the students, and these questions exemplify the various possible trouble spots in task completion. Note, for example, in Interest Box 4.5, the statements that exemplify the problem of identification of invalid testimonial. This phase of instruction is presented as practice that gives the teacher the opportunity to repeatedly question the students about the task.

In some scripts, there is a very clear delineation between the modeling, or direct instruction phase, and this phase, whereas in other materials the distinction is less clear. Still, at some point, the student assumes the major responsibility for task completion. During this phase, the teacher provides immediate feedback to the student in order to prevent continuation of incorrect problem solution. This feedback is one of the cornerstones of direct instruction, as feedback of this nature was heavily emphasized in the effective teaching research.

Independent Practice. After the child has demonstrated some competence on the teacher-directed practice, a series of tasks are assigned for independent practice (Baumann, 1984). At this point in the lesson, the script instructs the teacher to present various worksheets and task assignments to the students. Generally, the tasks will require no more than half of the total lesson time. The child will work on these tasks alone and show the completed work to the teacher for checking. In some direct instruction curriculum materials, this phase of instruction may be done as homework, though most of the commercially available materials include some independent practice in the recommended class lesson time. The student's success rate is monitored on a daily basis on these independent practice problems. As you will recall, monitoring of student behavior is another of the effective teaching behaviors discussed in Chapter 1. Figure 4.5 presents a monitoring record from the early direct instruction research, as presented by Meyer, Gersten, & Gutkin, 1983).

Efficacy of Direct Instruction

Follow Through Research. The increasing influence of direct instruction as an instructional procedure is directly linked to a major evaluation of the effectiveness of federally funded Follow

Direct Instruction Group Summary Form

Circle One:
Reading (I) II III
Arithmetic I II III
Language I II III

Test Section 8
Lesson Number 82
Group 11
Teacher Allen
Date 12/7/80

Names	Items 1	2	3	4	5	6	7	8	9	10	Percent Passed
1. David	+	+	+	+	−	+	+				86%
2. Sally	+	+	+	+	−	−	+				72%
3. Tom	+	+	+	+	+	−	−				72%
4. Josh	+	+	+	+	−	+	+				86%
5. Sara	+	+	+	−	−	−	−				57%
6. Steve	+	−	−	+	+	−	−				43%
7. Louise	Absent										
8.											
9.											
10.											
Percent Passed	100	93	93	93	33	33	50				

FIGURE 4.5 The Monitoring Record

Through Programs for lower socioeconomic level children (Meyer, Gersten, & Gutkin, 1984). The Follow Through Programs were initiated in 1968 by the federal government to assist low income children in their preparation for, and success in, the elementary grades. The program was designed as a "follow through" for the earlier success in Head-start programs. Each of the 180 Follow Through Programs implemented was assigned a sponsor at the local level, such as a University, an educational laboratory, or a state Department of Instruction. Because of this approach, a wide array of educational models were utilized in the different Follow Through Programs, because each local sponsor was responsible for selection and implementation of an educational approach to assist low income children.

The federal government selected an outside agency—Abt Associates—to evaluate the effectiveness of these diverse programs (Stebbins, 1976; Stebbins, St. Pierre, Proper, Anderson, & Cerva, 1977), and the research reports written by that agency have come to be known as the Abt Report (Gersten & Carnine, 1984).

The evaluation looked at the comparative success of the various programs on both academic achievement variables and affective variables. The affective variables included such things as improved self-concept and improved attitudes about school. The evaluation used several groups of children from each location in a comprehensive longitudinal design that compared the effectiveness of the different instructional models (a longitudinal research design is a research study that studies effects of a treatment over a long period of time, at least several years). These early results indicated that direct instruction was clearly superior to all other programs in achievement in math, reading, and language arts (Gersten & Carnine, 1984; Meyer, Gersten, & Gutkin, 1983). Also, direct instruction was among the three highest programs on all of the outcome measures (Gersten & Carnine, 1984). Clearly, the direct instruction model provides evidence of federal dollars that appear to be well spent. With this type of strong comparative research support available, numerous researchers became very excited about the potential benefits of direct instructional procedures.

The research on the Follow Through Programs did surprise a number of researchers in one important way. The study included several affective dependent variables: self-concept and locus of control (Gersten & Carnine, 1984). Self-concept refers to the view one has of oneself, and locus of control refers to the degree of control one believes one has over one's life. These were areas of concern because the government was very sensitive to educational programs that might make underprivileged children feel less than adequate about themselves.

Actually, it was quite surprising when direct instruction resulted in measurable positive gains in self-concept and locus of control (Gersten & Carnine, 1984). As you recall, numerous educational programs were used in Follow Through Programs, and several of these were aimed explicitly at improvement in affective areas, whereas direct instruction was primarily aimed at improvement in academic achievement in the basic skill areas. Consequently, to find that direct instruction outperformed the affective curriculums on improvement of affective variables was quite startling. It must be noted, however, that these affective research results have not been fully investigated in more recent studies, and, therefore, these positive results may not be obtained when direct instruction is used with other groups of children.

Current Research: Achievement Outcomes. The more recent research that has investigated the academic outcomes of direct instruction has been very positive: Direct instruction may be used to teach basic skills in reading, math, and language arts to very diverse groups of school children with a stunning success rate (Baumann, 1986; Darch & Gersten, 1986; Gersten, Woodward, & Darch, 1986; Hare & Borchardt, 1984; Polloway et al., 1986). Most of these studies compared a direct instruction curriculum materials package to an instructional approach recommended in basal reading or math texts, and the results consistently favored the experimental group receiving direct instruction. It should also be mentioned, however, that research on direct instruction has included examples where the researchers themselves write a set of curriculum materials that adhere to the direct instructional principles, rather than use a commercially available direct instruction script (Baumann, 1984; Darch & Gersten, 1986). Results on this type of direct instruction curriculum have been positive as well.

As every experienced teacher knows, instructional strategies that work with average children may not work for children with mild and moderate disabilities. However, research using direct instruction with these learners has shown the same frequency of positive results as research involving nondisabled children (Gersten, Woodward, & Darch, 1986). Studies using subjects with mild and moderate intellectual disabilities, as well as severe intellectual disabilities, have demonstrated positive results of direct instruction (Gersten, Woodward, & Darch, 1986).

For example, Gersten and Maggs (1982) reported on a study that investigated the effects of *DISTAR Language* and *DISTAR Reading* programs on the educational achievement of students with mild intellectual disabilities. The dependent measures for the project included the monitoring tests administered in the educational program and IQ changes. Results were very positive. After 18 months, most of the students had mastered the basic language components of the *DISTAR Language Program* and the ability to follow instructions in an academic setting. They then began the reading program. By the end of the five-year evaluation study, most of the students had mastered through Level III of both the language and reading programs. Level III is intended for average third grade level readers. This is quite a stunning success for children whose average IQ was 41. Furthermore, the IQ score demonstrated an increase, and by the end of the project the average IQ was 50.6. Clearly, direct instructional principles will work with students with moderate intellectual disabilities, as well as with low-achieving groups and economically deprived children.

Although there are studies that fail to document success in using direct instruction on students with disabilities (Kuder, 1990), these studies seem to be a decided minority of the available research. In addition, many of the studies that have shown the success of direct instruction in teaching academics have used groups of children who were functioning well below grade level academically. The similarity between these groups and students with mild disabilities may suggest the appropriateness of a similar instructional program.

Current Research: Combination Treatments. More recent research has begun to incorporate newly acquired knowledge from other research areas as well. For example, research on strategies for learning (discussed in detail in Chapter 5) has been incorporated into direct instruction scripts in recent years. This type of cross-fertilization of ideas represents a major strength of the more recent research.

Baumann (1984) provided an example of the efficacy of strategy instruction combined with direct instruction. He conducted a treatment study in which the goal was to teach comprehension of main ideas. He used 66 sixth grade students, randomly assigned to one of three treatment groups. One group used the instructional strategies suggested by a basal reader, and another group—the control group—used vocabulary lessons that had nothing to do with comprehension of main ideas. The third group—the strategy group—was taught a learning procedure that emphasized lessons on identification of the main ideas and supporting details in reading sections. The lessons emphasized explicit texts in which the main idea was stated in a sentence in the text, and implicit texts in which the main idea was not explicitly stated but incorporated into the sentences in the text. Each group received eight lessons of 30 minutes each, spread over a two-and-one-half-week period. At the end of the eight lessons, students in each of the groups were assessed on how well they could identify the main ideas and supporting details in text. Also, a test of free recall of main ideas was included.

Results demonstrated that the students in the strategy group outperformed students in the basal and control groups on ability to recognize main ideas and supporting details. Also, the strategy group was more able to construct a main idea outline for passages. There were no differences between the groups on free recall of main ideas. This research demonstrates that direct instruction can be used in combination with learning strategy training as well as other types of tasks. Also in this study, students learned higher-level skills than merely reading recognition and math operations, which were emphasized in many of the early research studies. Chapter 5 discusses learning strategy instruction in more detail.

Advantages of Direct Instruction

The advantages of a direct instruction approach are numerous and some are fairly obvious. For example, direct instruction works with different groups of children, including both the underprivileged and students with disabilities. As you are aware, basic skill instruction forms the foundation of educational curriculums for most students with mild disabilities in the lower grade levels, and the need for effective instructional strategies in these basic skill areas has prompted many special educators to look favorably at direct instruction.

Direct instructional materials generally come in a well organized format that requires little advance preparation on the part of the teacher. Although teachers may need encouragement to "stay with the script" and not wander off on verbal tangents in response to students' questions, these materials are generally fairly easy to use. Training may be done in a series of brief workshops, as teachers begin to use direct instruction materials.

A third advantage, which may be less obvious, is the fact that direct instruction works in mainstream classes and inclusive classes as well as special education classes (Gersten, Woodward, & Darch, 1986). Because of recent federal initiatives that may result in increased inclusion for students with mild disabilities, this advantage of direct instruction may become more important in the near future.

Disadvantages

Nevertheless, there are several disadvantages to direct instruction programs. First, many teachers feel that the use of such structured scripts removes the spontaneity and value from teaching. These teachers indicate that teacher's aides can read scripts and conduct lessons in this format as well as teachers (Gersten & Carnine, 1984). Also, many teachers believe their role is to respond independently to student errors, and not to read a response from a script. In short, some teachers resent this teaching format. However, proponents of direct instruction who have trained teachers on this method report that when the results are in, the teachers decide that direct instruction works and become more favorably disposed toward this instructional strategy. Even teachers who were very negatively disposed toward direct instruction initially have changed their minds completely when implementation of this approach worked with particular students while every other plan lead to no success.

A second disadvantage is the fact that most of the early research investigated effectiveness of this strategy only on lower-level academic skills in reading, math, and language arts (Kameenui et al., 1986). This is because the early commercially available materials all concentrated in basic skill areas, and researchers tended to use these materials rather than prepare their own. However, more recent studies have begun to use direct instruction in higher level math and reading comprehension problems, and the early evidence suggests that direct instructional strategies are very successful on these higher-level tasks as well (Kameenui et al., 1986). More research will, no doubt, be forthcoming on this issue.

A final problem with direct instruction is the limited number of commercially available materials that teachers may access. Although a researcher may have the time to develop higher-level materials to teach, for example, caution with invalid testimonials in reading (see Interest Box 4.5; Darch & Kameenui, 1987), teachers rarely have time to sit and write a script for lessons with such detail. Consequently, use of direct instruction will probably not increase until additional commercially prepared materials become available.

Implementation in Your Classroom

Like many of the strategies that have been reviewed in this text, direct instruction may be implemented in your classroom with a little additional time and investment on your part. Should you choose to use a direct instructional strategy with your students, you should probably start with some of the commercially prepared materials (see the references at the end of this chapter for DISTAR and Corrective Reading). You should carefully select the materials so that there is an appropriate match between learner needs and curriculum. Many of the direct instruction materials have various pretests that may be used in this regard. These materials can be implemented in small reading groups, small math groups, or individually. You may wish to select one reading or math group and implement the lessons for a few days prior to beginning the lessons in other groups. You should recall that the script is written in complete form and every effort should be made to stay with the script, because getting off the script breaks up the pacing of the lesson. After several days, you may wish to implement direct instruction with other groups of students in various subject areas. Check to see that the materials are exactly at the correct level for the children and proceed.

After a while you may wish to prepare your own scripts for various lessons. Although this should be encouraged, you must prepare yourself for this task with additional readings on direct instruction and effective teaching behaviors. Also, review of the research studies in which the researchers prepared materials may be helpful.

SUMMARY

The behavioral model of learning has been the dominant model for learning for the last thirty years in education. The techniques associated with this model—modeling, stimulus fading, reinforcement, precision teaching, and direct instruction—are wide-ranging. However, all of these techniques are dependent upon accurate repeated measures of observable tasks. Thus, in one sense, behavioral thought underlies all of these instructional approaches.

The use of curriculum-based assessment has been presented as both an assessment and an instructional decision-making strategy for teachers of students with mild and moderate disabilities. CBA models generally have three assumptions in common: the belief that assessment should be based on the child's curriculum; the belief that assessment should be repeated frequently; and the belief that these assessments should be the sole basis for instructional decision-making.

Three different models for CBA have been discussed; precision teaching, criterion-referenced testing, and computer-based assessment. Precision teaching was discussed more thoroughly because that system provides a basis for daily monitoring of student performance, as well as instructional decision making that involves the student.

As is clear from the discussion of effectiveness, every teacher in special education—whether in self-contained classes, resource classes, consultative or inclusive class roles—should employ some type of CBA. In the context of the self-contained class, these charts can document progress for parents, and other professionals. For resource, consultative, or inclusive class teachers, these performance charts can serve as a vehicle of communication with other teachers about the efficacy of the instruction the student is receiving. This instructional strategy also represents a very effective motivational tool for use with the students themselves. Further, many commercially available materials are using these procedures. Clearly, you will see frequent use of precision teaching in special education classes in the future.

Direct instruction is generally thought to mean the scripts that incorporate effective instructional behaviors on the part of teachers into the curricular content. Although this definition is more confining than some theorists would like, most of the research on direct instruction has focused on curriculum materials that meet this definition. The research has demonstrated positive academic gains in reading, math, and language arts, as well as gains in self-concept and improved locus of control. Further, these programs outperformed the affective instructional programs in Follow Through that were explicitly designed to produce improved self-concept. Finally, more recent research has demonstrated the effectiveness of direct instruction on higher order cognitive skills, and various learning strategies have been used to supplement the direct instructional procedures.

Implementation of direct instruction in the classroom need not be cumbersome, but some curricular materials will need to be purchased. After some experience with this set of instructional procedures, teachers may wish to prepare their own materials. Also, additional materials that incorporate these instructional procedures will probably become available commercially in the near future.

Summary Points

- The behavioral model of learning, emphasizing antecedents, behaviors, and consequences has been the dominant model for education for the last 30 years.
- Learning is defined as a measurable change in observable behavior, and almost all instructional methods utilize that definition today.
- Modeling is one of the most frequently utilized behavioral strategies, and is incorporated into most innovative instructional approaches today.
- Errorless learning procedures involve the use of procedures that preclude the possibility of making errors.
- Positive practice involves the completion of problems correctly, as a consequence to incorrect problem completion.

- Curriculum-based assessment means assessment of skills from the students' curriculum on a periodic basis to be used for instructional planning.
- CBA is founded on three assumptions: (1) that assessment should be based on the curriculum the child is expected to master, (2) that frequent measurement must take place, and (3) that instructional planning should be founded on this type of measurement.
- CBA allows the teacher to respond immediately when a student begins to fall behind so that instructional planning is much more responsive to the needs of the student.
- Precision teaching is one form of CBA that has been shown to be highly effective for use with students with disabilities.
- Objectives for precision teaching instruction must be stated in terms of the rate of the behavior.
- Precision teaching charts present the number of correct problems, the errors, and some indication of the aim of the student.
- Criterion-referenced tests also demonstrate quite convincingly the particular types of problems the student has and has not mastered.
- Many computer-based instructional programs are designed to facilitate collection of CBA data.
- Direct instruction may be considered synonymous with effective teaching behaviors. However, when practitioners use the term, they are typically talking about the commercially prepared direct instruction materials.
- Direct instructional materials typically include a teacher script or a set of verbal questions and commands the teacher is supposed to read to the students. Many teachers initially react negatively toward these scripted lessons.
- When using a direct instruction approach, instruction is broken down into phases, including a direct instruction phase, a teacher-led practice phase, and an independent practice phase.
- Direct instruction is effective in improving the academic performance of lower socioeconomic level children in the basic skills areas. This research was conducted to evaluate the Follow Through Programs sponsored by the federal government.
- Direct instructional programs also outperformed other programs in enhancing socioemotional development, as measured by such variables as self-concept and locus of control.
- Recent research on direct instruction has shown that these techniques may be combined with other effective instructional practices.
- Implementation of direct instruction is fairly easy and typically results in improvement in the rate of learning for many students with disabilities.

QUESTIONS AND ACTIVITIES

1. Review Chapters 1, 2, and 3 with the definition of behavioral model of learning in mind. What examples of application of this model can you find?
2. Describe and demonstrate a time-delay instructional procedure in class. Have a class member role play a fourth grade child with mild intellectual disabilities who has difficulty with mathfacts multiplication, and arrange an instructional lesson for that person.
3. As a group, list the examples of "positive practice" types of learning situations that you can recall from when you were in elementary school. Were these experiences effective? Explain.
4. Prepare a set of 20 cards, using nouns from a sight word list, for instruction, based on the stimulus shaping instructional idea.
5. Review the efficacy studies presented in this chapter on time delay. What types of tasks are involved in those studies? Can you find other studies that teach other types of tasks or other content areas?

6. As a class, collect a number of CRTs and duplicate these for each class member. These may become one of the more useful projects, which you may use once you are employed in a school system. Also, you may wish to review some of the commercially prepared CRTs in your curriculum laboratory.
7. Invite the assessment specialist faculty member to your class to present further information on CBA models. You may wish to invite the faculty member who specializes in computer utilization in education to speak on computerized models.
8. Describe a precision teaching project designed to teach the times tables to a third grade student with intellectual disabilities.
9. Write a dialogue to describe a precision teaching project to a ninth grade student with behavioral disorders that is designed to teach that student long division.
10. Inquire in the local school system concerning precision teaching projects that may be underway locally. Visit a classroom that utilizes this procedure.
11. Present a role-play debate in which one "psychologist" defends the use of IQ assessment while another "psychologist" argues for the use of CBA. What arguments for each can be identified?
12. Visit you school's curriculum lab and identify some educational materials that provide some type of daily charting mechanism to monitor student performance. How many materials can you identify that employ precision teaching concepts?
13. Identify the two definitions of direct instruction. Which definition do the researchers in the field tend to use in their studies?
14. Write several lesson scripts to teach recognition of a topic sentence to a student with mild intellectual disabilities in the fourth grade.
15. Review the research that demonstrates the effectiveness of direct instruction on academic achievement and on affective development. In which area is there more research? Why?
16. Preview several lessons from DISTAR or Corrective Reading in your curriculum materials center and present some of these materials to the class.
17. Conduct a telephone survey of 10 local special education teachers and find out how many of these teachers have ever used direct instructional materials. Also, contact the nearest teachers' college or university education reading program. Ask if these programs have courses related to direct instruction.
18. Explain the development of direct instruction in light of the effective teaching behaviors discussed in Chapter 1.
19. Discuss the various components of a direct instruction script and how these relate to effective teaching behaviors.

REFERENCES

Alig-Cybriwsky, C., Wolery, M., & Gast, D. L. (1990). Use of a constant time delay procedure in teaching preschoolers in a group format. *Journal of Early Intervention, 14,* 99–116.

Baumann, J. F. (1984). The effectiveness of a direct instruction paradigm for teaching main idea comprehension. *Reading Research Quarterly, 20,* 93–115.

Baumann, J. F. (1986). Teaching third-grade students to comprehend anaphoric relationships: The application of a direct instruction model. *Reading Research Quarterly, 21,* 70–87.

Biederman, G. B., Davey, V. A., Ryder, C., & Franchi, D. (1994). The negative effects of positive reinforcement in teaching children with developmental delay. *Exceptional Children, 60,* 458–465.

Bohannon, R. M. (1975). *Direct and daily measurement procedures in the identification and treatment of reading behaviors of children in special education.* Unpublished doctoral dissertation, University of Washington, Seattle.

Browder, P. M., Morris, W. W., & Snell, M. E. (1981). Using time delay to teach manual signs to a severely retarded student. *Education and Training of the Mentally Retarded, 16,* 252–258.

Coles, G. S. (1978). The learning disability test battery: Empirical and social issues. *Harvard Educational Review, 48,* 313–331.

Darch, C., & Gersten, R. (1986). Direction-setting activities in reading comprehension: A comparison of two approaches. *Learning Disability Quarterly, 9,* 235–243.

Darch, C., & Kameenui, E. J. (1987). Teaching LD students critical reading skills: A systematic replication. *Learning Disability Quarterly, 10,* 82–91.

Dorry, G. W. (1976). Attentional model for the effectiveness of fading in training reading vocabulary with retarded persons. *American Journal of Mental Deficiency, 81,* 271–279.

Engelmann, S., & Carnine, D. W. (1972). *Distar Arithmetic III.* Chicago: Scientific Research Associates.

Engelmann, S., Hanner, S. (1982). *Reading Mastery, Level III: A Direct Instruction Program.* Chicago: Science Research Associates.

Engelmann, S., Osborn, S., & Hanner, S. (1989). *Corrective Reading: Comprehension Skills Comprehension B 2.* Chicago: Science Research Associates.

Espin, C. A., & Deno, S. L. (1984). The effects of modeling and prompting feedback strategies on sight word reading of students labeled learning disabled. *Education and Treatment of Children, 12,* 219–231.

Fuchs, L. S., & Deno, S. L. (1994). Must instructionally useful performance assessment be based in the curriculum? *Exceptional Children, 61,* 15–24.

Fuchs, L. S., Fuchs, D., Hamlett, C. L., Phillips, N. B., & Bentz, J. (1994). Classwide curriculum-based measurement: Helping general educators meet the challenge of student diversity. *Exceptional Children, 60,* 518–537.

Galagan, J. E. (1985). Psychoeducational testing: Turn out the lights, the party's over. *Exceptional Children, 52,* 288–299.

Gersten, R., & Carnine, D. (1984). Direct instruction mathematics: A longitudinal evaluation of low-income elementary school students. *Elementary School Journal, 84,* 396–407.

Gersten, R., & Maggs, A. (1982). Teaching the general case to moderately retarded children: Evaluation of a five year project. *Analysis and Intervention in Developmental Disabilities, 2,* 329–343.

Gersten, R., Woodward, J., & Darch, C. (1986). Direct instruction: A research-based approach to curriculum design and teaching. *Exceptional Children, 53,* 17–31.

Good, T. (1983). Research on classroom teaching. In L. S. Schulman & G. Sykes (Eds.)., *Handbook of Teaching and Policy* (pp. 42–80). New York: Longman.

Hare, V. C., & Borchardt, K. M. (1984). Direct instruction of summarization skills. *Reading Research Quarterly, 20,* 62–78.

Howell, K. W., & Morehead, M. K. (1987). *Curriculum Based Evaluation for Special and Remedial Education: A Handbook for Deciding What to Teach* (pp. 36–39). Columbus, OH: Merrill.

Jenkins, J. R., Deno, S. L., Mirkin, P. K. (1979). Measuring pupil progress toward the least restrictive alternative. *Learning Disability Quarterly, 2,* 81–91.

Johnson, K. M., Gutkin, T. B., Plake, B. S. (1991). Use of modeling to enhance children's interrogative strategies. *Journal of School Psychology, 29,* 81–88.

Kameenui, E. J., Carnine, D. W., Darch, C. B., & Stein, M. (1986). Two approaches to the development phase of mathematics instruction. *The Elementary School Journal, 5,* 633–650.

Karsh, K. G., & Repp, A. C. (1992). The task demonstration model: A concurrent model for teaching groups of students with severe disabilities. *Exceptional Children, 59,* 54–67.

Kinney, P. G., Stevens, K. B., & Schuster, J. W. (1988). The effects of CAI and time delay: A systematic program for teaching spelling. *Journal of Special Education Technology, 9,* 61–72.

Knowlton, H. E. (1980). Effects of picture fading on two learning disabled students' sight word acquisition. *Learning Disability Quarterly, 3,* 88–96.

Kowry, M., & Browder, D. M. (1986). The use of delay to teach sight words by peer tutors classified as moderately mentally retarded. *Education and Training of the Mentally Retarded, 21,* 252–258.

Kuder, S. J. (1990). Effectiveness of the *DISTAR Reading Program* for children with learning disabilities. *Journal of Learning Disabilities, 23,* 69–71.

Lindsley, O. R. (1971). Precision teaching in perspective: An interview with Ogden R. Lindsley (Duncan, A., Interviewer). *Teaching Exceptional Children, 3,* 114–119.

Linn, R. L. (1986). Educational testing and assessment: Research needs and policy issues. *American Psychologist, 41,* 1153–1160.

Marston, D., Tindal, G., & Deno, S. L. (1984). Eligibility for learning disabilities services: A direct and repeated measurement approach. *Exceptional Children, 50,* 554–556.

Matson, J. L., Esveldt-Dawson, K., & Kazdin, A. E. (1982). Treatment of spelling deficits in mentally retarded children. *Mental Retardation, 20* (2), 76–81.

McIntyre, S. B., Test, D. W., Cooke, N. L., & Beattie, J. (1991). Using count–bys to increase multiplication facts fluency. *Learning Disability Quarterly, 14,* 82–88.

Meyer, L. A., Gersten, R. M., & Gutkin, J. (1983). Direct instruction: A project follow through success story in an inner city school. *Elementary School Journal, 84,* 241–252.

Monda-Amoya, L., & Reed, F. (1993). Informal assessment in the classroom. In W. N. Bender (Ed.), *Best Practices in Learning Disabilities.* Reading, MA: Andover Medical Publishers, pp. 105–134.

Patching, W., Kameenui, E., Carnine, D., Gersten, R., & Colvin, G. (1983). Direct instruction in critical reading skills. *Reading Research Quarterly, 18,* 406–418.

Peterson, J., Heistad, D., Peterson, D., & Reynolds, M. (1985). Montevideo individualized prescriptive instructional management system. *Exceptional Children, 52,* 239–243.

Polloway, E. A., Epstein, M. H., Polloway, C. H., Patton, J. R., & Ball, D. W. (1986). Corrective reading program: An analysis of effectiveness with learning disabled and mentally retarded students. *Remedial and Special Education, 7* (4), 41–47.

Rinne, C. H. (1994). The skills system: A new interactive video technology. *Technological Horizons in Education Journal, 21* (8), 81–83.

Rosenshine, B. (1976). Classroom instruction. In N. L. Cage (Ed.), *The Psychology of Teaching Methods: The Seventy-Fifth Yearbook on the National Society for the Study of Education.* Chicago: University of Chicago Press, pp. 109–143.

Schloss, P. J., Schloss, C. N., Wood, C. E., & Kiehl, W. S. (1986). A critical review of social skills research with behaviorally disordered students. *Behavioral Disorders, 11,* 1–14.

Schuster, J. W., Stevens, K. B., & Doak, P. K. (1990). Using constant time delay to teach word definitions. *The Journal of Special Education, 24,* 306–317.

Singh, N. N., Singh, J., & Winton, A. S. (1984). Positive practice overcorrection of oral reading errors. *Behavior Modification, 8,* 23–37.

Stebbins, L. B. (Ed.). (1976). *Education as Experimentation: A Planned Variation Model.* Cambridge, MA.: Abt Associates.

Stebbins, L. B., St. Pierre, R. G., Proper, E. C., Anderson, R. B., & Cerva, T. R. (1977). *Education as Experimentation: A Planned Variation Model (Vols. 4 A–D). An Evaluation of Follow Through.* Cambridge, MA.: Abt Associates.

Touchette, P. (1971). Transfer of stimulus control: Measuring the movement of transfer. *Journal of Experimental Analysis of Behavior, 15,* 347–354.

Trap, J. J., Milner-Davis, P., Joseph, S., & Cooper, J. O. (1978). The effects of feedback and consequences on transitional cursive letter formation. *Journal of Applied Behavior Analysis, 11,* 381–393.

Vail, C. O., & Huntington, D. (1993). Classroom behavioral interventions for students with learning disabilities. In W. N. Bender (Ed.), *Best Practices in Learning Disabilities.* Boston, MA: Andover Medical Publishers, pp. 153–176.

Wesson, C. L. (1991). Curriculum based measurement and two models of follow-up consultation. *Exceptional Children, 57,* 246–256.

White, O. R. (1986). Precision teaching—precision learning. *Exceptional Children, 52,* 522–534.

Wilson, C. L., & Sindelar, P. T. (1991). Direct instruction in math word problems: Students with learning disabilities. *Exceptional Children, 57,* 512–519.

Wolery, M., Bailey, D. B., & Sugai, G. M. (1988). *Effective Teaching: Principles and Procedures of Applied Behavior Analysis with Exceptional Students.* Boston: Allyn & Bacon.

Wolery, M., Cybriwsky, C. A., Gast, D. L., & Boyle-Gast, K. (1991). Use of constant time delay and attentional responses with adolescents. *Exceptional Children, 57,* 462–473.

CHAPTER 5

METACOGNITIVE INSTRUCTION AND SELF-MONITORING IN THE CLASSROOM

OBJECTIVES

Upon completion of this chapter, you should be able to:

1. Define metacognitive instruction, and diagram the metacognitive model.
2. Describe the different types of learning strategies, and the common element that defines a learning strategy.
3. Describe several research studies that demonstrate the effectiveness of a learning strategy.
4. Describe the steps involved in the use of learning strategies.
5. Present suggestions that relate particular learning strategies to various instructional situations with children with disabilities.
6. Describe the theoretical roots of a learning strategies model.
7. Describe reciprocal teaching.
8. Discuss the efficacy of the Learning to Learn Curriculum.
9. Define self-monitoring.
10. Describe the methods of instruction used to teach self-monitoring.
11. Institute a self-instructional procedure in your class.

KEYWORDS

metacognition
inner language
learning strategy
visual imagery
Learning to Learn
generalization
RAP
reciprocal teaching
predicting
questioning strategies
summarizing
clarifying
self-monitoring
recording sheet
cue
self-instruction
Michenbaum's model
self-checking
academic productivity

Metacognition is a term that may be loosely translated as thinking about thinking. With the success of the behavioral model of learning, and the instructional principles founded on that model, some theorists sought a way to employ the human capability of language within the behavioral model. This has lead to increasing study of metacognition in educational psychology and special education. The relationship between this metacognitive learning process and the behavioral learning process discussed in Chapter 4 is presented in Interest Box 5.1.

Metacognition may be more accurately defined as awareness, and regulation, of one's own thinking processes (Palincsar & Brown, 1987). Metacognition thus involves understanding of (1) the task to be performed, (2) a strategy used to complete the task, and (3) awareness of self-performance on that task. For example, when an assignment is given (such as 5 pages of reading from a history text) some students with disabilities read each word of the text in the same fashion that one would read a novel; that is, without attempting in any way to retain understanding of the content. In a novel, the structure of the story

INTEREST BOX 5.1
Behavioral and Metacognitive Models of Learning

Behavioral Model

Antecedent Events → Response → Consequence
In this sequence the antecedent environmental events set up the response. For example, a teacher asks the question, "What is 2 + 2?" The child then responds, "4." The teacher then arranges consequences, by giving the child a reward if the response is correct or withholding the reward if the response is wrong. The antecedents and consequences control the behavioral response.

Metacognitive Model

Antecedent Events → Inner Language → Response → Consequence
In this sequence the antecedents, response, and consequences remain the same, but a new step is added based on the potential use of language. When asked the question, the child mentally tells himself or herself, "I hold up two fingers on one hand and two fingers on the other hand, then count all the fingers." The teacher using metacognitive instruction will influence this inner language process in order to give the child a strategy for completing the task. The typical instructional strategies include modeling of inner language during problem completion.

itself facilitates memory of the important points. That is not true of a history text, in which one section of the chapter may deal with an entirely different topic than previous or subsequent sections. The student who reads the history text "as a novel" demonstrates little understanding of the task, with no thought for an appropriate strategy for completing the task or self-performance on that type of task.

In contrast, a more capable student will realize that textbook reading is not pleasure reading, and that some method for retaining information will be necessary. That student will plan a strategy for the task—perhaps forming visual images of the material read, perhaps questioning himself or herself on the content of each page. Finally, that student will frequently pause for a moment and reflect on the information retained. Perhaps that student will summarize, mentally, the major points covered. Ellis (1994) described a writing organizational procedure whereby these reflections may be summarized. This interaction with the content of the text is the appropriate learning strategy for content reading in subject areas.

Instruction that is specifically designed to structure the student's inner language in order to create this "interaction" with the education task has come to be known as metacognitive instruction. Several different approaches to metacognitive instruction are discussed in this chapter. One of the most developed curricular models of metacognitive instruction, presented in the next section, is the "Learning Strategies Curriculum." Another approach that is particularly beneficial for students with disabilities is the use of self-monitoring of attention behaviors. Numerous alternative self-instructional techniques are also presented.

THE LEARNING STRATEGIES CURRICULUM

What Is a Learning Strategy?

Although several groups of theorists have developed memory devices to assist students with mild disabilities in metacognitive planning and monitoring of the educational task (Bender, 1985a; Gambrell, Pfeiffer, & Wilson, 1985; Heiman, 1985; Idol-Maestas, 1985; Montague, 1992; Montague & Leavell, 1994; Smith & Friend, 1986; Torgesen, 1977), much of the recent research has been associated with Dr. Donald Deshler and his co-workers at the University of Kansas Institute for Learning Disabilities (Clark, Deshler, Schumaker, Alley, & Warner, 1984; Deshler, Alley, Warner, & Schumaker, 1981; Deshler, Warner, Schumaker, & Alley, 1983; Deshler, Schumaker, & Lenz, 1984; Deshler, Schumaker, Lenz, & Ellis, 1984, Ellis, 1994; Ellis, Deshler, & Schumaker, 1989; Ellis & Sabornie, 1986). These researchers have developed a set of mnemonic devices that assist the student in understanding the academic task and the steps necessary to complete the task. These mnemonic devices usually take the form of an acronym that the student is to memorize and apply. Such acronyms are referred to as learning strategies, and numerous strategies have been developed commercially as the "Learning Strategies Curriculum." The research, cited above, has indicated that use of learning strategies can create dramatic increases in reading comprehension or improved performance on many other educational tasks.

A learning strategy may be thought of as a method of cognitively organizing or planning the performance of a learning task (Ellis, 1994; Scheid, 1994). Some strategies consist of a set of self-instructional steps that a learner may use in order to complete a task (Ellis & Sabornie, 1986; Ellis, 1994), others consist of an organizer or method provided by the teacher. Interest Box 5.2 presents a simple learning strategy designed by the Kansas group to facilitate word identification, a skill frequently needed by older students with intellectual and learning disabilities.

The steps in this strategy form a heuristic the student memorizes in order to complete the task

INTEREST BOX 5.2
A Sample Learning Strategy

DISSECT: A word-identification strategy

D = Discover the context
I = Isolate the prefix
S = Separate the suffix
S = Say the stem
E = Examine the stem using the rules of 2 & 3*
C = Check with someone
T = Try the dictionary

*Rules of 2 & 3: If a stem or a part of the stem begins with a vowel, divide off the first two letters, if a consonant, divide off the first three letters.

Source: Ellis (1994).

Information on learning strategies is available from a large variety of sources. See Alley and Deshler (1979); Clark, Deshler, Schumaker, Alley, and Warner (1984); Ellis and Sabornie (1986); Lenz and Hughes (1990); Lenzo, Schumaker, Deshler, and Beals (1984). Training in the learning strategies approach is available through the University of Kansas, Lawrence, KS.

(Ellis & Sabornie, 1986). This particular strategy, as an example, would be used by middle school and secondary school students with disabilities to decode words in content areas and in reading classes.

As this example should make clear, a learning strategy approach may be differentiated from a "study skills" approach. Whereas study skills include such things as writing down assignments and allocation of time for homework, a learning strategy approach encompasses a metacognitive plan for completing the task itself and structuring the inner language (through use of the acronym) in order to help complete the task.

Note in Interest Box 5.3 the strategies that may be used to increase reading comprehension, and contrast those learning strategies with the types of "organizational" assistance typically provided in study skills classes. The learning strategies model is much more heavily dependent upon the student's use of inner language in planning and completing the task.

The researchers at the University of Kansas have produced a large number of strategies (Deshler et al., 1983; Ellis, 1994). These provide insight into various types of tasks, including test taking skills, word identification, utilizing pictures in texts, chapter assignments in content based classes, visual imagery to improve reading comprehension, self-questioning, searching for answers in text, and many others. Some strategies are independent, others include substrategies for various steps, as presented in Interest Box 5.4.

Strategies developed by many researchers do not provide an acronym, but do assist the student in cognitively organizing the task at hand (Bender, 1985a; Heiman, 1985; Smith & Friend, 1986). For example, the participatory organizer concept discussed by Bender (1985a) aids the student of history in understanding the content of the material during lectures and reading assignments. The student is required to participate by completing the information in the organizer from listening to lectures and readings. A sample participatory organizer is presented in Interest Box 5.5.

INTEREST BOX 5.3
Two Strategies for Improving Reading Comprehension

FIST: A self-questioning strategy

F = Read the *first* sentence in a paragraph
I = *Indicate* a question based on the sentence
S = *Search* for the answer to your question
T = *Tie* the answer to the question with a paraphrase

RIDER: A visual imagery strategy

R = *Read* the sentence
I = Make an *image* in your mind
D = *Describe* how the new image is different from the image for the last sentence
E = *Evaluate* to see that the image contains everything that is necessary
R = *Repeat* this strategy as you read the next sentence

Source: Ellis (1994).

Information on learning strategies is available from a large variety of sources. See Alley and Deshler (1979); Clark, Deshler, Schumaker, Alley, and Warner (1984); Ellis and Sabornie (1986); Lenz and Hughes (1990); Lenzo, Schumaker, Deshler, and Beals (1984). Training in the learning strategies approach is available through the University of Kansas, Lawrence, KS.

INTEREST BOX 5.4
IQWHO, with RASPN: A Mini-Strategy for Sizing Up Important Information in a Chapter

I = Illustrations interpreted
Q = Questions at chapter end, read and paraphrased
W = Words in italics defined
H = Headings: for each heading do a RASPN
R = read a heading
A = ask self a question based on heading
S = scan for the answer
P = put answer in own words
O = Other hints that chapter employed used

Source: Ellis (1994).

Information on learning strategies is available from a large variety of sources. See Alley and Deshler (1979); Clark, Deshler, Schumaker, Alley, amd Warner (1984); Ellis and Sabornie (1986); Lenz and Hughes (1990); Lenz, Schumaker, Deshler, and Beals (1984). Training in the learning strategies approach is available through the University of Kansas, Lawrence, KS.

INTEREST BOX 5.5
Participatory Organizer for World War I

1. List the major countries on each side.
2. Discuss the goals of each party.
3. List 4 major results of the war.

Allied Countries Goals
1.
2.
3.
4.

Axis Powers Goals
1.
2.
3.

Results of the War.
1.
2.
3.
4.

This participatory organizer concept is very similar to the semantic map promoted by the researchers at the University of Kansas (Ellis & Sabornie, 1986). Also, the Learning to Learn college curriculum, discussed below, has a version of this same concept, referred to as an information map (Heiman, 1985).

Learning Strategies and the Learner's Efficiency

As you learned in the introductory courses in special education, many students with mild and moderate disabilities are very inefficient as learners. For example, in discussing students with learning disabilities, Dr. Joseph Torgesen (1977) presented evidence to demonstrate that students with learning disabilities do not use efficient memory and attention strategies when completing school tasks. Other research has shown that students with intellectual disabilities and behavioral disorders do not attend to the educational task with the same frequency as nonhandicapped learners (Bender, 1985b, 1987; Brown & Alford, 1984). This has the effect of severely limiting the instructional time and opportunity to learn for these students; if students do not spend time attending to an educational assignment, they do not learn the material.

Research has also shown that students with disabilities do not use memorization strategies effectively (Palincsar & Brown, 1987). Specifically, students with disabilities do not attempt to glean understanding from reading assignments, lectures, or class discussions, and no attempt is made during the educational task to cognitively plan what to remember later.

As these learning characteristics demonstrate, students with disabilities are inefficient in their cognitive plans concerning how to accomplish almost every learning task. This inefficiency will reveal itself in homework assignments as well as seatwork in class. Also, this same inefficiency presents an opportunity for the teacher who can implement the learning strategies instructional principles. Many students with disabilities realize that they have special problems in learning, and they are usually appreciative of a "special" technique that can reduce their study time. The next section discusses how to present a learning strategy to a student with mild disabilities in a way that will gain his or her cooperation.

Using Learning Strategies

Although learning strategies can be used in various ways, the researchers associated with the University of Kansas suggest an 8-step model for instruction in any particular learning strategy (Ellis & Sabornie, 1986). These steps are intended to provide guidance for the special education teacher in implementation of a learning strategies approach. Training in the use of Learning Strategies is provided by the University of Kansas Center for Research on Learning in Lawrence, Kansas. The assumption behind the model is that the special education class will be the setting in which instruction in learning strategies takes place, though the strategy may actually be applied in special classes and in inclusive mainstream classrooms.

Step 1: Pretest and Commitment. First, the student with disabilities is tested to determine if he or she needs a strategy for a particular task. The results of the assessment are explained to the student, and he or she is informed about the level of performance the new strategy would make possible. A decision is then made determining whether the student will learn the new strategy. A student is free to choose not to learn a new strategy at that time. The model stresses the need for student involvement in this decision and student commitment to the decision to learn a new strategy. This step usually takes one instructional period—45 minutes.

Step 2: Description of the New Strategy. During the second implementation step, the components of the strategy are described to the student. This step focuses on the key elements of the strategy and how these are used. Also, the student is told where and under what conditions a strategy may be applied. This also usually takes one class period.

Step 3: Model the Strategy. On the next day, the teacher models each step of the strategy while discussing the use of the strategy out loud. Note the use of modeled "inner language" here, as discussed earlier. Each aspect of the strategy is modeled, and students are encouraged to ask questions. This instructional period may include several different tasks and the teacher may prompt students to model particular aspects of the strategy.

Step 4: Verbal Rehearsal of the Strategy. Students must learn to state the strategy steps quickly before they attempt to apply the strategy. The students identify the action to be taken in each step and tell why each step is important for the strategy overall. This step is intended to facilitate independence in strategy application, and can be completed in about 30 minutes.

Step 5: Practice with Controlled Materials. The assumption behind this step is that the difficulty of the material should not impair the student's ability to learn the strategy. Consequently, the strategy should be applied on controlled materials. If the DISSECT strategy was being taught, the student would first apply that strategy with known words, then with lower-level unknown words. The student would be coached by the teacher using explicit corrective feedback. Utilizing the CBA concept discussed in Chapter 4, a daily record of performance is also completed during this step. This step will be repeated over numerous instructional periods involving up to 20 hours of instructional time. This allows the student and teacher to chart progress on learning the learning strategy itself.

Step 6: Practice on Grade Appropriate Materials. The level of complexity on which the student practices is gradually increased until the materials approximate those grade level materials with which the student works. This step also involves the fading out of various prompts and cues the student used in earlier steps. This step usually takes between 5 and 20 instructional periods. Again, progress during this phase of instruction is charted to present a daily picture of the student's progress.

Step 7: Commitment to Generalize the Strategy. The student must be encouraged to see the value of generalizing the new strategy to other similar educational tasks. A commitment should then be forthcoming from the student to apply the strategy. This discussion with the student may take as little as a few minutes during one of the instructional periods.

Step 8: Generalization and Maintenance. This step, in many ways, is the most important. There is little advantage in spending the number of instructional periods discussed above to teach a student the DISSECT strategy unless that student is then taught how to apply that strategy throughout his or her schooling. However, if this strategy is mastered, the student then has a skill that can enhance learning in numerous classes in the future.

The generalization step involves three separate phases, the first of which is orientation to generalization. This is designed to make the student aware of situations in which the new skill may be tried. The student is encouraged to make adaptations of the original strategy. The second phase is activation, where the student is given specific assignments to apply the strategy in grade appropriate materials from the mainstream class. Throughout this process, the special education teacher is encouraged to work with the mainstream teacher in encouraging use of the strategy. The teacher then checks the output of the strategy.

Finally, a maintenance phase is implemented. The students who have been trained in a particular strategy should be periodically reminded to use that strategy and the teacher should check the work output.

A Learning Strategy Example

RAPs is a strategy for paraphrasing reading material, as presented in Interest Box 5.6. This was one of the first strategies to be marketed commercially, and has demonstrated effectiveness with students with disabilities. This section of the text traces the implementation of this strategy over a

INTEREST BOX 5.6
***RAP:* A Paraphrasing Strategy for Reading**

R = Read a paragraph
A = Ask self what were the main idea and two details
P = Put the main idea and details into your own words

Information on learning strategies is available from a large variety of sources. See Alley and Deshler (1979); Clark, Deshler, Schumaker, Alley, and Warner (1984); Ellis and Sabornie (1986); Lenz and Hughes (1990); Lenzo, Schumaker, Deshler, and Beals (1984). Training in the learning strategies approach is available through the University of Kansas, Lawrence, KS.

period of 35 school days in order to give a specific, hands-on example of learning strategy instruction. For this example, let's assume that the special education teacher, Mr. Jonas, has 6 students with disabilities in an inclusive classroom during the first period of each day. Ms. Rooten is the general education teacher for that class, which also includes 22 students without disabilities. The grade level of the students with disabilities ranges from 6 to 8 and the reading level ranges from 4 to 6.

On the first day, after Ms. Rooten and Mr. Jonas decide to utilize the learning strategy, Mr. Jonas gives out prepared readings of at least 5 paragraphs for each student at the student's grade placement. He tells the students that they are to read their paragraphs silently, and then record (on a cassette recorder) what they have read. He reminds the students that they will be tested on the material the next day. Overnight, he will score the materials (using detailed scoring instructions provided in the manual from the Learning Strategies Curriculum), and identify the percentage of correct, nonrepetitive statements. This becomes the students' pretest.

On the second day, Mr. Jonas administers the appropriate individual comprehension test on the passage each student reads. The percentage of correct responses becomes the comprehension score for that student. Also, on the second day, the test results are communicated to each student in order to demonstrate the need for a new strategy for reading comprehension. At this point the student is asked if he or she would like to learn a new strategy to help remember better what has been read. The student should then write a long-term goal stating this commitment. Also, a management chart that records daily performance is initiated for each student. These two daily lessons complete the first step for the paraphrasing strategy.

The lesson on the next day is a description of the strategy, using a cue card that displays the steps of the strategy. Mr. Jonas will first discuss the meaning of paraphrasing and the use of this skill in various subjects. He may include both students with disabilities and students without disabilities in this segment of the instruction. He will point out the advantages of the ability to paraphrase in terms of increased comprehension. Students are then encouraged to set goals for learning the strategy, with a suggested guideline provided by the teacher. Mr. Jonas will then discuss the strategy steps in order, carefully giving the students examples. First, reading is discussed, as attending to the meaning of the words. Second, several ways to find the main idea (such as looking for repetitive words in the paragraph or studying the first sentence) and details from the paragraph are provided. Next, the need to put the ideas into the student's own words is discussed. Finally, the criteria for a good paraphrase are presented in order for students to know how their work will be graded. This description lesson completes the second step in the strategy.

The fourth day provides the student with the opportunity to see the strategy modeled by the teacher. Mr. Jonas will read an appropriate passage of 5 paragraphs and implement the RAPs strategy. Before starting, he will verbally remind himself of the strategy. This is done in order for the students to see the metacognitive aspect of this step. He then reads the passage aloud and discusses the strategy with himself. "Now that I have read the first paragraph, I have to list the main idea and some details." After several ideas are specified, Mr. Jonas puts these in his own words on the tape. This is done for the first several paragraphs and students are involved in the last several paraphrasing attempts. This completes the third step for this strategy.

The next day is spent on verbal practice of the components of the strategy. Each student should be able to name the series of steps from memory and provide information on how to complete each step. With the cue card in front of the board, the students should be encouraged to state the next step of the strategy or to answer any question Mr. Jonas asks. For example, they should be able to give at least two suggestions for finding the main idea of a paragraph. This lesson completes step 4.

The next day begins step 5, or the controlled practice for the paraphrasing strategy. Each student is given a 5-paragraph reading at the student's independent reading level—the level at which a student has 95 percent mastery of the words. That reading section may be several grade levels below the grade level placement of the student. First, Mr. Jonas briefly reviews the steps in the strategy with the students. Then, the students are told to use the RAPs strategy with each paragraph, recording one main idea and two major details for each.

These worksheets are scored using the same criteria as the pretest. Depending upon the time, the students may also take the comprehension test for that reading (Mr. Jonas has the option of using the next day as a comprehension test day also). Each of these scores is placed on the student's individual progress chart.

The scoring of student work is used as an opportunity to provide corrective and positive feedback. You may recall that frequent feedback was one of the effective teaching behaviors discussed in Chapter 1. In order to provide appropriate feedback, Mr. Jonas will identify several things that each student did well and share these with the student. Also, he will review the requirements that were not met when a student did not receive credit for an answer on the paraphrasing evaluation. This daily lesson is continued until the student reaches mastery level in both paraphrasing and comprehension of the material at that grade level. On average, students may be expected to reach mastery of this step in three to six practice attempts, though some students with disabilities may take longer.

Step 6 emphasizes grade appropriate practice, and the students may reach this step on different days. The day after a student reaches the goal he or she will receive a reading passage one grade level higher than the first one. In this example, John will continue to use the strategy in the same way until he reaches mastery on this level and then will proceed to the next grade level. This continues until he reaches his grade level placement, at which time his final passage will be taken from a text he normally uses at his grade level.

Step 7 involves the posttest and student commitment to generalize the strategy. John will complete a paraphrase task and a comprehension test for a passage that consists of 5 paragraphs of reading from his grade placement level. Results of these will be noted on the progress chart. Mr. Jonas will discuss the entire learning procedure with John, in order to point out the progress depicted in the chart. He will then obtain a commitment from John to generalize the strategy to other textbooks. This step takes only one instructional period, but the commitment step must be done with each student individually.

The next day, Mr. Jonas begins step 8 with John—generalization. John is asked to use his textbook, and Mr. Jonas gathers reading material from other settings, such as the home, newspapers, magazines that interest John, and so forth. Mr. Jonas will discuss with John the use of each book and material. At this stage, Ms. Rooten should become involved by meeting with John and Mr. Jonas to discuss strategy application in the materials from the mainstream class. John will make cue cards for the strategy and tape these inside the front of each textbook, and other cues for using the strategy are discussed. Ms. Rooten will make an agreement with John to remind him to utilize the strategy whenever appropriate on a reading assignment.

The next day begins the activation phase of the generalization step. Mr. Jonas presents a "Report of Strategy Use" form that consists of a series of lines on which John will enter each use of the strategy from the mainstream class and/or other reading. The form also lists the date and the type of material on which the strategy was used: textbook, newspaper, novel, or magazine. Mr. Jonas will generate various assignments from these reading materials for the student to complete sometime within the next 24 hours. These are quickly graded by Mr. Jonas and corrective feedback is given where necessary. The student should complete 6 different activities of this nature. Mr. Jonas will also discuss the completion of the form for particular dates and John will keep a record for a two-week period on utilization of the strategy.

Maintenance is the last phase of the generalization step. This consists of a series of evaluations similar to the posttest; these are generally done one week after the student completes the activation phase. At this point, John has internalized a strategy that should facilitate his reading comprehension across grade levels and for all types of reading materials.

As can be seen, the example above uses a number of methods that have demonstrated effectiveness in teaching children, including modeling, use of inner language, corrective and timely feedback, and repeated guided practice. Use of effective teaching behaviors greatly enhances the efficacy of the learning strategies model of instruction.

METACOGNITIVE INSTRUCTION ALTERNATIVES

Although the Learning Strategies Curriculum is the most developed single approach to metacognitive instruction, there are other approaches. For example, Welch, Von Loeys, Bender, and Scott (in press) indicated that teachers should consider development of their own metacognitive instructional practices for particular students in the classroom. Also, other metacognitive instructional approaches have been developed and demonstrated in the special education research literature. These include reciprocal teaching, intended for use in public schools, and the Learning to Learn Curriculum for use with college students with disabilities.

Reciprocal Teaching

Reciprocal teaching is a metacognitive instructional method designed to promote metacognitive understanding of the material through structured dialogue (Palincsar & Brown, 1986; Palincsar & Brown, 1987). This method is metacognitive because the emphasis is placed on the correct dialogue in which a student must engage for successful task completion. Although the learning strategies presented earlier focused on the specific language a student should use during task completion, the reciprocal teaching method focuses on the things the teacher can do to facilitate the students' use of metacognitive strategy planning. Interest Box 5.7 presents a sample reciprocal teaching dialogue (Palincsar & Brown, 1986).

Implementation of Reciprocal Teaching. In reciprocal teaching, the teacher and the students take turns as instructional leader. Whoever is the "teacher" assumes the role of leading a dialogue about the task. We use an example here in which the task is a reading passage the students read silently. Using the reciprocal teaching approach, the common goals of each member of the group are predicting, question generating, summarizing, and clarifying. Each of these goals is taught separately.

First, the teacher discusses the benefits of prediction as a reading strategy. Prediction of what comes next in the text involves relevant background knowledge of the text and provides students with a reason to read further; that is, to con-

INTEREST BOX 5.7
A Sample Reciprocal Teaching Dialogue

Student 1: My question is, what does the aquanaut see when he goes under water?
Student 2: A watch.
Student 3: Flippers.
Student 4: A belt.
Student 1: Those are all good answers.
Teacher: Nice job! I have a question too. Why does the aquanaut wear a belt? What is so special about it?
Student 3: It's a heavy belt and keeps him from floating up to the top again.
Teacher: Good for you.
Student 1: For my summary now: This paragraph was about what aquanauts need to take when they go under the water.
Student 5: And also why they need those things.
Student 3: I think we need to clarify gear.
Student 6: That's the special things they need.
Teacher: Another word for gear in the story might be equipment, the equipment that makes it easier for the aquanauts to do their job.
Student 1: I don't think I have a prediction to make.
Teacher: Well, in the story, they tell us that there are many strange and wonderful creatures that aquanauts see as they do their work. My prediction is that they'll describe some of these creatures. What are some of the strange creatures you already know about that live in the ocean?
Student 6: Octopuses.
Student 3: Whales.
Student 5: Sharks.
Teacher: Listen and find out. Who will be our next Teacher?

This dialogue comes from an article by Palincsar and Brown (1986). A dialogue such as this is exciting for anyone who has ever attempted to involve students in discussions. Not only are numerous students participating, but the level of this small group instructional dialogue indicates a great deal of metacognitive understanding on the part of the students. Each of the students was aware of the four basic metacognitive goals included in reciprocal teaching, and even when the students could not complete one of the goals (Student 1—prediction) the student was still aware of the need to think about what may come next in the story.

Reciprocal teaching is a cognitive instructional intervention that can easily be incorporated into almost any classroom. You may wish to read several of the articles listed in the references and consider using this method in your class.

firm or refute their predictions. Therefore, this strategy involves both comprehension of material being read and comprehension monitoring of material that has already been read.

The second phase of reciprocal teaching is question generation. Question generation gives the student the opportunity to identify the type of information that may make up test questions. Also, this activity may provide an occasion to discuss the methods of study for various types of questions.

Summarizing is the third aspect. This step provides an opportunity to integrate information from different sections of the text. The most important ideas of the reading sections may be jointly identified and discussed.

Finally, the fourth phase, clarifying, forces students to identify the major points of the reading selection and to identify concepts that may be difficult. Identification of difficult concepts is one aspect of reading comprehension that is particularly troublesome for students with mild disabilities, because these students will often read a selection and not realize that they did not understand part of the passage. Seeking clarification also allows the student to ask questions without embarrassment, because the role of the students is to "question and clarify" the problem areas for other students.

Each of the four strategies is taught for a single instructional period, with the teacher conducting these lessons. Initially each strategy is explained and examples are given along with guided practice. By the fifth or sixth day, the teacher and students are using the strategies together to discuss reading material. At that point the teacher continues to model the strategies, praises the students for using the strategies, and prompts the students to use additional strategies. By the end of a two-week period, the role of "teacher" is rotated and the students become the facilitators.

Research on Reciprocal Teaching. Several studies have indicated that reciprocal teaching is useful in helping students understand written text (Brown & Palincsar, 1982; Palincsar & Brown, 1985, 1986, 1987). These studies used various groups of students and concentrated on reading comprehension in the basic skills areas. However, all of the research was completed by only one group of researchers. Although this is quite common for new areas of research, additional research by others is necessary before this strategy is fully accepted.

Learning to Learn Curriculum

Pelczar (1987) reports that many colleges and universities are beginning to use the Learning to Learn Curriculum—a learning strategies curriculum developed by Heiman (1983, 1985) at Boston College. Unlike the individual learning strategies approaches, the Learning to Learn Curriculum was developed and tested as a package. Generally, students take a three-hour course for one semester that discusses numerous learning strategies, including information mapping, comprehension, study skills, self-questioning, and test taking skills. The students bring in materials from their academic classes to use in the course. The results of research have demonstrated the effectiveness of this approach in retaining minority students in college and in improving the grade point average of students, compared to students who did not take the course. All of the studies have been positive, suggesting that even college age students with disabilities need these types of metacognitive instruction.

Research Base

School Age Students. Research on effectiveness of metacognitive instruction with middle school and high school students with mild disabilities has demonstrated that a metacognitive strategies instructional approach can increase achievement (Chan, Cole, & Barfett, 1987; Clark et al., 1984; Deshler et al., 1983; Gambrell, Pfeiffer, & Wilson, 1985; Lenz, Alley, & Schumaker, 1987). For example, Smith and Friend (1986) used 54 students with learning disabilities to determine the effectiveness of a metacognitive strategy approach based on determining text structure in aiding recall of ideas in text. The experimental group consisted of 30 students; 24 formed the comparison group. The students first took a pretest, consisting of three short passages that ranged from 91 to 134 words in length. The comparison group received training for the same length of time in a problem-solving technique unrelated to text structure. The experimental group was instructed in the identification of 5 types of text structure, including time-order, problem/solution, comparison, description, and cause/effect. Next, five different lessons on recognition of the text structure and recall of ideas from the texts were read. Finally a posttest and delayed recall test were administered. Results showed that the training in identification of text structure increased the student's ability to recall the main ideas in the text, both immediately after the reading and on a delayed recall test that took place one week after the students read the passage.

College Age Students. Although most of the research using learning strategies has used public school aged students with various types of mild disabilities, several groups of researchers have begun to explore the applications of learning strategies with college populations of students with learning disabilities (Ellis & Sabornie, 1986; Pelczar, 1987). For example, Ellis and Sabornie (1986) report on several studies which showed that various learning strategies were effective with students in junior colleges and universities. With the increasing numbers of students with learning disabilities and behavioral disabilities attending college, special educators and college faculty need to be aware of these metacognitive strategies.

SELF-MONITORING

Teachers in this century have often taken the perspective that education is a process done to and for students. Students have been viewed as passive recipients of the educational process, and active participation of students in planning their own learning has not been encouraged. This passive treatment of students has been particularly obvious in terms of the educational treatments recommended for students with mild and moderate disabilities. For example, as Hallahan and Sapona (1983) indicate, behavioral reinforcement strategies and drug interventions to control behavioral outbursts both suggest that the child is a passive recipient of educational treatments. However, this view of students runs contrary to the need for students to assume personal responsibility for their studies as discussed in Chapter 1.

In spite of this historic perception, educators now realize that the success of education is, in large measure, dependent on the responsibility students take for their own learning and behavior. In short, it is very difficult (if not impossible) to teach anyone anything unless they are willing to learn. The self-monitoring metacognitive strategy presented here addresses this recently perceived requirement for individual responsibility for educational and behavioral outcomes.

Self-monitoring means the ability to repeatedly check one's own task-oriented behaviors in order to effect positive change in those behaviors (Hallahan & Sapona, 1983; Fowler, 1986). The concept of self-monitoring is rooted in two widely distinct fields of thought: effective teaching research and metacognitive research. Although the effective teaching research (discussed in Chapter 1) demonstrated that close monitoring of student progress greatly facilitates learning, that body of research seemed to suggest that the teacher should do the monitoring. However, the metacognitive instructional model presented earlier strongly indicates that students with mild disabilities, when trained, can become more involved in responsibility for learning if a series of inner language strategies can be identified that facilitates such responsibility. Self-monitoring represents a merger of the need for monitoring with a metacognitive emphasis on inner language.

Self-monitoring has been used in a number of ways in special education classes. For example, Hallahan, his associates, and numerous others have trained students with learning disabilities, intellectual disabilities, and behavioral disabilities to monitor their own attending behaviors in class (Digangi & Magg, 1991; Hallahan, Lloyd, & Stoller, 1982; Hallahan & Sapona, 1983; McCarl, Svobodny, & Beare, 1991; Rooney & Hallahan, 1988). This use of self-monitoring is important for special education because so many of the students with mild and moderate disabilities have problems paying attention in class.

Self-Monitoring for Attending Behavior

Although all teachers have told children to, "Pay attention," very few teachers have ever taught a child exactly *how* to pay attention. The fact is, we all tend to assume that students know what we mean by that frequently used phrase. In spite of this assumption, most students with mild and moderate disabilities do not stay on-task as well as nondisabled children. Phrases such as attention deficit disorder, attention problems, and poor task orientation all suggest this deficit in the skill of paying attention.

Daniel Hallahan and his associates began to address this problem within the learning disabled population. During the early 1970s there were basically three types of treatments for poor attention skills: drug intervention, behavior modification, and reduced stimuli environments (Hallahan & Sapona, 1983). However, each of these treatments required that the child be a passive participant, and Hallahan argued that children with attention problems should be made active agents in their own treatment program (Hallahan & Sapona, 1983).

In order to make children more responsible for their own behavior, Hallahan used several ideas from the metacognitive school of thought, as well as the behavioral school (Glynn & Thomas, 1974; Michenbaum & Goodman, 1971; Hallahan & Sapona, 1983). For example, numerous metacognitive psychologists have suggested that students would perform better were they provided with a statement, or set of statements, that outline the steps in the task (Michenbaum & Goodman, 1971). This represents, again, emphasis on the use of inner language. Hallahan utilized this idea of changing attention behavior by instructing children to ask themselves the question, "Was I paying attention?"

Glynn and Thomas (1974) developed a set of procedures to encourage self-control of behavior for elementary school students, which included monitoring and cues that indicated when the students should monitor their behavior. The behavioral influence is apparent in the number of daily checkpoints students were encouraged to make in this monitoring process. These same procedures were applied to the specialized education of students with learning disabilities in a series of papers by Hallahan and his associates (see Hallahan & Sapona, 1983, for review). The next section reviews the self-monitoring procedures that may be used to improve attending behaviors.

Implementation of Self-Monitoring

Identification of the Student. As with many effective educational strategies, your first task as a teacher is to decide upon the right strategy for the right child. Hallahan and Lloyd (1987) have suggested several guidelines for identifying the type of children for whom self-monitoring may be an effective intervention. First, the self-monitoring strategy to improve on-task behavior, as described by Hallahan and his co-workers, is intended for students who demonstrate attention problems, such as poor task orientation and an inability to complete worksheets on time. This strategy is not effective for children who do not perform their schoolwork because of aggressive tendencies or noncompliance in the classroom, though variations of self-monitoring procedures have shown some success—more on those variations later.

Second, self-monitoring should not be used when a student is being introduced to a topic. Rather, self-monitoring is most effective when a student is in the independent, drill-and-practice phase of learning. Seatwork in any basic skill area is appropriate. Hallahan and Lloyd (1987) recommend that this strategy be used in seatwork settings in order to facilitate attention to task when the student is working independently of the teacher. Hallahan and Lloyd (1987) also recommend that self-monitoring be used in instances where the child is generally accurate on drill and practice work but has trouble completing that work because of attention problems. Self-monitoring is more effective in "speeding up" a child, rather than increasing a child's accuracy in problem completion (Snider, 1987). Finally, the strategy is appropriate for behaviorally disordered and emotionally disturbed children (McLaughlin, 1984; McLaughlin, Krappman, & Welch, 1985), as long as the problems are attentional in nature.

Components of Self-Monitoring. During a self-monitoring project, a child is trained to ask himself or herself a very simple question, "Was I paying attention?" The question may be printed on the recording sheet or the blackboard, or merely memorized by the student. This question provides the child with a simple memory technique that tells what should be done. Whenever the child is cued or told to consider the "attention behavior" he or she is exhibiting, this question must be asked. After the question is answered, the student should return to the seatwork.

Self-monitoring is dependent on counting or charting of attention behaviors (Hallahan & Sapona, 1983). Each student who has notable deficits in attending behaviors is trained to indicate whether he or she was paying attention at various times during an activity. The chart that was developed by Hallahan and his associates at the University of Virginia is presented in Figure 5.1 (Hallahan, Lloyd, & Stoller, 1982).

The chart indicates at the top the question the students are to ask of themselves; "Was I Paying Attention?" The columns indicate the answer for each instance and, after answering and marking the chart, the student should return immediately to the task at hand.

In some projects, the student is encouraged to use a wrist counter (or a golf counter) to indicate the number of on-task and off-task behaviors (Hallahan, Lloyd, & Stoller, 1982). This procedure may be more appealing for some students, because it seems a little "different" for the initial stages of the project.

In the effective teaching research, the teacher was expected to monitor the attention behavior of all of the children. In self-monitoring projects, this monitoring function is given to the student. However, a "cue" is needed to indicate when the student should consider his or her attending behaviors. Hallahan, Lloyd, and Stoller (1982) recommend that a cassette tape be prepared that has a series of bell tones. The time interval between these bell tones should vary from 10 to 90 seconds, but the average time interval should be around 45 seconds. At the sound of each bell tone, the student asks himself or herself the question, marks an answer, and returns to the educational task.

Initial Self-Monitoring Instruction

Hallahan, Lloyd, and Stoller (1982) have recommended a series of instructional steps by which the teacher actually teaches attention skills. On the first day, the teacher begins instruction by suggesting that the student could finish his or her work faster and more accurately by learning how to pay attention better. This possibility is discussed with the student in an attempt to have the student accept responsibility for the self-monitoring procedures. The dialogue presented in Interest Box 5.8 was recommended by Hallahan, Lloyd, and Stoller (1982).

This dialogue presents a discussion of exactly what paying attention means. The teacher is encouraged to sit at the student's desk and model eye contact with the educational task (workbook, reading book, or blackboard). Also, the teacher may model several off-task behaviors such as staring out the window, playing with a pencil, or talking to other students. This initial instruction takes about 15 to 20 minutes on the first day, and should be repeated in a brief form for the first several days. The student should use the self-monitoring procedure every day during the initial stage of instruction. This will require 10 to 15 days.

Weaning Procedures

The goal of self-monitoring is the establishment of good attentional skills based on habit rather than being outwardly dependent on behavior charts and tape recorders. Consequently, Hallahan and his coworkers have stressed weaning procedures by which the initial counting device and cues to record are withdrawn, leaving the "habit" of continually monitoring one's own attending behavior.

Initially, the teacher should wean the student from the cue to record. After a successful

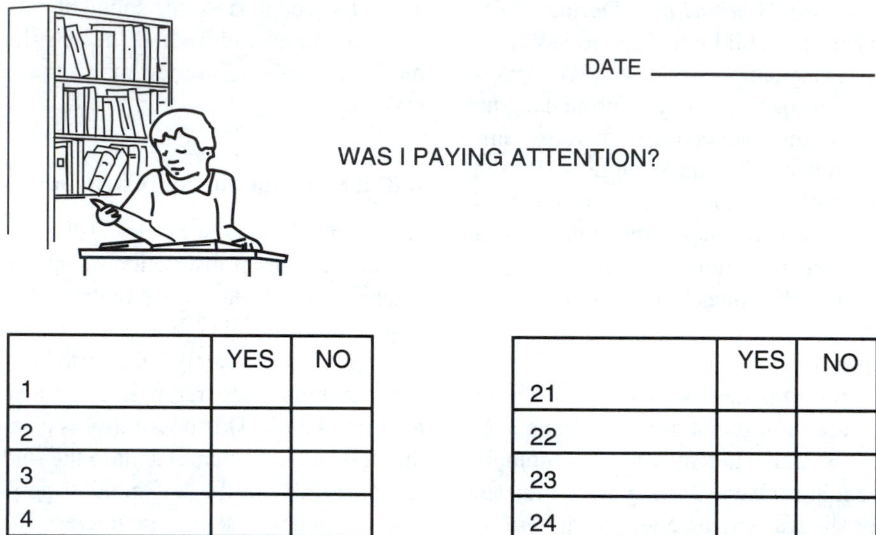

DATE ____________

WAS I PAYING ATTENTION?

	YES	NO
1		
2		
3		
4		
5		
6		
7		
8		
9		
10		
11		
12		
13		
14		
15		
16		
17		
18		
19		
20		

	YES	NO
21		
22		
23		
24		
25		
26		
27		
28		
29		
30		
31		
32		
33		
34		
35		
36		
37		
38		
39		
40		

FIGURE 5.1 Self-Monitoring Chart

intervention period (10 to 15 days, in most instances), the teacher simply indicates that the student's success has increased and that it is no longer necessary to listen to the taped cue to record. The student is encouraged to continue counting his or her on-task and off-task behavior for a few days in order to further ingrain the habit. The student is told to count his or her behavior,

INTEREST BOX 5.8
Self-Monitoring Instructions

"Johnny, you know how paying attention to your work has been a problem for you. You've heard teachers tell you, 'Pay attention,' 'Get to work,' 'What are you supposed to be doing?' and things like that. Well, today we're going to start something that will help you help yourself to pay attention better. First we need to make sure that you know what paying attention means. This is what I mean by paying attention." (Teacher models immediate and sustained attention to task.) "And this is what I mean by not paying attention." (Teacher models inattentive behaviors such as glancing around and playing with objects.) "Now you tell me if I was paying attention." (Teacher models attentive and inattentive behaviors and requires the student to categorize them.) "Okay, now let me show you what we're going to do. Every once in a while, you'll hear a little sound like this:" (Teacher plays tone on tape.) "And when you hear that sound quietly ask yourself, 'Was I paying attention?' If you answer 'yes,' put a check in this box. If you answer 'no,' put a check in this box. Then go right back to work. When you hear the sound again, ask the question, answer it, mark your answer, and go back to work. Now, let me show you how it works." (Teacher models entire procedure.) "Now, Johnny, I bet you can do this. Tell me what you're going to do every time you hear a tone. Let's try it. I'll start the tape and you work on these papers." (Teacher observes the student's implementation of the entire procedure, praises its correct use, and gradually withdraws his or her presence.)

Source: Hallahan, Lloyd, & Stoller (1982).

"whenever you think about it." If the student was paying attention when he or she monitored, self-praise should be given.

During the next phase, the student is weaned from the counting device—wrist counter or chart. The student is given instructions to ask the question whenever the thought occurs, and to praise himself or herself for being on-task and returning quickly to the task. Generally five or six days are recommended for each phase of the weaning process (Hallahan, Lloyd, & Stoller, 1982).

Efficacy Research on Self-Monitoring

The research on self-monitoring has demonstrated numerous positive effects of this instructional strategy. First of all, the primary goal of self-monitoring was to alleviate attention problems, and research indicates that this strategy works for many students with mild and moderate disabilities (Blick & Test, 1987; Digangi & Magg, 1991; Hallahan & Lloyd, 1987; McCarl, Svobodny, & Beare, 1991; Prater, Joy, Chilman, & Miller, 1991; Snider, 1987). The on-task behavior of some students has doubled (from 35 percent to over 90 percent), which is roughly like doubling the educational year for that child. This is no less than a profound effect, in terms of the learning opportunity provided for that child.

Hallahan, Lloyd, Kosiewicz, Kauffman, and Graves (1979) conducted one of the classic early studies in the self-monitoring research. A 7-year-old learning disabled boy was used in a single-subject, reversal design. The A phases were baseline phases in which both on-task behavior and academic productivity were measured. The B phases were self-monitoring treatments in which both the cue (a taped bell tone) and a record sheet were used. These phases were used to establish effectiveness of the treatment over the baseline phases. During the C phase the cue to record (bell tone tape) was withdrawn, and the child was instructed to record his behavior whenever he thought of it. During the D phase, the recording sheet was withdrawn and the child was instructed to praise himself whenever he was on-task.

To measure on-task behavior, several observers were trained to observe the child in class. Also, academic productivity in math and handwriting was measured by evaluation of the worksheets the child turned in. The results demonstrated that both on-task behavior and academic productivity improved during both of the treatment phases. The on-task behavior remained at relatively high levels during the weaning phases in which the tape and the recording sheet were withdrawn. This suggested that the child had internalized the habit of checking on-task behavior regularly by the end of the project.

This general result has been repeatedly demonstrated; self-monitoring works to increase the on-task behavior of many children with mild and moderate disabilities (Blick & Test, 1987; Digangi & Magg, 1991; McCarl, Svobodny, & Beare, 1991). Although much of the research has shown the efficacy of this technique with students who have learning disabilities, more recent research has shown this technique to be effective with children who demonstrate behavioral disorders, intellectual disabilities, and developmental disabilities during preschool (McLaughlin, Krappman, & Welch, 1985; Sainato, Strain, LeFebvre, & Rapp, 1990). If one of your students with mild or moderate disabilities demonstrates these types of attention problems, a self-monitoring intervention should certainly be employed in order to alleviate those problems.

One early concern of proponents of this instructional approach was the accuracy of the students in their self-monitoring. This was particularly true when self-monitoring procedures were being applied with preschool children with disabilities. This concern led to the concept of "matching" for monitoring accuracy. Basically, in this version of self-monitoring intervention, both the teacher and the child answer the question concerning paying attention, and the student is rewarded for accurately matching the teacher's perceptions of on-task behavior. Sainato, Strain, LeFebre, and Rapp (1990) provided an example of this type of matching intervention. Those researchers used a monitoring checksheet with a happy face to indicate on-task and a sad face to indicate off-task work. The results indicated that self-monitoring was effective with preschool children with moderate disabilities, when this matching component was added.

Self-Monitoring in Inclusive Classes. Because the early research was conducted almost exclusively in resource room programs, a number of research studies have been conducted in order to identify various instructional settings where self-monitoring instruction may be successfully applied. Hallahan, Marshall, and Lloyd (1981) conducted a study with several children which indicated that self-monitoring may be taught to groups of children together in either special classes or inclusive mainstream classes. Also, Rooney, Hallahan, and Lloyd (1984) presented data to demonstrate that self-monitoring instruction could be effective when conducted in mainstream classrooms. Clearly, this is an important question, since you may wish to employ this strategy in mainstream inclusive classrooms, or in a consultation situation with the mainstream teacher. The mainstream teacher, with your assistance, could implement this intervention for several children at once.

Academic Productivity. Another question regarding the efficacy of self-monitoring concerns the effects of self-monitoring procedures on academic achievement. Hallahan and Sapona (1983) reported that many of the early studies demonstrated that academic productivity (that is, the number of problems completed correctly) increased during self-monitoring procedures, though these results were challenged somewhat by Snider's later review of research (Snider, 1987). She pointed out that positive results of the self-monitoring studies on academic achievement were small and variable between the studies, and that the number of problems completed correctly may not be the best indicator of academic achievement. In response to this argument, Hallahan and Lloyd (1987) indicated that rate of correct problem solution was the best measure for drill and practice types of tasks where the desire is to improve the child's ability to complete tasks in a timely fashion. Also, more recent research has continued to suggest that self-monitoring does increase academic productivity as well as on-task behavior (Digangi & Magg, 1991).

Generalized Effects in Other Settings. More recent research on self-monitoring has investigated several potentially related effects of the treatment (Blick & Test, 1987; Rooney & Hallahan, 1988). For example, in the study by Blick and Test (1987), anecdotal evidence suggested that positive effects of self-monitoring were identifiable in both the training and nontraining settings. In other words, a student's academic productivity may have increased even on educational tasks when the student was not using self-monitoring. However, this result has not been supported by additional research.

Increased Instructional Interaction. Rooney and Hallahan (1988) investigated the effects of self-monitoring on the number of teacher interactions with children with learning disabilities. They reasoned that, if self-monitoring made the students with learning disabilities more independent, then the teacher's instructional time should be more flexible, since the teacher had fewer monitoring responsibilities. The results did demonstrate that teacher contact decreased when the students were trained in self-monitoring. This is important because many teachers function as "facilitators" in the special education class, and self-monitoring may free up some of their instructional time so they can work with other children.

Reducing Inappropriate Behaviors. A number of recent studies have documented the effects of self-monitoring on reduction of inappropriate behaviors (McCurdy & Shapiro, 1988; Morgan, Rhode, Smith, West, & Young, 1988). In these studies, the students are trained to monitor disruptive behavior or some other undesirable behavior in an effort to reduce that behavior. Some of the studies involve the "matching" procedure discussed earlier. This research has demonstrated that, when presented with a particular undesirable behavior on the part of a student, the teacher and the student can use a variation of self-monitoring and decrease that behavior significantly.

Summary of the Research

As is apparent, self-monitoring is quite effective. Teachers frequently report that a child's "inability to finish work on time," is one of the major problems in classroom management. If this is the case, it is difficult to imagine a more appropriate or effective educational intervention than self-monitoring. Self-monitoring interventions may be thought of as the single pill to cure all cancer, if indeed inattention is a major "cancer" in public school classrooms today. It would be difficult to overstate the importance of this educational treatment idea: Simply put, a cassette tape and a sheet of paper can double a child's meaningful instructional time.

SELF-INSTRUCTION

Self-instruction usually involves self-monitoring of some form, but the concept of self-instruction is broader and may include goal setting, use of other metacognitive strategies, and assessment. These interventions have been used to change academic and social behaviors (Blandford & Lloyd, 1987; Carlton, Hummer, & Rainey, 1984; Dunlap & Dunlap, 1989; Kiburz, Miller, & Morrow, 1985). For example, self-instructional systems usually involve some type of chart of past performance on particular types of tasks, combined with self-initiated goals (Neilans & Israel, 1981). Self-instruction is more comprehensive than merely self-monitoring of on-task behavior, as discussed previously. Self-instruction may involve any number of instructional activities, such as self-goal-setting, self-direction through tasks, self-monitoring of performance, self-checking, and self-reinforcement for task completion (Blandford & Lloyd, 1987; Carlton, Hummer, & Rainey, 1984; Dunlap

& Dunlap, 1989; Leon & Pepe, 1983; Neilans & Israel, 1981). Also, the term *self-instruction* may be used when a monitoring procedure is used to monitor instructional activities rather than merely on-task behavior (Kiburz, Miller, & Morrow, 1985).

Most self-instruction research is founded on the self-instructional model offered by Michenbaum and Goodman (1969). This model of instruction, with its emphasis on the use of inner language to structure the task for the child, is one of the early metacognitive models of learning. In Michenbaum's early model, a five-stage process for instruction was presented that provided the background for self-instruction. The five stages are presented in Interest Box 5.9.

These five stages may be used in the earliest instructional sequence, when a student is first learning a new task. In that respect, self-instruction is different from the self-monitoring procedure described earlier.

Implementation of Self-Instruction

You can easily implement a self-instructional procedure in your special education class merely by outlining the task and following the guidelines for the five stages. For example, imagine that you are introducing the topic of double-digit addition with regrouping in the tens' place to a student. First, you would have to task analyze the type of addition problem in order to generate the self-instructional statements. To complete such a problem one has to:

$$\begin{array}{r} 35 \\ +17 \end{array}$$

1. add the digits in the ones' place
2. write down only the first digit of the answer under the ones' place
3. write down the other digit in the answer above the tens' place
4. add the three digits in the tens' column
5. write that answer under the tens' column.

After the task is task analyzed, you proceed with the first step. Model performance of the task as you state these instructions out loud, in order for the child to see the task completed and hear the self-instruction. Stage 2 requires that the child carries out the task while the teacher verbalizes each step in the process. In stage 3, the child performs

INTEREST BOX 5.9
Self-Instructional Stages

1. The teacher completes the problem, reciting the independent step-by-step instructions for problem completion. This modeling step encourages the child to respond similarly in later steps.
2. The teacher and student complete the next problem while the student repeats the steps out loud.
3. The student completes the problem and uses overt self-instruction by repeating the steps out loud. The student gains confidence because the teacher is immediately available to help.
4. The student completes the problem relatively independently while whispering the step by step instructions softly. This is intended to approximate the last step using covert (inner speech) self-instruction.
5. The student completes the problem using inner speech to provide covert self-instructions.

Source: Michenbaum & Goodman (1969, 1988)

the task and does the outward verbalization of the task steps. In stage 4, the child again completes the task, but the steps are merely whispered. In stage 5, the child completes the task and says the steps using inner (silent) speech.

Almost any task can be taught in this manner. For example, language arts tasks, including identification of subject and predicate, locating the topic sentence, and rechecking paragraph structure during writing assignments, can all be task analyzed resulting in a series of steps to perform while doing the task. Consequently, all of these activities are appropriate for self-instructional procedures. Some suggested guidelines for using self-instruction in your class are presented in Interest Box 5.10.

Effectiveness of Self-Instruction

The early work on self-instruction used nonhandicapped children. However, research results concerning efficacy of this procedure among students with disabilities have been very positive (Blandford & Lloyd, 1987; Dunlap & Dunlap, 1989; Fowler, 1986; Kiburz, Miller, & Morrow, 1985; Leon & Pepe, 1983; Neilans & Israel, 1981). For example, self-instruction has been used with success in both reading and math (Leon & Pepe, 1983; Neilans & Israel, 1981). Also, self-instruction has been used to manage social skills instruction (Kiburz, Miller, & Morrow, 1985) and disruptive behavior (Fowler, 1986).

The Leon and Pepe study (1983), is one of the early studies on self-instruction. Leon and Pepe (1983) used 22 resource room teachers to study remediation of deficits in math achievement. From this group, 10 teachers were randomly selected to participate in training that emphasized the use of the self-instructional procedures presented above. In each teacher's class, 4 children were randomly selected to participate, and the dependent measures included assessment of math achievement for these 88 students. Pretests demonstrated no differences in achievement for the students in the two groups. However, posttest differences demonstrated that the students who were

INTEREST BOX 5.10
Guidelines for Use of Self-Instructional Procedures

1. Select a task for which several independent steps may be written down. Self instruction is less effective with rote memory tasks.
2. Use self instruction initially with children who do not demonstrate attention problems and can stay on a single task for more than a few seconds.
3. Accurately match the child to the task by making certain that the child has all of the required prerequisite skills necessary.
4. Prepare your teaching schedule so that you can sit with the child for 10 to 15 minutes during the self-instructional exercise and not be interrupted.
5. Prepare the child by saying, "We are going to learn this type of problem in a new way. We are going to learn to talk to ourselves while we do this problem. I'll show you how."
6. Go through the self-instructional stages during the next 5 to 10 minutes.
7. After the child completes phase five, encourage some independent practice work, and tell the child to do some additional problems for the next five minutes. Check back with the child every minute or so.
8. Repeat this procedure, including the five stages, for two or three days on the same type of problem as needed. Then the child should be ready for independent practice on that type of problem.

trained in self-instruction demonstrated significantly more achievement than the students in the control group. Also, the results of this study indicated that self-instructional strategy training on one skill may generalize to the use of self-instructional strategies on other skills as well. Like much of the research on self-instruction, this study supports the use of this technique with students who demonstrate mild and moderate disabilities.

CONSIDERATIONS IN USE OF METACOGNITIVE INSTRUCTION

Several considerations are involved in the use of metacognitive instructional strategies. First, the amount of instructional time that can be devoted to a particular learning task may limit implementation of various types of metacognitive instruction. For example, the strategies developed at the University of Kansas generally require a number of days devoted exclusively to the strategy training.

However, the use of other metacognitive approaches has been recommended without extensive periods of training for the teacher (Bender, 1985a; Clark et al., 1984; Gambrell, Pfeiffer, & Wilson, 1985; Johnson, Pittelman, & Heimlick, 1986; McCormick & Hill, 1984). For example, a cognitive or participatory organizer may be used for a particular assignment merely by providing the organizer for the student. Each teacher must decide how to work the metacognitive instructional concept into his or her instructional schedule for particular students with disabilities.

A second issue is the availability of the curricular materials associated with some metacognitive approaches. The model used by the Learning Strategies Curriculum group and the Learning to Learn group generally require participation in a workshop in order to get the materials. Although numerous teachers who have participated in these workshops have attested to their worth, other teachers may find this requirement expensive or cumbersome.

A third issue is the cognitive level of the students. Most of the research on metacognitive instruction has involved students with mild disabilities—predominantly learning disabilities—in the middle and upper grades, because most of the strategies assume a certain level of maturity, cognitive awareness, and reading ability. Some of these instructional approaches may be inappropriate for intellectually disabled children in grade 1, as one example. However, intellectually disabled children in grade 5 may find the RAP strategy very helpful in reading comprehension. In short, the students must be capable of understanding the strategy, the reason for it, and the mechanics of charting the behaviors. This ability to understand the progress chart provides the opportunity for reinforcement through the use of the chart.

Next, these techniques are not particularly useful when the task requires minimal cognitive involvement. For example, unlike the double-digit math problem described above, rote memory of multiplication tables cannot be task analyzed and broken into sequential steps. Consequently, a multistep self-instructional process should not be used with this type of memory task.

Next, metacognitive strategies can and do provide a good set of metacognitive skills for continued schooling. As such, it is appropriate to include the mastery of learning strategies as a long-term goal on the students' individualized education plan. For older students with a reading comprehension problem, the objective for mastery of a RAPs strategy is much more impressive—not to mention measurable—than merely stating an objective concerning improving reading comprehension with no indication of how this is to be done. The strong emphasis on daily curriculum-based assessment data in certain metacognitive instructional programs is a real plus for those programs.

Next, the evidence suggests that metacognitive strategy is more effective when the student takes responsibility for mastery of the strategy. This commitment is crucial for success and, with almost any teaching idea, can prove to be the single most important factor in successful implementation.

Self-monitoring of behavior and self-instruction are both instructional techniques that make the learner responsible for his or her own progress. Self-monitoring deals directly with the on-task behaviors of the student in the class, and research has shown that this technique is very effective. Self-instruction involves more than merely self-monitoring of behavior. Setting goals, self-instructional statements, and self-checking are all components of self-instructional procedures.

SUMMARY

Metacognitive instructional procedures may be used for a wide variety of instructional activities in the classroom, including any activity that involves a sequential set of steps which can be identified and verbalized by the student, any on-task behavioral problems for students in the independent practice phase of learning, and any academic tasks. You will want to remain current in your understanding of new metacognitive instructional techniques as they are developed.

Summary Points

- Metacognition may be broadly conceived of as thinking about thinking. The three components of metacognition are: (1) understanding the task, (2) selecting a series of steps to complete the task, and (3) monitoring the performance of the task.
- A learning strategy is a mnemonic device used by students to structure the inner language for the student in order to assist in completion of the task.
- The Learning Strategies Curriculum is the most highly developed of the metacognitive instructional systems.
- Learning strategies are independent of curricular content, and concentrate instead on particular types of tasks found in various curricular areas. Strategies have been used for numerous tasks, including test taking skills, word identification, utilizing pictures in texts, searching for answers in text, chapter assignments in content based classes, visual imagery, and self-questioning to improve reading comprehension.
- Research has shown that metacognitive instruction is effective in improving academic growth.
- Reciprocal teaching involves the student in a metacognitive plan by which students assume the teaching responsibilities.
- Reciprocal teaching uses four specific strategies: predicting, questioning, summarizing, and clarifying. Each student learns these strategies and is prepared to lead instructional discussions on these strategies for other students.
- Self-monitoring is usually taken to mean checking on classroom behaviors, usually the monitoring of on-task behaviors.
- Self-monitoring is effective for increasing on-task time, and there are numerous secondary effects, including some tendency to generalize, and some suggested increases in academic productivity.
- Self-instruction is more comprehensive than self-monitoring and may involve self-goal setting, self-directions through tasks, and self-monitoring of task performance.
- Self-instruction and self-monitoring have theoretical roots in both behavioral psychology and metacognitive instructional techniques.
- Michenbaum was one of the first theorists to develop a set of instructional practices that assist the student to internalize task directions. That five-step model is still utilized today.
- Research has supported the use of self-instructional strategies with many students with mild disabilities.

QUESTIONS AND ACTIVITIES

1. How does the Learning Strategies Curriculum developed by Dr. Deshler and his co-workers at Kansas compare to the Learning to Learn model developed by Heiman?

2. What does the present system for measuring cognitive abilities tell us about a student's metacognitive abilities?
3. What would a behavioral perspective on a learning strategy model consist of? How do behavioral psychologists respond to the "cognitive" aspects of the learning strategies model?
4. As a class project, select a particular type of learning task with which students have problems, and design a learning strategy for it. Include an acronym to facilitate memorization of the strategy and consider methods whereby the strategy may be taught.
5. What groups of students with disabilities cannot use learning strategies?
6. Contrast the types of tasks facilitated by the learning strategies model as compared to the precision teaching model of instruction discussed in Chapter 4.
7. Discuss a learning strategies approach to instruction for word problems in upper level mathematics. What would such a strategy consist of?
8. Pick one of the learning strategies presented in this chapter and write a set of lessons for presentation of the idea to a group of students with mild intellectual disabilities in a junior high school. How does using a learning strategies model with those children differ from such a model used with children with learning disabilities?
9. Sometimes professional journals publish a scholarly "argument" or "dialogue" between professionals, and Snider's (1987) article on self-monitoring presented such an opportunity. Review that paper from the *Learning Disability Quarterly* and discuss this professional disagreement in class.
10. Look through the various indexes in your library and identify studies that used self-monitoring or self-instruction with children with intellectual disabilities. Present these to the class.
11. Design a set of self-instructional statements that would assist a child in identifying the main idea of a paragraph. How are these instructional statements similar to the learning strategies concept?
12. Identify five school tasks in elementary language arts for which self-instruction would not be appropriate. Identify five tasks for which it would be appropriate.
13. Review Michenbaum and Goodman's (1971) research. Present a research review to the class on each of these studies.

REFERENCES

Alley, G. R., & Deshler, D. D. (1979). *Teaching the learning disabled: Strategies and methods.* Denver: Love Publishing.

Bender, W. N. (1985a). Strategies for helping the mainstreamed student secondary social studies classes. *The Social Studies, 76,* 269–271.

Bender, W. N. (1985b). Differential diagnosis based on task-related behavior of learning disabled and low-achieving adolescents. *Learning Disability Quarterly, 8,* 261–266.

Bender, W. N. (1987). Behavioral indicators of temperament and personality in the inactive learner. *Journal of Learning Disabilities, 20,* 280–286.

Blandford, B. J., & Lloyd, J. W. (1987). Effects of a self-instructional procedure on handwriting. *Journal of Learning Disabilities, 20,* 342–346.

Blick, D. W., & Test, D. W. (1987). Effects of self-recording on high-school students' on-task behavior. *Learning Disability Quarterly, 10,* 203–213.

Brown, R. T., & Alford, N. (1984). Ameliorating attentional deficits and concomitant academic deficiencies in learning disabled children through cognitive training. *Journal of Learning Disabilities, 17,* 20–25.

Brown, A. L., & Palincsar, A. M. (1982). Inducing strategic learning from texts by means of informed self control training. *Topics in Learning and Learning Disabilities, 2,* 1–17.

Carlton, G., Hummer, T., & Rainey, D. (1984). Teaching learning disabled children to help themselves. *The Directive Teacher, 6* (1), 8–9.

Chan, L. K. S., Cole, P. G., & Barfett, S. (1987). Comprehension monitoring: Detection and identification of text inconsistencies by LD and normal students. *Learning Disability Quarterly, 10,* 114–121.

Clark, F. L., Deshler, D. D., Schumaker, J. B., Alley, G. R., & Warner, M. M. (1984). Visual imagery and self-questioning: Strategies to improve comprehension of written material. *Journal of Learning Disabilities, 17,* 145–149.

Deshler, D. D., Alley, G. R., Warner, M. M., & Schumaker, J. B. (1981). Instructional practices for promoting skill acquisition and generalization in severely learning disabled adolescents. *Learning Disability Quarterly, 4,* 415–421.

Deshler, D. D., Warner, M. M., Schumaker, J. B., & Alley, G. R. (1983). Learning strategies intervention model: Key components and current status. In J. D. McKinney & L. Feagans (Eds.). *Current Topics in Learning Disabilities* (Vol. 1). Norwood, NJ: Ablex.

Deshler, D. D., Schumaker, J. B., & Lenz, B. K. (1984). Academic and cognitive interventions for LD adolescents: Part 1. *Journal of Learning Disabilities, 17,* 108–117.

Deshler, D. D., Schumaker, J. B., Lenz, B. K., & Ellis, E. S. (1984). Academic and cognitive interventions for LD Adolescents: Part II. *Journal of Learning Disabilities, 17,* 170–187.

Digangi, S., & Magg, J. (1991). Self-graphing of on-task behavior: Enhancing the reactive effects of self-monitoring on-task behavior and academic performance. *Learning Disability Quarterly, 14,* 221–229.

Dunlap, L. K., & Dunlap, G. (1989). A self-monitoring package for teaching subtraction with regrouping to students with learning disabilities. *Journal of Applied Behavior Analysis, 22,* 309–314.

Ellis, E. S. (1994). Integrating writing strategy instruction with content area instruction. *Intervention In School and Clinic, 29,* 169–179.

Ellis, E. S., Deshler, D. D., & Schumaker, J. B. (1989). Teaching adolescents with learning disabilities to generate and use task-specific strategies. *Journal of Learning Disabilities, 22,* 108–118.

Ellis, E. S., & Sabornie, E. J. (1986, October 12). *Teaching learning strategies to learning disabled students in post-secondary settings.* Paper presented at Rutgers University Symposium on College Students with LD.

Fowler, S. A. (1986). Peer-monitoring and self-monitoring: Alternatives to traditional teacher management. *Exceptional Children, 52,* 573–581.

Gambrell, L.B., Pfeiffer, W. R., & Wilson, R. M. (1985). The effects of retelling upon reading comprehension and recall of text information. *Journal of Educational Research, 78,* 216–220.

Glynn, E. L., & Thomas, J. D. (1974). Effect of cueing on self-control of classroom behavior. *Journal of Applied Behavior Analysis, 7,* 299–306.

Hallahan, D. P., & Lloyd, J. W. (1987). A reply to Snider. *Learning Disability Quarterly, 10,* 153–156.

Hallahan, D. P., Lloyd, J. W., Kosiewicz, M. M., Kauffman, J. M., & Graves, A. W. (1979). Self-monitoring of attention as a treatment for a learning disabled boy's off-task behavior. *Learning Disability Quarterly, 2,* 24–32.

Hallahan, D. P., Lloyd, J. W., & Stoller, L. (1982). *Improving Attention with Self-Monitoring: A Manual for Teachers.* Charlottesville: University of Virginia.

Hallahan, D. P., Marshall, K. J., & Lloyd, J. W. (1981). Self-recording during group instruction: Effects on attention to task. *Learning Disability Quarterly, 4,* 407–413.

Hallahan, D. P., & Sapona, R. (1983). Self-monitoring of attention with learning disabled children: Past research and current issues. *Journal of Learning Disabilities, 16,* 616–620.

Heiman, M. A. (1983). *Learning to Learn.* Joint Dissemination Review Panel, National Diffusion Network, U.S. Department of Education.

Heiman, M. A. (1985). Learning to Learn. *Educational Leadership, 43,* 20–24.

Idol-Maestas, L. (1985). Getting ready to read: Guided probing for poor comprehenders. *Learning Disability Quarterly, 8,* 243–252.

Johnson, D. D., Pittelman, S. D., & Heimlick, J. E. (1986). Semantic mapping. *The Reading Teacher, 39,* 778–783.

Kiburz, C. S., Miller, S. R., & Morrow, L. W. (1985). Structured learning using self-monitoring to promote maintenance and generalization of social skills across settings for a behaviorally disordered adolescent. *Behavioral Disorders, 10,* 45–52.

Lenz, B. K., Alley, G. R., & Schumaker, J. B. (1987). Activating the inactive learner: Advance organizers in the secondary content classroom. *Learning Disability Quarterly, 10,* 53–67.

Lenz, B. K., & Hughes, C. A. (1990). A word identification strategy for adolescents with learning disabilities. *Journal of Learning Disabilities, 23,* 149–163.

Lenz, B. K., Schumaker, J. B., Deshler, D. D., & Beals, V. L. (1984). *The word identification strategy.* Lawrence: University of Kansas.

Leon, J. A., & Pepe, H. J. (1983). Self-instructional training: Cognitive behavior modification for remediating arithmetic deficits. *Exceptional Children, 50,* 54–60.

McCarl, J. J., Svobodny, L., & Beare, P. L. (1991). Self-recording in a classroom for students with mild to moderate mental handicaps: Effects on productivity and on-task behavior. *Education and Training in Mental Retardation, 26,* 79–88.

McCormick, S., & Hill, D. S. (1984). An analysis of the effects of two procedures for increasing disabled readers' inferencing skills. *Journal of Educational Research, 77,* 219–226.

McCurdy, B., & Shapiro, E. (1988). Self-observation and the reduction of inappropriate classroom behavior. *Journal of School Psychology, 26,* 371–378.

McLaughlin, T. F. (1984). A comparison of self-recording and self-recording plus consequences for on-task and assignment completion. *Contemporary Educational Psychology, 9,* 185–192.

McLaughlin, T. F., Krappman, V. F., & Welch, J. M. (1985). The effects of self-recording for on-task behavior of behaviorally disordered special education students. *Remedial and Special Education, 6,* 42–45.

Michenbaum, D. H., & Goodman, J. (1969). The developmental control of operant motor responding by verbal operants. *Journal of Experimental Child Psychology, 7,* 553–565.

Michenbaum, D. H., & Goodman, J. (1988). Training impulsive children to talk to themselves: A means of developing self-control. *Journal of Abnormal Psychology, 77,* 115–126.

Montague, M. (1992). The effects of cognitive and metacognitive strategy instruction on the mathematical problem solving of middle school students with learning disabilities. *Journal of Learning Disabilities, 25,* 230–248.

Montague, M., & Leavell, A. G. (1994). Improving the narrative writing of students with learning disabilities. *Remedial and Special Education, 15* (1), 21–33.

Morgan, D., Rhode, G., Smith, D., West, R., & Young, K. (1988). Reducing the disruptive behavior of junior high school students: A classroom self-management procedure. *Behavioral Disorders, 13,* 231–239.

Neilans, T. H., & Israel, A. C. (1981). Towards maintenance and generalization of behavior change: Teaching children self-regulation and self-instructional skills. *Cognitive Therapy and Research, 5,* 189–195.

Palincsar, A. S., & Brown, D. A. (1985). Reciprocal teaching: Activities to promote reading with your mind. In E. J. Cooper (Ed.), *Reading, Thinking, and Concept Development: Interactive Strategies for The Class.* New York: The College Board.

Palincsar, A. S., & Brown, D. A. (1986). Interactive teaching to promote independent learning from text. *The Reading Teacher, 39,* 771–777.

Palincsar, A. S., & Brown, D. A. (1987). Enhancing instructional time through attention to metacognition. *Journal of Learning Disabilities, 20,* 66–75.

Pelczar, S. (1987, June). *Learning to Learn: A Process of Thinking Strategies for Learning Disabled College Students.* Paper presented at Rutgers University.

Prater, M., Joy, R., Chilman, J., & Miller, S. (1991). Self-monitoring of on-task behavior by adolescents with learning disabilities. *Learning Disability Quarterly, 14,* 164–178.

Rooney, K. J., & Hallahan, D. P. (1988). The effects of self-monitoring on adult behavior and student independence. *Learning Disabilities Research, 3,* 88–93.

Rooney, K. J., Hallahan, D. P., & Lloyd, J. W. (1984). Self-recording of attention by learning disabled students in the regular classroom. *Journal of Learning Disabilities, 17,* 360–363.

Sainato, D. M., Strain, P. S., LeFebvre, D., & Rapp, N. (1990). Effects of self-evaluation on the independent work skills of preschool children with disabilities. *Exceptional Children, 56,* 540–549.

Scheid, K. (1994). Cognitive based methods for teaching mathematics. *Teaching Exceptional Children, 26* (3), 6–10.

Smith, P. L., & Friend, M. (1986). Training learning disabled adolescents in a strategy for using text structure to aid recall of instructional prose. *Learning Disabilities Research, 2,* 38–44.

Snider, V. (1987). Use of self-monitoring of attention with LD students: Research and application. *Learning Disability Quarterly, 10,* 139–151.

Torgesen, J. K. (1977). The role of non-specific factors in the task performance of learning disabled children: A theoretical assessment. *Journal of Learning Disabilities, 10,* 24–34.

Welch, I., Van Laeys, O., Bender, W. N., & Scott, K. (in press). Teachers create learning strategies: Guidelines for classroom creation of strategies. *Teaching Exceptional Children.*

CHAPTER 6

TUTORING AND COOPERATIVE LEARNING IN INCLUSIVE CLASSES AND SPECIAL EDUCATION

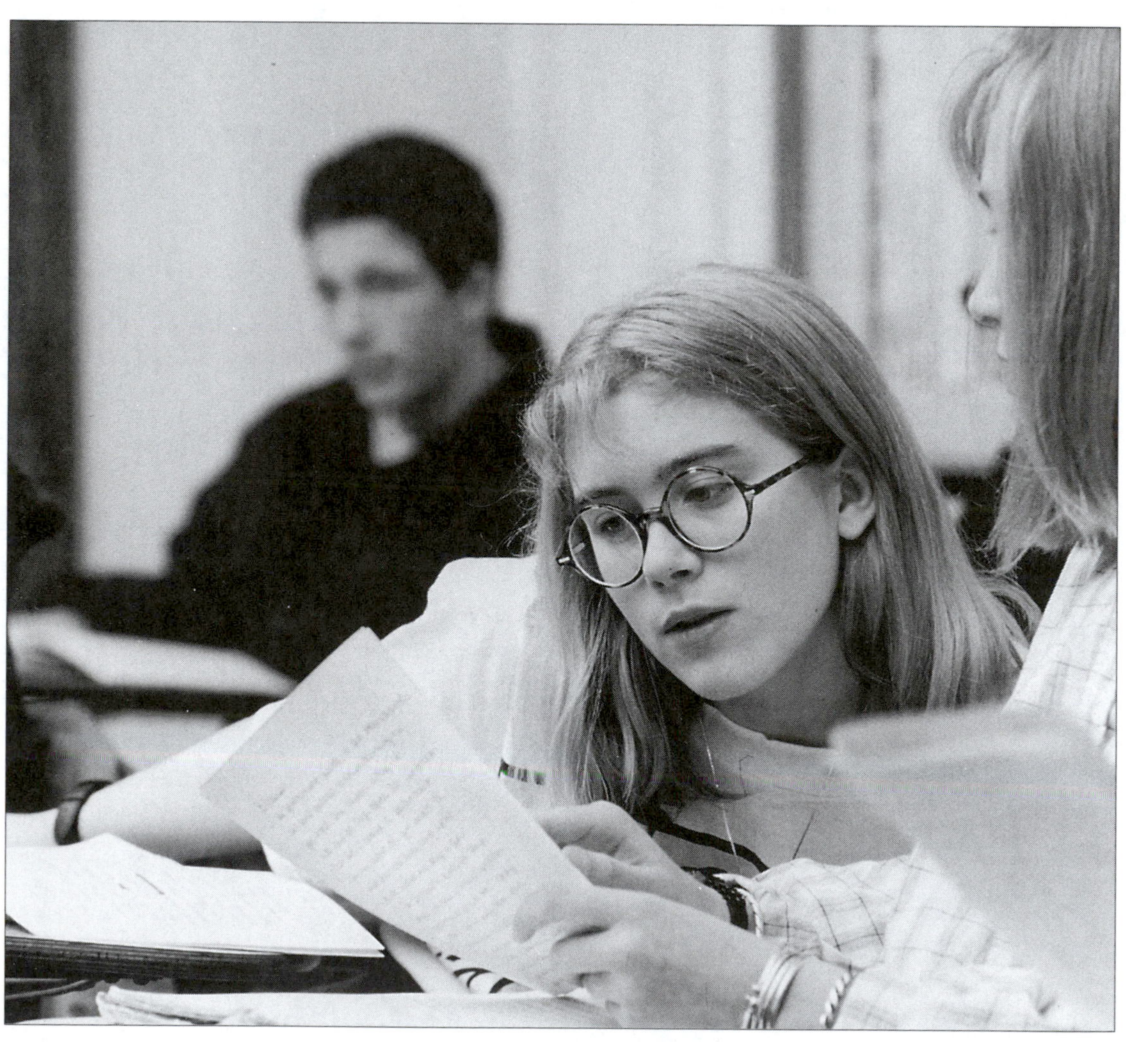

OBJECTIVES

When you complete this chapter, you should be able to:

1. Identify the guidelines for establishing a peer tutoring system in your class.
2. Discuss the interaction between the level of training of the tutors and the responsibility assigned to them.
3. Discuss the tasks a teacher's aide should be encouraged to do in a special education class.
4. Describe the types of tasks that should be reserved exclusively for the teacher in a special education class.
5. Discuss the efficacy of peer tutoring and cross age tutoring in special education.
6. Discuss the efficacy of cooperative instructional groups in special education.
7. Discuss at least three methods for implementing cooperative instruction in your class.

KEYWORDS

TAI	Level 1 Task	STAD
peer tutor	cooperative instruction	Jigsaw II
cross-age tutoring	Jigsaw	

One set of instructional strategies that has received widespread research support is the use of tutors in inclusive mainstream classes and special education classes (Beirne-Smith, 1991; Campbell, Brady, & Linehan, 1991; Delquadri, Greenwood, Whorton, Carta, & Hall, 1986; Russell & Ford, 1984; Scruggs, Mastropieri, Veit, & Osguthorpe, 1986; Scruggs & Richter, 1985). This instructional strategy is useful in numerous content areas including reading, math, language arts, science, history, and any of the other academic content areas. The potential applications of various tutoring programs is almost limitless.

As a special education teacher, you will have numerous opportunities to use tutoring approaches for the students in your class. Although most of the research has investigated the effectiveness of using peer tutors, many other tutoring opportunities are also available. For example, many special education classes and inclusive mainstream classes are assigned a teacher's aid, a grandparent tutor, or some other adult whose time can be utilized for individual instruction. It is unfortunate that many educational programs in special education do not prepare the special education teacher to manage the time of teacher's aids. Nevertheless, with the proper training, you can become skilled at using these tutors to maximum advantage. For purposes of this chapter, the strategies recommended for use of peer tutors may also be used for adult tutors and teacher's aids.

This chapter focuses on the utilization of tutoring in inclusive and special education classes. First, research on the efficacy of tutoring is presented in order to provide guidelines concerning the use of tutors. Next, a section is presented on the initiation of tutoring support for your class. Finally, cooperative instructional groups are discussed as a possible alternative to one-to-one tutoring.

EFFICACY OF TUTORING PROGRAMS

Research studies have demonstrated that use of tutors in both elementary classes and special education classes has numerous positive effects for both the students being tutored (referred to as the tutees) and the tutors (Beirne-Smith, 1991; Cohen, Kulik, & Kulik, 1982; Sasso, Mitchell, & Struthers, 1986; Scruggs & Richter, 1985). Generally, the research in this area has investigated several different types of effects. The primary effects of tutoring concern the effects of tutoring on the academic progress of the tutees, since academic progress is, first and foremost, the primary goal of tutoring. However, there are numerous secondary effects, or results of a secondary nature, that provide some rationale for implementing tutoring. These questions concern the effects of the tutoring on the tutors themselves, as well as positive emotional and social effects of tutoring.

Efficacy of Tutoring for the Tutees

Research has demonstrated that tutoring has numerous positive academic effects for the students who are being tutored (Carlson, Litton, & Zikngraf, 1985; Delquadri et al., 1986; Russell & Ford, 1984). Most of the tutoring studies have used basic skills subjects as the content for the tutoring programs, including exercises in reading, math problems, and vocabulary, and the evidence is quite convincing in this area—tutoring works.

A study by Carlson, Litton, and Zinkgraf (1985) is typical of this research. These researchers investigated the effectiveness of peer tutoring in word recognition tasks among children with mild intellectual disabilities. Twelve classes were used and six of these were randomly selected as the experimental group. These classes included 74 students. The other six classes (with 62 students) became the control group. A statistical comparison demonstrated that these two groups were comparable in reading ability before the experiment began. In the experimental group, the students were assigned the role of tutor or tutee based on their pretest reading score, with the higher-scoring students assigned the role of tutor. These tutors were then instructed in conducting a flashcard drill activity in order to assist their tutee in learning unknown words. The students in the control group were instructed by the teacher in the traditional fashion. Results demonstrated that both the tutors and tutees learned more words during the instructional phase than the students in the six control classes. Also, statistical comparison revealed that both the tutors and tutees in the experimental group made significant gains in reading comprehension as a result of the peer tutoring instructional activities. This type of result is intriguing because it suggested that results unrelated to the particular instructional activity may be a positive by-product of peer tutoring.

In addition to positive academic outcomes, research has suggested that numerous other positive results stem from peer tutoring. Research reviewed by Cohen, Kulik, and Kulik (1982) suggested that tutored students develop more positive attitudes toward the subject in which they are tutored. One study even suggested that peer tutoring was more effective than traditional instruction by the resource teacher (Russell & Ford, 1984).

In spite of these optimistic findings, research concerning the positive social and behavioral effects of peer tutoring on the tutees is less convincing than research that demonstrates positive academic benefits. For example, one major concern in special education is the social segregation of children with disabilities, and peer tutoring was discussed as one method whereby the teacher may help break down the social barriers that negatively impact students with disabilities. However, as Scruggs and Richter (1985) indicate, few studies have demonstrated that tutees are more adept socially or are more likely to socially interact than students who have not received tutoring. Therefore, the potentially positive social effects of tutoring on the tutees have not yet been fully demonstrated.

Effects of Tutoring on the Tutors

One happy consequence of tutoring—a secondary effect of most tutoring programs—is the effect on the academic achievement of the students doing the tutoring. Cohen, Kulik, and Kulik (1982), in a review of the literature on tutoring, reported that tutors performed better academically than students who were not involved in tutoring. Also, the tutors developed more positive attitudes toward the subject matter they taught. In retrospect, these data make sense, particularly if you consider the motivational aspect of instruction. Would you present yourself as an instructor (i.e., tutor) for a subject unless you were fully prepared to teach that subject? Also, instruction always involves motivation of the learner, and tutoring places the tutor in a position to defend the need for content mastery. Such a required "defense" can, and apparently does, affect the attitudes of the tutors.

Other secondary effects of tutoring include positive behavioral and social effects on the part of the tutors (Maher, 1982). Likewise, when students without disabilities are used to tutor students with disabilities, the attitudes of the tutors toward social integration of the students with disabilities change for the positive. These tutors are more likely to select a student with disabilities as a playmate.

Maher (1982, 1984) of Rutgers University has conducted a series of studies on the use of conduct problem adolescents as tutors. These studies present a major innovation for these "last chance" students, because very few educational interventions seem to work with this group of students. In the 1982 study, Dr. Maher used 18 adolescents identified as socially maladjusted and emotionally disturbed (11 males and 7 females). These subjects were selected randomly from a pool of 26 students, all of whom had behavioral problems in school. Three treatment groups were formed: a cross-age tutor group, a group receiving peer tutoring, and a group receiving counseling. Of the 18 students, 6 were randomly assigned to each group. The peer tutoring group received peer tutoring, and the counseling group received counseling for school problems. The cross-age tutoring group was trained to tutor young children with intellectual disabilities. Two tutoring sessions (30 minutes each) were held each week and the tutor also met with the elementary child's teacher once per week to review the child's progress. Results of this multiple-group research treatment study clearly revealed the success of the cross-age tutoring compared with the other interventions. The grades of the cross-age tutors improved significantly, the absences decreased, and the number of disciplinary referrals decreased compared to the other groups. Clearly this treatment must be judged a success.

Efficacy of Tutoring

As we have seen, the research on tutoring has been conducted in four basic areas and, in three of these diverse areas, the research results have been quite positive. Both tutors and tutees learn more in tutoring situations and develop more positive attitudes toward the subject matter. Also, when students with disabilities are the tutors, several studies have shown positive benefits in terms of the behavior of those students. Further, tutors develop more positive attitudes toward the social integration of students with disabilities. For these reasons, tutoring should be incorporated into every educational program for these students in some form.

INITIATING A TUTORING SYSTEM

You will want to ensure that students receive all of the individual instruction they require, and one of the best ways to provide this help for 6 to 8 students per period is to initiate a tutoring system that provides your class with tutors. The author of this text initiated such a system in a public school junior high resource class. Tutoring systems are easy to initiate, though certain tutoring systems require more time than others. Also, tutoring in inclusive mainstream classes may be harder to manage, because of the larger number of children. Finally, there are several specific decisions to make before you start. These are summarized in Interest Box 6.1.

What a Tutor Can Do

The first consideration in initiating a tutoring system is delineating the specific tasks you want a tutor to accomplish in your class. It may be helpful to think of the various tasks in terms of different level tasks, depending upon the level of complexity of the assignment, and the instructional skills a person should have before they attempt to teach a particular assignment to a student with disabilities. For example, with very little preparation, any tutor can enter your class and begin to assist in checking the students' objective answers to classwork. However, if you want a student to assist with reading comprehension questioning exercises, some training will be necessary. Likewise, if a tutor is to assist the students in a precision teaching charting exercise (as discussed in the last chapter) the tutor will require some training. Clearly, the types of tasks you need done will impact on the training the tutor requires.

As the teacher in charge of the classroom, you will take the final responsibility for deciding what the tutors do in the class. You should note the types of activities you typically have to do that do not require complex instruction. The list may include the following: checking student worksheets, rechecking the self-checking worksheets students

INTEREST BOX 6.1
Decisions in Preparation of a Tutoring System

I. What can a tutor do in your classroom?
   What types of tasks would save you the most time?
   What types of tasks require major training time?
   Do you use self-checking materials a great deal?
   Can tutors assist you in setting up equipment? How frequently do you use such equipment?
   Can tutors monitor the academic tasks in your class, such as listening to a child read?
   What guidelines should you give a tutor on when to request your assistance?

II. Who should you use as a tutor?
   Who is available to you? Can you, with a little public relations work, make other tutors available?
   Given your particular teaching style and methods of behavioral management, do you foresee problems sharing authority with a tutor? How does this affect the selection of tutors?

III. Can you provide the training necessary for tutors?
   What types of tasks should you train tutors for? Have you identified a good time for tutor training?
   Can someone else conduct the training? Perhaps a school principal, if the tutoring system involves the entire school?

IV. Have you identified a communication method?
   Do you have time for good communication about student progress if a tutor is conducting the instruction?

complete, listening to oral reading and correcting oral reading errors, assisting with dictionary skills, monitoring group art projects (while you work on a one-to-one basis with another student). Each of these activities can be accomplished with very little training for the tutor. For purposes of this text, this type of tutoring task will be referred to as a level 1 task.

However, certain activities require more training. These include assisting a student with comprehension of a math problem, using an advanced organizer to assist in reading comprehension (see Chapter 10 for a discussion of advanced organizers), and initial instruction in a new type of whole number operation in math. Because these skills are more complex, you will want the tutor to see how you accomplish them. Training in these skills can be as simple as having the new tutor observe you while you work with a student on one of these tasks. This type of task is referred to as a level 2 task.

Finally, there are certain types of tasks that you, as the teacher, should reserve for yourself. These are referred to as level 3 tasks, and are some of the more difficult decision making areas in teaching, which can have a very negative impact upon the child's development if the decision is not correctly made. These level 3 tasks would include reinforcing the student for completed work, punishing students for misbehavior, and planning the next set of instructional activities for the students.

Clearly, when contemplating a tutoring system, you should consider the level of task you want the tutor to do, and then make time for the appropriate training for your tutors. Nothing positive will be gained if you begin to use tutors for complex tasks for which they have received no training.

Who Do You Want as a Tutor?

Tutors may be obtained from any number of sources. For example, you may discover that a full-time teacher's aid is assigned to your resource class. Social agencies such as civic clubs, churches, and other organizations may have already initiated some type of "school assistance program" that results in a tutor in your class two mornings per week. You may use advanced students from other classes in your school. Also, as mentioned previously, research has demonstrated the effectiveness of having students with disabilities tutor other student with disabilities (Top & Osguthorpe, 1987). In short, the supply of tutors is truly endless.

If some type of tutoring system is not in place, you should consider starting one. The simplest method is to use students in your own class to tutor other students. Although using students with disabilities as tutors has been supported by research, this type of tutoring system requires more active monitoring of the tutor–tutee interactions (Maher, 1982; Scruggs et al., 1986). Still, with very little training, your own students can assist others in the class. Clearly, you should assure yourself that the student whom you assign as a tutor knows the material in the proposed lesson completely. You will also need to consider the sex of the tutors. At certain ages (generally grades 1 through 4) the sexes do not mix a great deal socially, and you may want to use only male tutors with male students and female tutors with female students. Beyond that age, you will need to consider the social acceptance of each student in the proposed tutoring pair. You should pair students together who have some history of working together, if at all possible. Tutors selected on this basis can begin to assist in level 1 tasks immediately.

It may be possible to obtain peer tutors from other classes in your school. For example, the author of this text implemented a tutoring system whereby study hall students who wished to tutor were assigned to the resource class for a particular period. Private instructions to the guidance counselor—who assisted in class assignments—assured that each tutor would be an academically capable student. These students began to assist with level 1 tasks immediately and, with very few observations, began to assist in level 2 tasks during the second week of their tutoring experience.

One unanticipated advantage of the peer tutoring system that involved nonclass tutors was the presence of academically capable students on a constant basis in the special education class. These students provided effective role models of behavior, as well as providing assistance academically. Also, because other students in the school saw these academically capable students going into the resource class, the social stigma that may sometimes be associated with special education classes was somewhat de-emphasized.

A word of caution is in order. As the teacher, you will have to maintain complete control over your tutoring system, and you may have to discipline the tutors discretely if they begin to overstep their responsibilities. Problems have been noted in tutoring situations involving grandparent tutors from a senior citizens' organization, who were used to a more stern disciplinary system than the one employed today in public schools. Also, in order to prevent this type of problem, you should not allow the parent of one of the students in your class to become a tutor in that class. You may, however, inform the parent of your need for tutors in other classes during different periods of the day, and assure the parent that, in the same fashion that they assist another student with disabilities, their own child is receiving assistance.

Training the Tutors

As noted previously, the task level you assign to tutors in your class has a direct bearing on the type of training you provide once your tutors are selected. Level 1 tasks can be assigned to any tutor on the first day of tutoring, whereas level 2 tasks may require complicated training. Also, the sex, social abilities, and attitudes of your tutors may affect the success of your tutoring program and must be considered.

For instructional situations that require training, there are two choices. First, observation combined with critical review may be enough of a training process for certain tutors. This generally involves three steps. In order for a tutor to be of benefit in conducting a precision teaching instructional lesson, for example, the tutor may be required merely to watch for several days as you conduct the timed exercises with the students. You may then discuss the purpose of the exercises with the tutor after class, answering any questions concerning the project. Finally, have the tutor conduct the timing exercise while you observe and critique the performance. The advantage of this type of training is that almost all of the training takes place in class, with very little time utilized for extra class training. Delquadri and his co-workers (1986) recommended this type of training for every student in the class in order to implement a classwide peer tutoring program.

The second type of tutor training involves extended extra-class training. For example, in order for a tutor to understand the purpose of a learning strategies instructional method, you may require the tutor to read certain materials on learning strategies. Also, you may take extra-class time and go over these materials with the tutor before he or she is considered ready to observe a learning strategies lesson in your class. After these steps, the in-class training exercises described above would be implemented. Much of the research on tutoring has used models of tutor training that require extra-class training time during the initial stages (Lazerson, Foster, Brown, & Hummel, 1988; Russell & Ford, 1984). For example, Russell and Ford (1984) trained tutors during a three-hour training session prior to implementation of the tutoring program. Beirne-Smith (1991) used a more involved tutor training to prepare tutors to teach math to students with learning disabilities. She had two instructional sessions of forty-five minutes each, during which tutors were trained in two different instructional methods. Clearly, the level of the task you want tutors to perform will determine the type and extent of necessary training, with level 2 and 3 tasks requiring much more training than level 1 tasks.

Finally, if extensive training of tutors for level 2 and level 3 tasks is necessary, you should prepare a set of detailed written instructions for the tutors to follow, in order to assure that their instructional presentation is standardized. As discussed in Chapter 6, direct instructional curriculum materials include teacher scripts for the teacher or tutor to use, and this type of scripted lesson format may be an appropriate choice for you in preparing the instructional session for your tutors to conduct. There are numerous examples in the literature of scripted lessons for tutors. Interest Box 6.2 presents a set of instructions for tutors that Beirne-Smith (1991) used in tutor training.

Communication with the Tutor

If the tutors in your class are merely conducting level 1 tasks, there is very little need for structured communication concerning student progress. These tutors merely do the types of activities you suggest, and these suggestions are generally made while class is in progress. For this type of tutorial assistance, you should require a written record of the student's performance on the task, such as collection of the worksheet the tutor has graded. This allows you to monitor the student's progress and plan the student's instruction appropriately.

However, in situations where the tutor is trained to conduct instructional, level 2 tasks, and in inclusive classes where two or more teachers may direct the tutor, additional and more structured communication about the student's progress may be necessary. For example, many teachers assign a particular time slot to the tutor each day for conducting an instructional assignment with a student. During the first 15 minutes of the period each day, the tutor or teacher's aid may be expected to work with Bill on spelling exercises. However, the basic responsibility for Bill's instruction rests with the teachers. Clearly, some form of daily communication between the aid and the teachers regarding Bill's performance is necessary.

One option is to require a brief written summary each day—usually a single paragraph—that summarizes the lesson and notes the number and types of errors made during the day. Some type of charting procedure is also helpful, as recommended by

INTEREST BOX 6.2
Instructional Session Plan for Tutor Training

In the Beirne-Smith (1991) study, students with learning disabilities received tutoring in addition facts from older students without learning disabilities. Training in mathfacts was based on 20 sets of three "related" mathfacts where the first addend in each set was held constant and the second addend was increased by one (e.g., 2 + 4 = 6; 2 + 5 = 7; 2 + 6 = 8). For each set a file folder was prepared showing the mathfact without the answer on the front and the mathfact with the answer on the back. With materials prepared in that fashion, the following task instructions were provided.

The tutor should display the file with answers, point to second addends and sums, and follow the five steps below.

1. Rule stating (e.g., "Each time the addend increases by one the sum increases by one. Say it with me.");
2. Demonstration (e.g., "My turn, 2 + 4 = 6; 2 + 5 + 7; 2 + 6 = 8");
3. Unison responding (e.g., "Say it with me: 2 + 4 = . . .);
4. Individual turns ("Say it by yourself");
5. Testing ("Say it again").

This type of task card, prepared for the instructional situations in which you expect your tutor to function (level 2 or level 3), will facilitate effective instruction.

Source: Beirne-Smith (1991).

both the precision teaching and the learning strategy instructional methods. In any case, it should be stressed to all concerned that the teacher is responsible for the instruction in his or her class, and needs to be fully informed of student progress.

Putting the Tutoring System Together

The four major concerns: who will do the tutoring, tasks of the tutors, tutor training, and communication with the tutor, are all interrelated, and once you decide on these factors you are ready to begin your in-class tutoring system. The steps in initiation of a tutoring system are presented in Interest Box 6.3. These steps are based on a tutoring system in which other students from the school (not in your class) are to be used as tutors. Nevertheless, these recommendations are generally appropriate during the initiation of most tutoring systems.

First, permissions should be obtained from the administrators, including your school principal and the director of special education in your district. You may wish to share some research articles or reviews of the literature on peer tutoring with these individuals. One fear concerning peer tutoring is the possibility of wasting the time of the tutors, and the research articles will clearly lay this fear to rest. As the research already cited demon-

INTEREST BOX 6.3
Checklist for Initiating a Tutoring System

Permissions:

__ Obtained permission from school administrators.
__ Obtained permission from each prospective tutor's parents.

Tutor Selection:

__ Identified time slots when tutors are needed.
__ Requested that the guidance counselor suggest some tutors.
__ Requested recommendations and support from other teachers.

Meeting with tutors:

__ Discussed your needs from tutors.
__ Outlined the prospective duties and privileges of tutors.
__ Elicited a commitment from tutors for one grading period.
__ Verified each student's parental permission.

Begin Tutoring System:

__ Have student observe in each task for which he or she will be utilized.
__ You observe the tutor while he or she conducts a tutoring session.
__ Tutors begin to conduct the sessions themselves.

Initiation of Tutor Training:

__ Identify which level 2 tasks you wish to have tutors conduct.
__ Identify the tutors whom you think capable of adequately conducting these tasks.
__ Identify method of training (reading, videotapes of you conducting the session) the tutor is to engage in.
__ Begin in-class training after the tutor completes tasks.

strates, a tutoring program is usually quite beneficial for all persons involved; the tutors learn better and develop better attitudes toward the work.

Second, you will want to involve the guidance counselor in your school in order to discuss the students who may become tutors. For example, this person may be able to identify any potential behavior problem students among your pool of potential tutors. Likewise, this person will be able to identify students who may make very effective tutors. If your school has a "Future Teachers of America" club, you may wish to make your tutoring system known by the advisor and ask for volunteers.

Third, you should choose more tutors than you can use. You should meet with the tutors themselves, explain the proposed job, and elicit their cooperation. Some will choose not to participate, and this is fine if you have selected more than enough. You should elicit an agreement to act as tutors for at least one grading period, and every student tutor should have the option of leaving the tutoring program at that time. At this point, you should send a parental permission letter home to the parents of the tutors, explaining the system, the time involvement of the tutors, and the advantages of tutoring. You should use students as tutors only after parental permission has been obtained.

Fourth, begin the tutoring responsibilities with level 1 tasks on the first day of tutoring. Generally, all students in schools can check a paper when an answer key is provided. These level 1 tasks from the first week of the tutoring program let you observe the tutors and their relationships with the students in your class. At this point, you may have to counsel some student tutors to withdraw from the tutoring program, explaining that not everyone has the personality to be a teacher or tutor. However, this should be a fairly rare occurrence. More common is your decision to use some tutors exclusively for level 1 tasks and to train others for more complex tutoring tasks. This decision may be made through observation of the tutors in their early experiences.

Finally, after several weeks, you should know which tutors are likely to be successful with more complex tutoring tasks. At that point you may wish to begin a training session designed to prepare some of your tutors for monitoring of comprehension through the use of advanced organizers, precision teaching charting, and other complex instructional strategies. As discussed previously, you may use some combination of modeling the lesson format, required readings, and scripted lessons as the basis for your training.

Disadvantages of Peer Tutoring

Several disadvantages of peer tutoring programs are readily apparent. First, as the discussion above indicated, training of tutors may take some out-of-class time, depending on the types of tasks your tutors are required to do. Also, eliciting the support of other professionals in the school may take some time. This last problem is somewhat alleviated if you use your own students as tutors.

Also, as a teacher you must not lose control of the instruction and disciplinary decisions in your class. If an aide, adult tutor, or peer tutor begins to overstep the responsibilities that have been delineated for the tutor, you may have to intervene and reassert the role responsibilities of the tutor.

Finally, you must be sure that parents are fully informed and give consent to use of their children as tutors, particularly if those students are spending instructional time tutoring on a daily basis. Most parents will be unaware of the evidence that demonstrates that tutors learn while they are engaged in tutoring. You may need to make these advantages of tutoring clear to these parents.

COOPERATIVE INSTRUCTIONAL GROUPS

The use of cooperative instructional groups is similar to tutoring, in the sense that students are teaching other students. However, in this system, no single student is designated as a tutor. Rather, small groups (usually 3 to 5 students) are identified and given a common project or task. Further, the work is structured such that every student has to participate in accomplishing the goal.

One early goal of mainstream programs has been to socially integrate students with disabilities and nondisabled students. Schools have traditionally operated competitively, or at least individualistically, in that every student worked alone on almost every assignment. Clearly, this type of work would not facilitate the integration of students with disabilities in mainstream classes. Theorists began to seek a combination of individualistic and cooperative instructional procedures, and the movement for cooperative instruction took root. For example, perhaps a combination of cooperation and competition results in the most interaction between these groups.

Johnson, Johnson, Warring, and Maruyama (1986) provided one of the first multigroup comparisons along these lines. Seventy-two students in sixth grade classes were used in the first study in the series (Johnson et al., 1986). These students were assigned to three conditions: cooperative controversy, cooperative debate, and competitive instruction (individualized work). In the first condition, the students were provided with information on wolves and then were randomly assigned to argue a position, as discussed below. After several days, the roles of the students were changed to the other position. Finally, a group report was required as a measure of comprehension. In the cooperative debate, the students were assigned roles and remained with those roles for the entire project, including the preparation of the group report. Finally, in the competitive condition, the students studied alone, and then wrote a group report. These three treatments thus varied in the degree of cooperation—from complete cooperation to no cooperation during the study and learning periods. The dependent variable for the study was a self-report questionnaire in which each student indicated the other students with whom he or she had been socially engaged. Four general types of engagement were compared: structured time, unstructured time (both of which took place in the classroom), out-of-class time, and play time at home. On the first two variables, there were significant differences favoring students in the cooperative controversy condition. In other words, students in the cooperative controversy condition (the most cooperative treatment condition) were more likely to choose playmates with disabilities than were the students in the other two conditions. Also, students in the cooperative debate condition (with a moderate level of cooperation) were more likely to choose students with disabilities than were students in the totally competitive condition. In short, having some cooperative tasks works better than having none for integrating students with disabilities, but completely cooperative tasks work measurably better than mixed cooperation and competition to facilitate such integration.

Cooperative Instructional Procedures

Different theorists have used different methods of cooperative instruction (Schniedewind & Salend, 1987; Slavin, 1983; Webb, 1982). These procedures are not difficult to implement, and the brief description below should allow you to begin the procedures. For additional information, you may wish to consult some of the references in this section of the text.

One fairly common method is the jigsaw (Schniedewind & Salend, 1987). In this method, the members of the cooperative group are each provided with certain information that other group members do not have, and the task for each group member is to learn all of the information. Students from different jigsaw groups who have been provided with the same information meet in "expert groups" to discuss how to teach their information to other group members. Then the original jigsaw groups meet and instruct each other. Groups may meet for 45 minutes each day for a period of five to ten days. Students then take an individual quiz and are graded on their comprehension of all of the material.

Aronson and his colleagues (1978) developed a procedure whereby four students were given different roles to play in a debate, and each role description presented different information on the topic. Johnson et al. (1986) used this jigsaw debate strategy as follows. Four students on a team were each given a role to play in an open debate concerning extermination of wolves. Two roles supported the hunting and killing of wolves (a hunter and a dairy farmer), whereas two roles argued against such practices (a conservationist and a scientist studying wolves). Each student was given an individual goal of learning all of the information during a seven-period debate, after which each student would prepare a written report. The jigsaw presentation of information is apparent, in that each student receives only certain information but is required to master all of the information presented.

The STAD, or student team achievement division, is another common cooperative instructional method. In this method, 5 or 6 students are assigned to learning groups. First a pretest on the new material is given to each student. Then, after the teacher introduces the material to be learned, worksheets are provided to team members. The teams study together and take another test individually. Each student's gain between the pretest and the posttest is averaged to provide a team score. High scoring teams and individual students are recognized.

Numerous other methods of organizing cooperative instruction have received research support. Like the methods discussed above, these may be implemented in any subject area merely by structuring the necessary educational materials (test, worksheets, etc.). A number of these methods are briefly described in Interest Box 6.4.

Efficacy of Cooperative Instruction

Research has indicated that cooperative instruction is a very effective instructional method (Anderson, 1985; Webb, 1982). These positive results can be identified in at least three areas. First, numerous studies report academic gains for all of the students when cooperative instructional procedures are used (Johnson et al., 1986; Slavin, 1983; Webb, 1982).

Second, cooperative instruction results in improved attitudes toward the subject matter (Slavin, Madden, & Leavey, 1984). Slavin (1983) reported that an experimental group exposed to cooperative instruction developed more positive attitudes toward the subject matter than the control group, even when a pretest of attitude toward the subject was taken into account.

Finally, cooperative instruction has been used in mainstream classes in an attempt to facilitate the integration of students with disabilities into these classes (Johnson, Johnson, & Maruyama, 1983). Although this particular result has not been proven

INTEREST BOX 6.4
Alternative Cooperative Instructional Methods

Jigsaw II: This method differs from the original jigsaw (described in text) only in that both a pretest and posttest are given to each student, and these are compared to yield a gain score for each child. The average gain score for the group becomes each group member's score.

Team Assisted Individualization (TAI): Heterogeneous groups of 4 to 5 students are formed. Based on a diagnostic assessment (this strategy is usually employed in math only), each student is given specific unit materials. Each unit consists of an instruction sheet, worksheets, checklists, other activities, and a final test. Working in pairs, students check each other's worksheets, and a score of 80 percent or better means that a student can take the final test for that unit. Teams are reinforced together for exceeding preset standards and for completing units.

Group Investigation: Students self-select into groups of 2 to 5 students and choose a topic from a potential list of topics for study. The group decides who should prepare what materials on subtopics in the group, and a final project, demonstration, or report is prepared for presentation to the class.

in inclusive education settings, at least one study indicated that social relationships in a special education class may be improved by the use of cooperative instruction (Anderson, 1985). Clearly, such improvement in social relationships must be one goal of every special education teacher.

SUMMARY

The use of peer tutoring and cooperative instructional arrangements in special education has been demonstrated to be an effective procedure. In utilizing a tutoring procedure, the level of task you want the tutors to perform is one of the crucial concerns. In that sense, utilization of tutors and teacher's aides is very similar. Clearly, the more complex tasks must be reserved for the teacher, whereas level 1 and level 2 tasks may be performed by the tutor if proper training is provided.

The positive effects of both tutoring and cooperative instruction are numerous. Positive effects in both academic achievement and attitudes have been demonstrated. These are strategies that may be implemented in almost every special education class at some point during the year, and the use of tutors or cooperative instructional groups frees the teacher for more individual instruction in problem areas. For these reasons, you will want to employ some type of tutoring and/or cooperative instructional program in your class.

Summary Points

- Peer tutoring has been shown to be effective in a number of studies in improving the academic performance of students with disabilities.
- Peer tutoring also has a number of secondary effects that are quite positive. These include improved academic performance and behavior on the part of the tutors, as well as more positive attitudes toward school.
- Cross-age tutors involves the use of a group of tutors from a different (usually older) age bracket to tutor students. This procedure has resulted in positive behavioral improvements on the part of adolescents with behavioral disorders.
- The type of task you want your tutors to perform will dictate the level of training necessary for those tutors. Appropriate training is necessary for complex instructional tasks.
- Cooperative instruction involves the use of cooperative instructional procedures. This technique generally sprang from the need to integrate students with disabilities into mainstream classes.
- Jigsaw procedures involve providing only some of the necessary information to each pupil in the group, then requiring the group to complete a common project.
- STAD stands for Student Team Achievement Division, and involves group and individual tutoring to enhance performance of all students in the group.

QUESTIONS AND ACTIVITIES

1. Imagine that you are a teacher in the high school from which you graduated. You know the scheduling procedures and the routine. If you were teaching in a resource room at that school, how could you implement a peer tutoring system? What organizations could you contact? Write out a two-page plan concerning implementation for such a system and discuss it in class.
2. Review the research articles in the text on peer tutoring, in addition to other articles. Can you find any negative effects of peer tutoring? Do tutors end up wasting their instructional time?
3. Interview several special education teachers locally and identify any tutoring or cooperative instructional procedures they might use.

4. Theoretically speaking, this chapter could have been titled "Cooperative Instruction and Tutoring." What is the relationship between the two? Is cooperative instruction a "special case" of peer tutoring, or the other way around?
5. Design some role-play materials for use in a debate jigsaw for four mildly handicapped children. How can materials already available in the class be used for this purpose?
6. Review the research on the efficacy of cooperative instruction. Are there additional positive effects that have not been discussed in this chapter?

REFERENCES

Anderson, M. A. (1985). Cooperative group tasks and their relationship to peer acceptance and cooperation. *Journal of Learning Disabilities, 18,* 83–86.

Aronson, R., Blaney, N., Stephan, C., Sikes, & Snapp, M. (1978). *The Jigsaw Classroom.* Beverly Hills, CA: Sage Publications.

Beirne-Smith, M. (1991). Peer tutoring in arithmetic for children with learning disabilities. *Exceptional Children, 57,* 330–337.

Campbell, B. J., Brady, M. P., & Linehan, S. (1991). Effects of peer-mediated instruction on the acquisition and generalization of written capitalization skills. *Journal of Learning Disabilities, 24,* 6–13.

Carlson, M. B., Litton, F. W., & Zinkgraf, S. A. (1985). The effects of an intraclass peer tutoring program on the sight word recognition ability of students who are mildly mentally retarded. *Mental Retardation, 23* (2), 74–78.

Cohen, P. A., Kulik, J. A., & Kulik, C. C. (1982). Educational outcomes of tutoring: A meta-analysis of findings. *American Educational Research Journal, 19,* 237–248.

Delquadri, J., Greenwood, C. R., Whorton, D., Carta, J. J., & Hall, R. V. (1986). Classwide peer tutoring. *Exceptional Children, 52,* 535–542.

Johnson, D. W., Johnson, R., & Maruyama, G. (1983). Interdependence and interpersonal attraction among heterogeneous and homogeneous individuals: A theoretical formulation and a meta-analysis of the research. *Review of Educational Research, 53,* 5–54.

Johnson, D. W., Johnson, R. T., Warring, D., & Maruyama, G. (1986). Different cooperative learning procedures and cross-handicap relationships. *Exceptional Children, 53,* 247–252.

Lazerson, D. B., Foster, H. L., Brown, S. I., & Hummel, J. W. (1988). The effectiveness of cross-age tutoring with truant, junior high school students with learning disabilities. *Journal of Learning Disabilities, 21,* 253–255.

Maher, C. A. (1982). Behavioral effects of using conduct problem adolescents as cross-age tutors. *Psychology in the Schools, 19,* 360–364.

Maher, C. A. (1984). Handicapped adolescents as cross-age tutors: Program description and evaluation. *Exceptional Children, 51,* 56–63.

Russell, T., & Ford, D. F. (1984). Effectiveness of peer tutors vs. resource teachers. *Psychology in the Schools, 21,* 436–441.

Sasso, G. M., Mitchell, V. M., & Struthers, E. M. (1986). Peer tutoring vs. structured interaction activities: Effects on the frequency and topography of peer interactions. *Behavioral Disorders, 11,* 249–258.

Schniedewind, N., & Salend, S. J. (1987). Cooperative learning works. *Teaching Exceptional Children, 19,* 22–25.

Scruggs, T. E., Mastropieri, M., Veit, D. T., & Osguthorpe, R. T. (1986). Behaviorally disordered students as tutors: Effects on social behavior. *Behavioral Disorders, 11,* 36–43.

Scruggs, T. E., & Richter, L. (1985). Tutoring learning disabled students: A critical review. *Learning Disability Quarterly, 8,* 286–298.

Slavin, R. E. (1983). *Team assisted individualization: A cooperative learning solution for adaptive instruction in mathematics.* Unpublished paper, Center for Social Organization of Schools, John Hopkins University, Boston.

Slavin, R. E., Madden, N. A., & Leavey, M. (1984). Effects of cooperative learning and individualized instruction on mainstreamed students. *Exceptional Children, 50,* 434–443.

Top, B. L., & Osguthorpe, R. T. (1987). Reverse-role tutoring: The effects of handicapped students tutoring regular class students. *The Elementary School Journal, 87,* 413–423.

Webb, N. M. (1982). Student interaction and learning in small groups. *Review of Educational Research, 52,* 421–445.

CHAPTER 7

COMPUTER-BASED INSTRUCTION

GARY ROSS
WILLIAM N. BENDER

OBJECTIVES

Upon completion of this chapter, you should be able to:

1. Identify and discuss the unique features of computer-based instruction (CBI) that may enhance the educational process for individuals with mild disabilities.
2. Identify learning situations in which CBI may improve the educational progress of individuals with mild disabilities.
3. Describe the appropriate use of CBI with students who have mild disabilities.
4. Defend the proposition that computers should supplement rather than replace teacher instruction.
5. Identify, using proper evaluation techniques, software that will meet the needs of individuals with disabilities.
6. Discuss computer management programs for IEP preparation.

KEYWORDS

Software	Digitized Speech	Hypermedia
Wait time	Interactive Videodisc	Computer-Based Management
Speech Synthesizer	Multimedia	Computer-Managed Instruction
Branching	CD-ROM	
Interface	Liquid Crystal Display	

At various periods in the history of education, proponents of technology have suggested that a particular type of technology will revolutionize education in the classroom, and these prognostications have frequently been incorrect. For example, when the filmstrip projector first became widely available, media specialists envisioned a major revolution in classroom education. Likewise, educational television was described as another revolutionary force on the educational scene. Unfortunately neither of these technologies fulfilled the initial prophecies (Lieber & Semmel, 1985). Educators are understandably skeptical when theorists suggest, once again, that a relatively new technology, microcomputers, may revolutionize education.

However, important aspects of computer-based instruction (CBI) suggest that microcomputers are beginning to have this type of impact. First, unlike the first two technologies identified above, microcomputer usage is typically under the control of the classroom teacher. Whereas teachers of the 1970s had to schedule their classes around educational television schedules or check out films/videos several days in advance, the teacher with a computer can integrate computer-based instruction (CBI) throughout the curriculum. When teachers have computers in their classrooms they are free to schedule the utilization of the computers to suit the needs of the students and curriculum (Kascinski & Gast, 1993; Montague & Fonseca, 1993). Additionally, many unique features of CBI, such as interactivity (i.e., the capability of the computer to interact with students' input), enhance the learning environment, especially for students with disabilities (Littauer, 1994). It is this flexibility of planning, coupled with the unique features of computers, that impacts on learning in ways that earlier technologies do not.

Research has indicated that CBI is an effective instructional tool (Bottge & Hasselbring, 1993; Caftori, 1994; Hudson, Lignugaris-Kraft, and Miller, 1993; Perry & Garber, 1993). In academic areas as wide-ranging as spelling, mathematics, writing, and the secondary content areas, CBI has been shown to be at least comparable to traditional instruction and in certain types of tasks, more effective. Caftori (1994), although supporting use of CBI, did indicate that the overall effectiveness of CBI depended upon not only the quality of the software, but on how the software was utilized; if the "Gaming" format is emphasized too heavily, academic progress may suffer.

More recent applications of computers have surpassed the rather mundane drill and practice applications through the development and integration of multimedia technology. Today, the student can, using the new CD-ROM technology, interact with the lessons, and selectively view brief filmstrips/video on various topics at the computer screen. If the teacher chooses, the actual selection of which content to review may be determined for the student, with the student selecting the format from a wide array of available media possibilities.

The computer has also been proven useful as a classroom management tool (Kascinski & Gast, 1993). In this role the computer is capable of assisting with the "paperwork" and the manipulation of numerical data required in classroom and behavior management. Some school districts use computerized packages that produce finished IEP goals and objectives, and track student performance, once the appropriate assessment information has been identified. This form of computer-managed instruction is discussed in a later section.

There are many unanswered questions concerning the use of microcomputers. For example, Goldman, Semmel, Cosden, Gerber, and Semmel (1987) surveyed special education administrators in California to find out such basic information as how many special education programs used microcomputers. Those data indicate that 51 percent of the administrators surveyed reported that their school district owned microcomputer hardware. A classroom observation of computer use (Cosden, Gerber, Semmel, Goldman, & Semmel, 1987) confirms that microcomputers are found in both resource and self-contained special classes. Finally, 79 percent of the students in resource rooms had potential access to microcomputers (Lieber & Semmel, 1985). There is every indication that CBI use has increased and will continue to increase in the years to come.

Practitioners report that acquisition of microcomputers typically follows a predictable pattern. First, the computers are made available to the advanced (perhaps gifted) math and science classes. Next, microcomputers have been purchased for the elementary classes. Finally, microcomputers have been made available for the children in special education classes. This pattern may affect your decisions about the level of CBI integration you choose to pursue. However, you may be assured that use of the microcomputer will only increase in the years ahead, and the teacher who is not proficient with CBI integration will be at a great disadvantage.

This chapter is intended to acquaint you with the fundamentals of computer usage in special education. An overview of CBI design and integration is presented first, followed by a brief discussion on applications of computer-based technology. Then research on the effectiveness of CBI among students with mild disabilities is described. Next, guidelines for purchasing software are presented, and problems encountered in using CBI are explored.

UNIQUE FEATURES OF COMPUTER-BASED INSTRUCTION

Computer-Based Instruction offers many unique features that enhance the presentation of instruction, especially for individuals with disabilities (Littauer, 1994; Montague & Fonseca, 1993). Some of these features are inherent within the technology. For example, the computer will patiently wait for an answer and then provide immediate reinforcement for a correct answer or corrective feedback for an incorrect answer. Computers use a multimodal presentation, animation and graphics, sound, varying type sizes, and small sequenced steps for information presentation, all of which help meet the needs of students with various disabilities. Also, computers facilitate the use of adaptive devices to control various forms of computer input and output. Other features include control of and involvement in the learning process by student and/or teacher, increased motivation to keep the learner on task, hands-on experience through tutorials, and cooperative learning among students. Interest Box 7.1 presents these advantages of CBI.

When considering the unique features of technology, it is important to remember the components of CBI systems. Software refers to instructions contained on a disk that tell the computer what to do. Hardware is the computer itself—that is, just a machine that will sit and do nothing without appropriate software. Therefore, the quality of the software used influences the effectiveness of the CBI lesson and determines which of these unique instructional features will be employed. The balance of this section details many of these features.

Nonthreatening Presentation

Computers are patient and nonthreatening as they wait for student input (Hannaford, 1987). The computer can be programmed to present a problem and then wait patiently for the student to answer. The wait time, a period of time from the presentation of a problem to presentation of the next problem, can be adjusted to meet the needs of all individuals. For example, the wait period can be indefinite, several seconds long, variable, sequentially shortened, or any combination of these. Whatever wait period is chosen, a good software program will allow the teacher or student to adjust the period as needed. Some programs will automatically adjust the period to improve fluency. The flexibility offered by being able to adjust the rate of presentation and sequence of material makes CBI the ideal tool for meeting the individual needs of individuals with disabilities.

INTEREST BOX 7.1
Instructional Features of CBI

Computers will:

—patiently wait for an answer
—provide immediate reinforcement
—provide corrective feedback
—present multimedia instruction
—hold student's attention
—facilitate use of adaptive devices
—increase motivation to learn
—present information in different ways (speech, text, video, graphics)
—facilitate instructional flexibility

Source: Littauer (1994); Montague and Fonseca (1993).

Motivational Advantages

Although motivation, as a construct, is difficult to measure, the motivational increases produced through the use of technology in special education are evident in increased time on task, increased quantity of products produced, and the improved quality of those products (Montague & Fonseca, 1993; MacArthur, 1988). There are a number of reasons for the increased attention. It may be something as simple as the text appearing on the screen immediately as a student types, or the CBI referring to the student by name. However, CBI uses combinations of text, graphics, color, sound, and animation to provide a motivating, multimodal learning environment in which to present information. It is this total environment that keeps students interested and on task. For example, students with learning disabilities have shown improvements in their written work through the use of a combination of modes on the computer (Montague & Fonseca, 1993). Students experiencing difficulties getting their thoughts down on paper through handwriting are able to use the keyboard of the computer effectively so that the quality and quantity of their work improves dramatically (MacArthur, 1988). This improvement is perhaps produced by many differing factors, but a combination of the ease of text manipulation and the interactivity of the computer is certainly a major factor. It is quite easy to visualize a student with mild disabilities throwing the paper he or she is working on into the trash, because of making the same mistake for the third time. However, that same student, given a computer and some basic word processing skills, will be able to turn in the paper without extensive revisions—those revisions will have been done on the computer.

Another feature that is used in combination with the ease of text manipulation afforded by the word processor is the speech synthesizer, which generates speech output. The addition of speech output during the typing phase will enhance the accuracy of the first draft for many students. With speech output by the computer the student can hear the letters, words, sentences, or paragraphs spoken as he or she types. This combination of visual and auditory feedback provides the enhanced environment some students with mild disabilities need.

For other students, motivation may come through the use of sound, graphics, and/or animation in the program presentation. Indeed, the appropriate use of sound, graphics, and/or animation can hold the attention of students with disabilities at various ages. Preschool aged children, for example, are fascinated with zany little characters that help present information and reinforce correct responses. Older students may need fewer characters, but those students may continue to be reinforced by sound and animation, especially in the form of a game. Secondary students often find sufficient motivation in the products they are able to produce with the computer. These products may take the form of text-based documents with a word processor, graphics-based computer art, text and graphics combinations such as a newsletter, or interactive programs on the computer itself.

Reinforcement

Students seem to improve more in academic performance when using well designed computer programs to increase fluency or mastery in various academic and functional skills, compared to instruction using worksheets and flashcards (Hasselbring & Goin, 1989; Montague & Fonseca, 1993). One of the reasons for this improvement may be the reinforcement provided by CBI. As the student correctly answers problems, effective CBI programs will immediately provide reinforcement with graphics and/or sound. Upon answering a set number of problems, the student is treated to a larger portion of reinforcement, sometimes in the form of a short game. In the case of incorrect answers, a CBI program may ignore the answer, provide corrective feedback, tell the student to call the teacher for assistance, or change to a part of the program that gives the student additional practice in the concept. The immediate reinforcement and feedback CBI programs provide is a major reason for the increased achievement associated with CBI use.

Program Flexibility

Providing a flexible learning environment within a CBI program is accomplished through the use of branching. Branching is a powerful programming tool that allows a program to select from several types of instructional avenues or branches. It can be invoked either automatically within a program or controlled by the user or teacher. For example, a student working with a math program may reach a level where he answers three problems in a row incorrectly. Through branching, the CBI program will take the student back to a lower level of content or to some additional problems of less difficulty in the same content area for practice. When the student reaches proficiency in the lower level, an effective CBI package will return the student to the selected content level.

The method of teaching can also be controlled by branching. Many programs offer methods of teaching that address the stages of learning. In the acquisition stage the student will use the training module of the program, whereas in the fluency or mastery stages the student will use the practice and testing modules. Finally, in the generalization stages the student will use the generalization module. An example of this type of branching is found in the Attainment Company's *Survival Signs Program* (1988). In the training or acquisition stage the student is presented with signs on the screen and the name of the sign is spoken by the speech synthesizer. The next screen presents the sign in context with background scenes and the name is spoken again. The practice or fluency/mastery stage presents a sign and asks the student to press the enter key when the name of the sign is heard as several signs are flashed slowly on the screen. Generalization is tested by presenting two signs at once and asking the student to choose the correct sign.

Branching also comes into play in interactive programs where giving a certain answer will automatically take the student to another area of the program. For example, if a student is operating a program on mammals and selects the picture of a dog, the program then jumps to a portion of the program that will lead the student through a tutorial about various breeds of dogs. Thus, the CBI package allows for some student exploration through branching.

More and more programs are being developed to take advantage of this branching technique. It is this feature that allows a CBI package to break instructional tasks down into small sequenced steps for presentation and allows the student and/or teacher to control the sequence of these steps and the pace of presentation. For many students with disabilities this flexibility is an important aspect of the individualized instruction offered by a CBI package. Therefore, branching has proven to be a powerful tool as the program moves the student among content areas, levels of content difficulty, mode of presentation, or method of teaching.

Interface Modes

Standard Interface Modes. Interface modes are a combination of input and output devices that facilitate interaction between the computer and human user. These devices include the keyboard, a mouse, a monitor, printers, scanners, speech recognition, and speech synthesizers. These devices are described below.

A mouse is a device that is rolled around on the table to position the cursor on the screen and to select objects or text. Most computers now come equipped with either a mouse or one of the variants (such as a trackball) as a standard feature.

The monitor or display screen is the device that looks like a television and provides a visual output of what the computer is doing. It may be either black and white or color, which, although more expensive, is preferable for many programs.

Scanners come in two styles, hand-held or full-page, and allow the user to enter printed material into the computer without having to type it. Scanners also enter pictures or graphics into the computer. The hand-held scanner is dragged across the material to be entered and the computer receives the information. The full-page scanner works just like a copier except that the image is entered into the computer instead of being reproduced on paper.

Speech recognition allows the user to speak to the computer and the computer receives the input just as if it had been typed on the keyboard. Less sophisticated voice recognition systems require that all input be trained (e.g., spoken three times), before the computer accepts it as input. More sophisticated and expensive systems learn to recognize speech patterns based on one example.

Speech synthesizers produce speech based on the input from other modes, typically the keyboard. These devices allow the CBI package to "talk" to the students. Of course this is a tremendous help when a nonreading student with a disability wishes to use the computer.

The interface system, consisting of a keyboard, monitor, and a mouse, seems to be relatively standard today. Plate 7.1 shows these standard interface systems.

The individual requirements of students with disabilities should dictate which type of system is utilized in the class. For example, a student with a strength in auditory learning would benefit from a presentation that combines speech or sound output with text and graphics. A visual learner may likewise benefit from a presentation based primarily on text and graphics. A visually impaired learner, on the other hand, would perhaps benefit from enlarged text, talking programs, speech-based interfaces, Braille printers, voice recognition, and/or word prediction programs. These basic adaptations require additional expense, but may greatly enhance a student's educational outcomes. Also, many small computers today will accommodate some of these enhancements. For example, every Macintosh computer by Apple incorporates the ability to present a magnified version of the screen presentation, and several computers exist that allow programs to "speak."

Sophisticated Interface Modes. Sometimes it is desirable to provide other adaptations to the input or output of the computer. These adaptations can be made with the addition of adaptive devices, such as the *TouchWindow,* by Edmark. The *TouchWindow,* shown in Plate 7.2, is a device that attaches over the screen of the computer and allows interaction with

PLATE 7.1 Standard Interface Systems

the computer by touching the screen. In the IBM family of computers and the Macintosh this interaction means that a student or teacher is able to control most mouse driven programs and control most of the computer functions, except the entering of text, just by touching the screen. This mode of interaction is particularly effective with younger children during the prereading years. Of course, this adaptation has also been used effectively with older students who have reading problems.

Other adaptive devices include expanded and programmable keyboards that allow the control of the CBI lesson through a larger surface than the standard keyboard. This is a real advantage for students with fine motor problems. These keyboards can be programmed so that they contain all the functions of a standard keyboard or just the functions that are needed for a particular software program. For example, many programs require just the cursor controls keys and the return key to run them. Expanded keyboards can be set up to contain just these keys. This type of a setup is beneficial to the student who has difficulty isolating the keys on a standard keyboard or gets confused by the numerous stimuli presented on a standard keyboard. Keyboards in this group are the *PowerPad,* by Dunamis, and the *Unicorn Keyboard,* by Unicorn Engineering.

Some students benefit from hearing information presented by the CBI package as well as seeing it. This process is facilitated by the use of a speech synthesizer. Speech output mechanisms come in two basic forms, speech synthesis and digitized speech. Synthesized speech requires specialized electronics called a speech synthesizer, which is addressed by the software to produce a robotic sounding "speech." Speech synthesizers can be internal (within the computer) or external. The Echo family of speech synthesizers, by Street Electronics, is the most widely used. Because synthesized speech is converted from text in the computer, it requires very little memory and addresses an unlimited vocabulary. However, the words translated by the speech synthesizer are based upon known phonics rules and therefore are sometimes mispronounced by the synthesizer.

PLATE 7.2 *TouchWindow*

Digitized speech, on the other hand, is essentially recorded speech stored in a digital format and therefore is limited in vocabulary to what is recorded and takes extensive amounts of memory. As computers come on the market with larger memory capacities, more of this type of speech is being incorporated into programs, creating a more natural sounding interface for the user.

TYPES OF SOFTWARE

Traditionally, the classification of instructional software has been based upon functions that the particular program performed. Examples of this classification scheme include drill and practice, simulation, tutorial, problem solving, and assessment software (Malouf, Jamison, Kercher, & Carlucci, 1991). All of these fulfilled the function specified by the title, and each software type could be further categorized by the academic subject area addressed. That is, if a program was designed to provide practice in mathfacts then the classification would be "math drill and practice," and so on for language arts, reading, writing, or any other subject.

This classification scheme makes it possible to identify software that meets the instructional goals of the teacher. For example, instructional activities generally include some tutorial work designed to increase the rate of acquisition within new topics of study, drill and practice work on topics that have already been introduced, problem solving through critical thinking and knowledge applications, simulations designed to promote the use of skills in different situations, and assessment of new skills. Each of these areas of instruction represents a major potential application of computer-based instruction. When considering the following descriptions of types of software it is important to remember that, historically, the computer was used only rarely to introduce new information or material. Instead, the computer has been used primarily in later stages of learning to enhance fluency, mastery, and generalization. This is still true today, though newer innovations such as multimedia—discussed later in this chapter—suggest that this may change.

Tutorials

Microcomputers may be used to provide guided practice or sequentially ordered information to the student (Malouf, Jamison, Kercher, & Carlucci, 1991). For example, software designed to provide tutoring in double-digit division would begin with a brief review of single-digit division and of the relationships between the divisor and dividend. From this point, the screen display would present the newer type of problem and lead the student through a series of instructional and/or practice activities. These activities would include graduated guidance, where an example of how to work the problem is presented, followed by examples of partially completed problems. Problems would be presented in increasingly less complete fashion until the student was working the entire problem. As the student worked, the CBI program would address the individual needs of the student by monitoring progress and adjusting the instruction as necessary. For example, if the student were to exhibit difficulty in a practice session, the CBI program might automatically drop back to an explanation of how to work the problems. In short, tutorial software increases fluency and mastery in much the same way a teacher would, by building new understanding on recently acquired knowledge.

Guided Practice

The most frequently used type of CBI by far is guided practice, sometimes referred to as drill and practice (Cosden et al., 1987). After initial instruction the pupil is usually required to perform the new skill repeatedly in order to gain practice. The presentation of this type of repetitive practice, with corrective feedback, is one of the strong points of effective CBI (Malouf, Jamison, Kercher, & Carlucci, 1991; Vockell & Mihail, 1993), and many students choose to participate in guided practice game formats in their spare time (Caftori, 1994). Guided practice software is often referred to as "electronic flashcards," and in many ways that is an accurate description. However, such software developments as graphics, sound reinforcement, and immediate feedback have enhanced the concept far beyond that of mere flashcards. In the more developed CBI programs the student is rewarded for correct responses immediately and competes with his or her earlier performance, with the CBI package itself, or with another student. Rewards for successful problem completion have gone much further than the earlier "smiling face" formats. Some current software uses very elaborate graphic and/or sound displays to indicate the successful completion of a problem, and many students with mild disabilities respond quite favorably to that type of reinforcement.

In many cases, CBI programs are designed to provide drill and practice in a game format. Generally, modern game formats also have a built in "counter" that will allow the teacher to see the total number of problems attempted, the total number correct, type of problem incorrect, and in some cases recall the incorrect problems in order to do these with the student at the end of the computer lesson. Thus, an error analysis of the student's work would be possible. Finally, some guided practice CBI games tally the daily completion rate that may be used to provide a running record for several weeks on problem completion. Note the similarity between this idea and the precision teaching procedures discussed in Chapter 4.

Problem Solving

Problem solving software is designed to provide practice for students in working through a problem. Many forms have been developed that present various situations in which the student has to use a combination of skills to find solutions to the problem. One of the more famous CBI programs of this type is *The Oregon Trail,* by MECC (1991), which is based on a group of pioneers crossing the country from Saint Louis, Missouri, to Oregon. The students have to make a multitude of decisions that affect the outcome of the journey. For example, if the student chooses to ford the river when the river is too deep the wagon and contents may be lost. Or if the student does not go hunting, or secure food some other way, before running out of food he may starve to death. Through these and other situations students learn to work through problems and think ahead about consequences. Younger students may have to have peers or teachers help with the reading on some programs or help the student think through the process to reach solutions.

Simulations

Simulation software provides skill practice in simulated real-life situations. These situations are, of course, not as realistic as many practitioners would like, but can be designed to present the information and allow practice that will generalize to real situations. For example, in a secondary chemistry class, a mixture of certain chemicals may result in vapors harmful to students, or even explosions. Use of simulations that allow such mixtures affords the students the opportunity to experiment in these areas without danger.

With advances in memory and presentation techniques, software is being designed that provides very realistic simulations in the business world. As these improvements are incorporated into educational software, teachers will have access to teaching tools that could only be dreamed about a few years ago. Although the computer is somewhat limited in its ability to present simulations with large amounts of real-life video, there are new technologies that when used in conjunction with the computer are achieving promising results. Multimedia technologies, which present video, sound, and film along with the more standard text and graphics, are becoming more available in public school classrooms, and foremost among these at present is the interactive videodisc technology. Interactive videodisc technology combines computer programming with motion video on a computer-controlled videodisc. This combination affords the means to have extensive simulations because the video portion is not dependent upon the computer memory. Technology advances, such as the interactive videodisc, promise to open new frontiers in the education of individuals with mild disabilities.

A second multimedia technology is the CD-ROM, a small CD read as input software in the same fashion that a disc is read. The CD-ROM can store so much more information than the standard disc that interaction is possible whereby the student may choose the next learning activity (e.g., a text screen on the topic, a short video, or a combination of these). The CD-ROM does not store as much information as the videodisc.

Assessment on the Microcomputer

Although many CBI programs include some type of assessment of the skills taught, there are also CBI programs intended exclusively as assessment packages. However, there is some reason for caution in use of these CBI packages. Varnhagen and Gerber (1984) compared a spelling assessment package to traditional assessment in spelling. Twenty-seven students, nine of whom were mildly disabled, were assessed using both traditional assessment and a computer assessment software program. Both the students with mild disabilities and the nondisabled students took longer and made more errors on the computerized version of the assessment, a result that obviously raised some questions concerning the effectiveness of computerized assessment programs. Because of this research, teachers should exercise caution in using a computerized assessment program, at least until additional evidence is available.

An Updated Classification System

Although the above classification scheme is accepted by most of the industry and has worked well in the past, many factors seem to indicate the need for an alternative means of software classification (Hasselbring and Goin, 1989; Langone, 1990). One major factor warranting such a change is the evolution of software. With many software packages being designed today the differences between the above classification types wane as more and more programs utilize a combination of elements from several software types (Hasselbring and Goin, 1989; Langone, 1990). For example, few educational programs are developed today that are strictly "drill and practice." Likewise, it is sometimes quite difficult to determine the difference between a problem solving CBI package and a simulation.

It may be more appropriate today to consider the acquisition and use of software based upon the relationship of the software to the four learning stages: acquisition, fluency, mastery, and generalization (Hasselbring and Goin, 1989; Langone, 1990). Using the learning stages to assess the appropriateness of a software package helps address the requirements of the concept of curriculum-based assessment discussed in Chapter 4.

This proposed model suggests that "guided practice" software should not be used in the acquisition of a new skill. In fact, CBI in general is not appropriate as a single source for the acquisition of a new skill, unless multimedia CBI materials are utilized. Other forms of CBI can be thought of only as tools to assist the teacher in the instruction process and should not be considered as a stand-alone panacea for all the ills of special education (Hannaford, 1987). Therefore, it is important to remember that, regardless of the method used to choose or classify software, CBI is only a tool.

SUBJECT AREA CBI APPLICATIONS

In consideration of CBI use, teachers need to remember that there has not been a great deal of research on the efficacy of CBI with students with mild disabilities (Lieber & Semmel, 1985), and some questions have been raised concerning appropriate utilization of software (Caftori, 1994). However, the available research does indicate some positive outcomes for CBI (Bottge & Hasselbring, 1993; Chiang, 1986; Howell, Sidorenko, & Jurica, 1987; Hudson, Lignugaris-Kraft, & Miller, 1993; Keene & Davey, 1987; Littauer, 1994; Trifiletti, Frith, & Armstrong, 1984; Torgesen, Waters, Cohen, & Torgesen, 1988), as well as some equivocal results (McDermott & Watkins, 1984). Most of this research has investigated the effectiveness of CBI programs on academic achievement of a general nature. In this section information on the use of CBI in particular subject areas is presented.

Writing

Writing seems to be a major problem for individuals who have mild disabilities. Imagine the following scenario. A student is trying to write a paper for a mainstream class and makes mistake after mistake, many in the same place, so that soon a hole is erased through the paper. The student is frustrated, wads up the paper, throws it over his shoulder, and ends up in detention for misbehavior. When allowed to write on a computer with a word processor the student may, for the first time in his life, be able to turn in a paper with no mistakes on it. Many educators see potential for the word processor on the computer in overcoming these obstacles.

The text editing capabilities of the computer are seen as an enhancement to the writing process (Graham & MacArthur, 1988; MacArthur, 1988; Montague & Fonseca, 1993). For example, MacArthur (1988) noted an increase in motivation, increased quantity of work, improvement in social interaction, and improved quality of work. He also identified five ways by which word processors affect the writing process—these are presented in Interest Box 7.2.

Desktop publishing is another option that may be used to enhance writing skills. It is used to combine text and graphics to create products that can range from greeting cards to school newspapers.

INTEREST BOX 7.2
Improvements in the Writing Process by Using CBI

1. Flexible editing, where text can be manipulated with just a few key strokes.
2. The visibility of the writing process on a computer generates more interaction among the teacher and other students.
3. Neat printed copies are seen as a power not often enjoyed by individuals who have great difficulty getting their thoughts down on paper.
4. For students with poor handwriting, typing on a keyboard can be an efficient way of producing a paper (although they will need training in typing skills).
5. There are now appropriate word processors for all ages and disabilities (although the operation of a word processor must be taught).

Source: MacArthur (1988).

Just as the personal computer has opened this field to the business world, students with disabilities are now able to participate in creating these products.

A liquid crystal display (LCD) is a device that, when placed on an overhead projector, projects what is seen on the computer monitor onto a large screen for all the class to see. With this device the students may engage in collaborative composition and editing activities. Students may be assigned in small groups to compose and/or edit papers. A single student may serve as typist for the group and others can offer suggestions as to what should be written or changed. Observations of this procedure with students who demonstrate mild disabilities have indicated very positive interactions (MacArthur, 1988; Montague & Fonseca, 1993). Students who under different circumstances may have trouble staying in the same room can now be expected to work together, producing high quality work as they interact as a team.

Specialized story writers, such as *Big Book Maker* and the *Creative Writing Series,* by Toucan Software (1988), lead young writers through the creation process by providing graphics that can be combined with text to produce a story. This type of program is available for several age and intellectual levels. Programs like *Big Books* often include sound and speech output as enhancements to the writing process. Teachers and/or students using these programs can add graphics to a page and require the students to write about what they see. While being lead through the writing process students are free to create any story that strikes their fancy.

Extension activities or enhancements of the basic word processor identified by MacArthur (1988) include spelling checkers, grammar analyzers, interactive prompting, and speech output. Some teachers view spell/grammar checkers with disdain and feel that these devices will not help their students learn. However, the corrective feedback provided by these CBI packages and devices affords a form of teaching that traditional instruction is unable to match unless one-to-one instruction is provided. For example, the computer makes no judgment of the individual, just the mistake. Also, the student has a chance to correct the work before anyone can call attention to the fact that an error was made. MacArthur (1988) states that there is need for more development in the educational use of these instruments, because they were primarily designed for business uses. However, many students seem to make advances in spelling and grammar skills based on these devices. Just being reminded that a word is misspelled is often impetus enough to seek the correct spelling. Additionally, these checkers do not correct mistakes. Rather, for the most part, these devices only call attention to the mistake and ask the student to make corrections. Even when the checker provides a list of possible corrections, the learner still has to choose the right one and this in and of itself becomes a learning experience.

FrED Writer, by CUE SoftSwap (1986), is an example of a prompted writing program. With *FrED Writer* a teacher can develop a series of questions or prompts to guide the student through the development process of a writing project. The students are unable to change the prompts during their session. Additionally, the prompts do not have to print out with the paper. Therefore, by looking at the final paper no one can tell that the student was prompted through the writing stage. This type of program is good for individuals who have poor organizational skills or who cannot visualize the steps of development. The prompts take the form of (1) "Tell me about your favorite place," (2) "Tell me what your place looks like," (3) "Tell me what your place smells like," and so on. These prompts can be as detailed as the teacher wishes. The prompts can also occur after a segment of writing and take the form of "Does this paragraph say what you want it to?" Prompting programs used within an effectively developed writing curriculum will provide just the tool needed by many students with disabilities.

Some students have problems getting their thoughts down on paper due to processing difficulties, such as reversals. These students may be helped through the use of talking word processors that speak the letters, words, sentences, and/or paragraphs as they are entered. *Key Talk,* by PEAL Software (1986), and *Dr. Peet's TalkWriter,* by Dr. Peet Software (1991), exemplify this type of software. These programs use a speech synthesizer to "say" the letters or words typed on the computer. Students can hear what they have written as they type, and make corrections. Users of talking software learn to recognize the robotic sounding output from the computer quickly and can often access the feature of the speech synthesizer that speeds up the rate of speech output. The speeded up output sounds like a fast-talking salesman we have all seen and heard in advertisements. This is often disconcerting to the adult personnel in the classroom, but can be routed through headphones in order to lessen the disturbance.

Another group of individuals that may be helped by talking software consists of those who have strong receptive language skills, but may not have adequate spelling and typing skills. A talking word processor may enable these individuals to be more precise in their typing, thereby creating higher quality papers. For these individuals the "spoken word" becomes the source of confirmation that a word is spelled or typed correctly. In these ways talking software, which was originally developed for individuals with visual disabilities, helps individuals with mild disabilities by providing an additional sensory feedback.

Reading

Reading instruction with CBI reading programs offers many advantages over the use of traditional printed materials. The repeated practice required by many individuals with mild disabilities is in itself one of the strong attributes of CBI. That is, the computer is capable of delivering instruction in repeated trials at a pace that is comfortable for the student. During delivery of this instruction the computer is patient and nonthreatening. Therefore, the student is able to practice or review a set of instructions as often and as fast as he or she needs to. This paced practice will build fluency in the identified skills. For example, Jones, Torgesen & Sexton (1987) studied 20 elementary students who were identified as having learning disabilities, using a program from DLM Teaching Resources called *Hint and Hunt II* (1986). This program presented words in text on the screen and "spoke" them in a natural sounding digitized format. In this way the students heard the sounds of various vowels as they moved through the CBI program and thus were able to make more correct choices. These researchers reported significant increases in decoding skills through the use of this program.

Programs are also available to build fluency in letter recognition, letter sounds, sight word recognition, vocabulary, root words/affixes, cloze systems, and comprehension. An example of a program to build fluency in phonological decoding is *Word Munchers,* by MECC (1987). *Word Munch-*

ers is based upon a game format in which students help munchers locate words sounding like the sample, which the munchers then eat. The students have the option of hearing the correct pronunciation of the vowel sound they are working on. The *Edmark Reading Program* from Edmark (1987) is an extensive sight word recognition program that is based upon Edmark's popular printed version. The program uses extensive digitized speech output to guide the student through the lessons.

In the area of reading comprehension there are many programs that utilize various features of the computer to increase comprehension. One of these, *Readable Stories* from Laureate Learning Systems, Inc. (1989), offers combinations of graphics, speech, text, and animation to lead the student through the story. Probes for comprehension are conducted, the student is assessed, and opportunities for review are provided as the student completes sections of the program. As with other areas of Special Education CBI integration, research into the efficacy of reading based CBI is still being compiled. Therefore an increased emphasis on treatment research is needed as teachers include additional CBI in their curriculum.

Math

The appropriate instruction of mathematics with children who have mild disabilities will follow similar patterns to that of reading and writing. That is, the students will require additional trials or repeated practice with a program that addresses as many modes as possible. Therefore, CBI in math instruction will again be only a part of the entire instructional program. The total program will include other parts such as manipulatives that are used in conjunction with the computer to provide input from the tactile/kinesthetic modalities of learning. Although individual programs may not suggest or require the use of manipulatives as enhancements to the program, the teacher needs to plan for their use, especially with younger students.

Although functional skills such as money management and measuring may be the final goal of a mathematics educational plan for students with mild disabilities, several prerequisite skills need to be taught. Matching and sequencing are just two of these skills where CBI can be used to build fluency and mastery. The teacher introduces the skill and then the student uses CBI in combination with other tools, such as manipulatives (colored blocks for matching or counting), for practice toward fluency and mastery. For example, if matching were the concept being taught, the teacher would teach the basic concept and then use programs like *Math Rabbit,* by The Learning Company (1989), *Talking Math and Me,* by Davidson & Associates, Inc. (1989), or *Math Magic,* by Mindplay (1986), to provide guided practice for the student. Manipulatives are used beside the computer to provide additional examples of skill and to facilitate the connection between concrete examples (blocks on the table) and more abstract examples (blocks on the computer screen). The addition of speech output enhances the motivational factors of the program and addresses another learning modality.

As the student progresses from one level of instruction to another additional skills may be addressed within the same program or require the use of more advanced programs. For example, *Talking Math and Me* by Davidson & Associates (1986) addresses shapes, patterns, numbers, and simple addition. After the student masters these concepts he or she can then use *Math Blaster Plus,* by Davidson & Associates, Inc., to practice higher-level skills through fractions and percents.

Some programs are being designed to be comprehensive and include many options that relieve the teacher of additional chores. Such a program is the *DLM Math Fluency Program,* by DLM Teaching Resources (1989). Developed by Dr. Ted Hasselbring of Vanderbilt University, this program provides for the assessment of current levels of achievement, designs an individualized program for the student based upon that assessment, and tracks student performance through the program. The teacher is afforded extensive control of various functions within the program so that she may customize the presentation for each student. The program covers both the elementary and secondary levels of instruction. It is advances in technology such as this that will help individuals with mild disabilities reach their full potential.

Problem Solving and Critical Thinking

Software designed to enhance the problem solving skills of individuals with mild disabilities is available in several formats and for all age levels. For younger students, *LogicMaster,* by Dunamis, Inc. (1990), is a program in which students are guided with feedback and clues to a solution of a problem. *Memory Machine,* by Sunburst Communications (1989), uses gears, pulleys, trolleys, and levers in a concentration type game to improve memory and problem solving skills. As students master memory and deduction skills they can move on to programs like *Factory,* by Wings for Learning, Inc. (1989), which requires students to use or design a simulated assembly line to create products. A three-stage format is used where, in the discovery mode, the students learn what each machine does. Then, in the "make a product" stage, students design a product using various machines. Finally, in the "challenge" stage, the students match a product designed by the computer. In this stage students have to figure out which machine was used, in what way, and in what sequence. Thus students are led through the process and have to rely on reasoning to reach a solution.

For students with a higher level of skill in problem solving, but who still seem to need additional guidance to correctly identify the solution to problems, programs like *Discrimination, Attributes, and Rules: Second Step in Problem Solving,* by Sunburst Communications (1989), can be the tool they need. This program leads students through scenarios that help develop an understanding of rule meanings and decision making processes and gives practice in applying these skills. Likewise, *Blueprint for Decision Making,* by MCE (1989), is a program designed for secondary students needing high-interest low-vocabulary programming. The students are asked to investigate decision making and the consequences of decisions by examining several scenarios. The correct and incorrect solutions are given and the consequences of each decision are presented. This is one area of instruction that has benefited from advances in hardware capacity because of the enormous amount of information needed to present the scenarios. Again, empirical data to prove the efficacy of this use of CBI is lacking.

EMERGING TECHNOLOGIES

Preschool Applications

There are several areas in which various features of CBI are showing promise. The first of these is the area of preschool instruction. Software designed for the preschool setting is being developed at a rapid rate, and several programs that fall in the category of exploratory play are available now. These programs allow the student to explore various options within the program. *Playroom,* published by Broderbund (1990), is one example of this type of program. With *Playroom* the student is presented with a screen that looks like a playroom. The screen contains several buttons that cause different actions to take place or branch out to other modules within the program. For example, there is a clock on the wall of the playroom and when the student selects the clock he is presented with a subprogram that gives practice in telling time. Other options from the main screen include moving objects on that screen that make sounds. Virtually everything on the main screen causes some kind of action to take place or branches to a subprogram. In this way the student is led through an exploratory play type of environment with many successful experiences.

Another example would be *Millie's Mathhouse,* by Edmark (1992). *Millie's Mathhouse,* as the name implies, is designed to enhance number skills in preschool students. This program is also based upon the exploratory play format. The student has several options right from the start and each choice leads to a different subprogram. An example would be the Shoestore. A student who makes this choice is taken to a shoestore to choose shoes for customers. The customers come in big, little, and medium sizes and the shoes also come in these sizes. When the student makes a choice the computer complies. That is, if the student chooses small shoes for a large customer then the computer shows the large customer with small shoes. Without being told "You are wrong," the student knows that this combination will not work.

These programs utilize a combination of speech output, graphics/animation, and color to provide a motivating presentation for preschool children. From these examples it is easy to see why CBI works so well with preschool individuals who have mild intellectual disabilities. The instructional areas of early learning, discovery, cause and effect, language development, and basic skills are all areas in which CBI enhances educational activities and improves the basic quality of life for preschool children.

Multimedia and Hypermedia

Multimedia is best described as an environment on the computer that allows for mixing various media to make an interactive program for the students (Byrom, 1990). Multimedia is so easy to use that, with little or no formal training, teachers and students across the world are utilizing programs. Common characteristics among multimedia systems include the ability to use text, graphics, sound, animation, and speech output in any combination desired. The typical multimedia screen contains graphics, written information or "text fields," and buttons. The buttons are areas of the screen that allow for selection of subsequent screens; each has an individual function and each is associated with a picture or icon on the screen. Selection of a button causes something to happen on that screen or the computer to branch to another part of the program.

If multimedia is exciting, hypermedia is even more so. To understand hypermedia, one should consider a stack of index cards, with each card in the stack presenting certain information about the topic of choice (Byrom, 1990). In this analogy, a single index card would be the information contained on a single computer screen. Imagine a hypermedia stack where the first card is a map of the United States. The user would use a "button" area on the screen to select the state of choice. The student would then be presented with a map of that state, a brief text about the state, and additional buttons. The buttons on this card might access information about the state, such as the capital city or the major industry. Selection of the button marked "county" would result in a map of the county, with the same buttons on it for further selections.

The choice of some buttons would result in text presentations, whereas others might result in a brief filmstrip or a three-minute video presentation on the computer screen. Whereas multimedia allows for the mixing of different media (e.g., film, text, video, sound) with student selection of the topics to be studied, hypermedia allows teachers and students to create sophisticated "buttons" to interact with the instructional content, as well as more involved branching options.

Another example would be an interactive yearbook where each student's picture is scanned in and biographical information is stored behind different buttons. The possibilities for working with hypermedia are unlimited, and many are just now being discovered. Three of the most used hypermedia authoring systems are *HyperCard,* from Apple Computer (1988), *LinkWay,* from IBM Educational Systems (1989), and *Hyperstudio,* from Hypertech, Inc. (1990). *HyperCard* for the Macintosh computer is the most widely used of the three.

Interactive Videodisc

The third area of interactive technology is videodisc. Interactive video combines the power of the computer with the instantly accessible video segments on the videodisc. Without this option, multimedia is limited to text and graphic presentations. However, multimedia coupled with videodisc technology dramatizes situations. These video segments can be accessed randomly through the CBI program when the student selects a particular button; that is, the computer program controls the videodisc player. The computer program can direct the player to display a single frame on the disk, a motion sequence of up to 30 minutes, or any combination of these. The combination of a well designed program on the computer and video segments become an interactive video program that leads the student through the process of learning. Simulations, which include actual video sequences of real life situations, are at present the most promising uses of interactive video.

For example, workplace behavior may be best taught through experience in the actual workplace. In fact, this is how most of us learn this type of behavior. For many students with mild disabilities, it is sometimes difficult to acquire a skill by being told about it, and any approximation of "real experiences" through videodisc technology tends to enhance their understanding of the workplace. If students with disabilities are given the opportunity to explore the options that face an individual in the workplace in any given situation, they may be able to grasp an understanding of the correct and incorrect decisions and the consequences of those decisions. However, taking each student to the workplace and orchestrating several scenarios would be expensive and time consuming. This is precisely where interactive video can be utilized. A double-sided videodisc containing 1 hour of video sequences or 60,000 still frames can be combined with a computer program to lead the student through several different outcomes.

Imagine the following video scenario: A worker has been partying all weekend and is reluctant to get up Monday morning to go to work. The multimedia program and videodisc technology can present the student with several choices and show the consequences for each decision. Those choices may be to call in sick, get up and get to work on time, or sleep a little longer and get in late. Using this program, the student gets to see the actual situation and participate in the decisions. The student becomes aware of the consequences of various decisions without leaving the classroom.

Interactive video has been integrated into many teaching experiences and the initial research is quite promising (Bottge & Hasselbring, 1993; Hasselbring and Goin, 1989; Langone, 1990). However, additional technologies may enter the educational field soon, the most prominent of which is the compact disk interactive. This technology offers up to 76 minutes of video on a six-inch disk. Using various compression systems, this technology will be able to store even larger amounts of video, film, movies, etc., on smaller disks. The methods of interaction will most likely remain similar to those described above. Technology advances such as these promise to open new frontiers in the education of individuals with mild disabilities.

LIMITATIONS OF CBI

As teachers consider the integration of CBI it must be remembered that CBI is only a tool teachers can use to enhance the learning environment (Caftori, 1994). During the 1980s there seemed to be a feeling that this newly developed technology would provide a panacea for numerous education problems. However, just as it was falsely predicted that filmstrip projectors and television would revolutionize the classroom, the promises of CBI have remained largely unfulfilled. As more research is completed it appears that the use of this technology will reach its full potential as a tool within a well developed instructional environment. The teacher must be well informed about the attributes and possibilities of CBI and then use CBI to maximize those possibilities within the curriculum and in harmony with his or her teaching style. Further, teachers must be cognizant that there is only a small body of empirical data to show what works in the design of instruction to integrate the use of CBI in the curriculum, particularly for students with disabilities (Malouf, Jamison, Kercher, Carlucci, 1991).

THE MATCHING GAME OF SOFTWARE EVALUATION

The Evaluation Process

Every beginning teacher needs some knowledge of how to select appropriate CBI software. Although selection of the computer hardware is usually not under the control of the teacher, many teachers do have the responsibility to select appropriate software for their classes. In order to ensure that the software purchased relates to the needs of the students, teachers must consider numerous aspects of the CBI program.

Proposed software may be evaluated in several ways to determine if it will meet the needs of the students. First, one must understand the difference between external and internal evaluations. External evaluations are those completed by persons outside the teacher's local school. These would include evaluations completed by magazines or journals, computer clubs, professional organizations, software publishers, and computer companies. Many external evaluations are useful in narrowing the field of software in question. However, caution must be exercised when considering the reliability of external evaluations. Some external evaluations may contain evaluator bias. For example, an evaluation written by a software publisher may contain valid information or may be embellished beyond the point of usefulness, since that information is used for sales purposes. Other evaluations, although reporting valid information, may not have included individuals with disabilities in the sample group when the CBI program was developed. These CBI programs, therefore, may not address issues that are a major consideration for students with certain types of disabilities.

With these cautions in mind, some external evaluations merit consideration. Various computer companies have software and curriculum guides that address various curriculum areas and levels of performance. Apple Computer (1994), for example, has several guides that give excellent overviews of many software packages. (You may also call 1-800-600-7808 to request a free disc called *Macintosh Access Passport.*) Also, special-interest group newsletters like *Closing the Gap* provide excellent guides for software acquisition and/or selection.

Internal evaluations are those conducted by someone within the local school. These may be completed by the teacher, other teachers, or a media specialist. This type of evaluation normally contains more detail than external evaluations and is directed at the population in question. It is reasonably easy to develop internal evaluations in an organization and to make these available to various teachers within that organization. Someone, perhaps a media specialist, collects other members' evaluations that have been completed on a standardized form. These evaluations are then made available to other teachers so that everyone interested in a particular CBI package does not have to do an extensive individual evaluation of this software. Rather, a teacher would merely check the evaluations already completed and then determine whether this software meets the particular needs.

The above procedure is recommended as an efficient method of evaluating software because most teachers will have neither access to sufficient software titles nor the time necessary to complete adequate evaluations on several CBI programs. Therefore, screening of software prior to a more in-depth evaluation should be accomplished by examining completed evaluations. One may use either external or internal evaluations for that purpose. At the very least such a screening will determine which titles seem to meet the needs of the individuals in question. Such screening involves merely a quick read-through of the available evaluation.

If the screening results are kept in a central place like the media center, this will save time for everyone. Once a teacher screens the available CBI packages, he or she may select a small group of CBI titles to review in depth. These CBI programs should be evaluated in more detail. The detailed evaluation should be completed using an evaluation form that is standard for the organization and addresses the important factors to be considered for individuals with disabilities and nondisabled children.

Several forms are available in the current literature base. Some of these are overly extensive in the factors they evaluate and others are decidedly lacking. The form in Interest Box 7.3 may be used as a guide for the process.

Type of Software and Content

One of the first considerations in software selection is the type of CBI you wish to employ (Clark,

INTEREST BOX 7.3
Software Evaluation Form

Program Name: ______________________________

Publisher: ______________________________

Address: ______________________________

Copyrighted __________ Price __________ Public Domain __________

Shareware __________ Fee __________

TYPE OF SOFTWARE:

___ Drill/Practice ___ Game ___ Tutorial

___ Problem Solving ___ Simulation ___ Other:

HARDWARE REQUIRED:

Computer Type: __________ Memory Needed __________

Peripherals required: ______________________________

Adaptive Devices Supported: ______________________________

Color Required: ______________________________

Color Recommended ? Yes No

----------------- Circle GRADE RANGE estimates -----------------

CONTENT Grade Levels	Pre/K	1	2	3	4	5	6	7	8	9	+
INTEREST Grade Levels	Pre/K	1	2	3	4	5	6	7	8	9	+
READING Grade Levels	Pre/K	1	2	3	4	5	6	7	8	9	+

STATED OBJECTIVES:

1985; Malouf, Jamison, Kercher, & Carlucci, 1991). The type of instruction, content, form of presentation, use of text and graphics, and disability of the student are the most important considerations for selection of software. For example, building number recognition fluency in an elementary student with mild intellectual disabilities requires different software than does improving survival reading skills for a secondary student with moderate intellectual disabilities. Such determi-

BRIEF DESCRIPTION:

MODES USED:

Graphics Sound Text Animation

Other: ____________

Is there a student management component? YES NO

Is there a teacher management component? YES NO

Is Documentation Available? YES NO

Availabe How? ___ PRINT ___DISK

APPROPRIATE FOR WHICH STUDENTS?

LD ED/BD MR P/OHI HI^G SLI OTHER:

COMMENTS:

Inappropriate for: LD ED/BD MIMH MOMH P/OHI

SMH PMH VI HI^G SLI OTHER:

Comments:

nants as age appropriateness, functional skills, learning modality, and adaptations for disability become important here.

Additionally, the format of the material is a consideration (Clark, 1985). As the teacher you will want to note how the material is presented by the software. Does a particular type of reading comprehension exercise meet your students' needs? Are the materials visually pleasing? Are the visual display reinforcements age appropriate? Are the concepts presented one at a time or several together, and does this meet the needs of your students? You will want to consider all of these format questions prior to selection of a particular program (Lee, 1987).

Instructional Presentation

In order to use CBI effectively, part of the evaluation should focus on the instructional presentation (Clark, 1985; Vockell & Mihail, 1993). You need to consider the length of time the instructional sequence takes, and relate that to your scheduling concerns. Consider the motivational aspects of the programs, and the types of reinforcement offered.

You will want to carefully consider the presence of destructors, which are intentionally built into many software programs specifically to hold student interest. Are these "bells and whistles" distracting for your students with learning disabilities or mild intellectual disabilities? What effect do these CBI aspects have on the attention behaviors of your students? Further, it is possible that many of the "high interest" pictures on the display screen may merely confuse certain children with disabilities (Lee, 1987).

Also, you will want to determine what the software program instructs the child to do when an incorrect answer is given. Some programs merely reroute the child's work to include another set of the same problems. However, if the child misses two or three of these, he or she may be stuck in a never-ending cycle of problems that are completed incorrectly. This is potentially very destructive, because the end result is that the student gains a lot of fun and exciting practice completing problems incorrectly. More advanced programs either instruct the child to request assistance from the teacher after several incorrect attempts or branch to a review section on the content in question, rather than merely continue to present problems. All of these features when correctly addressed contribute to the instructional integrity of the CBI package and must be considered in a thorough evaluation.

Technical and Management Aspects

The last major concern deals with the technical and management aspects of the software program (Clark, 1985). Although some programs allow relatively easy entry and exit, other programs require that a student finish an entire lesson or "lose" all of the work that has been completed when the bell rings. Obviously, the more sophisticated programs will allow a student to store partially completed lessons and to start at the point of exit the next time.

A management system that allows the teacher to check daily progress after class is beneficial in tracking student performance. Furthermore, the instructional advantages of daily data-based instruction are apparent, and computers make such instruction quite time efficient for the teacher. Although this feature was not included in many of the earlier software packages, such systems are more frequently included in software today. Data are stored on the number of problems answered, how many correct, and what kind of mistakes, as well as how long the student accessed a certain part of the program, the wait time before response, and various other pieces of information.

Also, the length of time the program takes may be varied by the teacher in some of the more complex software programs. Any managerial aspect that gives the teacher and the student more control is generally more desirable. Some of the control features you will want to look for are length of time given before response, rate of problem presentation, sound on/off, length of flash for flashcard-type presentations, number of problems, number of problems correct before reinforcement, and other conditions that may be peculiar to a given program. In the best CBI programs, these features are under the teacher's control.

Finally, prior to purchasing a software package, make certain you have the necessary hardware compatibility. Printers, voice synthesizers, color monitors, hard disk drives and/or extra disk drives may be required to realize the full potential of particular programs, and it would not be useful to buy a program that has capabilities that go beyond your hardware capabilities.

EFFICACY OF CBI

Some recent research has investigated the types of critical thinking skills and learning strategies that may be effected by CBI (Bottge & Hasselbring, 1993; Goldman & Pellegrino, 1987; Keene & Davey, 1987; Torgesen et al., 1988; van Daal & van der Leij, 1992). For example, Keene and Davey (1987) conducted a research study on computerized instruction using 51 high school students with learning disabilities. The question in this study concerned not only achievement differences, but also differences in the learning processes that may result from CBI usage. The students were randomly assigned to either a computer reading comprehension task or a traditional reading comprehension task. All of the subjects were encouraged to use six critical reading strategies, including looking back over the material, asking questions, saying difficult words to themselves, looking ahead in text, noting underlined text, and making mental pictures to assist comprehension. The results of this study demonstrated no differences in overall reading comprehension and no differences in frequency of use of five of the six strategies. However, students in the CBI group did employ the look back reading strategy more than the students using traditional reading instruction. This type of difference may suggest that CBI encourages development of more appropriate learning strategies even when no differences are apparent in achievement scores.

Lally (1981) conducted a study to determine the effectiveness of CBI in sight word instruction with children with mild intellectual disabilities. Two groups of students were used, with 8 students in each group. The 8 students in the CBI group were instructed using a computer program that included presentation of the words and assessment. The 8 students in the control group received traditional instruction in recognition of sight words. There was no attempt to equate the length of instructional time between the groups, and this is one drawback of the study. Lally explains this by stating that the research was intended to determine the effectiveness of CBI as a supplement to, rather than as a substitute for, traditional instruction. The results did indicate that the number of sight words recognized by the CBI group increased from 38 to over 70; recognition by the traditionally instructed group increased from 38 to 47. This is a clear difference favoring the use of CBI to supplement traditional instruction.

Related research has suggested other tentative answers concerning the efficacy of CBI. For example, one issue concerned the use of the computer essentially to replace the teacher. In other words, should computers be used for the entire instructional process, as was done in the Trifiletti, Frith, and Armstrong (1984) study, or should this technology be used merely as a supplement to the instruction the teacher provides? The results presently available may be used to argue for either position, though the best results seem to be obtained when CBI is used as a supplement to traditional instruction provided by the teacher (Lieber & Semmel, 1985).

Another question of concern is the relationship between CBI and the attitudes of the students toward schoolwork (Lieber & Semmel, 1985; Keene & Davey, 1987). For example, in the Keene and Davey (1987) study reviewed above, the CBI group and the traditional instruction group were required to complete an attitude survey, and the results demonstrated that the CBI group demonstrated a stronger desire to repeat the learning task than did the traditional instruction group. There was no difference in two other attitude variables. This type of attitude result may reflect the novelty of the CBI experience compared to traditional instruction (Lieber & Semmel, 1985), and conclusions regarding effectiveness of CBI on changing attitudes toward instruction must remain tentative for the present.

Summary of Research Results

As we have seen, the first type of research on efficacy of CBI dealt with effectiveness of CBI on achievement outcomes or product variables. Most of this research was concerned with effectiveness of guided practice tasks, though certain studies used combinations of the several types on CBI instructional activities, and most of the research demonstrated positive results. The early studies also suggested that computers may be best used to supplement traditional instruction.

The more recent studies have asked more complex questions, dealing with process variables or how students complete a task. Also, attitudes toward schoolwork have been investigated, and although some positive results in each area have been noted, the research is still very tentative. In total, although initial results look promising, much more research is needed.

PROBLEMS IN IMPLEMENTATION OF CBI

Several problems have been noted anecdotally in the literature (Caftori, 1994; Cosden & Abernathy, 1990; Goldman & Pellegrino, 1987). First, scheduling computer time is a major concern, and careful thought must be given to various methods of making computer time accessible to all of the students in your class. In some cases, teachers may group several students together at the computer, though the effectiveness of CBI used in this fashion has not yet been determined (Cosden et al., 1987).

Next, research has not yet answered questions completed regarding the effectiveness of CBI on learning strategies and automaticity (the ability to complete problems with relatively little cognitive energy—automatically). Careful attention should be given to the software characteristics that may impact on learning strategies. Also, as a beginning teacher, you will want to keep informed about further research on the effectiveness of CBI in developing these higher-level cognitive processes.

As noted earlier, some programs reprogram themselves in response to an incorrect answer from the child and present another problem of the same type. You must make sure that the software you use does not do this more than several times because practicing incorrect answers is detrimental to learning (Goldman & Pellegrino, 1987). The program should instruct the child to request assistance from the teacher when several problems are completed incorrectly.

Finally, the game format of many drill and practice programs may have negative affective consequences for children with disabilities (Goldman & Pellegrino, 1987). Care should be taken to assess the student's affective response to CBI, and game CBI formats should not be used with students who consistently respond negatively to them.

COMPUTER MANAGEMENT

Grade Management Capabilities

Certain computer-managed instructional programs are capable of managing the instruction of entire elementary classes, such that daily grades, test grades, homework grades, and quizzes are programmed into the computer memory and the six-week grade is generated. Certain programs give the teacher the option of assigning a different weight to each grade so that daily grades count less than unit test grades when figuring the average. Finally, certain programs will also allow the elementary or secondary teacher to compare all of the students to the class average.

In some programs assessment scores may be programmed in, such that the computer knows what actual questions were missed, and prints out a list of objectives the student should master for those questions. Although many of the class-grade management functions of computer software may be unnecessary for the special education teacher because of small class size, this last function is very helpful when compiling recommended goals and objectives for an IEP. Generally, the goals and objectives for the commercially available computer packages are written to be comparable to IEPs that are generated by hand.

IEP Management Capabilities

Generally, use of the computer to generate IEPs is relatively straightforward. You will be expected to conduct formal and informal assessments of the student in order to identify specific areas that should be included on the IEP. Then you will check specific objectives or sets of objectives from the master list. The master list of objectives is a list of all of the objectives in the computer program in each academic and social area. Most IEP programs include such a master list and some of these may be quite comprehensive, including social skills, study skills, functional skills, self-help skills, and academic skills in each area of the curriculum. You turn in the checklist for the student to the secretary and that person programs the information. The computer then prints an IEP with only those objectives from the master list you have selected.

However, there are IEP programs that use a format that allows for more complete individualization of the IEP. An example of this type of program is the *PennStar* program by the Pennsylvania Department of Education (1986). *PennStar* allows the development of objectives by choosing an objective stem (e.g., "will be able to identify color red"); then adds conditions ("independently, without prompt"); then adds schedule of evaluation ("daily, weekly"); and finally adds the method of evaluation ("teacher observation"). The completed objective is then added to the IEP for printing. Because the various parts of the objective are chosen from menus with several choices, the resulting objective can be extremely individualized. In this fashion the teacher can enjoy the benefits of computer generation of IEPs and still not have to settle for a "canned" IEP.

As a special education teacher, you will be exposed to these types of reports and IEPs at some point. Even if your school system does not yet use the computer for IEP preparation, you may get a transfer student who has such a report in his or her file. Therefore, you should be aware of some of the advantages and disadvantages of computer-managed instructional programs designed to produce these reports.

One obvious advantage is the time savings involved in writing out each assessment report, each goal, and each objective. Many special education teachers complain of the time it takes to prepare IEPs well, and the computer, if used appropriately, can save a great deal of time over having to write out a long list of objectives by hand.

Next, computer formats may serve to "remind" teachers to assess and write objectives for areas that would otherwise be overlooked. For example, a standard IEP format already programmed into the computer may list objectives in social and affective areas that may be included in the student's IEP, and the presence of these objectives may encourage teachers to include them where applicable.

However, as is often the case, this advantage may turn into a disadvantage. Overinclusion of very minor concerns on the IEP may encourage some teachers to de-emphasize more important objectives, and even when the teachers do exercise initiative in selecting those objectives on which to concentrate, the teachers themselves may be evaluated by a supervisor regarding the degree to which every objective on the IEP has been emphasized. The ease of computer-generated objectives for the IEP should not make IEPs prohibitively long and cluttered with minor concerns.

A final disadvantage is the flexibility of computer-generated IEPs. For example, programs such as those mentioned above, which allow the teacher to write a "special objective" for a particular child and add it to the master list of objectives, can result in cluttered IEP objective lists. Other programs do not have that flexibility. Clearly, the more flexible the program, the more useful it is in terms of generating practical, applicable IEPs, but teachers should realize that more objectives do not necessarily result in better IEP development.

Computer-Managed Assessments

Several of the commonly used tests in special education have computer-generated assessment reports in which the test administrator merely inputs the student's scores, and a 5- to 10-page assessment report is written. Some of these packages include specific goals and objectives, whereas others merely report the score comparisons in the different cognitive and academic areas. Other programs, such as *Sheri,* by Performance Monitoring Systems (1989), can assist the teacher in tracking student's behavior. This program will provide the teacher with graphs of student progress in either academic or behavior domains. We can expect to see more of this type of program in the future as programmers begin to take advantage of the additional power offered by the new generation of computers.

SUMMARY

The unique features of computer-based instruction that enhance the educational process for individuals with mild disabilities have been discussed in detail. As discussed, many concerns about access for individuals with mild disabilities can be addressed through the built-in adaptations of newer computers. There are also a number of external devices that adapt the input or output of the computer to meet the needs of these individuals. Additionally, software programs now include more of the features that address the needs of individuals with disabilities.

The successful use of CBI in various special education domains has been illuminated. These domains include reading, writing, math, pre-vocational, and other functional areas. It is clear from the discussion on the effective integration of technology into the curriculum that teachers must have an understanding of appropriate software evaluation procedures. The software must be evaluated to assure that it is able to meet the needs of the students. Also, many aspects of a software package make it applicable to the education of students with disabilities. Therefore, the best way to assure an appropriate evaluation is to use a form as a guide.

Most of the research on CBI has demonstrated the effectiveness of this technology, but not all of the research results are positive. CBI seems to be most effective when used as a supplement to traditional instruction provided by the teacher. As a teacher, you will want to be familiar with future research on the effectiveness of CBI and appropriate uses in your classroom.

Computer-generated IEPs do help with the time-consuming work of writing goals and objectives, and many school districts are employing computers in this capacity. You should be aware of both the advantages and the disadvantages of these IEP generation programs, and remember to never let the computer program generate anything but the most individualized and appropriate IEP for the student.

Summary Points

- Computer-based instruction has been proven effective in increasing student's performance on academic tasks.
- Computer-based instruction has many unique features that enhance the educational process.
- Computer-based instruction provides various input/output modes to meet the needs of students with disabilities.
- Software is advancing in quality and sophistication.
- Current thinking on software classification is leaning toward a system based on the four stages of learning: acquisition, fluency, mastery, and generalization.
- Emerging technologies such as preschool applications, hypermedia, and laserdisc programming promise to bring new capabilities to the classroom teacher.
- Software evaluation is a skill that every computer user needs to acquire.
- Although efficacy studies on computer-based instruction report successful integration results in most areas, there is still a need for expanded research on its applicability for students with disabilities.
- Computer-based management is an area of application that is still developing and promises to provide teachers with powerful tools as the power of new machines is tapped.

QUESTIONS AND ACTIVITIES

1. Check the local school districts in your area and identify as many different types of computer-generated IEPs as you can. Are those local districts using the same program? What computers are they using?
2. Search the professional journals and identify as many studies as you can that employed comprehensive CBI packages rather than merely drill and practice. How many of these studies used children with disabilities?

3. What cautions can you identify in generalizing research results on CBI use from populations without disabilities to groups with disabilities?
4. Identify the five types of CBI and describe the rationale for use of each type.
5. Compare the elementary and the special education resource class in terms of CBI needs. What setting characteristics suggest different CBI needs?
6. Find studies in the professional literature that assess the effectiveness of tutorial CBI packages. Why are these studies so few?
7. Interview several local school principals and find out which teachers obtained microcomputers first in the local schools. Does a pattern emerge? Why?
8. Among local school districts in your area are there any that utilize some of the new technologies, such as hypermedia and/or interactive videodisc? Are those districts also heavily invested in the integration of CBI?
9. How many colleges and universities in your area offer programs in the integration of special education technology? How extensive are those programs?

REFERENCES

Apple Computer, Inc. (1994). *Apple Computer's Disability Resources.* Dallas, TX: Apple Computer, Inc.

Apple Computer, Inc. (1988). *HyperCard* (computer program). Cupertino, CA.

Attainment Company (1988). *Survival Signs Program* (computer program). New York, NY.

Bottge, B. A., & Hasselbring, T. S. (1993). A comparison of two approaches for teaching complex, authentic mathematics problems to adolescents in remedial math classes. *Exceptional Children, 59,* 556–566.

Broderbund (1990). *Playroom* (computer program). San Rafael, CA.

Byrom, E. (1990). Hypermedia (multimedia). *Teaching Exceptional Children, 22* (4), 47–48.

Caftori, N. (1994). Educational effectiveness of computer software. *Technological Horizons in Education Journal, 22* (1), 62–65.

Chiang, B. (1986). Initial learning and transfer effects of microcomputer drills on LD students' multiplication skills. *Learning Disability Quarterly, 9,* 118–123.

Clark, F. L. (1985). Evaluation of software for handicapped students. *Learning Disabilities Focus, 1,* 50–59.

Cosden, M. A., & Abernathy, T. V. (1990). Microcomputer use in the schools: Teacher roles and instructional options. *Remedial and Special Education, 11* (5), 31–38.

Cosden, M. A., Gerber, M. M., Semmel, D. S., Goldman, S. R., & Semmel, M. I. (1987). Microcomputer use within micro-educational environments. *Exceptional Children, 53,* 399–409.

CUE SoftSwap (1986). *FrED Writer* (computer program). Los Angeles, CA.

Davidson & Associates, Inc. (1986). *Talking Math and Me* (computer program). Torrance, CA.

DLM Teaching Resources (1986). *Hint and Hunt II* (computer program). Allen, TX.

DLM Teaching Resources (1989). *Math Fluency Program* (computer program). Allen, TX.

Dr. Peet's Software (1991). *Dr. Peet's TalkWriter* (computer program). San Diego, CA.

Dunamis, Inc. (1990). *LogicMaster* (computer program). Suwannee, GA.

Edmark (1987). *The Edmark Reading Program* (computer program). Redmond, WA.

Edmark (1992). *Millie's Mathhouse* (computer program). Redmond, WA.

Goldman, S. R., & Pellegrino, J. W. (1987). Information processing and educational microcomputer technology: Where do we go from here? *Journal of Learning Disabilities, 20,* 144–154.

Goldman, S. R., Semmel, D. S., Cosden, M. A., Gerber, M. M., & Semmel, M. I. (1987). Special education administrators' policies and practices on microcomputer acquisition, allocation, and access for mildly handicapped children: Interfaces with regular education. *Exceptional Children, 53,* 330–339.

Graham, S., & MacArthur, C. (1988). Improving learning disabled students' skills at revising essays produced on a word processor: Self-instructional strategy training. *Journal of Special Education, 22* (2), 133–152.

Hannaford, A. (1987). Microcomputers are powerful learning tools with proper programming. *Teaching Exceptional Children, 14* (2), 54–56.

Hasselbring, T., & Goin, L. I. (1989). Enhancing learning through microcomputer technology. In E. A. Polloway, J. R. Patton, J. S. Payne, & R. A. Payne (Eds.), *Strategies for Teaching Learners with Special Needs* (4th ed., pp. 147–164). Columbus, OH: Merrill.

Howell, R., Sidorenko, E., & Jurica, J. (1987). The effects of computer use on the acquisition of multiplication facts by a student with learning disabilities. *Journal of Learning Disabilities, 20,* 336–341.

Hudson, P., Lignugaris-Kraft, B., & Miller, T. (1993). Using content enhancements to improve the performance of adolescents with learning disabilities in content classes. *Learning Disabilities Research and Practice, 8* (2), 106–126.

Hypertech, Inc. (1990) *Hyperstudio* (computer program). St. Paul, MN.

IBM Educational Systems (1989). *LinkWay* (computer program). Atlanta, GA.

Jones, K. M., Torgesen, T., & Sexton, T. (1987). Using computer-guided practice to increase fluency in learning-disabled children. A study using the Hint and Hint I program. *Journal of Learning Disabilities, 20,* 122–128.

Kascinski, S. T., & Gast, D. L. (1993). Computer-assisted instruction with constant time delay to teach multiplication facts to students with learning disabilities. *Learning Disabilities Research and Practice, 8* (3), 157–168.

Keene, S., & Davey, B. (1987). Effects of computer-presented text on LD adolescents' reading behaviors. *Learning Disability Quarterly, 10,* 283–290.

Lally, M. (1981). Computer assisted teaching of sight-word recognition for mentally retarded school children. *American Journal of Mental Deficiency, 85,* 383–388.

Langone, J. (1990). *Teaching Students with Mild and Moderate Learning Problems.* Boston, MA: Allyn & Bacon.

Laureate Learning Systems, Inc. (1989). *Readable Stories* (computer program). Winooski, VT.

The Learning Company (1989). *Math Rabbit* (computer program). Freemont, CA.

Lee, W. W. (1987). Microcomputer courseware production and evaluation guidelines for students with learning disabilities. *Journal of Learning Disabilities, 20,* 436–438.

Lieber, J., & Semmel, M. I. (1985). Effectiveness of computer application to instruction with mildly handicapped learners: A review. *Remedial and Special Education, 6* (5), 5–12.

Littauer, J. (1994). A "How to . . ." on using courseware in the classroom. *Technological Horizons in Education Journal, 2* (1), 53–54.

MacArthur, C. (1988). The impact of computers on the writing process. *Exceptional Children, 54* (6), 536–542.

Malouf, D. B., Jamison, P. J., Kercher, M. H., & Carlucci, C. M. (1991). Integrating computer software into effective instruction. *Teaching Exceptional Children, 23* (3), 54–56.

McDermott, P. A., & Watkins, M. W. (1984). Computerized vs. conventional remedial instruction for learning disabled pupils. *The Journal of Special Education, 17,* 81–87.

MCE, Inc. (1989). *Blueprint for Decision Making* (computer program). Kalamazoo, MI.

MECC (1991). *The Oregon Trail* (computer program). St. Paul, MN.

MECC (1987). *Word Munchers* (computer program). St. Paul, MN.

Mindplay (1986). *Math Magic* (computer program). Tucson, AZ.

Montague, M., & Fonseca, F. (1993). Using computers to improve story writing. *Teaching Exceptional Children, 25* (4), 46–49.

PEAL Software (1986). *Key Talk* (computer program). Calabasas, CA.

Pennsylvania Department of Education (1986). *PennStar* (computer program). Philadelphia.

Performance Monitoring Systems (1989). *Sheri* (computer program). Cambridge, MN.

Perry, M., & Garber, M. (1993). Technology helps parents teach their children with developmental delays. *Teaching Exceptional Children, 25* (2), 8–11.

Sunburst Communications (1989). *Memory Machine* (computer program). Scotts Valley, CA.

Sunburst Communications (1989). *Discrimination, Attributes, and Rules: Second Step in Problem Solving* (computer program). Scotts Valley, CA.

Torgesen, J. K., Waters, M. D., Cohen, A. L., & Torgesen, J. L. (1988). Improving sight-word recognition skills in LD children: An evaluation of three computer program variations. *Learning Disability Quarterly, 11,* 125–132.

Toucan Software (1988). *Big Book Maker* (computer program). Fairfield, CT.

Toucan Software (1988). *The Creative Writing Series* (computer program). Fairfield, CT.

Trifiletti, J. J., Frith, G. H., & Armstrong, S. (1984). Microcomputer versus resource rooms for LD students: A preliminary investigation of the effects on math skills. *Learning Disability Quarterly, 7,* 69–76.

van Daal, V. H. P., & van der Leij, A. (1992). Computer based reading and spelling practice for children with learning disabilities. *Journal of Learning Disabilities, 25,* 186–195.

Varnhagen, S., & Gerber, M. (1984). Use of microcomputers for spelling assessment: Reasons to be cautious. *Learning Disability Quarterly, 7,* 266–270.

Vockell, E. L., & Mihail, T. (1993). Instructional principles behind computerized instruction for students with exceptionalities. *Teaching Exceptional Children, 25* (3), 39–43.

Wings for Learning, Inc. (1989). *Factory* (computer program). Scotts Valley, CA.

CHAPTER 8

READING RECOGNITION INSTRUCTIONAL STRATEGIES

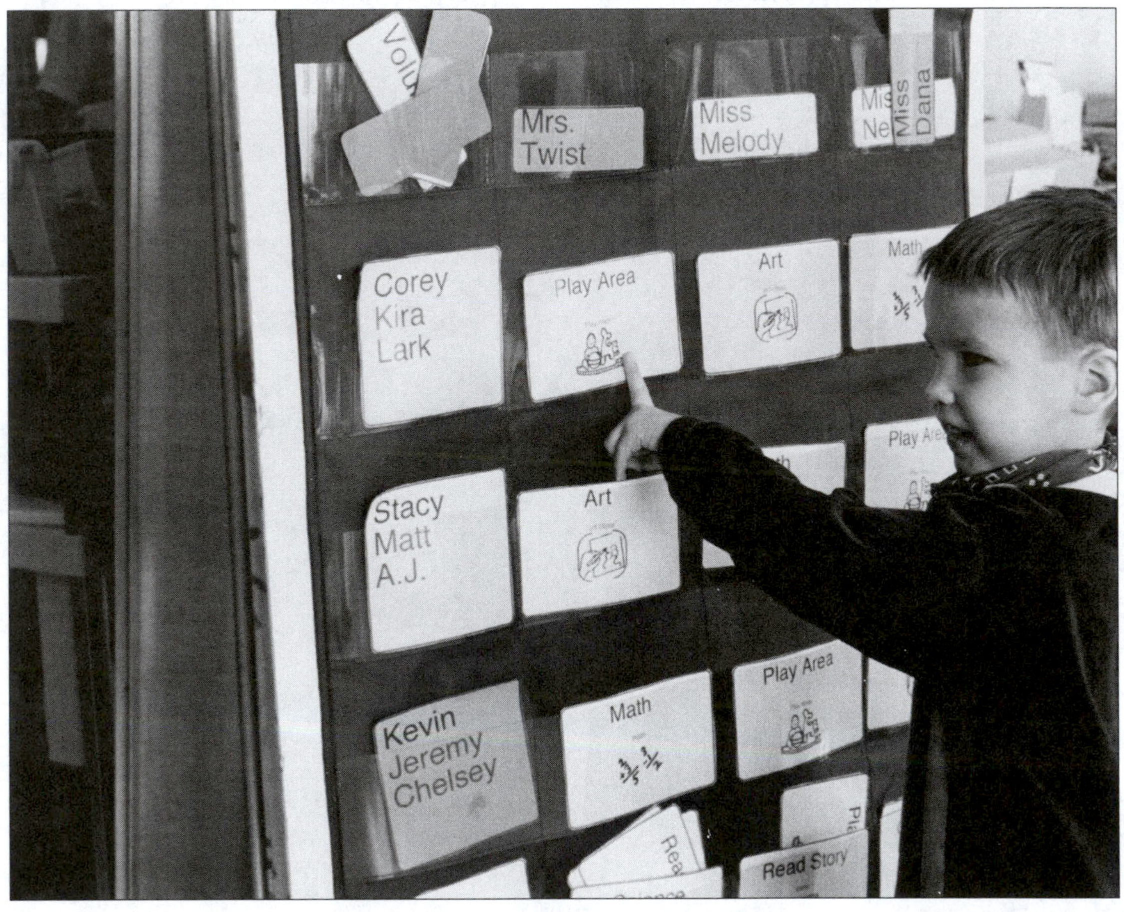

OBJECTIVES

When you complete this chapter, you should be able to:

1. Describe a language experience instructional approach and contrast that to a basal reading instructional approach.
2. Describe several word comprehension strategies.
3. Identify the types of decoding skills necessary in identification of unknown words.
4. Describe one metacognitive method for decoding content words in upper grade levels.
5. Describe a word bank instructional approach.
6. Compare and contrast the efficacy of phonics instruction and sight word instruction.
7. Describe a whole language approach to reading instruction.

KEYWORDS

paired associate learning	decoding	syllabication
configuration clues	sight words	structural analysis
context clues	picture fading	patterned language
language experience	word bank	cloze procedure
story starters	Fernald Method	DISSECT
basal	VAKT	*Edmark*
whole language	phonics	rebus

Reading instruction tends to take up a great deal of the instructional time in many special education classes. Needless to say, reading is also very prevalent in inclusive classes. Even more than math and language arts—the other basic skill instructional areas—reading is an essential skill and, as such, has been the focus of a great deal of research over the years.

Many of the fundamental questions concerning reading instruction have been addressed. What is the most appropriate method of reading instruction: phonics or sight word? Does pairing of pictures and words assist students in learning new words? What types of metacognitive strategies facilitate word recognition and word comprehension? These and other research questions have been addressed over the years, and this research will be reviewed as a backdrop for discussion of the teaching strategies in the last sections of the chapter.

This chapter presents numerous instructional methods based on this body of research. The relative effectiveness of phonics instruction, as compared with instruction in sight words, is presented as a historical review of many of the research issues. Next, two different instructional approaches used in mainstream and special educational classes are presented: basal instruction and language experience instruction. Then strategies for word recognition and word comprehension are presented.

PHONICS OR SIGHT WORD INSTRUCTION

Phonics Instruction

Historically, there have been two different approaches to instruction in reading (Ross, 1976). Phonics involves instruction in sound–symbol relationships such that the student is expected to master the names and various sounds of the letters in the alphabet prior to mastery of a wide variety of words. First, the consonants are taught, and then short vowel sounds are generally introduced. Simple words that follow certain pronunciation rules are then introduced. For example, in a consonant–vowel–consonant word, the vowel sound is usually short (cat, bed, him, etc.). During this phase, initial and final consonant sounds are stressed, and emphasis on consonant–vowel–consonant, silent "e" words (e.g., cape and bake, where the silent "e" controls the vowel sound, usually making it a long vowel sound) and consonant blends (ch, sh, th, etc.) comes next. Interest Box 8.1 presents several general pronunciation rules, though one must remember that these rules are not universally applicable.

Mastery of such sound–symbol relationships enables a student to decode, or decipher the sound of, unknown words that appear in the reading material. Theoretically, by production of the various sounds and application of certain pronunciation rules involving syllabication, the student should be able to produce a reasonable likeness for an unknown word. If the student's receptive vocabulary included the word, then the production of a reasonable likeness should trigger memory of the correct pronunciation of the word.

The obvious advantage in this method of instruction is the ability to decode new words in a text that have not been explicitly taught. When trained in this method, students have a tool that can unlock new doors of meaning in difficult texts. However, a major disadvantage of this approach is the irregularity of many words in the English language. (Approximately 15 percent of the English words are irregular in that they do not follow a predictable pattern of pronunciation.) Consequently, knowledge of phonics will not typically help with these words.

Another disadvantage is the use of letters with multiple sounds (e.g., *g* and *c*), which are very confusing for many beginning readers. Each of the sounds must be taught, and this can become quite laborious.

Finally, instruction in phonics may not be appropriate at upper grade levels. Phonics instruction is typically included during the first three grade years in basal readers and spelling texts, and is usually dropped after that in order to move on to more complex word attack skills, such as syllabication rules. However, in some special education classes, one can find instructional activities on final consonants and consonant blends during the junior high school years, and no research has demonstrated the effectiveness of phonics at that late period in a student's schooling. Although phonics is effective in the early years of school for nondisabled students, no research has demonstrat-

INTEREST BOX 8.1
Pattern Word Structures

1. In vowel–consonant words, the vowel sound is usually short (e.g., *at, in, on, am*).
2. In consonant–vowel–consonant words, the vowel sound is usually short (e.g., *cap, bat, dad, ham*).
3. In consonant–vowel–consonant, silent "e" words, the vowel sound is usually long (e.g., *cape, came, game, role*).
4. In two-syllable words where each syllable is formed from a consonant–vowel–consonant pattern, the vowel sounds are usually short (e.g., *butter, happen*).

ed its effectiveness during the middle school and/or later years for students with disabilities, even though use of this method during those years is fairly common.

Sight Word Instruction

Early reading scholars identified certain words that seemed to do most of the work in the English language (and, an, the, come, etc.). Mastery of these words at an early age was assumed to give reading students an advantage. The Fry Instant Word List (Fry, Fountoukidis, & Polk, 1985) is one of the better known lists of common available words, though numerous scholars and textbook companies have published other lists of the "most common" words. The first section of the Fry list is presented in Interest Box 8.2.

The sight word approach involved sight memory of whole words, so that a student would be trained in instant recognition of these words. For example, the word "cat" was taught as a whole, without breaking the word into letter sounds. In many instances words were taught by pairing them with pictures that represent them. This method of instruction, referred to as paired associate learning, concentrated on mastery of the basic words used in English, and irregular words were just as easy to master using this approach as more regular words.

Instruction in sight words resulted in mastery of numerous words during the early months of instruction. Also, sight word instruction was usually paired with instruction in configuration clues (drawing boxes around letters in words to concentrate on the shape of the word) and on using context clues (pictures presented in the text, preceding sentences, and other clues from context) to master new words. These techniques, along with a growing vocabulary of words that were explicitly taught, gave the student a method for approaching new words in text.

Another major advantage of the sight word approach is the interdependence between this technique and the use of other reading techniques. For

INTEREST BOX 8.2
Most Common Words: The Fry Word List

the	of	and	a	to	in
is	you	that	it	he	was
for	on	are	as	with	his
they	I	at	be	this	have
from	or	one	had	by	word
but	not	what	all	were	we
when	your	can	said	there	use
an	each	which	she	do	how
their	if	will	up	other	about
out	many	then	them	these	so
some	her	would	make	like	him
into	time	has	look	two	more
write	go	see	number	no	way
could	people	my	than	first	water
been	call	who	oil	now	find
long	down	day	did	get	come
made	may	part	over		

Source: Fry, Fountoukidis, and Polk (1985).

example, attention to context clues is a skill effective readers use at every grade level, and sight word approaches tended to emphasize this skill much sooner than phonics approaches, since phonics instruction would involve large amounts of time teaching the various letter sounds in isolation during the early grades. Further, sight word tasks will enable special needs students to master a variety of techniques such as word configuration, which may then be applied to mastery of other more complex sight words, such as those found on survival word lists ("bridge out," "danger," "inflammable," etc). As Ross (1976) indicated, sight word strategies teach some children to read in the same way that more experienced readers read.

The major disadvantage of this model for reading instruction is that the student is left with a less-than-effective method to attack unknown words in isolation. Clearly, use of the context of the sentence and use of available pictures does not prepare one to decode unknown words as well as extensive knowledge of letter sounds and syllabication rules. Also, the use of the context surrounding the word may not be enough to trigger word recognition and understanding, and context clues—although helpful for detecting the general meaning of a new word—are not terribly useful in decoding the correct pronunciation of new words.

Relative Research Efficacy

The research has demonstrated that phonics instruction is probably the most effective reading instructional technique for most children without disabilities, though careful qualification of this statement is necessary (Ross, 1976). As you may well imagine, a number of variables may indicate growth in reading. For example, the sight word method generally results in mastery of more words during the first two years of schooling than does phonics instruction, because in sight word instruction little time is spent on letter sounds. Consequently, almost all of the reading instructional time is spent in learning new words. However, students without disabilities who are instructed in phonics generally catch up to sight word readers by the end of grade 2, and during later years there is no difference in the number of words recognized. Also, after grade 2, students instructed in phonics generally exceed sight word readers in reading comprehension of unknown text, presumably because of their mastery of techniques that enable them to decode unknown words (Ross, 1976). For this reason, almost all reading materials today emphasize a phonics approach, supplemented by certain sight word activities, and few modern scholars recommend reading instruction that is dependent exclusively on sight words for readers without disabilities.

As a teacher of children with disabilities, you will become painfully aware of the fact that many students with disabilities do not learn using the same methods that are successful with nondisabled students. Although almost all curriculum materials available today present phonics instruction, this method may be inappropriate for some children. Some students with learning disabilities, for example, may require a sight word approach, without a great emphasis on phonics. Likewise, some children with mental retardation may profit from certain sight word techniques that emphasize paired associate learning, as described previously.

It will be your task to identify the appropriate method for reading instruction for every child in your class, independent of the fact that the text materials available to you will probably emphasize phonics most heavily. In that regard, precision teaching procedures will be useful, because, as you recall from Chapter 4, these procedures allow you to follow a student's progress on a daily basis and change techniques when no academic growth is forthcoming.

READING INSTRUCTIONAL SYSTEMS

Basal Reading Instruction

Historically, public schools have used a basal reader as the instructional approach, and this is still the most widely used instructional system in reading. The basal reader approach is dependent on a set of reading texts that are grade appropriate and are usually accompanied by a teacher's manual that lists additional activities. In spite of the fact that many students with disabilities have not succeeded in this type of curriculum, many resource rooms, special education classes, and inclusive classes use this type of reading instructional approach. Although such instruction may be appropriate for some, it is probably inappropriate for others, and teachers are seeking new methods for teaching early reading skills that are not dependent upon the basal reader curriculums.

The heart of the basal reader approach is a set of student tasks designed to promote word recognition and comprehension skills. The activities and the accompanying word lists are usually specific to a particular story. For example, the teacher may introduce a story with certain "interest heightening" questions, designed to arouse the students' curiosity. Next, some type of questioning activity may be undertaken, in which students are encouraged to look at pictures that accompany the text and make hypotheses concerning the topic of the story. At some point prior to reading, new vocabulary words may be introduced. The students then read the story, either individually or in some group format. Postreading comprehension activities are undertaken, either by group questioning and discussion or as individual seatwork assignments. Perhaps the students would be expected to answer questions about the story, or use an encyclopedia to seek further information on the story topic. Finally, some type of test is used to measure student comprehension.

Many modern basal readers apply some of the instructional strategies discussed previously. Many strategies that involve metacognitive planning of educational tasks, such as those discussed in Chapter 5, are found today in basal reading texts. For example, use of advanced organizer questions, or questions read in advance of the story that help the student focus on certain important aspects of the story, represent an attempt to elicit metacognitive planning on the part of the student. The student may then be taught a strategy for self-questioning as he or she reads the story. These strategies for improving reading comprehension are discussed more completely in the next chapter; they are mentioned here in order to give you a complete understanding of the scope of basal reader curricula.

Certain scholars have criticized many basal reading instructional approaches as too inexact for meaningful instruction (Darch & Gersten, 1986). As discussed in Chapter 4, scholars promoting direct instruction indicate that basal reading lessons tend to be initiated with nonspecific interest heightening activities designed to capture the student's curiosity. These scholars have indicated that this type of activity is less effective in promoting reading comprehension than are direct instructional methods (Darch & Gersten, 1986).

One final criticism of the basal reading approach is the relatively static nature of this instructional design. For example, the companies that publish the basal readers generally assume that the vocabulary level of the children in each grade is relatively homogeneous, even though such rigid homogeneity is clearly nonexistent. Also, little use is made of the student's own receptive and expressive language, in spite of the fact that reading is dependent on language usage. This static nature of the basal approach has led several scholars to suggest use of an approach to reading instruction that is much more flexible and adaptable to the child's language level.

The Language Experience Approach

The language experience approach is dependent on the expressive vocabulary of the students to be taught (Fry, 1977; Stauffer, 1970). In this method, a student is encouraged to tell a story about any topic he or she is interested in. In some cases, teachers have used "story starters," interesting pictures or story titles that promote the creative storytelling process. The student is expected to tell a brief story and then write it down. For beginning readers, a one- or two-line story may be considered enough, whereas more experienced readers would write more. The story is not graded; instead, the teacher circles errors that may prohibit other students from understanding the story. Because of the reinforcement of having one's stories read by others, most students will willingly spend the next day trying to correct the errors. The teacher reviews the story with the student and assists in spelling, looking up new words, capitalization, and punctuation. Through several rewrites over several days, the story becomes more and more correct in each of these areas. Once a correct and neat copy is available, the story is added to the student's storybook to become reading material for the student. Students enjoy producing their own "books" and generally enjoy reading books written by others. Figure 8.1 presents a sample language experience story.

There are numerous variations on this instructional idea. Fry (1977) discussed a group activity that used a language experience chart to enable several students to write a story together. The teacher may modify the sentences produced by the students as they are written on the chart. This makes participation of several students possible. Numerous CBI programs are available that will allow for such group writing on the computer. Also, students may "sequence write" a story by selecting teams, each of which writes the next section of a story and then sends it to the next team for preparation of another section.

Several advantages of this instructional approach are apparent. First, the student language level is considered in the reading and language arts instruction. Whereas stories in a basal reader may be too advanced for some students in the class, the language experience approach puts each student in the position of writing his or her own reading material. Second, there are motivational advantages to reading material that is self-produced. Finally, unlike the basal approach, which concentrates exclusively on reading, the language experience approach concentrates on all forms of language arts in a holistic fashion. Students are trained to see the value of correct spelling and skills such as capitalization, because these skills are necessary in order to allow others to read and understand the stories the student wants to share with his or her peers.

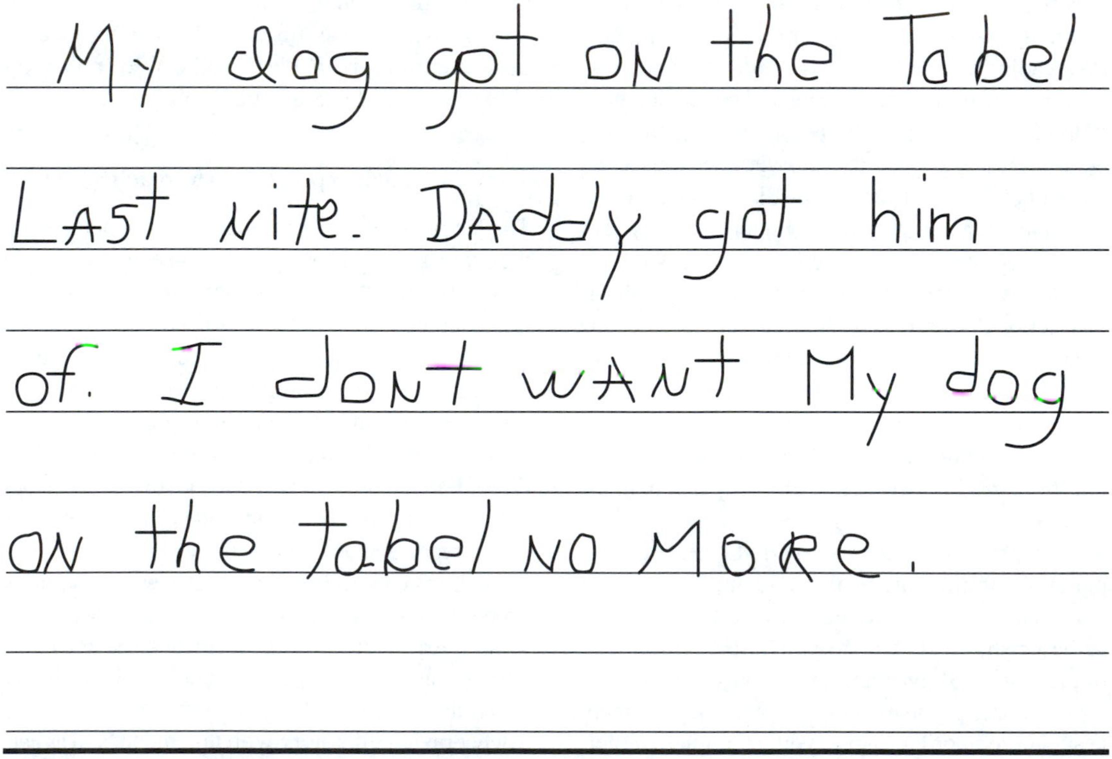

My dog got ON the Tabel
LAst Nite. DAddy got him
of. I doNt wANt My dog
ON the tabel NO MoRe.

FIGURE 8.1 Language Experience Story

One major disadvantage of the language experience approach is the fact that no text materials are available. Although this may sound like an advantage to some, the fact is that completion of a basal reader is one indication of successful progress in school over the year, and most principals would not consider writing several storybooks indicative of reading progress. Also, teachers seem to prefer completion of the activities in the basal readers rather than the unknowns of planning successful language experience reading classes. Some teachers indicate that the language experience approach is more difficult than other approaches. Still, many elementary teachers and special education teachers include language experience reading approaches in their total reading curriculum.

Whole Language Approach

A more recently developed approach used in many inclusive classrooms is the whole language approach (Mandlebaum, Lighthouse, & Vandenbrock, 1994; Stull, 1992; Wilde, 1992). In this reading instructional approach, the emphasis is on reading for meaning, as opposed to performance of reading, phonics, and/or language arts exercises. The major concern is that students begin at the earliest age possible to understand that reading and language arts skills are, in reality, methods of communication (Altwerger, Edelsky, & Flores, 1987; Wilde, 1992). This method thus features the use of real literature rather than basal reading stories that have been intentionally constructed for teaching purposes. Again, the emphasis is on the intentional nature of reading, that is, reading in order to understand something, and only in that context are specific skills such as decoding, phonics, and syllabication presented.

Perhaps an example is in order. Chow, Dobson, Hurst, and Nucich (1991) offered the following suggestions for conducting a whole language reading lesson. First, the "shared" nature of the reading experience is emphasized by having many students read the story and retell it. Students should be encouraged to compare their reading understandings between themselves, and perhaps act out parts of the story. The teacher should encourage elaboration of material, including elaborations from the various versions of the story. Finally, the "theme" or lesson of the story should be highlighted in order to emphasize to the students that writers write for a specific purpose—to communicate a specific message.

Obviously, this type of "reading for meaning" instruction tends to break down the traditional barriers between reading instruction, speaking, communication skills, writing instruction, and language arts instruction. Goodman (1986) suggested that students should be encouraged to dictate stories they create to an adult, and then use those stories for reading and language arts instruction. Another technique involves structured silent reading activities, in which students are guided by a study guide. Subsequent to the reading activities, reading conferences are held to ascertain that the student has understood the material. Similarly, Hetfield (1994) described the formulation of a student newspaper in order to practice writing skills. She also indicated that such a practical activity tended to build self-esteem and helped to motivate students with mild disabilities.

Numerous researchers have suggested a combined approach that incorporates whole language instruction and certain other methods (Chiang & Ford, 1990; Mather, 1992). For example, Chiang and Ford (1990) suggested that this emphasis on whole language be used in a combination approach with direct instructional practices such as those discussed in Chapter 4. Such a combined approach would allow teachers to focus on the functional holistic aspect of reading in their instructional practices, while simultaneously providing for instruction on specific skills when necessary. Chiang and Ford's (1990) guidelines for implementation of a whole language approach are presented in Interest Box 8.3.

Numerous curriculum materials and instructional techniques associated with the whole language approach are becoming available (Chow et al., 1991; Stull, 1992; Wilde, 1992). For example, Stull (1992) uses pictures of animals, and the young learners' natural curiosity about animals, to

INTEREST BOX 8.3
Implementation of Whole Language Programs

1. Read aloud to students regularly.
2. Devote a few minutes each day to sustained silent reading.
3. Introduce students to predictable books with patterned stories.
4. Use writing activities that provide opportunities for the teacher to model writing strategies and skills.
5. Include journal writing as part of the students' individualized educational programs.
6. Provide meaningful printed materials in the instructional setting (e.g., simplified dictionaries, categorized lists of words).
7. Establish a network to communicate with other teachers using holistic techniques in working with students with learning problems.

Source: Chiang and Ford (1990).

initiate reading instruction coupled with simple language arts activities and art activities. The children are encouraged to color and cut out various pictures of animals. Wilde (1992) recommends numerous spelling and punctuation activities for whole language instruction.

In addition to the "teacher idea" books discussed above, several reading instructional programs are currently on the market, including *Learning Through Literature* (Dodds & Goodfellow, 1991) and *Victory!* (Brigance, 1991). However, there is very little literature on the efficacy of these programs, or indeed, efficacy for the whole language approach itself. Although many teachers who attempt this type of instructional approach for students without disabilities seem to love it, evidence that shows the efficacy of whole language instruction for students with disabilities is particularly difficult to find. Consequently, caution in implementation of this reading and language arts instructional approach for children with mild disabilities is certainly in order.

STRATEGIES FOR WORD RECOGNITION

Understanding words in reading material is fundamental to the overall goal of comprehending the meaning of the reading material. Consequently, many strategies for teaching word decoding, word attack, and word comprehension have been proposed. This section presents the strategies whereby word attack skills may be taught. Suggestions for including the strategy in the planning and organizational framework discussed in earlier chapters are also included.

Sight Word Recognition

Some strategies do not involve decoding or "sounding out" unknown words. As previously mentioned, these strategies are commonly referred to as sight word strategies because of the historical relationship with early sight word approaches to reading instruction. Use of word configuration is one example that has already been discussed.

Picture Fading. The paired associate method discussed earlier involved pairing a picture and a word together. Picture fading is built on this concept but goes one step further by fading the picture out gradually over time (Corry & Shamow, 1975; Dorry, 1976; Knowlton, 1980). The picture fading technique usually involves a series of cards with a word–picture pair on each card. The cards may then be placed on a board to which several pieces of translucent plastic are attached. The plastic allows the teacher to cover the picture without covering the word. The teacher asks the child to pronounce one of several such words and then covers the picture associated with each word with one sheet of plastic. This plastic partially fades the picture, and after several pieces of plastic cover the picture, it will fade entirely from view. This allows the teacher to gradually fade out the pictures, as dictated by the student's instructional responses. Complete fading usually takes five to seven trials. This approach could easily be paired with precision teaching, discussed in Chapter 4, to chart the student's acquisition of new vocabulary words over time.

Picture fading techniques work best with lower-level words during the early grades, though this technique may be appropriate for content pictures in upper grade levels. Obviously, nouns are easier to "picture" than other types of words, but a creative teacher may find interesting ways to draw certain action words. Many teachers apply this technique by drawing or locating pictures of common household and classroom objects and then making picture fading cards for them. For a particular student on a particular day, the assignment may require that he or she complete 5 different cards.

Word Bank Instruction. Many teachers use a word bank, in which 5 to 10 unknown sight words are utilized every day. Generally, the teacher begins by having the student read a sight word list. The teacher marks the errors and stops reading when 10 words are marked. This list is dated and filed, and will be used as an informal assessment measure for future reference. The 10 unknown words become a part of the child's word bank. The words are written on cards and placed in a word can or folder for the child to use each day. On some days the child merely writes each word several times and reads these to the teacher. On other days, the child may look up the words, use them in sentences, use them in a story, locate them in a story he or she is reading, or any other activity that involves each of those 10 words.

After about two weeks, the student will be able to read these words with very little problem. At that point, the student is told to take the words home and share them with his or her parents. The word list is utilized again, and another 10 words are selected for the word bank. At the end of the year, the student will have learned a large number of new words, and the teacher will be able to show the word list, which indicates specifically the vocabulary level of the child at the first of the year, and the succeeding mastery of various groups of words throughout the year, to the parents. Parents generally respond quite favorably to specific evidence of academic growth, such as that represented by this word list. Interest Box 8.4 presents a list of other activities that may be used to master the words that have been in the word bank during the year.

Precision teaching provides one of the best methods for monitoring progress on sight word recognition for word bank activities. Such a project is presented in Interest Box 8.5.

Functional/Survival Words

Some words are essential for survival and functional living. Words such as "bridge out" or "men's

INTEREST BOX 8.4
Activities for Word Bank Words

1. Look for words that have the same spelling.
2. Look for words that rhyme.
3. Look for words that may mean the same thing (i.e., synonyms).
4. Write words on cards and play a "dominoes" game by matching the first two or the last two letters of each word.
5. Categorize words by their type: nouns, pronouns, verbs, etc.
6. Have students write stories together using all of their words.

INTEREST BOX 8.5
Precision Teaching Project on Sight Word Recognition

This describes a precision teaching project used to monitor sight word recognition. This type of project works well, regardless of the specific types of activities the child uses each day to study his or her words from the word bank. First, as described in text, the teacher should identify only those words the child does not know. Approximately 10 words should go in the word bank. In order to get an accurate count on reading rate for the 10 words in the word can, the teacher must prepare a reading sheet that lists those ten words in random order, with each word listed at least 12 times. This should provide enough words for the child to be able to continue reading through a one-minute timing. After the child's word bank activity for the day is finished, the teacher and the child sit together and, at the beginning of the timing period, the child begins to read the words. During this see-to-say activity, the child reads as many words as possible in one minute. Words read correctly and errors are counted and charted; the teacher should mark corrections and errors on another sheet.

After the child reaches the goal, the teacher may wish to change words. If a word has proven to be particularly hard, it may be kept, along with nine new words. Remember that each change of words should be indicated as a phase change line on the precision teaching chart. You may wish to review Chapter 4.

room" certainly serve to make life safer and more comfortable. Therefore, there is some justification for teaching these words as instant sight recognition words, even though they are considerably longer that the words that comprise most sight word lists. In some cases, students with disabilities who did not read above a first or second grade level have performed well, indeed saved lives in life and death situations, because the teacher had taught certain survival skills words to those students. Interest Box 8.6 presents a selection of the most common survival words (Fry, Fountoukidis, & Polk, 1985). Generally these are taught using the same techniques discussed above for other sight words.

Fernald Method

The Fernald method (Fernald, 1943) is a whole word identification method that uses visual, auditory, kinesthetic, and tactile sensations to teach students to read and write words. Sometimes this method is referred to as the VAKT method. It involves a series of activities that includes writing a word in sand (to get the sense of movement and of touch), tracing the word, saying the word, hearing the word, and eventually writing the word from memory. The process is long and laborious, but research has demonstrated the effectiveness of this method for some readers with moderate to severe reading problems (Thorpe & Borden, 1985). Interest Box 8.7 presents the types of activities included in the Fernald Method.

Linguistic Approach

In the linguistic approach, words composed of similar phonemes are introduced together, often before the student is expected to do any reading. The approach was first introduced by Bloomfield and Barnhart (1961) for students who had failed in the basal approach. Generally, words of a consonant–vowel–consonant pattern are introduced first (cat, bat, hat, etc.). Also, words that emphasize a short vowel sound pattern are introduced before words that include long vowels. This grouping of words allows the student to detect the patterns and similarities between words.

INTEREST BOX 8.6
Selected Survival Words

acid	alarm	blasting	exit	caution
combustible	danger	dispensary	do not drink	warning
don't walk	electrical	elevator	entrance	taxi
explosives	fire escape	first aid	flammable	hospital
keep off	keep out	no admittance	notice	one way
out of order	perishable	poison	private	railroad
stop	telephone	warning	tow away zone	

Source: Fry, Fountoukidis, and Polk (1985).

INTEREST BOX 8.7
Activities Recommended by Fernald during Initial Mastery of New Words

1. Elicit student's commitment to learn.
2. Have the student select a new word to learn.
3. Write the word on a 4" x 11" card and say the word as you write it. When you finish, say the word again as you move your fingers over the letters.
4. Model tracing the word as you say the word. Say the word in parts as you trace it, without sounding out the individual letters. The sound should be a natural approximation of the actual sound of the word.
5. Have the student trace the word, saying it. Stop the student if an error is made.
6. Have the student continue to say the word while tracing it until it is learned, and the child can write the word from memory.
7. Add the word to the word file.
8. Have the student type the word in order to establish a link between the written word and the typed word.

During later stages of this activity, the student learns the new words without tracing them and, finally, without having them written on a word card.

Source: Fernald (1943).

Corrective Feedback

Finally, corrective feedback on oral reading errors can improve a student's word recognition skills. As you may recall from the chapter on direct instruction, corrective feedback that is immediate can improve a child's academic performance on many tasks. Pany and McCoy (1988) utilized this principle of corrective feedback by having the teacher immediately correct any oral reading errors the student made. The teacher correctly said the word and the student repeated it correctly. This resulted in fewer oral reading errors on reading recognition than the no feedback condition.

The meaning of this type of research is clear for the teacher; when a student does not know a word, the teacher should tell the student the word and have the student repeat it. The teacher may also make a note of the word and review those words with the student after the lesson.

WORD ATTACK STRATEGIES

Because of the regularity of word pronunciation in English, and the general rules of word formation, several specific word attack skills can be of benefit in decoding new words. In addition to the phonics skills mentioned previously, these include skills in structural analysis and syllabication. The techniques described below may be of benefit for some of the children in your special education resource class or inclusive classroom.

Syllabication

The ability to divide a long word into syllables enhances a student's ability to read unknown words. Such division often enables a student to apply phonics skills to each syllable separately. A number of syllabication rules are generally applicable, and may be taught as general guidelines. Although no single set of rules is comprehensive enough to cover every situation in English, several of the most common rules for syllabication are presented in Interest Box 8.8.

Syllabication skills are generally taught using these general rules. One may think of them as a metacognitive strategy that enables a student to recognize the likely positions of syllables in words. Instruction would proceed, as described in Chapter 5, by eliciting cooperation, modeling the rule application with known words, application to unknown words, and daily checks of progress. The creative teacher may find some acronym to represent each of these rules. Use of a direct instructional approach would also be of benefit in teaching these general rules.

Structural Analysis

For students beyond grade 3, the use of structural analysis of words is recommended. Structural analysis involves specific instruction in the ability to recognize prefixes, suffixes, and root words, and may be considered a form of syllabication since many prefixes and suffixes form separate syllables. For example, the word "playing" looks considerably longer and more complicated to many second graders than the more common word "play." Identification of the suffix syllable "ing" will aid in recognition of the word.

There are some suffixes and prefixes that are not separate syllables, such as the suffix "s," often used to make a noun plural. Interest Box 8.9 presents a list of the most common prefixes and suffixes in English (Fry, Fountoukidis, & Polk, 1985).

Teaching the most common prefixes and suffixes will thus assist in the overall reading performance

INTEREST BOX 8.8
Common Syllabication Rules

1. When two consonants come between two vowels, as in *hammer* and *slumber,* divide the word between the two consonants: *ham/mer, slum/ber.*
2. When a single consonant comes between the two vowels, divide the word after the first vowel: *be/gan.*
3. When a word ends in a consonant followed by *le,* as in *table,* the final syllable is made up of the consonant and the *le: ta/ble.*
4. Generally, multiletter suffixes are syllables by themselves: *head/ed, load/ing.*

Source: Portions of these guidelines were taken from Rude and Oehlkers (1984).

for most students. Various strategies may be used in which prefixes and suffixes are taught. Interest Box 8.10 presents a worksheet that uses a visual scanning technique to identify prefixes and suffixes. Completion of this type of worksheet on a daily basis would result in a total number of corrects and errors that could then be plotted on a precision teaching chart for evaluation of the student's performance.

Gillingham–Stillman Method

The Gillingham–Stillman Method (Gillingham & Stillman, 1973) is based on the work in language development done by Orton (1937). This approach is a highly structured, phonetically oriented reading program that incorporates multisensory instruction similar to the Fernald Approach discussed above. The method involves repeated associations between the look and speech production of a word. Also, a key word is used to represent each of the initial letter sounds ("fun" for "f," etc.). Ten letter sounds are introduced initially and once these are mastered simple words using those sounds are presented. This method has been criticized for being overly rigid, though research has supported use of this method with very low level readers.

INTEREST BOX 8.9
Common Prefixes and Suffixes

Prefixes	Meaning	Suffixes	Meaning
in, en,	into or not	er, or	action or actor
re	again	tion, sion	action taken
de, dis	from, away	ble, able,	capable of being
ex	out of	ment	result of action
con	together	ic, ics	pertaining to
pro, pre	before	ous, ious	full of, alike
di	double	s, es	more than one
	to separate		

Source: Fry (1977).

INTEREST BOX 8.10
A Visual Scan Worksheet for Locating Prefixes/Suffixes

Directions: You should look at each word, identify the prefix or suffix, and circle it.

helping	draw	load	predate	women
used	helped	biparty	remove	prewash
working	inside	beside	proactive	inform
school	restless	schooled	pencil	pencils

This listing could continue, including more advanced suffixes and prefixes. Also, a worksheet such as this would be appropriate for use on a timed precision teaching task in order to document mastery of suffixes and prefixes.

WORD COMPREHENSION

Whereas the techniques reviewed earlier concentrated basically on recognition of words, the following techniques address the issue of word comprehension in text. In some of the strategies, correct pronunciation of the word is not addressed, because this skill is seen as less important than deriving meaning from the word in context. There are numerous methods that address word comprehension. Some of these are useful for lower level readers in the earlier grades, whereas other techniques may be used in higher grade levels in subject content areas.

Comprehension for Lower-Level Readers

Rebus Approach. The rebus approach to reading and word recognition involves substitution of pictures for words in sentences to be read. Eventually, the word will be placed in the sentence in addition to the picture, and the picture dropped. Note that this is another form of paired associate learning. The correct word identification is facilitated by teaching the use of picture clues that accompany each stimulus. Figure 8.2 presents several examples of rebus word sentences. Note that the number of rebus words and the percentage of rebus words to printed words in a sentence may vary.

Many parents may recall use of this approach with their own children during preschool reading at bedtime. This is an effective technique for students, even before they have been introduced to the alphabet, and many books are available to parents in toy stores that utilize this approach.

Patterned Language. The patterned language approach involves use of the metacognitive strategy of prediction in the story (Bridge, Winograd, & Haley, 1983). The teacher reads the material and invites students to join in at any point where they can predict what may come next. The reading materials are structured to be highly predictable and numerous opportunities are provided for teachers and students to read together. Also the materials incorporate various picture cues that the students are encouraged to interpret, as the reading lesson progresses.

One major advantage to the patterned language approach is the dependence on the types of reading skills that successful readers in the higher grades use. For example, successful readers become increasingly proficient at interpretation of context and picture clues. Also, the concept of pre-

FIGURE 8.2 Rebus Sentences

dicting the next sequence of events in the story is a metacognitive reading comprehension technique used in numerous reading programs, and early practice at this skill is certainly useful. Interest Box 8.11 presents several types of activities that have been incorporated into the patterned language approach.

Word Comprehension Techniques for Older Readers

Cloze Procedures. A cloze procedure is a structured fill-in-the-blank activity that emphasizes word comprehension and context clues. The semantic and syntactic clues aid in selection of the correct term. In some cases, every content word in a particular sequence is omitted, and the student's task is to complete the reading section by filling in the blanks. Teachers may structure a cloze procedure from almost any reading section by selecting every seventh word (omitting words such as "a" "and" and "the"), and deleting them. The prepared reading selection should be checked to assure that the blanks may be completed by use of the available clues. This activity can easily be modified in inclusive classes for low level readers, merely by providing a "word list" from which the correct terms may be selected. These terms would then be matched to the particular blanks by the students. As you may imagine, an activity of this nature, completed every day during a particular unit of instruction, would quickly yield information on the student's progress in building the vocabulary for that unit. Again, the daily scores for corrects and incorrects may then be charted using a precision teaching approach, in order to demonstrate progress.

This type of activity is frequently used in late elementary and higher grades to teach vocabulary particular to the subject area. Historically, this technique has been used to assess reading comprehension, though comprehension of words in text may be a more accurate description of this particular skill.

A Word Identification Learning Strategy. As discussed in Chapter 5, the University of Kansas researchers have produced a number of learning strategies that stress metacognitive approaches to various learning situations. The DISSECT strategy (Lenz, Schumaker, Deshler, & Beals, 1984) was developed to enable secondary students to identify the meaning of unknown words in text. This strategy would be presented to the students in the same fashion as discussed in Chapter 5, including presentation of the strategy, modeling, teaching of known words, applying the strategy to unknown words, and generalization of the strategy. Interest Box 8.12 presents the steps in the DISSECT strategy.

INTEREST BOX 8.11
Steps in a Patterned Language Approach

1. Read the story aloud. Reread, inviting the students to join in when they know what will come next. Have students read the book together.
2. Put the text on large paper. Read the story and then have the students read it chorally. Give the students sentence strips from the story and have them match the strips to the story chart.
3. Give the students word cards and have them match those to the words in the story.
4. Chorally read the story from the chart.

Source: Bridge, Winograd, and Haley (1983).

INTEREST BOX 8.12
The *DISSECT* Learning Strategy

D = Discover the word's context. Reread the sentence before and after the word. Look at the pictures.
I = Isolate the prefix. Look for common prefixes the student already knows.
S = Separate the suffix.
S = Say the stem. See if the stem is recognizable in isolation (without prefix or suffix).
E = Examine the stem. If the stem is not immediately recognizable, the student may have to sound it out, or at least sound out the pronounceable parts.
C = Check with someone. If the student has some idea of the word, he or she should check that out.
T = Try the dictionary. If a student has no one to ask, or if that person doesn't know, the dictionary should be referred to.

Source: Ellis (1994).

Information on learning strategies is available from a large variety of sources. See Alley and Deshler (1979); Clark, Deshler, Schumaker, Alley, and Warner (1984); Ellis and Sabornie (1986); Lenz and Hughes (1990); Lenzo, Schumaker, Deshler, and Beals (1984). Training in the learning strategies approach is available through the University of Kansas, Lawrence, KS.

INSTRUCTION IN READING RECOGNITION

Instructional Ideas for Word Recognition

1. These activities may be used for words in a word bank. You may have the student write a short story using each word or use the words in a series of sentences the teacher has prepared (based on a fill-in-the-blank type of activity). Also, the child may be encouraged to write the words on the chalkboard and draw boxes around each letter. Discuss the shape of the word.
2. Using a dictionary is cumbersome, but students can learn a large set of vocabulary words in that fashion. You should have dictionaries that are appropriate for your grade level instruction (e.g., first grade dictionaries, elementary dictionaries).
3. Students can learn vocabulary words by seeking words in a story. Discuss with the students which definition is used in that story.
4. A word notebook can help students master particular vocabulary terms that are new to them. They keep a notation of each time they see a word in reading. You may then have students call out their words to each other, and suggest to each other various ways to remember words.

Commercially Available Curriculum Materials

Edmark Reading Program. The *Edmark Reading Program* (Bijou, 1977), is designed to teach 150 sight words and various suffixes such as "ing," "ed," and "s." The materials include 227 lessons that involve direct instruction principles. Generally, new words are introduced two at a time, and activities involve matching words and pictures, oral reading, and match to sample tasks. Research has demonstrated the effectiveness of this material with very low level readers, but the time commitment for mastery of 150 sight words may be excessive for students who can learn the words more quickly using other methods. Nevertheless, this set of materials is quite popular and you may find an *Edmark* program in your classroom during your first year of teaching.

DISTAR. The *DISTAR* program (*Direct Instructional System for Teaching Arithmetic and Reading,* Engelmann & Bruner, 1974), is a direct instructional approach to word attack that involves basic phonics decoding skills, sound blending skills, and rhyming tasks. The lesson formats usually involve 30-minute daily lessons for small homogeneously grouped learners. The manual specifies the teacher's instructional statements and possible responses from the students, as discussed in Chapter 4. Immediate feedback and corrective procedures are included in every lesson format. This material is quite popular and found in many special education classes.

Corrective Reading. The *Corrective Reading Program* (Engelmann et al., 1978) incorporates the same components of direct instruction as the *DISTAR* program. This program is geared to remedial work with older students in grades 4 through 12, and emphasizes both decoding and comprehension. This set of materials presents 340 lessons in three levels of skill development.

Peabody Rebus Reading Program. The *Peabody Rebus Reading Program* (Woodcock, Clark, & Davis, 1979) includes three programmed workbooks and several readers that employ rebus words to teach a sight vocabulary of 120 of the most common words. This material is designed to prepare a child for the premier level of reading in traditional basal reading programs.

CBI MATERIALS

Computer-Based Instructional Programs

Reader Rabbit. *Reader Rabbit,* by the Learning Company, is a mastery practice program that builds early reading skills for short pattern words. Emphasizing the CVC pattern, one option is the "sorter" program, in which a mallet on the screen pushes out the words one at a time and if the newly presented word matches the stimulus word, the student is to select that word. Pacing can be varied by pressing a number during program selection. Also, the teacher can adjust the response time to between 1 and 5 seconds. The program is appropriate for students ages 5 to 7. Reinforcement (in the form of the rabbit dancing) is offered when the student correctly selects five words, though the teacher doesn't have control over the level of reinforcement offered.

First Letter Fun/Phonics Prime Time. MECC produces a number of high quality phonics programs. In *First Letter Fun* students select initial consonants and short vowels in a number of different types of activities. In the Circus activity, the student must select the correct letter for the initial consonant in the word "tiger." Each program offers several teacher options, and students' performance data can be reviewed on screen or printed out. These software packages use only a few commands and those are relatively consistent from one program to the next. This software is somewhat older, and this company has established a good reputation in the industry.

SUMMARY

This chapter presented a brief review of the reading research in the areas of phonics and sight words. Although most of the educational materials in use today rely predominately on phonics, almost all of the materials do include some "whole word" or "sight word" techniques. As a teacher of children and youth with disabilities, part of your responsibility is to select a method of instruction to which the individual students respond positively. Consequently, it is not enough for you to merely teach each student in your class from the available curriculum materials. Rather, you must carefully select the reading strategies that work for particular students. In inclusive classrooms the mainstream member of the co-teaching team will typically look to the special education person (i.e., you!) to make selections for students with disabilities and other slow readers in the class.

Some students may learn best using exclusively a sight word and context clue approach, whereas others may need only phonics instruction coupled with syllabication and structural analysis rules. Your task is to individually teach each student in the manner most appropriate for that person. Daily curriculum based assessment and precision teaching progress charts will assist you in forming an effective instructional plan for each student.

The chapter reviewed two traditional approaches to reading instruction, the basal approach—by far the most common—and the language experience approach. As a special education teacher, you may wish to combine these approaches in order to maximize each student's reading progress. A more recent approach—the whole language approach—was also discussed.

Finally, the most commonly used strategies for word identification and comprehension were presented. You may find any or all of these strategies in use in a particular school system. Also, the media center in most schools has many of these materials available for you to use on a short-term basis. Over the first several years of teaching, you should try to utilize as many of these methods as possible in order to find out which methods seem to fit best with your individual teaching style and the needs of your students. As indicated in the discussion, any of these methods may be readily adapted in the organizational framework described earlier for resource, self-contained, or inclusive classrooms.

Summary Points

- Historically sight word instruction and phonics instruction were the two methods used to teach word recognition.
- Research has shown that most students without disabilities respond most favorably to phonics and most reading programs today emphasize that approach. However, this general conclusion may not apply to students with disabilities, and certainly will not apply to all of your students.
- The basal reader approach is the basic instructional approach used today to teach reading. However, the language experience approach may offer several advantages for reading instruction for many children with disabilities.
- Sight word instructional strategies are quite common in many curriculum materials. These include context clues, word configuration, and other strategies.
- The whole language instructional approach has captured the attention of numerous researchers and teachers, but there is currently little evidence that supports use of this instructional approach for children with mild disabilities.
- More sophisticated sight word approaches have been devised, including picture fading, word bank activities, the Fernald Method, the linguistic approach, and corrective feedback.
- A number of word attack strategies utilize phonics and other "rule based" instructional approaches for vocabulary development. These include study of syllabication rules, structural analysis, and the Gillingham–Stillman Method.
- Word recognition and word comprehension are not necessarily the same skill. Two methods of study are used for word comprehension for young readers: the rebus approach and patterned language.
- Word attack strategies for more mature readers include cloze procedures and a learning strategy called *DISSECT.*
- In inclusive classrooms the special education teacher will typically be expected to initiate individual reading programs for students who do not seem to learn in the same fashion as the other students.

QUESTIONS AND ACTIVITIES

1. Describe the steps in teaching a learning strategy such as the *DISSECT* strategy.
2. Check the curriculum laboratory in your school or college of education. Do you have access to *DISTAR, Corrective Reading,* the *Peabody Rebus Reading Program,* or other materials mentioned in this chapter? Check these out and present the materials to the class.
3. Review the research on the effectiveness of the Gillingham–Stillman method. Present a brief summary to the class.
4. This chapter presented various ideas for using precision teaching strategies. Can you think of others? Write a brief description of these examples and share these with the class.
5. Select a secondary history text or science text and prepare a cloze procedure for use with a particular unit.
6. Review the research on picture fading. Can you think of useful methods to utilize this strategy?
7. Describe a direct instructional approach to word identification. What components of the direct instructional theory are incorporated into this approach?
8. If a laboratory placement is available to you, use the language experience approach for several days with a low-level reader. Do you notice any motivational advantages associated with this approach? Share your impressions with the class.
9. List the advantages and disadvantages of phonics and sight word instruction.

REFERENCES

Altwerger, B., Edelsky, C., & Flores, B. M. (1987). Whole language: What's new? *The Reading Teacher, 41,* 144–154.

Bijou, S. W. (1977). *Edmark Reading Program.* Bellevue, WA: Edmark.

Bloomfield, L., & Barnhart, C. L. (1961). *Let's Read, a Linguistic Approach.* Detroit: Wayne State University Press.

Bridge, C. A., Winograd, P. N., & Haley, D. (1983). Using predictable materials vs. preprimers to teach beginning sight words. *The Reading Teacher, 39,* 884–891.

Brigance, A. H. (1991). *Victory!* East Moline, IL: Linguisystems.

Chiang, B., & Ford, M. (1990). Whole language alternatives for students with learning disabilities. *LD Forum, 16* (1), 31–34.

Chow, M., Dobson, L., Hurst, M., & Nucich, J. (1991). *Whole Language Practical Ideas.* Markham, Ontario: Pippin.

Corry, J. R., & Shamow, J. (1972). The effects of fading on the acquisition and retention of oral reading. *Journal of Applied Behavior Analysis,* 5, 311–315.

Darch, C., & Gersten, R. (1986). Direction-setting activities in reading comprehension: A comparison of two approaches. *Learning Disability Quarterly,* 9, 235–243.

Dodds, T., & Goodfellow, F. (1991). *Learning through Literature.* Chicago: Science Research Associates.

Dorry, G. W. (1976). Attentional model for the effectiveness of fading in training reading-vocabulary with retarded persons. *American Journal of Mental Deficiency, 81,* 271–279.

Engelmann, S., & Bruner, E. (1974). *DISTAR: An Instructional System.* Chicago: Science Research Associates.

Engelmann, S., Johnson, G., Hanner, S., Carnine, L., Meyers, L., Osborn, S., Haddox, P., Becker, W., Osborn, W., & Becker, J. (1978). *Corrective Reading Program.* Chicago: Science Research Associates.

Fernald, G. (1943). *Remedial Techniques in Basic School Subjects.* New York: McGraw-Hill.

Fry, E. B. (1977). *Elementary Reading Instruction.* New York: McGraw-Hill.

Fry, E. B., Fountoukidis, D. L., & Polk, J. K. (1985). *The New Reading Teacher's Book of Lists.* Englewood Cliffs, NJ: Prentice-Hall.

Gillingham, A., & Stillman, B. W. (1973). *Remedial Training for Children with Specific Disability in Reading, Spelling, and Penmanship.* Cambridge, MA: Educators Publishing Service.

Goodman, K. S. (1986). *What's Whole in Whole Language.* Portsmouth, NH: Heinemann.

Hetfield, P. (1994). Using a student newspaper to motivate students with behavior disorders. *Teaching Exceptional Children, 26* (2) 6–9.

Knowlton, H. E. (1980). Effects of picture fading on two learning disabled students' sight word acquisition. *Learning Disability Quarterly, 3,* 88–96.

Lenz, B. K., Schumaker, J. B., Deshler, D. D., & Beals, V. L. (1984). *The Word Identification Strategies.* (Learning Strategies Curriculum). Lawrence: University of Kansas Press.

Mandlebaum, L. H., Lighthouse, L., & Vandenbrock, J. (1994). Teaching with literature. *Intervention in School and Clinic, 29* (3), 134–150.

Mather, N. (1992). Whole language reading instruction for students with learning disabilities: Caught in the cross fire. *Learning Disabilities Research and Practice, 7,* 87–95.

Orton, S. T. (1937). *Reading, Writing, and Speech Problems in Children.* New York: W. W. Norton.

Pany, D., & McCoy, K. M. (1988). Effects of corrective feedback on word accuracy and reading comprehension of readers with learning disabilities. *Journal of Learning Disabilities, 21,* 546–550.

Ross, A. O. (1976). *Psychological Aspects of Learning Disabilities and Reading Disorders.* New York: McGraw-Hill.

Rude, R. T., & Oehlkers, W. J. (1984). *Helping Students with Reading Problems.* Englewood Cliffs, NJ: Prentice Hall.

Stauffer, R. G. (1970). *The Language-Experience Approach to the Teaching of Reading.* New York: Harper & Row.

Stull, E. S. (1992). *Alligators to Zebras! Whole Language Activities for the Primary Grades.* West Nyack, NY: Center for Applied Research in Education.

Thorpe, H. W., & Borden, K. F. (1985). The effect of multisensory instruction upon the on-task behavior and word reading accuracy of learning disabled students. *Journal of Learning Disabilities,* 18, 279–286.

Wilde, S. (1992). *You Kan Red This! Spelling and Punctuation for Whole Language Classrooms: K–6.* Portsmouth, NH: Heinemann.

Woodcock, R. W., Clark, C. R., & Davis, C. O. (1979). *Peabody Rebus Reading Program.* Circle Pines, MN: American Guidance Service.

CHAPTER 9

READING COMPREHENSION

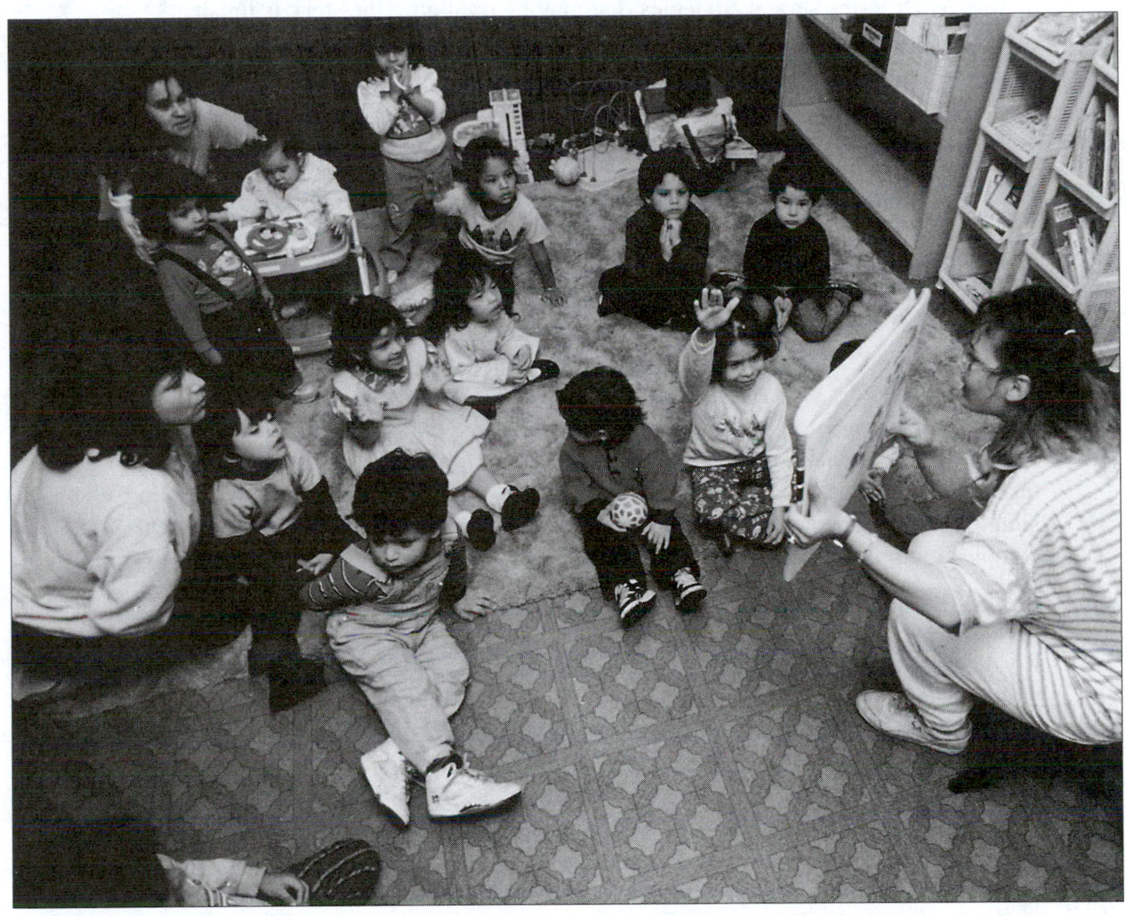

OBJECTIVES

When you complete this chapter, you should be able to:

1. Describe several metacognitive strategies that may be used to increase reading comprehension.
2. Identify a learning strategy that is utilized before reading the story to improve comprehension.
3. Describe reciprocal teaching.
4. Describe a story frame.
5. Describe a text structure strategy.
6. Describe several strategies that may be used after the story is finished to improve comprehension.
7. Describe the different skills involved in reading comprehension.
8. Describe the different methods whereby reading comprehension is typically measured.
9. State four general guidelines to be used when selecting a reading comprehension improvement method for a particular child.
10. Identify several advanced reading comprehension improvement techniques for use with older students in the upper grades.

KEYWORDS

literal comprehension	advance organizers	reciprocal teaching
inferential comprehension	visual imagery	critical reading
testwiseness	schema	interactive reading
simple multiple choice (SMC)	story map	trait-by-treatment
complex multiple choice (CMC)	story frame	

Reading is the act of searching for and understanding the meaning of the printed or written word. All of the skills discussed previously in this volume that involve word recognition and word comprehension are merely the prerequisite skills for reading. The true meaning of reading is gathering the meaning, or reading comprehension—that is, understanding what is read.

This chapter presents information on reading comprehension skills. A number of different skills are included in reading comprehension, and these will be discussed first. Next, the methods of measuring reading comprehension are presented. Finally, a number of strategies designed to improve reading comprehension are discussed. Although numerous strategies are covered in this chapter, there is such a wide array of available strategies that no single chapter on reading comprehension could include them all. Instead, this chapter gives an overview of the types of instructional ideas and materials available and includes specific suggestions for instructional use of several of the more prominent strategies.

As a special education teacher, you will spend a large percentage of your time involved in reading instruction, either at the elementary level or in secondary subjects. You should be aware of the types of strategies and instructional approaches available for all grade levels. Also, you may wish to undergo additional training in reading comprehension strategies, and further course work in this area is certainly recommended for all special education teachers who deal with instruction for students with disabilities.

READING COMPREHENSION SKILLS

Most scholars involved with studies of reading suggest that a number of different skills are involved in completely comprehending a reading passage. For example, literal comprehension merely involves recall of facts and main ideas whereas evaluation of reading material involves a qualitative judgement of the merits and literary quality of the reading material. Clearly, the latter skill is of a higher order than the former, in the sense that the student must be able to perform the former in order to successfully perform the latter. Consequently, when most scholars speak of comprehension skills, they generally refer to a hierarchy of comprehension skills.

Literal Comprehension

Literal comprehension involves recall of facts from the text; these usually include recall of the main idea and several supporting details. Comprehension questions referring to specific details in the reading material may be considered literal comprehension questions. Likewise, questions that address the main concept of the paragraph, dealing with conclusions directly stated in text, are literal comprehension questions.

This is the first level of comprehension skill, and is a prerequisite for all the higher levels. Because of the basic nature of this level of comprehension, this aspect of comprehension is relatively easy to measure. Any question that refers to the major facts

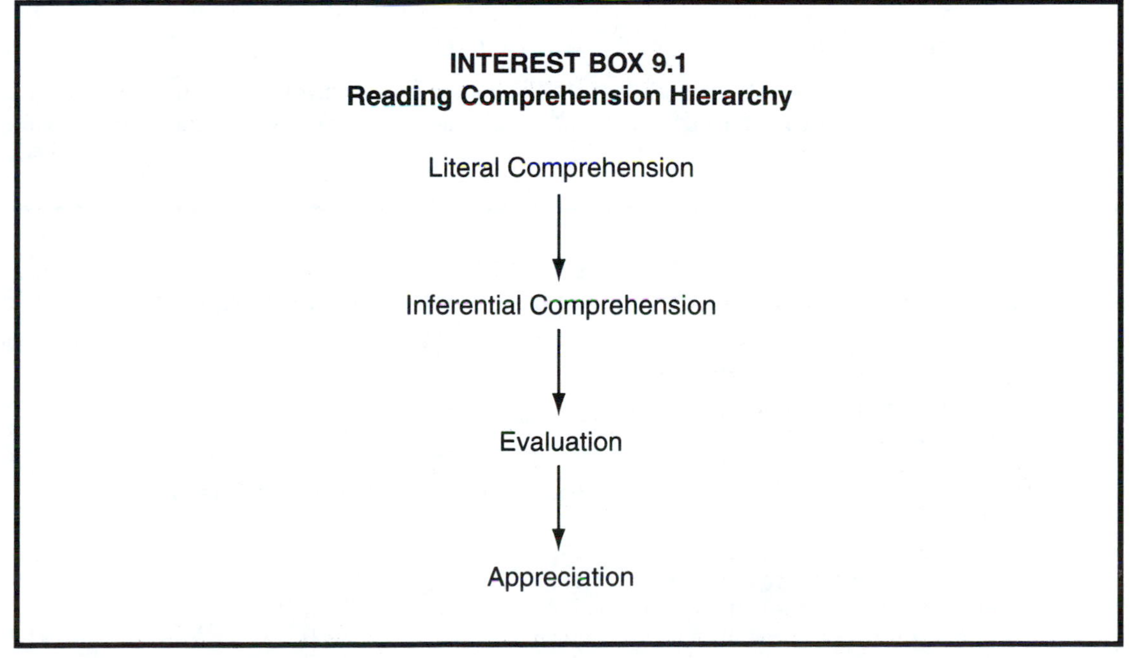

and ideas in a text provides a measure of literal comprehension. Also, because of the ease of measurement, this aspect of comprehension is the most frequently measured on most reading tests. For example, on one of the commonly used reading assessments in special education—the *Peabody Individual Achievement Test, Revised* (*PIAT-r,* Markwardt, 1989)—around 70 percent of the reading comprehension questions are literal comprehension questions (it was 72 percent in the original version of the *PIAT,* Dunn & Markwardt, 1970; Lillie & Alberg, 1986). This test is widely used in special education for reading comprehension assessment.

Finally, a number of strategies are available that increase literal comprehension skills. Because of the low reading level of many students with disabilities, many special education teachers find that they spend a great deal of time using strategies intended to increase literal comprehension. Questioning strategies, advance organizer strategies, and visual imagery are a few of the strategies discussed later in this chapter that improve literal comprehension, though these strategies may improve other areas of reading comprehension as well.

Inferential Comprehension

Inferential comprehension refers to the ability of the student to draw inferences from the text. In many reading situations, a student is required to bring his or her background knowledge into play, along with information provided from the text, in order to understand the true meaning of the story or reading selection. Interest Box 9.2 presents a set of questions or subskills that represent different aspects of inferential comprehension.

As you can see from the subskills listed above, this level of comprehension is dependent on literal comprehension, because it is not possible to draw valid conclusions or inferences from text unless one has understood the text. However, this level of comprehension is relatively easy to measure in a question and answer format, and most reading tests include some measure of this type of comprehension. In many reading assessments used in special education, about one-third of the comprehension questions are inferential questions (Lillie & Alberg, 1986).

Strategies that improve inferential comprehension generally involve stating conclusions not explicitly stated in the text, or prediction of what may come next in a reading passage. Several strategies of this nature are discussed below, including reciprocal teaching and prereading questions.

Evaluation

Evaluation of text involves a higher order set of skills than either literal or inferential comprehen-

INTEREST BOX 9.2
Subskills Representing Different Aspects of Inferential Comprehension

Drawing conclusions not explicitly stated in text
Ability to differentiate fact from opinion
Ability to generalize knowledge gained from text
Ability to predict events that may come next
Making inferences about character or plot
Ability to accurately paraphrase text, or answer questions phrased in a fashion different from the text
Recognition of traits and motivations of characters
Recognition of emotional reactions of characters
Recognition of cause and effect relationships

sion. Evaluation of texts involves detection of the author's purpose, the literary style the author selected, and an ability to qualitatively grade or evaluate the written material. Does this story hold my interest? Is this a good poem or a bad poem? These questions involve the evaluation of the reading material. Interest Box 9.3 presents an extended list of the types of subskills usually included under evaluation.

Many commonly used achievement texts include a few questions that measure some aspects of evaluation. For example, one could easily write a question that addresses understanding the purpose of the author or illustrator. However, other evaluation skills are not so easy to measure on standardized tests. For example, evaluation of the overall quality of a particular poem is frequently debated among professional poets, and few teachers can say with certainty which poems may be effective for particular students. Likewise, evaluation of opinion or position papers in the upper grades is often a subjective process. Consequently, at this level of the comprehension skills hierarchy, the specific subskills are less likely to be measured on standardized comprehension tests.

In spite of this measurement difficulty, there are instructional strategies that will improve evaluation skills. For example, both elementary knowledge of text structure and critical reading instruction will tend to make students with disabilities more aware of the intention and purpose of the authors. Each of these strategies is discussed below.

Appreciation

Because one end goal of reading instruction should be personal fulfillment on the part of the student through reading activities, appreciation is included in this reading comprehension skills hierarchy. Appreciation goes beyond merely identification of the literary style of the author or understanding the unwritten purpose of a manuscript. Appreciation involves the enjoyment a student should receive from reading, and increased appreciation of reading material should be one goal of every reading instructional activity.

It is very difficult to conceptualize subskills for this particular level of the comprehension skills hierarchy, because specific behaviors that indicate enjoyment of reading are few. One may note how many books, magazines, or stories a student freely chooses to read, but that is not a measure that can be easily obtained in a standardized test format. Consequently, this level of comprehension is usually not measured at all on most standardized tests of reading.

Likewise, it is very difficult to identify particular reading instructional strategies that are intended to improve a student's appreciation of reading. Many teachers do offer incentives for reading a certain number of books of interest to the child, and that practice can lead to increased appreciation of reading. It is crucial for teachers to remember at all times that one of their responsibilities is to encourage students to choose to read. Careful selection of high interest materials, or

INTEREST BOX 9.3
Reading Comprehension Evaluation Subskills

Compare quality of writing styles
Determine author's purpose
Compare quality of message
Search for bias in message
Determine the knowledge bases of author
Determine the integrity of the author

reading materials that directly relate to personal questions with which the student is struggling, may be helpful. The effective teacher in this regard is the one who can show a student some reading materials the student wants to read, independent of any assignment. Also, identifying the types of instructional situations in which particular students seem to enjoy reading (group or individual, with or without teacher assistance, with a tutor, for a particular time of day, etc.) may increase the likelihood of improving a student's appreciation of reading as a pleasurable activity. Part of your responsibility as a teacher is to structure the environment so that your students enjoy reading.

ASSESSMENT OF READING COMPREHENSION

Several different methods are commonly used for assessment of reading comprehension, and these are used in both special education classes and inclusive classrooms. As a teacher of students with disabilities, you will need some understanding of these several methods and the differences between them in order to correctly interpret test data to students, parents, and other teachers.

Text/Question Format

The most common measurement paradigm for assessment of reading comprehension is the format that requires the student to read a selection of text and then read and answer several comprehension questions. Many commonly used tests in education employ this measurement approach.

There are several concerns with this type of question format. First, the student may correctly understand and comprehend the information in the text, but may misunderstand the question. Consequently, an incorrect answer on the question does not indicate an inability to read and comprehend text. This issue is of particular concern as many test publishers are moving to increasingly complex question formats. In short, does the reading test really measure reading comprehension or does it measure test taking skills? The particular skills that enable a student to take a test are referred to as testwiseness, and can include understanding of question formats, efficient use of time, inferencing skills, and the ability to glean information from one question in order to answer another.

An understanding of common question formats is one example of testwiseness. Most of the text/question format tests use some type of multiple-choice question format. This type of question can be either a simple multiple choice (SMC) or a complex multiple choice (CMC). The SMC format is the most frequently used type. Generally, this type of question has a stem, or question, and four choices for the answers, as shown in Interest Box 9.4.

Of the four possible answers in the standard SMC question format, two are irrelevant distractors because they are, typically, unrelated to the question. One other distractor is usually tangentially related to the correct answer. If a student has no knowledge of the answer, it is usually better to invest time on the other questions, but if a student can identify the two irrelevant distractors, he or she then has a 50/50 chance of correctly guessing which of the two remaining answers is correct on most SMC questions. Thus, knowledge of both test question format and of the two distractor items can greatly enhance the possibility of choosing the correct answer. For example, in the SMC in Interest Box 9.4, note that neither John Calhoun nor Henry Clay was ever president. If the student has that much information, he or she can then make a guess at the answer with a 50 percent chance of being correct. This knowledge of how to eliminate distractor items based on partial information is one of the testwiseness skills that can be specifically taught to students with disabilities. Further, some research suggests that certain students with disabilities may be deficient in these testwiseness skills (Scruggs & Mastropieri, 1986, 1988).

A second type of multiple-choice question is the complex multiple choice (CMC). The CMC format is being used increasingly on many reading comprehension tests, even though very little research has been done to investigate the fairness of this question format on the text performance of

INTEREST BOX 9.4
Types of Multiple Choice Questions on Reading Comprehension Tests

1. A simple multiple choice (SMC) question format:
   The president of the United States during the Civil War was

   a. John C. Calhoun
   b. Henry Clay
   c. Jefferson Davis
   d. Abraham Lincoln

2. A complex multiple choice (CMC) question format:
   The United States has elected several generals to the office of president over the years. These include

   1. Dwight D. Eisenhower
   2. Franklin Roosevelt
   3. Ulysses S. Grant
   4. Lyndon Johnson

   a. 1 and 2 above
   b. 1 and 3 above
   c. 2 and 3 above
   d. 3 and 4 above

children with disabilities or low-achieving students. The CMC format is composed of a stem question, several answer choices, and an answer set—that is, the actual answers in the answer set force the student to choose from several correct answer choices, as shown in Interest Box 9.4. The testwiseness skills for completing the CMC question are much more complicated than for the SMC question. In this example, the students must have some knowledge of each of the answers, and must use a fairly complicated process of elimination in order to determine the correct answer. This type of test question requires the same type of metacognitive planning discussed in Chapter 5, and many students with mild disabilities are deficient in those metacognitive skills.

Another concern with many of the tests utilized today is the timed nature of these tests. Many tests allow only a certain number of minutes for completion of the comprehension section. If a student has read two text sections, completed each of the questions for those sections, and completed reading the third section without having completed any questions when time is called, he or she will be penalized for the questions in the last section, even though he or she may have comprehended the information. It is conceivable that the student could have answered some of those questions correctly, but the nature of the test format (read the section first, and then answer) prohibited the student from completing any questions. This represents a bias in the test that may penalize students with disabilities unjustly, because many of these students do read more slowly than nondisabled students.

Also, this set of instructions run counter to what is now known about effective reading strategy. The effective reader interacts with the reading material, and that interaction may involve continually flipping from the text to the questions to be completed in a "searching" mode, in order to complete the questions as quickly and accurately as possible. Many of the strategies discussed later in this chapter encourage this type of interactive reading, which involves simultaneous use of both questions and text. However the instructions on some reading comprehension tests actually prohibit use of these effective strategies. These problems with test construction have resulted in reduced use of this assessment format for individualized assessment in recent years.

Multiple Choice with Pictures

The *Peabody Individual Achievement Test, Revised* (Dunn & Markwardt, 1970; Markwardt, 1989) has been one of the most widely used assessment devices in special education, primarily because this test has eliminated several of the problems discussed above. First, there is no time limit on the reading comprehension section. Next, in order to remove the possibility of error due to misreading the questions, the written answers have been replaced by picture answers. The student merely reads a section of text, and then selects the most accurate picture representation of the passage from among four pictures. The answers themselves involve no reading.

Cloze Procedure

Two widely used assessments in special education, the *Woodcock Reading Mastery Test, revised* (Woodcock, 1987), and the *Woodcock Johnson Psycho-Educational Battery* (Woodcock & Johnson, 1977), use a cloze procedure in assessment of reading comprehension. This is the same procedure described in Chapter 8. Generally, the student reads a brief section of text and is expected to complete a fill-in-the-blank answer space embedded within the text.

This format eliminates some of the problems discussed in other test formats. The test is not timed, which eliminates one possibility of inaccurate measurement. Also, because the answer is embedded within the reading passage, there is no issue concerning possible misreading of the question itself. Also, the student will not be penalized by "not getting to the answer section" on this test. Because of these improvements in test design, these tests are likely to be utilized more widely in the future.

Curriculum-Based Assessment

As discussed in Chapter 4, assessment using a precision teaching paradigm seems to be the preferred method for monitoring achievement. Using a precision teaching approach, the student would be given sentences and brief paragraphs that incorporate a cloze exercise. The student would read as many sections as the time allowed and complete the blank answer sections verbally. This assessment would be conducted on a daily basis. Phase changes may involve moving to an increasingly difficult grade level passage, or changing to a higher level of comprehension at the same grade level. This type of daily assessment would yield a chart of assessment data based on daily performance, and use of such data in instructional planning is strongly encouraged by most scholars today. Clearly, this assessment approach results in the most accurate picture of reading progress of any of the assessment approaches.

ELEMENTARY READING COMPREHENSION IMPROVEMENT

There are literally scores of comprehension improvement strategies that work with various children in elementary reading activities, and many of these are useful for students in special education classes and inclusive classes (Bristor, 1993; Mathes & Fuchs, 1993). Some of these strategies are widely known and used, whereas others are not; discussion of each of the possible strategies would require a complete reading text. However, there are several ways in which reading comprehension improvement strategies may be grouped for study. First, some strategies are dependent on language-based exercises to enhance understanding, whereas others use visual imagery, spatial organizers, or pictures. This may be an important consideration in instruction of a child who seems to respond well to imagery but not to linguistic analysis of stories, and the special education teacher, whether in a special education class or an inclusive class, will have to make the final determination about which type of strategy seems to work for particular children with disabilities.

Another method in which comprehension improvement strategies may be grouped is based on the time of application of the strategy. For example, some strategies are initiated prior to reading a story or reading selection. Other strategies are used as the student reads the material, and still more strategies are generally used after a story or reading section is complete. This is the method of organization used in the text below. However, some of the strategies discussed below may be used at any time during the reading process, and thus do not fit easily within this time utilization model.

Prereading Activities

As defined in Chapter 5, metacognition involves being aware of the assigned task, the strategy used to complete the task, and self-performance on the task. Many of the currently recommended prereading instructional strategies are based on this metacognitive approach (Paris & Oka, 1989). The strategies below may be considered as metacognitive strategies because the activities are intended to make the student aware of the task components before he or she begins the reading section.

Advance Organizers. The advance organizer may be defined as organizational material that is presented in advance of, and at a higher level of, generalizability and abstraction than the learning task (Ansubel & Robinson, 1969). The similarity between this higher level of organization and the metacognitive instructional approach is clear from this definition; metacognitive instruction has largely been founded upon the advance organizer concept. Ansubel is credited with the early development of the advance organizer concept, and use of advance organizers has received increasing support in the research literature (Darch & Gersten, 1986; Lenz, Alley, & Schumaker, 1987).

In using an advance organizer approach, the student is presented with an outline of the important information in a reading section prior to reading the section. The teacher reviews the outline with the student, questioning the student on why certain material is important. In some organizers, the student is expected to predict what the story may entail. Afterward, the student reads the story or reading section and reviews the outline again, and then completes the comprehension questions (Darch & Gersten, 1986). Note, again, the interactive nature of reading, based on the advance organizer concept. The student doesn't merely sit down with a text and begin to read; rather, certain advance organizer activities are completed to "set up" the reading comprehension question that may come later.

Lorna Idol-Maestas (1985) demonstrated the use of an advance organizer learning strategy called "TELLS, Fact or Fiction." Two experiments were reported in which 6 subjects were included in an ABA multiple baseline design. In other words, daily performance data on reading comprehension was taken for each subject, and the length of the baseline was varied for each subject. During each baseline phase, the subjects read a story each day and answered 10 comprehension questions. After a few days of baseline data, each student was introduced to the TELLS, Fact or Fiction strategy. One experiment involved elementary-age children and the other involved secondary students.

Like many of the learning strategies described in Chapter 5, these letters represent steps a student is to go through in completing the task. The steps in the strategy are as follows: *T* means that the student should examine the title of the reading passage for clues; *E* means examine the page in the passage for clues concerning content; *L* means to look for important words; the second *L* means to look for hard words, practice them, and think about what they mean; *S* means to consider the setting of the story. *Fact or Fiction* means to decide whether the story is true.

The results demonstrated that, for each of the 6 subjects, the comprehension scores improved when the TELLS, Fact or Fiction, strategy was in use. One student went from 36 percent correct during baseline to 85 percent correct during the intervention phase. Every student improved. Also, the comprehension scores for 5 of the 6 students went down after the student stopped using the strategy, indicating that the strategy caused the positive effects.

As a special education teacher, you will want to use some type of advance organizer strategy for many students, and you may wish to consider the TELLS, Fact or Fiction concept. This strategy can be readily applied in almost any class and will work nicely in inclusive classes, because it is different from more traditional methods. The strategy is fairly simple to implement, and reading the Idol-Maestas (1985) article should provide you with enough information to begin to use this idea. For implementation, the teacher would merely prepare an outline of the major points, concepts, and details in the reading section prior to assigning a particular story. Of course, these outlines would be usable the next year for the same story.

Use of Spatial Organizers. Some advance organizers are not linguistically based, but are based on visual aides, illustrations, or maps (Chan, Cole, & Morris, 1990; Darch & Carnine, 1986; Hawk & McLeod, 1984; Mastropieri & Peters, 1987; Rose & Robinson, 1984). For example, in a comprehension exercise that involved listening to a brief story, students with learning disabilities responded positively to an advance organizer strategy that involved use of a spatially oriented map of the town in which the story took place (Mastropieri & Peters, 1987). In that study, the use of the map assisted the students more than merely pictures of various locations in the town viewed in a nonspatial fashion.

In fact, some research has demonstrated that the mere presence of pictures in reading text may be detrimental for certain readers with disabilities, because the pictures may direct attention away from the text (Harber, 1983; Rose & Robinson, 1984). These findings surprised many researchers because use of pictures to illustrate text generally helps students without disabilities comprehend the reading passage. However, for students with disabilities, pictures are particularly distracting if the pictures are not related to crucial aspects of the text, or if they are not utilized in an appropriate fashion by the students (Rose & Robinson, 1984).

This research certainly suggests that if pictures are present in the reading material for learners with disabilities, the teacher must discuss the pictures with the students in an attempt to demonstrate the relationship between the pictures and the printed text. Only those aspects of the pictures that illustrate important points should be discussed. Various strategies may be employed that facilitate the conceptual link between the pictures and the text, and use of pictures in such a structured fashion prior to reading a story should aid in comprehension. Also, spatial organizers and pictures represent strategies that may be used either before a text is read or during the reading itself. Students should be taught specifically how to search in the pictures for important ideas and supporting details from the text.

Questioning Strategies. Authors of texts have long recognized that use of questions after a student reads a passage can improve comprehension. However, evidence during the last decade has demonstrated that use of questioning strategies may also be employed as a prereading activity, or during the reading session itself, with beneficial effects (Clark, Deshler, Schumaker, Alley, & Warner, 1984; McCormick & Hill, 1984). In utilizing this strategy, the teacher asks questions that are generally included in the teacher's manual. Recently published reading materials generally have several questions located before the text and at regular intervals during the text in the teacher's manual.

For example, McCormick and Hill (1984) demonstrated that prereading questions designed to help a student relate his or her background to the story resulted in improved comprehension. Eighty children were participating in the resource rooms, and each child was selected for participation because of low reading scores. Four stories were selected at the children's general reading level, and 20 questions—10 literal comprehension and 10 inferential comprehension—were prepared for each story. The students were randomly divided into three groups. One group was used as a control group and was taught reading in the standard fashion, using questions printed at the end of the story. A second group—the inferencing group—was asked only questions that involved inferential comprehension at the end of the story. The third group—the strategy group—was trained to respond to several prereading questions that represent the main ideas of the story. For example, one of the stories included a boy, newly arrived from Greece, who spoke no English but attended an American school. The first question was intended to make the students relate their own background to the experience they would shortly be reading about: How do you feel when you are with a group and you can't do something they can do? The second question was designed to encourage the students to predict the story outcome: How would you feel if you couldn't speak the same language everyone in your class speaks? For each story, three main ideas were selected, which resulted in six prereading questions for each of the stories used in the study. Results indicated that both the strategy group, which used the prereading questions, and the inferencing group, which used the postreading inferencing questions, consistently outperformed the control group. This study demonstrates that questioning strategies can be one effective prereading activity.

Concurrent Comprehension Strategies

Almost all of the recent scholarship in the field of reading indicates that improvement of comprehension is based on encouraging meaningful interaction between the learner and the text materials. Consequently, few scholars recommend that reading should proceed from word to word, paragraph to paragraph, without some time for metacognitive reflection on the material that has been read. For this reason, the majority of recently recommended reading comprehension improvement strategies involve regularly planned activities that the student should engage in during the reading process.

Text Structure. Awareness of the structure of the text may help students to understand stories more completely (Bristor, 1993; Englert & Thomas, 1987; Griffey, Zigmond, & Leinhardt, 1988; Smith & Friend, 1986; Wong & Wilson, 1984). For example, even the simplest stories in basal readers usually include some type of story problem or rudimentary plot, a number of situational scenes that build the story plot further, a climax, and a closing section. In utilizing a text structure strategy, the teacher would indicate when each of the major features of the plot occurred and would briefly review each earlier story event. In other words, when the climax began, the teacher would indicate that the story had approached its climax. A brief synthesis of the initial story problem would be provided, with some supporting details. Then the teacher would encourage the student to continue reading in order to find out what happens. Bristor (1993) recommended this type of activity as a supplement to viewing videotapes of children's stories. This type of activity may be used with one child or with a group of children reading the same story, though the overall yearly goal would be to establish the skill of recognition of story structure by each student. With such a goal in mind, the teacher would be teaching the child a skill that would be useful in later years.

Research has demonstrated that certain students with mild and moderate disabilities are less able to recognize the structure of reading passages than nondisabled children (Englert & Thomas, 1987; Wong & Wilson, 1984). Clearly, this deficiency on the part of students with disabilities further suggests that effective teachers will specifically teach their students the various aspects of story structure and will use story structure as one strategy for improving reading comprehension.

Self-Questioning. Because of the effectiveness of questioning strategies, some scholars have begun to train students to ask themselves questions during the reading process (Clark et al., 1984; Malone & Mastropieri, 1992). As you may recall, the RAPs learning strategy discussed in Chapter 5 involved asking questions and paraphrasing text during reading. Another learning strategy developed at the University of Kansas Institute for Learning Disabilities involves a self-questioning strategy based on the five *wh* questions (Clark et al., 1984). The student is trained to read a passage and to constantly ask the five *wh* questions (who, what, where, when, and why). The student answers the questions as he or she reads.

In some classes this strategy has become the focal point for reading comprehension instruction. The five *wh* questions may be written on the board or a chart, and consistency in the use of the five questions will confirm the importance of them for the students. Whenever a student reads a passage, he or she should know that the first questions that will be asked are the five *wh* questions. Then if a teacher wishes to use the questions presented in the reading materials he or she is free to do so.

Visual Imagery. The use of pictures that are well integrated with text has been discussed previously. However, the learning strategy scholars have developed a more active process than simple use of pictures included in the text—the student is trained to develop his or her own pictures. Using a learning strategy called RIDER, the student develops a visual image of the passage as he or she is reading. The training for using this strategy proceeds along the same lines as the training described in Chapter 5. Research results have demonstrated the effectiveness of the procedure in improving reading comprehension (Clark et al., 1984). Interest Box 9.5 presents the RIDER learning strategy.

INTEREST BOX 9.5

The *RIDER* Learning Strategy

R = *Read* the first sentence.
I = Try to make an *image*—a picture in your mind.
D = *Describe* your image.
  a. If you cannot make an image, explain why you cannot and go on to the next sentence.
  b. If you can make an image, decide whether it is the same as an old image (one held in memory from the most recent image), the old image changed somewhat, or an entirely new image (not at all similar to the most recent image). Make a changed image by adding or subtracting things from the picture.
E = *Evaluate* your image for its completeness.
  a. Check to make certain your image includes as much of the sentence content as possible. If content is missing, adjust your image and continue.
  b. If your image is comprehensive, continue.
R = *Repeat* the preceding steps as you read the next sentence.

Source: Clark et al. (1984).

Information on learning strategies is available from a large variety of sources. See Alley and Deshler (1979); Clark, Deshler, Schumaker, Alley, and Warner (1984); Ellis and Sabornie (1986); Lenz and Hughes (1990); Lenzo, Schumaker, Deshler, and Beals (1984). Training in the learning strategies approach is available through the University of Kansas, Lawrence, KS.

Comprehension Monitoring. Several studies have investigated the use of comprehension monitoring activities to improve reading comprehension (Bowman & Davey, 1986; Chan, Cole, & Barfett, 1987). For example, Chan and his co-workers have demonstrated the effectiveness of teaching students to monitor the reading passage for inconsistencies as they read. Initially, students were trained using specially prepared materials that include two sentences per passage that do not fit with the remainder of the passage. In the Chan, Cole, and Barfett (1987) study, the search for anomalous sentences resulted in improved reading comprehension for students with learning disabilities, but not for the nondisabled comparison pupils. This is important because such differential effectiveness of instruction provides one indication of the types of instructional strategies that should be taught to students with disabilities. In other words, if nondisabled students are already employing this strategy, or a similar strategy to accomplish the same purpose, they do not need instruction in using the strategy. In contrast, children with disabilities would need such instruction. Interest Box 9.6 presents a more detailed discussion of this point, along with a review of the study itself.

Although this strategy is intriguing, the lack of commercially prepared materials that include anomalous sentences may inhibit the use of this approach for the immediate future. Nevertheless, research on this idea will continue, and you may find that at some future time you will be expected to teach reading skills that involve searching for anomalous sentences.

Participatory Organizers. As discussed previously, advanced and spatial organizers are presented prior to the reading material. However, the same idea may be modified so that the organizer is to be completed as the student does the reading lesson (Bender, 1985; Hawk & McLeod, 1984). Such participatory organizers may be as simple as a partially completed outline or map in which the student has to write or draw representations of facts as he or she reads them. The typical, and most common, example of a participatory organizer is the "lab sheet" many secondary science teachers require during laboratory procedures. In using this strategy for reading comprehension, the particular aspects of the participatory organizer would vary from one story to the next. Also, as a postreading activity, the participatory organizers themselves may be checked for accuracy and used as a discussion focal point during later classwork. The key is active student participation in completion of the organizer. Finally, students should be encouraged to use these organizers as study guides for later quizzes, in order to emphasize the importance of the material in the organizer.

Postreading Strategies

Certainly the most frequently used reading comprehension improvement strategies today are postreading activities. Typically, these include questions at the end of the chapter, fill-in-the-blank activities, and/or preparation of paragraph synopses of the reading passage. Frequent use of these postreading activities is encouraged by most publishers of basal readers, because this is the type of activity most teachers are used to using.

However, many of the prereading activities and concurrent activities may also be used after completing the reading passage. For example, self-questioning strategies, visual imagery, participatory organizers, and other strategies would work well as postreading strategies. Nevertheless, there are several strategies intended to be used after the reading passage. These include story retelling and story frames.

Story Retelling. Encouraging students to summarize and/or "retell" a story after reading it has been shown to enhance reading comprehension (Gambrell, Pfeiffer, & Wilson, 1985; Hansen, 1978; Jenkins, Heliotis, Stein, & Haynes, 1987). Although this technique was historically used as a method of assessing reading comprehension, recently scholars have noted that, rather than being merely an assessment of reading performance, this technique actually improves recall of the major points in the story.

INTEREST BOX 9.6
A Trait by Treatment Study

The study by Chan, Cole, and Barfett (1987) provides a strong indication that children with learning disabilities should be trained in strategies such as comprehension monitoring. This study also provides an example of a trait by treatment study. Thirty-two students with learning disabilities and 32 nondisabled students were randomly assigned to either a general instruction treatment or a specific instruction treatment that used a comprehension monitoring strategy. This resulted in four groups, one LD group in general instruction and one in specific instruction, and one non-LD group in each condition.

If the student was in the general instruction group, he or she was trained by reading passages that included several sentences which did not fit logically with the remainder of the reading passage. During the training, the teacher would merely indicate which sentences did not fit. In the specific instruction condition, the training included explanations of why the sentences didn't fit in the passage, as well as some work on identification of additional anomalous sentences. The students in both types of treatment then read a series of reading passages and were graded on both how many anomalous sentences they detected and reading comprehension. The specific instruction in comprehension monitoring improved the scores of students with disabilities, but not the scores of students without disabilities.

With a study designed in this fashion, experimenters can draw conclusions regarding the effects of a particular educational treatment on particular types of children. For example, with the four groups in this study, experimenters were able to demonstrate that an instructional approach such as comprehension monitoring was effective for students with disabilities but not for the comparison children. In effect, the study design allows the researchers to cross-tabulate the effects on the treatment with the educational traits of the two types of children involved—LD and non-LD. Hence, this type of study is referred to as a trait by treatment study, or an aptitude/treatment interaction study, because the aptitude (or the characteristics associated with a learning disability) is crossed with different types of treatment.

This trait by treatment interaction study is important in special education for one additional reason. If a particular treatment is useful for special education populations, but largely unnecessary for nondisabled children, that instructional idea should be used in a special education class rather than in a mainstream class, since most children in the mainstream do not need to learn that instructional strategy. Consequently, trait by treatment studies provide some rationale for continuing separate special education instruction and placements for children with disabilities. To be specific, the results of this study did demonstrate a trait by treatment interaction. Thus this study, and other trait by treatment studies like it, provide some indication of the continuing need for different types of instruction for children with disabilities.

The technique may be used easily in any inclusive classroom or special education setting, either for individual students or small groups of students who read the same story. In some cases a set of questions is given that encourages the student to list the main ideas and supporting details in the story, whereas other teachers merely encourage the students to retell the story in several sentences or a paragraph format. Because of the demonstrated effectiveness of this technique with children with disabilities, as well as the ease of use, this is one technique that each special education teacher should employ. After a student has completed a reading section, merely have him or her write a brief paragraph that summarizes the passage, then check the paragraph for comprehensiveness and accuracy.

Story Mapping and Story Frames. Because most new knowledge must be related in some fashion to old knowledge to be useful, scholars have begun to attend to the use of background knowledge that a child may bring to a story. Some scholars speak of schema, which may be defined as a presentation of ideas that allows for the incorporation of other new ideas. Using this approach, the teacher would ask questions to determine the level of understanding the student had of a particular important aspect of the story and, as the story progresses, further elaborations would be made in order to more closely approximate the story line.

The story mapping approach and the story frame approach are two methods for schema building comprehension improvement (Fowler & Davis, 1985; Idol, 1987; Idol & Croll, 1987). A story map is a picture constructed to illustrate the ideas and relationships between ideas in a story or reading selection. The story frame is a linguistic synopsis of the story schema. Interest Box 9.7 presents a simple story frame that may be used for most basal reader stories.

In utilizing this approach, the teacher would hand out the story frames after the reading is completed and request that the students complete each section. Students could be assigned to work individually or in groups.

Selection of a Comprehension Improvement Method

There are no proven guidelines to use when selecting a method to improve a student's reading comprehension. However, several suggestions may be offered. First, you will certainly need very frequent

INTEREST BOX 9.7
Story Frame

The problem in the story was ______________________________

____

It started when ______________________________

____

____

After that, ______________________________

____

Then, ______________________________

____

The problem is solved when ______________________________

____

____

The story ends ______________________________

Source: Fowler and Davis (1985).

measures of the comprehension progress of the student. Clearly, a precision teaching approach, or at least a biweekly reading comprehension assessment, is far superior for documentation of continued progress than less frequent assessment. Do not allow yourself to make the common mistake of depending on unit quizzes, spaced weeks apart, or on norm referenced assessments administered yearly, to monitor a child's growth in reading comprehension. Reading comprehension is simply much too important to loose track of progress for that length of time.

Second, in using various strategies with a particular child, coupled with frequent curriculum-based assessments, you should be able to determine what types of methods work with that child. With some children, methods dependent on pictures and visual imagery may be more useful, whereas other children may profit more from methods that are linguistically dependent, such as advance organizer outlines, paraphrasing strategies, and story retelling. Use the assessment information on particular children to make decisions about the most effective instructional methods for those children.

Third, do not become overly dependent on any instructional method. For example, many teachers use a postquestioning strategy merely because many basal readers include that strategy. Do not allow yourself to make instructional decisions based on the types of materials provided. Rather make instructional decisions based on daily measurement of the needs and growth patterns of the children in your charge, and work to secure appropriate instructional materials that facilitate those instructional methods.

Finally, strive to use instructional methods that are applicable beyond the immediate needs of today's reading assignment. If a child responds to advance organizer strategies, you should help the child progress, over the year, until he or she begins to develop those organizers when they are not provided without your assistance, because that skill can easily be transferred into other instructional situations. Do not let your use of, or dependence on, an instructional method limit the child. Rather, attempt to expand the child's understanding of these techniques, and encourage application of the techniques in various areas of instruction.

COMPREHENSIVE METHODS FOR COMPREHENSION IMPROVEMENT

Reciprocal Teaching

The reciprocal teaching method, as discussed in Chapter 5, is a combination of a number of reading strategies into an integrated system of discussion designed to facilitate reading comprehension (Bruce & Chan, 1991; Palincsar & Brown, 1986). The method is used when small groups of children share the same reading assignment. The role of "teacher" is reciprocal because the teacher and students share responsibilities for conducting the discussion concerning the reading topic.

Initially, the students are presented with four goals, including predicting, question generating, summarizing, and clarifying. First, students are expected to hypothesize about what the story may entail, based on use of pictures and story title as advance organizers. From these hypotheses, questions are to be generated. The students read part of the material, refine their predictions, and formulate questions. Afterward, the students together summarize the important points, and seek clarification for any unanswered questions.

As you can see, this method involves use of a number of the particular strategies discussed above, including advance organizers, questioning techniques, self-questioning, and retelling (summarizing), and each of these methods works well individually with some children. Also, the research that has been done on this combined method has demonstrated its effectiveness (Bruce & Chan, 1991; Palincsar & Brown, 1986). Interest Box 5.8 presents a dialogue that Palincsar and Brown (1986) use to illustrate the types of discussion this method can generate while reading a brief passage about aquanauts. Note the metacognitive understanding demonstrated in the student's contributions to the dialogue. This emphasis on the student's ability to metacognitively plan a task is a major strength of this method.

Holistic Instruction

Recently holistic reading has received a great deal of attention (Bender, 1987; McNutt, 1984). In using a holistic method, a teacher would choose the methods of reading comprehension instruction that seemed to work best together, and these would be combined with instruction in other language arts skills beyond reading comprehension. This concept has been likened to the whole language method described previously, though the holistic method emphasizes integrated language arts instruction rather than reading world recognized literature itself.

For example, a teacher may require that, before each story or reading passage is attempted, the student use the pictures in the story as an advance organizer and write out three sentences concerning what the story will be about. Next, the student would read the story, refining the predictions and asking questions concerning future events. After the story, the student may be expected to answer orally the five *wh* questions and/or the comprehension questions in the text. Finally, the student may be required to retell the story, either in paragraph format or orally. Upon checking the paragraph, the teacher may decide that some remedial work in certain areas (punctuation, capitalization, or subject/verb agreement) is needed, and appropriate assignments would be made.

As you can see, such an approach has the advantage of covering every aspect of language arts and reading instruction, and the instructional approach clearly goes beyond merely reading comprehension. Nevertheless, certain scholars are recommending an end to the presently disjointed nature of reading, speaking, writing, spelling, and language arts instruction (Bender, 1987; McNutt, 1984), and you may find at some future time that holistic instructional strategies have been implemented in your local school district.

ADVANCED READING COMPREHENSION INSTRUCTION SKILLS

Reading comprehension skills are generally taught directly in the public school curriculum until the eighth grade. However, comprehension of reading material is a requirement for all school subjects beyond the upper elementary grades. Consequently, there are several reading comprehension improvement methods intended for use during the later years of schooling, though each of these methods may also be used during the middle school years.

Critical Reading Skills

One of the more advanced comprehension skills students must learn is the set known as critical reading. Critical reading includes such skills as the ability to distinguish fact from opinion, identify faulty generalizations, detect false causality, and identify invalid testimonials (Bender, 1987; Darch & Kameenui, 1987; McNutt, 1984; Patching, Kameenui, Carnine, Gersten, & Colvin, 1983). For example, in the study by Darch and Kameenui (1987) three critical reading rules were taught, using a direct instructional script. The rules and relevant examples are presented in Interest Box 9.8.

Instruction in application of these rules led to improved critical reading skills among students with disabilities. However, some issues must be addressed prior to full implementation of this type of critical reading instruction. First, no research to date has demonstrated that these specific critical reading skills are related to standard measures of reading comprehension. Although no one doubts that critical reading skills are important in life (one look at modern advertisements will attest to that fact), today's reading comprehension assessments may not measure this skill, and this needs to be rectified.

A more important problem is the lack of reading materials that emphasize instruction in these skills. Very few commercially available education materials are currently published that emphasize critical reading, and those available are very recent. As a result, despite the obvious importance of critical reading skills in overall reading comprehension, instruction in these skills is still much less frequent than the standard comprehension instructional format of text and postreading questions. However, in

INTEREST BOX 9.8
Critical Reading Rules and Examples

1. Ability to detect faulty generalization.
   Rule 1. Just because you know about the part, it doesn't mean you know about the whole thing.
   Example: Sue has long legs. She must be a very good runner.
2. Ability to detect false-causality.
   Rule 2. Just because two things happen together, it doesn't always mean that one causes the other.
   Example: John's mother told him not to open the windows in the house at night. "If you open that window, someone we know will get sick." A week later, John opened the window in the house and that night his sister, Susie, became very sick. Opening the window must have done it.
3. Ability to detect invalid testimonial.
   Rule 3. Just because someone important in one area says something is good or bad in another area, you can't be sure it's true.
   Example: Dr. Smith is a very good doctor, and everyone likes him. He tells people why they are sick and helps them get better quickly. When I wanted to buy a lawnmower, Dr. Smith told me that I should.

Source: Darch & Kameenui (1987).

spite of these cautions, you should anticipate that you will be responsible for teaching some critical reading skills, should your class include students with disabilities from the middle or upper grades.

Content Area Reading

Reading content area material in secondary textbooks is quite different from reading a novel or a basal reading story. For example, chapters in textbooks are generally grouped such that the content across chapters is related. Understanding of the day's assignment is dependent on understanding the information given in earlier chapters. Accordingly, the researchers associated with the University of Kansas Learning Disabilities Institute developed a learning strategy that should enable a secondary student with mild disabilities to complete a chapter reading assignment and relate that new knowledge to earlier chapters (Ellis & Sabornie, 1986). This TISOPT strategy is presented in Interest Box 9.9.

Text Structure Comprehension Strategies

Although a simplified version of the text structure strategy was discussed for use with basal reading assignments, a more complex version of the text structure strategy may be applicable in certain subject area assignments in the upper grades. Smith and Friend (1986) examined five different types of text structure, including descriptive, time order, cause/effect, problem solution, and compare/contrast. An experimental group was trained in recognition of these text structures in five instructional sessions, and a comparison group was trained using an unrelated instructional procedure. Results demonstrated that training in complex text structure resulted in improved recall of facts, both immediately after reading and after a one week delay. For upper-level subject area instruction, you may wish to consider instruction in strategy training on how to recognize the text structure of particular reading passages.

INTEREST BOX 9.9
The *TISOPT* Comprehension Strategy for Reading Chapters in Content Area Texts

T = Title: Read and paraphrase the Title of the Assigned Chapter
I = Introduction: Read the introduction. Study it briefly and reread if necessary.
S = Summary: Read the summary. Relate the information presented to the information in the introduction.
O = Organization: Study the organizational headings in the chapter and relate those headings to the introduction and summary.
P = Pictures: Read each caption below the pictures. Study the pictures to identify the text information which they represent, and relate that information to the other information you have from the chapter.
T = Table of Contents: Examine the table of contents and identify the reasons why the information you have from the assigned chapter was placed at this particular point in the text. What is the relationship between the chapters?

Information on learning strategies is available from a large variety of sources. See Alley and Deshler (1979); Clark, Deshler, Schumaker, Alley, and Warner (1984); Ellis and Sabornie (1986); Lenz and Hughes (1990); Lenzo, Schumaker, Deshler, and Beals (1984). Training in the learning strategies approach is available through the University of Kansas, Lawrence, KS.

INSTRUCTION IN READING COMPREHENSION

Instructional Activities

1. In Directed Inquiry Activity, the children preview a part of the reading assignment and predict outcomes to the "who, what, when, where, how, and why" questions. After group discussion of the ideas take place, students read to confirm or alter their predictions. The teacher should write the words, "what," "when," "where," "how," and "why" on the board and enter each child's prediction beside each word. After reading the selection, discuss why those children who chose outcomes different from the events selected those ideas, and how facts or events would have to have been altered to accommodate their predictions.

2. Select a few newspaper articles. Ask students to read each article and answer:
   a. Who was involved?
   b. What took place?
   c. Where did this happen?
   d. When did it happen?
   e. How or why did it happen?

3. Select a newspaper article or item from a magazine that is appropriate for this activity and for which the children have mastered the vocabulary.

4. Laminate some of the student's favorite comic strips. Cut each frame apart. Place them in envelopes and ask the children to read them and place them in order.

5. Have the children write simple autobiographies. Create a life sequence for each child by

writing significant events in chronological order on a long piece of tagboard. Or make a scrapbook with one event on each page, and perhaps a family photo provided by the parents to illustrate the event. Be sensitive to the group, however, and do not include this activity if it is uncomfortable for any child.

6. Include written directions on *all* teacher made worksheets. Be sure to use mastered vocabulary and write the directions neatly, making certain that the directions say exactly what you intend that the student do.

7. Choose a project. A simple aquarium (10-gallon) is ideal for this. Using the local pet store as a resource, have students research which fish are most appropriate for the classroom environment, what equipment is needed, and how to care for the fish. Provide a simple manual (many are available) for assembling and caring for the aquarium and fish. Allow the students to take responsibility (with teacher supervision) for this ongoing project. Provide fish-care books for future reference and problem solving.

8. Plan a group activity, such as snack time. Do not *tell* the group what you are planning, rather write the necessary information on sentence strips that are numbered. Distribute the strips to the group and ask the students to arrange themselves according to the numbers on the strips. Depending upon the developmental level of the group, allow them to organize the activity following the directions on the strips.

9. Discuss how certain words create moods for stories, and identify words that create different moods; for example, gloomy, sobbing, gray, foggy, indicate a sad mood; flashing, sparkling, bubbly, giggles, indicate a happy mood. Have the children select passages and indicate the mood of each passage.

10. Smith and Dauer (1984) describe a strategy to help students monitor comprehension as they read content area materials. They provide an example of a code for reading a social studies selection: *A* = Agree; *B* = Bored; *C* = Confused; *D* = Disagrees; and *M* = Main Idea. As they read, students monitor their responses to the selection, writing the appropriate code letters on strips of paper attached to the pages. Later they participate in postreading discussions to clarify their thinking and discuss the feelings they had while reading the assignment.

11. Explain that understanding the text means comprehension and that knowing that you understand the text is called metacomprehension.

Commercially Available Materials

Celebration! In *Celebration!* (Alemany Press), oral language comprehension skills are the basis for the acquisition of reading and writing skills. Each topic is introduced by a group activity requiring directed, hands-on student response. The purpose of these activities is to motivate students' oral language communication. The students' oral language is written down, using the language experience approach in both group and individual stories. Differing proficiency levels notwithstanding, the students *can* read the stories.

Celebration! is a 3-level reading program for beginners that utilizes shared classroom activities to gradually lead students from action to print. It has four key components: the orientations manual, duplicatable exercise sheets with notes, a poster set, and 10 copies each of four readers. The total physical response activities and the language experience approach to stories, together with appropriate, well sequenced follow-up exercises make *Celebration!* an excellent set of materials for special education students.

Fact. The *Fact Reading Program* (Raintree) is a supplementary remedial reading program for underachieving readers in grades 5 and above. It is built around 24 high-interest books selected for their appeal to young readers. *Fact* is designed to provide opportunity to apply previously learned skills in the reading process. It focuses on fluency, attitude, comprehension, and taste.

The teacher who employs *Fact* is assigned the role of learning facilitator rather than director of learning. The program focuses on learning by discovery. The kit contains 20 audiocassette tapes with accompanying texts. The students select a tape and follow it, using the book. When they have completed this activity, they answer the "In Review" questions and check their answers. The activity is resolved with a "book" conference after they have completed the book.

Teaching Reading Skills. The purpose of the *Teaching Reading Skills* (Sauer-Bloser, Inc.) kit is to provide methods and activities for teaching and reinforcing word recognition, word analysis, and comprehension skills. The skills presented are appropriate for grades 1 through 3. The materials in the kit include alphabet charts, basic word cards, modality-specific word cards, alphabet cards, laminated spinners, and a teacher's manual. The teacher's manual provides a basic understanding of modality and how to use modality-based instruction in the classroom.

The Reading Comprehension Idea Book. *The Reading Comprehension Idea Book* (Scott, Foresman Co.) contains a wide variety of activities and ideas designed to get children actively involved in comprehending written material. An additional purpose is to encourage the development of divergent thinking strategies, rather than adhering to the right-answer syndrome commonly associated with comprehension workbooks.

The activities are organized around "getting the main idea," understanding sequence, grasping details, and drawing inference. These activities are designed for a broad range of students and abilities and may be adapted for each individual and allow for follow-up activity ideas from the class or individual.

Bill Martin's Instant Reader. The *Instant Readers* (Holt, Rinehart, & Winston) are a series of children's books with accompanying audiotapes that instill in children the belief that they can read and at the same time provide them with materials that allow them to decode and comprehend written language. For purposes of decoding, these books incorporate rhyme, rhythm, phrase-sentence-and-story patter, and, for purposes of comprehension, are illustrated to reflect the meaning of the passages. The books involve the children aesthetically, as well as intellectually, holding "whole book success as a basic purpose of reading instruction."

Reading for Understanding. The *Reading for Understanding* (Science Research Associates) program includes a series of individualized multilevel kits that are designed to develop critical thinking, inferential logic, and the ability to draw conclusions. The student reads a selection and chooses the appropriate ending from four suggested conclusions. Level I is designed for students in first through third grades; Level II, third through seventh; Level III, seventh through twelfth.

TR Reading Comprehension Series. Designed for remedial students in third through seventh grade who are two to three grades below level, the *TR Reading Comprehension Series* (DLM) features a framework for teaching comprehension skills through the use of 8 work texts that can be used with phonics/decoding programs and graded readers. There are 42 lessons in each work text that focuses on following such areas of skill development as vocabulary, main ideas, contrast and comparison, and study skills.

SRA Reading Laboratories. The *SRA Reading Laboratories* (SRA) are available for students from the first grade through secondary school. Comprehension, word attack skills, and vocabulary are covered, as well as study skills and reading-rate improvement. The materials are color coded and may be used as a supplement to provide individualized reading instruction.

Reading Comprehension Software

Ace Detective

Publisher: MindPlay

Skill Level: Elementary; secondary; adult

Hardware: Apple IIe, IBM PC

Description: Ace Detectives practice critical reading skills by organizing information and drawing conclusions based on their findings. Players read reports, conduct interviews, phone witnesses, and examine mug shots as they search for the suspect with motive, opportunity, and means. Sixty reading mysteries are included plus a Story Creator for adding original stories. Challenge Upgrade, a You-Control feature, offers options for game play, difficulty levels, and performance summaries. (Publishers: MindPlay; elementary, secondary, and adult skill levels; for Apple IIe & IBM PC).

Ace Reporter

Publisher: MindPlay

Skill Level: Elementary, secondary

Hardware: Apple IIe, IBM

Description: Students practice reading for main idea and details by reading teletypes and conducting telephone interviews to uncover the who, what, when, where, and why of each story. Then they select a "main idea" headline before the paper goes to press. Includes sixty stories plus a Story Creator for original stories. Challenge Upgrade, a You-Control feature, includes options for game play, difficulty levels, and performance summaries.

Comprehension Connection

Publisher: Milliken Publishing Company

Skill Level: Elementary, secondary, adult

Hardware: Apple IIe

Description: Program is designed to improve reading comprehension skills in grades 4–9. Readers have access to several levels of content and can instantly go to an easier version of the passage or access a help feature. There are graphics and an online dictionary to assist students with words and concepts they may not be able to understand. Teacher management features also help track student performance and control features of the program.

Comprehension Power

Publisher: Instructional/Communications Technology

Skill Level: Elementary, secondary

Hardware: Apple IIe, IBM

Description: An extensive program that includes 15 four-disk sets containing 180 low level–high interest age-appropriate selections for grade levels 1–12. The program helps improve comprehension and reading/study skills through a comprehensive reading practice. Each lesson consists of three steps: Vocabulary Introduction, which has the students look up definitions; Preview Skimming, in which the students discover pertinent facts about selection; and a Thorough Reading with comprehension activities interspersed throughout the text. The student and teacher have complete control of presentation rate and the student can re-read at will.

Explore-a-Classic Series

Publisher: Wm. K. Bradford Publishing Co.

Skill Level: Preschool, elementary

Hardware: Apple IIe, Mac, IBM

Description: Contains such familiar stories as "Stone Soup," "The Princess and the Pea," and "The Three Little Pigs." Students use combinations of animated graphics, dialogue bubbles, and narrative text to read existing stories or create their own versions or new stories. Students can use all story elements to modify scenes of existing stories or to develop their own original creations. After developing their stories the students can save them on disk and print them out. The Explore Series also includes *Explore-a-Folktale Series* and an additional 12 stories under the title of *Explore-a-Story Series.*

SUMMARY

Reading comprehension skills are one of the most important topics that most special educators are expected to teach, and a great deal of your time in special education instruction in resource, self-contained, or inclusive classes will probably be devoted to this skill. Comprehension is important, both in basal reading progress and in reading texts in content areas in the upper grade levels, and various strategies have been developed in each of these areas.

Most of the recently developed reading comprehension improvement strategies employ a metacognitive instructional perspective. Many of the strategies discussed also include a heavy emphasis on curriculum-based assessment in order to chart reading comprehension progress on a daily basis. You would do well to apply curriculum-based assessment measures and a variety of metacognitive strategies in your own teaching. You should let the frequently measured progress of a child indicate what types of strategies work best for that child, and then select strategies accordingly.

Summary Points

- Special education teachers spend a large percentage of their time in reading comprehension instruction.
- Reading comprehension can be broken down into a number of different kinds of comprehension, and may be so dissected in numerous ways. For our purposes, this text divided comprehension into literal comprehension, inferential comprehension, evaluation, and appreciation.
- In understanding reading comprehension, it is important that one understand the methods used to measure it. For example, the simple multiple choice or SMC format is, by far, the most common method, though complex multiple choice or CMC questions are becoming more common. Multiple choice questions with picture answers are becoming common in special education use, as are cloze procedure questions.
- Strategies to improve reading comprehension vary widely, and the teacher's role is to select a comprehension strategy that works for each individual student. These strategies can generally be divided into prereading, simultaneous, and postreading strategies.
- advance organizers, spatial organizers, and questioning strategies may be used before the reader is exposed to the story or reading selection.
- Concurrent strategies include review of text structure, self-questioning, visual imagery, comprehension monitoring, and participatory organizers.
- Postreading strategies include story retelling, story mapping, and story frames.
- A number of comprehensive strategies involve an entire teaching method. Reciprocal teaching and holistic instruction are two examples.
- Advanced comprehension skills include critical reading skills and reading of content area texts.
- Given this wide array of comprehension improvement methods, the teacher is responsible for selecting the appropriate method for each child, based on that child's performance.

QUESTIONS AND ACTIVITIES

1. In your class, identify a team of class members and role play a reciprocal teaching lesson. Write out the lesson to include each of the goals discussed and present the lesson to the class.
2. What is the relationship between the advance organizer concept and other organizer concepts discussed in the chapter?
3. Individually, use the TISOPT strategy presented in the text for your next chapter reading assignment in another course. Is this an effective strategy for you?
4. Select a basal reading text from the curriculum materials center, read an elementary grade story, and apply the visual imagery strategy. List the steps you would go through with elementary-age children to teach this strategy.
5. Obtain copies of the various reading comprehension tests discussed in the chapter, and share these with the class.

6. Review the critical reading skills and the examples presented. Write a series of samples to further illustrate each of these skills.
7. Describe a cloze procedure that may be used as a precision teaching rate sheet in a curriculum-based measurement approach.
8. Review one of the reading tests discussed in the chapter and identify the levels of reading comprehension as represented by the questions on the test.
9. Describe the interpretation of a trait-by-treatment study.

REFERENCES

Ausubel, D. P., & Robinson, F. G. (1969). *School Learning: An Introduction to Educational Psychology.* New York: Holt, Rinehart, & Winston.

Bender, W. N. (1985). Strategies for helping the mainstreamed student in secondary social studies classes. *The Social Studies, 76,* 269–271.

Bender, W. N. (1987). Holistic language arts: Remedial strategies and procedures. *Techniques, 3,* 273–280.

Bowman, J. E., & Davey, B. (1986). Effects of presentation mode on the comprehension-monitoring behavior of LD adolescents. *Learning Disability Quarterly, 9,* 250–257.

Bristor, V. J. (1993). Enhancing text structure instruction with video for improving reading comprehension. *Intervention in School and Clinic, 28* (4), 216–233.

Bruce, M. E., & Chan, L. (1991). Reciprocal teaching and transenvironmental programming: A program to facilitate the reading comprehension of students with reading difficulties. *Remedial and Special Education, 12* (5), 44–54.

Chan, L. K. S., Cole, P. G., & Barfett, S. (1987). Comprehension monitoring: Detection and identification of text inconsistencies by LD and normal students. *Learning Disability Quarterly, 10,* 114–123.

Chan, L. K. S., Cole, P. G., & Morris, J. N. (1990). Effects of instruction in the use of a visual-imagery strategy on the reading comprehension competence of disabled and average readers. *Learning Disability Quarterly,* 13, 2–11.

Clark, F. L., Deshler, D. D., Schumaker, J. B., Alley, G. R., & Warner, M. M. (1984). Visual imagery and self-questioning: Strategies to improve comprehension of written material. *Journal of Learning Disabilities, 17,* 145–149.

Darch, C., & Carnine, D. (1986). Teaching content area material to learning disabled children. *Exceptional Children, 53,* 240–246.

Darch, C., & Gersten, R. (1986). Direction-setting activities in reading comprehension: A comparison of two approaches. *Learning Disability Quarterly, 9,* 235–243.

Darch, C., & Kameenui, E. J. (1987). Teaching LD students critical reading skills: A systematic replication. *Learning Disability Quarterly, 10,* 82–91.

Dunn, L. M., & Markwardt, F. C. (1970). *Peabody Individual Achievement Test.* Circle Pines, MN: American Guidance Service.

Ellis, E. S., & Sabornie, E. J. (1986, July 23). *Teaching Learning Strategies to Learning Disabled Students in Post-Secondary Settings.* Paper presented at the Learning Disabled Students in Higher Education Faculty/Staff Development Program, Rutgers University, New Brunswick, NJ.

Englert, C. S., & Thomas, C. C. (1987). Sensitivity to text structure in reading and writing: A comparison between learning disabled and non-learning disabled students. *Learning Disability Quarterly, 10,* 98–105.

Fowler, G. L., & Davis, M. (1985). The story frame approach: A tool for improving reading comprehension of EMR children. *Teaching Exceptional Children, 17,* 296–298.

Fry, E. (1977). Instant Words. In. E. B. Fry, D. L. Fountoukidis, & J. K. Polk (Eds.), *The New Reading Teachers' Book of Lists.* Englewood Cliffs, NJ: Prentice-Hall.

Gambrell, L. B., Pfeiffer, W. R., & Wilson, R. M. (1985). The effects of retelling upon reading comprehension and recall of text information. *Journal of Educational Research, 78,* 216–220.

Griffey, Q. L., Zigmond, N., & Leinhardt, G. (1988). The effects of self-questioning and story structure training on the reading comprehension of poor readers. *Learning Disabilities Research, 4,* 45–51.

Hansen, C. L. (1978). Story retelling used with average and learning disabled readers as a measure of reading comprehension. *Learning Disability Quarterly, 1,* 62–69.

Harber, J. R. (1983). The effects of illustrations on the reading performance of learning disabled and normal children. *Learning Disability Quarterly, 6,* 55–59.

Hawk, P. P., & McLeod, N. P. (1984). Graphic organizers: A cognitive teaching method that works. *The Directive Teacher, 6* (1), 6–7.

Idol, L. (1987). Group story mapping: A comprehension strategy for both skilled and unskilled readers. *Journal of Learning Disabilities, 20,* 196–205.

Idol, L., & Croll, V. J. (1987). Story-mapping training as a means of improving reading comprehension. *Learning Disability Quarterly, 10,* 214–229.

Idol-Maestas, L. (1985). Getting ready to read: Guided probing for poor comprehenders. *Learning Disability Quarterly, 8,* 243–253.

Jenkins, J. R., Heliotis, J. D., Stein, M. L., & Haynes, M. C. (1987). Improving reading comprehension by using paragraph restatements. *Exceptional Children, 54,* 54–59.

Lenz, B. K., Alley, G. R., & Schumaker, J. B. (1987). Activating the inactive learner: Advance organizers in the secondary content classroom. *Learning Disability Quarterly, 10,* 53–67.

Lillie, D. L., & Alberg, J. Y. (1986). The PIAT: Error analysis for instructional planning. *Teaching Exceptional Children, 18,* 197–201.

Malone, L. D., & Mastropieri, M. A. (1992). Reading comprehension instruction: Summarization and self-monitoring training for students with learning disabilities. *Exceptional Children, 58,* 270–279.

Markwardt, F. C. (1989). *Peabody Individual Achievement Test–Revised.* Circle Pines, MN: American Guidance Service.

Mastropieri, M. A., & Peters, E. E. (1987). Increasing prose recall of learning disabled and reading disabled students via spatial organizers. *The Journal of Educational Research, 80,* 272–276.

Mathes, P. G., Fuchs, L. S. (1993). Peer mediated reading instruction in special education resource rooms. *Learning Disabilities Research and Practice. 8* (4), 233–243.

McCormick, S., & Hill, D. S. (1984). An analysis of the effects of two procedures for increasing disabled reader's inferencing skills. *The Journal of Educational Research, 77,* 219–226.

McNutt, G. (1984). A holistic approach to language arts instruction in the resource room. *Learning Disability Quarterly, 7,* 315–328.

Palincsar, A. S., & Brown, A. L. (1986). Interactive teaching to promote independent learning from text. *The Reading Teacher, 46,* 771–777.

Paris, S. G., & Oka, E. R. (1989). Strategies for comprehending text and coping with reading difficulties. *Learning Disability Quarterly, 12,* 32–42.

Patching, W., Kameenui, E., Carnine, D., Gersten, R., & Colvin, G. (1983). Direct instruction in critical reading skills. *Reading Research Quarterly, 18,* 406–418.

Rose, T. L., & Robinson, H. H. (1984). Effects of illustrations on learning disabled students' reading performance. *Learning Disability Quarterly, 7,* 165–171.

Scruggs, T. E., & Mastropieri, M. A. (1986). Improving the test-taking skills of behaviorally disordered and learning disabled children. *Exceptional Children, 53,* 63–68.

Scruggs, T. E., & Mastropieri, M. A. (1988). Are learning disabled students "Test-wise"?: A review of recent research. *Learning Disabilities Focus, 3,* 87–97.

Smith, P. L., & Friend, M. (1986). Training learning disabled adolescents in a strategy for using text structure to aid recall of instructional prose. *Learning Disabilities Research, 2,* 38–44.

Wong, B. Y. L., & Wilson, M. (1984). Investigating awareness of and teaching passage orientation in learning disabled children. *Journal of Learning Disabilities, 17,* 477–482.

Woodcock, R. W. (1987). *Woodcock Reading Mastery Tests—Revised.* Circle Pines, MN: American Guidance Service.

Woodcock, R. W., & Johnson, M. B. (1977). *Woodcock–Johnson Psycho-Educational Battery.* Boston: Teaching Resources.

Chapter 10

INSTRUCTIONAL METHODS FOR LANGUAGE ARTS

OBJECTIVES

When you complete this chapter, you should be able to:

1. Describe several methods for improving the spelling of children with disabilities.
2. Discuss several classroom techniques that provide practice in speaking.
3. Describe a learning strategy used to teach testwiseness skills.
4. Discuss the relationship between language and listening skills.
5. Identify several methods for improving the quality of written work of students with mild and moderate disabilities.
6. Describe the stages in the writing process.
7. Describe at least two methods for improving oral reading fluency.
8. Discuss methods to improve handwriting.
9. Describe a whole-language language arts curriculum.

KEYWORDS

pragmatics
declarative
interrogative
imperative
exclamatory
type/token ratio
descriptive
narrative
exposition
active listening
argumentative
whole language

Instruction in language arts skills is the second most frequent instructional activity for many special education teachers, regardless of the setting in which they teach—second only to reading skills. As a special education teacher, you will spend considerable time on language arts. However, the definition of language arts is rather elastic and may include many topics. Also, several topics could be considered language arts that most special education teachers do not teach.

First, for most students with mild and moderate disabilities, the role of the special education teacher does not typically include instruction in speech itself. Most special education teachers who work with these students do not have to elicit speech or reinforce each utterance of a child in order to encourage speech. If such services are needed, they are usually provided by a speech clinician. Of course, this is not true of special education teachers who specialize in working with students with severe disabilities. Also, even special education teachers who work with students with mild disabilities may, on occasion, assist the speech teacher with certain daily speech exercises for some pupils.

Still, the term language arts, when used by teachers of students with mild and moderate disabilities, generally includes a number of communication skills on which school success, and life success, is dependent (Weller, 1993). Many consultative, resource room, self-contained class, and inclusive class teachers teach higher-level speaking skills, which may involve speaking to a group to persuade, or participation in role play and debate activities. Likewise, listening skills are frequently taught by special education teachers. Certainly, most special education teachers have the occasion to teach handwriting skills, and many teachers teach sentence and paragraph writing as well. Others, depending upon the grade level, teach theme writing and creative composition. Other language arts skills include testwiseness—as defined in the chapter on reading comprehension—spelling, and oral reading. Although no single chapter can provide detailed information in each of these areas, this chapter provides some examples of instructional strategies in each area, and you will find that many of the teaching strategies discussed previously are useful in this area also.

Finally, some language arts skills have been included in traditional school curriculums for decades (spelling, composition, and narrative writing), whereas others have been emphasized more recently (listening and public speaking). This chapter indicates which skills represent a relatively new emphasis and why each skill is presently considered to be important.

SPEAKING SKILLS

As stated previously, instruction in language arts does not generally involve eliciting speech itself, but rather instruction in higher-order speech skills. The term "pragmatics" is used to represent the use of language in normal, everyday social situations; some research has shown that many students with mild disabilities demonstrate deficits in pragmatic language skills (Boucher, 1986; Feagans, 1983; Weller, 1993). Apparently, many of the children in special education are deficient in conversation skills and do not know how to conduct oral communication. Whereas the typical elementary-age child will adjust language according to the age level of the child to whom they are speaking, the student with a mild disability may not simplify language in conversation with younger children, thus demonstrating a lack of awareness of pragmatic language skills (Bryan, Donahue, & Pearl, 1981). For these reasons, many special education teachers include some activities that assist students with disabilities in developing these pragmatic language skills.

A number of instructional activities may be used that strengthen the pragmatic language abilities of students with disabilities. For example, role-play activities require that a student study and adopt the role or persona of a particular character, and then engage in conversation as that character would. This type of practice in the adoption of various "roles" will strengthen a child's ability in pragmatic language. This technique is particularly useful in the inclusive classroom, where students without disabilities can work in mixed groups with students with disabilities on role-play activities. Further, role-play activities typically involve various position statements that may then be discussed in some type of open forum, and that prelude activity to the actual role play itself may also strengthen a student's pragmatic language skills.

Debate types of activities may also give students with mild disabilities some experience in using language in situations in which they have to argue for or against a position. In addition to these structured activities, there are a number of unscheduled techniques a special education teacher may use to strengthen the pragmatic language skills of the students. These are presented in Interest Box 10.1.

LISTENING SKILLS

Efficient use of spoken language is dependent, in large measure, on listening skills. Most children learn speech through exposure to speech in others, and, contrary to popular belief, listening does not merely mean passively attending to the conversation. When one considers the types of activities most children are exposed to in schools that involve listening—such as listening to teachers, other students, and audiovisual materials—the importance of active listening skills becomes apparent. Because many children with disabilities have a particularly difficult time acquiring new knowledge through reading materials, listening skills may be even more important for these students (Forster & Doyle, 1989).

INTEREST BOX 10.1
Strengthening Pragmatic Language Skills

As a special education teacher, one goal you will specify for many of your students is that of strengthening their use of language in social situations. The structured activities such as role-play and debates will assist in this regard, but there are many brief, unstructured activities that will also help. Several of these guidelines are presented below.

1. When a student speaks to you, and his or her use of language is incorrect, repeat the sentence correctly and request that the student repeat it after you. This type of modeling will give the student an example of correct use of grammar.
2. Do not accept incorrect sentences in class discussions. However, rather than embarrass the student, you may wish to call him or her aside later on to listen while you correctly model the sentence.
3. When a child constructs a sentence incorrectly in a small group, you may be able to ask his or her friend in the group to help correct the sentence. Then the first child should restate the sentence correctly.
4. When you see a child miss a nonverbal clue during communication (such as the meaning of a facial expression or a hand gesture), stop the communication and call the child's attention to the clue. Discuss what that clue may mean.
5. When you communicate with your students, and they miss a nonverbal clue of yours, stop them and repeat the communication while emphasizing the clue, then discuss it.

Active Listening

Like most useful skills, listening involves active participation in the learning process. For example, an active listener frequently brings himself or herself back to attention in order to concentrate on the speaker. The active listener will, on occasion, politely interrupt the speaker to ask questions that, hopefully, lead to improved understanding. The active listener is frequently summarizing the major points in his or her words as well as listening to what the speaker is saying at present. As you can readily see, these skills are quite a bit more involved than merely passive attendance to someone else's speech. Also, these skills are very useful in the academic environment. They require active participation and some degree of planning, and those requirements would suggest that students with disabilities may not be successful at active listening.

Instruction in Listening

Informal Instructional Tips. No specific aspect of the current school curriculum includes direct instruction in listening skills. Consequently, many special education teachers utilize a number of creative methods for teaching such skills. Perhaps an example would illustrate. Forster and Doyle (1989) recommend the following set of activities to strengthen listening skills. First, the teacher makes an edited tape of a morning news broadcast, including only several stories that are of interest to the students. Generally, one lead story, a weather story, and a sports story are sufficient. The teacher then makes an information outline of the news, which includes the main ideas and several supporting details for each story. The teacher also develops a fill-in-the-blank quiz for the broadcast. Students are told that their first activity is to help them learn to listen. They are given a prelistening exercise that involves reading the prepared outline of the news and asking about any unknown words. Next the students listen to the edited broadcast. Afterward, each student is encouraged to ask questions about the news while reviewing the news outline. The outlines are put away, and the whole group attempts to reconstruct the several news stories from memory while one student makes notes on the board. Next, each student retrieves his or her outline and compares it with the notes about the news. As a final prequiz step, all the students together write a summary of the entire news broadcast. Finally, the teacher administers the quiz. The papers may be graded in the group and any unclear concepts discussed again. Each student's performance may be charted daily in order to show progress in listening skills. Because of the relatively loose structure of this activity, it could easily be managed as a group activity with a "panel" of students taking the final quiz together.

Storytelling as a Listening Activity. Bauer and Balius (1994) described a storytelling therapy for use with students with emotional disturbance. Storytelling involves the teacher in selection and presentation of a story that may illustrate an issue that needs discussion—for example, single parent homes or abusive foster care situations. Storytelling on the part of the teacher is undertaken for therapeutic reasons, and students with emotional disturbances who will not listen to traditional instruction will frequently begin to listen during storytelling time. In some cases, this can strengthen the relationship between the student and the teacher, and at that point, both the emotional problems and listening skills are being addressed.

These listening activities should result in continued improvement in each student's ability to listen for main ideas and supporting details. Should you use this activity, you should also point out to the students how it should help them in listening to class lectures and discussions even after the news activity is finished.

A number of other activities have been discussed previously that also develop listening skills. These include role-play, debates, participant discussions, and other activities in which students with disabilities are encouraged to actively listen and participate in information exchange. As a special education teacher you will wish to include specialized instruction in listening skills, if language arts subjects are included as one of your instructional responsibilities. Of course, in inclusive classrooms you may find that you conduct at least one listening activity for groups of children across the ability spectrum each week.

HANDWRITING

Beyond mere use of spoken language and listening skills, the growing child is expected to master use of written language. Of course reading skills, discussed in previous chapters, constitute a large part of mastery of the use of written language. However, the students in our society are also expected to master the ability to write for purposes of communication, and this requires instruction in writing techniques that involve letter formation and writing style. The importance of good handwriting cannot be overemphasized. For many teachers, good handwriting is synonymous with neatness, and this provides rationale enough to stress legible handwriting as a crucial school skill. Also, good writing skills will enable the student to take more complete and accurate notes on material in his or her lessons, and can thus lead to improved performance in numerous subjects during the later school years.

In most public schools, writing skills comprise a separate subject area for the first three years of school, unlike the two language arts skills discussed above. Also, during the early years of schooling, the young child is required to learn two forms of writing: manuscript, or letter-by-letter writing, and cursive, or handwriting in which the individual letters are connected. Generally, by the age of nine the student is expected to have mastered manuscript writing and be ready to move into cursive writing. Needless to say, this type of transition in learning can affect other school skills, such as spelling, sentence formation, and written reports. Finally, both manuscript and cursive writing must be explicitly taught. Although printed materials expose the young child to numerous examples of manuscript letters, cursive writing is far less frequent in most children's reading materials. As a teacher of language arts for students with disabilities, you may spend a considerable amount of time in instructional activities that involve handwriting skills.

Suggestions to Improve Handwriting

In order to improve the handwriting of students with disabilities, both the students and the teachers must be involved. First, before a written assignment is turned in, require that the student review the first two lines, the middle two lines, and the last two lines in each writing assignment in order to check exclusively for handwriting errors. The student should be given specific instructions concerning what to look for, including:

1. Are all of the short and tall letters consistent in height?
2. Is the slant of each letter the same?
3. Are the spaces between the words the same?
4. Are there any letters capitalized not usually capitals (such as Z or Q), and are these correct?
5. Is the paper smudged?

Next, as a paper is handed in, the teacher should make an instant judgement concerning the handwriting. If the writing does not meet a certain standard for legibility, the student should be required to recopy the work. You should give the student specific suggestions concerning where letter formation or distancing between words may be improved. If necessary, time may be allocated to instructional activities that improve a child's handwriting.

Finally, as a teacher you should reinforce good handwriting by displays of student's works, awards for the most neat papers, and notes to parents concerning how their child's handwriting has improved, complete with examples of before and after handwriting. This type of encouragement will generally motivate most students to improve their handwriting skills.

Specific Techniques

Letter Fading. In addition to the activities listed above, several specific techniques may be used to assist in handwriting skills. The first of these techniques comes from behavioral psychology and involves the use of model letters a student is to trace a specified number of times each day. The teacher should select the letters a particular student writes incorrectly and place these on a sheet of practice paper for the student to trace. The student spends a few minutes with each problem letter every day, then the model letters are gradually faded until only the command to write the letters is present. Such repeated practice, coupled with praise for correct letter formation, generally results in improved letter formation in just a few weeks. Interest Box 10.2 presents a sample of this letter fading technique.

A Metacognitive Strategy for Handwriting. In an innovative metacognitive approach to handwriting improvement, Blandford and Lloyd (1987) used a self-instructional approach to improve the handwriting of elementary-age students with learning disabilities. Using the Blandford and Lloyd procedure, students were required to write in a journal on a subject they chose for 5 minutes each day. These written assignments were scored for neatness, letter placement relative to the line, and letter formation. Students were aware of their scores for each day of the project. During the intervention phase, each student was instructed to use a self-instructional card that asked questions concerning the child's written work. The questions are presented in Interest Box 10.3.

Using the questions, the students began to instruct themselves in handwriting each day by checking their own work. Such self-monitoring of one's own performance can be a very influential and effective instructional procedure. The results demonstrated that the students' handwriting improved measurably during the first 10 days of intervention, and that these improvements generalized to other classes. This transfer of learning indicates that this method of self-monitoring of

INTEREST BOX 10.2
Letter Fading Techniques

If a child has a problem with formation of particular letters, a letter fading **[[AUTHOR: hyphenate? letter-fading technique?]]**technique may be appropriate. In this type of technique, the student is presented with a tracing activity in which he or she initially traces the letters correctly, while noting the height and slant of the correct letter. After this activity is used for several days, the letter (or letters) a particular student is working on is purposely faded so that only part of the letter is there. Generally the remaining part of the letter includes the turns and slopes that form the most difficult aspects of correct letter formation. After a few more instructional periods, these aspects of the letter are faded and only several hints at letter formation are left. The child traces these for several days, and then practices the letter without any stimulus. The lines below give several examples of the types of faded letters the student would trace.

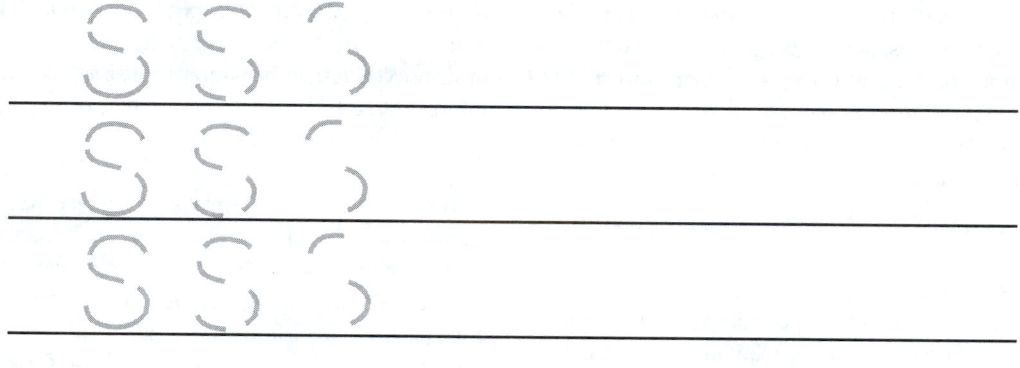

INTEREST BOX 10.3
Self-Instructional Writing Statements

1. a. Am I sitting correctly?
   b. Is my paper positioned correctly?
   c. Am I holding my pencil correctly?
2. a. Are all my letters sitting on the line?
   b. Are all my tall letters touching or nearly touching the top line?
   c. Are my short letters filling only 1/2 of the space?
3. Am I leaving enough, but not too much, space between words?

Source: Blandford and Lloyd (1987).

handwriting is a very powerful instructional technique. You may wish to compare this self-instructional task with the technique discussed in Chapter 5. At the very least, you will wish to employ this strategy with some of your students in order to improve their handwriting skills.

SPELLING SKILLS

One major focus of language arts instruction concerns spelling. Unlike some of the skills discussed previously, this area comprises a subject in and of itself in most elementary grades, and instruction is frequently a daily occurrence. However, like most language arts skills, this skill may also be taught in conjunction with early reading skills. For example, emphasis on phonics and decoding words involves some knowledge of spelling, because when a student knows what letters represent certain sounds, he or she can frequently spell the word or part of the word correctly.

General Spelling Techniques

To spell an unknown word, students use some combination of the following three strategies (Ehri, 1989). First, the student uses a knowledge of letters and letter sounds. Next, knowledge of the spelling system is utilized. This involves knowing how to break a word down into separate sounds and pronouncing those sounds. Finally, the student uses his or her knowledge of specific letter sequences in other similar words. These three tactics may be used in combination and in any order, depending on the student's spelling knowledge. These are important in this context because students with disabilities typically demonstrate deficits in each of these spelling strategies, and do not routinely use them in any systematic fashion. You may wish to teach these techniques to your students. A poster with these suggestions could be placed on permanent display and you would then remind students to use these ideas when they have a spelling task.

Often, when students with mild learning problems are given an assignment such as studying spelling words, the students merely look at the words repeatedly—a procedure that often results in wasted time. The effective teacher will specifically assign a study strategy, such as the one described above, in order to prevent this wasted time. You should employ this strategy, or some other study strategy that helps the student structure the study time, whenever you assign spelling words for study.

In both resource rooms and inclusive class settings, assigning "spelling partners" is one option for spelling practice. For example, students may take a "trial test" on the weekly spelling list on Tuesday, and on Wednesday the partners could practice the words they missed. This could easily be implemented in inclusive classes, pairing children with disabilities and children without disabilities.

Metacognitive Spelling Techniques

Much of the intervention research on spelling skills of students with disabilities has involved instruction in metacognitive spelling strategies (Gerber, 1984, 1986; Graham & Freeman, 1985). This parallels a similar trend in research on spelling instruction for nondisabled children (Sears & Johnson, 1986).

The educational treatments studies available strongly suggest that metacognitive instruction involving use of specific spelling strategies results in improved spelling performance (Graham & Freeman, 1985; Nulman & Gerber, 1984; Sears & Johnson, 1986). These learning strategies are patterned after the strategies discussed in Chapter 5. For example, in the Graham and Freeman (1985) study, students were taught to use a 6-step strategy. Specifically, students were trained to: say the word, write the word, check the word, trace the word while saying it, write the word from memory and check it, and repeat the first five steps as necessary (you could implement this strategy in your own class by making a poster of these 6 steps). Use of this strategy resulted in improved spelling performance. As an interesting aside, you may wish to note the similarity between this strategy and those discussed in the chapters on reading that involved modeling and tracing activities.

Sears and Johnson (1986) described a visual imagery instructional procedure similar to the visual imagery procedure for reading comprehension improvement discussed in Chapter 8. Using this visual imagery spelling technique, a child is trained to mentally imagine a large screen with the word printed on it. Children who are unable to imagine this screen can listen to descriptions from those children who can. This procedure was more effective than either auditory imagery (hearing the letter sounds), or copying the words in a research comparison (Sears & Johnson, 1986).

Nulman and Gerber (1984) demonstrated the effectiveness of an instructional strategy based on imitating a child's spelling errors. These authors suggest that the single most important teaching technique for spelling is the child correcting his or her own error under the direction of the teacher. This technique, quite obviously, employs the effective teaching behaviors emphasized in Chapter 1; specifically, this technique stresses both immediate feedback and modeling. Consequently, when a child makes an error, the teacher is to indicate that an error has been made and imitate it. The child then identifies the error, with the teacher's help, and corrects it. The teacher then models the correct spelling and encourages the child to repeat it.

WRITTEN EXPRESSION

Beyond handwriting, speaking, and spelling, most children with mild and moderate disabilities will require some instruction in written expression. Although a student may be able to copy sentences, fill in the correct answer on spelling exercises, and read a passage appropriately, he or she may not be able to write a coherent series of sentences about a selected topic, much less a single- or multiparagraph passage. According to Tompkins and Friend (1986), children with mild disabilities have a particularly difficult time when given a writing assignment. They may have problems getting their paper organized and in position, generating ideas for the topic, and/or putting those ideas down in any type of organized fashion. For these reasons, many special education teachers find that a great deal of instructional time is spent on written expression.

The Writing Process

Scholars have identified various stages in the writing process (Ellis, 1994; Englert, Raphael, Anderson, Anthony, Fear, & Gregg, 1988; MacArthur, 1994; Tompkins & Friend, 1986, Whitt, Paul, & Reynolds, 1988). The common elements in these analyses are numerous; Interest Box 10.4 presents a synthesized description of the stages in the writing process as utilized in this text.

Teacher's Decisions Prior to Writing

Prior to assigning a writing assignment, there are several things a teacher should consider. These include informal assessment of the writing skills of each student, the mode of discourse the assignment involves, the method of text production, and motivational approaches for reluctant writers.

Informal Assessment. First of all, very few commercially available assessments do an adequate job in identifying the weaknesses of written expression among children with mild and moderate disabilities. As a result, you may need to conduct an informal assessment of a student's written work in order to find out how to improve the child's work. Minner, Prater, Sullivan, and Gwaltney (1989) have provided some guidelines for informal assessment of a student's written expression. This type of assessment will yield specific instructional activities for inclusion on each student's IEP. The form for this evaluation is presented in Figure 10.1.

First, the teacher should look at fluency or quantity of writing a student produces. One common measure of fluency is the average sentence length. Nondisabled 8-year-old children generally average eight words per sentence, and this increases at a rate of one word per year until the child is 13. This rough guideline will give some indication

INTEREST BOX 10.4
Stages in the Writing Process

Many different scholars have discussed the stages in the writing process, and not all would agree that the stages listed below are complete or comprehensive. Still, these stages do describe the writing process from the decision making which the teacher does concerning assignments to the preparation of the final copy.

- Prewriting Teacher Decisions
  - Informal Assessment of Writing
  - Decision on the Mode of Discourse
  - Decision on the Text Production Method
- Motivation for The Writing Assignment
  - Use of Observation of A Particular Stimulus on the Topic
  - Sensory Exploration of the Environment
- Drafting the Composition
  - Brainstorming Techniques
  - Ignoring Errors
- Revision and Editing
  - Use of Editing Marks
  - Rereading for holistic content
- Teacher Checking Conference
- Final Rewrite for Perfect Copy

Sources: Ellis (1994); Englert et al. (1988); MacArthur (1994); Tompkins and Friend (1986): Whitt, Paul, and Reynolds (1988).

of where a child stands in relation to his or her peers in fluency of writing.

Next, the types and functions of the various sentences should be assessed. Sentence forms include sentence fragments, simple sentences, compound sentences, and complex sentences. Obviously, growth on this variable involves decreasing sentence fragments and increasing the frequency of other, more complex types of sentences. The informal assessment also includes a frequency count of the four sentence functions: declarative, interrogative, imperative, and exclamatory. Declarative sentences state one or more facts. Interrogative sentences ask a question. Imperative sentences give a command, and exclamatory sentences express heightened emotion and excitement. A writing sample should include a range of sentence types.

Vocabulary should also be assessed. This is typically done by a calculation called the type/token ratio. The number of different words used constitutes the type, and the total number of words constitutes the token. For example, "The red wagon rolled down the red clay hill" has 7 different words in a total of 9 words. The type/token ratio is 7/9 or .77. As this ratio becomes higher, the student's use of words has become more varied. You may also make a note of unusual or new vocabulary words a student uses.

In assessing grammatical correctness of the writing, Minner and his co-workers recommend the grammatical correctness ratio. To calculate this ratio, the number of grammatical errors is divided by the total number of words in the passage, and that product is multiplied by 100 to yield a percentage figure. Then an error analysis is conducted to identify the common types of errors.

Student's Name ______________________ Date ________ Teacher ______________________

Fluency

ASL Number of Words ____________ Number of Sentences ____________

Number of words/number of sentences ____________ (ASL)

Comments:

Sentence Types

Sentence Forms	Frequency	Sentence Functions	Frequency
Fragments		Declarative	
Simple		Interrogative	
Compound		Imperative	
Complex		Exclamatory	

Comments:

Vocabulary

TTR Number of different words (types) ______

Number of total words (total) ______ Types /Total= _____(TTR)

Comments:

Unusual Words (number of words not used in previous writing sample)

Comments:

Structure

GCR Total number of errors ______________ Total number of words ________

Number of words - errors/number of words x 100 = ____ (GCR)

Comments:

Structural Error Analysis

Types of Errors	Frequency

Comments:

Ideation: (circle one) Excellent Good Needs Additional Thought

Questions:

Is the writing sample relevant to the selected or assigned topic?	Y	N
Does the writing sample represent original thinking?	Y	N
Are the child's personal perspectives expressed in the sample?	Y	N
Are the ideas in the sample expressed in a logical and appropriate sequence?	Y	N
Does the student appear to have a basic interest in the topic and does he/she seem to be motivated to commit ideas to written form?	Y	N

FIGURE 10.1 Informal Assessment of Written Expression Form

Finally, the teacher should consider the content and ideation behind the written work. Is the work well conceived and well organized? Have the major points that should be covered been covered? These questions, and those on the bottom of the form in Figure 10.1, should allow a teacher to fully evaluate the quality of the writing sample.

As a special education teacher, you will want to keep a clean copy of the evaluation in Figure 10.1 and use it with those children who experience writing difficulties in any educational setting. Further, this assessment should be performed on a continuing basis, perhaps twice a week throughout the year, in order to document progress regularly.

Mode of Discourse. When a teacher makes a writing assignment, he or she should consider the mode of discourse to be used (Blair & Crump, 1984). For example, in many beginning-to-write activities, the student is merely expected to write a descriptive statement concerning the event or topic. Sometimes students are provided with a "story starter"—a picture or an incomplete sentence—and told to write a description of it. Descriptive discourse is generally the first type of written assignment made in the lower grades. This type of discourse mode tends to be characterized by a high frequency of declarative sentences and fewer compound or complex sentences. However, by the middle school years, students are expected to be able to write several other types of discourse.

The narrative discourse mode is slightly more complex than the descriptive mode, because the former includes the responsibility of developing a story theme or plot in a logical sequential fashion (Crealock, 1993). Sentences tend to begin with words that suggest sequential ordering (e.g., Next, Then, After that). Also, more ideas tend to be expressed in narrative discourse than in descriptive discourse.

The exposition discourse mode represents the student's attempt to expose some unusual aspect of, or explain a process within the topic to be discussed. This requires the student to utilize logical discussion and indicate why a particular point should be exposed, as well as sequential logic in the timely presentation of the various events in the process.

Finally, the argumentative discourse is much more complex than the earlier discourse modes. This discourse mode is sometimes referred to as thesis writing or position papers. The student is expected to take a position and present that position in a convincing way. This type of discourse is characterized by more complex sentence forms than the earlier types of discourse.

In a comparison of descriptive and argumentative discourse production among elementary students with learning disabilities, Blair and Crump (1984) found that the students used longer thought units and included more subordinate clauses in the argumentative discourse mode. Also, there was some evidence that those students may not cognitively differentiate between the various modes of discourse until several years later than nondisabled students. This suggests that special education teachers in the upper grades should specifically teach these four types of discourse (using both spoken and written products) to students with mild disabilities. One interest group activity assignment would be to give the same general topic to four students and assign each of them a different mode of discourse. The students should then compare the written assignments in order to discuss the purposes of each type of written work.

Mode of Text Production. With the advent of the microcomputer many new instructional strategies for writing have become available (Kerchner & Kistinger, 1984; MacArthur, 1994; MacArthur & Graham, 1988; Outhred, 1989). For example, rather than being provided with an open writing assignment, many children now learn to write using various simplified word processing programs, such as *Logo* (Papert, 1980) and *Bank Street Writer* (1980). Word processing programs make the transition from first draft to finished product much less time consuming. Editing is also done more quickly. Several of the general advantages of using computer assisted instruction were discussed in Chapter 7.

Research has generally demonstrated that students with mild disabilities who use word processing programs achieve writing proficiency more quickly than students taught in more traditional ways (MacArthur, 1994; Kerchner & Kistinger, 1984; MacArthur & Graham, 1988). For example, Kerchner and Kistinger (1984) used the *Bank Street Writer* in an experiment to determine the effect of word processing on the writing skills of middle-grade learning disabled children. An experimental group and a control group were pretested using the *Test of Written Language* (Hammill & Larsen, 1978) at the beginning of a school year. The control group studied writing in either the language experience approach or in traditional reading or writing instruction. The experimental group used a writing method that incorporated word processing. On each writing assignment day, a prewriting conference was held at which each student selected a topic and the teacher asked questions to facilitate thought about that topic. The student then composed his written work at the keyboard. During that phase, the students could make obvious corrections, but were encouraged not to worry about mistakes. Then the student printed a draft. An editing conference was then held including the writer, the teacher, and the student's peers. This group edited for spelling, sentence structure, punctuation, and clarity of the ideas. After this conference the student went back to the keyboard and edited the draft. Then a final copy was printed. Posttest results at the end of the year demonstrated the advantage of the writing instruction received by the experimental group. This study, among others, demonstrates the efficacy of using word processing as an instructional tool for improving writing skills.

As a special education teacher you will wish to use word processing instructional programs with your students when those options become available in your school. You should use some type of daily assessment procedure, as discussed in Chapter 4, to identify the students for whom word processing works best; for other students you should continue to use more traditional forms of instruction.

Motivating the Reluctant Writer. A number of scholars have presented instructional methods that should assist a reluctant writer to begin the assignment and complete the first several steps in the writing process (Fortner, 1986; Tompkins & Friend, 1986; Whitt, Paul, & Reynolds, 1988). For example, Tompkins and Friend (1986) recommend several different approaches that should provide some information about which a student may write. First, the teacher may instruct the student in observation skills, by selection of an interesting picture with numerous details included. The students should be encouraged to discuss the picture among themselves, and try to explain what the picture represents. Students may be further exposed to observation skills by having them observe various interesting objects (flowers, seashells, household objects), or various events (such as a candle burning or a fish swimming).

Next, students may be trained to discuss sensory exploration. The five senses are introduced, then a single type of object (popcorn is recommended) may be used by exposing the object to each of the senses. The students look at the object, listen to it, touch it, smell it, and taste it. Afterward, they describe each of the sensations.

Finally, in order to motivate reluctant writers and provide some material for written compositions, Tompkins and Friend (1986) recommend that students be trained to interview others. They may interview parents about their jobs, other teachers, or other students. Specific questions should be provided for the students to ask, and the interviewer should also be trained to generate his or her own questions during the interview.

Drafting the Composition

After teacher consideration of these preliminary issues drafting of the written work begins. Preparation of the first draft of a written composition is one of the early stages in the writing process. Generally, students should be told that drafting is a brainstorming activity during which they should get as many ideas down as possible in coherent form. Students should be encouraged to "keep their pencils moving" and not to stop to correct mistakes during their first draft (Whitt, Paul, & Reynolds, 1988). Such correction can prohibit the flow of ideas in reluctant learners. If a student realizes that a sentence should have been placed earlier, or that a new paragraph should have been started, he or she may indicate this with a pencil mark drawn vertically at the place where the break in thought is located. It is also possible to use the computer in this prewriting phase (MacArthur, 1994).

Revision and Editing

Although teachers generally assist in the checking, revision, and editing of written compositions, one goal of instruction should be for each student to learn to edit his or her own works. At a minimum, after the first draft is finished, the student should be encouraged to go back, prepare a second draft, and correct these obvious mistakes. Kerchner and Kistinger (1984) refer to this emphasis as a process approach to writing instruction because the teacher is instructing the student in the entire process of drafting, editing, and rewriting. Consequently, use of certain standardized editing symbols (Whitt, Paul, & Reynolds, 1988) will assist many students in this process. After the student decides that the first draft is completed, he or she should be encouraged to review the written work and search for possible errors. Each error should be indicated with one of the symbols presented in Interest Box 10.5.

INTEREST BOX 10.5
Use of Editing Symbols

Many scholars have recommended the use of editing symbols to identify errors in written work. Also, use of these symbols tends to make children feel more "professionally" involved in attempts to correct their mistakes, since these editing symbols may be taught as a "secret code" that many students in the school cannot read. Whitt, Paul, and Reynolds (1988) recommended use of the following basic editing symbols.

Symbol	Explanation	Example
(circle)	Circle words that are spelled incorrectly.	My freind and I went to the zoo last week.
/	Change a capital to a small letter.	Mary and Jim watch the Television for one hour.
≡	Change a small letter to a capital letter.	bob loves the way I play.
∧	Add letters, words or sentences.	My friend lives in the ∧ brick house next door.
⊙	Add a period.	My dog and I are private detectives⊙
(delete mark)	Take out letters, words, or punctuation.	Last summer Bob went and flew in a airplane.
(comma caret)	Add a comma.	Bob visited Alaska Ohio and Florida.

Source: Whitt, Paul, and Reynolds (1988).

Also, in addition to searching for errors in word placement and spelling, the student should be encouraged to read each part of the composition for meaning. This process may be thought of as reading for holistic content, or the relationship between the numerous ideas and topics in the composition.

A 3-step strategy may be used for this phase of the revision and editing process. First, students should read each sentence individually to make sure that it is correctly worded. Next, the sentences should be read in two- or three-sentence units, in order to assure that each logically follows from the previous sentence, that no contradictions are present, and that each sentence leads into the next in a clean and concise fashion with no breaks in the logic. If contradictions or large gaps in logic are found, these should be corrected by rewriting sentences or adding additional information where necessary. Finally, each paragraph in longer compositions should be read as a whole, in an effort to assure that each logically follows the one above.

After editing and checking the logic of the sentences and paragraphs, the students should be required to rewrite the composition in a form that may be turned in to the teacher. This draft should be free of mistakes.

Teacher Conference

Whitt, Paul, & Reynolds (1988) recommend that teachers plan an evaluation conference with students in order to check written work. Because of the small numbers of students in many special education classes, such conferences may be utilized for almost every written assignment. However, this may become impractical in inclusive classes. Still, with two teachers in the class, some students could benefit from a teacher conference on each assignment, and such conferences could then be held with other students on the next written assignment.

In preparation for the conference, the teacher should require that students submit both the first draft and their final composition. The first draft should be reviewed to identify the ideas and to check on correct use of editing and revision procedures. Next, the final draft should be checked. Students should be praised for identifying mistakes and correcting them on the final draft. Also, the teacher should point out any additional mistakes the students have overlooked.

Final Rewriting

Although many teachers stop instruction after the teacher conference, others find that students are quite willing to continue working on the composition until it is letter perfect. Even after the grading at the teacher conference many students will be prepared to rewrite their composition to correct the final few mistakes, if they are reinforced for that work. Personally, I found that almost every student I taught in a junior high school resource room would recopy work in order to make a corrected copy for public display on the wall in the room or the bulletin board outside in the hallway. Special education students rarely have their work publicly displayed, and the reinforcement of such a display was often the motivational factor to which my students responded. Also, it is very impressive during parent visits to show parents displays of their children's work.

The last point cannot be overemphasized. Student work display was, singularly, one of the most important things I did in my class for parents and students alike. I well remember one parent in tears one evening, when she reported that she had never seen her daughter's written work on display before in the hallway of any school (her daughter was then in junior high). She commented repeatedly—over a series of meetings, over a series of years—how much it meant for her daughter to show that paper to her mom. It is those moments, so few and so very precious, that make teaching a joy. At any rate, students will recopy work several times, for that type of reinforcement.

TEST-TAKING SKILLS

One relatively new concern in language arts instruction is training in the skills involved in taking tests (Ritter & Idol-Maestas, 1986; Scruggs &

Mastropieri, 1986). Although this set of skills is useful for certain texts in math and other subject areas, it is most frequently taught as a language arts topic, since these skills involve efficient use and manipulation of language. As you may recall, certain test-taking skills were discussed in Chapter 9.

One strategy for instruction in test-taking skills that has received some research support is the use of a learning strategy called SCORER (Carman & Adams, 1972). The strategy itself is presented in Interest Box 10.6.

Research has shown that the SCORER strategy, and other similar strategies, may be taught to students with mild disabilities as early as the third grade (Scruggs & Mastropieri, 1986). For example, Scruggs and Mastropieri (1986) conducted a study that demonstrated the effectiveness of instruction in test-taking skills. Seventy-six third and fourth grade students with learning disabilities and behavioral disorders were randomly assigned to either an experimental group or a control group. Students in the experimental treatment condition were trained for two weeks on test-taking strategies relevant to reading achievement tests. These strategies included attending to directions, marking answers carefully, choosing the best answer, using error avoidance strategies, and deciding appropriate situations for soliciting teacher assistance. The students were further trained in several specific strategies related to word recognition reading subtests. Specifically, the students were trained to employ seven sequenced strategies, presented in Interest Box 10.7.

The results demonstrated that the students in the experimental group scored significantly higher than the students in the control group on word study skills, and this study shows that specific training related to the skills measured by a test does result in improved performance.

ORAL READING SKILLS

One final skill that is often included in a rather offhand way in the language arts curriculum is oral reading. Although many teachers routinely require oral reading in their classes, not many teachers allocate instructional time specifically to those skills unique to oral reading. Many beginning teachers assume that oral reading skills are roughly the same as silent reading skills, though many experienced teachers know that this is not the case.

In oral reading, unlike silent reading, the student does not have the option of skipping a new vocabulary term and using the context to determine the meaning. Each term must be pronounced, and

INTEREST BOX 10.6
A Test-Taking Learning Strategy

Carman and Adams (1972) developed a test taking strategy which is used to help students understand how to complete questions on a multiple choice test. The steps are presented below.

S = Schedule your time
C = Clue words
O = Omit difficult questions
R = Read carefully
E = Estimate your answer
R = Review your work

Source: Carman and Adams (1972).

INTEREST BOX 10.7
A Seven-Step Test-Taking Strategy

1. Read the first word.
2. Pronounce it to yourself and think of the sound of the underlined letter.
3. Carefully look at all the answer choices and choose the word with the same sound as the underlined letter.
4. If you don't know all the words, read the words you do know or read parts of individual words that you may know.
5. If you are not sure of the answer, see if there are some answers that you are sure are not correct, and eliminate those.
6. Color in the answer quick, dark, and inside the line.
7. Guess if you are not sure; never skip an answer.

Source: Scruggs and Mastropieri (1986).

that requirement necessitates highly developed decoding skills as well as word attack skills. Also, there is the potential for embarrassment should the new word be mispronounced.

If you choose to require oral reading in your classroom, you should investigate the research on oral reading. For example, Gottlieb (1984) presented research that suggested that students with learning disabilities have fewer oral reading errors when reading in a group of similar ability peers. This would suggest that oral reading should be employed only in relatively homogeneous groups, and that has obvious implications for the inclusive classroom. Alternatively, if oral reading will be required on a given day, a prereading review (or a silent read-through) of the material to be read orally can alleviate many errors and thus most of the embarrassment associated with oral reading.

There are a number of instructional strategies that improve the oral reading performance of students with disabilities. Rosenberg (1986) demonstrated that error correction procedures in which drills on correct pronunciation were used improved oral reading more than a phonics procedure. Freeman (1984) demonstrated that a taped word treatment also improved oral reading. Finally, Rose and Sherry (1984) have demonstrated that a previewing strategy that involves listening to the passage can reduce the oral reading errors demonstrated by some students with mild disabilities. Each of these strategies are easily employed in almost any classroom.

WHOLE LANGUAGE INSTRUCTION

As discussed in Chapter 8, whole language instruction has received increasing attention (Altwerger, Edelsky, & Flores, 1987; Chiang & Ford, 1990; Goodman, 1986). Perhaps this new instructional approach is best understood in contrast to traditional instruction in language arts, and some discussion of this contrast is necessary here.

The traditional language arts texts approach instruction in a rather disjointed manner. For example, the use of words in sentences is governed by numerous rules involving word type (nouns, adjectives, etc.), verb tenses, dominant and subordinate clauses, pronoun referents, and many other aspects. In traditional language arts classes these skills have been taught in a rather piecemeal fashion and have not been systematically interwoven into a complete holistic understanding of the use of language. You may recall from your own elementary education the tasks that involved only one of these skills: a worksheet requiring students to underline all of the subjects and predicates or to connect the pronoun and its referent. This type of activity, although necessary on occasion, generally left students with a very disjointed picture of language arts competence.

The Whole Language Perspective

Today, however, many scholars recommend a whole language approach to language arts instruction, in which reading, writing, and speaking are all integrated and included as part of the total curriculum (Altwerger, Edelsky, & Flores, 1987; Chiang & Ford, 1990). The constant focus remains the desire to communicate meaningfully, and these skills, which have traditionally been the matter for separate instruction, are now integrated for successful communication (Bender, 1987; McClure, 1985; McNutt, 1984). In a whole language classroom, the student is required to perform each of the language arts skills based not on textbook reading but rather on the use of published literature. For example, novels and published poetry would be used to teach reading, with various instructional tasks in speaking and writing based on those assignments. This instruction may involve silently reading a brief selection from a novel, retelling that subplot so that the teacher may check for comprehension, and then writing and editing a synopsis of the selection. Specialized worksheets are still utilized, but only when the student has consistently demonstrated a problem in one particular area, and those worksheets never become the major focus of the language arts instruction time period. Instead, the focus remains on effective communication, whichever mode is used—reading, speaking, or writing.

Whole Language Instructional Activities

The following instructional example would be appropriate for whole language instruction in a resource room for junior high school students with mental retardation, learning disabilities, and behavioral disorders. This example incorporates every major aspect of the language arts curriculum into one comprehensive whole language instructional system.

At the beginning of the school year, the students should be told of the importance of useful communication between themselves and others. Next, students should be encouraged to select reading material they wish to know more about. The teacher should provide a set of reading materials in which great literature has been rewritten at an appropriate grade level. Topics could be changed for each grading period.

Students would then be instructed to read a section (that would take between 5 and 15 minutes) each day from their selected material. After reading, the students would be expected to answer questions on the section and retell the reading content to the teacher verbally. The advanced organizer technique referred to as the five *wh* questions, or a similar technique, could be used each day. If this technique is used, the questions "Who? What? When? Where? Why?," printed on a poster, should be displayed all year, and the first thing every student should do after reading is answer these questions to the satisfaction of the teacher. If the student cannot answer each of the questions, he or she should be encouraged to return to the reading to find the answers. This instructional phase would last from 3 to 8 minutes each day, and the teacher could then evaluate the student's verbal expression skills. The teacher should listen to amend any incorrect language on the part of the child. Also, more advanced students should be expected to speak more clearly and be encouraged to speak in complete sentences and paragraphs. The teacher should note any consistent speech or grammatical errors, and these should be recorded each day. About 5 minutes would be required to complete this phase each day.

Finally, the students would be required to write one or two paragraphs about the reading section that summarized the material. These are intended to be comprehensive and should include each of the major points in the verbal summary discussed above.

After the student has completed the summary, he or she would bring it to the teacher for an editing conference. Errors would then be recorded and the student would be expected to return to his or her seat and correct each error. While this correction is taking place, the teacher would compare the written errors on the paper with the early drafts of paragraphs from the previous several weeks. These drafts should be saved in a special file for each student for this comparison. Any consistent error patterns should be pointed out to the child in order to encourage particular attention to situations in which those errors may arise.

This corrected writing sample would then be shown to the teacher, and the student would be encouraged to copy the perfected paper for display on the class bulletin board. In order to emphasize the importance of this display, the teacher should indicate the student's work to parents during parental visits. Also, on occasion, the teacher may wish to invite the principal to make a "surprise visit" and to complement a particular student regarding the work on display.

As you can see, the whole language approach incorporates almost every major aspect of language arts into the curriculum in a comprehensive fashion (Chiang & Ford, 1990). This direct relationship between the student's reading comprehension of quality literature and the written products and speaking skills motivates students who understand the reason for particular assignments and the importance of those assignments in enhancing communication skills. Using this whole language approach, the language arts curriculum would not seem so disjointed (Goodman, 1986).

INSTRUCTION IN LANGUAGE ARTS

Instructional Activities

1. *Verbal directions:* Prepare on a piece of tagboard a diagram similar to the following example:

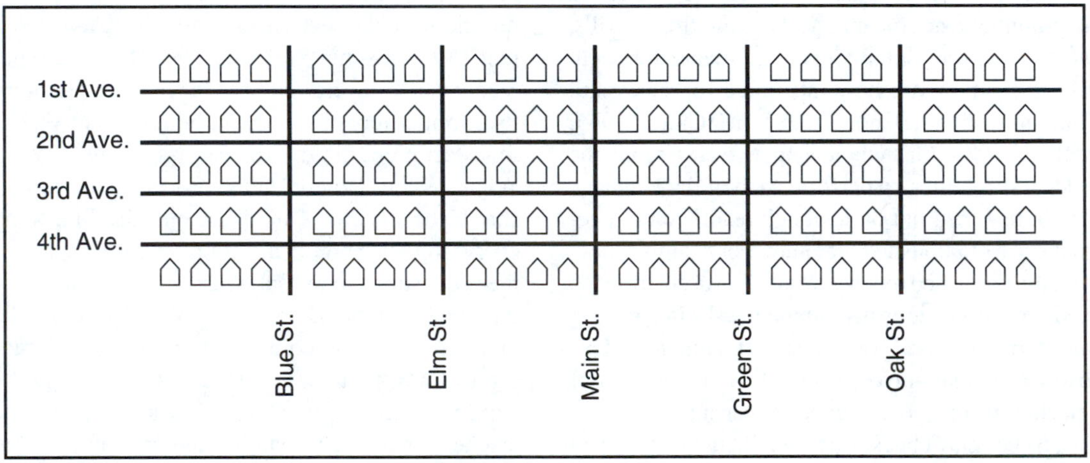

1st Ave.
2nd Ave.
3rd Ave.
4th Ave.
Blue St.
Elm St.
Main St.
Green St.
Oak St.

Direct the child to drive a miniature car to an area on the diagram. For example, "Drive two blocks on Blue Street, turn right and drive three blocks on 2nd Avenue." The directions may be written on index cards to be read or given orally.

2. *Puppet stories.* Use this as a follow-up activity for stories that have been read to the group, or have the group create its own stories, and then create the puppets to act out the story. Materials needed are tagboard, construction paper, rubber cement, and tongue depressors.

   Puppets are made of tagboard and/or construction paper. The figures are cut out and mounted on a stick with glue. A cardboard stage made out of a box or a table with a cloth that will hide the children could be used. Children move their puppets along the upper edge of the stage. Cue cards may be necessary for some children. Taped music or sound effects can be used to add to the production.

3. *How would you feel?* This activity allows the child to express his ideas and feelings verbally concerning various situations. Materials include 3 pieces of white tagboard, magazines, cartoons, magic markers, paste, and scissors. Select pictures from magazines or newspapers. Laminate these pictures and place on tagboard. Photographs of the children themselves are also very effective. Under the pictures write with magic marker, "How would you feel . . . ?" Have the children take turns expressing their responses to the pictures. Encourage them to be specific.

4. *Mystery pictures.* Select pictures with several objects or activities in them. Laminate them and mount on black construction paper, then on tagboard. On separate cards (4 × 5) write questions concerning the pictures. Make a pocket of tagboard and attach it to the back of each picture with masking tape. Show the picture for fifteen seconds, then take the picture away and ask the prepared questions.

5. *"Thinking" pictures.* Select pictures of abstract designs, unusual social situations, and mature scenes. Place each picture on the left-hand side of a 12" × 18" piece of tagboard. Fold the tagboard in half, with the picture on the inside. Design an attractive cover. On the right side of the folded tagboard write a question or an unfinished sentence. Have the student record his or her response on a tape recorder. Save the tape, and on another day allow the student to look at the pictures and listen to the previously taped response. Adding to or deleting from the original response if the student chooses is allowed. If the response is altered, ask why the student has changed his or her thinking.

6. *Haiku poems.* Read some Haiku poems to the students and then present them with this formula:

1. Noun
2. Two words to describe
3. What does it do? (3 words)
4. How does it make you feel? (4 words)
5. Repeat the original noun.

First compose some group poems. On the chalkboard write whatever noun a child suggests, then decide what descriptive words to use. An example:

Girls.
Pretty, pretty
They're nice sometimes
I feel funny then.
Girls.

Allow the children to write poems of their own. Display them on a bulletin board with an oriental motif. (This would be good to use in a unit on Japan.)

7. *Following directions.* On a large tagboard make a racetrack with four lanes. Make each lane about 3/4" to 1" wide. Divide each lane into equal parts. Along each lane scatter various signs, for example: Flat tire—skip 1 turn; red light—lose 1 turn; Four-lane—advance 2 spaces; Wrong turn—go back 2 spaces. Be sure each lane has the same number and types of road signs. Mark one end of the track "Start" and the other "Finish." Use the concept cards, adding to them as new concepts are learned. For example:

1. Give 5 compound words.
2. What holiday comes in December?
3. How many minutes in an hour?
4. Give 5 good safety habits.
5. Free question. Make up your own question and answer.
6. What do A.M. and P.M. mean?
7. Give the opposites of hot, long, small, good.

Each child selects a miniature car and places it at the starting line. The concept cards are placed in the center of the game board. The first child rolls the die and draws a card. If he answers the question correctly he moves the number of places on the die, if he does not answer correctly, he does not move. If the student lands on a road sign, he must obey the sign.

8. *Vocabulary building.* You will need 52 tagboard playing cards. Make 13 sets of four cards each. Each set shows four matching synonyms. Sample sets are:
   1. buoyant, cheerful, happy, joyous
   2. thin, slender, lean, narrow
   3. castle, palace, mansion, alcazar
   4. defy, disregard, resist, disobey
   5. cash, money, funds, currency
   6. menace, danger, threat, peril
   7. priest, deacon, cleric, minister
   8. mistake, inaccuracy, error, fault
   9. neophyte, beginner, novice, greenhorn
   10. witchcraft, sorcery, magic, voodoo
   11. truth, candor, honesty, verity
   12. idol, image, statue, totem
   13. parch, scorch, sene, dry

   Vary the difficulty of the synonyms to fit the ability level of your group. Two or more players may enjoy this game. Deal all the cards evenly among the players. Each player puts his or her cards face down in a stack. The players in turn take their top cards and turn them face up. If any player's card is a synonym of a face-up card in an opponent's stack, either of these players may say, "SNAP!" The player who says "SNAP" first gets all of the cards in the opponent's face-up stack, and the game continues. The object is to collect all of the cards.

Commercially Available Materials

***Distar Language,* Science Research Associates**

The *Distar* language program is designed for students in preschool through third grade. The program focuses on expressive and receptive language as well as on cognitive development. Level I is designed to give students practice in word use and sentence building, as well as in asking and answering questions. Level II students continue practice in sentence development and begin to focus on questioning and reasoning skills. Level III introduces the rules of grammar and students begin to formulate the concept of using these rules to communicate effectively. The program is highly structured and uses drill and repetition to teach language concepts. The teacher follows a script and models appropriate responses. The students respond rapidly and the teacher corrects incorrect responses, or reinforces the correct responses.

***All-Purpose Photo Library,* Development Learning Materials**

This "library" contains lifelike photos divided into two sets. Set 1 has 12 categories that include "body parts," "transportation," and "tools and hardware." The 16 categories in set 2 include "musical instruments," "sports," "birds," and "school." There are a total of 626 photo cards. In addition, each category contains a question card pertaining to the basic characteristics of the categories. This set of materials is designed to reinforce and expand language skills and vocabulary and to increase the student's awareness of functions and attributes of common objects and other various items.

***"American Storytelling Series,"* The H. W. Wilson Company**

This series presents 6 audio cassettes of 21 colorful, compelling stories told by some of America's finest storytellers. Myths, legends, folk tales, and fairy tales come alive in the telling. Each of the 8 volumes in the series is introduced by storyteller David Holt. The background music that accompanies the stories, composed especially for the *American Storytelling Series,* is performed on a wide range of instruments including those of the traditional orchestra, the bansuni, the bamboo flute of India, and many other fascinating acoustical delights. The stories range from the fanciful, rhythmical language of "Frogs, Dodge City," for beginning "story listeners," to "The Twelve Huntsmen," a story of two people's journey from adolescence to adulthood.

***Vocabulary Boosters,* Fearon Press**

Vocabulary Boosters are reproducible worksheets for a language enrichment program that focuses on use of a dictionary, using context clues, use of a thesaurus, and analogy practice. Each book includes a glossary, worksheets, crossword puzzles, and a final test for each level.

***The Literature Experience*, Houghton Mifflin**
The Literature Experience is a program organized into themes for students in kindergarten through eighth grade. It is accompanied by activities and response materials that ensure that every student is actively involved. The kindergarten package is composed of two levels, "All About Me" and "Let's Be Friends." Each level is organized by theme to give students the experience of listening to literature read aloud, participating in shared reading, and reading independently. The first grade materials include instructional strategies for all ability levels incorporated into a group of teaching materials that include student journals, student resource books, activity cards, and theme and writing center posters. The second through fifth grade materials include books about adventure and humor, heroes and history, mystery and achievement. The middle school series includes anthologies that parallel the content areas in junior high school and expand and enrich the themes that are meaningful for upper-level students.

***Crayola Creativity Program*, Binney & Smith Educational Products Division**
Crayola Creativity Program is a unique approach to early childhood education and carries a heavy emphasis on language arts skills. This program introduces activities that enhance children's natural curiosity while reinforcing fundamental skills. Center-based activities are for use in six learning centers traditionally found in early childhood classrooms: arts and crafts, blocks, language and listening, manipulatives, science and nature, and dramatic play. Skill-based activities encourage development in four broad skill areas: language, physical, thinking, and social/emotional. This program includes a director's manual, teacher's guide, activity book, skills assessment record, and training video.

***One Hundred Twenty-Six Strategies to Build Language Arts Abilities: A Mouth-by-Mouth Resource*, Allyn & Bacon**
This is a resource book designed to help increase the effectiveness and efficiency of language arts instruction. One of the most prominent features is that it provides new strategies to teach the more difficult communication and conceptual skills. Special elements of this book were included to increase the student's retention of class objectives while reducing the amount of time spent in instruction. This book departs from a more holistic approach to targeted skill development. In addition, this book illustrates many ways language arts can be integrated across the curriculum, as each lesson is based on a social science, sociological, or scientific theme.

Language Arts Software

Academic Skill Builders in Language Arts
Publisher: DLM Teaching Resources
Skill Level: Elementary, secondary
Hardware: Apple IIe, IBM
Description: The six programs in this series provide drill and practice in vital language arts areas: *Verb Viper* for subject–verb agreement, *Word Invasion* for six parts of speech, *Word Man* for word building, *Spelling Wiz* for commonly misspelled words, *Word Radar* for sight words, and *Word Master* for antonyms, synonyms, and homonyms. The programs each use a different game format that reflects their name. For example, *Verb Viper* has students match a verb with its subject by shooting the verb. All areas of the program are editable and controllable, including the content and the speed at which the students must answer questions. Also included are extensive instructional and student tracking features.

Bank Street Writer Plus
Publisher: Broderbund Software, Inc.
Skill Level: Elementary, secondary, adult
Hardware: Apple IIe, IBM
Description: Bank Street Writer Plus is an easy-to-use, nontechnical word processor developed by educators for children and adults of any age. Its features include a 6,000 word automatic

spelling corrector, on-line dictionary, option to add personalized dictionary, and macro command. This program allows the use of enlarged text for use with younger individuals.

Big Book Maker: Favorite Fairy Tales and Nursery Rhymes

Publisher: Pelican Software, Inc.

Skill Level: Secondary, adult

Hardware: Apple IIe

Description: This program allows the user to create mini to big books, write original fairy tales or recreate traditional ones to encourage writing. Each "page" is a two-screen scrolling area consisting of a picture with room to write in. Goldilocks can visit the three little pigs or Humpty Dumpty can climb up the beanstalk. Students can design their pages any way they want to with graphics and text. Graphics from other sources may be imported to create additional sequences. Prints out in strips you easily tape together to make big books. *Big Book Maker* comes in many other editions besides Fairy Tales. It includes six typestyles and font printout sizes.

Capitalization

Publisher: Hartley Courseware, Inc.

Skill Level: Elementary, secondary

Hardware: Apple IIe

Description: This program introduces the basic rules of capitalization. Each lesson includes examples and 25 randomly presented items on which a student can practice applying the rules.

Children's Writing and Publishing Center

Publisher: Learning Company

Skill Level: Preschool, elementary

Hardware: Apple IIe, IBM, Macintosh

Description: Children's Writing and Publishing Center features sophisticated word processing, picture selection, and page design capabilities. The program can readily be integrated into many curriculum areas. Contains clip art that students can use to create reports, stories, letters, publish newsletters, awards, and more. Elements are added to a "page" and the program works the text around the graphics. Looks like a mini desktop publishing program.

Co:Writer

Publisher: Don Johnston Developmental Equipment, Inc.

Skill Level: Elementary, secondary, adult

Hardware: Macintosh

Description: Co:Writer empowers your word processing program with word prediction capabilities. The program improves grammar skills and productivity for writers with disabilities. Grammar-intelligent word prediction reduces keystrokes to improve production and stimulate creativity. Loaded with such features as capitalization, spacing, and many other routine activities, the program helps students learn sentence structure and other writing mechanics. For example, when a student types a period indicating the end of the sentence, the program automatically enters two spaces and capitalizes the next word. The language structure features of the program help put the right words in the right places. Prediction of words is determined by sentence location, subject–verb agreement, recency, redundancy, frequency, and other user preferences.

Creature Capers

Publisher: Laureate Learning Systems, Inc.

Skill Level: Preschool

Hardware: Apple IIe, speech synthesizer

Description: Creative Capers is designed for very low cognitive functioning populations. It can be used with a single switch, the keyboard, or TouchWindow. Upon the user's command, different creatures perform animated routines. The game can be used to teach cause and effect, turn-taking, and use of a single switch.

Early Learning 3.5

Publisher: MarbleSoft

Skill Level: Preschool, elementary

Hardware: Apple IIe

Requirements: Color monitor

Description: Programs control level of difficulty, rate of advancement, program speed, response to incorrect answers, and amount of verbal and visual feedback. Compatible with keyboard, hand controls, PowerPad, TouchWindow, IntroVoice, Echo, Cricket, and DoubleTalk. Has built-in management system. Includes the programs *Matching Colors, Learning Shapes, Counting Numbers, Letter Match, Early Addition I/II, Sequencing Up/Down, Sorting Fun, Count the Shapes, Match the Shapes, What Comes Next, Coin and Bills, Counting Money,* and *Making Change*. Includes keyboard overlays.

FrED Writer

Publisher: CUE SoftSwap

Skill Level: Elementary, secondary, adult

Hardware: Apple IIe

Description: A word processor that allows students to use either 40- or 80-column text. The 40-column text is larger and easier for some students to work with initially. The program has all the standard utilities and comes with instructions right on the disk that can be accessed as a help file from anywhere in the program. Prompted writing is an important feature in the program and allows the teacher to embed prompts within the file to elicit student responses. The prompts are not editable by the student and are embedded blocks that stand out from the rest of the text. When the program is in prompted mode the student uses the down cursor arrow to get to the next prompt and then follows the prompt there. For example, a teacher may want the students to write short essays on their favorite places. The first prompt may ask the student to answer the prompt "my favorite place is . . .".The next prompt may be "my favorite place looks like . . ." and the third prompt, "my favorite place smells like . . ." In this fashion, the student is prompted through the writing process and can then print their essay out. The printing function offers the standard options and includes a choice of whether to print the prompts or not. Lesson disks are available to help teachers work through the prompted writing process.

McGee

Publisher: MCE, A Division of Lawrence Productions

Skill Level: Preschool

Hardware: Apple IIe, IBM

Description: McGee is an independent exploration program with no words, using realistic sounds and speech output. Rising with the sun, McGee goes exploring while mom is asleep. Students guide McGee on his adventure by selecting one of four choices at the bottom of the screen. The program contains no menus or words of any kind (other than the title screen). Colorful rooms and animated sequences are drawn from a child's perspective. As McGee feeds the dog, crawls under an ornamental rug, watches TV, bounces a ball, plays with a puppet, goes into the bathroom, and more, the program talks and plays all the appropriate sounds. For example, when McGee goes to the bathroom he closes the door for privacy and all the student hears is the flushing of the toilet. Further, when he goes into mom's room and picks up the music box, the user hears the music and mom waking and sleepily saying "McGee put that back." Each time McGee is taken into a different environment the choices at the bottom of the screen change. This program has two sister programs that function in the same way but offer different environments and characters: *Katie's Farm*, in which McGee visits Katie's family's farm, and *McGee at the Fun Fair*, which McGee visits with his parents.

Predict It: A Word Processing Program

Publisher: Don Johnston Development Equipment, Inc.

Skill Level: Preschool, elementary, secondary

Hardware: Apple IIe

Description: Predict It is a word processing program with a predictive word feature. The user types the first letter of a word and several choices appear at the bottom of the screen. The user then types in the number corresponding to the correct word, or presses the space bar if the correct choice is at the cursor, and that word is placed on the screen. Sending a final punctuation mark inserts the sentence into a document screen and automatically places two spaces and capitalizes the next word. *Predict It* also provides rapid access to grammatically correct endings such as -ing, -ly, etc. The choices are made from a base of 1,500 words and utilize grammatical or letter probability factors to select the words. *Predict It* has all the features needed in a word processor program, such as cut, copy, and paste. Can be used with the Adaptive Firmware Card.

Writer Rabbit

Publisher: Learning Company
Hardware: Apple IIe

Description: Writer Rabbit is a tool for developing writing skills and reinforcing reading comprehension. Students identify sentence parts and construct sentences in a motivating atmosphere. Over the course of six sequenced games, students learn grammar concepts and build up to higher writing levels. The activities also reinforce reading comprehension as students read the sequences to identify correct sentences. The program includes a Silly Story Party, which allows students to create their own letters and stories.

SUMMARY

Instruction in language arts skills will consume a great deal of the typical special education teacher's time. These skills are necessary for functional literacy, for success in other classes at school, and for later vocational success. Although many special education classes and inclusive classes emphasize reading skills, more and more time is being spent on other language arts areas as well, including listening, speaking, writing, and spelling.

As a special education teacher you will make decisions concerning which of these language arts skills to emphasize in your class with particular students. The overall guiding principle in your decision should be the needs and abilities of the individual student. However, do not let the historical concern for one language arts skill—reading or writing—overshadow the need for meaningful instruction in such other skills as speaking, listening, and oral reading. You should find the appropriate balance to meet the needs of each student in your class.

For this reason, many teachers today are investigating a whole language approach to language arts. A whole language approach involves all of the language arts skills each day, but instruction is flexible enough to emphasize particular curricular aspects as the needs of each student indicate. You may wish to take additional coursework in whole language arts instruction should your schedule allow.

Summary Points

- Language arts instruction has been expanded beyond spelling and writing to include listening skills, speaking skills, test-taking skills, and oral reading skills.
- Role play and debate activities can be used to strengthen a child's speaking skills.
- Active listening involves a set of specific behaviors children should be taught. These behaviors increase the interaction between speaker and listener.
- Handwriting skills may be improved by either behavioral techniques—such as letter fading—or metacognitive instruction–such as self-checking questions about handwriting legibility.
- General spelling strategies involve knowledge of letters, knowledge of the spelling system, and knowledge of standard sequences of letters. A number of metacognitive techniques are also effective in spelling instruction.
- The writing process involves several stages, including prewriting activities, drafting, revision and editing, and a teacher conference for evaluation.
- Information assessment of writing should involve some consideration of the types of discourse, the types of sentences used, the elaboration included in the sentences, and the overall expression of the general theme.
- The mode of discourse determines the types of sentences and the general complexity of the written assignment. For example, a writing assignment in the argumentative mode will be more complex than one in the descriptive mode.

- Word processing writing programs such as *Logo* or *Bank Street Writer* assist learners with disabilities in mastery of writing skills.
- Use of concrete objects and group projects can motivate the reluctant writer.
- During the drafting phase of writing, the student should be encouraged to put ideas down and to worry about organization and error correction later.
- The revision and editing process is the process of error correction and checking for completion of ideas.
- Students with mild disabilities can profit from instruction in test-taking skills such as SCORER.
- Oral reading is expected in some classrooms, and a number of strategies have been used to decrease the frequency of oral reading errors. These include imitation of the errors and immediate feedback to correct the errors.
- A whole language instruction procedure is utilized to emphasize the communicative skills in total, rather than specific language arts skills in isolation. This instruction typically proceeds from reading classic literature and should involve each of the major language arts skills, including reading, writing, oral expression, and listening.

QUESTIONS AND ACTIVITIES

1. Obtain several writing samples from elementary students with disabilities and edit the samples using the editing symbols. Then complete the informal assessment for that sample. What types of errors do you see?
2. Invite a local elementary school teacher to speak to your class concerning his or her language arts curriculum. What aspects of language arts are emphasized?
3. Review the research on spelling techniques. Form debate teams and stage a debate concerning the most effective strategies.
4. List several guidelines for taking tests. Can you think of a learning strategy acronym that would help students memorize these strategies?
5. Review the research on the mode of discourse employed by students with disabilities. What are the characteristics of the different modes? What types of discourse are most frequent among the writings of these students?
6. Why are listening skills important?
7. Define active listening and give examples of the various skills involved.
8. Develop a language arts lesson plan for a role-play activity that involves students with disabilities. How would this lesson plan be different from a lesson plan for a similar activity in the elementary class?
9. Review the special education journals and find several methods for teaching handwriting. Present these to the class.
10. Describe the theory and instructional procedures used in a whole language instructional approach.

REFERENCES

Altwerger, B., Edelsky, C., & Flores, B. M. (1987). Whole language: What's new? *The Reading Teacher, 41,* 144–154.

Scholastic Inc. (1980). *Bank Street Writer* (computer program). Lyndhurst, NJ.

Bauer, M. S., & Balius, F. A. (1994). Storytelling: Integrating therapy and curriculum for students with serious emotional disturbances. *Teaching Exceptional Children, 27* (2), 24–29.

Bender, W. N. (1987). Holistic language arts: Remedial strategies and procedures. *Techniques, 3,* 273–280.

Blair, T. K., & Crump, W. D. (1984). Effects of discourse mode on the syntactic complexity of learning disabled students' written expression. *Learning Disability Quarterly, 7,* 19–29.

Blandford, B. J., & Lloyd, J. W. (1987). Effects of a self-instructional procedure on handwriting. *Journal of Learning Disabilities, 20,* 342–346.

Boucher, C. R. (1986). Pragmatics: The meaning of verbal language in learning disabled and nondisabled boys. *Learning Disability Quarterly, 9,* 285–295.

Bryan, T. S., Donahue, M., & Pearl, R. (1981). Learning disabled children's peer interactions during a small-group problem solving task. *Learning Disability Quarterly, 4,* 250–259.

Carman, R. A., & Adams, W. R. (1972). *Study Skills: A Student's Guide for Survival.* New York: Wiley.

Chiang, B., & Ford, M. (1990). Whole language alternatives for students with learning disabilities. *Learning Disabilities Forum, 16,* 31–33.

Crealock, C. (1993). The grid model for teaching narrative writing skills. *Teaching Exceptional Children, 25* (3), 33–37.

Ehri, L. C. (1989). The development of spelling knowledge and its role in reading acquisition and reading disability. *Journal of Learning Disabilities, 22,* 356–365.

Ellis, E. (1994). Integrating writing strategy instruction with content-area instruction. *Intervention in School and Clinic, 29* (3), 169–179.

Englert, C. S., Raphael, T. E., Anderson, L. M., Anthony, H. M., Fear, K. L., & Gregg, S. L. (1988). A case for writing intervention: Strategies for writing informational text. *Learning Disabilities Focus, 3,* 98–113.

Feagans, L. (1983). Discourse processes in learning disabled children. In J. D. McKinney & L. Feagans (Eds.), *Current Topics in Learning Disabilities,* Vol. 1. Norwood, NJ: Ablex.

Forster, P., & Doyle, B. A. (1989). Teaching listening skills to students with attention deficit disorders. *Teaching Exceptional Children, 22,* 20–22.

Fortner, V. L. (1986). Generalization of creative productive thinking training to LD students' written expression. *Learning Disability Quarterly, 9,* 274–282.

Freeman, T. J. (1984). Effects of a taped words treatment procedure on learning disabled students' sight-word oral reading. *Learning Disability Quarterly, 7,* 49–53.

Gerber, M. M. (1984). Orthographic problem-solving ability of learning disabled and normally achieving students. *Learning Disability Quarterly, 7,* 157–164.

Gerber, M. M. (1986). Generalization of spelling strategies by LD students as a result of contingent imitation/modeling and mastery criteria. *Journal of Learning Disabilities, 19,* 530–537.

Goodman, K. (1986). *What's Whole in Whole Language?* Portsmouth, NH: Heinemann.

Gottlieb, B. W. (1984). Effects of relative competence on learning disabled childrens' oral reading performance. *Learning Disability Quarterly, 7,* 108–112.

Graham, S., & Freeman, S. (1985). Strategy training and teacher vs. student controlled study conditions: Effects on LD students' spelling performance. *Learning Disability Quarterly, 8,* 267–274.

Hammill, D., & Larsen, S. (1978). *Test of Written Language* (Rev. ed.). Austin, TX: Pro-Ed.

Kerchner, L. B., & Kistinger, B. J. (1984). Language processing/word processing: Written expression, computers and learning disabled students. *Learning Disability Quarterly, 7,* 329–335.

MacArthur, C. (1994). Peers + Word Processing + Strategies = A powerful combination for revising student writing. *Teaching Exceptional Children, 27* (1), 24–29.

MacArthur, C. A., & Graham, S. (1988). Learning disabled students' composing under three methods of text production: Handwriting, word processing, and dictation. *The Journal of Special Education, 21,* 22–42.

McClure, A. A. (1985). Predictable books: Another way to teach reading to learning disabled children. *Teaching Exceptional Children, 17,* 267–273.

McNutt, G. (1984). A holistic approach to language arts instruction in the resource room. *Learning Disability Quarterly, 7,* 315–320.

Minner, S., Prater, G., Sullivan, C., & Gwaltney, W. (1989). Informal assessment of written expression. *Teaching Exceptional Children, 22,* 76–79.

Nulman, J. A. H., & Gerber, M. M. (1984). Improving spelling performance by imitating a child's errors. *Journal of Learning Disabilities, 17,* 328–333.

Outhred, L. (1989). Word processing: Its impact on children's writing. *Journal of Learning Disabilities, 22,* 262–264.

Papert, S. (1980). *Mindstorms: Children, Computers, and Powerful Ideas.* New York: Basic Books.

Ritter, S., & Idol-Maestas, L. (1986). Teaching middle school students to use a test-taking strategy. *Journal of Educational Research, 79,* 350–357.

Rose, T. L., & Sherry, L. (1984). Relative effects of two previewing procedures on LD adolescents' oral reading performance. *Learning Disability Quarterly, 7,* 39–44.

Rosenburg, M. S. (1986). Error-correction during oral reading: A comparison of three techniques. *Learning Disability Quarterly, 9,* 182–192.

Scruggs, T. E., & Mastropieri, M. A. (1986). Improving the test-taking skills of behaviorally disordered and learning disabled children. *Exceptional Children, 53,* 63–68.

Sears, N. C., & Johnson, D. M. (1986). The effects of visual imagery on spelling performance and retention among elementary students. *Review of Educational Research, 79,* 230–233.

Tompkins, G. E., & Friend, M. (1986). On your mark, get set, write. *Teaching Exceptional Children, 19,* 82–89.

Weller, C. (1993). Building a pragmatic language. In W. N. Bender (Ed.), *Learning Disabilities: Best Practices for Professionals.* Boston: Andover Medical Publishers.

Whitt, J., Paul, P. V., & Reynolds, C. J. (1988). Motivate reluctant learning disabled writers. *Teaching Exceptional Children, 20,* 37–39.

Chapter 11

INSTRUCTION IN MATHEMATICS

OBJECTIVES

Upon completion of this chapter, you should be able to:

1. Describe the concrete to abstract instructional sequence recommended for instruction in early math operations.
2. Present a rationale for instruction in functional math.
3. Describe several metacognitive strategies for calculation.
4. Define automaticity and discuss the importance of this skill.
5. Describe several math curricula such as *Touch Math, DISTAR,* and *Project Math.*
6. List the types of activities that may be included in a functional math curriculum.

KEYWORDS

conservation	seriation	face-times-place
readiness skills	numeration	automaticity
one-to-one correspondence	STAR approach	*Touch Math*

Mathematics is one essential skill often de-emphasized in public school curriculums for students with mild disabilities, because of the substantial needs these children demonstrate in reading and language arts. For example, research by Carpenter (1985) indicated that only about one-third of the instructional time in most resource rooms is devoted to mathematics, even though most teachers indicate that this skill is second in importance only to reading. Although no research is available on instructional time in math in inclusive classrooms, there is every reason to believe that students are not overloaded with instructional opportunities in math in that setting either.

RESEARCH ON MATH INSTRUCTION

Research has shown that children and adolescents with disabilities tend to perform better on mathematics skills that require literal manipulation of numbers and worse on skills that require applications of mathematical knowledge (Algozzine, O'Shea, Crews, & Stoddard, 1988). Of course, the last type of problem is much more similar to the mathematics problems faced in real world situations, and thus students with disabilities have difficulties in their daily lives because of math deficits. If one considers the routine daily life skills dependent to some extent upon math (balancing a checkbook, tax payment, shopping, and making change), one can readily see the importance of math for students with disabilities. Clearly much more attention should be given to mathematics in most special education classes and inclusive classes, and researchers are beginning to address this lack of knowledge on how to teach math to students with disabilities (Boom & Fine, 1994; Mayer, 1994; Montague, Applegate, & Marquard, 1993; Scheid, 1994).

However, this does not mean that students with mild or moderate disabilities should follow the same curriculum in mathematics as nondisabled children (Zentall, Smith, Lee, & Wieczorek, 1994). Although the same curriculum may be appropriate for many students with disabilities, certain adaptations will be necessary for others (Boom & Fine, 1994; Lambie & Hutchens, 1986; Mayer, 1994). For example, Zentall and her coworkers (1994) demonstrated that a group of boys with attention deficit hyperactivity disorders demonstrated less adaptive math computation strategies than nondisabled students, and the authors recommended specific adaptations for students with that disorder.

Further, the research evidence indicates that many students with mild disabilities will not progress as quickly as nondisabled students in mathematics, nor will they go as far in overall math achievement, even when their computational skills are similar to the skills of the nondisabled (Algozzine et al., 1988; Bilsky & Judd, 1986; Cawley & Miller, 1989). Because of this need for adapted instruction in mathematics for many students with mild and moderate disabilities, this chapter presents information in several basic areas of mathematics instruction. These instructional areas include math readiness, early math skills, operations, word problems, and functional math skills. Although these areas do not exhaust the mathematics curriculum by any means, understanding of the types of instructional adaptations in each of these areas should prepare you to effectively meet the mathematics instructional needs of most students with disabilities in every instructional setting.

Prior to presentation of information on the various instructional areas, a word is necessary about assessment of these areas. Generally, neither the student's placement test scores nor the school records will include enough information concerning mathematics achievement to allow you to prepare an effective instructional plan. As discussed previously, math is often de-emphasized in both assessment and instruction, and even if a math assessment is included in the battery of tests used for placement decisions, it may not be specific enough to use as a basis for planning daily instructional activities.

Consequently, you will probably need to conduct several informal assessments in various areas. This chapter includes specific suggestions for assessment in each of the areas discussed, and several assessment instruments are presented. One general rule when using an informal assessment is to write a brief paragraph describing the task you asked the child to perform and his or her performance. Also include the date and your signature. This documents the informal assessment for later use in communication with parents or to show progress later in the year. Next, you should consider routine use of criterion-referenced assessments in math to assist you in identifying the problems experienced by students with disabilities. Finally, numerous commercially available math curriculum materials include criterion-referenced tests. If you use such a curriculum in your instruction, you should certainly consider using the assessments that accompany that curriculum. These informal measures could alleviate the need for formal testing in preparation for the next IEP.

MATH READINESS AND COGNITIVE ABILITY

Readiness for instruction in math depends to some degree on the cognitive development of the child, and math readiness may depend more on the development of different cognitive skills than does reading readiness. For example, Rourke and Finlayson (1978) concluded that children with a learning disability specific to mathematics generally demonstrated a profile of cognitive abilities characterized by low nonverbal skills. Alternatively, students who demonstrated learning disabilities in both reading and math had cognitive profiles characterized by low scores on both verbal and nonverbal cognitive assessments.

A second cognitive ability area related to mathematics readiness is the concept of conservation. Because of the pioneering work of Jean Piaget (1965), mathematicians have begun to attend more to this concept. Basically, conservation means that certain numerical or quantitative properties of an object do not change simply because the shape or appearance of the object changes. In the early conservation work, a certain amount of water was poured from a tall thin glass into a short, larger glass, and the child was asked if the same amount of water was present. Clearly, the water in the thin glass filled more of the glass than the same amount of water in the larger glass, and if a child indicated an understanding that the amount of water was the same, that child had achieved the cognitive understanding of conservation of quantity—that is, the quantity had not changed.

This skill impacts on early mathematics in numerous ways. For example, when teachers use counters or sticks to illustrate a math problem, they may draw a circle and move the counters from place to place to illustrate place value. You will find numerous examples of this technique later in the chapter. The child's understanding of conservation will affect the degree to which he or she understands this reconceptualization of the numerals, because a circled group of sticks appears to be different from the same number of sticks when they are pictured individually.

Beyond these few generalizations very little is known about the impact of cognitive ability on mathematics achievement. Undoubtedly, future research will shed more light on this relationship.

READINESS SKILLS

In addition to the cognitive abilities discussed above, early success in math is also dependent on certain prerequisite skills that do lend themselves to instruction. These prerequisite skills are generally referred to as math readiness skills, and include a number of diverse areas, each of which is discussed below. Informal assessment of these readiness skills is fairly simple, and is discussed within each section.

Classification Skills

First, children must learn the skills involved in classification. This involves awareness of likenesses and differences between numbers or sets of objects and instructional activities that generally include sorting objects into specific groups according to the characteristics of the objects. Nondisabled children can generally sort objects into different groups by the age of 5 to 7 years, and many kindergarten instructional activities or preschool activities involve this type of sorting by color, shape, or texture.

Various simple games and activities may be used to assess and reinforce this skill. For example, merely give the child a number of objects and request that he or she place them in groups according to some attribute, such as color. Remember to keep a signed and dated record of your task instructions and the child's performance.

One-to-One Correspondence

Next, children must learn to identify a one-to-one relationship before they can be taught to count. That is, they need to understand that an object in one set of objects has a corresponding member in another set of objects. For example, Mercer and Mercer (1983) described an activity in which a child was required to place one large button in one glass for every small button placed in another glass. After a few moments, when the glass with the larger buttons appears more full, one should ask the child, "Does each glass have the same number of buttons?" If the child responds in the affirmative, then the child has acquired the concept of one-to-one correspondence. Of course, a negative response indicates that the child is using visual cues to answer the question.

The importance of one-to-one correspondence is apparent when one considers the skill of counting. The child must realize that one sound or word (such as the word "one") represents the first of the numerals in the number line, whereas the second sound (two) represents the second numeral, and so forth. Understanding of one-to-one correspondence is generally considered to be one of the most important of the math readiness skills. Interest Box 11.1 presents several instructional suggestions for teaching one-to-one correspondence.

INTEREST BOX 11.1
Strategies for Teaching One-to-One Correspondence

Each of the ideas below may be used to teach one-to-one correspondence. Likewise, if you write out an adequate description of the questions you ask each child, and sign and date it, these activities may be used as informal assessments of the child's understanding of one-to-one correspondence.

1. Draw two large circles on a sheet of paper. Draw an *X* in one circle and request that the student draw an *X* in the other circle. When this is done indicate that the two circles have the same number of *X*s in them. Then draw two more *X*s in the first circle. Encourage the child to draw two in the other circle. At first these should be widely spaced in the circle, so that even the child who does not count can readily tell the number of objects in the teacher's circle. Repeat the process, drawing between one and three *X*s in the teacher's circle.
2. Use a set of coins which are all the same (all dimes). Give one to the child and tell the child to keep it for a time, and then give one to another child. Ask the first child if both have the same number of coins. Give two coins to the second child, and one to the first child, and enquire again. Make sure that each child openly displays the coins.
3. Use body parts to illustrate one-to-one correspondence. Show a child two extended fingers on one hand. Ask the child to show you the same, and hold the hands together, matching finger for finger. Repeat the steps with any number of fingers.

Seriation

Seriation, or the ability to place objects in order based on some attribute of the objects, is another prerequisite math skill. For example, objects may be ordered by weight, length, overall size, or any other property in which a progression of ordering guidelines may be established. Many preschool manipulative toys involve seriation. For example, when a child is asked to place the rings on a peg according to the size of the ring, the concept of seriation is being taught, and this concept leads directly to understanding that some numbers are "small" and "come before" other numbers. Teachers in higher grades may reinforce this concept by assigning activities that involve sorting objects from smallest to largest or longest to shortest. Pattern games that require the child to complete patterns of letters of numbers (e.g., X X X O X X X O X X X _, or R S T U) also teach this skill (Mercer & Mercer, 1983).

EARLY MATH SKILLS

In addition to the math readiness skills, teachers in special education must often instruct students in certain early math skills. Some of these early math skills must be mastered before or during the earliest work in mathematics. An example of this type of skill would include numeral recognition. However, instruction in many of these early math skills, such as place value and memorization of mathfacts, overlaps with early work in calculation. Instructional suggestions for each of these early math skills are discussed below.

Numeration

Numeration may be defined as the child's understanding of numbers, number sequences, and counting. Success in later mathematics exercises is largely dependent on numeration skills, and many students with disabilities have not mastered these early math skills.

Numeral Recognition. Instruction in number recognition generally proceeds in much the same way as letter recognition. Activities that involved matching manipulative numerals to sample numerals on a page are involved. Many children's books that assist in numeral recognition may be used. Students are first taught to recognize the ten digits and then place them in order.

Assessment of this skill is simple and may be accomplished by asking the child to name several numerals that you write on a piece of paper. As in all informal assessments, the paper should then be dated and signed, with a brief description of the task added so that the informal assessment may be documented at a later date, or at the end of the year, to show progress. All informal assessments should be saved in the student's folder.

Writing Numerals. Sometimes students experience difficulty, not in recognition itself, but in reproduction (i.e., writing) of numerals. To address this problem with young children, Boom and Fine (1994) utilized a metacognitive approach with a kindergarten child. These researchers utilized the structured 8 steps recommended for strategy instruction (see Learning Strategy in Chapter 5), to teach the student how to write the basic numerals. The STAR (Sayings for Forming Numerals) approach prepared the student with written instructions for formation of the basic numerals. Use of these scripted statements by the student resulted in improved numeral formation. The sayings are presented in Interest Box 11.2.

Counting. Many nondisabled children enter the first grade with certain counting skills, because most kindergarten curricula include some number recognition and counting activities. Instruction in counting proceeds rather smoothly if the child has mastered the prerequisite skills discussed above. For example, if the child has a good understanding of seriation as well as one-to-one correspondence he or she should be able to point to sequenced objects and verbally run through the numbers. Generally, children are taught to count

INTEREST BOX 11.2

***STAR* Statements for Numeral Writing**

To make a **0**: The woman went around the circle until she got back home.
To make a **1**: The man went straight down, like a stick.
To make a **2**: The woman went right and around, slid down the hill to the left, then made a line across the ground.
To make a **3**: The man went right and around, then around again.
To make a **4**: The woman went down the street, turned to the right, then back to the top for a straight ride down.
To make a **5**: The man went down the street, around the corner, and his hat blew off.
To make a **6**: The woman made a curve and then a circle at the bottom.
To make a **7**: The man made a line across the top, then he slid down the hill to the left.
To make an **8**: The woman made a half circle to the left, another to the right, and then she found her way back up to the top again.
To make a **9**: The man made a small circle and then a straight line down.

Source: These statements are from Boom and Fine (1994).

up to 10 objects, and then are taught to count from 10 to up to 20 objects. Many special education teachers encourage children to use their fingers to count, and although this may need to be discontinued at a later time, finger counting is one method by which this process can be made very concrete for children with disabilities. Assessment of this skill involves requesting that the child count several sets of objects verbally.

Many children learn to "count" their fingers during parental reading sessions prior to school. Although such parental involvement should certainly be encouraged, the teacher should not assume that a child who can "count" to 10 using fingers has a complete understanding of the sequential order of the numerals, or knows the written numerals. Some children merely "count" along these lines by memorizing the sound of the numerals and repeating them. Should a teacher encounter a young child who can "count" using fingers, it is always wise to informally check the child's understanding of counting and the other prerequisite math skills.

Older children should be required to count objects past twenty in order to demonstrate understanding of the gradual progression of groups of tens. A final milestone is reached when a child can count up to 100.

Number Sequences. Many math curricula and assessment instruments in mathematics stress the importance of number sequences during the first and second grades. For example, problems that present an incomplete sequence and require the student to fill in the blanks are common, even when the sequence does not include every number (two examples are: 1 2 3 4; and 3 6 9 12). Each of these examples is dependent on the child's understanding of the concept of the number sequence. Assessment of this skill is accomplished by presenting several number sequences, such as those above, and requiring that the child complete them. Also, time spent on number sequences often pays benefits later. For example, counting by twos, threes, or fives often aids the student in later multiplication work.

Place Value

Understanding of place value is one of the most important of the early math skills because students must develop this understanding in order to master early operations. This skill is generally taught during the first grade, and reviewed during each grade thereafter. Students must understand that the digit "3" in the ones' place is different from the same digit in the tens' or hundreds' place. This skill is initially taught by using concrete examples and grouping or regrouping those objects as the student watches. Place value instruction also is usually taught in concert with early addition. Several examples of these grouping techniques for teaching place value are presented in the discussion of addition later in this chapter.

Some recent research using students with disabilities has indicated that place value instruction should begin with very concrete examples, such as actual manipulatives (Hudson, Peterson, Mercer, & McLeod, 1988; Peterson, Mercer, & O'Shea, 1988). Hudson and her co-workers (1988) recommended the use of one-inch plastic cubes as counters to enable students to identify the number of tens and ones in a specific double-digit number. An intermediate step, using semiconcrete examples (picture sticks, hash marks, or pictures of blocks on paper as counters), followed the instruction for concrete examples. Finally, instruction on the abstract level was conducted in which no manipulatives or pictures were used. Criterion-referenced posttests indicated that this method of concrete, semiconcrete, and abstract instruction worked for students with disabilities. Interest Box 11.3 presents an example of how place value assessment and instruction generally proceeds.

The experienced teacher soon realizes that instruction in place value, though initiated quite early in the math curriculum, continues throughout the early and middle elementary school years. For example, instruction in place value during the middle grades may involve use of decimals, the implied addition of digits in multidigit numerals, and the verbal names of multidigit numerals. Many math curricula include activities that involve multiplication of

INTEREST BOX 11.3
Place Value Instruction

Begin instruction with concrete manipulatives. First, obtain at least 40 small objects which do not vary in size or color. These counters should be stackable. Draw two circles side by side on a sheet of paper with the circle on the right labeled the "ones' circle" and the one on the left labeled the "tens' circle." Place that paper on the desk above a group of objects for the child to count—the number should range between 11 and 19.

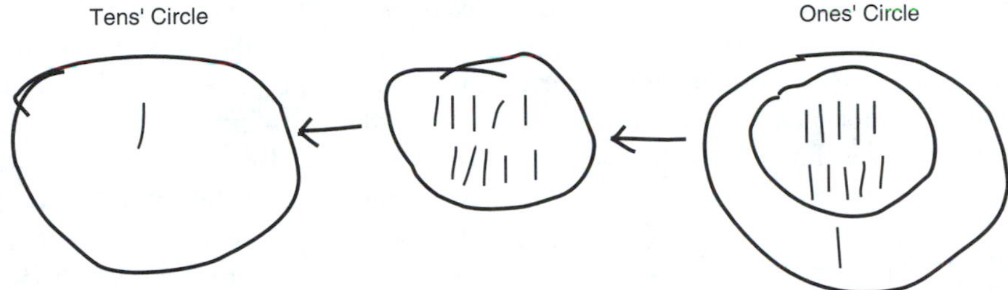

Elicit the child's cooperation in counting the objects, and for each object the child counts place another object in the circle on the right. When the circle on the right has ten objects, stop the child, and indicate that the circle is "filled up." Ask if the child has any ideas concerning what to do about the problem, and (if no ideas are forthcoming) suggest that the child move the objects out of the ones' circle, and draw a hash mark (|) in the tens' circle to represent that group of objects. Help the child count in this fashion using several numbers between 11 and 19.

When the child is first grasping the representation of groups of objects as marks in the tens' circle, you may wish to use hash marks in both the ones' and tens' circles. This represents the semiconcrete nature of the instructional plan discussed in text. However, as the child grows in his or her understanding of the representation of groups of ten objects, you should begin to use numerals. Finally, the numerals may be written without the use of the circles and the child will understand that a digit in the tens' place represents a different number from the same digit in the ones' place.

At this point, you may wish to use written terms for the labels of the tens' and ones' places. This type of example is very common in math curricula for elementary school children. The examples below demonstrate this type of exercise.

64 = 6 tens and 4 ones.

32 = 3 tens and 2 ones.

Finally, you should explore the curriculum this child is using in mathematics and find examples of the place value instruction provided there. As a final step in your place value instruction, you should teach the child to perform the place value tasks using the same types of examples he or she will encounter in the curriculum.

the face value of a digit by the place of the digit in the numeral, or face-times-place. For example, the value of the digit 5 in the numeral 537 is discovered by multiplying the face value of "5" by the place value of the "hundreds" place. This allows the elementary students to understand that the total value of the numeral is "5 hundreds + 3 tens + 7 ones." These types of exercises are frequently found in math assignments in upper grades, and they represent some of the more advanced forms of instruction in place value concepts. Clearly, although place value instruction begins early in the math curriculum, understanding place value is a math skill that permeates the elementary grades.

Mathfacts

Use of Counters. Instruction in the early facts generally begins before formal training in school. As mentioned previously, many children learn to count using the fingers, and early parental instruction in addition often takes the same form. For example, a parent may hold up a hand and ask a child to count the fingers on that hand, then the fingers on the other hand, and then place the two hands together while the child counts all of the fingers together. Instruction in addition generally begins during kindergarten or first grade and proceeds in the same fashion, though counters and hash marks (sticks drawn on the page) are usually used rather than fingers. For example, in the picture below 3 sticks and 4 sticks are placed together to demonstrate the total of 7 sticks.

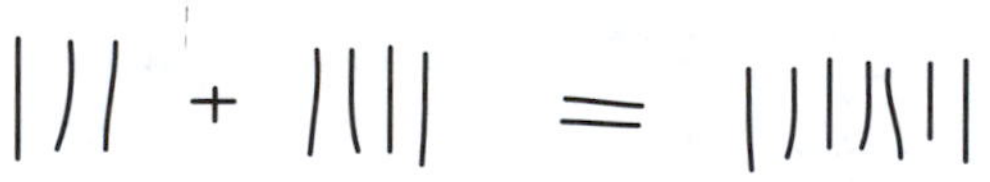

||| + |||| = |||||||

Concrete examples of this sort may likewise be used to illustrate basic mathfacts in the other operations. For example, in the illustration below, multiplication is illustrated by the grouped sets of three squares.

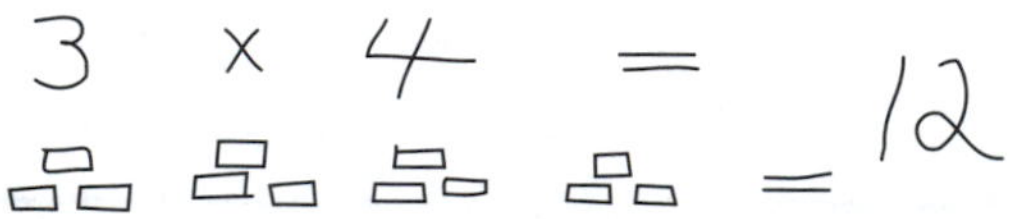

3 x 4 = 12

Use of this type of semiconcrete example is the most frequently used method of instruction for mathfacts. Interest Box 11.4 presents several examples of the use of sticks for both assessment and instruction in the basic mathfacts.

Using Metacognitive Strategies. Many children begin very early to use metacognitive strategies to ascertain the answer to certain mathfacts. For example, if a student knows the fives times tables, and wishes to find the answer to 5 x 6, the student need only recall 5 x 5 = 25 and add another 5 to that product to find the answer (Thornton & Toohey, 1985). Use of this type of strategy should be encouraged from the earliest years in order to give children an additional set of tools for mathfacts calculations. Several other strategies of this nature are presented in Interest Box 11.5.

Automaticity in Mathfacts. The concept of automaticity is crucial to understanding the relationship between mathfacts and use of mathfacts in more complex calculations. As basic mathfacts are practiced repeatedly, the execution of these math problems requires less cognitive processing capacity and the processes become more or less automatic (Hasselbring, Goin, & Bransford, 1987). Such automaticity greatly enhances a child's ability to do calculations that involve multiple-digit work.

Development of automaticity is certainly one goal of every special education teacher who is confronted with a child who is still using counters to calculate basic mathfacts. Automaticity in mathfacts is also crucial in inclusive classes, where teachers would expect most mathfacts recall to be automatic. Hasselbring, Goin, and Bransford (1987) present several recommendations for assessment and instruction intended to develop automaticity. These are described in Interest Box 11.6.

OPERATIONS

Assessment of Early Operations

Addition and subtraction are the operations usually taught first, and instruction generally begins

INTEREST BOX 11.4
Counters for Math Facts

Instruction in math facts usually is based on semiconcrete examples that employ the use of hash marks for instructional purposes. These examples may be used for either instructional or initial assessment purposes.

Addition

$3 + 4 = \underline{7}$

||| |||| |||||||

Subtraction

$9 - 4 = \underline{5}$

||||| (||||) |||| |||||

Multiplication

$7 \times 3 = $ ||| ||| ||| ||| ||| ||| ||| $= 21$

7 groups of |||

Division

$12 \div 3 = \underline{4}$

$=$

INTEREST BOX 11.5
Metacognitive Strategies for Mathfacts Instruction

The strategies below are metacognitive strategies that many students spontaneously develop as they progress through the elementary math curriculum. These strategies have been discussed by a number of different authors (Boom and Fine, 1994; Bos and Vaughn, 1988; Thorton and Toohey, 1985; Bullock, Pierce, Strand, and Branine, 1981), and may be taught as metacognitive instructional strategies to assist children with disabilities in simple calculations.

Students may be taught in addition and subtraction to start counting from the first number in the problem. For example, in the problem 6 + 7, the child should say the word "six," and then begin counting from that point and say seven additional numbers, as he or she holds up a finger for each number spoken. When seven fingers are up, the child has arrived at the answer. Subtraction problems involve starting with the first number and counting backward. These ideas are utilized in a math curriculum called *Touch Math* (Bullock, Pierce, Strand, and Branine, 1981).

Using doubles involves the computation of math facts relative to known mathfacts that contain the same number (or a double). For example, 5 + 4 may be calculated by remembering that the double 5 + 5 = 10, and 5 + 4 has to be one less than that (i.e., 5 + 4 = 9).

Even when the problem presented doesn't allow one to think in terms of "doubles," the student may be able to think one more (or one less) than a known fact. For example, 4 + 9 has to be one less than 4 + 10, and students remember that 4 + 10 = 14 rather easily. Thus, 4 + 9 = 13.

One common strategy for multiplication involves counting by 2s, 3s, 4s, 5s, or 10s. Although some students learn to count by 6s, 7s, 8s, and 9s, this is much less common than counting by the lower numbers. After exposure to the first several years of the elementary math curriculum, many students "recall" multiplication facts that involve lower numbers by using this strategy, of counting by the multiplier.

Boom and Fine (1994); Bos and Vaughn (1988); Thorton and Toohey (1985); Bullock, Pierce, Strand, and Branine (1981).

during the first grade. You, as the teacher, should know exactly what types of problems the child has difficulty with. Interest Box 11.7 presents a brief criterion-referenced assessment in addition that may be used to identify the specific types of problems with which students have difficulty. If you find that a student needs instruction in basic operations you should be prepared to use this assessment or something similar.

Addition and Subtraction

Once the student has mastered most of the mathfacts, instruction in multidigit addition and subtraction begins, usually following the same form as the example described earlier. For example, counters or concrete examples are typically used, and the digits that represent each set of counters are written at the side of the problem. The diagram presented below illustrates both addition and subtraction problems that may be easily illustrated using semiconcrete examples. If children in your class need instruction in these operations, you may wish to use this strategy by creating worksheets that present numerous examples of problems and the counters (sticks, boxes, circles) to go with them.

3 + 2 = 5   4 − 1 = 3

INTEREST BOX 11.6
Strategies to Develop Automaticity

1. Develop a "fast facts" matrix for each mathfact in addition (or any other operation). Use a set of flash cards to assess the speed and accuracy of a student on each mathfact. If it takes a student more than two seconds to answer, or if the student uses an obvious counting strategy, the fact is not automatic. In the sample matrix by Hasselbring, Goin, and Bransford (1987), the colored facts are automatic.
2. New facts are taught by building upon previously known facts. For example, because the child knows 1 + 9 = 10, he or she may readily learn that 9 + 1 also equals 10. Generally, you should select the fact that includes the lowest addend for which the matrix is incomplete. In the matrix above, you should first teach 1 + 9 and then move on to 2 + 5, the higher 2s, 3s, and 4s.
3. Help the student to focus on a small set of mathfacts, involving two or three facts and their reciprocals. This becomes the fast fact set of problems for the day or the week. Various games may be used to teach these facts, and a precision teaching project should be initiated to demonstrate the growth of the child's understanding.

6x1	6x2	6x3	6x4	6x5	6x6	6x7	6x8	6x9	6x10
7x1	7x2	7x3	7x4	7x5	7x6	7x7	7x8	7x9	7x10
8x1	8x2	8x3	8x4	8x5	8x6	8x7	8x8	8x9	8x10
9x1	9x2	9x3	9x4	9x5	9x6	9x7	9x8	9x9	9x10
10x1	10x2	10x3	10x4	10x5	10x6	10x7	10x8	10x9	10x10

Source: Hasselbring, Goin, and Bransford (1987).

Regrouping Problems

The next skill in the math curriculum is generally calculation of addition and subtraction problems that involve regrouping. This skill is often introduced during the first or second grade, though practice in it extends over the first several years of school. It is very difficult for many students with mild and moderate disabilities to understand the issue of regrouping unless the student has a firm understanding of the earlier place value concepts. Generally semiconcrete examples of addition and subtraction problems that illustrate regrouping are of assistance; this type of problem is illustrated below.

33 =
+ 18 =
= 5 groups + 1 = 51

INTEREST BOX 11.7
Criterion Referenced Assessment for Early Addition

1. When presented with addition mathfacts up to ten, the child will complete the problems with 80 percent accuracy.

3	5	7	2	4
+ 6	+ 1	+ 2	+ 3	+ 4

2. When presented with addition mathfacts between 10 and 20, the child will complete the problems with 80 percent accuracy.

8	6	3	8	6
+ 6	+ 8	+ 9	+ 7	+ 5

3. When presented with addition problems involving single- and double-digit addends resulting in double-digit sums, the child will complete the problems with 80 percent accuracy.

13	21	7	15	8
+ 6	+ 5	+ 12	+ 3	+ 11

4. When presented with addition problems involving double-digit addends that do not require regrouping, the child will complete the problems with 80 percent accuracy.

24	52	61	37	25
+ 45	+ 46	+ 25	+ 44	+ 64

5. When presented with addition problems involving single- and double-digit addends that require regrouping in the tens' place, the child will complete the problems with 80 percent accuracy.

16	37	8	59	35
+ 8	+ 7	+ 15	+ 4	+ 6

6. When presented with double-digit addition problems that involve regrouping in the tens' place, the student will complete the problems with 80 percent accuracy.

38	26	39	43	47
+ 27	+ 59	+ 38	+ 29	+ 35

7. When presented with double-digit addition problems that involve regrouping in both the tens' place and the hundreds' place, the student will complete the problems with 80 percent accuracy.

48	56	69	83	95
+ 86	+ 97	+ 37	+ 49	+ 16

8. When presented with double-digit addition problems that involve regrouping in the hundreds place, but not in the tens' place, the student will complete the problems with 80 percent accuracy.

83	95	72	85	64
+ 31	+ 82	+ 64	+ 53	+ 63

The grouped sticks in the diagram illustrate an addition problem that involves regrouping in the tens' place. Instruction would usually take the form of a teacher completing this problem and modeling the types of self-instruction that explain the regrouping process.

As you may imagine, picturing objects that demonstrate regrouping in the hundreds' or thousands' place is quite cumbersome, but children generally understand the concept if semiconcrete examples are used in problems involving the ones' and tens' places. However, once this concept of regrouping is established by using semiconcrete examples of regrouping in the tens' place, you should provide your students with problems that involve regrouping in the hundreds' place in order to reinforce the concept that regrouping is basically the same for three- or four-digit numerals. Finally, you should provide some practice in problems that involve regrouping in various places. For example, some students understand problems that require regrouping in both the tens' and hundreds' place, but do not understand that a problem may involve regrouping in the hundreds' place but not in the tens'. For those students, practice in that specific type of problem should be provided, in addition to worksheets that have several types of problems that require the student to discriminate where regrouping is necessary and where it isn't.

Multiplication

Mathfacts in multiplication are generally introduced during the third grade. The illustrations in this chapter depicted one way to use counters to illustrate mathfacts in multiplication. Also, many teachers require students to memorize the multiplication mathfacts through the tens times tables, and some require memorization through the twelves times tables.

Eich (1981) described a multimodality approach to multiplication facts in which the student is taught to "count" by fives as the first step to multiplication. Five dots are drawn on each finger on a child's hand to represent the five objects the students count. The fingers then become cues to the numbers the students should say as they count by fives. While counting, students will hear the number, see the representation on their fingers, and move their fingers. Students may be encouraged to count a set of objects by ones and then fives. Although they should reach the same answer, counting by fives will be quicker and more fun. From this type of concrete cue (dots on the fingers) the teacher should move the students to written problems based on the fives times tables, and finally, to the other times tables.

After the basic mathfacts in multiplication are mastered, the initial instruction for one- and two-digit multiplication may be taught initially by referring to addition. For example, the problem 4 x 12 may be taught as "adding 12 four times," or 12 + 12 + 12 + 12. The example below demonstrates how this type of problem may appear on a worksheet.

$$3 \times 6 = 6 + 6 + 6 = 18$$

However, after this level of multiplication is mastered, multiplication becomes increasingly complex. For example, once two-digit multipliers are introduced, the multiplication problem requires not only multiplication, but also mastery of addition, regrouping, and place value concepts. Interest Box 11.8 illustrates the various stages of a multiplication problem that involves a two-digit multiplier.

Informal assessment of multiplication can take many forms. However, at the very least, the teacher should ascertain how the child performs on each of the major types of multiplication problems. The informal assessment in Interest Box 11.9 includes several different levels of multiplication, and use of this or a similar assessment should provide both the teacher and the student with an accurate picture of the student's level of mastery in multiplication.

Division

Division problems require understanding of the process of division, multiplication, subtraction, regrouping, and place value. For this reason, long division is considered one of the most difficult

INTEREST BOX 11.8
Complexity of Two-Digit Multiplication

Two-digit multiplication is unlike simple multiplication, addition, or subtraction in that it involves another operation for completion. When one completes an addition problem, for example, the only operation one performs is addition. This is true even in double- or triple-digit addition with regrouping. However, in double-digit multiplication, both multiplication and addition skills are used. Also, the double-digit multiplication problem is further complicated by place value considerations and regrouping considerations. These complications are illustrated by the example below.

$$\begin{array}{r} 36 \\ \underline{\times 25} \end{array}$$

The first step in this problem is to multiply the 5 by the 6, resulting in 30. The 0 is placed under the 5, whereas the 3 is placed above the other 3. Then 5 is multiplied by 3 and the "regrouped 3" is added to that product. The next step is to multiply the 2 by the 6, but here the student has to consider where that product should be written. The first digit in the product is written under the 2 (or in the tens' place) and the next digit is regrouped in the hundreds' place while the product of 2 x 3 is found. Finally, the multiplication problem becomes a multiple-digit addition problem, and the student has to contend with the usual place value and regrouping considerations. Because of these complex problems, double-digit multiplication is often very difficult for many students with disabilities.

operations and is generally taught later in the school curriculum, beginning around the fourth grade. Specifically, students are usually introduced to division during the third grade, and long division is introduced during the fourth grade.

As in all other operations, early division problems can be illustrated using concrete examples. Mercer and Mercer (1983) recommend illustrating the problem in a semiconcrete fashion and pairing that instruction with the abstract numerical problem, as shown in the following example:

22 ÷ 3

= 7 groups of 3 + r = 1

Generally, longer division requires extended instruction over a period of time, and the large numbers used in long division problems usually prevent the use of concrete examples to illustrate the problem. Instruction in this operation generally proceeds much the same way in instruction for nondisabled children. However, you should be prepared for instruction to take longer for students with mild and moderate disabilities. Also, many special education teachers tend to deemphasize this skill because time requirements demand that instructional time be spent on other, more frequently used skills, such as counting money, measurement, and purchasing. Interest Box 11.10 presents a discussion of the decision concerning which math skills to emphasize for a particular child.

INTEREST BOX 11.9
Criterion-Referenced Assessment for Multiplication

1. When presented with multiplication mathfacts involving the 2s, 3s, 4s, and 5s times tables, the student will solve the problems with 80 percent accuracy.

3	7	8	4	9
x 6	x 2	x 5	x 4	x 3

2. When presented with multiplication mathfacts involving the 6s, 7s, 8s, and 9s times tables, the student will solve the problems with 80 percent accuracy.

6	8	9	4	7
x 5	x 7	x 4	x 8	x 6

3. When presented with multiplication problems involving one-double digit and one single-digit numeral, the student will complete the problems with 80 percent accuracy.

13	7	46	9	25
x 6	x 27	x 7	x 32	x 7

4. When presented with multiplication problems involving two-digit numerals, the student will complete the problems with 80 percent accuracy.

24	47	83	78	59
x 36	x 24	x 15	x 26	x 53

5. When presented with multiplication problems involving three-digit numerals, the student will complete the problems with 80 percent accuracy.

354	268	594	472	480
x 385	x 482	x 174	x 385	x 285

SPECIALIZED MATHEMATICS SKILL TOPICS

Fractions

Instruction in fractions is included in the elementary school curriculum from the third or fourth grade level on. However, children in the first or second grade may learn concepts such as $^{1}/_{2}$ or $^{3}/_{4}$. At a minimum, every student with mild and moderate disabilities should be instructed in recognition, and understanding of, the most common fractions ($^{1}/_{2}$, $^{3}/_{4}$, $^{4}/_{5}$, $^{2}/_{5}$, etc.). Social discourse often includes reference to these numbers and the student should not be prevented from understanding these. Recognition of the meaning of these terms may be taught using concrete or semiconcrete examples as pictured next.

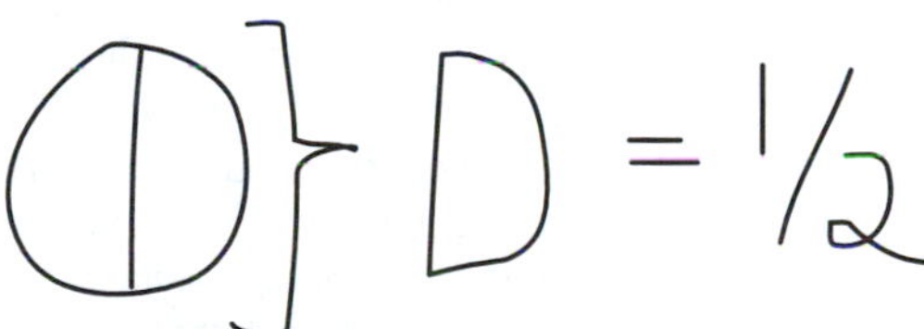

Addition and subtraction of fractions with like denominators is fairly easy once a student has mastered basic addition and subtraction facts. The concrete examples above may easily be modified to depict addition problems involving like denominators.

However, students tend to experience difficulty when the fractions include unlike denominators. In this type of problem, the student must

INTEREST BOX 11.10
Decisions of Skills to Be Included in the Mathematics Curriculum

More than any other teacher in the school, the special education teacher has responsibilities for making decisions concerning what skills to include in a particular child's curriculum. Although many elementary teachers make decisions to de-emphasize one aspect of the curriculum in order to devote more time to other aspects, the special education teacher has the responsibility to make these decisions for each child individually. Consequently, one of the decisions that must be made involves the types of math skills which should be stressed for a particular child.

As an example of this, you may wish to consider the difference between two students, both of whom are functioning at about the fourth grade level in math. Both have basically mastered the times tables, simple multiplication, and division, but both are having problems with fractions. Both students have some math instruction in the mainstream class, as well as in the resource room.

The first child is in the ninth grade, and comes to your resource room one period per day. The second child is in the sixth grade. Because of the grade level difference, you may have to make different decisions concerning what skills to stress for each student even thought these students are in about the same place in achievement. For the first student, with several years of failure in mainstream instruction concerning fractions behind him, you may wish to de-emphasize fractions and spend more time on functional math skills for tax returns, banking, etc. You may wish to merely teach that student to convert all fractions into decimals and then to work with decimals. As you realize, decimals are much easier to work with than other types of fractions because the operations with decimals involve basically lining up the dots and then performing standard operations. With the agreement of the mainstream math teacher, this modification of the curricular expectations for that student should work out well.

With the second student, you may wish to retain more instructional time for operations involving fractions for several reasons. First, that child will continue to encounter fractions for another six years in mainstream classes rather than for merely another couple of years. Next, that student may not have developed the strong negative attitudes toward fractions that many students develop after years of failure.

As this example demonstrates, math goals for each student with disabilities may vary greatly and you should be constantly on guard in order to assure that each student progresses in each math area as far as his or her abilities will allow. You should not let your zeal for instruction in daily living math skills overshadow a student's need for instruction in complex multiplication, long division, or fractions, if the student's ability suggests that these skills are attainable. Likewise, you should not blindly instruct a child in these complex math skills merely because some curricular materials dictate such instruction. It is your responsibility to decide what to emphasize based on the individual needs of the children whom you teach.

Decisions in the math curriculum such as this should be reflected in each child's individualized education program, and you should make clear to parents and mainstream teachers why you feel such a shift of emphasis is necessary. If the committee approves, you will wish to demonstrate progress at the end of the year in the areas that have been emphasized.

first identify a common denominator and convert each fraction to that common term. Although many teachers in special education in elementary settings teach fractions with like denominators, only a few elementary special educators make major time commitments to operations that involve fractions with unlike denominators. However, such instruction may become more common in inclusive classes. The decision concerning instruction in fractions should depend on the needs and abilities of each individual child.

Decimals

Decimals are a special type of fraction and are typically introduced to the elementary grade child during the fourth and fifth grades. Decimal numerals are one type of fraction that should be taught to every student with mild disabilities. Ability to work with decimal numerals makes addition and subtraction of money possible, and these skills allow for other skills, such as comparative shopping, purchasing, and making change. Also, many teachers find that decimals are fairly easy to understand and manipulate compared to work with other types of fractions. Generally, for addition and subtraction, the procedure involves no more than "lining up the dots." Multiplication and division are a bit more complicated, but these skills are still considerably easier than comparable procedures involving other types of fractions.

Money

The skills of counting money, making change, adding and subtracting money, and using money to shop are crucial daily living skills. Students in special education classes and inclusive classes should be required to engage in each of these skills frequently. It is difficult to think of a particular area of mathematics more fundamental to living. In spite of this, acquisition of skills in using money is too often viewed as a tangentially related subject, rather than a central component of the mathematics curriculum.

Money Recognition. For many students with disabilities, recognition of coins and bills is the first step in money instruction. A teacher can usually assess a student's skill and money recognition by presenting real coins and bills to the student and asking what they are. A brief record should be kept of the coins and bills a student recognizes, and when that record is dated and signed it should be saved in the student's file.

Various memory games may be used to instruct children in coin and bill recognition. Also, some CBI software is available for money recognition activities on the computer. Finally, use of "play money" for a classroom token economy is certainly useful for both special education and inclusive class settings. However, teachers should ensure that the play money utilized looks enough like real money that the students gain the necessary discrimination skills, which will then generalize to real money in the real world.

Counting Money. Money counting skills are dependent on counting skills as well as on knowledge of the denominations of coins and bills. Generally, if these skill areas are mastered there should be no additional problems in counting money, unless the money to be counted involves a mixture of different bills and coins. The procedure for the latter situation involves arranging the bills and coins in piles that include only one denomination of bill or coin. The piles should be sorted in order from largest to smallest, and the money in each pile is counted. At that point, an addition procedure is used to find the total sum of the money in the piles.

After the student has practice in this procedure, he or she should be instructed in a simpler procedure that involves "counting on." In that procedure, the piles of bills and coins are arranged from largest to smallest, and after a student counts one pile (e.g., $1.75 in quarters) he or she switches to counting by tens' to count the dimes, and "counts on" to the initial total (by saying "$1.85, $1.95, $2.05 . . ."). Then the student counts on by fives for the nickels. This counting on procedure is fairly easy to teach if the child has the prerequisite skills. This is also the way in which most adults count change.

Addition and Subtraction of Money. Students must learn to add and subtract both coins and bills, and instruction in decimal fractions that involve two decimal places is the best instructional method. Once the decimals are lined up, the place value problems take care of themselves. In fact, the necessity for counting money is so apparent for even young children in special education that many teachers reverse the procedure and teach "money counting" as an introduction to decimal fractions, rather than the other way around. Clearly, repeated practice on each of these skills should be available in every special education class and every inclusive class.

Telling Time

The ability to read a clock may help determine which students with mild or moderate disabilities will be employable. Most entry-level jobs are dependent on working a set number of hours each day or week, and the ability to arrive on time is one concern to the prospective employer.

With the recent popularity of digital clocks, the ability to read a standard clock face may have been de-emphasized by some teachers. However, there is no assurance that a digital clock will be available for every student with mild or moderate disabilities whenever one is needed. Consequently, many special education teachers should spend some time instructing students in reading a clock.

Should you choose this as one curricular goal for a particular student, the instructional procedure is fairly simple, though practice on a daily basis is usually required. First, point out the differences between the hour hand and the minute hand. Next, teach the student to tell the time when the minute hand is straight up (on the hour). Half hours are introduced next, then quarter hours, five-minute segments between the quarter hours, and, finally, minute by minute time-keeping. You should always strive to teach the child every possible name for a particular time. For example, 2:45 is also "a quarter to three," "fifteen 'til three, or "fifteen minutes to three."

One daily living skill founded on the ability to tell time is the use of schedules. Even for someone who never rides a bus or flies in an airplane, schedules are often used. For example, reading a TV guide or selecting a ferry route are dependent on schedule reading and time skills. The creative teacher can make a number of interesting games and assignments that involve reading schedules in order to teach students with mild disabilities this important set of skills.

Measurement

Instruction in the most common weights and measurements is crucial for daily living for most individuals with disabilities. For example, in many classes for students with moderate or severe mental impairment, cooking procedures are taught that are dependent on measurement skills. Also, skill in using a ruler or the ability to calculate distance in yards, feet, and inches may enable a student with mild disabilities to attain employment in carpentry or some related building industry. Because measurement with weights and common measures is generally taught to nondisabled students by using concrete examples, very little modification in instructional technique is usually required for students with disabilities. However, more time should be allocated for students with disabilities to attain mastery of these important measurement skills.

WORD PROBLEMS

A word problem is a mathematical problem represented by words or a brief story. The student has the task of translating the terms within the problem into one or several mathematical calculations, conducting the calculations, and arriving at the correct answer.

Instruction in word problems usually begins during the early elementary school years, though predecessors to this type of problem can be found in math curricula as early as kindergarten. One obvious limitation on the introduction of word problems is the child's reading ability. A second limitation is the child's ability to conduct the operations that may be required. Consequently, word problems are generally introduced after early work has been done in both reading and math operations. Of course, these limitations are a crucial concern for special education teachers, because many students with disabilities demonstrate problems in both reading and math operations. Consequently, development of these prerequisite skills is essential in special education.

Single and Multiple Operation Problems

Word problems taught during the elementary grades may be classified in several different ways. The basic classification deals with the number of operations involved. However, other classification systems are also available. Interest Box 11.11 presents a classification system based on cognitive instructional strategies.

During the early instruction in word problems, word problems that have one operation are introduced:

> *Mary has 7 pennies. John has 2 pennies. How many pennies do they have altogether?*

This type of problem involves translation of the various cue words in the problem (such words as "how many" and "altogether"). After such translation of the problem from verbal to mathematical terms, the student has only one mathematical operation to perform. As problems become more complex, two or more operations may need to be performed, as demonstrated below:

> *John had 4 pieces of candy in his lunch box. His friend Tom had 6 pieces of candy. Together they decided to share the candy equally with each of their friends at the lunch table. There were 3 other boys at the table. If all of the boys got an equal share, how many pieces of candy did each boy get?*

This problem demonstrates the need for clear understanding of the translation process. First, the total number of pieces of candy must be calculated. Then, the total number of boys at the table must be found. Finally, the number of pieces of candy must be divided by the number of boys to arrive at the correct answer. Thus, two addition operations and one division operation are necessary to determine the answer.

The translation process involved in word problems is based on the student's ability to identify cue words that may suggest certain mathematical operations. Comprehension of the operations necessary for successful problem completion seems to be the critical skill for many learners with disabilities. For example, Bilsky and Judd (1986) demonstrated that, compared to nondisabled students, adolescents with mental retardation performed poorly on verbal math problems even when the groups were comparable on a computation screening test. Clearly, the skill of identification and translation of the cue words in word problems is one of the more important aspects of problem solution. Interest Box 11.12 includes a list of these cue words and suggestions for teaching them.

One final stumbling block to the correct solution of word problems is the use or misuse of irrelevant information. In the translation process students will often select facts that are not relevant at a particular point in the problem/solution process and calculate based on those facts. Likewise, some problems include irrelevant linguistic and numerical information that should not be used at all, and some evidence suggests that this type of irrelevant information may present special problems for students with disabilities. For example, in a group comparison study by Englert, Culatta, and Horn (1987), students with learning disabilities were negatively affected by the presence of irrelevant numerical information in a set of word problems, though irrelevant linguistic information had no demonstrable effect. Because of this type of evidence, it is becoming increasingly clear that students with mild disabilities must often be taught which information to ignore in the solution of word problems.

Problem Format

Cawley and his co-workers (Cawley, Fitzmaurice, Shaw, Kahn, & Bates, 1979) indicated that the

INTEREST BOX 11.11
A Metacognitively Based Classification of Word Problems

Goldman (1989) described a classification system based on metacognitive thought. The system depends on the number of schema the child must activate in order to solve the problem. A schema may be defined as a mental diagram, or concept, of a particular aspect of the problem. Word problems may then be divided into static "comparison-of-quantities" problems, which involve the overall schema of comparison or more dynamic-change problems in which several schema are involved. Take the following comparison problem as an example:

John has 4 apples. He has 3 more apples than Paul. How many apples does Paul have?

In order to solve this problem, the child must have a comparison schema or mental concept that includes three pieces of information: two reference quantities (the numbers presented in the problem) and a derived piece of information involving the comparison answer. Note also that the verbal cue (more) usually means that a child should add, although in this example it indicates subtraction.

A second type of problem is the one that requires a change schema. These problems will include a set of information that indicates change in other information in the problem.

John had some apples. Paul gave him 3 more apples. Now John has 7 apples. How many did John have in the beginning?

The change information (3) must be subtracted from the resultant set of information (7) in order to determine the start set.

More complex problems involve the use of multiple schema, which may include both a change schema and a comparison schema. Consider the following:

Paul had 4 apples. Peter gave him seven more. Now Paul has 2 more apples than John. How many apples does John have?

The change schema in the problem above involves the addition of 4 and 7. The comparison schema involves subtraction (11 - 2).

The spontaneous use of metacognitive planning required by problems such as these is often quite beyond students with mild or moderate disabilities. However, many of these children can be instructed in various metacognitive steps that may facilitate such planning. A more detailed explanation of these metacognitive planning steps and this classification of word problems may be found in Goldman's work.

Source: Goldman (1989).

format of various word problems may be used as the basis for instruction. Although word problems are very common in daily life, they come in formats that are very different. The most common type of word problem format is that in which the word problem is written out, as in the examples above. A second format, frequently found on achievement tests in mathematics, is the story format, in which a child reads a story and then answers several questions about it, based on reasoning and calculations

INTEREST BOX 11.12
Use of Cue Words

Word problems generally involve translation of cue words into mathematical operations. Many teachers find that students are more motivated when they are taught that solving word problems really involves a "secret code," or set of cue words that the teacher can teach them. Although these words do not always have the same meaning in all word problems, the teacher can assure the student that they often indicate a particular operation. The list of cue words below may be helpful, although it is not a exhaustive list.

Operation	Cue Words
Addition	altogether, sum, and, more, plus, finds
Subtraction	left, lost, spent, remain, gave away, take away
Multiplication	rows, groups, altogether
Division	share, each, cost per month, per

Initially during instruction involving cue words, the teacher should select only problems in which the cue words mean the operation specified above. The student should be trained to write a "number sentence" to represent a one operation problem. Then multiple operation problems that require multiple number sentences are introduced. When grading this work, you may wish to assign a certain number of points to correctly identifying this number sentence, independent of problem solution.

Finally, you should require that the student complete some problems in which the cue words represent different operations from those they typically represent, and offer instruction on how the meaning was changed based on sentence construction in the problem.

applied to information presented in the story. A third format is the display, which involves obtaining information from charts, graphs, etc. Each type of format is critical for daily living, and instruction in mathematics for students with disabilities should involve some word problems of each type.

Metacognitive Approaches

A number of researchers have begun to use various metacognitive strategies in instruction of word problems (Boom & Fine, 1994; Hutchinson, 1993; Machida & Carlson, 1984; Montague, Applegate, & Marquard, 1993; Montague & Bos, 1986; Scheid, 1994). Instruction in these techniques usually involves a set of advanced organizer questions that the student uses to prepare himself or herself to complete the problem. Use of these advanced organizer questions is taught by the same basic methods described in Chapter 5 on learning strategy instruction.

As one example, Hutchinson (1993) used a metacognitive self-questioning strategy in which 20 adolescents with learning disabilities were taught a series of self-questions concerning problem solution. The questions were placed on prompt cards, as shown in Interest Box 11.13. Results of this strategy indicated that the adolescents' performance improved relative to the control group, and that the skills generalized into other settings.

Montague and Bos (1986) utilized an 8-step strategy that prepared 6 adolescents with disabilities to solve word problems involving two operations. The students were taught the steps, which included reading the problem aloud, paraphrasing it aloud, visualizing the problem or drawing a

INTEREST BOX 11.13
Self-Questions for Word Problems

Self-Questions for Representing Algebra Word Problems

1. Have I read and understood each sentence? Are there any words whose meaning I have to ask?
2. Have I got the whole picture, a representation, for this problem?
3. Have I written down my representation on the worksheet? (goal; unknown(s); known(s); type of problem; equation)
4. What should I look for in a new problem to see if it is the same kind of problem?

Self-Questions for Solving Algebra Word Problems

1. Have I written an equation?
2. Have I expanded the terms?
3. Have I written out the steps of my solution on the worksheet? (collected like terms; isolated unknown(s); solved for unknown(s); checked my answer with the goal; highlighted my answer)
4. What should I look for in a new problem to see if it is the same kind of problem?

diagram, stating the information given and requested, hypothesizing the steps needed to solve the problem, estimating an answer, calculating the answer, and checking the work. Although no particular acronym was used, the strategy training steps discussed in Chapter 5 were applied. The students were taught the steps and practiced them, first on controlled materials and later on more complex word problems. Of the 6 students, 5 were able to reach high levels of success after training.

You may wish to review Chapter 5 and think about the integration of this type of metacognitive strategy training into your classroom work on word problems. Also, in order to enable you to compare various metacognitive strategies, Interest Box 11.14 presents two additional strategies.

INSTRUCTIONAL SUGGESTIONS IN MATHEMATICS

Instructional Activities

1. Collect 9 clear plastic containers large enough to hold 9 one-inch cubes. When the numeral 1 is introduced label the first container 1. Place one colored one-inch cube in the container. After the child has mastered the concept of one, introduce two as a concept. Label the second container with 2, placing two cubes of a different color in it, and so on. Keep these containers as reference. Allow the student to use the containers for counting practice.

2. Create a set of cards with the numerals 1 through 9 written in bold black magic marker. Give the child a paper plate and a box with 9 identical objects. Ask the child to pick a card, say the number, and place the correct number of objects on the plate. This can be played as a game with a small group, depending upon the developmental level of the children.

   For children who have mastered groups 2 through 9 and who are ready to manipulate concrete objects to build an understanding of addition, a variation is: place 0, 1, 2, 3, 4, 5, 6, 7 or 8 objects on the plate, then hold up a card and ask the child to add the number of objects needed to represent the number. The card that

INTEREST BOX 11.14
Metacognitive Strategy Instructions

Fleischner, Nuzum, and Marzola (1987) presented the following metacognitive strategy to facilitate word problem solution. As students learn to complete each of these five steps, their success with word problems should grow.

Read	What is the question?
Reread	What is the necessary information?
Think	Putting together means addition; Taking apart means subtraction Do I need all the information? Is this a two-step problem?
Solve	Write the equation.
Check	Recalculate, label, and compare.

Bos and Vaughn (1988) also presented a set of metacognitive steps. Review these and compare them with the steps in text and above.

I. Read the Problem.
  a. Find unknown words.
  b. Find cue words.
II. Reread the problem.
  a. Identify what is given.
    1. Is renaming needed?
    2. Are there unit changes?
  b. Decide what is asked for.
    1. What process is needed?
    2. What unit or category is asked for in the answer?
III. Use objects to show the problem.
  a. Decide what operation to use.
IV. Write the problem.
V. Work the problem.

is displayed should be more than or equal to the number of objects on the plate. After the child has developed the concept of addition and equal to, this same activity can be used to introduce subtraction by holding up a card that is less than the number of objects on the plate.

3. Cut six circles 4 inches in diameter from tagboard. Cut petals that will, when placed around the circumference of the circle, make a flower. Write a number 4, 5, 6, 7, 8, or 9 in the middle of each circle. Have the child add the correct number of petals to make a flower.

4. To practice grouping, use domino configurations. One activity is matching spots. Materials include six white cards with spots 1 through 6; six blue cards with identical markings; six red cards with numerals 1 through 6.

Have children match groups *without* counting. When the child has mastered matching the cards without counting, have him assign the correct numeral to the groups.

5. A "clothespin fact board" can be used for practicing many different facts. For use with number facts, acquire a piece of cardboard 7" × 7". Divide the board into eight even triangles (pie shapes). Write a number fact in each triangle. With a black magic marker, write the answers on clothespins. Have the child select the correct answer from a "clothespin box," then clip the answer to the corresponding number fact.

6. "Numbers have many names" is a game that can be used to develop the concept of numeral, number word, and groups of numbers 1 through 10. Materials include 30 circular cards each 2" in diameter. These make ten sets of three cards each. In each set, one card bears the numeral, another the number word, and the third the appropriate number of spots in a domino pattern (e.g., 2, two, and **). Ten sets of different-colored circles are placed on the back of the cards for "self-checking." Have the student match the number word, the numeral, and the domino grouping. He or she may self-check by turning the cards over. If the colored circles on the back are the same, the cards are matched correctly.

7. Geometric Bingo is a game to develop knowledge about shapes and the names of shapes. Materials include six 9" × 9" game boards, each with a different arrangement of 9 shapes and colors; sixteen 2" × 2" cards bearing one colored shape for each game board; thirty 3" × 3" cards for each caller, each bearing one colored shape. The game is played by 2–6 players and one caller. Children use the small cards with shapes that match the shapes on the boards to mark the identified shape. The game is played following the rules of Bingo.

8. Make a paper chain using alternating colors. Number the links. If a student reads only the numerals on the second color, he will be counting by twos.

9. Make a caterpillar with 10 feet for the bulletin board with pipe cleaner legs. The 10 numbers may be printed on the feet or shaped out of pipe cleaners. The student arranges the feet in correct order.

10. To provide practice with addition facts, collect sixteen 2" × 3" tagboard cards and twenty-five 4" × 6" tagboard cards. Write a numeral from 0 to 16 on each small card. Write a numeral from 0 to 16 on each large card. On the back of the large cards write all the addition combinations in which the sum is on the front of that card. The first player holds up a large card and shows the side with the large number to the second player. The second player makes equations (as many as possible) with the small cards. The first player checks the second player's equations by looking at the back of the large card.

11. To provide practice with subtraction facts, cut tagboard into the shape of 16 stepping stones to play "Over the River." Put a numeral on 12 of the stones and mark 2 stones with (-) and two with (=). Lay the "stepping stones" on the floor representing various subtraction problems. Have the children find the correct path across the river.

Specialized Math Curricula

Project Math. Cawley and his associates (Cawley, 1977; Cawley, Fitzmaurice, Shaw, Kahn, & Bates, 1979; Cawley & Miller, 1989) developed a set of curriculum materials that may be used to teach elementary math to students with disabilities. The entire program includes four separate kits, each of which covers about $1^1/_2$ years of the typical elementary math curriculum. The skills taught range between first and sixth grade level skills, though numerous teachers have used the higher-level kits with remedial math students and students with disabilities in high school.

The curriculum is divided into six strands, including patterns, sets, geometry, numbers and operations, measurement, and fractions. Each strand and lesson provides the teacher with multiple presentation options that vary according to input and output modes. The materials are designed to make the mathematics curriculum available to students of very low reading ability.

DISTAR. Englemann and Carnine (1972, 1976) designed a set of math materials utilizing the direct instruction principles discussed in Chapters 4 and 8. Three separate *DISTAR Arithmetic Kits* are available, which include skills from early math to such fifth grade level skills as column multiplication and long division. The materials are intended to be used with small groups of children. Each kit contains a teacher's guide, teacher's presentation books, take-home activities, workbooks for students, and various manipulative materials to be used with some of the lessons. As in all direct instruction materials, the lessons require constant output from students in both oral and written form.

Corrective Mathematics Program. Englemann and Carnine (1982) also designed a direct instructional mathematics program for remedial math skills. This curriculum includes instruction in the basic operations, regrouping, and word problems. The material is intended for use with students from grades 3 to 12. There are 65 lessons in each operation area, and each lesson takes between 25 and 45 minutes.

Structural Arithmetic. Stern (1965) developed a set of materials intended for use in grades kindergarten through 3. There is one kit for each of those four grade levels. The kits contain the teacher's manual, students' workbooks, and manipulative materials. The lessons in each kit are set up along the discovery model, which encourages children to make mathematical discoveries and generalizations concerning early operations. These materials have been used successfully with children with disabilities.

Touch Math. If assistance is needed for instruction in the basic operations, you may wish to explore a set of materials developed by Bullock, Pierce, Strand, and Branine (1981) called *Touch Math.* In that program, the lower numerals have dots on them that correspond to the number represented. Higher numerals (6, 7, 8, and 9) have individual dots and dots that are circled, and the circled dots are counted twice. The student counts as he or she touches the dots on the numbers.

In the *Touch Math* system, addition is a matter of counting the dots and counting forward whereas subtraction is taught by having the child count out the first number and then count backward. Sample addition and subtraction problems are illustrated below. Multiplication is taught by skip counting (counting by threes, fours, etc.), as is division. This is a very effective math instruction system for students with disabilities.

Mathematics Software

Academic Skill Builders in Math:

Publisher: DLM Teaching Resources

Skill Level: Elementary, secondary

Hardware: Apple IIe, IBM

Description: The fast-action and colorful graphics of these math programs provide drill and practice in the four basic math operations and speed combinations of operations. Game control options include speech, content, run time, and paddle, joystick, or keyboard control. Programs available include *Alien Addition, Meteor Mission, Meteor Multiplication, Demolition Division, Alligator Mix,* and *Dragon Mix.* Each program addresses the different math content the title indicates and the material is presented in the game format suggested by the title. For example, Alligator Mix presents problems dealing with a mixture of addition, subtraction, multiplication, and division, and the game format is a screen with an alligator that eats the correct answers. The games are a little dated in their design, but students continue to find them exciting.

Arithmetic Critters

Publisher: MECC

Skill Level: Elementary

Hardware: Apple IIe

Description: Once children have learned basic skills, they're ready for this delightful package. Four programs help them master simple math skills. Students practice drills on place values to 99, single-digit addition and subtraction, and basic measurement. Instructive feedback with each program gives additional help to children having difficulty.

Big and Small Concepts Package

Publisher: Vocational and Rehabilitation Research Institute

Skill Level: Preschool, elementary

Hardware: Apple IIe, Echo speech synthesizer

Description: This package provides remedial instruction in the concept of size relationships. Tutorials on the concepts of big and small are reinforced by a drill and practice program. Speech output is available with the Echo.

DLM Math Fluency Program

Publisher: DLM Teaching Resources

Skill Level: Elementary; secondary

Hardware: Apple IIe

Description: Designed for children in special and remedial education who need additional help prior to the customary drill and practice. The teacher has the ability to control program options. The program assesses students on their current mathfact knowledge. After assessment, the program designs an individualized course of study. Students are introduced to from one to three mathfacts at a time. Completion of each session allows each student to enjoy game-play to reinforce the facts.

Math Blaster Plus / Talking Math Blaster Plus

Publisher: Davidson & Associates, Inc.

Skill Level: Elementary

Hardware: Apple IIe, IBM, Macintosh

Description: Math Blaster Plus builds basic math skills using colorful graphics and animation to motivate students. The program covers all fundamental math skills in addition, subtraction, multiplication, division, decimals, fractions, and percents in five learning activities. It features an easy-to-use editor, test maker, printable certificates of excellence, scorekeeper, optional sound effects, pull-down menu, and re-take option for missed items. Students may use mouse, joystick, or keyboard. *Talking Math Blaster Plus* is Apple IIGS specific.

Millie's Math House

Publisher: Edmark Corporation

Skill Level: Preschool

Hardware: Macintosh, IBM

Description: Students choose from six activities on various math concepts; for example, "Little, Middle, and Big" is an activity in which the student has to choose different sizes of shoes for each different size of character. If the student chooses the wrong size shoe the character puts the shoe on anyway and the student can see very graphically why it is the wrong size and is told to try another. In Bing & Bong the student creates musical pieces by putting different shapes and/or characters together in various sequences. Students may also try to complete sequences developed by Millie. Each shape and character has a different note and the sequence then becomes a musical piece. In the section of the program called "Mouse House" the student builds houses for Frank Lloyd Mouse by putting shapes together. There are triangles, squares, rectangles, and circles to choose from. In "Build a Bug" the student can build bugs out of parts such as ears and eyes. The student can drag parts to locations where they normally wouldn't be. For example, the student may put eyes on the legs so the bug doesn't trip over boulders. Another activity, called the "Number Machine," resembles a cash register; when the student presses one of the keys, the drawer opens and little creatures count off the number. For instance, if the student presses 3, the drawer will open and three mice, for example, will count, "1 mouse, 2 mice, 3 mice: 3 you found 3 mice." As with the other activities, there are two phases of the activity that can be attempted: exploration, and question and answer. In the exploration phase the student just picks some numbers, shapes, or objects and creates the object or gets a response. The question and answer phase sets the activity and asks the student to do something like find a number, get a shape, or pick a shoe. The student then does what is asked and is rewarded or given corrective feedback. The program speaks all the requests, responses, questions, and directions. The last activity is the "Cookie Factory." In the Cookie Factory the student makes cookies by squirting some dough on a conveyor belt and then adding jelly beans. The parts of the factory produce action in the discovery/exploration mode. In the question mode students need to produce cookies with the right amount of jelly beans. There are extensive teacher control features, including a scanning mode for students who require it.

Money Skills

Publisher: MarbleSoft

Skill Level: Preschool, elementary

Hardware: Apple IIe

Description: Money Skills teaches students to count money and make change using coins and bills. The programs feature teacher control of level of difficulty, rate of advancement, program speed, response to incorrect answers, and amount of verbal and visual feedback. It is compatible with keyboard, hand controls, PowerPad, TouchWindow, Echo, and Cricket, and has a built-in management system. It includes the programs *Coins and Bills, Counting Money,* and *Making Change*. The program will display either American or Canadian money.

Number Munchers

Publisher: MECC

Skill Level: Elementary, secondary, adult

Hardware: Apple IIe, Macintosh, IBM

Description: An active game format that builds fluency in identifying factors, primes, multiples, equalities, and inequalities. Students must navigate a matrix that contains correct and incorrect expressions. However, they must also watch out for munchers that gobble them up. Teacher editing features are included so that teachers can add their own content and track student performance.

SUMMARY

In spite of the importance of mathematics in the daily living of persons with disabilities, mathematics is often de-emphasized when compared to reading and language arts instruction in special education and inclusive classrooms. Still, students with disabilities need a large percentage of time devoted to various mathematics instructional activities.

Mathematics instruction begins with the mathematics prerequisite skills and early math skills, and proceeds to operations with whole numbers, fractions, decimals, and word problems. Each section of this chapter presents examples of assessment techniques that should allow you to adequately identify any deficiencies in a child's math skill. The instructional techniques presented in this chapter encourage use of both concrete and semiconcrete examples in each of these areas. Use of these assessment and instructional suggestions should foster growth for most students with disabilities in overall mathematics achievement.

Summary Points

- Math is often shortchanged, and more math instruction is needed, particularly in daily skills and practical application areas, such as counting money, making change, measurement, and telling time.
- Use of instructional procedures that progress from concrete to semiconcrete to abstract are the most effective procedures for students with disabilities.
- Informal assessments are probably more necessary in math than in any other area because

both assessment and instruction in this area are shortchanged. Use of regular informal assessments and CRTs is recommended.

- Instruction in word problems involves recognition of cue words in the problem, determination of what operations are needed, calculation, and presentation of the answer. This is a very complex skill for some students with disabilities to master.

QUESTIONS AND ACTIVITIES

1. Describe the process whereby use of math-facts becomes automatic.
2. Visit the curriculum laboratory of your college or university (the local school district may also have a curriculum laboratory for you to visit) and check out the *DISTAR, Corrective Arithmetic,* and *Structural Arithmetic Programs.* Present these to the class.
3. Write a lesson plan for using advanced organizer questions in solving a word problem that involves multiple operations. What types of questions must be included in the lesson? (Hint: some questions must deal with cue words, whereas others deal with order of the operations; how are these questions ordered?)
4. Visit a local kindergarten class and interview the teacher concerning math readiness activities. Does that teacher share the view of readiness skills presented in this text?
5. Review the research on the use of irrelevant information in word problems by students with disabilities. Present a report to the class on how irrelevant information affects children with disabilities compared to nondisabled learners.
6. Obtain another text on instructional methods in special education and compare the techniques discussed in that text with the techniques presented here of a particular area. What differences do you find?

REFERENCES

Algozzine, B., O'Shea, D. J., Crews, W. B., & Stoddard, K. (1988). Analysis of mathematics competence of learning disabled adolescents. *The Journal of Special Education, 21,* 97–102.

Bilsky, L. H., & Judd, T. (1986). Sources of difficulty in the solution of verbal arithmetic problems by mentally retarded and nonretarded individuals. *American Journal of Mental Deficiency, 90,* 395–402.

Boom, S. E., & Fine, E. (1994). STAR: A number writing strategy. *Teaching Exceptional Children, 27* (2), 42–45.

Bos, C. S., & Vaughn, S. (1988). *Strategies for Teaching Students with Learning and Behavior Problems.* Boston: Allyn & Bacon.

Bullock, J., Pierce, S., Strand, L., & Branine, K. (1981). *Touch Math Teacher's Manual.* Colorado Springs, CO: Touch Math, Inc.

Carpenter, R. L. (1985). Mathematics instruction in resource rooms: Instruction time and teacher competence. *Learning Disability Quarterly, 8,* 95–100.

Cawley, J. F. (1977). Curriculum: One perspective for special education. In R. D. Kneedler & S. G. Tarver (Eds.), *Changing Perspectives in Special Education.* Columbus, OH: Charles E. Merrill.

Cawley, J. F., Fitzmaurice, A. M., Shaw, R. A., Kahn, H., & Bates, H. (1979). Math word problems: Suggestions for LD students. *Learning Disability Quarterly, 2,* 25–41.

Cawley, J. F., & Miller, J. H. (1989). Cross-sectional comparisons of the mathematical performance of children with learning disabilities: Are we on the right track toward comprehensive programming? *Journal of Learning Disabilities, 22,* 250–259.

Eich, J. (1981). Multimodality multiplication for mildly handicapped students. *Teaching Exceptional Children, 13,* 156–157.

Englemann, S., & Carnine, D. (1972). *DISTAR Arithmetic, Level I.* Chicago: Science Research Associates.

Englemann, S., & Carnine, D. (1976). *DISTAR Arithmetic, Level III.* Chicago: Science Research Associates.

Englemann, S., & Carnine, D. (1982). *Corrective Mathematics Program.* Chicago: Science Research Associates.

Englert, C. S., Culatta, B. E., & Horn, D. G. (1987). Influence of irrelevant information in addition word problems on problem solving. *Learning Disability Quarterly, 10,* 29–35.

Fleischner, J. E., Nuzum, M. G., & Marzola, E. S. (1987). Devising an instructional program to teach arithmetic problem solving skills to students with learning disabilities. *Journal of Learning Disabilities, 20,* 214–217.

Goldman, S. R. (1989). Strategy instruction in mathematics. *Learning Disability Quarterly, 12,* 43–55.

Hasselbring, T. S., Goin, L. I., & Bransford, J. D. (1987). Developing automaticity. *Teaching Exceptional Children, 19,* 30–33.

Hudson, P. J., Peterson, S. K., Mercer, C. D., & McLeod, P. (1988). Place value instruction. *Teaching Exceptional Children, 18,* 72–73.

Hutchinson, N. (1993). Effects of cognitive strategy instruction on algebra problem-solving of adolescents with learning disabilities. *Learning Disability Quarterly, 16,* 34–63.

Lambie, R. A., Hutchens, P. W. (1986). Adapting elementary school mathematics instruction. *Teaching Exceptional Children, 16,* 185–189.

Machida, K., & Carlson, J. (1984). Effects of a verbal mediation strategy on cognitive processes in mathematics learning. *Journal of Educational Psychology, 74,* 1382–1385.

Mayer, R. W. (1994). Understanding individual differences in mathematical problem solving: Towards a research agenda. *Learning Disability Quarterly, 16* (1), 2–5.

Mercer, C. D., & Mercer, A. R. (1983). *Teaching Students with Learning Problems,* 2nd ed. Columbus, OH: Merrill.

Montague, M., Applegate, B., & Marquard, K. (1993). Cognitive strategy instruction and mathematical problem-solving performance of students with learning disabilities. *Learning Disabilities Research and Practice, 8* (4), 223–232.

Montague, M., & Bos, C. S. (1986). The effect of cognitive strategy training on verbal math problem solving performance of learning disabled adolescents. *Journal of Learning Disabilities, 19,* 26–33.

Peterson, S. K., Mercer, C. D., & O'Shea, L. (1988). Teaching learning disabled students place value using the concrete to abstract sequence. *Learning Disabilities Research, 4* (1), 52–56.

Piaget, J. (1965). *The Child's Conception of Number.* New York: Norton.

Rourke, B. P., & Finlayson, M. A. J. (1978). Neuropsychological significance of variations in patterns of academic performance: Verbal and visual–spatial abilities. *Journal of Abnormal Child Psychology, 6,* 121–123.

Scheid, K. (1994). Cognitive-based methods for teaching mathematics. *Teaching Exceptional Children, 26* (3), 6–10.

Stern, C. (1965). *Structural Arithmetic.* Boston: Houghton Mifflin.

Thorton, C. A., & Toohey, M. A. (1985). Basic math facts: Guidelines for teaching and learning. *Learning Disabilities Focus, 1* (1), 44–57.

Zentall, S. S., Smith, Y. N., Lee, Y. B., & Wieczorek, C. (1994). Mathematical outcomes of attention-deficit hyperactivity disorder. *Journal of Learning Disabilities, 27,* 510–519.

CHAPTER 12

INSTRUCTION IN SUBJECT CONTENT AREAS

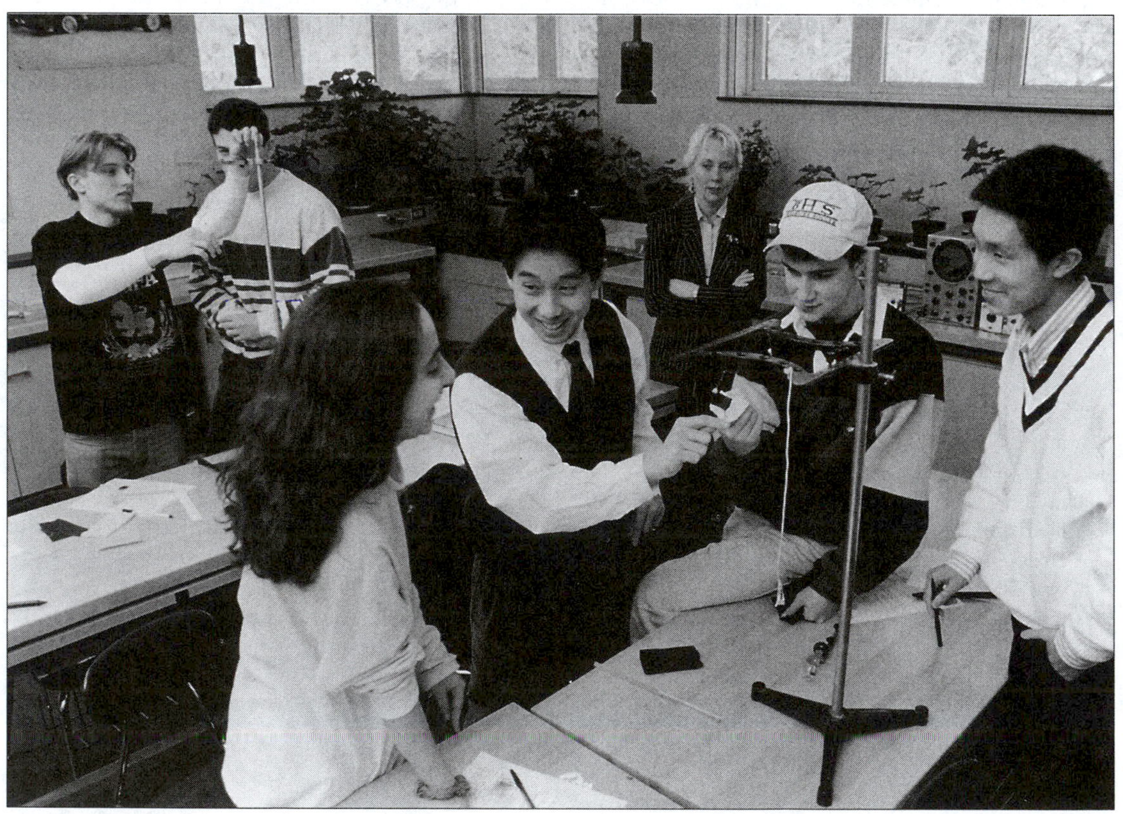

OBJECTIVES

Upon completion of this chapter, you should be able to:

1. Identify three learning characteristics that affect the types of instructional strategies used in subject content instruction.
2. Discuss the recommendations for adaptations for content instruction.
3. Describe the types of strategies that allow a child to repetitively practice the skills and knowledge acquired in subject content courses.
4. Describe a reconstructive elaboration.
5. Describe a participatory organizer strategy.
6. Describe an advanced organizer strategy.
7. Discuss the use of visual displays and research that demonstrated their effectiveness.

KEYWORDS

basic skills
ENIGMA
reconstructive elaborations
study guide

One role of the school in our society is to give persons a broad education in numerous fields considered essential for successful life in modern society. Although reading, language arts, and math may be considered "basic skills" or "tool skills" in the sense that they allow for acquisition of knowledge, other subjects are taught for the sake of gaining content knowledge in those specific subjects. A great deal of instructional time in school is spent on content areas, such as geography, health, science, history, civics, literature, and fine arts. Although research on various instructional approaches in these areas for children with disabilities has been slow to emerge, some research is available in most of them (Kinder & Bursuck, 1993; Mastropieri & Scruggs, 1994). This chapter is intended to provide some information on instructional techniques that may be used in these subject content areas.

Several limitations should be mentioned at the outset. First, special education teachers generally spend a great deal more time on instruction in the basic skills than on subject content areas. In many special education classes, the teacher's instructional responsibilities are limited to instruction in basic skills, and the students study subject area content in their mainstream classes. These factors have served to de-emphasize research on instruction in the subject content areas and much more research on instructional techniques for children with disabilities is available in basic skill areas. The information presented here, although based on research, is certainly much more tentative than research suggestions presented elsewhere in this text. Of course, with the recent advent of more inclusive class instruction, the questions about how to teach students with disabilities in curricular content areas have taken on a new importance. Much research is currently under way, and more articles on appropriate instruction in content areas will certainly be forthcoming.

Second, some areas, for which no research-based instructional strategies are available, deal directly with the instruction of students with disabilities. For example, in the area of fine arts there are simply no available studies that indicate how instruction in art or music for these students should be conducted. Therefore, although some of the ideas presented in this chapter may be appropriate in the fine arts instructional areas, you should utilize these suggestions at your own discretion.

Finally, many of the ideas presented are excellent instructional techniques for all students, and should be utilized in inclusive mainstream classes as well as in special education classes. You may find that you can assist your co-teacher in the inclusive class in applying one or several of these techniques in order to facilitate inclusive instruction for students with disabilities.

INSTRUCTIONAL PROBLEMS IN SUBJECT CONTENT AREAS

For this chapter, the subject content areas will be defined as those instructional areas that involve reading, language arts, and math activities in an effort to acquire knowledge in particular subject content areas rather than skill in the basic skill area itself. This definition is consistent with most definitions of subject content areas, and includes subjects like health, science, literature, history, geography, civics, and politics.

Reading Skills

Within these subject content areas, there are certain common expectations of students that impact on the instructional techniques used. For example, students are generally expected to be able to acquire information through reading material in texts. As one may well imagine, students with mild disabilities are not proficient at acquiring information from many middle school and upper grade textbooks (Espin & Deno, 1993). Deshler and his associates (Deshler, Schumaker, & Lenz, 1984) have indicated that the average reading level of secondary learning disabled students is between the fifth and the seventh grade. This means that many students with disabilities would not be competent at acquiring information from textbooks written at a tenth grade reading level.

This problem is further compounded by the reading level of the texts themselves. Although the content level in middle school and secondary textbooks may be appropriate for particular grade levels, many textbooks require reading skills beyond the grade for which the text is intended (Johnson & Varidan, 1973). For example, it is not uncommon to find a seventh grade science book written at a tenth or eleventh grade reading level. This further compounds the problem, particularly when the reading comprehension skills of a particular student with mild disabilities may be in the third grade range. Consider a not untypical situation in which a 13-year-old child with mild mental retardation demonstrates reading comprehension around a second or third grade level but is in an inclusive sixth grade class, and the science text for that class is written at an eighth grade reading level. Clearly, such placement is not fair or reasonable for that child unless very significant accommodations are made to make that science content accessible.

Reasoning Skills

Even when concerned teachers provide reading material for the subject content areas written at the appropriate grade level for students with mild disabilities, the issue of cognitive skill is still a major concern. For example, the reasoning skills of students with learning disabilities or mental retardation may not allow for understanding of the subject content itself even when the material is presented in some "high interest–low readability" format. Understanding conceptually from reading material that the planets revolve around the sun may be difficult for some students without the use of concrete examples, even in the middle and upper grades. It may be even more difficult for some students to grasp the fact that they themselves are standing on one such planet. This problem is further compounded by the fact that many secondary content teachers use few concrete examples, based on the assumption that such concrete displays are not necessary by the middle and upper grades.

For many students with mild and moderate disabilities the use of concrete examples is essential (Lambie & Hutchens, 1986; Sachs & Banas, 1987). Although many math teachers in the middle and upper grades already use concrete examples for these students, all teachers, regardless of content area, should be encouraged to use them. For this reason, there has been an increase in the number of researchers who are investigating methods for making content instruction concrete for students with disabilities. As an example, Interest Box 12.1 presents a method whereby use of a map/puzzle procedure may be used to assist students in learning geography.

Note-Taking Skills

Because of the frequent use of lecture formats in middle school and secondary classes, students are expected to be proficient at taking notes from lectures. Such note-taking involves a number of skills that tend to be weaker areas for students with disabilities. For example, note-taking is dependent on a number of abilities, including organizational skills, memory skills, and metacognitive planning skills. When a middle school teacher or a secondary mainstream teacher is presenting information in a lecture format for the history class, the students, including those with disabilities, must utilize auditory memory skills to take in the information. Next, the students must discriminate the important informational points and selectively attend to the most important aspects of the information—a step involving metacognitive planning and organization. These are the points on which notes should be based. Finally, the students must organize what they write so that the notes are usable in the future. All of these tasks must take place relatively automatically, because the content area teacher has continued to present information, often at a brisk pace, that must also go in the notes. Needless to say, note-taking in secondary classes is a complex skill, and teachers today have begun to teach note-taking skills. If you serve as an inclusive special education teacher, note-taking is one of the more important skills you will facilitate in the inclusive classroom.

GENERAL CURRICULAR ADAPTATIONS

Recommended Adaptations

Given these problems in middle school and secondary content instruction, there are a number of general adaptations in content curricula that may facilitate the success of mainstreamed pupils (Bender, 1985; Bergerud, Lovitt, & Horton, 1988; Lambie & Hutchens, 1986; Lovitt & Horton, 1994; Monti, Cicchetti, Goodkind, & Ganci, 1994; Munson, 1986). As a rule, these adaptations are not particularly esoteric and teachers generally originate many of these ideas in discussions among themselves. In fact, these strategies tend to evolve when teachers discuss inclusive instructional strategies specifically, because use of these ideas will enhance the instruction in content area classes both for many students with disabilities and for nondisabled students. One list of adaptations was presented in Chapter 2. Additional ideas for the content areas are presented in Interest Box 12.2.

Although the general adaptations and specific strategies presented above are useful throughout the content areas, a number of instructional ideas particular to specific content areas will benefit students with disabilities. These adaptations, presented in Interest Box 12.3, are relatively self-explanatory. However, you should review all of the ideas in each subject area, as you may devise a method whereby an idea in the social sciences may be modified for use in science or health classes.

Use of Adapted Curricula

The special education teacher will use these curriculum adaptation strategies in several ways. First,

INTEREST BOX 12.1
The *ENIGMA* Approach to Geography Instruction

ENIGMA stands for Engineering Individual Growth through Manipulative Associations (Sachs and Banas, 1985). This instructional concept is based on use of visual images and concrete examples to build comprehension. Sachs and Banas (1987) recommend the following procedures for teaching geography using the ENIGMA system.

1. Prepare a map by laminating it after the location names have been blocked out. The map should then be cut into approximately 10 horizontal pieces.
2. On a set of small yellow cards, print general names of certain map features (words such as east, west, ocean, and mountain). On a set of small white cards, print specific place names such as countries or important cities.
3. The map is placed in an envelope and the envelope is labeled with the name of the country or continent. The yellow and white cards are placed in a smaller envelope, and those envelopes are placed in the larger envelope with the map.

The instructional activity should include a small group of students who have little mastery of the geography of the country or continent under study. These students should be seated around a worktable so that each student can see the map area.

1. The teacher places the pieces of the map on the table in random order and instructs the students to put the map together by locating the lines of the country or continent on one piece and comparing that with other map pieces, much like a jigsaw puzzle.
2. After the map is assembled, the teacher picks up a white card, pronounces the word on the card, and asks one of the students where the card should go on the map. If the student does not respond immediately, the teacher provides the correct answer and shows the student where to place the card on the map. The teacher then picks another card and repeats the procedure with the next student.
3. The procedure is repeated as necessary until the white cards are all correctly placed by the students with little teacher assistance.
4. After the students are fluent with locations of the white cards, the teacher begins the procedure using the yellow cards. The yellow concept cards should be discussed in terms of the general meaning, and students should be given mnemonic strategies to assist in placement of these cards. For example, a student may be taught to remember that west is on the left of the map and east is on the right by using the word *WE.* Imagine the word *WE* written in big letters in the center of the map. The *W* is closer to the left side and should go there, while the *E* is closer to the right side and should go there. These associative memory techniques provide a method for students to concretely picture the correct response.
5. The yellow concept cards should all be placed correctly on the map in that fashion. However, these cards should then be removed and placed on the map again on another correct region. For example "ocean" may be placed correctly on the map several times. The teacher should encourage quick response.

The ENIGMA system is one method whereby geography studies may be made very concrete for students with disabilities. Also, this type of group activity is generally more fun than the typical "color the map" type of individual activity. Finally, you can easily vary this activity so that the entire group responds in order to locate the cards on the map, thus placing the students in a position to learn from each other.

Source: Sachs and Banas (1987).

each lesson activity planned for the special education student should incorporate these strategies in some fashion. As indicated in Chapters 1 and 2, many resource room teachers find that their responsibilities include instruction in the content areas, and these adaptations will facilitate this instruction, and special education teachers in inclusive classes are expected to adapt the curriculum for all children who require such adaptations.

Next, these recommendations may be provided to middle school and secondary mainstream teachers who are experiencing difficulty in working with students with disabilities in their mainstream classes. A special word of caution is in order, however. Many of the adaptations recommended may seem to give the student with disabilities an unfair advantage over the other students in the class, and mainstream teachers will, on occasion, question the wisdom of such practices. Consequently, if you recommend any of these adaptations to a mainstream teacher, you should be prepared to defend its use. Generally, merely a reminder of the fact that students with disabilities suffer from inherent unfairness each day at school will be enough to persuade the mainstream teacher that minor adaptations are warranted.

The final, perhaps the major, issue that must be dealt with is the mainstream teachers' instructional time. Whereas special education teachers have limited numbers of students in their classes and can be expected to apply time-consuming instructional modification techniques, mainstream teachers typically deal with 25 to 30 students at any given time. Consequently, the recommendations for adaptations you make to mainstream teachers must be very time efficient. For example, you should point out that if a mainstream teacher develops a simplified laboratory worksheet for students with disabilities this year, that same worksheet will be usable next year also. Likewise, a modified unit test on Civil War history will be reusable for several classes, and usable next year for the same course. In making recommendations for curricular adaptations, you must be sensitive to the time those adaptations take.

In inclusive classes, the special education teacher and the mainstream teacher will make these adaptations together, with the special education teacher typically taking the lead. Thus, in the best of circumstances, the two teachers begin to "resource" each other with instructional ideas for adaptations.

Adaptations Currently in Use

Munson (1986) investigated the types of adaptations mainstream teachers make for students with mild or moderate disabilities. The results must be viewed as tentative, because only 26 mainstream teachers participated. Also, this research was not conducted in an inclusive classroom where a special education teacher was present. However, the 26 teachers interviewed indicated that they modified their content instruction in terms of giving directions, assignment requirements, and testing requirements fairly frequently. When giving directions for an assignment, many teachers provided additional, specific directions for students with disabilities. Also, in many cases time frames were extended for those students and/or fewer problems were assigned. Finally, numerous testing alternatives were reported, including giving exams orally, allowing students with disabilities to complete the test in the special education

INTEREST BOX 12.2
Common Adaptations in Content Area Instruction

Adaptations to Assist Reading

1. Have advanced pupils underline the topic sentence and two important details in every reading assignment they do, and use that prepared text for students with disabilities in succeeding years.
2. Have students "read in pairs" in the class, and pair a capable reader with a student who has reading problems.
3. Present a list of questions that emphasize major points in reading assignments, and differentiate the questions according to the level of abilities of the students. The questions should be completed during reading assignments.
4. Have the students read the same content from a text written at a lower reading level. For example, when studying the solar system in ninth grade science, you may wish to visit the old book room in the school, borrow several fourth and sixth grade books that have a chapter on the solar system, and assign these to students with disabilities. One problem with this recommendation is the potential embarrassment of these students when they are required to read "baby books." This issue may be deflated somewhat by using a wide diversity of books for the unit. For the advanced students you may wish to obtain books that are written above grade level, and you may use several different books written on grade level for the average students in the class.
5. Make large print books available to students who request them.
6. Obtain copies of auditory tapes of the textbook, and provide these for the students who may benefit from them. Many organizations such as the National Organization for the Blind may be able to make these tapes of common textbooks available.

Adaptations in Lecture/Whole Class Discussion

1. Use an outline and make the outline available to students before the presentation. Refer to the outline frequently to assist students in understanding what the next topic is.
2. Pair students together for note-taking and have them review each other's notes at the end of the class.
3. Use audiovisual materials and multimedia materials, if available, to illustrate various points.
4. Frequently refer to text material, such as pictures and charts in the reading material, as one way to illustrate points in the lecture and discussion.
5. Use cue words that help students organize their notes, such as, "The next point," or "Point number four is. . . ."
6. Tell students the major points to emphasize by reminding them, "In your notes, remember to state that. . . ."
7. Shorten lectures to two thirds of the academic period, and provide students time to complete some type of study guide on the lecture/discussion material for the rest of the class time.
8. Teach students to check their notes for accuracy, using the outline that was provided as a self-checking check-sheet.

Adaptations in Class Management

1. Always give directions in both verbal and written form. If this is too time-consuming for the

teacher, assign one above-average student each week to write down directions on the board each time the teacher gives them.

2. Hold directions to one or two tasks at any given time. Do not give multiple instructions that involve finishing one task, putting materials away, retrieving other materials, and beginning a new task.
3. Appoint a class "teacher's helper" each week. This person will help the teacher by providing assistance to those students who do not understand the directions.
4. Encourage all students to write down the instructions for homework assignments on an assignment pad, and frequently check this assignment pad to ensure that the directions are clear. You may use a "buddy" system in the upper grades to encourage students to check each other's assignment pad and, where necessary, require that the students have their parents sign the homework pad, indicating that the work was completed.
5. Provide on the blackboard an organization time frame for each period, which lets the students know the planned activities for that period or that day.
6. Do not vary the planned activities simply to be varying them. Students generally understand and respond positively to a similar structure each day. Vary the activities just enough to prohibit boredom.

Adaptations for Testing

1. Allow the students extended time to take the test.
2. Write a different test for low-achieving students. This may be explained by indicating that different students used different reading and study materials during the unit.
3. Allow students with disabilities to take the test on an "open book" basis.
4. Allow students with disabilities to take the test in the special education class, where help with directions may be offered.
5. Allow the special education teacher to read the questions for students who need that assistance.
6. Use simplified assessment formats. For example, if you choose to use a multiple choice test, you should use only simple multiple choice items and not complex multiple choice test items.
7. Allow students with writing difficulty or spelling difficulty to take essay tests in the computer room using a word processor.
8. Assess rote memory skills as little as possible. Memory skills comprise one aspect of a cognitive disability, and testing students with memory problems on memory tasks is similar to requiring a student with one leg to run a hundred yard dash unassisted. Instead, base your assessment questions on applications of knowledge that are relevant to the life of the individual with disabilities.

room, or varying the types of questions and using simpler question formats.

In contrast to the frequent use of minor adaptations in the three areas discussed above, the mainstream teachers did not indicate frequent use of more "substantive" adaptation options. For example, only 4 teachers reported that grading requirements were changed, and several teachers expressed some concern for issues of fairness in grading relative to both students with disabilities and nondisabled students in the class. Only 5 of the 26 teachers indicated any variation in instructional materials. Finally, only 8 of the 26 teachers indicated that they increased the use of oral presentation by reading

INTEREST BOX 12.3
Adaptations for Specific Content Areas

History and Social Science

1. Use a piece of butcher paper or any long sheet of paper (6 ft. or more in length). Have a group that includes both students with and students without disabilities demonstrate their understanding of historical events by locating various events in historical sequence on a time line and writing the time line at the top of the paper. Then have the students draw pictures to represent each of the major events of the period.
2. Stress lifestyle issues concerning how different persons lived. Knowledge of these issues may be illustrated by various art projects. For example, in the typical fort in the "Old West," the U.S. Army quickly learned that barracks and officer housing should be built next to the external wall whereas powder magazines and stables should be built on the interior of the fort, because during battle the fire arrows the Indians used could do much more damage to the latter structures than to the former. This type of insight can be illustrated by building a fort using small sticks and labeling the various buildings.
3. Stress the aspects of government with which the student may have contact. Where does one obtain a driver's license? Why does that particular government branch issue them? What jurisdiction does the local police hold, compared to the highway patrol? From whom does one get speeding tickets, and why? Where is the county court, the county jail? Visit these locations on field trips, if possible.

Science

1. Stress those aspects of science that are readily observable in the student's environment. For example, discussion of leaves decomposing is much more interesting when paired with a one-period field trip to the nearest woods to see that phenomenon than discussion of elephants using only pictures in books.
2. Stress those aspects of science that directly involve the students. For example, many students with disabilities are more interested in learning about their own bodies than about those of other creatures. Also, in studies of the human body, you may be able to relate important information to the students concerning their own physical well-being (e.g., what they should eat, and why).
3. Use several different versions of laboratory worksheets for each lab class. Emphasize that these different sheets are used for numerous students in the class, including the brightest students. Although the preparation time for the first laboratory will be considerable, these lab sheets will be usable next year and the year after that.

Fine Arts (Music, Dance, Art)

1. Encourage free expression of students with disabilities. Although these students may not respond well to highly structured performance tasks, they will often create beauty if left to their own devices in a medium of their choice.
2. If you can establish rapport with the student in a manner that allows the student to comfortably discuss his or her disability, you may wish to encourage expression of feelings about the disability in art or performance. Powerful artistic statements have resulted from this technique, as well as great insight into the nature of the student's perception of the disability.

3. Insist that a pupil with disabilities perform at his or her best level, and remember that a cognitive, emotional, or behavioral disability does not necessarily prevent a student from creating or performing at a level consistent with the best in the school. Many persons who have a low IQ can play the piano beautifully, and emotionally disturbed persons can and do create inspiring works of art. Accept nothing less than the best from each individual.

aloud to the students. Clearly, these adaptations are not as common as the ones discussed previously, at least for this group of teachers. Until research on inclusive classrooms is forthcoming, few conclusions may be drawn concerning specifically what types of adaptations are currently being made in those environments.

SPECIFIC INSTRUCTIONAL STRATEGIES

Recently, researchers have begun to attend to instructional strategies that facilitate academic achievement in the instructional content areas (Hawk & McLeod, 1984; Horton, Lovitt, & Slocum, 1988; Mastropieri & Scruggs, 1988, 1989; Monti, Cicchetti, Goodkind, & Ganci, 1994). These adaptations are generally more involved than those presented previously, and are specifically supported by research in the field. Also, the specific strategies discussed below generally take some degree of time to implement, unlike many of the relatively simple adaptations discussed above. Nevertheless, with these cautions in mind, use of these research supported strategies does facilitate achievement in content areas for students with mild disabilities. Also, special education teachers in inclusive classes have more time to implement these specific strategies.

Advance Organizers

As discussed in Chapter 9, an advance organizer enables a student to comprehend the basic organization of the material to be learned prior to actually studying the material. An advance organizer may be defined as material presented "in advance of and at a higher level of generality, inclusiveness, and abstraction than the learning task itself" (Ausubel & Robinson, 1969). The presentation of this type of material allows the student to mentally organize his or her studies of the material to be learned. The advance organizer may seem similar to the learning strategies discussed in Chapter 5, because the concept was one of the predecessors to the full development of those instructional techniques.

Research has indicated that advance organizers improve the content learning of students with mild disabilities (Darch & Carnine, 1986; Darch & Gersten, 1986; Lenz, Alley, & Schumaker, 1987; Lovitt & Horton, 1994). Whereas Chapter 10 discussed the use of advance organizers only in reading comprehension activities, the body of research cited above indicates that advance organizers work very well in other instructional activities in the content areas as well. advance organizers should be provided for lectures, homework assignments, classwork assignments, and other content area instructional activities. In many inclusive classes, the special education teacher will develop the advance organizer. Alternatively, in resource programs, special education teachers will assist the mainstream teacher in developing these organizers for particular content areas. The research has indicated that advance organizers worked in subject content instruction for students with disabilities from the fourth grade through high school.

Darch and Carnine (1986) demonstrated the effectiveness of using advance organizers during content instruction in the middle school grades. Twenty-four students with learning disabilities in grades 4, 5, and 6 were randomly assigned to either an experimental group or a control group. A statistical comparison of these two groups demonstrated no differences in IQ and reading achievement between the groups of students prior to treatment. The control group was taught using traditional text and teacher-initiated group discussion. The experimental group was taught the same science content, by the same teacher, using advance organizers in the form of visual displays. During the first day of unit instruction, the teacher of the experimental group would show a visual display of the various concepts to be learned. For example, one concept involved how the vegetation on mountains differs as a result of elevation. A display was shown in which a mountain was divided into different shaded areas. Within each shaded area a description of the types of vegetation for that area was written. At the bottom, the description stated "Bigger trees at the bottom of the west side." The shaded area above was labeled "Smaller trees." The area above that was described as "No trees, just meadows." The top of the mountain was labeled "Snow."

The experimental group received this type of visual display on the first day of each 3-day unit of instruction. The students were instructed in this content for 50 minutes on each of 9 days. After the nine days of instruction, the students were assessed on both achievement and attitude. Results indicated that the group taught using the advance organizers outperformed the control group on each of several achievement probe tests given during the unit instruction. Also, one of the attitude questions demonstrated that the group using the advance organizers believed that they learned more than the control group. There was no difference on the students' overall enjoyment of the instruction between the experimental and the control group. However, these results do demonstrate that advance organizers can result in higher achievement, and possibly a better attitude toward learning.

In addition to advance organizer strategies for particular tasks, the TISOPT learning strategy, presented in Chapter 9, is often useful for content instruction. TISOPT can serve as an advance organizer for reading assignments in almost any secondary subject content area. You may wish to review the information on that learning strategy and consider its application in secondary subjects.

Study Guides

Research has demonstrated the effectiveness of the use of study guides for students with mild and moderate disabilities (Hudson, Lignugaris-Kraft, & Miller, 1993; Lovitt & Horton, 1994; Lovitt, Rudsit, Jenkins, Pious, & Benedetti, 1985). Study guides differ from advance organizers in that the work on a study guide is to be completed during the study of the material rather than prior to it. Thus, the study guide may be considered one form of participatory organizer, discussed in Chapter 9 (Hawk & McLeod, 1984).

The study by Lovitt et al. (1985), as one example, indicated that provision of a study guide for junior high school science students resulted in greater gains in achievement than did traditional instruction. This was true for high achieving, normally achieving, and low achieving students, as well as for students with learning disabilities in the experimental classes. Clearly, provision of study guides facilitates increases in achievement for all students.

This last point cannot be overemphasized. All students benefit from the use of study guides. Should you ever recommend this strategy to a mainstream teacher, you should point out this advantage. Consequently, the mainstream teacher should not view preparation of study guides as additional work that benefits only students with mild disabilities in the mainstreamed class. In both the traditional mainstream class and inclusive classes with co-teachers working together, study guides will enhance learning for all students. Interest Box 12.4 presents a sample study guide format from the study by Lovitt and his co-workers (1985).

Although many study guides are based on words and reading skill, as is the sample in Interest Box 12.5, study guides may also be based on charts, or pictures to complete or label. Research by Bergerud, Lovitt, and Horton (1988) indicated that study guides in the form of visual displays may work better for some students than reading-

INTEREST BOX 12.4
Sample Study Guide

The study guide below is a sample of a study guide used by Lovitt and his co-workers (1985). The science students were to complete this study guide during the science lecture.

Name ______________________

Learning About Molecules Framed Outline.

A. Molecules

1. ______________ is made up of ______________.
2. A piece of ______________ is an ______________ when all the ______________ are ______________.
3. A ______________ ______________ is made up of ______________ atoms of the same kind.
4. The molecules for ______________ is O_2. This ______________ is made up of ______________ oxygen ______________. It is ______________ ______________.
5. The word kinetic means ______________.
6. There is a ______________ that all ______________ are always ______________. It is call the kinetic ______________.
7. Many years ago Robert Brown discovered the ______________ ______________. He observed ______________ grains ______________ in a ______________ pattern over surface of ______________.
8. Some examples of molecules moving are ______________.

Source: Lovitt et al. (1985).

based study guides. In a follow-up study, additional research indicated that study guides used in mainstream classes are more effective than self-study for students with disabilities as well as nondisabled children (Horton, Lovitt, & Bergerud, 1990).

Structured Presentation Technologies (SPT)

Because many secondary teachers utilize the lecture/class discussion teaching format, researchers have suggested methods whereby lecture presentations may be enhanced via structured presentation technology, or SPT. Monti et al. (1994) described the use of SPT as an enhancement of the now current use of some audiovisual media in most lectures.

For example, many teachers currently use transparencies to illustrate points in the lecture. Other teachers require their students to refer to pictures in the text during the lectures. These strategies may be thought of as advance organizer approaches, because the points are typically illustrated on the transparency and then discussed. However, as Monti et al. (1994) point out, SPT allows the lecturer access to many new interactive media options. For example, when discussing a volcano in science or geography, the new technologies allow all of the class to view an eruption while the teacher describes the processes that lead to it.

However, these SPT technologies allow for much more than merely a moving transparency or video show. For example, another phase in SPT allows different students in the class to pursue different inquiry topics, based on their interests. These students would then share their inquiry material with the class in an exposition phase. This is particularly advantageous in inclusive classrooms, because both students with disabilities and gifted students can work through this phase at their own pace. Finally, a review phase ties the various points together.

Clearly, as these technologies become more common in today's classrooms, the traditional concept of the teacher who imparts knowledge through a lecture will become increasingly outdated, in view of these much more effective presentation formats. Both mainstream and special education teachers will need a full understanding of what these technologies can do in order to adapt the classroom for students with disabilities.

Computerized Instruction

As reported in Chapter 7, the use of microcomputers in classrooms is increasing drastically. As a result of this increase, newer and more sophisticated computer programs are available for use. Horton, Lovitt, and Slocum (1988) compared two instructional approaches: a computer presented tutorial in geography and a traditional work-map instructional format. The two instructional treatments were used with ninth grade pupils with learning disabilities. The work-map format may be considered a form of participatory organizer, because the students were required to write in names of cities and countries as they studied the atlas.

The computer program used five instructional elements when introducing a geographical fact. The computer presented a map on the screen with a prompt arrow pointing to the city to be taught. Next, the prompt disappeared, revealing the name of the city on one side of the map. The student then moved the cursor to position it on the location of the city. This simple program resulted in much higher rates of learning than the work-map condition. The authors suggest that this result was based on the increased repetition, immediate corrective feedback, and cumulative review features found in computer-based tutorial instruction. Clearly, CBI can enhance the content instruction for students with disabilities.

However, the advent of recent multimedia technologies (discussed in Chapter 7) can increase the utility of CBI in the subject content areas. In fact, multimedia applications have a way of breaking down the artificial barriers between subject areas, and can enhance the instructional excitement in almost any classroom.

For example, the Sunburst Company (Pleasantville, NY) has developed award winning multimedia software called *The Voyages of the Mimi* (1994). The *Mimi,* a tall-masted sailing and research vessel, provides a backdrop for studies of rainforest environments, whales and their environments, maps and navigation, Mayan mathematical systems, and numerous other topics. The various programs were developed by the Bank Street College of Education, with federal funding, and this software has won numerous awards for state-of-the-art education programs.

As one example, the *Maya Math* program challenges students in grades 4 through 8 to become "math archaeologists." Students must apply their mathematical understanding to decipher the mysterious Maya base-20 number system. Thus, this could be an appropriate lesson for either a math or a social studies class. Also, the video segments presented in the many different voyages greatly enhance the applicability and excitement generated by this software. Clearly, all teachers should become increasingly proficient in multimedia applications, because use of these instructional applications will be the norm in the very near future.

Precision Teaching

Chapter 4 presented a detailed review of precision teaching instructional formats. As reported, most of the early research that demonstrated the effectiveness of precision teaching involved instruction in the basic skill areas for younger children or children with disabilities who were functioning below grade level. However, Lovitt et al. (1985) demonstrated that precision teaching may be used for higher-level content instruction for students with mild disabilities. In that study, precision teaching procedures were used to teach science facts to seventh grade children in three different ability groups: high achieving, normally achieving, and low achieving. Precision teaching practices were found to be more effective than traditional instructional approaches for each of the three groups. Interest Box 12.5 presents a sample precision teaching practice sheet from that study.

Precision teaching does involve the use of special materials—rate sheets that present the data to be learned. However, these rate sheets are relatively simple to prepare, and many teachers use workbook pages in various curriculum areas as the rate sheets.

Reconstructive Elaborations

Mastropieri and Scruggs (1988, 1989) have recommended a mnemonic strategy for content instruction that involves elaborations on the central theme in order to facilitate recall. Reconstructive elaborations provide more concrete information in a meaningful fashion than do the typical types of examples in text. For example, a typical history text concerning World War I may report that many soldiers died in trenches because of disease rather than combat. However, the typical pictures in those texts would show soldiers in trenches, but not the living conditions in those trenches. Mastropieri and Scruggs (1989) recommend using a picture cue that shows soldiers dying in the trenches, because such an elaborative reconstruction aids the memory of students with mild disabilities. Another example of an elaborative reconstruction is presented in Interest Box 12.6.

There is one problem with this method of instruction for most teachers. Development of the pictures and teacher scripts takes time, and most current textbooks do not include reconstructive elaborations. In inclusive classes, this time concern is somewhat abated because the teacher pairs can allow some flexible time for one teacher or the other to develop these reconstructive elaborations. Also, you may find that this approach to content instruction is more frequent in textbooks published in subsequent years, because the use of the reconstructive elaborations does facilitate content learning.

INSTRUCTION FOR CONTENT AREAS

Instructional Activities

1. Have groups create murals depicting scenes from different, successive eras or illustrating events from segments of history, such as the industrial revolution, and display them as a timeline.

2. How do plants grow? Place porous paper inside a glass and put one-half an inch of water in the glass. Put a seed between the paper and the glass. Keep the seed wet and watch the seed grow.

3. So plants need sunlight? Use two flowerpots. Plant six corn or bean seeds in each pot. Give each pot the same amount of water daily.

INTEREST BOX 12.5
Sample Precision Teaching Pages

These sample precision teaching pages are similar to the one used by Lovitt and his coworkers (1985).

Name________________ Date______ Count Correct______ Errors______ Min.______

See-Say or See-Write: Learning About Molecules

Directions: Review the definitions on this page. Then, on the next page, say or write the correct word for the given meaning.

molecules—most are made up of 2 or more different kinds of atoms

element—all the atoms in a piece of matter are alike

diatomic—made up of 2 atoms that are joined together

kinetic theory—idea that all the molecules in matter are moving

Brownian movement—molecules moving in a zig-zag pattern

matter—made up of atoms

O_2—O stands for oxygen, $_2$ stands for number of atoms

Diffusion—mixing of atoms or molecules because of random motions

Leave the plants in the sunlight until they are five or six inches tall. Then place one plant in a dark cabinet or under a box. Continue watering both equally. Watch the two plants daily for two weeks and compare them.

4. Ask each student to bring in one newspaper article about something that has happened on a continent other than the United States. Have them share the article with the class. Make a list on the chalkboard of the continents written about in the articles. Assign each continent a color and tape a square of that color construction paper onto the board beside the name of the continent (use a masking tape loop). Have pins with the same colored heads to locate the continents on a map that is displayed on the bulletin board.

5. Have students work in groups to design a flag. Emphasize that the flag should be symbolic, having something to do with their school or class. Have each group agree on an individual design. One student should draw an outline of the design, another should color the design, and a third group member should present the flag to the class.

6. Make nutrition placemats. You will need construction paper, old magazines, scissors, paste, and clear adhesive paper or laminating equipment. Have children cut out pictures of foods that would be part of a nutritious breakfast, lunch, or dinner. Paste these pictures to the construction paper and laminate with clear adhesive paper.

most are made up of 2 or more different kinds of atoms	idea that all the molecules are moving	all the atoms in a piece of matter are alike
mixing of atoms or molecules because of random motion	made up of two atoms that are joined together	made up of atoms
molecules moving in a zig-zag pattern	made up of 2 atoms that are joined together	Many are made up of 2 or more different kinds of atoms
O stands for oxygen 2 stands for the number of atoms	all the atoms in a piece of matter are alike	made up of 2 atoms that are joined together
idea that all the molecules in matter are moving	most are made up of 2 or more different kinds of atoms	all the atoms in a piece of matter are alike
molecules moving in a random zig-zag pattern	made up of atoms	mixing of atoms or molecules because of random motion

Source: Lovitt et al. (1985).

Commercially Available Materials

***Merrill Science Readiness*, Merrill Publishing Co.**
This readiness program includes a student text, a "big book," and a teacher edition that provides all of the necessary information needed to plan and teach science successfully. A "lesson plan" section found next to each corresponding student text page in the teacher's edition organizes information and enables the instructor to present individual lessons in a logical format. Lesson options are found below each corresponding student text page. The options include science background information and specific reinforcement, enrichment, challenge, curriculum integration, and technology and society activities. Part I is "All About Me," and includes My Senses, My Body. Part II, "All About My World," includes Seasons, Plants, Air, Water, Land, Weather, Animals, Space, and Caring for Our World.

***Wonders of Learning*, National Geographic**
Wonders of Learning targets the primary level and is a flexible teaching unit to be used individually, by small groups, or by an entire class. Each kit contains a teacher guide, booklets for instruction, background information, activity sheets, and follow-up activity. *Wonders of Learning* is a self-contained flexible teaching program designed to increase knowledge of social studies and science.

***I.D.E.A.L. Science Curriculum*, Opportunities for Learning**
The content in this self-directed program is suitable for junior and senior high school students with a fifth

INTEREST BOX 12.6
Sample Reconstructive Elaboration

The following reconstruction elaboration was presented by Mastropieri and Scruggs (1988) as an example of an acoustic reconstruction.

> *Woodrow Wilson was elected president in 1913. Foreign affairs became an important part of this administration. He selected William Jennings Bryan to be Secretary of State. Bryan was opposed to all wars, or a peacemaker. Someone opposed to all wars is called a pacifist. Between 1913 and 1914, Bryan negotiated 30 "cooling off" or peace treaties among the nations of the world.*
>
> *(Show Overhead) To remember that Bryan was the Secretary of State who opposed all wars, think of the keyword for Bryan: lion. What is the keyword for Bryan? (Elicit responses.) Remember this picture of a lion who is a secretary at a desk saying, "Please, no fighting," to the other animals, to help you remember Bryan was the Secretary of State who opposed all wars. Tell me what you think of when I ask who Bryan was. (Elicit responses and provide feedback.)*

Source: Mastropieri and Scruggs (1988).

grade reading level. The focus is on the human body and health sciences. Each booklet contains reading, writing, and lab activities as well as objectives, directions, and review tests. The teacher's manual contains instructions, 150 reproducible worksheets, tests, and answer keys. Each student completes the first three books (Introduction, Methods, and Cells to Systems), and then chooses from the seven remaining books (Nervous System, Excretory System, Circulatory System, Skeletal System, Digestive System, Respiratory System, Musculatory System).

Brains and Parker McGoohan, Sundance

Brains and Parker McGoohan is a paperback adventure series that introduces students to important scientific figures such as Galileo, Benjamin Franklin, and John James Audubon. Each book features two young teenagers, Brains and Parker, who use a time machine to travel to the past. The set also includes a teacher's guide and a "scientist's notebook" that includes background articles and suggestions for hands-on science activities.

Junior Geologist, United Learning

Junior Geologist is a series of four 8-minute videotapes and accompanying teacher's guide, designed to answer young students' questions about the planet Earth. The tapes are broken into segments, each of which starts with a question. The series answers questions about earth structure, the rock cycle, erosion, minerals, and more. Original music and animated graphics fully illustrate each topic.

A Sound History of America, Developmental Learning Materials

The ten audiocassettes in this program feature important historical events that are included in the traditional curriculum. The time frame covers the discovery of America to the 1980s. The lessons are 10 to 15 minutes long and the accompanying scripts can be used as a read-along activity. The tapes present factual information, dramatizations, period music, and sound effects.

World History and You, Steck and Vaughn

This series is designed for older students with reading problems. The consumable two-book survey is written on the fourth grade reading level. The emphasis is on world history, but the process also includes reading comprehension, vocabulary expansion, and other language skills. Book 1 presents ancient civilization, the growth of major religions, exploration, and the colonization of the new world. Book 2 begins with the industrial revolution, continues through the growth of democracy, and ends with contemporary world history.

Science and Social Studies Software

Ant Farm

Publisher: Sunburst Communications

Skill Level: Elementary, secondary, adult

Hardware: Apple IIe

Description: Students study an ant's pattern of movement and identify its work station. The goal is to place the ant into the ant farm to execute its pattern. In doing so, students use problem-solving strategies of successive scanning, pattern, or sequence-examining assumptions as well as information gathering.

Explore-a-Science Series

Publisher: Wm. K. Bradford Publishing Co.

Skill Level: Preschool, elementary

Hardware: Apple IIe, Macintosh, IBM

Description: The series contains stories on such science topics as the desert, tracks, wolves, whales, weather forecasting, and *Tyrannosaurus rex* both on the computer and in an accompanying book. These topics are explored through active inquiry and creative activities. The students explore the story content on screen and can use interactive components in the program to add text, labels, characters, and objects to the stories. All stories can be saved and printed. There are also interactive activities that the students can use to increase their understanding of the topics.

Fast-Track Fractions

Publisher: DLM Teaching Resources

Skill Level: Elementary, secondary

Hardware: Apple IIe

Description: High-interest graphics, appropriate reinforcement, and three response modes motivate the students as they solve problems in comparison, addition, subtraction, multiplication, and division of fractions. The students can choose scanning, matching, or fill-in-the-blank modes of responding. Teachers are able to edit content, and the program automatically computes the answers when editing. Worksheets can be generated and printed for additional practice. A student tracking system includes a top ten listing and response analysis so the teacher can determine where the student is having trouble.

Geography Adventure: USA

Publisher: SouthWest Ed Psych Services, Inc.

Skill Level: Elementary, secondary

Hardware: Apple IIe

Description: This program combines a colorful high resolution graphics adventure game with arcade action. It allows the player to use knowledge of U.S. geography and game skills to track down and capture a foreign agent at large in the United States. Multiple difficulty levels accommodate players from grade 4 through adult. It features a database of more than 1,400 unique U.S. geography facts and allows users to insert their own geography facts.

Learn About Animals

Publisher: Wings for Learning, Inc.

Skill Level: Elementary

Hardware: Apple IIe, Muppet Learning Keys, Apple mouse, Koala Pad, joystick (optional)

Description: Students use this illustrated, animated program to explore the natural habitats, foods, homes, sizes, and offspring of a variety of animals. They practice such skills as counting, matching, and classifying.

Occupations

Publisher: UCLA Intervention Program for Handicapped Children

Skill Level: Preschool, elementary, secondary

Hardware: Apple IIe

Description: Students explore the work environment and identify workers. Two levels let the student select individual workers and see their environment or answer the question "Who works here?" Workers are presented on the PowerPad,which the student also uses as an input device. The program is not as sophisticated as some others, but does a good job at presenting workers and their environments.

Oregon Trail

Publisher: MECC

Skill Level: Elementary, secondary, adult

Hardware: Apple IIe, Macintosh

Description: Students learn about the westward movement and frontier life in nineteenth-century America. They learn and practice decision-making skills applicable to everyday living: planning before starting an activity, dealing with an emergency, budgeting money and supplies, etc.

Where in the World is Carmen Sandiego?

Publisher: Broderbund Software, Inc.

Skill Level: Elementary, secondary, adult

Hardware: Apple IIe, IBM, Macintosh

Description: Players are introduced to world geography in an exciting game situation. Gameplay combines elements of graphic adventures, trivia games, mysteries,and arcade animation. Together, players help the detective decipher clues by looking up facts in the *World Almanac.* There are ten possible suspects, 30 cities, and nearly 1,000 clues.

SUMMARY

Although research on content instruction for students with disabilities in middle and secondary school is somewhat limited, there are a number of useful strategies that may be employed. First, a number of common adaptations may be made in any content area class that includes students with disabilities. These adaptations work in either the mainstream classes or the more recently established inclusive classrooms. You may wish to make the suggestions in Interest Boxes 12.2 and 12.3 available to all of the mainstream teachers in your school who request assistance. It would be relatively easy to use these adaptation lists as handouts for those teachers.

In addition to these general adaptations, several specific instructional strategies are supported by research. A number of these strategies represent ideas first introduced in earlier chapters, and with minor modifications such strategies as the use of advance organizers, CBI, precision teaching, multimedia applications, and study guides may be readily applied in most content area classes.

Although no single technique presented in this chapter will alleviate every academic problem of secondary students with disabilities in content instruction, the consistent use of these strategies should facilitate more achievement for most of these students. Also, if more and more classes move toward inclusive instruction, these strategies will take on increasing importance.

Summary Points

- There is less research on instructional methods in content areas for students with disabilities than on the basic skill areas.
- The reading skills, note-taking skills, and reasoning skills of some students with disabilities severely limit their ability to master academic work in the content areas. Thus, many adaptations to the curriculum are necessary in order for these students to succeed.
- Although many teachers adapt the curriculum in minor ways, few teachers make substantive adaptations.
- In recommending adaptations for either mainstream teachers or co-teachers in the inclusive class, the special education teacher must address two issues: fairness to all students and the amount of teacher time required to make the adaptation.
- Specific instructional strategies may include many discussed previously, such as the use of advance organizers, study guides, precision teacher procedures, and computerized educational materials.

QUESTIONS AND ACTIVITIES

1. Form an interview team and visit a local high school. Interview several different teachers in different content areas and inquire about the use of the adaptations presented in the interest boxes in this chapter. Find out if those teachers use other adaptations not mentioned here. Find an inclusive classroom and interview those teachers about which adaptations are made, and then compare the answers.
2. Conduct a telephone interview with several elementary and several secondary special education teachers in your local area. Ask about their responsibilities for teaching content area curriculum to students with disabilities.
3. Review the instructional ideas presented in Chapter 10, and identify any other ideas that may be adapted for use in content area learning activities such as lecture and group discussion.
4. Why are instructional strategies for content areas receiving research attention only recently?
5. Prepare a study guide such as the one found in this chapter. Present it to the class, along with suggestions about how to prepare such a study guide.
6. Review the research on reconstructive elaborations and present a report to the class.

REFERENCES

Ausubel, D. P., & Robinson, F. G. (1969). *School Learning: An Introduction to Educational Psychology.* New York: Holt, Reinhart, & Winston.

Bender, W. N. (1985). Strategies for helping the mainstreamed student in secondary social studies classes. *The Social Studies, 76,* 269–271.

Bergerud, D., Lovitt, T. C., & Horton, S. (1988). The effectiveness of textbook adaptations in life science for high school students with learning disabilities. *Journal of Learning Disabilities, 21,* 70–76.

Darch, C., & Carnine, D. (1986). Teaching content area material to learning disabled students. *Exceptional Children, 53,* 240–246.

Darch, C., & Gersten, R. (1986). Direction-setting activities in reading comprehension: A comparison of two approaches. *Learning Disability Quarterly, 9,* 235–243.

Deshler, D. D., Schumaker, J. B., & Lenz, B. K. (1984). Academic and cognitive interventions for LD adolescents: Part I. *Journal of Learning Disabilities, 17,* 108–117.

Espin, C. A., & Deno, S. L. (1993). Performance in reading content area text as an indicator of achievement. *Remedial and Special Education, 14* (6), 47–59.

Hawk, P. P., & McLeod, N. P. (1984). Graphic organizers: A cognitive teaching method that works. *The Directive Teacher, 6* (1), 6–7.

Horton, S. V., Lovitt, T. C., & Bergerud, D. (1990). The effectiveness of graphic organizers for three classifications of secondary students in content area classes. *Journal of Learning Disabilities, 23,* 12–22.

Horton, S. V., Lovitt, T. C., & Slocum, T. (1988). Teaching geography to high school students with academic deficits: Effects of a computerized map tutorial. *Learning Disability Quarterly, 11,* 371–379.

Hudson, P., Lignugaris-Kraft, B., & Miller, T. (1993). Using content enhancements to improve the performance of adolescents with learning disabilities in content classes. *Learning Disabilities Research and Practice, 8* (2), 106–126.

Johnson, R. E., & Varidan, E. B. (1973). Reading, readability, and social studies. *The Reading Teacher, 26,* 483–487.

Kinder, D., & Bursuck, W. (1993). History strategy instruction: Problem–solution–effect analysis, timeline, and vocabulary instruction. *Exceptional Children, 59,* 324–335.

Lambie, R. A., & Hutchens, P. W. (1986). Adapting elementary school mathematics instruction. *Teaching Exceptional Children, 22,* 185–189.

Lenz, B. K., Alley, G. R., & Schumaker, J. B. (1987). Activating the inactive learner: Advance organizers in the secondary classroom. *Learning Disability Quarterly, 10,* 53–67.

Lovitt, T. C., & Horton, S. V. (1994). Strategies for adapting science textbooks for youth with learning disabilities. *Remedial and Special Education, 15* (2), 105–116.

Lovitt, T., Rudsit, J., Jenkins, J., Pious, C., & Benedetti, D. (1985). Two methods of adapting science materials for learning disabled and regular seventh graders. *Learning Disability Quarterly, 8,* 275–285.

Mastropieri, M. A., & Scruggs, T. E. (1994). Text versus hands-on science curriculum: Implications for students with disabilities. *Remedial and Special Education, 15* (2), 72–85.

Mastropieri, M. A., & Scruggs, T. E. (1988). Increasing content area learning of learning disabled students: Research implementation. *Learning Disabilities Research, 4* (1), 17–25.

Mastropieri, M. A., & Scruggs, T. E. (1989). Reconstructive elaborations: Strategies that facilitate content learning. *Learning Disabilities Focus, 4* (2), 73–77.

Monti, D., Cicchetti, G., Goodkind, T., & Ganci, M. T. (1994). SPT: A new methodology for instruction. *Technological Horizons in Education Journal, 22* (1), 66–69.

Munson, S. M. (1986). Regular education teacher modifications for mainstreamed mildly handicapped students. *The Journal of Special Education, 20,* 489–502.

Sachs, F. G., & Banas, N. (1987). Using the ENIGMA reading program to teach geography more effectively. *Techniques, 3,* 121–124.

Sachs, F. G., & Banas, N. (1985). The "ENIGMA" reading program. *Academic Therapy, 20,* 481–485.

Sunburst (1994). *The Voyages of the Mimi: Innovative Multimedia for Active Learning* (computer program). Pleasantville, NY.

CHAPTER 13

INSTRUCTIONAL METHODS FOR INCREASING SOCIAL COMPETENCE

OBJECTIVES

When you complete this chapter, you should be able to:

1. Discuss the rationale for instruction in social competence.
2. State the distinction between social skills and social competence.
3. Compare the deficit model with the contextualist model of social competence.
4. Identify four components of social competence.
5. Discuss several measurement approaches for various aspects of social competence.
6. Describe two types of instructional approaches used to teach social competence.
7. Describe the general research conclusions regarding social competence instruction.
8. Describe several commercially available packages designed to improve social competence.

KEYWORDS

social competence	noxious behavior	self-report
social rejection	primary cause hypothesis	ACCEPTS
peer acceptance	secondary cause hypothesis	FAST
social skills	observation checklist	RECESS
contextualist	peer nomination method	skill-streaming
social cognition	roster rating	

This chapter presents information on instruction in social competence. Although the construct of social competence is defined more thoroughly later in the chapter, a preliminary definition should aid your understanding. Social competence is a multifaceted construct that indicates one's general level of social success and includes such things as the social skills that may be demonstrated by a child with a disability, self-perceptions, perceptions of motivations and feelings of others, peer acceptance, and appropriate social behaviors.

Unlike certain other instructional chapters included in this section of the volume, this chapter presents information on the theoretical background that underlies instruction in social competence. Instruction in social competence is a relatively new phenomenon, and an understanding of its historical background is necessary. Information on the commercially available assessments and instructional programs is provided later in the chapter.

THE SOCIAL COMPETENCE CONCEPT

Rationale for Study of Social Competence

Instruction in social competence is receiving a great deal more attention today for a number of reasons. First, research within the last two decades has shown decisively that many children and youth with disabilities demonstrate deficits in social competence (Bryan, 1994; Gresham, 1981; Gresham & Elliott, 1989a; McConnell, 1987; Vaughn

& Hogan, 1994). This evidence includes studies of students with mental disabilities, learning disabilities, and behavioral disorders, and each of these groups demonstrates measurable deficits in social competence.

Second, deficits in social competence among children with disabilities severely affects their success in school mainstreaming and inclusive class programs (Gresham, 1981; Nelson, 1988). Historically, one reason for mainstreaming was to provide appropriate role models of social behavior for these children, but research has demonstrated that social interaction between students with disabilities and their peers does not automatically increase when these students are placed in the same class. Consequently, even when placed in today's inclusive classes, a child with a mild or moderate disability may not be adequately exposed to appropriate role models he or she can emulate. Also, the sought after friendships between students with and those without disabilities may not develop. Without some instruction to promote social competence, the youngster with the disability is likely to remain "segregated" for all practical intents and purposes, even within the mainstream class.

Finally, researchers have concluded that deficits in social competence affect later success in life (Bryan, 1994; Parker & Asher, 1987; Vaughn, McIntosh, & Spencer-Rowe, 1991). For example, Parker and Asher (1987) reviewed the literature on social competence and found a strong relationship between poor peer relationships and dropping out of school. A relationship was also noted between poor peer relationships and juvenile crime during later years.

With these reasons in mind, much more attention is now given to instruction in social competence than was ten years ago. This emphasis represents a major shift within the field of special education. Whereas special education teachers in the 1940s and 1950s were providing instruction in reading, math, and vocational skills, training in social skills and social competence is a relatively new phenomenon. Today, special education teachers must be trained to teach social competence at every grade level, and instructional methods for social skills ranging in grade level from preschool through high school have been proposed (Bishop & Jubala, 1994; Brown, Ragland, & Bishop, 1989; Capone, Smith, & Schloss, 1988). This chapter presents information on the theoretical background of social competence in order to enable you to make informed choices concerning the available instruction strategies.

History of Social Competence Research

Historically, research on social competence began among populations of children with mental retardation. As early as the 1940s and 1950s, some research on teachers' ratings of adaptive behavior of students with mental retardation included indicators of social acceptance or rejection. This variable indicates how well students with disabilities are socially accepted by their peers, and is, perhaps, the most well-researched variable in the area of social competence (Vaughn & Hogan, 1994). The earliest studies demonstrated that children with mental retardation were not accepted socially by their peers in mainstream classes (see Semmel, Gottlieb, & Robinson, 1979, for a review). Later, research on peer acceptance of students with learning disabilities and behavioral disorders was conducted that demonstrated the same lack of social acceptance by nondisabled students in mainstream classes (Bryan, 1978; Johnson & Johnson, 1980; Vaughn & Hogan, 1994).

These indicators of low social acceptance became more important as the movement for mainstreaming grew during the 1960s and early 1970s, because increased mainstreaming resulted in increased placement of children with disabilities in regular classes. Some researchers saw this as one way to provide effective role models for students with disabilities, while other researchers feared that increased mainstreaming might result in increased social isolation for those students (Goodman, Gottlieb, & Harrison, 1972).

The general belief at the time was that the lower social acceptance of students with disabilities was caused by a lack of specific social skills among those students. The particular social skills typically discussed included such things as sharing behavior, joining in conversation, asking for help, verbal problem solving, and listening to others. This belief has been referred to as the "deficit model" or "social skills deficit model" of instruction, because the problem was believed to reside within the child (Vaughn, McIntosh, & Spencer-Rowe, 1991). Children with disabilities were believed to be deficient in skills that facilitate social acceptance, and it was believed that instruction in those particular skills would result not only in improved social skills but also in improved peer interactions and increased social acceptance in mainstream classes.

The early research on social skills training demonstrated that students with disabilities could learn these skills, but that their mastery of the skills did not generalize to situations outside of the instructional environment (Gresham, 1981; McConnell, 1987; Shepard & Koberstein, 1989). Also, the anticipated result of higher levels of social acceptance by mainstream class peers was not realized, even when the training on particular social skills was successful.

This research resulted in reconceptualization of the entire concept of social competence. Clearly, there was very little point in spending instructional time teaching social skills unless that instruction would result in the generalized use of those skills and increased social acceptance in mainstream situations.

Components of Social Competence

Four Components. As a result of this lack of success in social skills training, researchers began to reexamine the concept, resulting in increased attention to the more inclusive concept of social competence. In contrast to the social skills deficit model described above, researchers have recently adopted a contextual model that describes the multifaceted construct of social competence as an interaction between various child- and environment-based factors. Thus the contextualist perspective involves discussion of the entire context of social competence—child deficits in particular social skills, peer group perceptions, interpretations of each others' social cues, and other factors (Bryan, 1994; Vaughn & Hogan, 1994; Vaughn, McIntosh, & Spencer-Rowe, 1991).

Vaughn and her associates have provided strong leadership in this reconceptualization (Vaughn & Hogan, 1994, 1990; Vaughn, McIntosh, & Spencer-Rowe, 1991). They identified four interdependent factors that comprise social competence, each of which must be considered in order to construct an educational intervention to change a child's social competence. Each of the four factors is measured by different means and requires a different type of intervention for meaningful positive change to occur.

The first of these components is social skills knowledge. Obviously, a student's knowledge and use of acceptable social skills has some effect on overall social competence and thus is one component of social competence. The presence of particular social skills is generally measured by observation, teacher rating, or self-report measures, as discussed later in the chapter. Interventions for social skills deficits involve training the child in specific social skills or social problem solving strategies. Curriculum and instructional strategies for these areas are presented in more detail later.

The second factor concerns the child's relationships with others. This typically involves peer status, friendships, relationships with family and teachers, and, at later stages, intimate relationships (Vaughn & Hogan, 1994). Measures of peer acceptance generally should involve the use of the peers in the class for assessment. Such assessment is referred to as sociometric rating. Interventions for peer acceptance typically involve those in which the peers participate along with the target child, and increased structured interactions do tend to lead to development of peer acceptance and friendships that involve students with and without disabilities (Bishop & Jubala, 1994).

A third factor involves accurate age appropriate social cognition. This is the ability to cognitively interpret the social dialogue and understand the feelings, motivations, and behaviors of oneself and others (Vaughn & Hogan, 1990). Interpretations of one's own feelings may be measured by self-reports. However, the degree to which a socially incompetent child accurately interprets the social cues, moods, and emotions of others is not easily measurable. Intervention for this type of social cognition usually involves role-play activities in which the target child is taught to consider the feelings of others.

Finally, the absence of maladaptive behaviors is considered one aspect of social competence (Vaughn & Hogan, 1994). This includes serious behavior problems and noxious social behavior as well as development of self-control. An uncontrollable nose drip has been used as one example of a socially noxious behavior. This measure strongly affects social competence because these indicators can affect the peer's perceptions of the social desirability of interaction with a particular student. For example, if a student's nose is continually running, that noxious behavior—intentional or not—is likely to affect the social desirability of that child in the eyes of his or her peers. Typically, noxious behaviors and maladaptive behaviors are measured through observation or teacher rating, and interventions are structured to decrease or eliminate the inappropriate behavior whenever possible.

Two Practical Examples. These four components of social competence are important because any or all of these components may require attention in particular cases. Imagine the following situation: As a special education teacher in an inclusive classroom, you are participating on a committee that is designing an individualized educational program for a child in that class. Suppose that, as in the example above, a child's nose runs for uncontrollable medical reasons. A psychologist, however, has conducted a series of assessments that indicate that the student is socially isolated, and has recommended including social skills in the instructional plan. Clearly, the wrong aspect of social competence is being addressed by that recommendation; unless social skills are a demonstrable deficit, the problem leading to low social acceptance is the nose-running itself and not the lack of social skills. As an educator with responsibility for how that child spends time in the inclusive class, you should indicate that other interventions may be more appropriate for that child.

Imagine that there is a second child with low social acceptance in the same class, but this child sometimes demonstrates aggressive, maladaptive behaviors. At other times, the child may be polite, easygoing, and able to get along with peers very well. Again, instruction in social skills will probably not help. Clearly this child has the necessary social skills, but needs instruction in self-management of inappropriate behaviors. Rather than instruction in social skills themselves, institution of a behavioral management program (on a self-monitoring basis, see Chapter 5) should be considered to decrease the aggressiveness and maladaptive behavior.

In order to increase social competence for any child, each of the components of social competence must be considered, and any intervention design must address deficits found in all of the separate areas. As you can see from these examples, social competence is a very complex construct, with many factors to consider.

Causes of Deficits in Social Competence

There are a number of potential causes for low social competence among students with disabilities, though these causes tend to be associated with only one or two aspects of social competence. First, researchers have identified several potential causes for deficits in social acceptance. Since the beginning of the 1960s, researchers have been concerned with the potentially negative effects of labeling a child as disabled, including the potential that such labeling will result in low social acceptance. Some states have changed terminology for various disability groups to move away from "negative" labels, only to find that the newly proposed term results in the same labeling effect after a few years. North Carolina, for example, changed its terminology from "mentally retarded" to "mentally handicapped" during the 1977 school year, and by 1978 the new term had acquired all of the potentially negative effects of the old.

A second cause of low social acceptance consists of deficits in social skills, as mentioned above (Gresham & Elliott, 1989a; Vaughn & Hogan, 1990). The bulk of research during the last ten years in the area of social competence has dealt with measuring social skills and devising instructional programs for these skills. With this emphasis on research in the area, the recent question has become, "What causes deficits in the acquisition of social skills?"

One cause may be termed the "primary cause" hypothesis—that the same neurological dysfunctions or cognitive processing problems that caused the disability also caused the deficits in social skill deficits (Gresham & Elliott, 1989b; Vaughn & Hogan, 1990). Social competence is based, in part, on cognitive interpretation of social dialogue with others, as well as on interpretation of nonverbal social cues regarding the feelings and motivations of others—described above as a major component of social competence. The "primary cause" hypothesis, then, suggests that the cognitive processes that cause retardation or learning disabilities are also the primary cause for deficits in social competence (Gresham & Elliott, 1989b).

Another potential cause of deficits in social skills may be identified as the "secondary cause" hypothesis. This hypothesis suggests that deficits in cognitive abilities cause deficits in achievement, and that students who have obvious deficits in achievement are likely to be less popular, and thus less likely to have opportunities to practice acceptable social skills. Here, the deficit in social skills is seen as a secondary or indirect result of the cognitive process difficulties that caused the disability (Gresham & Elliott, 1989b; Vaughn & Hogan, 1990). At the present time, there is little evidence for the accuracy of either the primary or secondary cause hypothesis (Gresham & Elliott, 1989b). More research will be forthcoming on this issue in the hope that, at some future point, educators will have a more complete idea of how to provide instruction to improve both social skills and social competence.

ASSESSMENT OF SOCIAL COMPETENCE

The assessment of social competence is directly linked to the components of social competence discussed above. Several different methods are used, depending upon which aspect seems to be presenting the most problems (Fiedler & Chiang, 1989).

Teacher's Ratings

Teachers are generally good observers of certain types of behavior in their classes (Bailey, Bender, & Montgomery, 1983). They can generally determine the level of disruptive behaviors, maladaptive behaviors, and off-task behaviors of students, and these are the types of behaviors that comprise the fourth component of social competence. A number of teacher rating scales are commercially available (see Gresham and Elliott, 1989a, for a review), and you will see these behavior rating scales used frequently. For example, many school districts routinely require that the referring teacher complete one of these behavior rating scales for a target child as a part of the referral procedure.

Teachers may also be expected to measure the student's use of the particular social skills that comprise the first component of social competence. Many commercially available social skills training packages include teacher ratings of students' social skills to be used on a pre- or posttraining basis. Several of these commercially available curricula are discussed at the end of this chapter.

Observation Checklists

The observation checklist comprises a list of social behaviors (both positive and negative may be included) observed in role-play situations. These checklists are typically completed by teachers, and are used to measure the same components of social competence as the more formal teacher ratings discussed above: social skills and maladaptive behavior. When using the checklists, the social situation is "staged," and the observation checklist offers the opportunity to observe low frequency behaviors that may not be readily observable in free observations taken at random times in the classroom.

One concern with this type of assessment format is the relationship between social behaviors in a contrived situation such as a role-play and social behaviors in real world settings. Gresham and Elliott (1989a) suggested that there may be little or no correspondence between social behaviors in these different situations. Certainly, such results call into question the use of observation checklists. However, this assessment tool is more frequently used in research than in assessment practices in public schools, and more research on this issue will certainly be forthcoming.

Sociometric Ratings

Although teachers are generally good observers of certain types of problem behaviors, they are not as adept at assessing the second component of social competence—disturbed peer relationships. For that reason, techniques were developed whereby the peers in the classroom could be used to assess those behaviors. Sociometric ratings involve the use of the peer group within the classroom to rate the social acceptance, peer rejection, and/or specific behaviors of the target child. This sociometric rating method is considered the preferable method for measuring all aspects of peer relationships, though some teacher ratings will also yield measures of peer relationships.

It should be noted here that peer rejection and social acceptance are not exact opposites, as one might imagine. Many children with disabilities are not widely accepted socially because the majority of the children in the peer group ignore them. However, that does not necessary mean that those ignored children are actively rejected in social situations. In other words, social acceptance is generally a positive measure that indicates the degree to which a student has friends, the opposite of which is social isolation—that is, being ignored in the peer group. Peer rejection, on the other hand, indicates active dislike of a particular child (Hollinger, 1987). Of course, different researchers use these terms in different ways, and, as a consumer of research in the field, you should always seek clarification of the exact definition used by the author of the research or the curriculum materials you are using.

Generally, three types of sociometric measures are available (Gresham & Elliott, 1989a). In the peer nomination method, every student in the class nominates several class "stars" based on a question such as, "In this class, whom would you most like to play with?" A count of the nominations would reveal something about the more accepted and less accepted students in the class.

However, there are often students in the class who do not fall into either category. Further, if you wish to have information about the social acceptance of a particular child who has been referred, the peer nomination method may not yield any votes at all relative to that particular child.

For that reason, a second method was developed. The second method is called a roster rating method, and requires every student in the class to rate every other student on a question like, "How often would you like to play with this person?" or "How often would you like to sit with this person at lunch?" The names of every student in the class are listed down the side of a sheet of paper and the students are rated on a Likert scale (where the ratings range from 1, meaning almost never, to 5, almost always). By averaging the ratings for each child, you can determine the social acceptance score for that target child relative to the group mean. Interest Box 13.1 presents a sample of such a roster rating scale.

In the third type of sociometric, the peers in the class are asked to nominate or rate class members on specific behavioral characteristics, rather than the general "like or dislike" questions above. Unlike the other two methods, this method provides information on which students within the class fit particular behavioral categories, such as "brightness" or "dullness" (Gresham & Elliott, 1989a).

Each of these sociometric formats are used periodically in public school situations to assess social acceptance. You may find these results on an occasional assessment report for certain children in your special education program. Therefore, you should have some understanding of these assessment tools.

INTEREST BOX 13.1
Sample Roster Rating

How often do you like to play with this person?

	Almost Never		Sometimes		Almost Always
Tony Ramirez	1	2	3	4	5
Sherry Grissom	1	2	3	4	5
Tommy Packard	1	2	3	4	5
Roy Taylor	1	2	3	4	5
Amy Grant	1	2	3	4	5
Billy Johnson	1	2	3	4	5
Alfonzo Thomas	1	2	3	4	5
Justine Prichard	1	2	3	4	5
Leroy Joseph	1	2	3	4	5

Note: The list of names in the left column would include every student in the class. For any student who has been referred, Billy Johnson as an example, the results could be averaged. For comparison purposes, you may wish to average the score of several other randomly selected boys in the class. Higher scores indicate higher levels of social acceptance. You may wish to review the Bailey, Bender, and Montgomery (1983) study that employed this type of sociometric.

Self-Report Measures

Self-report measures are not as frequently used as teacher ratings, checklists, and sociometric rating procedures because of the obvious potential for bias (Gresham & Elliott, 1989a). Typically, this type of assessment will tell you more about a child's emotional well-being than about his or her overall social competence. Nevertheless, this type of self-report may be used to assess the second component of social competence—social cognition of self- and others. For example, the *Piers Harris Children's Self-Concept Scale* (Piers, 1983) includes a subscale score to measure the child's perception of his or her own popularity.

Other self-report measures assess particular social skills (see Gresham & Elliott, 1989a, for a review). Numerous social skills instructional programs require the target student to complete a self-report checklist of social skills, and these may be used as a type of pre- or posttest on social skills instruction. You may expect to use this type of measure if you choose to utilize one of the commercially available social skills training packages.

Parent Ratings

Parent ratings have been used to assess adaptive behavior of children, and to assess atypical behaviors, though less research is available on the use of parent ratings to assess social competence itself (Gresham & Elliott, 1989a). A further concern is the distinction between the environments in which parents and teachers observe behavior. For example, behavior tends to be specific to setting, and if social behaviors on the playground are a problem, will assessment of social skills by the parent (presumably based on parent observations at home, rather than on the school playground) really help? However, some research has recently demonstrated that parent ratings do reflect the social skills behaviors seen in other settings (Gresham & Reschly, 1986). At present, this question is far from settled. For these reasons, parent ratings of social competence and social skills are relatively infrequently used in public schools, though the occasional assessment folder and/or IEP will include a parent assessment of behavior or some component of social competence.

SOCIAL COMPETENCE INSTRUCTION

Two major instructional approaches are used to teach social competence (Hollinger, 1987). The first approach, developed over the last 15 years, is a direct instructional approach, and includes the typical instructional techniques emphasized by direct instruction: modeling, performance feedback, and rehearsal of specific social skills, among others. This approach centers on a set of specific social skills as the basis for instruction, and most of the commercially available materials available today utilize this instructional approach. The materials developed by Walker and his associates, reviewed below, are representative of this type of instructional approach.

The second instructional approach, developed more recently, is based on social cognitive problem solving, and may be conceived of as a metacognitive approach (Hollinger, 1987). Although this method may use some of the instructional strategies from direct instruction—for example, modeling or role-playing—the emphasis is on development of a metacognitive strategy that may be applied to all social problem situations, rather than development of a specific set of social skills themselves.

Direct Instruction Social Skills Training

The direct instruction social skills materials generally provide some set of social behaviors believed to facilitate social competence (Hollinger, 1987). Typically these discrete behaviors are taught using direct instructional techniques that include modeling, role-play, positive feedback, guided and independent practice, and positive consequences for use of the skills. The focus is on mastery of a discrete set of behaviors.

Although some commercial packages may include activities for each component of social competence discussed above, others may not. For example, some instructional programs include the peer group in the instruction, others do not. Some packages address only prosocial or positive behaviors, others include information on reduction of problem behaviors. Consequently, you should review each type of activity offered in a particular program or instructional package in an attempt to identify the specific components of social competence that are addressed.

The *ACCEPTS* (Walker, McConnell, Walker, Holmes, Todis, & Golden, 1983) social skills instruction program is typical of those programs that employ direct instruction methods. *ACCEPTS* stands for *A Curriculum for Effective Peer and Teacher Skills.* It was designed to teach social skills to children with mild and moderate disabilities prior to integration into a mainstream classroom. Thus, this program will probably be more widely applied as schools move toward increased inclusion for students with mild and moderate disabilities. The *ACCEPTS* program uses a direct instructional format—described in Chapter 4—to teach 28 specific social skills. These include such skills as listening, starting work, using the right voice, taking turns, using polite words, and sharing. Role-play examples of some of these skills are included on video cassette. The program includes a pre-assessment, the *ACCEPTS Screening Checklist.* Also included are scripted lessons that involve 9 steps following the basic direct instruction model. These include definition and guided discussion, modeling of positive and negative examples, review skill definition, role-play practice, and informal contracting to elicit generalization. As you can see from this brief description, this curriculum is heavily based in the direct instruction model.

There are three major components of *ACCEPTS* (McConnell, 1987). The first component is a set of instructional materials designed to teach 24 social skills to improve interactions with peers and 4 skills to improve interactions with teachers. This last aspect, designed to enhance interactions with teachers, is a strength of this program because success in inclusive mainstream environments is partially dependent on successful relationships with teachers.

A second component of *ACCEPTS* is an emphasis on recess coaching, which provides adult praise and prompting with group oriented contingency management. This component is intended to increase the use of the social skills in various social situations in the student's life (McConnell, 1987). In other words, this component of *ACCEPTS* is intended to facilitate generalization to a setting beyond the instructional one. Children without disabilities from the target child's mainstream class are also included in this recess coaching to enhance generalization.

The third component is a classroom-based individual contingency program in which the child is reinforced for appropriate classroom interactions with teachers and peers (McConnell, 1987). Note that this component, along with the second component of the program, addresses the use of the peer group within the instructional model. Not only is the peer group of the target child included in the instruction, but reinforcement is available for those peers, based on improved social competence of the target child. This program, therefore, attends to issues such as peer acceptance, and self-perceptions of social situations, that is, the other components of social competence.

A number of other social skills training programs presently on the market are based on direct instructional principles. A brief description of several commercially available social skills materials may be found later in this chapter.

Efficacy of Direct Instruction for Social Skills. The preliminary research on various direct instructional social skills training packages has generally been positive (Epstein & Cullinan, 1987; McConnell, 1987). Studies demonstrate that children can be taught to master certain social skills. However, as mentioned previously, successful use of newly learned social skills does not necessarily improve the child's overall social acceptance, and that single fact is the most telling criticism of the social skills approach. Also, over the years, several other issues became apparent when the overall efficacy of social skills instruction was reviewed in the broader context of social acceptance of children and youth with disabilities.

The first issue concerns the selection of the social skills for a particular child's curriculum. How should specific social skills be selected for inclusion on a target child's educational program? This is no simple question when one considers the numbers of social skills covered by some of the commercially available programs—some of the programs include instructional ideas for over 100 specific skills. Does every child need every skill? Does every child need this level of instruction in social skills?

Assessment and/or self-assessment of social skills would appear to be one answer. However, although some of the educational programs include a skills assessment as a part of the materials, others do not, and many teachers are still using their own judgment in selecting social skills for instruction. Interest Box 13.2 includes a sample self-assessment page from a social skills instructional program called *Skill-Streaming.*

Other, more complex methods have been recommended for selection of appropriate social skills. For example, the Cone method, discussed in detail in Interest Box 13.3 (Cone, 1979), presents a method whereby the socially accepted behaviors most highly desired by the peer group form the basis of assessment. This concept has initial appeal because it includes the peer group in the social skills assessment and training at the outset. However, more research is necessary before matching particular social skill instructions to particular students is common practice.

A second issue in the effectiveness research concerns the generalization of social skills that have been taught. Mastery of specific social skills does not necessarily mean that the students will use them outside of the instructional setting, and numerous researchers have raised the issue of how well these discrete social skills generalize to other settings in the target child's life (Epstein & Cullinan, 1987; Hollinger, 1987; McConnell, 1987). Clearly, interventions that involve the peer group in the training itself result in an increased likelihood for generalization of social skills, and you should keep this in mind when deciding which intervention materials to use.

Some recent research has indicated that generalization can occur when the social skills instruction

INTEREST BOX 13.2
Sample Assessment Checklist for Social Skills

Name: ______________________ Date: ______________

Directions: Each of the questions will ask you about how well you do something. Next to each question is a number.

Circle the number 1 if you *almost never* do what the question asks.
Circle the number 2 if you *seldom* do it.
Circle the number 3 if you *sometimes* do it.
Circle the number 4 if you do it *often*.
Circle the number 5 if you *almost always* do it.

There are no right or wrong answers to these questions. Answer the way you really feel about each question.

Ratings:

1	2	3	4	5
Almost Never	Seldom	Sometimes	Often	Almost Always

	Almost Never	Seldom	Sometimes	Often	Almost Always
1. Is it easy for me to listen to someone who is talking to me?	1	2	3	4	5
2. Do I ask for help in a friendly way when I need the help?	1	2	3	4	5
3. Do I tell people thank you for something they have done for me?	1	2	3	4	5
4. Do I have the materials I need for my classes (like books, pencils, paper)?	1	2	3	4	5
5. Do I understand what to do when directions are given and do I follow these directions?	1	2	3	4	5
6. Do I finish my schoolwork?	1	2	3	4	5
7. Do I join in on class talks or discussions?	1	2	3	4	5
8. Do I try to help an adult when I think he/she could use the help?	1	2	3	4	5
9. Do I decide what I don't understand about my schoolwork and ask my teacher the question in a friendly way?	1	2	3	4	5
10. Is it easy for me to keep doing my schoolwork when people are noisy?	1	2	3	4	5
11. Do I fix mistakes on my work without getting upset?	1	2	3	4	5
12. Do I choose something to do when I have free time?	1	2	3		5
13. Do I decide on something I want to work for and keep working until I get it?	1	2	3	4	5

Source: Goldstein, Sprafkin, Gershaw, and Klein (1980).

INTEREST BOX 13.3
Cone's Template-Matching Procedure

Cone (1979) proposed a process whereby the issues of social skill instruction and peer acceptance were directly linked, thus addressing two components of social competence. In this method, the peer group actually identifies the specific social skills desired in a particular situation, and the target child who is not accepted socially is then trained in those specific skills. This procedure was based on work in the field of social psychology (Bem and Lloyd, 1979).

As seen in the earlier examples, social skills instruction may not result in increased social acceptance because the particular skills taught may not address the real reason for low social acceptance. Cone's idea is to create a model or "template" of a hypothetical child with appropriate social skills who would be socially accepted. This template is created by having the peers of the target child choose certain behavioral descriptors that identify the hypothetical, socially accepted child. The template then forms the basis for selecting the specific social skills to be included in instruction. The target child is compared to the hypothetical child (the template) and deficit areas are identified. These deficit social skills are then included in the instruction for the target child. Note that this procedure initially involves the peer group of the target child, but only in the generation of social skills to be taught.

Research on this procedure has just begun, and no efficacy studies are presently available. However, as a preliminary research step, Hoier and Cone (1987) demonstrated that students are capable of developing appropriate template behavior descriptors to which those same students respond positively. Certainly more research will be forthcoming on this idea of template matching, based on social skills desired by the peer group.

Source: Cone (1979).

program is geared to result in generalization (Clement-Heist, Siegel, & Gaylord-Ross, 1992; Misra, 1992; Stewart, Houten, & Houten, 1992). Although the research is very tentative, it appears that certain types of instruction facilitate generalization of the targeted social skills. For example, Clement-Heist, Siegel, and Gaylord-Ross (1992) presented evidence to indicate that instruction in social skills is more likely to be generalized when some of the instruction takes place in the setting in which the social skills must be employed, rather than in the public school class. Also, Misra (1992) indicated that a self-monitoring procedure on application of particular social skills may facilitate generalization.

Metacognitive Instructional Methods

Vaughn and her co-workers developed a model of instruction based on the social cognitive problem solving concept (Vaughn & Hogan, 1990, 1994; Vaughn, Lancelotta, & Minnis, 1988; Vaughn, McIntosh, & Spencer-Rowe, 1990). In the description below, note how this model addressed each of the four components of social competence, either directly or indirectly.

First, students with learning disabilities who demonstrated low social acceptance were identified using sociometric ratings. Those students were provided with training outside of the mainstream classroom for four weeks. This training was generally provided in two or three 30-minute instructional sessions. During those sessions, the students were taught a problem solving strategy called *FAST* (Vaughn, McIntosh, & Spencer-Rowe, 1990). This is a cognitively based learning strategy similar to the strategies discussed in Chapter 5, in which each letter indicates a step in a problem solving activity. Students were taught the strategy through a combination of modeling, role-playing, and rehearsal. The metacognitive strategy is presented in Interest Box 13.4.

For the next 16 weeks, the target students were given "informant status," in the mainstream classroom and actually became the teachers of the *FAST* strategy to the remainder of the class. The students in the class contributed notes on social problems, and the "trained" student taught the *FAST* strategy, selected a different problem each week, and guided the group through the use of the strategy. Clearly, this "informant status" addressed the components of the model that deal with social acceptance and self-acceptance, both of which are likely to improve when the socially unaccepted student becomes the social problem solving expert in the class.

Also, during the last 16 weeks of the intervention, the mainstream teachers arranged instructional activities in which the target students would be seen as actively working, contributing members of the class. The socially unaccepted students were paired with a highly accepted member of the class, and work was assigned on that basis. This type of instructional activity is also likely to lead to improvements in both peer acceptance and self-acceptance.

The results of use of this instructional model demonstrated that positive changes in social status occurred for 5 of the 10 target students (Vaughn & Hogan, 1990). Although the authors state that these results are not overwhelmingly positive, they do demonstrate that social competence is alterable in some cases, based on social cognitive problem solving techniques.

Efficacy of Metacognitive Instruction. Research on the efficacy of metacognitive techniques has generally demonstrated some measurable gains in application of the problem solving techniques (Hollinger, 1987). However, similar to the results on direct instruction of social skills, there is some question as to whether the gains resulting from learning social cognitive problem solving skills lead to increased social acceptance overall (Hollinger, 1987). Again, generalization seems to be a problem.

INSTRUCTION IN SOCIAL SKILLS

Instructional Activities

1. Cut a circle 12" in diameter using cardboard or tagboard. Cut a spinner in the shape of an

---

INTEREST BOX 13.4
The *FAST* Strategy for Social Cognitive Problem Solving

The following social cognitive problem-solving strategy was used by Vaughn, McIntosh, and Spencer-Rowe (1991). Note the similarity to the metacognitive strategies discussed in Chapter 5 of this text.

F = Freeze and Think	What is the problem? State the problem in behavioral terms.
A = Alternatives	What are the possible behaviors I could do to solve the problem? List the alternatives.
S = Solution	Which alternatives will solve the problem in the long run and are safe and fair? Select the best alternative.
T = Try it	How can I implement the solution? If this does not solve the problem, return to the second step.

Source: Vaughn, McIntosh, and Spencer-Rowe (1991).

arrow from a piece of tagboard. Divide the circle into eight triangles. In the triangles, write a brief description of a situation that might arise in the school environment (e.g., "someone accidently bumps into you"). Have each child take a turn. When the spinner stops, have the student discuss an appropriate way to deal with the situation.

2. Collect or draw pictures of four faces depicting "happy," "sad," "angry," and "afraid." These are your title cards. Find eight or more pictures from a magazine that the child can react to. Mount each on cardboard and laminate. Examples are "happy": a circus, a picnic, a birthday party; "sad": a child crying, falling down. Place the four title cards in a row. Ask the child to study each picture and decide how it would make him or her feel. Place each picture under the appropriate title card.

3. Have children choose a friend or family member. If the children feel comfortable drawing, ask them to think of things that their friends enjoy or like to do. Then allow them to draw these things on art paper. Display the drawings on a bulletin board with the friend or family member's name below. If children prefer, allow them to cut pictures from magazines and paste them on the art paper.

4. Take individual and group pictures of the children in the classroom as they are engaged in different activities. Have the group discuss the pictures in terms of facial expressions and interaction. Have the group choose titles for the pictures and include them in a class scrapbook.

5. Develop a set of "what is wrong with this picture" cards (e.g., a child who has too much food in his mouth). Have a start-to-finish game board with markers for each child. Have children take turns drawing the cards and identifying the inappropriate behavior. Each correct answer earns one move forward on the game board.

6. Create negative social scenarios. For example, one child accidentally trips and bumps into another child. The second child responds by hitting. Identify alternative appropriate behaviors, such as the first child saying "Excuse me" and the second child saying "Are you o.k.?" Have the children role play both scenarios and record them on videotape. Use these as teaching aids, and also, when similar situations arise in the classroom, play the tapes and have the children discuss desired behavior.

7. Use "good manner" medals. Create your own design for the good manner medal of honor. When a child is observed in an act of kindness or positive social interaction, note the time and situation. Then, during group time, describe the situation and award the medal.

8. Post "Rules of the Board." At trouble spots such as the water fountain, passageways, and work tables, display both written rules stated positively for those who are readers and graphic reminders for nonreaders. Refer to these reminders before a negative interaction begins.

9. Select a behavior on which the group is focusing, such as sharing or taking turns. Collect pictures of adults engaged in such activities as waiting at a checkout line or carrying items for disaster relief. Discuss each of the pictures with the children, then have them make a collage of the pictures and label them for display.

10. Begin a "special journal" for each child. Place the child's picture at the beginning of the journal. Write an account of what the child likes and does not like, the child's pets, favorite activities, etc. Throughout the year record developmental milestones, such as "John is learning to wait his turn. Today he waited for Anne to take her turn on the playscape." Include special events, such as a family outing, and field trips from school. At the end of the year, include a current picture and record descriptions of developmental and social growth.

Social Skills Curriculum Materials

RECESS. *RECESS* stands for *Reprogramming Environmental Contingencies for Effective Social Skills* (Walker, Street, Garrett, Crossen, Hops, & Greenwood, 1978). This program is designed to decrease negative/aggressive behavior and simultaneously increase positive, cooperative interaction of school-age children. This program is implemented primarily in playground settings, though some activities may be used in the classroom. Four components are included in the program: first, discrimination training, in which children are taught to identify appropriate versus inappropriate social behaviors; next, a response cost point system that is designed to decrease negative behaviors; third, a systematic process for receiving adult praise for appropriate social interaction behavior; and finally, a system of group reinforcement, in which the target child's behavior results in positive or negative contingencies for the entire group. Like all of the social skills programs by Walker and his associates, this program is founded on direct instruction principles. Modeling, role-play, frequent feedback, and teacher-scripted lessons are included.

This program includes certain aspects that address both the social skills as well as the social acceptance components of social competence. Preliminary research on the use of this instructional training package has been quite positive (Dougherty, Fowler, & Paine, 1985; McConnell, 1987). The early field trials of this program demonstrated that group contingencies in which the peer group shared in the positive reinforcement for appropriate behavior was a major factor in the success of this program (Walker et al., 1978).

ACCESS. The *ACCESS* program was also written by Walker and his associates (Walker, Holmes, Todis, & Horton, 1988). *ACCESS* stands for *Adolescent Curriculum for Communication and Effective Social Skills.* The program teaches 31 social skills in three domains: peer related, adult related, and self-related. The skills included are generally a higher level of the skills from some of the programs intended for younger children. For example, the skills in this program include negotiating with others, being left out, handling pressure from peers, expressing anger, coping with aggression, and disagreeing with adults.

A direct instructional format is used, similar to the *ACCEPTS* program described above. Each separate skill is accompanied by a teacher scripted lesson, and all of the lessons follow the direction instruction sequence of activities.

Skill-Streaming: Adolescent. The Skill-Streaming instructional materials are designed to teach prosocial skills—skills that promote positive social interactions. The earliest book is intended for use in secondary classrooms (Goldstein, Sprafkin, Gershaw, & Klein, 1980). This book uses a direct instruction model, though the authors refer to this as a "structured learning approach." The same components are used in each lesson as in direct instruction, including modeling, role-playing, performance feedback, and instruction for generalization. The book provides several sample teacher scripts, but a script is not provided for every lesson.

There are 50 specific skills in 6 groups: beginning social skills, advanced skills, skills for dealing with feelings, skill alternatives to aggression, skills for dealing with stress, and planning skills. Beginning skills include such things as listening, saying thank you, and giving a compliment. Advanced skills include joining in and asking for help. A skills checklist is included that requires a rating (on a Likert scale) on each of the 50 skills. This serves as both a pretest and a posttest in documenting the effectiveness of the instruction.

The book does provide suggestions for a group instruction base for either homogeneously selected groups who demonstrate the same skill deficiencies or for larger groups. However, there is no mention of group contingencies or group reward. Consequently, the issue of inclusion of the target child's peer group is only partially addressed.

Skill-Streaming: Elementary. Similar to the Skill-Streaming adolescent instructional manual, this book presents social skills instructional materials for the elementary school student (McGinnis,

Goldstein, Sprafkin, & Gershaw, 1984). A direct instruction format is used to present 60 specific skills that include being honest, avoiding trouble, expressing affection, apologizing, saying thank you, beginning a conversation, and giving a compliment. A skill checklist is included that allows for a pretest and posttest.

Getting Along with Others. *Getting Along with Others* (Jackson, Jackson, & Monroe, 1983) includes instructional strategies to teach 17 social skills. Various subskills are included for each skill. For example, the skill "joining a conversation" includes such components as using a pleasant voice, looking at the person, and waiting for a pause, (Epstein & Cullinan, 1987). The instructional technique for each skill follows a common plan, including introducing the skill, demonstrating both positive and negative examples, practicing the skill using role-play, and reviewing the rationale for use of the skill. No mention is made in this instructional program of involvement of the peer group (Epstein & Cullinan, 1987).

ASSET. *Asset: A Social Skills Program for Adolescents* (Hazel, Schumaker, Sherman, & Sheldon-Wildgen, 1983) presents instructional materials to teach 8 areas of social skills to adolescents. These include giving positive feedback, giving negative feedback, resisting peer pressure, problem solving, negotiation, following instructions, and conversation. Video cassettes depict teenagers acting appropriately with others, and that activity is followed by a group discussion that focuses on the specific skill. The specific skills are then taught using modeling, practice, feedback, and reinforcement procedures.

Personal and Social Skills Software

Blueprint for Decision Making

Publisher: MCE, A Division of Lawrence Productions

Skill Level: Elementary, secondary, adult

Hardware: Apple IIe

Description: This high-interest, low-vocabulary program is designed for secondary and adult students who need help in decision making and problem solving. While students see and discuss problems faced by others, they use the utility section of this program to solve their own problems. With the program's help, students generate a variety of ways to solve a problem and predict the consequences of each action.

Body Awareness

Publisher: Mindscape, Inc.

Skill Level: Preschool, elementary

Hardware: Apple IIe

Description: Young students will enjoy learning about parts of the body and seasonal clothing with these self-directed activities and engaging graphics. Students fit body parts to a body, practice matching the pictures of body parts to the names for them, and learn the appropriate clothing for each season.

Following Directions: One- and Two-Level Commands

Publisher: Laureate Learning Systems, Inc.

Skill Level: Preschool, elementary

Hardware: Apple IIe, speech synthesizer

Description: This two-diskette program helps students learn to follow one- and two-level commands. A natural-sounding voice and colorful graphics make it ideal for learning disabled persons. Eight activities and three types of commands are included: one-level, sequential, and two-level.

Factory

Publisher: Wings for Learning, Inc.

Skill Level: Elementary, secondary

Hardware: Apple IIe, IBM

Description: Using color graphics and animation, this three-level program challenges students to create geometric products on a simulated machine assembly line that they design. Students develop inductive thinking abilities. This program works with TouchWindow.

Terrapin Logo

Publisher: Terrapin Software, Inc.

Skill Level: Preschool, elementary, secondary, adult

Hardware: Apple IIe, IBM, Macintosh

Description: Terrapin Logo is a programming language used in grades K–12 as well as by adults to learn programming, problem solving, and mathematical concepts. Because Logo is an exploratory language, the user works at his or her pace. Graphics are performed in Logo with very simple commands, such as forward and right, to move the cursor (a turtle) and draw. The *Instant* program included allows the user to draw using single key commands, such as F to move the turtle forward.

SUMMARY

Instruction in social competence is a multifaceted endeavor that involves several interdependent components. Interventions designed to address particular social skills may or may not result in improved social acceptance, particularly when the reason for the low social acceptance involves one of the other components of social competence. The best social skills will not result in high social acceptance for someone who (like a child with the noxious behavior of a constantly runny nose) is socially rejected for other reasons.

However, the need for instruction in social skills for many students with disabilities is apparent. Also, research within the last several years has made some headway in identifying the types of programs likely to result in improved social skills, as well as improvement in the broader construct of social competence. Consequently, as a special education teacher in the future, you will almost certainly be responsible for instruction in social competence at some point. You should remain constantly aware of the most recent research in the area, and investigate new social skills curriculum packages as they are made available commercially.

Summary Points

- Interventions to improve social competence have been undertaken for three reasons: many students with disabilities have deficits in social competence; those deficits affect success in school; and those deficits affect success in life after school.
- The deficit model of social competence suggests that social skills deficits on the part of the child with a disability cause the low levels of social acceptance of that child. According to this model, the teacher merely had to teach the child certain social skills and the social acceptance would improve. Research did not support this last hypothesis.
- The contextualist model of social competence is much broader than the deficit model, and looks at the social skills deficits in the context of the peer-group environment.
- The four components of social competence are social skills knowledge, relationships with peers, social cognition, and the absence of noxious behaviors.
- The primary cause hypothesis suggests that the psychoneurological deficit that caused the learning problem also causes a deficit in social skills.
- The secondary cause hypothesis suggests that deficits in cognitive abilities cause deficits in academic work and that children with academic work are less likely to be popular. This lack of social popularity, in turn, prevents those children from having the opportunity to practice social interaction, leading to the development of deficits in social skills.
- Assessment of social skills may use teacher ratings, sociometrics (such as a nomination system or a roster rating), observation checklists, self-report measures, or parent ratings.
- Instruction in social competence involves one of two strategies, either direct instruction on social skills or metacognitive instruction.
- Although particular social skills can be taught to many children with disabilities, generalization of these skills remains a major concern. Strategies to improve on generalization of social skills include self-monitoring of generalization and instruction of social skills in the setting where they should be applied.

QUESTIONS AND ACTIVITIES

1. List the several points in the rationale for instruction in social competence. Explain each point.
2. What is the difference between social skills and social competence as described in this chapter?
3. Describe the components of social competence.
4. Describe the several assessment techniques and indicate which particular aspect of social competence is addressed by each.
5. Describe three types of sociometric ratings. Find several studies in the research literature that exemplify each type of sociometric rating and present these to the class.
6. Explain the "primary cause" and "secondary cause" hypotheses.
7. Visit the curriculum materials center in your college and check out several social skills training packages. Present a sample lesson from each to the class.
8. Compare the instructional techniques from *ACCEPTS* and *Skill-Streaming*. What similarities and differences do you notice?

REFERENCES

Bailey, D. B., Bender, W. N., Montgomery, D. L. (1983). Comparison of teacher, peer, and self-ratings of classroom and social behavior of adolescents. *Behavioral Disorders, 8,* 151–160.

Bem, J. D., & Lloyd, C. G. (1979). Template matching: A proposal for probing the ecological validity of experimental settings in social psychology. *Journal of Personality and Social Psychology, 37,* 833–846.

Bishop, K., & Jubala, K. (1994). By June, given shared experiences, integrated classes and equal opportunities, Jamie will have a friend. *Teaching Exceptional Children, 27* (1), 36–41.

Brown, W. H., Ragland, E., & Bishop, N. (1989). A naturalistic teaching strategy to promote young children's peer interactions. *Teaching Exceptional Children, 23,* 8–11.

Bryan, T. H. (1978). Social relationships and verbal interactions of learning disabled children. *Journal of Learning Disabilities, 11,* 58–66.

Bryan, T. (1994). The social competence of students with learning disabilities over time: A response to Vaughn and Hogan. *Journal of Learning Disabilities, 27,* 304–308.

Capone, A. M., Smith, M. A., & Schloss, P. J. (1988). Prompting play skills. *Teaching Exceptional Children, 22,* 54–56.

Clement-Heist, K., Siegel, S., & Gaylord-Ross, R. (1992). Simulated and *in-situ* vocational social skills training for youths with learning disabilities. *Exceptional Children, 58,* 336–345.

Cone, J. D. (1979, March). *Inductive behavioral assessment.* Paper presented at the meeting of the Southern Psychological Association, New Orleans.

Dougherty, B. S., Fowler, S. A., & Paine, S. C. (1985). The use of peer monitors to reduce negative interaction during recess. *Journal of Applied Behavior Analysis, 18,* 141–153.

Epstein, M. H., & Cullinan, D. (1987). Effective social skills curricula for behaviorally disordered students. *The Pointer, 31* (2) 21–24.

Fiedler, C. R., & Chiang, B. (1989). Teaching social skills to students with learning disabilities. *LD Forum, 15,* 19–21.

Goldstein, A. P., Sprafkin, R. P., Gershaw, N. J., & Klein, P. (1980). *Skill-Streaming the Adolescent.* Champaign, IL: Research Press.

Goodman, H., Gottlieb, J., & Harrison, R. H. (1972). Social acceptance of EMRs integrated into a nongraded elementary school. *American Journal of Mental Deficiency, 76,* 412–417.

Gresham, F. M. (1981). Social skills training with handicapped children: A review. *Review of Educational Research,* 51, 139–176.

Gresham, F. M., & Elliott, S. N. (1989a). Social skills assessment technology for LD students. *Learning Disabilities Quarterly, 12,* 141–152.

Gresham, F. M., & Elliott, S. N. (1989b). Social skills deficits as a primary learning disability. *Journal of Learning Disabilities, 22,* 120–124.

Gresham, F. M., & Reshley, D. J. (1986). Social skills deficits and low peer acceptance of mainstreamed learning disabled children. *Learning Disability Quarterly,* 9, 23–32.

Hazel, J. S., Schumaker, J. B., Sherman, J. A., & Sheldon-Wildgen, J. (1983). *ASSET: A Social Skills Program for Adolescents.* Champaign, IL: Research Press.

Hoier, T. S., & Cone, J. D. (1987). Target selection of social skills for children: A template matching procedure. *Behavior Modification, 11,* 137–163.

Hollinger, J. D. (1987). Social skills for behaviorally disordered children as preparation for mainstreaming: Theory, practice, and new directions. *Remedial and Special Education, 8* (4), 17–27.

Jackson, N. F., Jackson, D. A., & Monroe, C. (1983). *Getting Along with Others.* Champaign, IL: Research Press.

Johnson, D. W., Johnson, R. T. (1980). Integrating handicapped students into the mainstream. *Exceptional Children, 47,* 90–99.

McConnell, S. R. (1987). Entrapment effects and the generalization and maintenance of social skills training for elementary school students with behavioral disorders. *Behavioral Disorders, 12,* 252–263.

McGinnis, E., Goldstein, A. P., Sprafkin, R. P., & Gershaw, N. J. (1984). *Skill-Streaming the Elementary School Child.* Champaign, IL: Research Press.

Misra, A. (1992). Generalization of social skills through self-monitoring by adults with mild mental retardation. *Exceptional Children, 58,* 495–507.

Nelson, M. (1988). Social skills training for handicapped students. *Teaching Exceptional Children, 21,* 19–23.

Parker, J. G., & Asher, S. R. (1987). Peer relations and later personal adjustment: Are low-accepted children at risk? *Psychological Bulletin, 102,* 357–389.

Piers, E. V. (1983). *The Piers–Harris Children's Self-Concept Scale, Revised, Manual.* Los Angeles: Western Psychological Press.

Semmel, M. I., Gottlieb, J., & Robinson, N. M. (1979). Mainstreaming: Perspectives on educating handicapped children in the public school. In D. C. Berliner (Ed.), *Review of Research in Education,* Vol. 7. American Educational Research Association.

Shepard, R., & Koberstein, J. (1989). Books, puppets, and sharing: Teaching preschool children to share. *Psychology in the Schools, 26,* 311–316.

Stewart, G., Houten, V., & Houten, J. (1992). Increasing generalized social interactions in psychotic and mentally retarded residents through peer-mediated therapy. *Journal of Applied Behavior Analysis, 25,* 335–339.

Vaughn, S., & Hogan, A. (1990). Social competence and learning disabilities: A prospective study. In Swanson, H. L., & Keogh, B. K. *Learning Disabilities: Theoretical and Research Issues.* Erlbaum, Lawrence, KA.

Vaughn, S., & Hogan, A. (1994). The social competence of students with learning disabilities over time: Q Within-Individual examination. *Journal of Learning Disabilities, 27,* 292–303.

Vaughn, S., Lancelotta, G. X., & Minnis, S. (1988). Social strategy training and peer involvement: Increasing peer acceptance of a female LD student. *Learning Disabilities Focus, 4* (1), 32–37.

Vaughn, S., McIntosh, R., & Spencer-Rowe, J. (1991). Peer rejection is a stubborn thing: Increasing peer acceptance of rejected students with learning disabilities. *Learning Disabilities Research & Practice, 6,* 83–88.

Walker, H. M., Holmes, D., Todis, B., & Horton, G. (1988). *The ACCESS Program.* Austin, TX: Pro-Ed.

Walker, H. M., McConnell, S., Walker, J., Holmes, D., Todis, B., & Golden, N. (1983). *The ACCEPTS Program.* Austin, TX: Pro-Ed.

Walker, H. M., Street, A., Garrett, B., Crossen, J., Hops, H., & Greenwood, C. R. (1978). *RECESS: Reprogramming environmental contingencies for effective social skills. Manual for consultants.* Unpublished manuscript, University of Oregon; Center at Oregon for Behavioral Education of the Handicapped, Eugene.

CHAPTER 14

INSTRUCTION IN VOCATIONAL EDUCATION

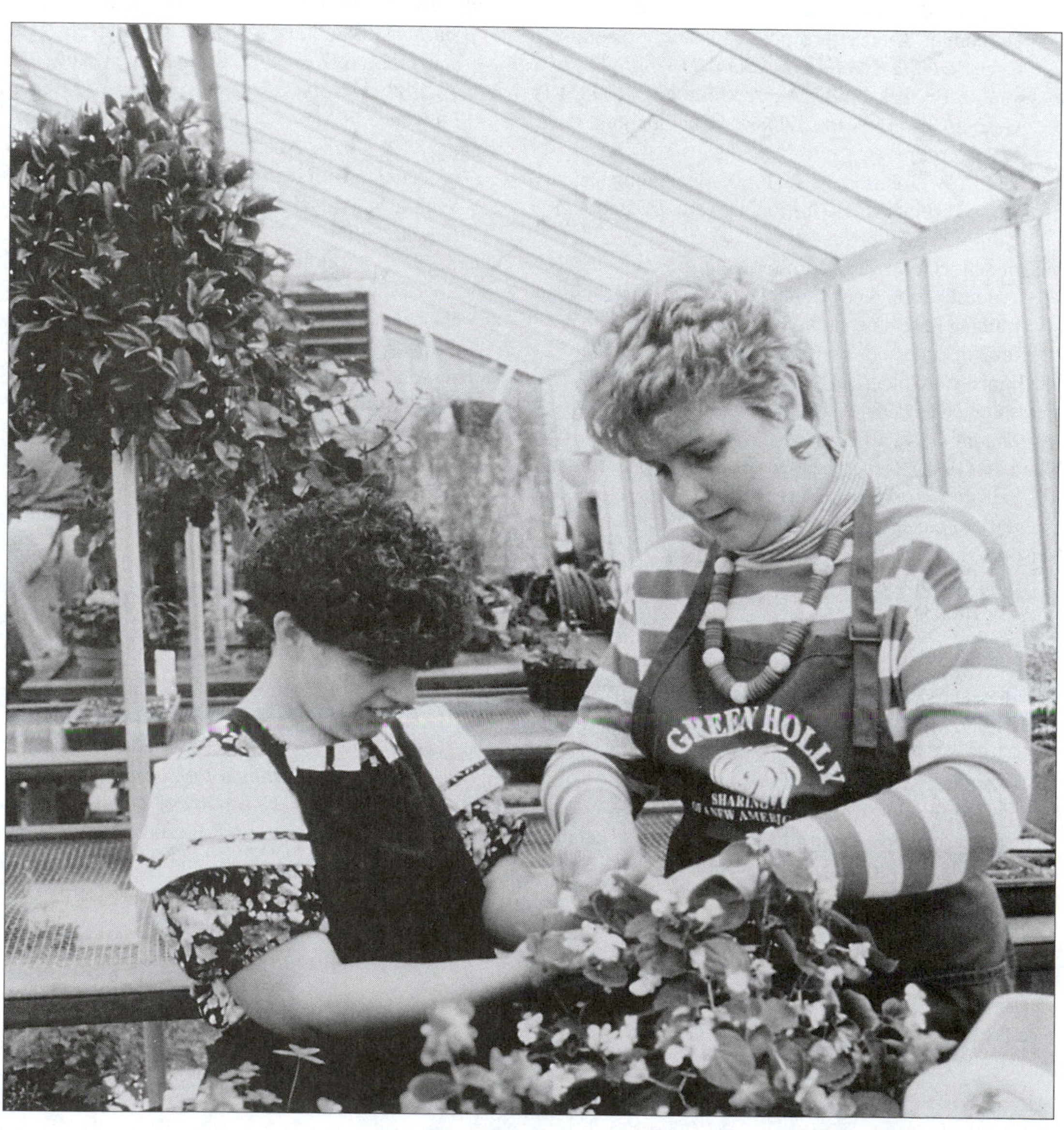

OBJECTIVES

Upon completion of this chapter you should be able to:

1. Discuss at least four reasons why special educators need to be aware of vocational educational instructional options.
2. Describe five models of vocational instruction.
3. Describe the research results from the follow-up studies.
4. Explain the primary instructional roles and the supporting roles of the special educator in the vocational educational instruction for students with disabilities.
5. Describe the three different aspects of vocational education and the appropriate time of study for each aspect.
6. Describe the three recent emphases of vocational studies.

KEYWORDS

career awareness
career orientation
vocational training
vocationally related academic skills
interpersonal skills
vocational high school
work study program
transition teaching
community-based instruction
Job Training Partnership Act
individual transition plan
Americans with Disabilities Act (ADA)

The majority of instruction in vocational education is typically handled by vocational education teachers in junior and senior high schools. At first glance, many special education teachers may wonder why this chapter is included at all in a methods book for special education. However, a quick review of the relevant research indicates a great need for special educators and regular educators to work together to ensure that students with disabilities receive effective instruction in vocational education. There are a number of reasons for special educators to study vocational education instructional methods.

First, because vocational education is so very important for students with disabilities (Adelman & Vogel, 1994), many school districts are initiating inclusive vocational education classes in junior and senior high schools. Even for special education teachers who are not working in those types of inclusive vocational education classes, however, vocational educational concerns will be apparent in future special education teaching assignments.

Next, students with disabilities are not as successful in obtaining full-time employment after school as most professionals would like (Adelman & Vogel, 1994; McLaughlin & Martin, 1993; Okolo, 1988; Okolo & Sitlington, 1986). The need for some useful societal role for individuals with disabilities is paramount, and vocational education programs, along with special education, must prepare these students for the world of work.

Third, students with mild and moderate disabilities are enrolling in vocational education programs in increasing numbers (Okolo, 1988). For example, the number of secondary school students with disabilities enrolled in vocational classes increased from 20 percent in 1977 to 40 percent in 1983 (Okolo, 1988).

Finally, should you teach in a secondary high school where students with mild and moderate disabilities have access to numerous vocational class options, you will be expected to discuss these choices with the students, the parents, and the vocational teachers in order to identify the appropriate educational program. For that reason, you should have some knowledge of the instructional approaches in this field.

EMPLOYMENT OF STUDENTS WITH DISABILITIES

Research on vocational education and employment of students with disabilities has increased recently. Some understanding of these research results is necessary in order to understand the instructional approaches presented later in the chapter.

Importance of Vocational Education

One may expect that vocational education classes play a major role in the success or failure of students with disabilities during the postschool years. In fact, numerous studies, using several different research approaches, have emphasized the crucial nature of vocational education in postschool success (Adelman & Vogel, 1994; Levine & Edgar, 1994; McLaughlin & Martin, 1993; Okolo, 1988; Okolo & Sitlington, 1986; Schalock, Wolzen, Ross, Elliot, Werbel, & Peterson, 1986). First, most of the studies that investigate postschool success of students with disabilities indicate that the majority of these students work after they complete high school (Hasazi, Gordon, & Roe, 1985; Haring, Lovett, & Smith, 1990; Mithaug, Horiuchi, & Fanning, 1985; Neel, Meadows, Levine, & Edgar, 1988). Between 55 percent and 69 percent of students with mild disabilities who graduate enter the job force, a statistic that indicates the importance of vocational education for these students. In short, vocational education can better prepare these students for life after school.

Information such as the data reported above comes from studies that collect information on students with disabilities after they leave school. Hasazi, Gordon, and Roe (1985), as one example, published one of the early follow-up studies. Initially, nine school districts in the state of Vermont were randomly selected to be representative of rural, urban, and metropolitan districts in the state. All of the special education students who graduated, dropped out, or left school between 1979 and 1983 were identified, resulting in a sample of 462 students. From that group, data could be obtained concerning 459 students by using a structured interview procedure. This selection procedure was a major strength of the study for several reasons. First, the random selection procedure used suggests that this sample represents the state population. Second, identification of the selected districts as urban, rural, or metropolitan allowed the researchers to compare the follow-up information on job placement based on the rural or urban nature of the home district. For example, after high school more rural students (34 percent) obtained jobs in agriculture than urban (15 percent) or metropolitan (0 percent) students—a statistic that makes sense only when viewed according to the geographic characteristics of the home district. Were this data reported on a statewide basis, it would suggest that 16 percent of the population received jobs in agriculture—a misleading figure.

Fifty-five percent of the sample were holding paid jobs, though only 67 percent of those employed held full-time jobs. The results indicated that vocational education was helpful in obtaining and keeping a job. Also, the majority of the subjects were employed in either clerical/sales positions or service occupations.

Although this is one of the more influential studies in the current special education literature, there are several weaknesses in this follow-up study. First, this study included no comparison group—a weakness that, unfortunately, tends to be true for a number of the follow-up studies. For example, in our interpretation of the fact that 55 percent of the sample held jobs, it would be helpful to know what percentage of low achieving nondisabled students obtain employment after school.

A second weakness is the tendency to lump all students with disabilities together for analysis. Grouping all students together may mask important differences between students with different disabilities. For example, do students with intellectual disabilities obtain jobs after graduation as easily as do students with behavioral disorders? Do students with learning disabilities have more success in the job market than others? Clearly, when the data are reported in grouped fashion, some of the most interesting questions are left unanswered.

As a special educator, you should remain current in your reading of the transition follow-up research. Also, more recent studies that eliminate some of the problems mentioned above are becoming available in the literature.

In another study, Schalock and his co-workers (1986) examined the postschool employment success of 108 students with disabilities. A number of variables were used to predict success, including the characteristics of the students (age, sex, race, etc.), the amount of time in certain school subjects (vocational education, math, etc.), and community variables, such as the types of jobs that were locally available. This study indicated the importance of vocational education; the results suggested that the number of vocational courses taken by the students during high school was one of the major indicators of successful job performance during the postschool period.

In a different type of study, Mithaug, Horiuchi, and Fanning (1985) investigated the postschool success of 234 students with disabilities who graduated from the public school in Colorado in 1978 and 1979. When asked to evaluate the usefulness of the classes taken during high school, 57 percent of these students indicated that vocational education was very useful in later employment and success in life. Fifty-five percent of the students indicated that special education classes were very useful, whereas only 39 percent of the students felt that their other classes were useful in success later in life. The fact that more students thought that vocational education was useful indicated the importance of this curriculum area.

These studies, taken together, underscore the need for vocational education. First, many students with disabilities do enter the job force after school. Second, some research indicated that the number of vocational courses taken predicts job success and other data indicated that the students themselves felt that vocational education was the single most important aspect of their high school education. In this instance, several different studies, each employing a different research perspective and methodology, indicated the same thing—that vocational education is one of the most important aspects of the education of students with disabilities.

Postschool Success of Students with Disabilities

In discussions of vocational education, one issue that continually arises is the postschool success of students with disabilities and the relationship between postschool success and vocational education. Unfortunately, the available information on postschool success is not entirely positive. First, over one-fourth of the students with disabilities drop out of school before graduation (Edgar, 1985). Of those who stay, only 60 percent graduate. The remainder of the students apparently finish the course work, but may be unable to complete exit exams such as the minimum competency tests many states require prior to awarding the diploma for graduation. Obviously, these depressing figures do not speak well for the vocational programs currently offered to many students with disabilities, because, if school was really of assistance to these students, one would expect them to drop out no more frequently than other students.

Some evidence is available concerning how students with disabilities find jobs after high school. Hasazi, Gordon, and Roe (1985), in the study reviewed above, also presented data from Vermont that indicated that students who were employed in part-time jobs during the summer and after school had a higher employment potential after finishing school. Sixty-nine percent of the students who had jobs during the summer and the school year were employed after finishing school, whereas only 37 percent of the students who had no summer work experience were employed after graduation. Clearly, working during the summer and after school hours is one factor that correlates with successful postschool employment.

Other information on finding work is also available. For example, the vast majority of individuals with disabilities find work through self-initiative or the help of family and friends rather than through agencies such as vocational rehabilitation or job services (Hasazi, Gordon, & Roe, 1985; Neel et al., 1988). Given the efforts our society makes to assist persons to obtain work, one may well wonder why this is so. Why do students with disabilities not utilize the social service agencies and employment services sponsored by various government agencies more? It may be that these students are unaware of these services and/or unskilled at the types of paperwork that these services require. Perhaps one aspect of vocational education could include training in utilization of the agencies society has available for job searches.

We have also gained some information concerning the types of postschool jobs students with disabilities acquire. Some studies have reported that many students with disabilities did not find work in the areas in which they had received vocational training (Shapiro & Lentz, 1991), and this raises some questions concerning the overall adequacy of the vocational education programs that are offered (Adelman & Vogel, 1994). Other data indicate that most students with disabilities who graduate and find jobs end up working in the service or the clerical sales sector (Hasazi, Gordon, & Roe, 1985; Neubert, Tilson, & Ianacone, 1989), though this varies somewhat for rural, compared to metropolitan, school districts. Needless to say, these types of positions do not offer great opportunities for advancement and research indicates that students with disabilities tend to earn minimum wage and remain in entry-level positions (Adelman & Vogel, 1994). Also, the specific reasons for these job selections are unclear. For example, vocational courses may be preparing these students only for low paying entry-level positions in sales and service jobs. Clearly this would be unfortunate, because some students with disabilities can go far beyond these limited entry-level jobs. More research will certainly be forthcoming on this question.

Unanswered Questions

A number of other questions regarding vocational education and postschool employment have not been answered. For example, Edgar (1985) suggested that the level of severity of the disability may affect performance in vocational courses and postschool employment, but no evidence has yet supported that contention (Neubert, Tilson, & Ianacone, 1989). Although one may initially assume that students with moderate disabilities would perform less well than students with mild disabilities, the types of jobs both groups obtain after school are not cognitively demanding, and one group may perform as well on most of those jobs as the other. We simply do not know if students with moderate disabilities perform less well on the job than students with mild disabilities.

There is some limited evidence that students with different disabilities have different levels of employment after high school. Students with intellectual disabilities are less likely to find postschool employment than are students with either learning disabilities or behavioral disorders. In one study, approximately 38 percent of students with intellectual disabilities are shown as employed, compared to 64 percent of the students with learning disabilities and/or behavioral disorders (Edgar, 1985). Still, little is known concerning the mechanism that causes employment failure among students with intellectual disabilities compared to the other groups, and information such as this could be vital to restructuring vocational programs. For example, if research demonstrated that students with intellectual disabilities were employed less frequently because of a fine motor inability to manipulate hand tools compared to other individuals with disabilities, more occupational therapy services could be offered to those students who required such services. Clearly, much more research on the postschool employment of students with disabilities needs to be done, and such research will probably restructure our current thinking about the curriculum content of effective vocational programs.

In a recent study, Levine and Edgar (1995) presented data from a longitudinal study on postschool outcomes for individuals with disabilities–The Decade Project. This study compared postschool outcomes for students with mental retardation, those with learning disabilities, and nondisabled students. These data indicate that there are some differences in outcomes between students in the various disability areas relative to attendance in postsecondary educational programs, but no postschool employment differences were found. The Decade Project is a federally funded long-term study, and this type of systematic research can be very beneficial for understanding youth with disabilities. You should watch for additional reports from this project in the literature.

Summary of Current Knowledge

The research available has demonstrated several facts relevant to vocational education. First, the majority of students with disabilities work after the school years, with most of those persons accepting service or clerical jobs. Also, the evidence indicates that vocational education is very important to the postschool employment success of these students. Finally, most persons with disabilities who work found their jobs through self-initiative or with the help of family and friends rather than through service agencies. Thus, work experience during the summer and after school is important for successful postschool employment. Still, the prognosis for many students with disabilities is not positive. Only 60 percent of these students graduate from high school, and over 1 in 4 students with a disability drop out. Hopefully, increasing knowledge of these data will allow professionals to restructure special education and vocational instruction to more completely meet the needs of students with disabilities.

COMPONENTS OF VOCATIONAL EDUCATION

Vocational education has historically included at least three different types of activities: career awareness, career orientation, and vocational training. The first of these activities may begin as early as kindergarten or the primary grades, followed by the orientation activities during the junior high years and the vocational training during the senior high years.

Because of the changing nature of public school instruction, the role of the special educator changes during the school years. Depending on the grade levels for which you are responsible, you may do all of the vocational education for your students or you may merely play a supporting role. The discussion below gives several examples of the types of activities special education teachers may engage in, in order to improve the vocational education program for students with disabilities. These are appropriate for the special education resource room and the self-contained class, as well as the inclusive classroom.

Career Awareness

First, career awareness activities are those that introduce certain jobs or groups of jobs to students. As early as kindergarten, many school programs have some emphasis on the different types of jobs a pupil may want to consider. Typically, the teacher will hold up a picture of a working person and discuss with the children the job that person is doing. Because very few schools employ vocational education teachers for younger children, this type of career awareness activity is often the responsibility of the elementary teachers and/or the special education teachers in the elementary schools. If your teaching responsibility includes a self-contained class of young students with disabilities, you will want to complete some type of instructional unit on career awareness at least once each year.

For instructional purposes, various professions are grouped together into job clusters. Most researchers use the job clusters suggested in the *Dictionary of Occupational Titles,* published by the U.S. Employment Service (1965). In that classification, service sector jobs (kitchen helper, cook, laundry worker, janitor) are grouped together for study, whereas jobs involving clerical sales (sales clerk, stock clerk, shipping clerk) comprise another group. Managerial jobs are typically grouped with professional jobs (doctor, lawyer, etc.). Agriculture, fishery, and forestry jobs comprise another job cluster. Machine trades, such as automobile mechanic and machine worker are also grouped together.

Activities that involve young children in discussion of the types of activities in which various persons are engaged represent the first emphasis in vocational education. Further, these types of career awareness activities help young students begin to think about the types of activities that interest them. Interest Box 14.1 lists several types of instructional activities you may employ in your class.

Career Orientation

Career orientation is the second phase of vocational education, and this phase typically begins during the middle school or junior high school years, though certain school districts have made an effort to make this phase available even earlier during the school program. This phase of vocational education involves the matching of a student's interests and abilities with the requirements of particular jobs. For example, for a student with low reading ability, a job as an attorney in a law firm may not be a realistic possibility, whereas jobs in wildlife conservation or fire-fighting may be conceivable.

Guidance counselors in the schools typically perform this function of matching students to potential job clusters, because these same individuals help junior high school students register for various courses that may lead into particular professions. For example, for students with the potential and interest for an extended undergraduate and

INTEREST BOX 14.1
Career Awareness Activities

1. Discuss pictures of various persons in various roles. You should select "action" pictures that represent the individual involved in an interesting situation. Also, select pictures that represent individuals with whom your students come into contact.
2. Use media presentations to represent different jobs.
3. On local field trips, point out the jobs of the different persons visited by the class. Discuss those jobs when you finish the trip.
4. Invite persons who have interesting jobs to come into your class or speak to a school assembly regarding their jobs.
5. Show elementary school children how to obtain information about various jobs from the school or local library.
6. Invite the high school guidance counselor to share information on job search activities for older elementary children.
7. Have "job fair" art projects in which the children draw a picture about various persons in selected jobs.

graduate higher education program, a course of study that includes introductory algebra and foreign language during the middle grades or junior high may be appropriate. It should be pointed out that such counseling in relation to various courses of study is not intended to limit a student's capacity or attainment. Rather, many students find that this early advice will save them precious time and, in some cases, failure experiences in courses that are not appropriate for them.

Further, career orientation is more than merely scheduling the appropriate classes. As the special education teacher, your role during this phase would include a number of different activities. First, you should relate the student's academic work to his or her chosen job cluster or clusters. This should result in higher motivation and better academic performance. Next, you should make information available to the student regarding the job cluster choice. Various reading materials may be made available and used for the assignments in class. You may be able to arrange guest speakers to come and speak to some of your students, and many of the other activities in Interest Box 14.1 would be appropriate during this phase as well. Any activity that gives students information about their initial job selections could be included.

Vocational Training

The final phase of traditional vocational education is the vocational class or "job skills" phase. This includes various classes during the junior high and secondary school period, which are intended to train students in vocation skills. For example, carpentry is one of the more common courses taken by the students with disabilities in the nation's high schools, whereas welding and small engine repair are less common. Various courses in auto mechanics, retailing, agriculture, secretarial work, computerized data management, and building trades are also frequently offered. The thrust of these programs is to teach the students the skills needed on particular jobs. Although information on vocational class selections is not available for all types of disabilities, Cawley, Kahn, and Tedesco (1989) provided some information on vocational course selection by students with learning disabilities, as presented in Interest Box 14.2.

Of course, should you be assigned to co-teach in an inclusive vocational education class, your responsibilities would be considerably involved with vocational training. However, this arrangement is fairly rare, and implementation of vocational programs is not typically handled by special educators, because students with mild and moderate disabilities are often placed in the same vocational classes with other students. Therefore, the special education teacher in the high school is usually in a secondary or supporting role for these aspects of vocational education.

This traditional instructional program, unfortunately, may tend to create a schism between special education and vocational education for students with disabilities. For example, the special educator may or may not have any input into the instruction offered in vocational classes. Further, the vocational education instructor may or may not be aware of instructional practices appropriate for students with disabilities. Okolo (1988) indicated that less than half of the surveyed vocational education teachers indicated that special educators consulted with them on a regular basis, and this certainly would not indicate that students with disabilities were receiving a well integrated vocational program.

Some difference of opinion between special educators and vocational educators is a natural offshoot of the training of each group. Special educators are trained to emphasize basic skills remedial instruction, whereas vocational educators have typically been trained to emphasize job related vocational skills (Okolo & Sitlington, 1986). Still, this lack of information and mutual involvement is not productive for students with disabilities, and more involvement between the special educator and the vocational educator should result in a higher likelihood of success in the vocational education programming for students with disabilities.

As a special education teacher, you can encourage increased involvement between your-

INTEREST BOX 14.2

Vocational Course Selections by Students with Learning Disabilities

Cawley, Kahn, and Tedesco (1989) presented information on the vocational course selections of 500 secondary students with learning disabilities who were attending vocational high schools. Because of the extensive vocational curricula in that type of school, the students in this study had a wide choice of courses. In most high schools, the choice would be more limited. Still, it is interesting to note the types of courses these students selected.

Trade	Number	Trade	Number
Carpentry	73	Fashion design	4
Plumbing	34	Masonry	10
Drafting	21	Painting	3
Mechanical drafting	12	Major appliance repair	5
Air conditioning	13	Health sciences	3
Exploratory	41	Sheet metal	13
Automotive	92	Building maintenance	1
Machine tool	39	Environmental systems	1
Food/culinary	22	Ship building	1
Hair dressing	18	Welding	1
Cosmetology	18	Small engine repair	1
Graphics	8	Heating/pipe fitter	1
Pattern drafting	1	Chemistry	1

As these data indicate, many students choose automotive, machine tool, carpentry, plumbing, and hair dressing/cosmetology jobs. These data are similar to data from other follow-up studies.

Source: Cawley, Kahn, and Tedesco (1989).

self and the vocational instructors in your school. First, communicate with them by written notes in order to let them know that you are interested in helping students with disabilities in the vocational education classes. Next, identify ways in which you may be able to help the vocational education teacher. For example, you may be able to work on vocational education vocabulary words in the special education class. Vocational teachers should be able to provide you with a vocabulary list from various units that will be covered, and students with disabilities could use such lists to learn dictionary skills, sentence and paragraph construction, or alphabetization in the special education class. Finally, as the relationship between you and the vocational educator develops, you may be able to suggest particular strategies to the vocational education teacher for use with students with disabilities. Obviously, this type of suggestion must be made tactfully, and supported by your offer of assistance, should the vocational education teacher desire it. Interest Box 14.3 presents an additional list of support activities.

RECENT EMPHASES IN VOCATIONAL EDUCATION

For the most part, vocational education classes were offered in the public schools prior to legislation that included students with disabilities in the

INTEREST BOX 14.3

Support Activities for Vocational Education Teachers

When building an effective working relationship between yourself, as the special education teacher, and the vocational education teachers in your school, you should offer some of your time and assistance to the vocational education teachers. The following activities may assist those teachers in working with students with disabilities.

1. When problems arise in the vocational class, offer to come to that class and observe the student during one or two class sessions. You may be able to identify a cause for the problem of which the vocational teacher is not aware.
2. Offer to conduct team-taught lessons with the vocational teacher. You help prepare the worksheets to be used in a class on, for example, engine repair. Show the vocational education teacher how to prepare lessons that challenge the students with disabilities in the class without frustrating them. You may need to let the vocational teacher know that it is permissible to have several different worksheets for the same diagram on engine parts, with some of the students receiving a more challenging work task, while others receive a lighter load.
3. Take joint field trips with the vocational teacher. Visit an automotive repair shop, a local hairdresser, a computer shop, and any other local industry. Discuss job possibilities in each setting and follow up on those discussions when you return to school.
4. Implement training in interpersonal skills, as needed.
5. Invite the vocational education teacher to your class so that he or she may observe how you work with the students in each class. Demonstrate how you prepare several levels of work on the same task or unit in order to allow for students' differential abilities.
6. Prepare materials for the student to complete that are applicable to both the vocational and the special education class. Suggest that both teachers grade the work. This would provide a mechanism by which both teachers can share and compare their expectations concerning the level of the student's work.

school population. As a result, vocational classes were set up and operating before these students were included, and the unique vocational education requirements of students with various disabilities have been considered in vocational programming only "after the fact." Moreover, recent research has demonstrated that students with disabilities need more from this final phase—the vocational training phase—of vocational instruction than merely job related skills (Okolo & Sitlington, 1986). In fact, some have questioned the overall efficacy of vocational education for students with disabilities (Adelman & Vogel, 1994). At the very least, the vocational education requirements of students with disabilities are somewhat different from the vocational education requirements of the nondisabled students.

Okolo and Sitlington (1986) identified several separate emphases that should be included during this third phase of vocational education instruction for students with disabilities: specific vocational skills, vocationally related academic skills, and interpersonal skills. Although some of these emphases are included in traditional vocational curricula, others are not. Consequently, in many cases it is the responsibility of the secondary special education teacher to make certain that the various skills are taught to each student who has a disability, according to the needs of that student.

Specific Vocational Skills

Students with disabilities tend to succeed more in job placements that involve the use of the same tools and techniques utilized in the vocational education class. A nondisabled student may be able to take a class in rough framing for home-building (which usually involves construction of the wooden frame of the home—that is, the floor, walls, and roof) and then be able to transfer some of those skills to other more specialized aspects of the building trades (metal building construction, drywall instillation, roofing, air conditioning services). Students with disabilities, however, are much less likely to be able to make such a transfer of knowledge. Therefore, these students should use the exact techniques and tools during vocational training that they anticipate using after graduation (Okolo & Sitlington, 1986).

The vocational teachers will typically be responsible for the decisions involving the use of particular tools and techniques. The role of the special educator in that aspect of vocational education will typically include extended discussions with students concerning the particulars of the jobs to which they aspire. Of course, any information about the types of jobs that are of interest to students should be shared with the vocational teacher. Further, if a special student already has a job and wishes to continue that job in some capacity postschool, then the skills, the abilities, and the tools needed for that job should be one cornerstone of that student's vocational program.

Vocationally Related Academic Skills

Academic skills present a problem for many students with disabilities in vocational curricula. Not only do secondary students with disabilities demonstrate deficits in both reading and math skills, but those deficits tend to be compounded by the type of material included in vocational education courses.

Vocational curricula include a number of academic tasks that are not emphasized in the traditional academic subjects. Vocational texts tend to include a higher concentration of charts, graphs, diagrams, and detailed instructions for machine assembly and other highly technical work than do the texts in other courses. Furthermore, the ability to glean information from these sources is crucial for success in the vocational program. Although some instruction in charts and graphs is included in modern math curricula, most students with disabilities do not receive nearly enough instruction in these skills to allow them to successfully complete the vocational curriculum. In fact, when one considers the types of reading skills necessary to complete a vocational education curriculum, coupled with the noted reading deficits of many secondary students with disabilities, one wonders how those students succeed at all in vocational courses. If you have ever been frustrated by the directions for assembly of a child's toy or a model airplane, you can certainly empathize with a student with a disability who is confronted with a complicated diagram, chart, or set of directions in a vocational education text.

Of course, this is one area in which you, as the special education teacher, can truly help. You should obtain these charts, graphs, diagrams, and so forth, in advance of the unit instruction from the vocational education teacher, and teach these basics to the students with disabilities before they start that unit in the vocational classroom. This will greatly assist the students and the vocational education teacher.

A number of academic skills are not job skills per se, but are essential for successful employment. Such activities as completing a job application or a tax form, banking, and monetary skills are "academic" skills that have, only within the last ten or fifteen years, been included in the math and vocational education curricula in public schools (Johnson, 1984). These academic skills are also included in a number of special education curriculum materials. Generally, such skills are discussed under the label of "daily living," "functional skills," or "survival skills." Instruction in these skills is vital for successful employment and daily living as an adult. Finally, because these skills have been included in both the math and the special education curricula, many vocational education teachers do not attend to them, even though acquiring and retaining a job may be dependent upon them. You may find, as the special education teacher, that your role is to instruct the student in the academically related vocational skills, whereas the vocational teachers teach the actual vocational skills.

Preferably, vocationally related academic tasks such as those described above should be viewed as the joint responsibility of the vocational teacher and the special educator, because both of those teachers have particular expertise to bring to bear on the instruction of students with disabilities. The special education teacher can include work with general charts, graphs, diagrams, directions, job applications, and tax forms in the special education class. The vocational educator can demonstrate the relationship between the diagram of the internal parts of a two-cycle engine and the actual parts of that engine. This type of instruction should facilitate the student's understanding of these academic skills so crucial for vocational success.

Should you find yourself in a secondary teaching position, you will want to develop a clear understanding of the types of vocationally related academic tasks covered by the vocational education instructors and those tasks that must be covered during your instructional time with the student. Only then can the vocational needs of students with disabilities be met. You should make every effort to understand which of these areas are not covered in the vocational classes, and then cover those areas in your own class instruction with the special needs students.

Interpersonal Skills

Interpersonal skills represent one of the most recent emphases in vocational education. Indeed, most vocational education programs do not currently include instructional components intended to foster successful interpersonal skills, because the needs of the original nondisabled vocational education populations did not dictate the inclusion of these skills in the curriculum. In spite of this negative history, most theorists in special education have indicated that interpersonal skills should be included in the vocational curriculum for students with disabilities (Okolo & Sitlington, 1986).

Upon a moment's reflection, inclusion of these skills makes a great deal of sense. Many persons with disabilities lose jobs, or fail to get jobs, because of poor interpersonal skills. Brown (1976) surveyed 5,213 employers in the state of Texas in an attempt to identify the reasons for rejecting job applications from persons with disabilities. Of the 10 most frequently cited reasons for rejecting an application, 9 dealt with interpersonal relationships. Needless to say, employers seek applicants who can get along well with other workers, and who do not cause personal problems in the workplace. Obviously, students with disabilities who lose jobs, or fail to obtain jobs, because of poor interpersonal skills could benefit from instruction in interpersonal skills.

For this reason, certain interpersonal skills may need to be included in educational programs for these students. It is unlikely that all vocational education curricula will be revised to include these skills, and, consequently, this is one emphasis that should be included in the secondary special education program. The role of the special educator, then, would be one of primary instruction in interpersonal skills.

Several of the instructional programs discussed in Chapter 13 could be used to develop appropriate interpersonal skills. Further, the commercially available programs include skills that may be more or less appropriate for various jobs. As the primary instructor for these skills, you may have to select certain ones for instruction, based on the type of job a student has. For example, should a student with a disability choose a job in the fast food industry, the skills that emphasize politeness when working with people would be more appropriate than the skills that stress extended conversation, because the waiter at a hamburger chain restaurant is required to be polite, but is only infrequently required to conduct extended conversation.

Role of the Special Educator

The several skills discussed above represent the recent emphases in vocational training of students with disabilities. Whereas vocational programs traditionally included only job related skills, the newer demands of students with disabilities indicate that vocational education must be expanded to include other areas as well. For example, vocationally related academic skills must be covered at some point in the curriculum for most of these students. Likewise, interpersonal skills should be stressed because these skills are essential in both obtaining and keeping a job.

The role of the special educator ranges from a tangential support role—in relation to job skills—to a primary role for instruction in interpersonal skills. The lines of communication between the vocational educator and the special educator must be kept open in order to ensure that the expanded vocational education needs of individuals with disabilities are being met. Typically, this responsibility for fluent communication will become the responsibility of the special educator, because teachers who are prepared in special education receive more training in communication with other professionals than do vocational education teachers. Many of the suggestions on working with mainstream teachers and working in inclusive classrooms, covered in Chapter 2, may be of benefit here as well. In short, you should do everything possible to ensure effective communication between yourself and the vocational education teachers with whom you work. Only through such a close working relationship can the entire spectrum of vocational needs for students with disabilities be met.

THE TRADITIONAL VOCATIONAL EDUCATION MODELS

In order to encourage more effective vocational education outcomes, several traditional models of vocational instruction have been developed (McLaughlin & Martin, 1993; Gaylord-Ross, Siegel, Park, & Wilson, 1988; Sands, Able-Boone, & Margolis, 1994; Tindall & Hedberg, 1987). The major thrust of all these models is an attempt to place students with disabilities in as realistic a setting as possible for vocational instruction. The traditional models include classroom-based vocational studies, vocational classes, vocational high schools, and postsecondary vocational training.

Classroom-Based Vocational Studies

A number of vocational educational studies may be offered in the public school classroom. For example, both job awareness and job orientation studies may be offered in almost any classroom during the early grades, as discussed above. Also, career counseling may be offered by school personnel, such as a vocational or guidance counselor. These types of instructional and guidance activities require no particular equipment or specialized classroom and may therefore be offered at any grade, in any classroom.

Finally, two of the newer emphases in vocational education—vocationally related academic skills and interpersonal skills—require no specialized equipment beyond a set of curriculum materials that may be purchased commercially. Therefore instruction in these areas may also be offered in the classroom.

Vocational Classes

Many junior and senior high schools include some vocational class options for their students. Although most secondary schools do not specialize in vocational studies, they do offer some of the most common vocational classes in classrooms that are especially equipped. Small engine repair, auto mechanics, drafting, home economics, construction, data processing, office management, and horticulture are some of the more common types of vocational classes offered by most secondary schools.

In some cases, the vocational classes will include only students with disabilities. In other cases, students are in mixed groups that include students with and without disabilities. There are inclusive programs in which special educators and vocational educators team-teach this type of class, so that the expertise of both the special educator and the vocational educator may be available for the students. However, in other vocational classes, students with disabilities are mainstreamed with nondisabled students. Obviously, mainstreamed placements are preferred for students with disabilities, as long as that placement meets the needs of each student.

Vocational High Schools

Although most secondary schools offer some vocational education classes, many school districts have found economic advantages in creating vocational high schools. The curriculum at vocational high schools typically includes some academic courses (required courses such as English, general math, etc.), but the focus is on an extensive list of vocational classes. Whereas many secondary schools offer one course in automotive mechanics, the vocational high school offers several courses, with advanced levels of study available to prepare students for higher-level positions (Cawley, Kahn, & Tedesco, 1989). Such courses may include brake, alignment, or transmission specialists. Also, the curriculum at the vocational high schools includes a number of additional vocational courses not available at most high schools.

Several states have adopted plans that make vocationally oriented high schools available to almost every student who chooses such a curriculum. For example, in New Jersey, many vocational high schools are set up and supported by a group of several school districts. The secondary students from those districts who choose a vocationally based secondary curriculum would then be transported daily out of their home districts to the vocational high school in order to take advantage of the extensive course work available.

The models of instruction and the instructional interaction between the special educator and the vocational educator range much as they did in vocational classes at most secondary schools. In some cases, the vocational teacher and special educator teach in separate classes; in other cases inclusive co-teaching is practiced. Also, only a small percentage of the population of students who attend these vocational high schools is disabled—in the Cawley, Kahn, & Tedesco study (1989) the figure was 7 percent. Although all of the students at the vocational high school have chosen a vocational rather than a college preparatory curriculum, there will still be major differences in the abilities and academic performance between some of the students with disabilities and other students in the school, and these differences must be attended to in order to ensure success for students with disabilities.

Postsecondary Vocational Training

In a statewide follow-up of the study completed in Colorado, around 8 percent of all individuals with mild disabilities attended vocational schools after the completion of high school (Mithaug, Horiuchi, & Fanning, 1985). Many counties and school districts have established vocational and technical colleges in order to make vocational education available. Typically, these institutions were established before a national effort had been made to provide educational services to students with disabilities, and the curricula of many of these colleges and technical schools does not include a great number of courses these students may need, such as the interpersonal skills discussed earlier.

Further, there may be less assistance offered in the postsecondary setting for the students with disabilities than would be available in the secondary school, because vocational and technical schools tend to employ fewer special educators than the public schools. However, there are postsecondary vocational and technical schools that have excellent programs of support for students with disabilities, and this aspect of service for these students would certainly vary from one technical school to another. In spite of these limitations, these schools do make postsecondary education available to some students with disabilities. The classes typically offered are similar to those offered by vocational high schools, though the postsecondary instruction classes tend to be more rigorous.

Reflections on the Traditional Models

The traditional models of instruction in vocational education are similar in many ways. First, many of the instructional needs of students with disabilities may be met in classroom settings, and certain areas of instruction in each of these models take place in the classroom. Next, these models of instruction were developed prior to a national effort to educate students with disabilities, and thus students with limited cognitive, perceptual, and motor abilities were not considered in formulating these models of instruction. Still, these instructional approaches can be successful with learners with disabilities for certain areas of vocational instruction, such as vocational awareness, vocational orientation, and vocationally related academic or social skills.

The traditional models do have one major disadvantage. Each of the instructional models discussed above provides instruction in vocational skills in a setting other than the workplace. Because students with disabilities often have some problems in transferring a learned skill into different settings, the disassociation between the setting in which vocational education instruction was held and the actual job cite created problems for some of these learners.

RECENT MODELS OF VOCATIONAL INSTRUCTION

Work–Study Programs

During recent decades, a number of vocational education students have participated in various work–study programs. In these programs a student may attend school for half of the school day to take traditional course work, such as English, math, and history, and then be excused from other classes in order to report to work at a job site in the local area. On-the-job training such as this would comprise the basis for the vocational program.

Work–study programs have met with some success because of the nature of the experiences the students receive. Obviously, the optimum result would be permanent employment of the student with a disability, who after graduation would stay with the same company doing the same job. Even when such employment is not offered, however, the student has gained some job experience that may assist in future placements, and the letters of reference from such work–study programs can assist in finding a job at another location.

One problem with the traditional work–study program has been the lack of emphasis on both vocationally related academic skills and interpersonal skills. In most work–study programs, there is little follow-up between the actual needs of the student in those areas and the academic work offered. For this reason, many special educators are now employed in a "transition teaching" role that involves coordination between the school and the workplace environments for students with disabilities. In many schools this person is not at all responsible for any direct teaching of students, but spends time observing students with disabilities on the worksite and indicating to the other special education/vocational education team members what types of instruction would help. Among the recent models of vocational instruction, this is one of the more useful ones for vocational education of students with disabilities.

Community-Based Instruction

Community-based instructional models represent a response to the limitations of the traditional instructional models discussed previously. In a community-based model, instructional activities take place in the community itself in order to minimize the negative effects of the transition between school and the workplace. Also, community-based instructional approaches differ from the work–study programs discussed above because the former are typically characterized by attention to a working partnership among the employers, special educators, and vocational educators to ensure that all of the vocational instruction needs are met—including vocationally related academic skills and interpersonal skills. Initially, the community-based instructional model was used for job-related skills, but the effectiveness of this model of instruction was soon demonstrated for vocationally related academic skills and interpersonal skills also. For example, both work–study programs and shopping trips to local stores are typical in community-based instructional programs.

Sands, Able-Boone, and Margolis (1994) reported on a live-in training experience for students with mild and moderate mental retardation. In this program, a consortium of agencies actually rents an apartment and moves students into a communal living arrangement (with several professionals for supervision), with the clients remaining there during the week. Job placement is handled by coordination with the division of vocational rehabilitation and the clients are employed in full-time positions Monday through Thursday. Initial evaluations of this program look very positive. Of course, a live-in situation such as this is the extreme example of community-based placement, but this arrangement allows not only study of work skills on the job, but also practice in the skills of getting up and to work on time, crucial for students with disabilities.

Initial research on the efficacy of community-based placement has been positive, indicating that this model of instruction is an effective method for providing vocational education to students with disabilities (McLaughlin & Martin, 1993; Gaylord-Ross et al., 1988; Neubert, Tilson, & Ianacone, 1989). Although this research may be challenged on certain methodological grounds—many of the studies include no control group whose vocational instruction was done in the classroom (Neubert, Tilson, & Ianacone, 1989)—the initial results seem to indicate that community-based instruction is quite effective.

Tindall and Hedberg (1987) presented several examples of community-based instruction in vocational skills. In the SELPAS Project in California, 100 high school students with disabilities were placed in jobs, with services provided by both special and vocational educators. The strength of this community-based project was the nature of the team effort. Orientation meetings were held that included the educators, the students, prospective employers, and parents. The employers received some financial incentive under the Job Training Partnership Act (discussed in Interest Box 14.4) for their participation in this project. A mutually satisfactory plan was prepared that included the work schedule as well as instructional suggestions for any vocationally related academic skills required by the job. Skills such as the use of public transportation to and from the job site, interviewing skills, and other vocationally related or interpersonal skills were often included in a student's course of study. The educators, parents, and employers composed a support team for each student, and this team effort resulted in a notable success. Of 150 students placed since 1983, 111 are still on the job.

Other community-based instructional programs have resulted in similar successes (Gaylord-Ross et al., 1988, Neubert, Tilson, & Ianacone, 1989; Tindall & Hedberg, 1987). For this reason, the community-based model of vocational instruction represents the future direction of vocational education for students with disabilities.

The Individual Transition Plan (ITP)

Numerous researchers have begun to attend to the transition period between school and the adult world of work for students with disabilities, and most of these persons recommend development of an individual transition plan (ITP) to facilitate it (Langone, 1990; McLaughlin & Martin, 1993). This plan should become a major component of the individual education plan for students in secondary school. The ITP should be developed during the last several years of the high school curriculum, and must include goals and objectives to facilitate the postschool transition. Langone (1990) recommends a three-point focus for the ITP: appropriate vocational education programs during the last two or three years of secondary school, instruction in community-based vocational environments, and paid, part-time work.

Sample goals from one student's ITP are presented in Interest Box 14.5 (McLaughlin & Martin, 1993). These sample goals should give some indication of the types of skills that would be included on the ITP.

INTEREST BOX 14.4
The Job Training Partnership Act

The Job Training Partnership Act (JTPA) is a piece of federal legislation, passed in 1983, which provides funds to prepare youth and unskilled adults for entry into the labor force. Approximately $3 billion are spent annually, with around 10 percent of that figure spent on youth with disabilities (Tindall and Hedberg, 1987).

Most JTPA programs involve five steps:

1. Students are identified and enrolled in the program.
2. A vocational assessment is conducted.
3. Based on the assessment, training is selected and developed to meet each student's needs.
4. Practical experience involving on-the-job placement is provided.
5. The training and other experiences result in permanent job placement.

One major reason for the success of the JTPA is the direct involvement of employers. In many of the model programs funded under this act, the employers are involved from the earliest stages in development of the job skills training and vocationally related academic training that participants receive. Also, one major incentive to the employer results from the fact that some funds may be used to pay a portion of the student's wages during the training period—in some cases, up to 50 percent. This type of incentive to employers has resulted in a very successful program for enhancing the employability of students with disabilities.

As these goals indicate, a number of variations in teachers' work assignments must be made in order to fully implement a comprehensive ITP. Teachers who are involved in transition teaching must be able to leave the school building to supervise the student in the community-based placement. Also, extended-day contracts will be necessary for some teachers for supervision at the worksite after school hours. Further extensive collaboration among the vocational teacher, the special education teacher, and the employer is necessary for this plan to work. However, the research has indicated that this type of comprehensive community-based placement is much more successful during the transition period than were the traditional models of vocational instruction. Further, the specific delineation of responsibilities on the ITP should facilitate the type of collaboration between professionals necessary for this type of program to work.

The Americans with Disabilities Act (ADA)

With the passage of the Americans with Disabilities Act (ADA)—a law that became effective in 1992—it is expected many more employers will be willing to consider employing students with disabilities. This law has a number of provisions intended to prohibit discrimination against persons with disabilities in employment. In simple terms, the law states that, if a person can perform the "essential functions" of the job for which they are being considered, then an employer may not discriminate against that employee. Further, employers must make some efforts to adapt the workplace to the needs of the individual with disabilities, at least as far as is reasonable, and standard adaptations may be required for the general public. This legislation should assist in the overall employment efforts on behalf of individuals with disabilities.

INTEREST BOX 14.5
Sample ITP Goals

Vocational Education Program
John will enroll in the small engine repair class. He will learn to service, maintain, and repair starting systems of wind-up type and electric type small engines. Mr. Smith, a vocational education teacher, is responsible for this instruction. Ms. Jones, a special education resource room teacher, will help by providing related instruction in her class. The related instruction will include helping John with assigned textbook readings and monitoring workbook assignments.

Community-Based Instruction
John will use the public transportation system to go to and from his part-time job. He will learn to use bus schedules so he can get on the correct bus to arrive at work on time. He will also practice correct conversational skills with the bus driver and fellow passengers. Ms. Jones is responsible for this instruction. The instructional activities will be carried out primarily in the community (i.e., at the bus stop and on the bus). This will require that Ms. Jones work outside the school building during a portion of the instructional day.

Paid, Part-Time Employment
John will work from 3:00 until 6:00 P.M. on Mondays, Wednesdays, and Fridays at Sloan's Small Engine Repair. He will start by doing basic cleaning of engine parts and by stocking the parts department shelves. He will also practice appropriate social skills with co-workers. John's work will be monitored by Mr. Smith and Ms. Jones. Both teachers have extended day contracts in order to provide on-the-job supervision.

Source: McLaughlin and Martin (1993).

INSTRUCTION SUGGESTIONS IN VOCATIONAL EDUCATION

Instructional Activities

1. Collect materials that are associated with specific jobs. Mount pictures of the people who perform these jobs on cards. Place all of the pictures in a row on the floor or on a table. Have the student match the appropriate objects to the pictures of the workers (e.g., badge, policeman, stethoscope, nurse).

2. From magazines, cut out small action pictures (e.g., a boy running, a policeman holding a hand up to stop). Glue these pictures on pieces of felt. Cut yellow, gold, green, white, and red flannel pieces into the shape of traffic signs. Place these safety signs on a flannel board. Have the child find the appropriate picture to pair with each sign.

3. To help children orient themselves to their surroundings, create maps of the school grounds and building. Have the children move through their environment and identify their location on their maps.

4. Have students identify local buildings by taking Polaroid pictures of areas and attaching the pictures to a bulletin board. Complete the environment by representing streets and roads with tagboard.

5. Collect pictures of everyday situations in a community, such as a scene in a department store or people at a football game or laundromat. Mount the pictures on tagboard and have the children identify work situations and leisure activities. Discuss the participants in the activities: "Who is buying?" "Who is taking up tickets?" "Who is working?"

6. To help develop the concept of community, develop a scrapbook of pictures of local schools, churches, and businesses.

7. Create a relief map using play dough of the child's state depicting the state capital and geographical features such as rivers and mountains.

8. Build a puppet theater and have children create puppets of community helpers. Help them develop scenarios to portray through the use of puppets (e.g., "If you were lost, who would be a good person to ask for help?").

9. Select professional roles such as doctors, dentists, and judges. Collect pictures of these professionals and pictures of their working environments, such as hospital, dentist office, courtroom. Laminate the pictures and have the children match the professionals to their surroundings.

10. Ask professional people or individuals in the community help services to volunteer for an interview. Help the children to develop questions to ask about the individual's job or service. Role play with the student before the interview. Receive written permission from the student's parent and the volunteer to video the interview.

11. Use the sun as a source of heat. Focus the sun's rays on a sheet of paper with a magnifying glass. Discuss the outcome.

12. Use collision as a source of heat: Hit a piece of brad or wire repeatedly with a hammer. Touch the metal. Discuss the outcome.

13. What causes sound? Stretch a rubber band over a box. Pluck the rubber bank. Discuss how vibration causes sound and the vibration of the rubber band moved particles of air around it back and forth, enabling the sound to be heard.

14. Construct a workboard on a 1" × 1" square piece of plywood. Attach hinges with locks and keys. Have the child practice manipulating these devices.

15. Collect nuts and bolts of varying sizes. Have the student match and attach the nuts to the corresponding bolts.

16. Assemble a tool box with household tools. Teach the proper names, use, and maintenance of these tools. Observing safety precautions, allow responsible students to use these tools in the classroom for assembly and repair.

17. Have a current daily newspaper in the classroom. Each day, review the want ads and discuss available positions and the qualifications for those positions.

18. Assemble a collection of types of nails. Teach the student to recognize and name the different types, such as box nail, common nail, finishing nail, casing nail, cut nail, and wire brad. Identify nails by size (penny) and length.

19. Obtain schedules and maps for local public transportation. Identify the most appropriate conveyance and have students identify the correct time and location on the time schedule and the map of the route.

20. Replicate common rebus symbols found in the workplace, such as "No Smoking." Teach the student the meaning of each symbol.

21. Have samples of linen and towels. Provide practice folding and counting designated numbers and items.

22. Have digital and conventional alarm clocks. Teach the student to set the clocks. Develop a daily wake-up schedule from the estimation of the time needed to leave home for work or school.

23. Assemble peat pots in flats, potting soil, and seeds. Have students plant seeds and water them on schedule. Have the next size container available for transplanting the seedlings. Instruct the student by placing a peat pot into the soil of the next size container. Cover the peat pot with additional soil and press firmly, then water the plant.

Vocational Software

Babysitting Basics

Publisher: MCE, a Division of Lawrence Productions

Skill Level: Elementary, Secondary, Adult

Hardware: Apple IIe

Description: A number of issues are presented in this interactive program designed to prepare students at any age with the responsibilities of child care.

Community Signs

Publisher: Conover Company

Skill Level: Elementary, secondary, adult

Hardware: Apple IIe, Echo speech synthesizer

Description: Community Signs is similar in format to other programs in the *Survival Skills System*. The subject mater in this program focuses on the signs commonly found within the community. Signs generally found within the community can be broken down into three categories: places, information, and safety. *Community Signs* covers places; *Information Signs* covers information; and *Safety Signs* covers safety. This program should be used in conjunction with *Information Signs* and *Safety Signs*.

Math on the Job

Publisher: Conover Company

Skill Level: Secondary, adult

Hardware: Apple IIe

Description: Math on the Job was developed to allow special needs and at-risk students an opportunity to explore careers and practice basic math skills, as well as to provide diagnostic and remedial occupationally related math skills information. Students discover how various math skills and concepts are used in occupations, learn how to apply different math skills, and consider the educational and training requirements for occupations.

Safety Signs

Publisher: Conover Company

Skill Level: Elementary, secondary, adult

Hardware: Apple IIe, Echo speech synthesizer

Description: Safety Signs is similar in purpose and format to *Information Signs*. The only difference is the subject matter. In this program safety signs commonly found in most community settings are covered. Understanding of these signs is important for the safety of the individual.

SUMMARY

Vocational instruction was implemented prior to the national effort to educate students with disabilities. Consequently, the scopes of traditional models of instruction, as well as traditional curriculum emphases in vocational education, were not broad enough to adequately meet the needs of students with disabilities. Vocational education was initially conceptualized as career awareness, career orientation, and job related skills, and this limited set of curriculum areas did not meet the needs of students with disabilities. Instruction in the career awareness area now begins in the early grades, and instruction in the other two areas proceeds throughout school.

Vocational training historically included only vocational skills training. However, because of the needs of students with disabilities, it has been expanded to include vocationally related academic skills and social interaction skills on the job. With these new curriculum emphases in place, vocational education is now in a position to meet the needs of a higher percentage of individuals with disabilities.

The new vocational instructional model of community-based placement includes emphasis on all of these areas. Also, placement of individuals with disabilities directly in the job setting has resulted in better job retention for these individuals. This model of instruction, supplemented by classroom-based studies, results in the best vocational prognosis for students with disabilities.

Summary Points

- Vocational education is important for students with disabilities because 55 percent to 69 percent of students with mild disabilities enter the work force after school.
- The postschool success of students with disabilities overall is not positive. One in four students with a disability drops out of school, and only 60 percent graduate.
- Most students with disabilities find early employment through their own or their family's initiative.
- Vocational education was initially conceptualized as career awareness, career orientation, and job related skills.
- Vocational education has now been expanded beyond merely vocational training to include activities such as vocationally related academic skills and social interaction skills on the job.
- The traditional models of vocational instruction included classroom-based vocational instruction, vocational classes, vocationally oriented high schools, and postsecondary vocational training.
- The more recently developed models include work–study programs and community-based placements for vocational instruction. In the latter type of model, the teacher actually follows the student into the vocational setting for evaluation purposes.
- Preparation of an ITP during the secondary school years may help to focus on the student's vocational instruction needs.
- The ADA should ensure that employers are much more willing to employ individuals with disabilities.

QUESTIONS AND ACTIVITIES

1. Review the information available in the literature on the Job Training Partnership Act and the Americans with Disabilities Act, and report back to the class. Should these bills be continued?
2. Contact the Department of Education in your state and inquire about community-based instructional programs in your area. If a program is operating locally, interview the vocational and special education teachers in that program and report the success of that program to the class. What modifications were necessary, if any, in the teacher's workday?
3. Why did new emphases have to be added to the traditional vocational education curriculum to meet the needs of students with disabilities?
4. Discuss with local elementary teachers the types of activities they use for instruction in career awareness.
5. Review the curriculum materials in the curriculum materials center of your college or university that deal with vocationally related academic skills and share some of these materials with the class.
6. Form a group to read the various follow-up studies on the vocational outcomes for students with disabilities that have been completed to date. Prepare a report of results and present it to the class.

7. Invite a local attorney to speak to the class about the new provisions of the ADA.
8. Review the goals for the ITP presented in this chapter. For each of these areas (and for other areas that should be included) prepare a set of specific behavioral objectives for inclusion on the ITP.

REFERENCES

Adelman, P. B., & Vogel, S. A. (1994). Issues in the employment of adults with learning disabilities. *Learning Disability Quarterly, 16,* 219–232.

Brown, K. W. (1976). What employers look for in job applicants. *Business Education Forum, 30,* 7.

Cawley, J. F., Kahn, H., & Tedesco, A. (1989). Vocational education and students with learning disabilities. *Journal of Learning Disabilities, 22,* 630–640.

Edgar, E. (1985). How do special education students fare after they leave school? A response to Hasazi, Gordon, and Roe. *Exceptional Children, 51,* 470–473.

Gaylord-Ross, R., Siegel, S., Park, H. S., & Wilson, W. (1988). Secondary vocational training. In Gaylord-Ross, R. (Ed.), *Vocational Education for Persons With Handicaps.* Mountain View, CA: Mayfield Publishing.

Haring, K. A., Lovett, D. L., & Smith, D. D. (1990). A follow-up study of recent special education graduates of learning disabilities programs. *Journal of Learning Disabilities, 23,* 108–113.

Hasazi, S. B., Gordon, L., & Roe, C. A. (1985). Factors associated with the employment status of handicapped youth exiting high school from 1979 to 1983. *Exceptional Children, 51,* 455–469.

Johnson, C. L. (1984). The learning disabled adolescent and young adult: An overview and critique of current practices. *Journal of Learning Disabilities, 17,* 386–391.

Langone, J. (1990). *Teaching Students with Mild and Moderate Learning Problems.* Boston: Allyn & Bacon.

Levine, P., & Edgar, E. (1994). Respondent agreement in follow-up of graduates of special and regular education programs. *Exceptional Children, 60,* 334–343.

Levine, P., & Edgar, E. (1995). An analysis by gender of long-term postschool outcomes for youth with and without disabilities. *Exceptional Children, 61,* 282–300.

McLaughlin, P. J., Martin, M. A. (1993). Vocational and independent living skills. In W. N. Bender (Ed.), *Learning Disabilities: Best Practices for Professionals.* Boston: Andover Medical Publishers.

Mithaug, D. E., Horiuchi, C. N., & Fanning, P. N. (1985). A report on the Colorado statewide follow-up survey of special education students. *Exceptional Children, 51,* 397–404.

Neel, R. S., Meadows, N., Levine, P., & Edgar, E. B. (1988). What happens after special education: A statewide follow-up study of secondary students who have behavioral disorders. *Behavioral Disorders, 13,* 209–216.

Neubert, D. A., Tilson, G. P., & Ianacone, R. N. (1989). Postsecondary transition needs and employment patterns of individuals with mild disabilities. *Exceptional Children, 55,* 494–500.

Okolo, C. M. (1988). Instructional environments in secondary vocational education programs: Implications for LD adolescents. *Learning Disability Quarterly, 11,* 136–148.

Okolo, C. M., & Sitlington, P. (1986). The role of special education in LD adolescents' transition from school to work. *Learning Disability Quarterly, 9,* 141–155.

Sands, D. J., Able-Boone, H., Margolis, H. (1994). Live-in training experience (LITE): A transition program for youth with disabilities. *Teaching Exceptional Children, 27* (2), 19–23.

Schalock, R. L., Wolzen, B., Ross, I., Elliott, B., Werbel, G., & Peterson, K. (1986). Post-secondary community placement of handicapped students: A five-year follow-up. *Learning Disability Quarterly, 9,* 295–303.

Shapiro, E. S., & Lentz, F. (1991). Vocational–technical programs: Follow-up of students with learning disabilities. *Exceptional Children, 58* (1), 47–60.

Tindall, L. W., & Hedberg, S. B. (1987). Job training partnership act. *Teaching Exceptional Children, 19* (3), 43–45.

U.S. Employment Service (1965). *Dictionary of Occupational Titles* (3rd ed.). Washington, DC: U.S. Department of Labor.

CHAPTER 15

WORKING WITH PARENTS

OBJECTIVES

Upon completion of this chapter you should be able to:

1. Describe the parents' reaction to the child's handicap.
2. Discuss the stress points in a parent's life.
3. Describe the steps in conducting conferences involving parents.
4. Describe the several different types of meetings necessary in the delivery of special education service.
5. Describe the information that can be provided by various participants in team meetings.
6. Describe methods of increasing meaningful parental participation in child study team meetings.
7. Describe the procedures to implement a parent tutoring program.

KEYWORDS

shock
denial
doctor shopping
adjustment
acceptance
departmentalized curriculum
team meeting
parent tutoring
coincidental teaching
graduated prompting

One of the major responsibilities of special education teachers is working with parents. The legal mandate in the Education for All Handicapped Children's Act, Public Law 94–142, requires schools and parents to work together, and there is no analogous situation in the entire educational system; in special education the parent and teacher, along with others, are required to jointly write a child's educational program for the next year.

More recent legislation has even provided some governmental services to parents and families of children with disabilities (Krauss, 1990). Public Law 99–457 stipulates that an individualized service plan be provided for every preschool child with a disability, and that the services be extended not only to the child but to the family of the child. Such services must be documented and included on an Individualized Family Service Plan. In effect, the special educator, at least in the preschool service delivery years, is a service delivery agent for the entire family. With this strong and growing emphasis on involvement of families in the education of children with disabilities, special education teachers must have some understanding of the skills necessary to work with parents.

One of your major responsibilities as an inclusive class or special education class teacher is working with parents. Although this requirement is sometimes frustrating, it always presents opportunities to make a positive difference in the lives of the students. A knowledgeable teacher can open new possibilities of effecting a meaningful change in the ways in which parents interact with their children. Further, unsuccessful parental interactions can lead to criticisms of the teacher as well as interruption of the child's education. Because of these possibilities, it is in the special education teacher's best interest to understand parental interactions.

This chapter presents some useful information on indirect instructional responsibilities with parents. First, a brief discussion of parental reactions to the child's disability is provided to prepare you to understand, to whatever degree possible, what parents may be feeling.

Next, information on parents as participants in educational planning is described, including the legal mandate for parental involvement and some research on parental participation. Then guidelines for conducting effective meetings with parents are presented. The several steps shown here provide a process whereby meetings can be conducted efficiently, with the maximum possibility of successful outcomes.

Finally, the increasing responsibilities of parents in the education of children with disabilities are discussed. Parents are expected to carry some of the instructional burden for children with and without disabilities alike, but there is more of a burden when they have children with disabilities. For this reason, several "parents as tutors" programs are discussed.

One preliminary note deserves special attention in dealing with parents of children with disabilities. Although all parents will initially feel somewhat uncomfortable about discussing their child's disability, this may be especially true for minority parents. Obiakor (1992) and Harry (1992) discussed several concerns in dealing with African-American parents, and their suggestions would seem applicable to interactions between the special education teacher and all minority parents. Basically, every professional should consider cultural differences in dealing with parents from minority backgrounds, and every effort should be made to facilitate the meaningful involvement of those parents in the educational endeavors of their children. Interest Box 15.1 provides some suggestions on enhancing this involvement.

PARENTAL REACTIONS TO DISABILITY

The stress associated with having a child with a disability is much greater than the stress associated with normal family life (Waggoner & Wilgosh, 1990). Feelings of anger, denial, and embarrassment are not at all uncommon during the period in which a parent becomes aware of the disability. Consequently, special educators should have some understanding of the types of difficulties parents and families go through during that turbulent time.

Stages of Grief

Although severe problems (severe intellectual disability, cerebral palsy, etc.) are diagnosed many years prior to involvement of most school personnel, many mild disabilities are first suspected by school teachers, psychologists, and special education teachers. You may find that during your first year of teaching, you sit in a committee meeting in which parents are informed that their child is considered disabled. The stress parents experience at such a point is almost overwhelming, and special educators must be sensitive to that stress.

When informed that their child is considered disabled, most parents go through a set of stages associated with grief. You may have read about the stages of grief, because these stages are somewhat common for many of the unpleasant occurrences during life. For example, much of the literature on grief was developed in relationship to dealing with death. However, these stages also provide some insight to how parents react when they are first informed that their child has a disability. Although it is true that most parents react to the initial diagnosis of the disability in fairly predictable ways, the individual reactions will vary widely.

INTEREST BOX 15.1
Facilitating Involvement of Minority Parents

Numerous suggestions for facilitating more active involvement of minority parents have been presented by various scholars.

1. Create a meaningful role for minority parents. Request that they engage in assessment of particular behaviors. For example, parents can, with relative ease, count the number of times they have to remind their children to refocus on their homework, and that can provide one measure of "distractibility."
2. Utilize the knowledge and insight of the parents. Parents can often provide useful information for teachers that teachers may be unaware of. Harry (1992) suggests that parent reports be incorporated into the file for the students.
3. Incorporate the suggestions of these parents into the IEP for the child. Realize that parents are true partners in planning their child's education, and encourage input.
4. Utilize parents as "peer support" for other parents, and recommend that they participate in advocacy groups together.
5. Invite the parents into the classroom for frequent observations, if their schedules allow. Encourage them to ask questions about materials in your class or the books their child uses.
6. Utilize the parents as tutors. Model the tutoring behaviors you wish the parents to engage in and request that they keep a record of their tutoring activities with their children.

Sources: This list stems from Dangle (1993) and Harry (1992).

The first reaction most parents experience is one of shock. Shock may be best understood as an initial emotional impact upon the person receiving the news, and it may involve actual physiological symptoms, such as nausea, dizziness, or even fainting. As you may imagine, it is not easy for caring parents to hear the information that their child may have a behavioral disorder, a learning disability, or mild intellectual disabilities. Shock takes place almost immediately, and can last for some time, depending on the parents, and their level of surprise at hearing this information. The parents may seem numb to receiving any additional information, or they may merely sit very still. It is not uncommon for parents to cry.

Clearly, when parents are first experiencing this shock, professionals must not force signatures for program changes or even continued consideration of the issues to be addressed at the meeting. Depending upon the level and depth of the parental reaction, the meeting may need to be postponed because of this type of reaction. The only thing that teachers and professions should do for parents during this phase is provide information. As a special educator, you should give the parents the names and phone numbers of various organizations that can support parents of children and youth with disabilities. Interest Box 15.2 presents a list of organizations that may have local chapters.

Parents should also be provided with written information on the disability and the program the school proposes. This will provide something for the parents to digest as they consider the issues while "burning the midnight oil." Parents will then have the opportunity to assimilate this information prior to the next meeting.

After parental shock, most parents experience some denial stage. This may happen almost instantaneously, after the parent is first informed of the existence of the disability. Or it may happen a

INTEREST BOX 15.2
Organizations for Parental Participation

1. Council for Exceptional Children (CEC): an advocacy group comprising numerous special interest divisions, with one division associated with each major disability. Parents may wish to select CEC membership and membership in one of Councils, such as the Council for the Gifted, or the Council for Children with Behavioral Disorders. This group has also been very effective in organizing student chapters at various colleges and universities.
2. Association for Retarded Citizens (ARC): an organization of scholars and parents who seek appropriate education and treatment of the mentally handicapped. Numerous chapters are organized in cities throughout the nation.
3. Council for Learning Disabilities (CLD): an independent group of parents and scholars who provide information to parents about children, youth, and adults with learning disabilities.
4. American Association of Mental Deficiency (AAMD): a group comprised of scholars interested in research on the mentally and intellectually disabled.
5. Children with Attention Deficit Disorders (CHADD): an advocacy group, comprised of both parents and professionals, concerned with children with attention problems.

day or a week later. This stage involves actual denial that there is a problem, and may involve anger at the professionals involved, including verbal disagreements with the diagnosis and any recommendations. At times parents may begin to engage in "doctor shopping" or in seeking other professionals who offer promises of a more positive diagnosis. Also, because some disabilities are more socially acceptable than others (learning disabilities vs. intellectual disabilities is one example) parents may seek a diagnosis that seems consistent with their beliefs about what society will accept. It is not uncommon for professionals to have their credentials challenged during the denial stage.

The professionals should understand that the denial and anger is not directed at them, but rather is a natural reaction to a painful and major stress. If asked to do so, you should be prepared to give the parents names of other professionals who could assist in a reassessment. Be helpful and understanding, but do not allow the parents to mislead themselves. Above all, do not allow the parental anger to engender anger on your part; remain professionally detached and provide all of the information requested.

The next step in the parental reaction is some sort of mental adjustment. Whereas shock and denial happen very quickly, adjustment is a much longer process. In some cases adjustment to the existence of the handicap may take years. Nevertheless, at some point during the shock and/or anger phases, parents may seem for the first time to be reaching out to find information or options. Research has shown that parents are worried about the long-term prognosis, as well as the child's social life (Waggoner & Wilgosh, 1990). Questions about prognosis should give the special educator the opportunity to point out that the prognosis is not so bleak as one may have thought. Indicate to the parents that most children with mild disabilities lead relatively normal, adjusted lives after school. Indicate that many of the students with mild disabilities take and hold a job, initiate a social life, marry, and raise children themselves. The long-term prognosis is not entirely rosy, but it is not entirely bleak either, and parents need to know this. At this point, you may wish to provide additional information on points the parents ask about.

The final phase in parental reaction is acceptance of the disability. This phase is attained when the parents can love and accept the child as a full family member, fully cognizant of the strengths and weaknesses of the child, and the future problems that may arise because of the disability. This phase usually takes some years to reach, and represents the parents' full appreciation of their child.

Family Reactions to the Disability

Even after the parents reach the stages of adjustment and acceptance, there continue to be some problems. Waggoner and Wilgosh (1990) interviewed parents about some of the difficulties.

One major theme that emerged from the parental interviews was the effect of the disability on the entire family. For example, parents of the child with the disability may assist with the child's homework, and such a nightly chore can be more time consuming than it would be with a nondisabled child (Waggoner & Wilgosh, 1990). Further, the child may not wish to engage in homework because of repeated failures, and may be quite resistant. Arguments may occur that disrupt the home life of the family.

Also, parents are concerned with the effects of this type of strife on the siblings of the child with the disability. When the other children in the family notice that parents are giving an unequal amount of time to the child who has a disability, resentment can result. The attention that seems to be offered to that child, necessary though it may be, can make other children in the family feel unloved and less than worthy of parental attention (Foster, Berger, & McLean, 1981). As Waggoner and Wilgosh (1990) indicate, siblings of the child must begin to accept the disability, and the demands that it will make on family life, in the same slow process of adjustment as the parents.

Each family will have to work out these problems as they occur, and no set of explicit guidelines can be provided that account for all of the contingencies. As a professional involved with these families, your responsibilities include providing as much support and information as you can. Membership in the parent groups mentioned previously may provide support for families who are experiencing these stresses, and many professionals find that they encourage parents to join and participate in these advocacy groups. Also, various communities and community organizations may provide some support in the form of a "mother's morning out," or "respite weekends." Professional teachers will maintain a file of such community support organizations and should encourage parents to seek out these options in their local community.

Stress Points during Childhood and Youth

There are certain decision points within the child's life that cause apprehension for parents. Because parents realize the difficulties their child has, some of these stress points may be more problematic for certain families than others. Nevertheless, the professionals who work with parents can relieve some of this stress by giving parents information to help prepare for these periods. As a special education teacher, your role is to provide this information to help parents think of the options they and their child have at each of these periods in life.

Obviously, the first stress point is associated with the parents' initial awareness of the disability. The last several pages have presented information on the stages most parents go through at that point, and special education teachers are frequently called upon to assist in that process.

The next stress point is around the age of 4 or 5. Because of recent preschool legislation that requires services for children with disabilities between 3 and 5 years of age (Krauss, 1990), many parents are used to having their 3- or 4-year-old child in some type of program for young children with disabilities. Still, when the kindergarten age comes many parents feel some stress because they wish their child could be included in the mainstream kindergarten. Clearly, preschool teachers of children with disabilities can foresee this type of stress on the part of the parents and prepare the parents for this transition. If parents frequently hear the preschool teacher refer to skills the child is learning in order to master the curriculum for kindergarten next year, they will be less inclined to experience a stressful reaction when their child begins kindergarten.

Because of the increasing mobility in our society, many children with disabilities change schools. Furthermore, even if a child with a disability remains in the same school district, the parents may find that upon entering the fourth grade, sixth grade, or the seventh grade, the child is expected to change schools. This represents some stress for the parents, because for several years the parents may have worked with one resource teacher and one mainstream teacher each year, whereas the next year, at the new school, the child may be working with not only a new mainstream teacher but also a new resource teacher. Also, when a child enters the departmentalized curriculum years (in which children change classes between each subject content area) the child will be expected to work with numerous mainstream teachers. This may also cause stress for both the child and the parents.

Another major stress point during the school years comes when the child chooses the courses for secondary school. Typically, choices of high school courses involve some decisions concerning either preparation for college, postsecondary vocational training, or vocational education courses, and parents are forced to assist the student in consideration of meaningful postschool work. At that point, parents are forced to consider (if they have not previously done so) the potential vocations for a student with a disability after school. Again, the best assistance a special educator can offer is to provide accurate information to the child and the parents to assist in those decisions. In some cases, it may become clear that a child with mild intellectual disabilities should consider a vocational program during the high school years, whereas a child with a learning disability in math may be quite capable of completing a modified college level curriculum. The special education teacher, in conjunction with the guidance counselor, should provide complete data for the parents and the student in order to assist with their decisions.

The final stress point is when parents face their own aging process or the death of a spouse, because at that point, parents are forced to consider what the individual's life will be like after both parents are gone. If the individual with the disability is still living at home, a choice must be made concerning his or her living arrangements when both of the parents are dead. Typically, mental health professionals deal with this type of problem more than teachers. Nevertheless, you may find that, because of the death of a parent of a student with a disability, you have to discuss this long-term care issue with the surviving parent.

Clearly, information is, again, the key. You must provide information on the types of long term care available in the local community and help the parent make informed choices, in conjunction with the wishes and needs of the individual with the disability. Again, it is wise to build a file on community resources for the occasions when you are asked about such topics. It is your responsibility, should you find yourself in this situation, to glean information from mental health specialists, state agencies and institutions, sheltered workshops, or group homes in your area. Seek the input of the school guidance counselor, principal, and the director of special education in your efforts to explore with the parent all the possible avenues. You will find that if you offer this type of assistance to parents while they are making these difficult choices, your assistance will be greatly appreciated. In fact, providing realistic information and suggestions at stressful times such as these will be one of the most rewarding activities you engage in during your career of service to individuals with disabilities and their families.

Death of a Child

Special education teachers are much more likely to face the death of one of their students than are other teachers in our nation's schools. With the increasing services available for medically fragile children—children who were, at one time, served in hospitals and institutions—and other children who may be more prone to illness and death, special education teachers should expect, at some point, to be confronted with such a loss. Furthermore, there is some evidence that children with disabilities are at higher risk for suicide than are nondisabled children (Huntington & Bender, 1993), and that only increases the possibility that a special education teacher may need to deal with parents during and after the death of a child with a disability.

Facing the death of a student is a risk for all teachers, but in addition to the increased risk for special education teachers, there is also the increased likelihood that special education teachers may be more negatively affected. Whereas mainstream elementary teachers deal with 20 to 30 children per day, the special education teacher may deal with only 4 or 6. It is possible for special education teachers to form stronger emotional bonds to the children they teach simply because they spend proportionately more time with each child. Also, mainstream teachers do not often attend to the biological functions of their students, whereas special education teachers may be quite involved in such assistance, as well as assistance in physical therapy, occupational therapy, and mobility training. The instructional attention to these needs may result in a closer bonding between special education teachers and their students than between mainstream teachers and their students. Each of these factors may make it particularly hard for the special education teacher to deal with the emotional demands when one of the children in the class dies.

Few, if any, teacher training programs deal directly with this issue. This is understandable for two reasons. First, medically fragile children were not included in special education settings until recently, so issues surrounding the death of a pupil are only now becoming increasingly relevant. Next, the death of the student removes the concern from the teacher in the sense that teachers are not counselors for the family or the siblings, and many texts and teacher education training programs have left out counseling information, under the assumption that these issues were more appropriately handled by school counselors or other professionals.

However, upon reflection, it is quite apparent that teachers need some understanding of how to deal with the death of a student for several reasons. At the very least, there are two distinct issues the teacher must address when a student who has been in the class dies. First, the teacher must identify appropriate coping strategies to assist himself or herself in dealing with one's own personal grief, a grief that can be considerable at times. Next, the teacher must specify activities that will assist the other children to understand and successfully deal with the death of their peer.

In addition to these two concerns, the teacher may also choose to assist the family in their grieving process. In many cases, the special education teacher may be perceived by parents as the professional who most understood the issues surrounding the life and death of a child with disabilities, and families may seek out that teacher rather than a minister or counselor. Although special education teachers are not clinically trained to provide in-depth counseling to parents and families relating to the death of a child, the teacher can share his or her presence as a sympathetic professional and friend.

Specific guidelines are very difficult to offer to the teacher who faces the death of one of the pupils in class. However, the list of suggestions in Interest Box 15.3 should provide a good place to start for the teacher when he or she learns of the death of a child. As these questions indicate, the specifics of the death should assist in making preparations. In addition to these strategies, teachers are encouraged to utilize their co-teacher, counselor, and/or the school psychologist for further assistance.

PARENTS AS PARTICIPANTS IN PLANNING

Parental Participation as a Mandate

In special education, perhaps more than in any other area in education, parents are considered full partners in the educational decision making process (Turnbull & Turnbull, 1982; Krauss, 1990; Kroth, 1972). For example, parents must sit on various committees to plan the educational program for the child, and parents of special education

INTEREST BOX 15.3
Questions and Strategies for Dealing with the Death of a Student

1. What was my relationship with the student? How much of a loss will I feel? Will I stay awake at night grieving? If you answer yes to any of these questions, you may wish to consider talking with a friend about your personal loss. The school guidance counselor or psychologist may also be a resource in this regard.
2. How close am I to the family of the deceased? Do I feel a need to talk to the parents of the child? Talking with parents whom you know well may assist them in their grieving process, and you, as the involved professional, may wish to offer that assistance. Many teachers choose to attend the funeral of a child, depending, once again, on the relationship between the parents and the teacher.
3. How close was the child to other children in the class? Who were his or her best friends? Is some form of class discussion needed for the other children? Children are curious about, and often afraid of, death, and some meaningful answer will need to be provided when students inquire about classmates who are absent.
4. How did the child die? Was the death "expected" based on a medical problem, or was it unexpected (e.g., suicide or accident)? Many school districts utilize an impressive array of resources when one or more suicides take place in the district. Various groups may be formed in which the school psychologist meets with the close friends or siblings of the deceased. Clearly, a suicide is much more traumatic than the anticipated death of a medically fragile child, and, as an advocate for children with disabilities, you should encourage major efforts along these lines when a suicide occurs.
5. Inquire about measures that may identify children who are becoming depressed as a result of the death of a classmate. Various depression inventories are commercially available and may be utilized as a sort of screening measure after the death of a child. The school psychologist should have some recommendations along these lines, and you will certainly want that individual—who has the appropriate background for the assessment of emotional problems—to administer and interpret those data for the other children in the class.
6. Did the child have siblings in the school? Do those students need help in dealing with the loss? You may wish to discuss the death directly with the siblings, or recommend that the guidance counselor do so, in order to gauge the initial reactions of the child, particularly if the sibling is also one of your students.
7. Would memorial services at the school be appropriate? Depending upon the type of death and the visibility of the student, some school districts hold memorial services at school. Although this is a decision that will be made by the administrators, you can provide input.
8. What types of services can be provided through the school counseling office? Inquire of school counselors, psychologists, and other teachers concerning any ideas they might have for facilitating acceptance of the death by the other students in your class.

children are contacted more by teachers than are parents of nonhandicapped children (Yanok & Derubertis, 1989). Although evidence has suggested that parents do not utilize their decision making authority as much as was originally hoped (Glass, 1988; Vaughn, Bos, Harrell, & Lasky, 1988), the fact is that they are legally considered full participants in the decision making process.

Historically, the participation of parents in the special education process took place in the educational planning conferences. Parents can provide certain types of information about adaptive behavior of the child with a disability and about the child's functioning at home or in nonschool social settings. Parents may also make educational programming suggestions, given their particular knowledge of a child's abilities. One real world example of this involved a meeting (attended by this author) in which school personnel and a single parent—the father—were deciding on a junior high school course schedule for a student with mild intellectual disabilities. The choices included several pre-vocational and vocational classes, and the father suggested a class on two-cycle engine repair. This was considered an advanced vocational course, and would clearly not have been the choice of this author or of the other educational professionals at the meeting. However, the father was aware that the student had begun a grass cutting business that had led him into repairing two-cycle gasoline engines (lawn mowers, chain saws, etc.). The school professionals were unaware of that, and the student tended not to voice such preferences for himself. Consequently, the input of the father allowed the student vocational participation in a course in which the student both learned a great deal of useful knowledge (which resulted in a job after the school years) and experienced success in a mainstream vocational course because of his special knowledge and experience.

Because of this type of potential parental contribution, parents have been encouraged to participate in the special education conferences that resulted in a description of their child's educational plan. This expectation can be dated as beginning at least as early as the passage of Public Law 94–142 in 1975.

Research on Parental Involvement

Even though parents have the right to participate in the various conferences with special education personnel designed to result in an educational plan, research has shown that many parents participate only passively in the decision making meetings (Glass, 1988; Harry, 1992; Vaughn et al., 1988). As discussed previously, this is particularly true of minority parents (Harry, 1992).

Vaughn and her co-workers (1988) observed 26 conferences with parents of children who had been referred for services as learning disabled. Observations were taken of the time parents spent asking questions, commenting, and responding to other team members. The results indicated that parents asked, on average, less than five questions per meeting. Further, parents spent less than 6 percent of the conference time in responding to questions asked by others. These results indicate that parents are not particularly involved in the educational planning sessions.

Other research supports the suggestion that parents are, at best, passive participants in the educational planning meetings (Glass, 1988; Meyers & Blacher, 1987). This research suggests that parents feel poorly equipped to participate, and meetings with teams of professional educators, psychologists, and principals tend to make parents uncomfortable (Glass, 1988). It also indicates that parents with higher incomes and higher levels of education tend to participate more than other parents (Glass, 1988; Meyers & Blacher, 1987), and this result may suggest some type of socioeconomic bias.

However, there are some positive results in the research on parental participation, suggesting that parents of children with more severe disabilities participate slightly more, probably because the level of severity dictates that those parents have more experience in various conferences involving their children (Glass, 1988). This may suggest that, as parents become more experienced in meeting participation, they may actively contribute more frequently. Also, among parents of students with severe disabilities, results indicate that parents have been highly satisfied with their child's educational program.

For the special education teacher today, these research results have a distinct message. Teachers must structure the parental conferences in such a way as to encourage parental participation. First, parents should be fully informed in advance of the purpose of the meeting, the information that might be provided by the parents in order to facilitate the meeting, and the desired outcome of the meetings. Interest Box 15.4 presents a letter requesting a

INTEREST BOX 15.4
Sample Letter to Parents about a Conference

Dear Ms. Davidson:

We would like to invite you to come to a meeting concerning the educational plan for your son, Tommy, for next year. The meeting is planned for 2:00 PM on September 24, 1996, in room 138 at Evansville Elementary School.

We have been pleased with the progress which Tommy has made this year, particularly in the area of social skills. We hope to build on this strength in the year ahead.

The specific purpose of the meeting is to design an educational plan for Tommy. This will entail considerable thought about what social and academic skills we wish to stress next year, and you may wish to think of suggestions along these lines. Does Tommy have any weaker areas that you have noticed, and should an emphasis on these be included? Can you think of other needs that should be stipulated? You may wish to bring in some of his work from the past and share it with the committee.

The meeting will include his teacher from this year, myself, the principal, the school psychologist who tested Tommy, and perhaps several other professionals. You should plan on thirty minutes to an hour.

We look forward to seeing you, and thank you for your time.

Yours,

William N. Bender

meeting with the parents of a child with disabilities that exemplifies the types of information that may lead to greater parental participation.

Next, the meetings with parents should be structured in such a way as to encourage parental participation. See the section on organizing a parental conference later in this chapter, which provides some general guidelines for conducting the conference in order to encourage parental participation.

Finally, parents should be repeatedly shown how and where their contributions to educational planning meetings have made a difference in the education of their child. Although special educators and other school professionals do have the expertise and responsibility for the education of the child, a wise professional is constantly reminding himself or herself that the parents have the ultimate responsibility for the child with the disability. It is quite a humbling experience to actually consider what living with a child with a disability can be like, and if a parent requests that a certain academic or adaptive behavioral skill be placed on the individual educational plan, and that request is realistic given the child's needs and abilities, it should be honored, even at the cost of leaving out other skills that would normally be taught. This type of response can only encourage greater parental participation and overall parental satisfaction with the educational program that the child receives.

Organization of the Parent Conferences

One of the most important methods of increasing parental participation in planning conferences is effective organization of the meeting. There are many types of meetings in which parents may be involved (Kroth, 1972). The most common meetings involving parents are intended to produce an individualized educational plan. Other meetings may be called to review assessment results with parents, or because of particular problems a child is having at school. These meetings will involve different participants, depending on the nature of the meeting, but the overall structure of the meeting should remain fairly constant.

Even beginning teachers may occasionally have to chair a meeting that involves parents and other professionals in a discussion of some aspect of the education of a child with a disability. Although this requirement is quite common, 48 percent of the teacher preparation programs in special education do not offer any training in interdisciplinary team meetings (Courtnage & Smith-Davis, 1987). Nevertheless, you should have some understanding of the structure of effective meetings in order to maximize parental participation. The following guidelines should help you in your responsibilities for conducting meaningful parent conferences. For further information, you may wish to consult Dangle's work (1993).

First, whenever possible, meet the parents at the door of the school, rather than wait for them to enter the school, find the correct room, and approach you. This is a courtesy, and this simple action may help stimulate an atmosphere conducive to effective problem solving.

Next, in order to begin the meeting, introduce everyone around the table to the parents. Use the names and position titles of the various professionals. Also, during your introduction, tell the parents the purpose of everyone's presence. Because some educational professionals may not have wide experience working with students with disabilities, you can utilize these introductory statements, as needed, to let other professionals know what is expected of them. For example, introduce the principal as the legal decision maker at the school. When certain disciplinary options need to be considered, the principal's responsibilities require that he or she be present. Do not forget to introduce the parents to the other professionals, with a statement like, "These are Mr. and Mrs. Lomax. They have come to share some information on how Bobby behaves at home, how he does when completing his homework, and they probably also have some ideas on other things that may need to be taught to Bobby this year." Interest Box 15.5 presents several sample introductory statements that may help parents understand the presence of everyone in the room.

After the introductions, you should state the propose of the meeting in terms of the issues to be decided. These should be roughly the same issues presented in the introductory letter that was sent to the parents. The statement of purpose is the indication that the meeting is getting down to business. In some cases, it may be necessary to disclaim an intention to punish the child, because many parents expect that, if they are called for a meeting at the school, there must be some disciplinary problem requiring attention. Consequently, parents may enter some of these meetings in a defensive mood. If possible, state the purpose of the meeting in a positive way in order to defuse this type of defensive stance. Next, you should open the floor for contributions from each participant. Generally, each person present should contribute something, and each contribution should be a brief summary of the involvement with the child, including recommendations on the issues to be decided. The chairperson of the meeting should never allow the various professionals to merely read their assessment report on the child. Reports should be briefly summarized, and may be referred to later as needed. If possible, each participant's contribution should be kept to a maximum of three to five minutes.

As you hear similar recommendations from the various participants, you, as chairperson, should highlight these by pointing out the similarities, and asking for comments on those similarities. If several professionals have the same type of idea, that idea certainly has merit for further discussion. Also, this turns the meeting into an open discussion rather than a "report reading" meeting. As a general consensus begins to emerge, start to make written notations of the ideas discussed. As

INTEREST BOX 15.5
Sample Introductory Statements

For the Principal: "This is Ms. Cheri Harness, our school principal. Ms. Harness has known Jeremy for almost four years now, and has worked with Jeremy on his behavior in school. Ms. Harness is here to share her instructional leadership experience and to make certain that the legal stipulations in the state educational guidelines are followed."

For the Mainstream Teacher: "This is Mr. Johnson, who, as you know, was Tamara's second grade teacher. Mr. Johnson has several papers that Tamara completed recently in his class, and he will share these with the group to show how she is doing presently on her work."

For the Guidance Counselor: "This is Ms. Grayson, our school guidance counselor. Ms. Grayson will share with us the group test scores that represent John's achievement last year, and we will see how these compare with the individually administered tests from last week."

For the Parent: "This is Mr. Everson, Belinda's father. Mr. Everson has come to talk with us about how Belinda behaves at home and to suggest several things we may wish to consider putting on the individualized education plan."

chairperson, you should also keep a fairly extensive set of notes as the meeting progresses, and you may utilize these to complete the necessary forms at the end of the meeting.

After each participant has spoken, note again the general agreements and suggest that these agreements be incorporated into the final summary of the meeting. Then highlight the disagreements, and suggest discussion on each of these. Some of these issues may already have been resolved by the agreements just stated. If possible, try to resolve each issue raised. As chairperson, if you feel progress is not being made on an issue, you may suggest that the group move on to another issue and seek resolution on it. You may have to agree, as a group, to wait for a decision on some issues until a later meeting, after more information has been collected.

As a final step, the chairperson should summarize the meeting for all of the participants. The summary should include the issues discussed, the resolution of each, various points of agreement and disagreement, and the recommended future action. This helps the meeting come to a meaningful close, and will encourage the various participants to focus on the progress made. Also, many professionals choose to write a letter that summarizes the meeting and send it to the participants. Some school districts have a form letter for that purpose. When you are employed in a school district, you should inquire about district form letters for that purpose.

PARENTS AS TUTORS

In addition to the historic role of parents as participants in the team meetings, parents are now called upon for tutoring their child with disabilities. Because of this recent change, researchers have begun to explore the use of parents as tutors in their child's education (Mehern & White, 1988; Schulze, Rule, & Innocenti, 1989; Thurston & Dasta, 1990). This direction has been actualized most obviously in education of the preschool students with disabilities. With the recent passage of Public Law 99–457, the special educator must now prepare an intervention plan for the entire family of the preschool child with disabilities that stipulates the types of training the parents will require in order to teach the child (Krauss, 1990). Thus, special educators must be aware of the facts of parental involvement in tutoring children with various disabilities.

Rationale for Parent Tutors

Although parents of children with disabilities have always assisted in homework, as one example, the move to train parents as tutors is fairly recent. Involving parents as tutors has seemed desirable for several reasons (Mehern & White, 1988; Schulze, Rule, & Innocenti, 1989). First, parents spend a great amount of time with children, and are much more constant in their child's life than a teacher whom the child may have for only a year or so. Economically, using parents as tutors makes a great deal of sense because of the time some parents have available to interact with their children. Next, the use of parents as tutors is consistent with national policy supporting the role of the family; also, teaching in the natural setting of the home and community is believed to be more "applicable" than teaching in a classroom environment. Finally, only nonclassroom environments such as the home or other community settings offer the opportunities to teach certain types of skills—community living skills, for example.

Research on Parent Tutors

Unfortunately, the early research evidence has not demonstrated widespread support for the concept of parent tutoring and the evidence that does support parent tutoring is usually anecdotal or self-report evidence rather than randomly controlled experimental studies (Mehern & White, 1988; Thurston & Dasta, 1990). However, some studies are available in the literature that show positive results (Lazzari, Bender, & Kello, 1987; Mehern & White, 1988; Slater, 1986). In one of the more recent experimental studies on the efficacy of parent tutoring, Mehern and White (1988) used 76 students identified as at-risk for reading problems during the spring of their kindergarten year. The students were rank ordered and paired, with one member of each pair assigned to the control group and one member assigned to the experimental group. The students in the control group received reading instruction in the first grade compensatory education program, which provided 30 minutes of supplementary reading instruction each day. The children in the experimental group also attended the compensatory reading program each day. However, parents of the experimental group children were requested to tutor their child in reading for three 15-minute sessions each week. Reading materials for those tutoring sessions were provided, and the parents were trained in tutoring skills during two 4-hour sessions. Follow-up meetings were also held each week during the year. Parents were requested to keep logs of their tutoring sessions. A battery of reading tests were used as pre- and posttest measures.

Results of this study are more detailed than those of other parent tutoring studies, because the tutoring logs allowed the researchers to subdivide the experimental group students according to the level of tutoring received. Results showed that tutoring resulted in improved reading scores for the experimental group, above the gains evidenced by the control group receiving only compensatory education. More importantly, the students whose parents generally met the goal of a full three sessions each week evidenced the greatest academic gains. These results clearly indicate that even minimal parental tutoring (three sessions of 15 minutes each per week) can result in substantial gains in student achievement. Therefore, if a special educator has the opportunity to encourage parental tutoring, that opportunity should not be missed.

Guidelines for Using Parents as Tutors

Parental tutoring programs can be divided into two basic types: highly unstructured or highly structured. Needless to say, the structured type of tutoring is more likely to generate specific academic gains among pupils with disabilities. Whenever a teacher encourages a parent to "work with" a child on his or her assignments, the teacher is encouraging a form of unstructured tutoring. However, no specific guidelines are provided for the tutoring time and, consequently, there is no assurance that the tutoring time is useful. For example, many parents may feel that the appropriate way to study spelling is to have the child look at the words for 15 minutes and then the parent will call them out to the child. Although such a procedure may work for children without disabilities, children with disabilities may not have the types of cognitive skills that allow them to stay actively engaged with such a task, and their minds may merely wander for 15 minutes.

In a structured tutoring approach, the teacher offers specific tutoring suggestions to the parents. The teacher may choose to use a "configuration clue" spelling approach in which the pupil is told to draw boxes around the short letters and tall letters and to remember the shape of the word based on a visual image of those boxes. To facilitate a structured tutoring approach, the teacher must provide some type of instructional guidelines to the tutor. Many of the instructional ideas presented in Chapters 10 through 16 of this text can be easily translated into parent tutoring suggestions. Also, many of the tutor training suggestions discussed in Chapter 6 would be applicable here.

A review of the parent tutoring instruction in the Mehern and White (1988) study indicates the types of tutor instruction that may be desirable. Thirty-eight mothers went through two sessions of training, each session lasting four hours. Reading materials were provided for the mothers, and each mother was instructed in specific procedures. Also, weekly instruction sessions were held in order to keep the mothers abreast of their tutoring responsibilities, and to help the new tutors solve any problems that may arise. Clearly, this level of tutor training exceeds anything an individual teacher can do. Nevertheless, an individual teacher can provide materials for parents and some written suggestions regarding study habits. Suggestions concerning implementation of a classroom-based parent tutoring program are presented in Interest Box 15.6.

INTEREST BOX 15.6
Implementation of a Parent Tutoring Program

The following guidelines should allow you to enlist the support of parents as tutors for their children. You may wish to implement this parent tutoring plan in your classroom.

1. Provide materials for parents to use at home, along with suggestions for their use. As you write a brief parenthetical set of "instructions" for tutoring on a particular worksheet or set of materials, copy these instructions for later use with other parents.
2. Whenever possible, model the tutoring for the parents. Demonstrate the use of the materials in at least one parent–teacher conference with the child. After modeling the use of the materials, encourage the parents to try one brief lesson in which you critique the tutoring.
3. Request that parents send you a weekly report on the tutoring progress, including the number of tutoring sessions each week, the material covered, and the parents' evaluation of student performance. Asking the parents to objectively evaluate the student's performance may result in the parents feeling more like equal partners in the child's education.
4. Contact parents frequently. Weekly telephone calls or brief notes of encouragement will result in more tutoring sessions and more commitment to the parental tutoring.
5. Be understanding of the circumstances that make parents miss tutoring sessions.
6. When several parents are tutoring their children, you may wish to schedule a "tutors' meeting" for brief additional training.

Another example of a structured parental tutoring approach was discussed by Schulze, Rule, and Innocenti (1989), who described a procedure called coincidental teaching. In that procedure parents were used to teach social skills at home and in the community. This type of parental tutoring results in skills that generalize from one setting to another. For example, when a teacher teaches sharing to the students in class, the sharing of various toys may be seen only during that class or in that setting. However, when a parent teaches the same skills, the daily life of the child and parent will allow the parent to teach those sharing skills in a number of different settings, and the skills are more likely to be generalized from one setting to another.

Parents taught skills such as sharing and greeting others to children with disabilities, and the coincidental tutoring procedure involved several steps. Parents were initially trained to identify situations in which certain social skills were necessary. Then parents participated in several training sessions that taught them a "graduated prompting sequence" involving a verbal prompt to use a particular behavior, modeling of the behavior, and a physical prompt for the behavior. The students did seem to learn these skills and the skills did generalize across settings. Both parents and teachers reported satisfaction with these procedures.

SUMMARY

Parents have responsibilities in the educational endeavors of children with disabilities, perhaps more than in any other area of education. Because of this mandate, special education teachers contact parents of disabled children more frequently than they do than parents of nondisabled children. Teachers in special education should have some knowledge of the types of stress parents will go through. The phases typically include shock, denial, adjustment, and acceptance.

Parents are required to participate in educationally planning for their child, though research has suggested that many parents participate only passively. Parents can provide certain types of information, particularly about the adaptive behavior of the child and the child's functioning at home or in the community. Active parental participation can be encouraged by a number of different actions, including effective structuring of the parental conferences.

Parental participation is also sought in tutoring children with disabilities in order to increase their level of learning. Although the early research was equivocal on the effectiveness of parental tutoring, more recent research has demonstrated that active parental tutoring does result in improved performance on the part of the children. If parents show any inclination to become active in tutoring their children, the special education teacher should utilize this potential resource by providing materials, support, encouragement, and reinforcement in terms of showing the parents the specific academic gains resulting from tutoring. Generally, structured tutoring sessions (three times each week for 15 minutes) are more effective than unstructured tutoring. Teachers should, at a minimum, provide some materials for the tutoring and some indications concerning the type of instructions the parent tutor should use.

Summary Points

- Parents go through a fairly predictable series of reactions to their child's disability. These include shock, denial, adjustment, and acceptance.
- Several stress points during a child's development may be particularly difficult for parents of children with disabilities. These include the transition from preschool age to school, any school changes, the decisions regarding curricular emphases during middle and high school, and whenever the parents consider their own demise and its effects on the student.
- The death of a child with a disability can provide an opportunity for teacher and parent to

offer comfort to each other. Special education teachers face that prospect more frequently than other teachers in the school.

- Effective team meetings can be facilitated by utilizing a certain set of steps. These suggestions will result in effective and efficient use of meeting time.
- Parenting tutoring programs are becoming much more frequent in special education because of recent legislation and the efficacy of such programs. As a special education teacher you should consider methods whereby you can encourage parents of your students to tutor them in the home setting.

QUESTIONS AND ACTIVITIES

1. Describe the stages of parental reaction to the child's disability.
2. Review the stress points in the parent's life relative to the life of the child with disabilities. Can you think of other points in a parent's life in which the parent may be unusually concerned about the well-being of the child with disabilities?
3. Describe the steps in an effective parental conference. Set up a role play in which different class members take the roles of psychologist, parent, child, mainstream teacher, special education teacher, and principal. Act out a parental conference with a parent who is "new" to the school and was dissatisfied with the special education program at the last school.
4. Review the suggestions provided here for increasing parental participation. Can you think of other suggestions? Discuss these in class.
5. What are the reasons for the passive parental participation at meetings with educators?
6. Describe the methods for implementing a parent tutoring program for the students in your class. Can you think of additional ideas that may be helpful?
7. Review the research on parental tutoring programs cited in this chapter. Present a brief report to the class that summarizes this research.
8. Describe the strategies for dealing with the death of a student. Can you think of additional strategies?

REFERENCES

Courtnage, L., & Smith-Davis, J. (1987). Interdisciplinary team training: A national survey of special education teacher training programs. *Exceptional Children, 53,* 451–458.

Dangle, H. L. (1993). Eligibility and team meetings. In W. N. Bender (Ed.), *Learning Disabilities: Best Practices for Professionals.* Reading, PA: Andover Medical Publishers.

Foster, M., Berger, M., & McLean, M. (1981). Rethinking a good idea: A reassessment of parent involvement. *Teacher Education and Special Education, 1* (3), 55–65.

Glass, I. (1988). *Teachers' and parents' perceptions of parental involvement in special education.* Unpublished doctoral dissertation. Rutgers University Graduate School of Education, New Brunswick, NJ.

Harry, B. (1992). Restructuring the participation of African-American parents in special education. *Exceptional Children, 59,* 123–131.

Huntington, D., & Bender, W. N. (1993). Adolescents with learning disabilities at risk? Emotional well-being, depression, suicide. *Journal of Learning Disabilities, 26,* 159–166.

Krauss, M. W. (1990). New precedent in family policy: Individualized family service plan. *Exceptional Children, 56,* 388–395.

Kroth, R. (1972). Facilitating educational progress by improving parent conferences. *Focus on Exceptional Children, 4* (7), 154–163.

Lazzari, A. M., Bender, W. N., & Kello, M. N. (1987). Parents' and childrens' behavior during preschool reading sessions as predictors of language and reading skills. *Reading Improvement, 24,* 89–95.

Mehern, M., & White, K. R. (1988). Parent tutoring as a supplement to compensatory education for first-grade children. *Remedial and Special Education, 9* (3), 35–41.

Meyers, C. E., & Blacher, J. (1987). Parents' perceptions of schooling for severely handicapped children: Home and family variables. *Exceptional Children, 53,* 441–449.

Obiakor, F. E. (1992). Embracing new special education strategies for African-American students. *Exceptional Children, 59,* 104–106.

Schulze, K. A., Rule, S., & Innocenti, M. S. (1989). Coincidental teaching: Parents promoting social skills at home. *Teaching Exceptional Children, 21,* 24–27.

Slater, M. A. (1986). Modification of mother–child interaction processes in families with children at-risk for mental retardation. *American Journal of Mental Deficiency, 91,* 257–267.

Thurston, L. P., & Dasta, K. (1990). An analysis of in-home parent tutoring procedures: Effects on children's academic behavior at home and in school and on parents' tutoring behaviors. *Remedial and Special Education, 11* (4), 41–52.

Turnbull, A. P., & Turnbull, H. R. (1982). Parental involvement in the education of handicapped children: A critique. *Mental Retardation,* 20, 115–122.

Vaughn, S., Bos, C. S., Harrell, J. E., & Lasky, B. A. (1988). Parent participation in the initial placement/IEP conference ten years after mandated involvement. *Journal of Learning Disabilities, 21,* 82–89.

Waggoner, K., & Wilgosh, L. (1990). Concerns of families of children with learning disabilities. *Journal of Learning Disabilities, 23,* 97–98.

Yanok, J., & Derubertis, D. (1989). Comparative study of parental participation in regular and special education programs. *Exceptional Children, 56,* 195–199.

CHAPTER 16

INSTRUCTIONAL TREATMENTS OF QUESTIONABLE EFFECTIVENESS

OBJECTIVES

Upon completion of this chapter you should be able to:

1. Describe the required research basis for recommended interventions for children with disabilities.
2. Describe a two-point rationale for study of unsupported treatments.
3. Describe the use of colored lenses for correcting reading problems.
4. Discuss the reasons why some parents encourage the use of unsupported treatments.
5. Describe the patterning approach.
6. List several examples of unsupported treatments.

KEYWORDS

visual training	multisensory	patterning
Irlen lenses	modalities	Feingold Diet
scotopic sensitivity	VAKT	
auditory perceptual training	neurological impress	

Historically, special education was criticized for utilizing numerous instructional methods that did not work (Glass, 1982). Previous chapters of this volume have presented the research evidence concerning numerous widely recommended instructional methodologies, and for each method discussed thus far the efficacy research has been overwhelmingly supportive. Both this text and your teacher preparation program have emphasized the professional approach to any new instructional idea: a critical review of the research evidence for the instruction. Most teachers today approach newly recommended instructional treatments with this critical review of evidence in mind, and because of the quality and quantity of good research on the effectiveness of various educational treatments, it is much less likely that unsupported instructional methods will be employed in special education classrooms today.

However, in the early history of the field, numerous instructional treatment methods were utilized that were questionable (Coles, 1978; Glass, 1982). Although some of these treatment approaches were recommended by theorists who are actively participating in the field of special education, others were recommended by theorists only tangentially related to the field. Also, recently recommended ideas sometimes garner wide public attention before they are substantiated by research. This is of special concern to special education teachers, because professionals should never willingly subject a student to an educational treatment that has not been supported by research.

This chapter presents information on certain unsupported, though widely publicized, instructional methods and treatments in special education. Each of the treatments and instructional methods presented in this chapter is currently either unsupported by research in special education or not widely accepted as common practice for children and youth with disabilities. The chapter does not cover all of these controversial treatment approaches, though an attempt has been made to discuss the rationale and evidence for the most popular of them, particularly ones that are supported by various books and parent's groups.

RATIONALE FOR STUDY OF UNSUPPORTED TREATMENTS

As a teacher, you will find that parents and other teachers ask about some of these approaches, and it will be important for you to understand something about each of these unproven instructional treatments in order to respond appropriately. You will want the parents to respect your knowledge of the field in general, and the only way to accomplish that is to be prepared to discuss any publicly available treatment with parents who are seeking help.

Further, professionals in any field of endeavor have a responsibility to let parents and the general public know of the research support for various ideas that may have been presented in the national press. As a teacher, you have a professional responsibility to discourage wide application of certain treatment approaches unless and until more evidence is forthcoming that is supportive of these methods. For example, you would not want a doctor using medical treatments on your child that have not been supported by the scientific establishment in medicine. Educators too have a responsibility to let parents and the public know of treatment approaches that are unsupported by research, and to discourage use of these treatments.

Use of Unsupported Treatments

In spite of the lack of scientifically acceptable evidence supporting these treatments, many parents encourage use of some of these unproven approaches. At first glance, this may be difficult to understand, but there are at least two reasons for the popularity of unsupported approaches: ignorance concerning what constitutes research and parental desperation. First, many nonprofessionals do not understand the distinction between "testimonial" evidence—the weakest type of treatment effectiveness evidence—and experimental evidence on which scientific arguments must depend. A number of "testimonials," or statements by parents concerning the effectiveness of some of the approaches, are presented later in this chapter. In some cases, books have been written about particular children who recovered or who compensated for their learning problems by using a particular treatment. However, a moment's reflection will remind one that testimonial evidence can be obtained for almost any proposition whatsoever, and such testimonials do not replace research treatment studies that have been recognized as acceptable research by others in the field.

Unsupported treatments are utilized for another, more personal reason. As discussed in the previous chapter, parents often have a difficult time accepting the fact that their child has a disability. The phenomenon of "doctor shopping" may lead to a desperate search for any instructional treatment, regardless of the lack of research support. Parents who are desperate enough may seek information on unsupported treatments. As a professional, you will need to be sensitive to the needs of parents who may wish to attempt one of these unproven treatments. You should share with them the information that indicates the lack of evidence for a particular treatment approach in a sympathetic manner, and then allow them to make their decision. When sharing information with them, it is wise to present one of the research articles that has included a critical analysis of the unsupported treatment the parents are considering. Parents are much more inclined to believe your assertions that a treatment is unsupported when such assertions are supported by a research article from the literature. Numerous articles are available that you may wish to use in this regard, and some of these are identified in the reference list for this chapter. You should obtain a copy of one or two of these articles and keep a copy permanently on file, to share with parents as the need arises.

VISION-BASED INTERVENTIONS

Visual and Perceptual Training

Rationale and Training Practices. In the field of learning disabilities, one group of researchers studied visual perceptual problems believed to underlie reading and language problems. Among this group, a number of theorists believed that the reading problems demonstrated by children with learning disabilities could be explained by inefficient vision (Busby, 1985). For example, the types of reading errors common among these students—reversals of letters or words, omissions, and so forth—may be a result of muscular control of the eye or misinterpretation of the visual stimulus. As a result of this belief, a number of theorists recommended specific training in visual and/or visual perceptual exercises in the belief that such training would enhance learning for many of these children (Busby, 1985).

Training in vision and visual perceptual performance involves many approaches. The training activities themselves usually involve some type of eye movement that requires fine visual discrimination. For example, stringing beads involves visually identifying the hole in a bead and inserting the string through the hole. Chalkboard activities include drawing lines between closely spaced lines on the chalkboard, or following a chalkboard maze in order to find an escape. Other activities involve finding hidden pictures or partially revealed stimuli embedded in other stimuli. These types of activities are frequent among the visual perceptual training approaches (Busby, 1985; Hammill & Wiederholt, 1973). Interest Box 16.1 presents a list of several of the most popular educational treatment programs of this type.

Efficacy of Visual Training. Evidence on the effectiveness of visual perceptual training may be divided into two separate questions. First, is the training effective for improving students' performance on the visual perceptual tasks themselves? Second, does the training work to improve performance on reading or other academic tasks?

The evidence on visual training clearly demonstrates that these approaches are not successful (Cook & Welch, 1980; Hammill & Wiederholt, 1973; Kavale & Mattson, 1983). In a major review of the research by Kavale and Mattson (1983), results from a number of studies were statistically treated so as to be comparable across studies. There was virtually no positive gain in the ability to complete visual perceptual tasks after students completed the visual perceptual training. Further, all of the major reviews have indicated that visual perceptual training does not positively affect reading or other academic work (Cook & Welch, 1980; Kavale & Mattson, 1983; Silver, 1987). As this research indicates, visual perceptual training should not be used as an educational intervention for students with disabilities.

Colored Light Filters

Irlen (1983) developed the concept of "scotopic sensitivity" by postulating that individuals with reading difficulties may react to particular frequencies and wavelengths of the white-light spectrum. This oversensitivity to certain frequencies of light was believed to be the cause of reading difficulties and certain other perceptual problems. Irlen (1983) recommended the use of colored lenses, selected according to the particular scotopic sensitivity of the individual student, in order to correct these reading problems.

INTEREST BOX 16.1
Popular Visual Motor Treatment Programs

Frostig–Horne Visual Perception Training Program
Getmans's Physiology of Readiness
Kirk and Kirk's Visual Perceptual Training
Kephart's Training Approaches

Efficacy of Colored Filters. At present a few efficacy studies are available that support this hypothesis (O'Connor, Sofo, Kendall, & Olsen, 1990; Robinson & Miles, 1987). In the study by O'Connor and his co-workers, 92 students were assessed according to the procedures developed by Irlen, and were then randomly assigned to treatment groups exposed to colored transparencies or clear transparencies. The students who received the appropriate colored overlays (as indicated by Irlen's recommended assessment procedures) improved significantly in several reading measures, compared to the other children.

With some research suggesting the efficacy of these treatments, there will certainly be more research forthcoming on this concept. At present, this treatment is not widely utilized in public school classes for children and youth with disabilities, but, at the very least, this treatment idea shows some promise. Should parents inquire about this concept you may wish to refer them to the available literature and let them know that this educational procedure is not yet widely accepted in the field.

AUDITORY PERCEPTUAL TRAINING

Components of Auditory Perceptual Training

Like the visual deficit perspective, the auditory/language deficit perspective was one of the early perspectives in the field of special education. Theorists who were proponents of this treatment approach believed that auditory perception deficits cause language delays in young children with learning disabilities, and that these language delays result in reading and language arts failures in school.

The treatment strategies recommended by the auditory deficit approaches were varied. For example, children were frequently trained to listen to a tape that presents words on a syllable-by-syllable basis, and the child's task was to "close" the word and pronounce the integrated whole. Other tasks were based on listening to words taped over competing sounds and trying to discriminate the word from the background noise. Completion of sentences that emphasize correct use of grammatical rules was another common task, as is listening to auditory stimuli—such as lists of digits—and writing them down after a brief time.

Efficacy of Auditory Perceptual Training

Although research has demonstrated some relationship between auditory skills and reading or language competence (Kavale, 1981), studies that assessed the effectiveness of auditory training have not shown positive results (Cook and Welch, 1980; Kavale & Mattson, 1983). Specifically, the treatment effects reported by Kavale and Mattson (1983) in a major review of the studies indicated no measurable gain for experimental groups who had been exposed to auditory training procedures. Like the visual deficit treatments discussed previously, auditory treatments are not effective for improving the reading and language skills of students with mild and moderate disabilities.

MULTISENSORY INSTRUCTIONAL APPROACHES

Development of Multisensory Approaches

With the attention that was given to visual and auditory perceptual training packages, it was probably inevitable that a method of instruction that combined these approaches would be developed. The use of combined sensory presentation to learn words, involving visual stimuli, auditory stimuli, tactile stimuli, and physical movement is called the multisensory approach. The various multisensory methods all involved imparting information to the student by multiple input modalities. In some cases, the child would hear the word "read," see the word, and trace the word on sandpaper letters in order to involve vision, auditory, tactile, and kinesthetic senses. This method is also called the VAKT method (for visual, auditory, kinesthetic, and tactile).

Some proponents of this method recommended identification of the "modality preference" for each child. Proponents of this concept believed that some children learn best through visual stimuli, whereas others learn using auditory stimuli or auditory stimuli combined with tactile sensation. Therefore, identification of the preferred modality would involve an attempt to identify the sense or "modality" through which a particular child seemed to learn best. Such modality preferences would then be considered in selection of daily work activities for particular children. This requirement to identify the modality preference may still be mandated by some state codes in the rules and regulations concerning the required information that must appear on the IEP.

Different theorists have been using this approach for decades (Fernald, 1943; Gillingham & Stillman, 1968), and you may see slightly different versions of this approach referred to by the names of these theorists (e.g., the Fernald method). Also, the "neurological impress" method involved a student reading words while the teacher read them simultaneously. Thus, the student saw the word and heard the word read at the same time.

This is not to suggest that all of these methods are similar. For example, the Fernald method stresses recognition of sight words and words as complete wholes, whereas the Gillingham–Stillman method involves blending different sounds. Nevertheless, the major thrust of these methods is the input of stimuli through different senses.

Efficacy of Multisensory Methods

The research evidence on the effectiveness of teaching language arts and reading with the multisensory approach has been equivocal (Blau & Lovelass, 1982; Borden, 1985; Kann, 1983). Although some studies have demonstrated that particular multisensory instructional strategies work for some children (Blau & Lovelass, 1982; Borden, 1985), other studies have indicated that these methods are not effective. A major drawback in this research has been the tendency for scholars to study only one multisensory approach compared to a control treatment group rather than having several different treatment groups with each exposed to a separate type of multisensory instruction. Studies of this type would assist practitioners in the field in deciding what type of multisensory approach—if any—works best.

Although the evidence is not conclusive that multisensory instruction works, it has been a widely accepted method of instruction in the past. At present, many teachers are using instructional approaches that depend on multisensory input, and you will probably see some type of application of this in your special education experiences. You should remain cautious regarding use of these methods unless and until more efficacy research is forthcoming that supports these strategies.

PATTERNING OR NEUROLOGICAL ORGANIZATION

The Neurological Organization Approach

This treatment approach was described by two authors (Doman & Delacato, 1968), and has become a widely publicized treatment approach, in spite of the complete lack of scientific evidence to support its use. The neurological organization approach, commonly referred to as patterning, involves the attempt to repattern the neurological connections in the brain by manipulation of various body parts in a manner that approximates the movements associated with certain physical reflexes among infants (Silver, 1987).

The approach was theoretically based on the concept that "ontogeny recapitulates phylogeny," or that the development of a single organism must progress through the same developmental stages as the development of the entire species. In other words, the reflexes of an infant are presumed to be based on the evolutionary history of our species, and children with learning problems for some reason did not progress through the developmentally "correct" set of reflexive movements. Consequently, the treatment consists, in large measure, of moving the arms, legs, and head of the child with learning problems in a manner consistent with early reflexive movements of the infant in an attempt to reorganize the neurological connections in the brain. Proponents of this method believed that this neurological reorganization would then permit normal learning to take place.

Specifically, the treatment typically included extended periods of bodily manipulations—in many cases 10 to 15 hours per day, every day, over a period of years. Furthermore, the treatment often required four or more adults standing around the child in order to move the bodily appendages at the same time. As you can see, this was a very involved process. Other aspects of the treatment included dietary restrictions and the breathing of expired air (i.e., by breathing into a bag) in order to reduce the oxygen supply to the brain (Silver, 1987).

An assessment based on this theoretical formulation, along with a recommended treatment schedule, may still be obtained at various treatment centers around the country for a considerable fee. This treatment may be obtained only through such an assessment, and the marketing of these assessment and treatment plans has been very lucrative for the originators of this idea. For this reason, it may be anticipated that these treatment plans will be available for the immediate future.

Efficacy Of Patterning

There are a number of books that are testimonials concerning the effectiveness of patterning for particular children. However, controlled treatment studies in which some children are randomly assigned to this treatment and others used for a control group have never been done. Furthermore, the proponents of this treatment idea have been reluctant to share their clinical data in professional journals. Consequently many scholars and professional groups have recommended that this treatment approach be discontinued because of the lack of evidence indicating positive outcomes (Silver, 1987). The American Academy of Pediatrics (1982) concluded that these treatment demands on families "are so great that in some cases there may be harm in its use."

The best source of information on the concerns with this treatment approach is a series of articles by Silver (1975, 1987). These articles should be shared with parents who are considering use of this treatment.

BIOCHEMICAL APPROACHES

In addition to certain recognized drug interventions to combat hyperactivity and behavioral disorders, a number of alternative biochemical approaches have been recommended as treatments for various educational problems (Baker 1985; Holborow, Elkins, & Berry, 1981; Kavale & Forness, 1983; Silver, 1987; Thatcher & Lester, 1985). Some of these interventions recommend increasing certain types of chemicals in the body in order to combat various behavior and attention problems (Baker, 1985; Thatcher & Lester, 1985). Other treatments involve the limitation or elimination of certain elements from the diet of the child with the learning problem (Holborow, Elkins, & Berry, 1981; Silver, 1987).

At the outset, it is apparent that these treatments are not "educational" in the sense that the teacher does not control the diet of the child. For example, it does little good for a teacher to understand that a dietary deficiency is causing learning problems if the parents are not receptive to the possibility of changing a child's diet. However, teachers may eventually play a monitoring role, similar to the role teachers play in prescribed drug interventions, should future research indicate that any of these dietary treatments hold promise as effective educational interventions.

The Feingold Diet

In 1975, Dr. Benjamin Feingold published a rationale for restriction of certain food additives such as artificial colors, flavors, and salicylates (Holborow, Elkins, & Berry, 1981). This work tied ingestion of these additives to hyperactivity in the classroom. Since that time a number of studies—many of which were poorly designed—showed that certain children may behave more appropriately when their dietary intake of these additives is controlled. This early series of studies resulted in a certain early optimism, which was quickly dispelled when more carefully designed studies were undertaken (Kavale & Forness, 1983; Silver, 1987). There may be a small group of children who respond positively to these dietary restrictions (Burlton-Bennet & Robinson, 1987; Silver, 1987), but the Feingold diet should not, at present, be used as a general treatment for all students with mild learning problems. Additionally, there is no manner in which children for whom this diet may be effective can be identified beforehand. As a result, the overall outlook for the efficacy of the Feingold diet in eliminating mild learning problems is not positive.

Refined Sugars

A number of clinical reports have indicated that ingestion of refined sugars may be related to hyperactive behaviors (Silver, 1987; Thatcher & Lester, 1985). However, a number of research studies have been done in which the ingestion of sugar was increased in children in order to identify any increase in hyperactive behaviors and/or other behavior problems. These studies have not demonstrated any measurable behavior change related to ingestion of sugar, though there are a number of variables that could influence these results, and these were not controlled in the available research. For example, the type of breakfast eaten may hamper or enhance the effect of sugar ingestion. Although it may be true that almost every member of American society could use less refined sugar in his or her diet, there is no clear evidence, at present, that reductions in refined sugars are particularly beneficial for children with mild disabilities. However, the research on this question is not yet conclusive (Silver, 1987), and more research will surely be forthcoming.

Megavitamins

Use of megavitamins for patients exhibiting certain mental disorders has been common for a number of years (Silver, 1987). Cott (1971) first recommended the ingestion of megavitamins for children with learning disabilities. Since that time, several researchers have recommended specific treatments that involve the use of megavitamins (Baker, 1985). At present, there is no evidence to support the use of megavitamins in controlling the behavior problems among children with any particular type of disability (Silver, 1987). In spite of this lack of support, this treatment is available in certain parts of the country, and parents will be exposed to articles in the national press that indicate occasional success of megavitamin therapy.

Trace Elements

Certain theorists have suggested that deficiencies in trace elements such as zinc, magnesium, chromium, and copper may be causally related to mild disabilities (Fishbein & Meduski, 1987; Moon, Marlowe, Stellern, & Errera, 1985; Struempler, Larson, & Rimland, 1985). At present, no published data supports the theory that deficiencies in these elements causes learning problems. Furthermore, there is no clear evidence that treatments involving replacement of these elements result in increased learning potential or improved behavior (Silver, 1987).

Certain studies have shown correlations between the presence of some of these elements and academic achievement (Moon et al., 1985). Further research will surely be done on this relationship, though the data at present do not support the use of treatments designed to replace these elements in attempts to improve the academic work of students with mild disabilities.

Chiropractic Interventions

Dr. C. A. Ferreri (1983) has indicated that certain types of chiropractic treatment may positively affect children with learning disabilities. Dr. Ferreri hypothesized that learning disabilities may be the result of pressure on the brain caused by two specific cranial bones. The chiropractic treatment is designed to ease this pressure and correct the learning disability. Dr. Ferreri claims measurable results after only one or two treatments. However, at present no evidence is available in the scientific journals to support this claim, and Dr. Ferreri himself presents only a one-page description of the technique as his research basis (Silver, 1987). This technique, because it involves physical manipulation of the body—and thus some potential for physical damage—should not be used unless some type of evidence that demonstrates the effectiveness of this treatment is presented (Silver, 1987).

SUMMARY

This chapter has presented a series of treatments that are unsupported by research evidence. Although some evidence, generally in the form of testimonials, is available for each treatment idea presented here, these ideas must be viewed as unsupported treatments at present. Further, some of these ideas have only the testimonial support of one or two proponents. Efficacy research on several of these treatment recommendations, especially patterning and chiropractic treatments, has not been subjected to peer evaluation in the literature in special education, because the proponents of these ideas have been hesitant to present their efficacy research data for peer review. However, because of the occasional testimonial support some of these ideas have received, these approaches will probably be with us for some time in the future.

The continuing work on certain biochemical treatments may eventually show results, and these treatments may eventually be considered important educational interventions for certain children with mild disabilities. However, at present none of the biochemical treatments may be confidently recommended for children with mild or moderate disabilities.

As a professional in the field, you will be expected to keep current with the changing treatments for children with mild disabilities. As illustrated by the discussion of the first several treatments, teachers must keep current or run the risk of using an educational intervention that has not proven useful. As the field of study matures, more effective treatments, such as those discussed in Chapters 10 through 16, will become available. Hopefully, these will eventually supplant the ineffective educational treatments discussed in this chapter.

Also, it is quite possible that further research on a particular instructional method will demonstrate the efficacy of these methods. For example, some research currently supports the use of colored filters and multisensory instruction. This ever-changing research base in special education demonstrates that all professionals must keep current with the ongoing research in the field.

Summary Points

- Teachers must be aware of the ineffective instructional approaches in the field because parents will frequently inquire about these approaches.
- Vision training was one of the early interventions in the area of learning disabilities, but research has demonstrated that visual training exercises are not notably effective in either improving performance on visual exercises or on reading tasks.
- The use of colored filters to correct reading problems has been supported by early research, and although this is not currently a widely accepted method, more research will certainly be forthcoming.
- Auditory training involves teaching students how to listen in order to "close" several syllables into a word. Research has not supported the use of auditory training programs.
- Multisensory training programs involve the use of numerous senses to input information. Research on this instructional approach has been equivocal, to date.
- Patterning is a method that is very time intensive, and has not been shown to be effective in improving reading problems. However, this is one of the more widely publicized methods,

and many parents have read testimonials to the efficacy of this treatment.

- The Feingold diet has been a widely publicized approach for controlling hyperactivity. Although some studies have suggested that this approach may be effective for some children, parents and teachers should exercise caution in application of this procedure, because it is not widely accepted in the field at present.
- A number of biomedical approaches have been suggested, including monitoring of trace elements, use of megavitamins, and reducing refined sugars. Research has not supported any of these treatments conclusively.

QUESTIONS AND ACTIVITIES

1. Explain the two reasons why some parents choose to utilize unsupported educational treatments.
2. Describe the theory behind patterning.
3. What biomedical interventions seem to hold any promise of yielding insight into potential treatment approaches?
4. Explain the questions that should be asked relative to the effectiveness of visual training.
5. Describe the types of exercises used in an auditory training program.
6. Describe the Feingold diet.
7. Compare the research support for direct instruction, as presented in earlier chapters, with the research support for patterning. What differences do you find?
8. Describe a treatment study on the efficacy of the use of colored filters to improve reading competence.
9. Differentiate between the Fernald method and the Gillingham–Stillman method.

REFERENCES

American Academy of Pediatrics (1982). The Doman–Delacato treatment of neurologically handicapped children. A policy statement by the American Academy of Pediatrics. *Pediatrics, 70,* 810–812.

Baker, S. M. (1985). A biochemical approach to the problem of dyslexia. *Journal of Learning Disabilities, 18,* 581–584.

Blau, H., & Lovelass, E. J. (1982). Specific hemispheric-routing-TAK/v to teach spelling to dyslexics: VAK and VAKT challenged. *Journal of Learning Disabilities, 15,* 461–466.

Borden, T. (1985). The effect of multisensory instruction upon the on-task behaviors and word reading accuracy of learning disabled children. *Journal of Learning Disabilities, 18,* 279–286.

Burlton-Bennet, J. A., & Robinson, V. M. J. (1987). A single subject evaluation of the K-P Diet for Hyperkinesis. *Journal of Learning Disabilities, 20,* 331–335.

Busby, R. A. (1985). Vision development in the classroom. *Journal of Learning Disabilities, 18,* 266–272.

Coles, G. S. (1978). The learning disability test battery: Empirical and social issues. *Harvard Educational Review, 48,* 313–340.

Cook, J. M., & Welch, M. W. (1980). Reading as a function of visual and auditory process training. *Learning Disability Quarterly, 3,* 76–87.

Cott, A. (1971). Orthomolecular approach to the treatment of learning disabilities. *Schizophrenia, 3,* 95–107.

Doman, G., & Delacato, C. (1968). Doman–Delacato philosophy. *Human Potential,* 1, 113–116.

Feingold, B. F. (1975). *Why Your Child Is Hyperactive.* New York: Random House.

Fernald, G. (1943). *Remedial Techniques in Basic School Subjects.* New York: McGraw Hill.

Ferreri, C. A. (1983). Dyslexia and learning disabilities cured. *The Digest of Chiropractic Economics, 24,* 74.

Fishbein, D., & Meduski, J. (1987). Nutritional biochemistry and behavioral disabilities. *Journal of Learning Disabilities, 20,* 505–512.

Gillingham, A., & Stillman, B. (1968). *Remedial Teaching for Children with Specific Disability in Reading, Spelling, and Penmanship.* Cambridge, MA: Educator's Publishing Service.

Glass, G. V. (1982). Effectiveness of special education. *Policy studies review, 2,* 65–78.

Hammill, D. D., & Wiederholt, J. L. (1973). Review of the Frostig Visual Perception Test and the related training program. In L. Mann & D. Sabatino (Eds.), *The First Review of Special Education.* Philadelphia: JSE Press.

Holborow, P., Elkins, J., & Berry, P. (1981). The effect of the Feingold diet on 'normal' schoolchildren. *Journal of Learning Disabilities, 14,* 143–147.

Irlen, H. (1983, August). *Successful treatment of learning disabilities.* Paper presented at the meeting of the 91st Annual Convention of the American Psychological Association, Anaheim, CA.

Kann, R. (1983). The method of repeated readings: Expanding the neurological impress method for use with disabled readers. *Journal of Learning Disabilities, 16,* 90–93.

Kavale, K. (1981). The relationship between auditory perceptual skills and reading ability: A meta-analysis. *Journal of Learning Disabilities, 14,* 539–546.

Kavale, K. A., & Forness, S. R. (1983). Hyperactivity and the diet treatment: A meta-analysis of the Feingold hypothesis. *Journal of Learning Disabilities, 16,* 324–330.

Kavale, K., & Mattson, P. D. (1983). "One jumped off the balance beam": Meta-analysis of perceptual-motor training. *Journal of Learning Disabilities, 16,* 165–173.

Moon, C., Marlowe, M., Stellern, J., & Errera, J. (1985). Main and interaction effects of metallic pollutants on cognitive functioning. *Journal of Learning Disabilities, 18,* 217–221.

O'Connor, P. D., Sofo, F., Kendall, L., & Olsen, G. (1990). Reading disabilities and the effects of colored filters. *Journal of Learning Disabilities, 23,* 597–603.

Robinson, G. L., & Miles, J. (1987). The use of colored overlays to improve visual processing: A preliminary survey. *The Exceptional Child, 34,* 65–70.

Silver, L. B. (1975). Acceptable and controversial approaches to treating the child with learning disabilities. *Pediatrics, 55,* 406–415.

Silver, L. B. (1987). The "magic cure": A review of the current controversial approaches for treating learning disabilities. *Journal of Learning Disabilities, 20,* 498–512.

Struempler, R. E., Larson, G. E., & Rimland, B. (1985). Hair mineral analysis and disruptive behavior in clinically normal young men. *Journal of Learning Disabilities, 18,* 609–612.

Thatcher, R. W., & Lester, M. L. (1985). Nutrition, environmental toxins and computerized EEG: A minimax approach to learning disabilities. *Journal of Learning Disabilities, 18,* 287–297.

INDEX